Essentials of
International Health

Essentials of International Health

Manoj Sharma, MBBS, CHES, PhD
Professor, Health Promotion and Education
University of Cincinnati

Ashutosh Atri, MD, MS
Resident, Department of Psychiatry
University of Texas Health Science Center

JONES AND BARTLETT PUBLISHERS
Sudbury, Massachusetts
BOSTON   TORONTO   LONDON   SINGAPORE

World Headquarters

Jones and Bartlett Publishers	Jones and Bartlett Publishers	Jones and Bartlett Publishers
40 Tall Pine Drive	Canada	International
Sudbury, MA 01776	6339 Ormindale Way	Barb House, Barb Mews
info@jbpub.com	Mississauga, Ontario L5V 1J2	London W6 7PA
www.jbpub.com	Canada	United Kingdom

Jones and Bartlett's books and products are available through most bookstores and online booksellers. To contact Jones and Bartlett Publishers directly, call 800-832-0034, fax 978-443-8000, or visit our website, www.jbpub.com.

Substantial discounts on bulk quantities of Jones and Bartlett's publications are available to corporations, professional associations, and other qualified organizations. For details and specific discount information, contact the special sales department at Jones and Bartlett via the above contact information or send an email to specialsales@jbpub.com.

Production Credits

Acquisitions Editor: Shoshanna Goldberg	Cover Design: Kristin E. Parker
Senior Associate Editor: Amy L. Bloom	Photo Research Manager and Photographer:
Editorial Assistant: Kyle Hoover	Kimberly Potvin
Production Manager: Julie Champagne Bolduc	Assistant Photo Researcher: Bridget Kane
Production Assistant: Jessica Steele Newfell	Cover Image: © Norman Pogson/
Associate Marketing Manager: Jody Sullivan	ShutterStock, Inc.
V.P., Manufacturing and Inventory Control: Therese Connell	Printing and Binding: Malloy, Inc.
Composition: International Typesetting and Composition, Inc.	Cover Printing: Malloy, Inc.

Photo Credits: p. 1 © Juan Manuel Ordóñez/ShutterStock, Inc.; p. 39 © Photodisc/Getty Images; p. 73 © Uros Ravbar/Dreamstime.com; p. 111 © Orange Line Media/Dreamstime.com; p. 155 © Lucian Coman/ShutterStock, Inc.; p. 193 © Uros Ravbar/Dreamstime.com; p. 219 © WizData, Inc./ShutterStock, Inc.; p. 271 © Muellek/ShutterStock, Inc.; p. 305 © Varina and Jay Patel/ShutterStock, Inc.; p. 341 © Pavalache Stelian/Dreamstime.com; p. 385 © Rafost/Dreamstime.com; p. 421 © Craig Hanson/Dreamstime.com

Library of Congress Cataloging-in-Publication Data
Sharma, Manoj.
    Essentials of international health / Manoj Sharma, Ashutosh Atri.
        p. ; cm.
    Includes bibliographical references and index.
    ISBN 978-0-7637-6529-3 (alk. paper)
    1. World health. I. Atri, Ashutosh. II. Title.
    [DNLM: 1. World Health. 2. Disease. 3. Internationality. 4. Public
Health. WA 530.1 S531e 2010]
    RA441.S53 2010
    362.1—dc22
                                        2009025541
                                                                    86

6048
Printed in the United States of America
13 12 11 10 09   10 9 8 7 6 5 4 3 2 1

CONTENTS

Contents

PREFACE

We are pleased to present this text, *Essentials of International Health*, to our readers. This is an introductory text in the area of international health for undergraduate students, introductory graduate classes, and practitioners interested in working in developing countries. This book offers an introduction to epidemiological, political, behavioral, sociological, cultural, and medical dimensions in the field of international health. Coverage includes problems concerning both developed and developing countries, but the emphasis is on problems confronting developing countries. Population-based public health approaches to solving international health problems are introduced. Topics include historical perspectives, health indicators, the role of culture and behavior, communicable and noncommunicable diseases, malnutrition, nutritional deficiencies and obesity, environmental health and population issues, the health of women and children, mental health, world health systems, and future issues in international health.

The outstanding feature of this book is its straightforward language, which is geared to enhance the understanding of undergraduate students and introductory graduate students regarding the subject. The book links health concepts to the international context, thereby enriching comprehension. Some of the pedagogic highlights of the book include:

- Key terms and a set of learning objectives help readers to focus their attention and retain important information.
- Each chapter includes a succinct introduction and a concise summary, which provide an opportunity for readers to prepare for exams and master key concepts by reinforcement.
- The book provides practical skill-building activities that help students gain mastery by applying concepts. These activities will enable students to hone their skills relating to planning and evaluation in international health.
- Boxed items emphasize important points and quotations to reinforce concepts.
- Focus Features within the chapters provide an account of interesting discoveries, anecdotes, or future directions being pursued on a particular topic, which should help to consolidate interest in a topic and foster further reading.
- Important terms are defined in the glossary at the end of the text, which provides the reader a useful resource for looking up concepts in international health.

- Each chapter provides a detailed list of references.
- Each chapter includes review questions to help the reader prepare for exams.
- Web exercises on the text's accompanying Web site include reliable links to Web sites related to each chapter. Each Web exercise provides interactive activities that directly relate to the chapter content and help students apply their new knowledge practically.

INSTRUCTOR RESOURCES

We have prepared a set of PowerPoint presentations for each chapter that instructors can use for classroom lectures. Instructors also have access to online TestBank questions for each chapter. These are available at http://health.jbpub.com/international.

ACKNOWLEDGMENTS

We are indebted to the Health team at Jones and Bartlett Publishers who aided the publication process at all stages: Shoshanna Goldberg, Acquisitions Editor; Amy Bloom, Senior Associate Editor; Julie Bolduc, Production Manager; and Jody Sullivan, Associate Marketing Manager. We would also like to thank Dr. John A. Romas, Professor and Chair at Minnesota State University; Dr. Bikash Nandy, Professor at Minnesota State University, Beth Miller, a doctoral student at University of Cincinnati; and Dr. Samita Gandhi at University of Texas Health Science Center for their review and feedback on the manuscript.

Manoj Sharma, MBBS, CHES, PhD, is a professor in the Health Promotion and Education program at the University of Cincinnati. He is a physician by initial training and completed his doctorate in Preventive Medicine/Public Health from The Ohio State University. He has worked in community health for more than 25 years at all levels: local (Columbus Health Department, Omaha Healthy Start Program, Lead Safe Omaha Coalition), state (Nebraska Health and Human Services, Ohio Department of Health), national (American School Health Association, Centers for Disease Control and Prevention), and international (India, Italy, Mongolia, Nepal, United Arab Emirates, United Kingdom, Vietnam). His research interests are in designing and evaluating theory-based health education and health promotion programs, alternative and complementary systems of health, and community-based participatory research.

Ashutosh Atri, MD, MS, is a third-year resident in the Department of Psychiatry and Behavioral Sciences at the University of Texas Health Sciences Center. He has completed postgraduate training in health education and health promotion from the University of Cincinnati. He has worked as a physician at SS Medical College, Rewa, India, and MGM Medical College, Indore, India. His research interests are in the field of international health, psychoeducation, mental health, and designing health education interventions for the mentally ill.

LIST OF ACRONYMS

ACSM	American College of Sports Medicine
ACT	artemisinin-based combination therapies
AFP	acute flaccid paralysis
AHA	American Heart Association
APA	American Psychiatric Association
ARI	acute respiratory infections
BAC	blood alcohol concentration
BB	midborderline leprosy
BCE	before Common Era
BCG	Bacille Calmette-Guérin
BL	borderline lepromatous leprosy
BMI	body mass index
BRFSS	Behavioral Risk Factor Surveillance System
BT	borderline tuberculoid leprosy
BTWC	Biological and Toxin Weapons Convention
BWC	Biological Weapons Convention
CARE	Cooperative for Assistance and Relief Everywhere, Inc.
CAST	Coalition to Abolish Slavery and Trafficking
CATW	Coalition Against Trafficking in Women–International
CBD	community-based distribution
CBR	crude birth rate
CDC	Centers for Disease Control and Prevention
CDM	clean development mechanism
CDR	crude death rate
CE	Common Era
CEDAW	Convention on the Elimination of All Forms of Discrimination Against Women
CFC	chlorofluorocarbon
CHD	coronary heart disease
CI	confidence interval
CIA	Central Intelligence Agency

CIDA	Canadian International Development Agency
CNS	central nervous system
COLD	chronic obstructive lung disease
COPD	chronic obstructive pulmonary disease
CRS	congenital rubella syndrome
CRY	Child Rights and You (formerly Child Relief and You)
CTBT	Comprehensive Nuclear Test Ban Treaty
CVD	cardiovascular diseases
CWC	Chemical Weapons Convention
DALE	disability-adjusted life expectancy
DALY	disability-adjusted life year
DDT	dichlorodiphenyltrichloroethane
DFLE	disability-free life expectancy
DOTS	directly observed therapy, short course
DM	diabetes mellitus
DSM-IV-TR	*Diagnostic and Statistical Manual of Mental Disorders* (4th edition, text revision)
DTP	diphtheria, tetanus, and pertussis vaccine
ECT	electroconvulsive therapy
ELISA	enzyme-linked immunosorbent assay
EMPOWER	Enabling Methods of Planning and Organizing Within Everyone's Reach
EMR	electronic medical record
EMTALA	Emergency Medical Treatment and Active Labor Act
EPA	Environmental Protection Agency
EPI	Expanded Program on Immunization
ERU	emission reduction unit
ETS	environmental tobacco smoke
FAO	Food and Agriculture Organization
FGM	female genital mutilation
FMF	Feminist Majority Foundation
FMR	fetal mortality rate
GAD	generalized anxiety disorder
GARD	Global Alliance Against Chronic Respiratory Diseases
GAVI	Global Alliance for Vaccines and Immunization
GMP	Global Malaria Program
GOARN	Global Outbreak Alert and Response Network

GOBI-FFF	growth monitoring, oral rehydration, breastfeeding, immunization, female education, family planning, and food supplementation
GOLD	Global Initiative for Chronic Obstructive Pulmonary Disease
HALE	health-adjusted life expectancy or healthy life expectancy
HBM	health belief model
HDL	high-density lipoproteins
HeaLY	healthy life year
Hib	*Haemophilus influenzae* type b
HIV/AIDS	human immunodeficiency virus/acquired immunodeficiency syndrome
I	incidence rate
IAEA	International Atomic Energy Agency
IAQ	indoor air quality
IARC	International Agency for Research on Cancer
ICAP	International Center for Alcohol Policies
ICRC	International Committee of the Red Cross
ID_{50}	infective dose 50 (median infective dose)
IDD	iodine deficiency disorders
IDF	International Diabetes Federation
IHR	International Health Regulations
ILO	International Labor Organization
IMCI	integrated management of childhood illness
IMPAC	integrated management of pregnancy and childbirth
IMR	infant mortality rate
IPCC	Intergovernmental Panel on Climate Change
IPV	inactivated poliovirus vaccine
IQ	intelligence quotient
IRF	International Road Federation
IRS	indoor residual spraying
ISPCAN	International Society for the Prevention of Child Abuse and Neglect
ISPTID	International Society for the Prevention of Tobacco Induced Diseases
ITN	insecticide-treated nets
JI	joint implementation

LDL	low-density lipoproteins
LL	lepromatous leprosy
MB	multibacillary leprosy
MDG	Millennium Development Goals
MDR-TB	multidrug-resistant tuberculosis
MDT	multidrug therapy
MMR	maternal mortality rate (ratio)
MMR	measles, mumps, and rubella vaccine
MNT	maternal and neonatal tetanus
MONICA	Multinational Monitoring of Trends and Determinants in Cardiovascular Disease
MPS	Making Pregnancy Safer
NAFDAC	National Agency for Food and Drug Administration and Control
NCA	Noise Control Act
NCCP	National Center for Children in Poverty
NGO	nongovernmental organization
NHANES	National Health and Nutrition Examination Survey
NIMH	National Institute of Mental Health
NMR	neonatal mortality rate
NPT	Nuclear Non-Proliferation Treaty
NSWP	Network of Sex Work Projects
NWS	nuclear-weapons state
OCD	obsessive-compulsive disorder
OECD	Organization for Economic Cooperation and Development
ONAC	Office of Noise Abatement and Control
OPCW	Organization for the Prohibition of Chemical Weapons
OPV	oral polio vaccine
OR	odds ratio
ORS	oral rehydration solution or salts
ORT	oral rehydration therapy
P	prevalence rate
PAP	Papanicolaou test (for screening of cervical cancer)
PB	paucibacillary leprosy
PEM	protein-energy malnutrition
PEN-3	person, extended family, neighborhood; perceptions, enablers, nurturers; positive, exotic, negative

PMR	perinatal mortality rate
PNMR	postneonatal mortality rate
POP	persistent organic pollutant
PRC	People's Republic of China
PRECEDE–PROCEED	predisposing, reinforcing, and enabling constructs in educational/environmental diagnosis and evaluation–policy, regulatory, and organizational constructs in educational and environmental development
PSA	prostate specific antigen
PTSD	post-traumatic stress disorder
QALY	quality-adjusted life year
RF	rheumatic fever
RHD	rheumatic heart disease
RT-PCR	reverse transcription polymerase chain reaction
RUTF	ready-to-use therapeutic food
SAMHSA	Substance Abuse and Mental Health Services Administration
SARS	severe acute respiratory syndrome
SARS-CoV	severe acute respiratory syndrome–associated coronavirus
SCHIP	State Children's Health Insurance Program
SCNT	somatic cell nuclear transfer
SEARO	South-East Asia Regional Office (of the World Health Organization)
SHS	secondhand smoke
SIA	supplementary immunization activities
SMHAI	Suicide and Mental Health Association International
SOC	stages of change model
STD	sexually transmitted diseases
STI	sexually transmitted infections
T_3	triiodothyronine
T_4	thyroxine
TB	tuberculosis
TFR	total fertility rate
TIA	transient ischemic attack
TPB	theory of planned behavior
TRA	theory of reasoned action
TT	tuberculoid leprosy
TTM	transtheoretical model

UN	United Nations
UNCED	United Nations Conference on Environment and Development
UNDP	United Nations Development Program
UNESCO	United Nations Educational, Scientific, and Cultural Organization
UNEP	United Nations Environment Program
UNFCCC	United Nations Framework Convention on Climate Change
UNFPA	United Nations Population Fund
UNHCR	United Nations High Commission for Refugees
UNICEF	United Nations Children's Fund
UNODA	United Nations Office for Disarmament Affairs
URI	upper respiratory infection
USAID	United States Agency for International Development
USA PATRIOT Act	Uniting and Strengthening America by Providing Appropriate Tools Required to Intercept and Obstruct Terrorism Act
USI	universal salt iodization
UV	ultraviolet radiation
WFMH	World Federation for Mental Health
WFP	World Food Program
WHO	World Health Organization
WMO	World Meteorological Organization
YLD	years lived with disability

Introduction and Historical Perspectives

AFTER READING THIS CHAPTER YOU SHOULD BE ABLE TO

- Define health, international health, and global health
- Differentiate between medicine and public health
- Describe common issues in international health
- Explain the salient contributions to international health from the ancient civilizations of India, Mesopotamia, Egypt, China, Greece, Rome, Mexico, and Central and South America
- Discuss the development of international health in the Middle Ages, Renaissance, early modern times in Europe, Industrial Revolution, and modern times
- Summarize the contribution of salient international organizations in the field of health

HEALTH

Before trying to understand international health, let us first begin by understanding what **health** means. *Health* is a very old term. In old English it was used as *haelen* (to heal), and in middle English as *helthe*, meaning to be sound in body, mind, or spirit. The word was related to the practice of medicine. In ancient Greek civilization the definition of medicine was to "prolong life and prevent disease," or, in other words, to keep people healthy (Cook, 2004). Similarly, medicine in ancient India was called **Ayurveda**, or the science of life or health. By the 17th century, the word *restoration* began to be used in most medical textbooks. By the end of the 19th century the word *health* was considered colloquial and was replaced with the word *hygiene*, which was considered more scientific (Cook, 2004).

After World War II, interest in the word *health* resurfaced with the formation of the World Health Organization (WHO), a global entity. Around the same time, the Hygienic Laboratory in the United States was renamed the National Institutes of Health. In 1948, the World Health Organization defined health in its constitution as "a state of complete physical, mental, and social well being and not merely the absence of disease or infirmity" (WHO, 1974). However, this definition of health has received much criticism over the years.

First, the use of the word *state* in this definition is misleading. Health is dynamic and changes from time to time. For example, a person may be healthy in the morning; in the afternoon, he or she develops a headache and is thus not in the "state" of health; in the evening, he or she may recover from the headache, thereby attaining the "state" of health again.

Second, the dimensions as mentioned in the definition are inadequate to capture variations in health. One such dimension is the political dimension. Do the rich get sick more often or is it the poor? Who controls greater resources for health? Which section of the population has a greater burden of mortality? All these and many more such questions pertain to the politics behind health. This dimension must be explicitly mentioned in the definition for it to be meaningfully complete. Another dimension that is not mentioned in the definition of health is the spiritual dimension (Perrin & McDermott, 1997). Bensley (1991) has identified six different perspectives related to the spiritual dimension of health, namely, sense of fulfillment, values and beliefs of community and self, wholeness in life, well-being, God or a controlling power, and human-spiritual interaction. These perspectives are not mentioned in WHO's original definition.

Third, the word *well-being* is very subjective in its connotation. A definition must be objective, and subjectivity must be minimized. Fourth, the way health is defined makes it very difficult to measure. McDowell and Newell (1987) point out that "just as language molds the way we think, our health measurements influence (and are influenced by) the way we define and think about health" (p. 14); in other words, health and measurement are inextricably linked. Fifth, the way health is defined presents an idealistic or utopian view. It would be impossible to find someone who embodies all the attributes presented in the definition. Thus, the definition of health needs to be more realistic. Sixth, health is presented as an end product in the definition, whereas most people perceive health as a means for achieving something that they value more. For example, a person may want to be healthy so that he or she can raise a family. Finally, the WHO definition of health is written from an individualistic perspective in which health is defined for one person. It lacks the community orientation that is needed for something that is as complex as health.

Since the original WHO definition was published, it has been further modified in subsequent discussions at the world level. In November 1986, the first International Conference on Health Promotion was held in Ottawa, Canada (WHO, 1986). The conference culminated with the drafting of the Ottawa Charter for Health Promotion, wherein health was defined in a broader perspective:

> [H]ealth has been considered less as an abstract state and more as a means to an end which can be expressed in functional terms as a resource which permits people to lead an individually, socially, and economically productive life. Health is a resource for everyday life, not the object of living. It is a positive concept emphasizing social and personal resources as well as physical capabilities.

PUBLIC HEALTH AND MEDICINE

Building further on the concept of health in order to appreciate international health, we have to understand the terms **public health** and **medical model**, two concepts that have shaped international health. Winslow (1920), a professor at Yale University, defined public health as:

> the science and art of preventing diseases, prolonging life, and promoting physical health and efficiency through organized community efforts for the sanitation of the environment, the control of communicable infections, the education of the individual in personal hygiene, the organization of medical and nursing services for the early diagnosis and preventive treatment of disease, and the development of social machinery, which will ensure to every individual a standard of living adequate for the maintenance of health; organizing these benefits in such a fashion as to enable every citizen to realize his birthright of health and longevity.

This definition makes it clear that public health deals with disease prevention and health promotion. It is also evident that an organized community effort is used as a fundamental approach in public health. Public health is also a profession and discipline. The ultimate aim of public health is to ensure social justice.

Medicine, on the other hand, is about diagnosing and treating diseases. Merriam-Webster's online dictionary defines medicine as "the science and art dealing with the maintenance of health and the prevention, alleviation, or cure of disease." The approach of medicine is different from that used in public health. In medicine the emphasis is on an individual patient, and the doctor is concerned with diagnosing and treating his or her illness; in public health, the emphasis is on populations.

In the medical model, the patient is usually absolved of personal responsibility and is prescribed an external agent, such as a drug, to rid himself or herself of the ailment. In public health, however, personal responsibility is greater and the person has to mobilize social and political forces in dealing with the problem. In the medical model, the focus is on the curative dimension, whereas in public health, the focus is on preventive approaches. The main work in medicine is that of the diagnosis and treatment of illnesses, whereas public health is more concerned with reducing risk factors for physical diseases as well as mental and social problems. In medicine the benefit to the individual is supreme, whereas in public health the philosophy of the greatest good for the greatest number holds. The medical model is very expensive—the cost for saving a single individual can go into millions of dollars—whereas the public health model is very inexpensive when one computes cost per person. The medical model is highly technocentric, whereas the public health model usually relies on people and indigenous technologies. The medical model creates dependency, whereas the public health model is liberating.

Philosophically, the medical model seeks to maximize the chance that the best possible outcome will occur, whereas the public health model seeks to minimize the chance that the worst possible outcome will occur. In medicine, the inputs of the basic sciences are narrow and focused, whereas in public health basic science inputs are broader. The medical sector is highly commercialized compared with the public health sector. Finally, whereas in medicine the primary goal is to rid a person of his or her suffering, in public health the goal is to ensure social justice. **Table 1.1** summarizes these differences between the public health model and the medical mode.

INTERNATIONAL HEALTH AND GLOBAL HEALTH

The terms *international health* and *global health* are often used interchangeably, although there are subtle differences between them. These terms have been defined in several ways in literature, and there is no consensus on their definition. Paul Basch (1999) has defined international health as "a systematic comparison of the factors that affect the health of all human populations." International public health has been defined as "the

TABLE 1.1	Differences Between the Medical Model and the Public Health Model	
Medical Model	**Public Health Model**
Emphasis on the individual	Emphasis on the population
No or minimum personal responsibility	The person is responsible for organizing and influencing societal and political forces
Focus on curative dimension	Focus on preventive dimension
Diagnosis and treatment of syndromes and diseases afflicting the physical condition of an individual (although extensions are made to mental and social problems)	Reduction of risk factors for physical diseases as well as mental and social problems
Benefit to the individual is supreme	Greatest good to the greatest number
Expensive	Inexpensive, especially in terms of investment per person
Highly technocentric	Relies on people and indigenous technologies
Creates dependency	Liberating
Seeks to maximize the chance that the best possible outcome will occur	Seeks to minimize the chance that the worst possible outcome will occur
Basic science inputs are narrow and focused	Basic science inputs are broader
High commercialization	Low commercialization
Ultimate goal: Rid a person from suffering	Ultimate goal: Social justice

application of principles of public health to health problems and challenges that affect low and middle income countries and to the complex array of global and local forces that influence them" (Merson, Black, & Mills, 2006, p. xiv). We define **international health** as the science and art of examining health problems in multiple countries, primarily those that are developing, and finding population-based solutions to their problems.

A related term is **global health**. The Institute of Medicine (1997) has defined global health as "health problems, issues, and concerns that transcend national boundaries, may be influenced by circumstances or experiences in other countries, and are best addressed by cooperative actions and solutions" (p. 11). The health problems addressed in global health are often outbreaks of communicable diseases, maternal and child health problems, population issues, natural disasters, war, environmental health issues, and other large-scale afflictions. These problems are very similar to those encountered in international health and, therefore, these two terms are often used interchangeably. In our opinion, however, there is a subtle difference between international health and global health, and the term *global health* should be used only when *all* countries are involved both in the problems and the solutions. Therefore, we define global health as the study of health problems and solutions affecting all people of the world.

ISSUES IN INTERNATIONAL HEALTH

This book is primarily concerned with issues confronting international health. Some of the questions that a student of international health needs to be able to address are as follows:

- What are some common international organizations? What role do these international organizations play in maintaining health around the world?
- How are various aspects of international health measured? What are the health indicators in international health?
- What is the role of culture in shaping health? How do behaviors influence health?
- What communicable diseases affect people of the world? Do developing countries have a greater burden of communicable diseases or do developed nations?
- What are lifestyle risk factors, and which noncommunicable diseases affect the people of the world?
- How does malnutrition affect the countries of the world? What are some specific micronutrient deficiencies and their distribution around the world?
- How does environment affect health? Is population explosion a problem in the world, and what are some measures being taken in this regard? How do air pollution and water pollution affect health for people around the world?
- What are some key concerns for women's health around the world?
- What are the determinants of children's health in different countries? How do infant mortality rates vary from country to country?
- What are the variations in mental health systems around the world?
- How do the health systems in developed and developing countries vary?
- What is the effect of globalization on health? What are some emerging diseases and what is their impact on human health around the world?
- How does poverty affect health? What are the threats of biological terrorism and warfare?

MEDICINE AND PUBLIC HEALTH THROUGHOUT HISTORY

The Indus Valley Civilization and the History of India

Modern humans evolved in Africa and have lived on our planet for about 150,000 years (Misra, 2001). The time during which there were no written records is called the **prehistoric period**. Humans learned writing only 5,000 years ago, at which point the **historic period** began. The prehistoric period is divided into three ages: the Stone, Bronze, and Iron Ages. The Stone Age, in which technology was based primarily on stone, is divided further into three periods: the Paleolithic, Mesolithic, and Neolithic. In the Neolithic period, humans started agriculture and animal husbandry. These developments led to urbanization; the first such urbanization is known as the Indus Valley or Harappan civilization, which flourished from 3500 to 1500 BCE. It was located around the Indus and Ghaggar-Hakra rivers in what is now northwestern India and Pakistan.

The Indus Valley civilization is among the three oldest civilizations of the world, the other two being Mesopotamia and Egypt. The economy of the Indus Valley civilization was based on wheat, barley, and millets. The Indus Valley civilization is known for its planned cities, which consisted of a citadel for the upper classes and a lower town for the common people. Both kiln- and sun-baked bricks were used in construction. The advanced architecture of the Indus Valley civilization is evidenced by dockyards, granaries, warehouses, brick platforms, and protective walls. From a sanitation perspective, it had an excellent drainage system consisting of both public and private drains (Marshall, 1931). There is evidence that municipal laws ensured the cleanliness of public areas and prohibited encroachment on them (Sharma, 1956). This civilization showed the first evidence of the practice of public health. Several factors led to the decline of this civilization, such as a shifting of the course of the river, a reduction in rainfall, foreign invasions, migration of the people, and environmental degradation (Misra, 2001).

This civilization in the Neolithic and Bronze Age paved the way for the Iron Age Vedic civilization (2000–600 BCE). The period is characterized by the development of *Vedas*, or the scriptures of teachings. Initially the Vedas were transmitted orally from one generation to another. They were eventually written in Sanskrit and primarily consist of four collections: the *Rig-Veda*, the *Sama-Veda*, the *Yajur-Veda*, and the *Atharva-Veda* (Hines, 1999). Collectively, these are referred to as the *Samhitas*.

It is believed that the system of Ayurveda, or the science of life or health, also originated during this time from the *Atharva-Veda* (Park & Park, 1986; Subbarayappa, 2001). Both the *Rig-Veda* and *Atharva-Veda* allude to the fact that diseases are caused by congenital factors (*ksetriya*), infection, seasonal change, or minute organisms or insects (*krmi*) residing in the body (Subbarayappa, 2001). The *Atharva-Veda* describes surgical operations to remove arrows. Ayurveda had eight branches: *Kay-acikitsa* (internal medicine), *Salya tantra* (surgery), *Salakya tantra* (ophthalmology and otolaryngology), *Kaumara brhtya* (pediatrics, obstetrics, and gynecology), *Agada tantra* (toxicology), *Rasayana* (geriatrics and nutrition), *Vajikarana* (sexology), and *Bhuta Vidya* (psychiatry and demonology) (Subbarayappa, 2001). Two classic texts of Ayurveda are the *Charaka* and *Susruta Samhita*. Ayurveda believes in *Pancha Bhutas*, or the five elements: space, air, fire, water and earth. A hallmark of Ayurveda is the **tridosha theory of disease**. The *doshas*, or humors, are *vata* (wind), *pitta* (gall), and *kapha* (mucus). Diseases were explained as disturbances in these three humors.

The system of **yoga** also originated during this time. The word *yoga* is derived from the Sanskrit word meaning "union." It is an ancient system of physical and psychic practice to maintain balance. In a more modern context, yoga has been defined as "a systematic practice and implementation of mind and body in the living process of human beings to keep harmony within self, within society, and with nature" (Maharishi, 1992, 1998). The first written records of this methodology appeared around 200 BCE in the *Yogasutra* of Patanjali (Singh, 1983). The system consisted of the eightfold path, or *Asthangayoga*. The eight conventional steps of *Asthangayoga* consist of *Yama* (rules for living in society), *Niyama* (self-restraining rules), *Asaana* (low physical impact postures), *Pranayama* (breathing techniques), *Pratihara* (detachment of the mind from senses), *Dharana* (concentration), *Dhyana* (meditation), and *Samadhi* (complete union with superconsciousness) (Romas & Sharma, 2010). The techniques of yoga are perhaps the most remarkable contributions of this era in the field of health.

> *One not knowing a land asks of one who knows it, he goes forward instructed by the knowing one. Such, indeed, is the blessing of instruction, one finds a path that leads him straight onward.*
>
> —*Rig Veda* 10.32.7

Ancient Civilization in Mesopotamia

The civilization in Mesopotamia (*meso* meaning "middle" and *potamia* meaning "river," implying a land between two rivers) flourished between the rivers Euphrates and Tigris in the period 6000 BCE to 400 BCE through the Neolithic Age to the Iron Age. It was located in the region where present-day Iraq is located, called the "cradle of civilization." The people who started the civilization were called Sumerians. They developed a system of cuneiform writing on wet clay tablets. Several medical texts, known as treatises, were written on these tables. Many of these were found in the library of the King of Assyria, Assurbanipal. When his palace was burnt by invaders, the clay tablets were baked and thus preserved. The longest treatise is known as the "Treatise of Medical Diagnosis and Prognoses" (Wolf, 1999). This text consists of 40 tablets studied by the French scholar Labat. The diagnostic treatise is arranged from head to toe and includes subsections on convulsive disorders, gynecology, and pediatrics. During that period it was believed that many illnesses were caused by ghosts, and magico-medical treatments were used to treat such illnesses (Scurlock, 2006). Ceremonial acts such as tying knots and wearing amulets were used as part of treatment (Bock, 2003). No treatises on surgery have been found, but it is believed that surgery was also practiced (Adamson, 1991). The art of bandaging was introduced in this civilization, as was the collection of medical treatises.

One of the great kings of Babylon was Hammurabi (1810–1750 BCE), who is well known for developing a set of laws called *Hammurabi's code*, or **Codex Hammurabi**. The code contained more than two hundred laws. Some of the laws governed the conduct of physicians and ensured that they got paid, the first example of the codification of medical practice. Spiegel and Springer (1997) draw a parallel between Codex Hammurabi and the managed care of present times. They argue that Codex Hammurabi, similar to present-day managed care, established a schedule of sliding fees for services and advocated the use of outcome measurements and, in the event they were not met, meted out severe penalties. The code required medical records to document diseases and therapies and included prescription benefits. It fully explained patients' rights. The model of managed care in those days was authoritarian, unlike present times, but there were definitive legal actions to ensure justice for everyone in the kingdom. Thus, Codex Hammurabi can be considered as a precursor of present-day managed care.

Ancient Civilization in Egypt

The civilization in Egypt developed in northeastern Africa around the river Nile in the period from 3000 BCE to 300 BCE. The civilization is known for its pyramids and sphinxes. A great deal is known about this culture because they invented picture writing and recorded it on papyrus. The main sources for studying Egyptian civilization have been surviving papyri, which have been translated into modern languages.

The **Edwin Smith papyrus**, dating back to around 1700 BCE, was discovered in 1862 outside of Luxor, Egypt (Stiefel, 2006). It is believed to be a copy of an original written in 3000 BCE. It is considered to be the oldest known surgical text in the history of civilization. This papyrus is divided into 48 cases, arranged by anatomic region, that primarily describe several traumatic injuries and their management. The unique feature of the text is that it describes the art of patient examination based on signs and symptoms and using logic and deductive reasoning.

Another papyrus is the **Kahun papyrus**, which dates back to about 1900 BCE and deals primarily with gynecological matters (Okasha, 2001). It talks about hysteria as a displacement of the uterus. It also talks about suggestion being an important part of all forms of treatment. One of the psychotherapeutic methods used in Ancient Egypt was "incubation," or "temple sleep," in which patients were placed in a deep sleep with the help of drugs such as opium. The originator of these forms of remedies seems to be Imhotep, physician of the pharaoh Zoser.

The **Ebers papyrus** was purchased in 1872 by the Egyptologist George Ebers, after whom it is named, and is believed to have originated in 1550 BCE. It is 110 pages long and is the lengthiest surviving medical papyrus. It has more than 800 paragraphs, each of which deals with a different medical ailment and its management.

In the area of public health, Egyptians built planned cities and public baths, had a system of collecting rain water, and built underground drains (Green & Ottoson, 1999; Park & Park, 1986). They also had knowledge of mosquito nets for the prevention of mosquito bites. Herodotus, a Greek historian, visited Egypt in the fifth century BCE and commented on the hygienic practices of Egyptians. He found Egyptians to be fond of cleanliness, taking frequent baths and using earth closets for human wastes (De Selincourt, 1962).

Ancient Civilization in China

China is one of the world's oldest continuous civilizations, dating back more than 6,000 years. There is evidence from inscriptions on tortoise shells that people dug wells for drinking water during the Xia (21st century BCE) and Shang (11th century BCE) dynasties (Green & Ottoson, 1999). Around the 14th or 13th century BCE, during the Shang dynasty, it was believed that ailments were caused by the curses of dead ancestors, and methods of healing such as prayers, offerings, and incantations were performed (Subbarayappa, 2001).

An emperor physician, Huang Di, or the Yellow Emperor of China (2695–2589 BCE) is credited with initiating systematic Chinese medicine (Cheng, 2001). Huang Di emphasized the importance of the principles of *yang* and *yin* everywhere in creation. *Yang* is the masculine principle, and *yin* the feminine principle. Balance between these two signifies good health. *Yang* and *yin* generate five phases: water, fire, earth, wood, and metal. Chinese herbal therapy was based on these five phases. Huang Di also supported the use of acupuncture in Chinese medicine, which arose around 2600 BCE (Cheng, 2001). He emphasized prevention of diseases, saying, "The superior doctor prevents diseases; the mediocre doctor attends to impending diseases; the inferior doctor treats full blown diseases." Another concept of Chinese medicine is that of *qi*, which is the basis of activities of body and mind and is the primordial entity of both material (body) and nonmaterial (mind) things, gross and subtle (Subbarayappa, 2001).

Lao Tse, or Lao Tzu (which literally means Old Master), who lived around the 6th century BCE, developed the philosophy of **Taoism** (Khoo, 1998). His teachings disseminated the philosophy of the *Tao* (or the Way), which refers to a reality that naturally exists from primordial time and gives rise to all other things. *Tao* can be found by experiencing oneness in all things. Taoists introduced the idea of healing by drugs and used alchemy. Another well-known Chinese philosopher who influenced Chinese medicine and public health is Confucius (541–479 BCE). His philosophy emphasized correctness of social relationships along with personal and governmental morality. Regarding traditional and modern treatments, Confucius said: "Because the new methods of treatment are good, it does not follow that the old ones were bad; for if our honorable and worshipful ancestors had not recovered from their ailments, you and I would not be here today" (Huth & Murray, 2000).

> *By nature the men are alike. Through practice they have become far apart.*
>
> —Confucius (541–479 BCE)

Greek Civilization

In early Greek civilization, Apollo, the Sun God, was considered to be the protector from epidemics such as plague. In Greek mythology, Aesculapius was the son of Apollo (Schmidt, 2007). He was raised by Charion, who taught him the art of healing. Aesculapius had two daughters: Hygiea, who was worshipped as the goddess of health, and Panacea, who was worshipped as the goddess of medicine. Thus we see an early dichotomy between prevention and cure in Greek thought. Around 776 BCE, the Olympic Games were founded; they initiated a movement toward good physique and physical fitness that had an influence on healthy living (Porter, 1997).

It is believed that the roots of medicine the way it is practiced today can be traced back to the 5th century BCE, when Hippocrates introduced a rational way of treating diseases (Cilliers & Retief, 2006). Hippocrates, often called the Father of Medicine, wrote a body of writings known as the **Corpus Hippocraticum**, a compilation of around 70 books. Classical Greek medicine involved four humors (blood, phlegm, black bile, and yellow bile), four elements (earth, air, fire, and water), and four qualities (hot, cold, moist, and dry). Any imbalance in these caused disease. The system was rational because it was devoid of superstition and religion and was based on experimentation.

> *Make a habit of two things: to help; or at least to do no harm.*
>
> —Hippocrates (460–357 BCE)

Also, the training of a physician was done by apprenticeship under another physician. Another important feature of Greek civilization was the development of an ethical code of conduct for physicians. The Hippocratic Oath is still used today in many parts of the world by physicians. Most physicians in Greek civilization were men (*iatroi*), but there were also women doctors (*iatrinai*).

Plato, a Greek philosopher, showed that medicine and philosophy were inextricably linked (Stempsey, 2001). He advocated holistic medicine, in which cure of the body alone without cure of the soul is not a whole cure. Holistic health involves uniting both body and soul; thus, along with medical technology, philosophy is needed for complete healing to take place. He also emphasized the role of personal responsibility in maintaining health and favored prevention rather than cure.

The urban sewerage and storm water drainage systems in ancient Greece during the Minoan period (second millennium BCE) were quite advanced (Angelakis, Koutsoyiannis, & Tchobanoglous, 2005)—comparable to modern urban water systems developed in Europe and North America during the second half of the 19th century CE. These advanced systems were exported to all parts of the Greek civilization in the Mycenaean, Archaic, Classical, and Hellenistic periods.

Roman Civilization

In earlier times, medicine in Roman civilization was based on folk remedies, herbs, religious influences, and superstition. Around the fourth century BCE, Greek medicine started entering Rome (Cilliers & Retief, 2006). In order to practice medicine in the Roman Empire, physicians only needed permission from a magistrate. Julius Caesar exempted physicians from paying tax and gave them citizenship. This practice was upheld by subsequent emperors such as Augustus, Vespasian, and Hadrian. The introduction of Greek practices also systematized medicine, including the process of childbirth. Use of rational, scientific techniques by midwives improved outcomes for both mothers and children (Todman, 2007). Galen (130–205 CE) was a well-known physician and medical teacher of the Roman civilization who contributed to the advancement of techniques in medicine. His approach was more analytic than the Hippocratic approach (Park & Park, 1986). He is the author of more than 500 treatises, which were considered authoritative during his time.

The great contribution of the Roman Empire was in the area of public health. The empire constructed the massive Cloaca Maxima in the sixth century BCE, which drained the marshes of central Rome and later served as a sewer (Cilliers & Retief, 2006). The Romans also had an elaborate system of aqueducts for water, which supplied about 50 gallons (189 liters) of water per person per day (Major, 1954).

Another development in the Roman Empire was that of an efficient health care system for the military. A team of physicians (*milites medici*), who were mostly Greek, accompanied the army. Soldiers were also given first aid training. Dioscorides, an army surgeon, wrote a pharmacopeia, *Materia Medica*, in 77 CE.

In 166 CE a plague broke out in Roman Empire that was one of the reasons for its downfall (Fears, 2004). The pandemic devastated the entire Roman Empire, extending from its eastern frontiers in Iraq to its western frontiers on the Rhine River and Gaul.

Middle Ages

European history is divided into three time periods: the classical civilization of antiquity, which covers the Greek and Roman civilizations; the **Middle Ages** (between 500 CE and 1500 CE); and modern times. During the Middle Ages there was very little progress in medicine and public health; it is, therefore, also known as the Dark Ages. During this period the influence of the Church and associated dogma increased in the lives of common people. Great expenditures were made on Crusades, or Holy Wars. The average life expectancy was a mere 31 years (Glasscheib, 1964). During these times the role of women as healers was challenged (Minkowski, 1992). They were excluded from admission to universities and professional schools of medicine. In addition, the Church branded women healers as witches, and many women healers were persecuted.

While Europe was passing through the Dark Ages, the Arabs, borrowing from the Greeks and Romans, developed their own medical system, known as the **Unani system**. Unani medicine is still practiced widely in the south and southeast parts of Turkey to Saudi Arabia and in other parts of Asia, such as India and Pakistan (Yesilada, 2005). The Unani system utilizes herbs and folk remedies and is also influenced by Ayurveda (Subbarayappa, 2001). Abu Bakr Muhmad Ibn Zakariya al-Razi (also known as Rhazes) (865–925 CE) wrote the book *Kitab al-hawi fi al-tibb*, also known as *Liber continens*, which became a standard reference medical compendium (Browne, 1921). The book contained the first accurate account of smallpox. Another well-known physician of those times was Abu Ali al-Husayn ibn Abd Allah ibn Sina (980–1037 CE), who is also known as Avicenna in the West. He wrote the book *Kitab al-Qanun fi al-tibb*, or *Canon of Medicine* (Shah, 1966). According to the Unani system, the human body and health were made up of seven components: elements (*Al-Arkan*), temperament (*Al-Mizaj*), four humors (*Al-Akhlat*), organs (*Al-A'da*), vital spirit (*Al-Arwah*), faculties (*Al-Quwa*), and functions (*Al-Afal*). The four elements were earth, fire, water, and air, and the four humors were blood, bile, phlegm, and black bile. Prevention and self health care were important components of this system.

Mayans, Incas, and Aztecs

Some of the civilizations of ancient peoples in the Americas have included those of the Mayans, Incas, and Aztecs. The Mayan civilization spanned five modern-day countries: Belize, El Salvador, Guatemala, Honduras, and Mexico. It is believed that the Mayans migrated from the north to the highlands of present-day Guatemala around 4000 BCE (Herrera, Rojas, & Terreros, 2007). Their civilization was village based and primarily agricultural. The culture of the Mayans originated from the earlier Olmec civilization, which flourished in the southern portion of North America. It is known that the civilization dug fresh water wells and used limestone in construction. They were well known for their advanced calendars and their knowledge of astronomy. Mayans also developed an elaborate system of herbal drugs based on having access to the world's third richest area in terms of diversity of plants (Borchardt, 2004). Recent studies have shown some of the plants used by Mayans to be helpful for gastrointestinal ailments, dermatologic conditions, and diabetes (Ankli et al., 2002). Some of the remedies developed by the Mayan civilization are still being used by modern practitioners (Blanchard & Bean, 2001).

The Inca civilization originated around the 13th century in modern-day Peru and spread to Ecuador, western and south-central Bolivia, northwest Argentina, north and north-central Chile, and southern Colombia. Medicine was well developed in the Inca Empire (Burneo, 2003). There is an account that melancholy was present in the family of the emperor (Elferink, 1999), which was treated with a combination of magic and empirical medicinal products composed of botanical compounds and minerals. Epidemics of smallpox, typhus, influenza, measles, and diphtheria between 1546 and 1618 were important pestilences that were a contributory factor in the decline of this civilization.

The Aztecs were an ethnic group that existed from the 14th through 16th century in Mexico. Aztec medicine, called *ticiotl*, used plants and herbs in the treatment of diseases (Pena, 1999). The Aztec doctors (*titicih*) knew about several diseases and dealt with the treatment of wounds and fractures methodically. Their system was different from that used in the Greek and Roman cultures. The public health system in Aztec society was well developed. Harvey (1981), in his paper on public health in Aztec society, notes that the cities in Mexico were beautiful and orderly and that Aztecs disdained noxious odors. Clay conduits were used to transport drinking water. In the houses of the nobility, water was stored in ponds, and *ajolotes* (a type of salamander) were kept in the water to keep it clean. Disposal of the dead was done by cremation.

Renaissance and Early Modern Times in Europe

The Middle Ages in Europe gave way to a cultural movement called the Renaissance (1420–1630), in which a revival of science, art, and culture occurred. This period dovetailed with the period from the 15th to 18th century that is also referred to as early modern times. During this time, Paracelsus (1493–1541), a Swiss-born physician who was known as the Luther of Medicine, publicly burned the work of Avicenna and tried to restore rational research to medicine (Debus, 1998). The Italian physician Hieronymus Fracastorius (1478–1553), who was also a poet, astronomer, and geologist, proposed the **theory of contagion** in his book *De Contagione* almost 300 years before the experimental development of the germ theory by Robert Koch. He proposed that the transfer of infection in epidemics occurred via minute imperceptible particles (Wright, 1930).

Andreas Vasalius (1514–1564) conducted several dissections of the human body and corrected the earlier notions of Hippocrates and Galen. Another well-known English physician during these times was Thomas Sydenham (1624–1689), who wrote the book *Medical Observations Concerning the History and Cure of Acute Diseases*, published in 1666 (Sydenham, 1666/1979). He is known as the English Hippocrates, or the Father of English Medicine (Low, 1999).

Anton van Leeuwenhoek (1632–1723), a Dutch city hall janitor, developed a microscope and saw bacteria in his dental scrapings (Shklar, 1998). However, he was never able to associate bacteria with disease. Edward Jenner (1749–1823), a British physician, developed the smallpox vaccine in 1796 (Stewart & Devlin, 2006). He took matter from pustules on the arm of a milkmaid who had developed cow pox and vaccinated that on a young boy. Later he demonstrated that the boy was immune when inoculated with smallpox. This marked the era of prevention of diseases by vaccination, a specific form of disease protection.

European Colonial Expansion

From 1600 to 1800, the Europeans (British, Dutch, French, Portuguese, and Spanish) colonized North America, Australia, Africa, Asia, and South America. The health of the people in the colonies was rather poor and epidemics were rampant. Action was taken only during epidemics and was in the form of isolation and quarantine (Green & Ottoson, 1999). The general tendency of the colonizers was to impoverish the natives and downplay their culture and medical systems.

Slavery was also at an all-time high during this period. The slave trade was very profitable for those who were involved in it, including Queen Elizabeth I of England (Basch, 1999). Slaves were primarily taken from Africa to America. Several diseases moved along with the slave trade from one continent to another. For example, treponemal disease (comprising syphilis, yaws, and bejel) originated in East Africa and was later transmitted to England (Rothschild, 2005). However, some diseases that required special animal hosts could not be transmitted, such as schistosomiasis, or flatworm disease. Urinary schistosomiasis is caused by *Schistosoma haematobium*, which was introduced in the Americas but could not get established for want of a suitable snail host (Basch, 1999).

The Industrial Revolution

The Industrial Revolution occurred in the late eighteenth and nineteenth centuries in Europe and North America. Industrialization in its early years led to poverty and disease among the masses. Working and living conditions for workers were poor, and sanitation was a problem. In 1832 there was a great cholera epidemic, which was investigated by a lawyer and "freelance civil servant," Edwin Chadwick (1800–1890). In 1838 to 1839, consumption (what is now known as tuberculosis) caused the deaths of 60,000 people in England and Wales (Brown, 2006). Fevers such as typhus and typhoid were endemic in most industrial towns and cities, and there were epidemics of influenza in 1837 and typhoid in 1838.

Edwin Chadwick was asked to carry out an investigation into sanitation, and in 1842 he published *The Sanitary Conditions of the Laboring Population*, a report in which he argued for improvement in sanitation. It is interesting to note that, fueled by this report, the first public health legislation in Britain was not for better wages or social welfare, but for sewerage (Brown, 2006). This was the Public Health Act of 1848 (Hamlin & Sheard, 1998). This act was developed well before the discoveries in bacteriology and pathology, but it was quite comprehensive (Calman, 1998). It covered poverty, housing, sewerage, water, safety, environment, and food. It had a strong component of local involvement and identified responsible people and penalties. What it did not cover was air quality and rural health. The act set out central and local boards of health with superintending inspectors and officers of health. These were linked to the Treasury for funds.

Another well-known public health physician during those times was John Snow (1813–1858), who studied the spread of cholera in London between 1848 and 1854 and led to its prevention. His contribution is summarized in Focus Feature 1.1. The Central Board of Health that was established in the Public Health Act of 1848 lasted until 1854 (Southgate, n.d.). The local boards wanted more power and that power was shifted to them by the Public Health Act of 1875. The 1875 act also gave additional tasks to local governments, such as construction and maintenance of parks, public houses, and special hospital isolation units for patients suffering from infectious diseases such as smallpox.

FOCUS FEATURE 1.1   John Snow and His Work with Cholera

John Snow (1813–1858) was the first of nine children in a farmer family in York, England (Lee, 1898). He was interested in medicine and apprenticed under William Hardcastle, a surgeon living at Newcastle-on-Tyne. He was admitted as a member of the Royal College of Surgeons of England in 1838 and a licentiate of the Royal College of Physicians in 1850. He was also an anesthesiologist and designed a chloroform inhaler. He administered chloroform to Queen Victoria during the birth of two of her children.

During his times the miasma theory (or spontaneous generation theory), which stated that diseases were caused by organisms that arose spontaneously from bad air, swamps, and putrid matter, was the common way of thinking. The greatness of Snow's work was that he was able to apply epidemiologic methods to discern the germ origin of cholera without knowing that *Vibrio cholerae* was the causative agent of cholera.

In 1854 an epidemic of cholera occurred in London, centered in the area of Broad Street, Golden Square, Soho Square, and adjoining streets in London. In between Golden Square and Soho Square was the Broad Street pump. John Snow began mapping the deaths resulting from cholera and was able to find that most had occurred near the Broad Street pump. He was thus able to link cholera to the drinking water supplied from the Broad Street pump. When he removed the handle of the pump, the number of cases of cholera dramatically declined. This example illustrates one of the first applications of epidemiology and its impact on preventing the spread of disease.

In North America, Lemuel Shattuck (1793–1859), a lay health professional working for the Massachusetts Sanitary Commission, issued the *Report of a General Plan for the Promotion of Public and Personal Health* in 1850 (Lemuel Shattuck, 1959). This report, influenced by Chadwick's report, recommended the development of a state health department and local health boards in each town. The report recommended a decennial census; uniform nomenclature of disease and death; and data collection by age, gender, race, occupation, economic status, and locality. In addition sanitary inspections were to be conducted. Control of food and drugs, research on tuberculosis, immigrant health, supervision of mental diseases, control of alcoholism, control of smoke nuisances, construction of public baths and wash houses, the teaching of preventive medicine in schools, and other issues were presented in the report. Although Shattuck died within nine years of writing this report, some of the changes he recommended have shaped public health in the United States and have come to fruition in the present.

Modern Times

Bacteriologic Revolution

Modern times start with the late 19th century, when the bacteriologic revolution took place. In 1860 Louis Pasteur (1822–1895), a French chemist, provided evidence for the **germ theory of disease**, which stated that microorganisms were responsible for some diseases. Pasteur demonstrated that microorganisms were present in the air, but were not created by the air, an idea at immediate odds with the then-popular notion of spontaneous generation (Tan & Rogers, 2007). Pasteur is well known for the process of pasteurization, which entails boiling milk to prevent it from getting spoiled, and the discovery of vaccines for rabies and anthrax.

> *Where observation is concerned, chance favors only the prepared mind.*
>
> —Louis Pasteur, inaugural address to Lille Faculty of Science, December 7, 1854

Another well-known physician was Robert Koch (1843–1910), a German whose first contribution was detecting the etiology of anthrax in 1876 (Zetterstrom, 2006). In 1884 he discovered the etiology of cholera. He also discovered that pulmonary tuberculosis was caused by *Mycobacterium tuberculosis*, for which he was awarded the Nobel Prize in 1905. He is known for Koch's postulates, which state that in order to prove the causal relation between a microorganism and a disease, (1) the microorganism must be found in those suffering from the disease, (2) the microorganism must be isolated from the diseased organism and grown in pure culture, (3) the cultured microorganism must cause disease when introduced in a healthy organism, and (4) the microorganism must be reisolated from the inoculated host and must be identical to the original causative agent.

A British surgeon who contributed to the germ theory was Joseph Lister (1827–1912), who introduced the concept of antisepsis (Tan & Tasaki, 2007). He developed the use of phenol (carbolic acid) as an effective antiseptic. He would disinfect incisions with carbolic acid, as well as disinfecting the instruments and hands of the surgical team. He also pioneered the use of catgut suture in surgery, which is self-absorbed by the body.

The idea of collaboration between countries on matters of health originated during these times. The first International Sanitary Conference was convened in 1851 in Paris, with the participation of 11 European nations (Howard-Jones, 1974). The purpose of this conference was to institute some uniformity in quarantine measures, which varied from country to country. The conference lasted 6 months and prepared an international sanitary code with 137 articles. Unfortunately, this code never came into effect because it was ratified by only three countries. This conference was followed by a series of conferences, which were also not able to reach a consensus on quarantine measures. In 1874 a proposal was made to establish a permanent International Commission on Epidemics, but it did not materialize immediately (Basch, 1999). The idea finally became reality in 1903 with the formation of the International Sanitary Bureau within the countries of the western hemisphere (later renamed the Pan American Sanitary Bureau in 1923). This was the world's first international health agency.

Another organization was set up in Paris in 1907: L'Office Internationale d'Hygiene Publique (OIHP), also known as the "Paris Office." The Paris Office was responsible for the administration of the international sanitary conventions and for collection and dissemination of data of public health importance to member states. The office was dissolved in 1946, and its epidemiologic functions were transferred to the World Health Organization in 1947.

World War I

Between 1914 and 1918, the world experienced a major war, called World War I or the Great War. The war was fought mainly in Europe, but because European countries had colonies all over the world, a large part of the world was involved. One of the parties to the war was the Entente Powers, comprising the United Kingdom and its colonies, France and its colonies, and Russia, and later joined by Italy and the United States. The other party was the Central Powers, comprising Germany, Austria-Hungary, the Ottoman Empire, and Bulgaria. The Netherlands, Spain, Switzerland, and the Scandinavian nations remained neutral. It is believed that over 40 million people died as a direct result of the war. Besides the negative effects of war, some demographers have argued that the war led to a drastic improvement in the living standards of the civilian population in Britain and Europe that would not have occurred if peace had prevailed (Winter, 1976, 1977).

War-torn countries were affected by several epidemics. More people died of epidemics than as a direct result of war. One of the most devastating pandemics of influenza occurred in 1918 and 1919. It is believed that between 50 and 100 million people died in that pandemic worldwide (White & Pagano, 2008). Most of the deaths occurred as a result of superadded bacterial infections because antibiotics were not yet available (Brundage & Shanks, 2007).

The League of Nations was created after the war in 1919. The primary purpose of the League was to prevent war, settle disputes between countries through negotiation, and improve worldwide welfare. In 1922, the League of Nations Health Committee and Health Section were formed in Geneva despite opposition and boycott by the United States (WHO, n.d). The Health Section acted as a link between national health administrations and governments. It has been considered the most successful auxiliary of the League. In 1926 it started publication of the *Weekly Epidemiological Record*, which continues even to present times through the World Health Organization (Basch, 1999). It spread its activities all over the world. An Eastern Bureau of Epidemiological Information was set up in Singapore, a State Serum Institute was established in Copenhagen, and a National Institute for Medical Research was formed in London. Through these institutions vaccination programs for diphtheria, tetanus, and tuberculosis were launched all over the world.

World War I on the whole left most of Europe in turmoil. There was economic crisis, hyperinflation, and unemployment, which led to a major depression in the 1930s. Under such circumstances and with economic issues at the forefront, health issues were relegated to a much lower priority.

World War II

The League of Nations failed in its purpose to prevent wars; another major global conflict took place between 1939 and 1945, namely, World War II. The world was divided into two groups: Allied and Axis Powers. The United Kingdom and its colonies, the United States, and the Union of Soviet Socialist Republics were "The Big Three" of the Allied Powers; France and China were also part of the Allies. The three major Axis Powers were Nazi Germany, fascist Italy, and imperial Japan. Over 60 million people died in World War II, making it the deadliest war in human history (Dunnigan, 1996). More civilians died than soldiers. Civilian deaths occurred from explosions, firestorms, suffocation, vaporization, and starvation. The war's direct cost in monetary terms was $4 trillion (in terms of then-current dollars), making it the costliest war of all times (Richman, 1991). In terms of positive effects of the war, democracies were established in Germany, Italy, and Japan, and Nazi and fascist governments were removed. Another positive effect of the war was a rapid advancement in science and technology. Antibiotics were discovered during this period, which helped save millions of lives.

One of the after effects of the war was the formation of the United Nations. The name "United Nations" was coined in 1942 by U.S. President Franklin D. Roosevelt in a declaration wherein representatives of 26 nations pledged their governments to continue fighting together against the Axis Powers (United Nations, n.d.). After the war, representatives of 50 countries met at the United Nations Conference on International Organization in San Francisco to draw up the United Nations Charter. The United Nations officially came into existence on October 24, 1945, when the charter was ratified by China, France, the Soviet Union, the United Kingdom, the United States (the five nations with veto power), and a majority of other signatories.

Another postwar effect was the independence of European colonies, starting with India and Pakistan in 1947, Myanmar (Burma) and Sri Lanka in 1948, several African nations in the 1950s through 1970s, and finally Zimbabwe in 1980 and Namibia in 1990. All these newly independent nations became members of the United Nations.

The United Nations has developed many programs and organizations. We will turn to a discussion of some of these organizations along with other important international health organizations.

WORLD HEALTH ORGANIZATION

Within the United Nations, the World Health Organization (WHO) is the directing and coordinating authority for health. Its constitution came into effect on April 7, 1948, which is celebrated as World Health Day. Work on the constitution began in 1946 when the Economic and Social Council of the United Nations established a Technical Preparatory Committee of Experts (Grad, 2002). WHO subsumed the functions of the League of Nations Health Committee and Health Section and L'Office Internationale d'Hygiene Publique in Paris.

Agenda

WHO has a six-point agenda:

1. Promoting development by working with poor, disadvantaged, and vulnerable groups
2. Fostering health security by fighting against outbreaks of emerging and epidemic-prone diseases
3. Strengthening health systems by providing for trained staff, sufficient financing, suitable systems for collecting vital statistics, and access to appropriate technology, including essential drugs
4. Harnessing research, information, and evidence by setting priorities, defining strategies, and measuring results
5. Enhancing partnerships between UN agencies, other international organizations, donors, civil society, and the private sector
6. Improving performance in terms of efficiency and effectiveness, both at the international level and within countries

Structure

The headquarters of the World Health Organization are in Geneva, Switzerland, and there are six regional offices (**Table 1.2**).

TABLE 1.2   Regional Offices of the World Health Organization

Region	City	Web Site
WHO African Region	Brazzaville, Congo	www.afro.who.int/
WHO Region of the Americas/Pan American Health Organization	Washington, DC, USA	www.paho.org/
WHO Eastern Mediterranean Region	Cairo, Egypt	www.emro.who.int/index.asp
WHO European Region	Copenhagen, Denmark	www.euro.who.int/
WHO South-East Asia Region	New Delhi, India	www.who.int/about/regions/searo/en/index.html
WHO Western Pacific Region	Manila, Philippines	www.wpro.who.int/

Governance

The World Health Assembly, comprising 193 member states, is the supreme decision-making body of WHO. The World Health Assembly appoints the director-general who heads the organization. The assembly also oversees the financial policies of the organization, including approval of the budget, and directs the executive board to take up matters for action, study, or investigation. The executive board is composed of 34 members who are technically qualified in the field of health. The Secretariat of the World Health Organization is staffed by approximately 8000 health and other experts and support staff who are on fixed-term appointments. They are based at the headquarters, at the six regional offices, and in different countries. Membership in WHO is open to all countries that are members of the United Nations and accept the WHO constitution. The proposed program budget for 2008–2009 was $4.22 million (WHO, 2007).

Functions

The functions of WHO are described in Article 2 of its constitution:

(a) To act as the directing and coordinating authority on international health work
(b) To establish and maintain effective collaboration with the United Nations, specialized agencies, governmental health administrations, professional groups, and such other organizations as may be deemed appropriate

(c) To assist governments, upon request, in strengthening health services

(d) To furnish appropriate technical assistance and, in emergencies, necessary aid upon the request or acceptance of governments

(e) To provide or assist in providing, upon the request of the United Nations, health services and facilities to special groups, such as the peoples of trust territories

(f) To establish and maintain such administrative and technical services as may be required, including epidemiological and statistical services

(g) To stimulate and advance work to eradicate epidemic, endemic, and other diseases

(h) To promote, in co-operation with other specialized agencies where necessary, the prevention of accidental injuries

(i) To promote, in co-operation with other specialized agencies where necessary, the improvement of nutrition, housing, sanitation, recreation, economic or working conditions, and other aspects of environmental hygiene

(j) To promote co-operation among scientific and professional groups that contribute to the advancement of health

(k) To propose conventions, agreements and regulations, and make recommendations with respect to international health matters, and to perform such duties as may be assigned thereby by the organization and are consistent with its objective

(l) To promote maternal and child health and welfare, and to foster the ability to live harmoniously in a changing total environment

(m) To foster activities in the field of mental health, especially those affecting the harmony of human relations

(n) To promote and conduct research in the field of health

(o) To promote improved standards of teaching and training in the health, medical, and related professions

(p) To study and report on, in co-operation with other specialized agencies where necessary, administrative and social techniques affecting public health and medical care from preventive and curative points of view, including hospital services and social security

(q) To provide information, counsel, and assistance in the field of health

(r) To assist in developing an informed public opinion among all peoples on matters of health

(s) To establish and revise, as necessary, international nomenclatures of diseases, of causes of death, and of public health practices

(t) To standardize diagnostic procedures as necessary

(u) To develop, establish, and promote international standards with respect to food, biological, pharmaceutical and similar products

(v) Generally, to take all necessary action to attain the objective of the organization

TABLE 1.3 Focus of World Health Reports, 1995–2008	
Year	**Focus**
1995	Bridging gaps between rich and poor and between those with and without access to health care around the world
1996	Strategies for combating infectious diseases
1997	Strategies for combating noncommunicable diseases
1998	Examination of trends over the past five decades and projection of how life would be until 2025
1999	Achievements of the 20th century and the problems that would be carried over in the 21st century
2000	Examination and comparison of health systems around the world
2001	Strategies for dealing with mental health
2002	Reducing risks and promoting healthy life
2003	Examination of the global health situation and the major threats to health in the world
2004	HIV/AIDS and its comprehensive strategy, involving prevention, treatment, care, and long-term support
2005	Maternal and child health
2006	Assessment of the health care workforce around the world
2007	Threats to public health security all over the world
2008	Individual health security and the role of primary health care and humanitarian action

Source: World Health Organization, http://www.who.int/whr/previous/en/index.html

World Health Reports

Every year WHO publishes a World Health Report. **Table 1.3** summarizes the focus of these reports from 1995 to 2008.

OTHER HEALTH-RELATED UNITED NATIONS AGENCIES

UNICEF

After World War II, children in Europe faced famine and disease. To provide food, clothing, and health care to them, the United Nations created the United Nations

FOCUS FEATURE 1.2   Primary Health Care

In 1978, the World Health Organization organized an international conference on **primary health care** in Alma Ata, in what was then the Soviet Union. The end result of the conference was the Declaration of Alma Ata (WHO, 1978). The declaration had ten clauses. The first clause affirmed that health was the right of all citizens of the world. The second clause declared that inequity existed between developed and developing countries in health status and that it was unacceptable. The third clause identified social and economic development as central to bridging the gap between developed and developing nations. The fourth clause affirmed individual and collective responsibility in planning and implementing health care. The fifth clause identified governmental responsibility and the role of primary health care.

The sixth clause defined primary health care as "essential health care based on practical, scientifically sound and socially acceptable methods and technology made universally accessible to individuals and families in the community through their full participation and at a cost that the community and country can afford to maintain at every stage of their development in the spirit of self reliance and self-determination." The seventh clause defined the attributes of primary health care as follows: (1) being based on social, biomedical, and health services research; (2) providing promotive, preventive, curative, and rehabilitative services; (3) including education about health problems, promotion of food supply and proper nutrition, adequate supply of safe water and basic sanitation, maternal and child health, family planning, immunizations, prevention of locally endemic diseases, appropriate treatment of common diseases and injuries, and provision of essential drugs; (4) being multisectoral, involving agriculture, animal husbandry, education, food, industry, housing, public works, communication, and so on; (5) involving individual and community participation; (6) having effective referral systems; and (7) utilizing a health team of physicians, nurses, auxiliaries, community workers, and midwives.

The eighth clause asked governments to formulate national policies to build an infrastructure for primary health care. The ninth clause asked for mutual cooperation between nations. The final clause urged the devotion of more resources for the health sector, with transference from current military spending.

Since the Declaration of Alma Ata many developing nations have embraced this philosophy and have made strides in improving the health of their citizens. The Declaration of Alma Ata wanted this to be a reality for all by 2000. However, that has not happened.

International Children's Emergency Fund (UNICEF) in December 1946. In 1953, when the program's emergency functions were over, the General Assembly extended its mandate indefinitely and renamed it the United Nations Children's Fund while retaining its acronym. In 1965 it was given the Nobel Peace Prize. The chief activities of UNICEF pertain to child survival and development; basic education and gender equality; HIV/AIDS and children (prevention of pediatric HIV/AIDS and care of orphaned children); child protection from violence, exploitation, and abuse; and policy advocacy and partnerships.

United Nations Development Program

The United Nations Development Program (UNDP) is responsible for a development-related network. It has offices in 166 countries, where it aims at building local capacity. It helps countries attract and use aid effectively. It is working toward achievement of the Millennium Development Goals by 2015: eradication of extreme poverty and hunger; achievement of universal primary education; promotion of gender equality and empowerment of women; reduction of childhood mortality; improvement in maternal health; combating HIV/AIDS, malaria, and other diseases; ensuring environmental sustainability; and developing a global partnership for development. The headquarter of UNDP is in New York, and it has liaison offices in Geneva (Switzerland), Brussels (Belgium), Copenhagen (Denmark), Tokyo (Japan), and Washington, DC (United States).

United Nations Population Fund

The United Nations Fund for Population Activities (UNFPA) began in 1969 as part of the UNDP and gradually became a separate entity. In 1987 its name was changed to the United Nations Population Fund, but its original acronym was retained. Its mission is to "promote the right of every woman, man and child to enjoy a life of health and equal opportunity. UNFPA supports countries in using population data for policies and programmes to reduce poverty and to ensure that every pregnancy is wanted, every birth is safe, every young person is free of HIV/AIDS, and every girl and woman is treated with dignity and respect" (United Nations Population Fund, n.d.).

Food and Agriculture Organization

The Food and Agriculture Organization (FAO) was formed in 1945 and has its headquarters in Rome. The FAO's mandate is "to raise levels of nutrition, improve agricultural productivity, better the lives of rural populations and contribute to the growth of the world economy" (FAO, n.d.). The FAO provides assistance such as the introduction of simple, sustainable tools and techniques to increase crop production in communities, relief in times of drought, and other such measures geared toward ensuring food security for all people of the world. The FAO budget for the biennium 2008–2009 was $929.8 million.

World Food Program

The World Food Program (WFP) is the United Nations' specialized agency with a mission to combat global hunger. According to some estimates, the problem of hunger affects one of every seven people in the world. The WFP was initially started as a 3-year experimental program in 1961 by the FAO, but has continued since then. It deals with both emergency relief and development efforts. In 2006, the WFP fed 87.8 million people in 78 countries.

United Nations Environment Program

The United Nations Environment Program (UNEP) is the United Nations agency for addressing environmental issues at the global and regional level. Its headquarters are in Nairobi, Kenya. The mission of UNEP is "to provide leadership and encourage partnership in caring for the environment by inspiring, informing, and enabling nations and peoples to improve their quality of life without compromising that of future generations" (UNEP, n.d.). The UNEP Governing Council has 58 members, who are elected by the UN General Assembly for 4 years. Some of the activities of UNEP include the following: evaluating global, regional and national environmental conditions; establishing international agreements and national environmental measures; consolidating institutions for the effective management of the environment; strengthening economic development and environmental protection; fostering transfer of knowledge and technology for sustainable development; and building new partnerships within society and the private sector.

United Nations High Commission for Refugees

The United Nations High Commission for Refugees (UNHCR) was established on December 14, 1950, by the United Nations General Assembly. Its mission is to lead and coordinate international action to protect refugees and resolve refugee problems all over the world. Its fundamental purpose is to safeguard the rights and well-being of refugees.

International Labor Organization

The International Labor Organization (ILO) was originally established in 1919 and then became the first specialized UN agency in 1946. The ILO's main aims are "to promote rights at work, encourage decent employment opportunities, enhance social protection and strengthen dialogue in handling work-related issues" (ILO, n.d.). ILO's activities are categorized under four objectives: (1) to promote and realize standards and fundamental principles and rights at work, (2) to create greater opportunities for women and men to secure decent employment and income, (3) to enhance the coverage and effectiveness of social protection for all, and (4) to strengthen cooperation and social dialogue.

United Nations Educational, Scientific, and Cultural Organization

The United Nations Educational, Scientific and Cultural Organization (UNESCO) was established on November 16, 1945. In the field of education, it promotes basic education for all, secondary education (including technical and vocational education), and higher education. In the field of natural sciences, it develops programs to assess and manage the Earth's resources and builds the capacities of developing countries in the sciences, engineering, and technology. In the field of social and human sciences, it helps to understand and interpret the social, cultural, and economic environment. In the field of culture, it helps in preserving and respecting the specificity of each culture. In the field of communication and information, it promotes sharing of knowledge and incorporating all the sociocultural and ethical dimensions of sustainable development.

ADDITIONAL HEALTH-RELATED INTERNATIONAL ORGANIZATIONS

Rockefeller Foundation

The Rockefeller Foundation was created in 1913 by John D. Rockefeller Sr. to promote the well-being of people around the world. In the early years it was mainly active in the area of public health and medical education. The foundation gives grants for projects that primarily focus on poor and vulnerable sections of the world. The major areas where the foundation has funded projects include global health, innovation for development, agricultural productivity, economic resilience, and urban life. It has assets of over $3.5 billion, making it a very powerful organization.

Ford Foundation

The Ford Foundation was created in 1936 through an initial gift of $25,000 from Edsel Ford, son of Henry Ford, the founder of the Ford Motor Company. The mission of the Ford Foundation is fourfold: (1) to strengthen democratic values, (2) to reduce poverty and injustice, (3) to promote international cooperation, and (4) to advance human achievement. The Ford Foundation supports programs in asset building and community development, peace and social justice, and knowledge, creativity, and

freedom. It has funded projects in arts and culture, civil society, community development, development finance and economic security, education and scholarship, environment and development, governance, HIV/AIDS, human rights, media, religion,
society and culture, sexuality and reproductive health, and workforce development.

CARE

CARE was created in 1946 as the Cooperative of American Remittances to Europe
for the purpose of sending food from American donors to war-distressed Europe. Today the acronym stands for Cooperative for Assistance and Relief Everywhere, Inc.
The present mission of this organization is to serve individuals and communities
struggling with poverty. The organization has a five-pronged strategy comprising the
following: (1) capacity building for self-help, (2) provision of economic opportunity,
(3) providing relief in emergencies, (4) influencing policy decisions at all levels, and
(5) eliminating discrimination at all levels. It has projects in 69 countries around the
world. CARE USA's budget in 2006 was more than $589 million.

International Red Cross

The International Red Cross is one of the world's largest humanitarian organizations
and has national offices in 186 countries. It includes the Geneva-based International
Committee of the Red Cross (ICRC) and the International Federation of Red Cross
and Red Crescent Societies (the International Federation). The mission of the International Committee of the Red Cross is "to protect the lives and dignity of victims of
war and internal violence and to provide them with assistance" (ICRC, n.d.). The
origin of this organization dates back to the Battle of Solferino in 1859, when a Swiss
businessman, Henry Dunant, was appalled by the suffering of injured soldiers on
both sides; he helped the soldiers and conceived the idea of the organization.

United States Agency for International Development

In 1961, the United States Agency for International Development (USAID) was created by President John F. Kennedy to provide economic development and humanitarian assistance programs all over the world in support of the foreign policy goals of the
United States. It is free from political and military functions; its purpose is mainly to
help developing countries. Its headquarters are in Washington, DC, but there are several field offices around the world. USAID works in agriculture, democracy and governance, economic growth, the environment, education, health, global partnerships, and

humanitarian assistance in more than 100 countries. Within the health field, USAID projects have been in the areas of environmental health, family planning, health systems, HIV/AIDS, infectious diseases, maternal and child health, and nutrition.

SKILL-BUILDING ACTIVITY

What kinds of careers are available in international health? To get a glimpse, visit the following sites:

- World Health Organization employment site (http://www.who.int/employment/en/)
- USAID careers site (http://www.usaid.gov/careers/)
- UNICEF careers site (http://www.unicef.org/about/employ/index.html)
- Peace Corps volunteers (http://www.peacecorps.gov/index.cfm)

What kinds of jobs interested you? Which country would you like to work for? Did any jobs look like dream jobs for you? What kinds of skill sets were required for those jobs? How can you shape your education to be able to fulfill those skill sets? Were there any internship or volunteer opportunities that appealed to you that will help you prepare for future jobs?

SUMMARY

Health can be defined as a means to achieve desirable goals in life while maintaining a multidimensional (physical, mental, social, political, economic, and spiritual) equilibrium that is operationalized for individuals as well as for communities. Medicine and public health are two disciplines that have shaped international health. Public health deals with disease prevention and health promotion through organized community effort, whereas medicine is about diagnosing and treating diseases. *International health* is defined as the science and art of examining health problems in multiple countries, primarily those that are developing, and finding population-based solutions to their problems. *Global health* is the study of health problems and solutions affecting all people of the world.

Among the oldest civilizations in the world are the Indus Valley civilization (3500–1500 BCE) and the Vedic civilization (2000–600 BCE) in India, which have given Ayurveda and yoga to the world. The ancient civilization in Mesopotamia (6000–400 BCE) is known for the Codex Hammurabi, the first set of written laws, including rules for health care. Ancient civilization in Egypt (3000–300 BCE) is known for medical texts on papyrus and for advancements in water and sanitation. Ancient civilization in China is credited with developing the Chinese system of medicine based on *qi, yang,* and *yin.*

Medicine the way it is practiced today can trace its roots to the fifth century BCE, when Hippocrates introduced a rational way of treating diseases. Galen (130–205 CE) was a well-known physician and medical teacher of the Roman civilization who contributed to the advancement of techniques in medicine. During the Middle Ages (500–1500 CE), the Arabs originated a system of medicine called the *Unani system* and had physicians such as Rhazes (865–925 CE) and Avicenna (980–1037 CE). Mayans, Incas, and Aztecs in Central and South America also had well-developed systems of medicine and public health. The Middle Ages in Europe paved the way for a cultural movement called the Renaissance (1420–1630), in which a revival of science, art, and culture occurred.

In 1842 Edwin Chadwick published a report on the sanitary conditions of the laboring population in Britain that led to the first public health legislation, the Public Health Act of 1848. John Snow in 1854 linked cholera to contaminated water, which led to prevention of the disease's transmission. Around the same time, Lemuel Shattuck wrote a public health report in Massachusetts, United States. In the late 19th century a bacteriologic revolution took place.

The period after World War I was marked by establishment of the League of Nations, the first entity designed for the collective action of nations. The period after World War II led to formation of the United Nations and the World Health Organization, along with several United Nations agencies related to health. Other international agencies working in the health sector include the Rockefeller Foundation, Ford Foundation, CARE, the International Red Cross, and USAID.

IMPORTANT TERMS

Ayurveda	prehistoric period
Codex Hammurabi	primary health care
Corpus Hippocraticum	public health
Ebers papyrus	*qi*
Edwin Smith papyrus	Taoism
germ theory of disease	theory of contagion
global health	*ticiotl*
health	*tridosha* theory of disease
historic period	*Unani* system
international health	*yang*
Kahun papyrus	*yin*
medical model	yoga
Middle Ages	

REVIEW QUESTIONS

1. Define international health. Differentiate it from global health.
2. Differentiate between medicine and public health.
3. Describe common issues in international health.
4. Discuss the contributions of the ancient civilizations of India to international health.
5. Explain the contributions of Greco-Roman civilization to international health.
6. Compare and contrast the Arabian *Unani* system of medicine with the Aztec *ticiotl* system.
7. Explicate the contributions of Edwin Chadwick and Lemuel Shattuck in their respective countries.
8. Summarize the key functions of the World Health Organization.

WEB SITES TO EXPLORE

Ancient Indus Civilization

http://www.harappa.com/har/har0.html

This Web site contains 1144 illustrated pages by leading scholars of ancient India and Pakistan and the ancient Indus Valley civilization. It has slides of recent excavations of these sites and provides a glimpse into the culture. *Explore this Web site and comment on public health structures found in the pictures from this Web site.*

John Snow

http://www.ph.ucla.edu/epi/snow.html

This Web site was developed by the Department of Epidemiology at the University of California, Los Angeles, in honor of John Snow (1813–1858). It has animated slide shows about the life and contributions of John Snow. Very detailed accounts can be obtained at this Web site. *Explore this Web site and watch and listen to the slide shows about John Snow. What did you learn?*

Rockefeller Foundation

http://www.rockfound.org/

The home page provides information about the Rockefeller Foundation's activities and news. From the home page one can link up to initiatives, other efforts, grants and ideas, and a library. Accounts about various initiatives of the foundation can be found, which make interesting reading. *Explore this Web site. In the Grants section, make a search for grants given out by the foundation on a topic of interest to you.*

UNICEF

http://www.unicef.org/

The official Web site of UNICEF provides information by country. It also has tabs about what UNICEF is, why it does what it does, people associated with UNICEF, voices of youth, its AIDS campaign, the Annual Report on the State of the World's Children, a press center, videos, and a newsletter sign-up. *Explore this Web site and read the most recent report on the state of the world's children. What were the salient points in this report?*

USAID

http://www.usaid.gov/

This Web site contains links explaining the kind and location of projects and activities done by USAID, as well as its policy, public affairs, business, and careers. *Visit this Web site and focus on careers. Did you find a career that interests you?*

World Health Organization

http://www.who.int/en/

The World Health Organization (WHO) was established in 1948 as a specialized United Nations Agency for health. The Web site contains information about WHO, its member countries, its publications, data and statistics, and programs and projects. The Web site also has links to information about international travel and the annual World Health Report. *Explore this Web site and read the latest World Health Report. What were the salient points in this report?*

REFERENCES

Adamson, P. B. (1991). Surgery in ancient Mesopotamia. *Medical History, 35*(4), 428–435.

Angelakis, A. N., Koutsoyiannis, D., & Tchobanoglous, G. (2005). Urban wastewater and stormwater technologies in ancient Greece. *Water Research, 39*(1), 210–220.

Ankli, A., Heinrich, M., Bork, P., Wolfram, L., Bauerfeind, P., Brun, R., et al. (2002). Yucatec Mayan medicinal plants: Evaluation based on indigenous uses. *Journal of Ethnopharmacology, 79*(1), 43–52.

Basch, P. F. (1999). *Textbook of international health* (2nd ed.). New York: Oxford University Press.

Bensley, R. J. (1991). Defining spiritual health: A review of the literature. *Journal of Health Education, 22*(5), 287–290.

Blanchard, D. S., & Bean, A. (2001). Healing practices of the people of Belize. *Holistic Nursing Practice, 15*(2), 70–78.

Bock, B. (2003). "When you perform the ritual of 'rubbing'": On medicine and magic in ancient Mesopotamia. *Journal of Near Eastern Studies, 62*(1), 1–16.

Borchardt, J. K. (2004). Medicine of the Maya Ameridians. *Drug News Perspectives, 17*(5), 347–351.

Brown, M. (2006). Making sense of modernity's maladies: Health and disease in the Industrial Revolution. *Endeavour, 30*(3), 108–112.

Browne, E. G. (1921). *Arabian medicine.* London: Cambridge University Press.

Brundage, J. F., & Shanks, G. D. (2007). What really happened during the 1918 influenza pandemic? The importance of bacterial secondary infections. *Journal of Infectious Diseases, 196*(11), 1717–1718.

Burneo, J. G. (2003). Sonko-Nanay and epilepsy among the Incas. *Epilepsy & Behavior, 4*(2), 181–184.

Calman, K. (1998). The 1848 Public Health Act and its relevance to improving public health in England now. *British Medical Journal, 317*(7158), 596–598.

Cheng, T. O. (2001). Hippocrates, cardiology, Confucius and the Yellow Emperor. *International Journal of Cardiology, 81*(2–3), 219–233.

Cilliers, L., & Retief, F. P. (2006). Medical practice in Graeco-roman antiquity. *Curationis, 29*(2), 34–40.

Cook, H. (2004). Historical keywords: Health. *Lancet, 364,* 1481.

Debus, A. G. (1998). *Paracelsus and the medical revolution of the renaissance: A 500th anniversary celebration.* Bethesda, MD: U.S. National Library of Medicine. Retrieved from http://www.nlm.nih.gov/exhibition/paracelsus/paracelsus_2.html

De Selincourt, A. (1962). *The world of Herodotus.* Boston: Little Brown and Company.

Dunnigan, J. F. (1996). *Dirty little secrets of World War II: Military information no one told you.* New York: Harper Paperbacks.

Elferink, J. G. (1999). Mental disorder among the Incas in ancient Peru. *History of Psychiatry, 10*(39 Pt. 3), 303–318.

Fears, J. R. (2004). The plague under Marcus Aurelius and the decline and fall of the Roman Empire. *Infectious Disease Clinics of North America, 18*(1), 65–77.

Glasscheib, H. S. (1964). *The march of medicine: The emergence and triumph of modern medicine.* New York: G. P. Putnam's Sons.

Grad, F. P. (2002). The preamble of the constitution of the World Health Organization. *Bulletin of the World Health Organization, 80*(12), 981–984.

Green, L. W., & Ottoson, J. M. (1999). *Community and population health* (8th ed.). Boston: McGraw Hill.

Food and Agriculture Organization of the United Nations. (n.d.). Mission, constitution and governance. Retrieved from http://www.fao.org/about/mission-gov/en/

Hamlin, C., & Sheard, S. (1998). Revolutions in public health: 1848, and 1998? *British Medical Journal, 317*(7158), 587–591.

Harvey, H. R. (1981). Public health in Aztec society. *Bulletin of the New York Academy of Medicine, 57*(2), 157–165.

Herrera, R. J., Rojas, D. P., & Terreros, M. C. (2007). Polymorphic Alu insertions among Mayan populations. *Journal of Human Genetics, 52*(2), 129–142.

Hines, R. (1999). Ancient Indian religion: The Vedas. Retrieved from http://www.wsu.edu/~dee/ANCINDIA/VEDAS.HTM

Howard-Jones, N. (1974). The scientific background of the International Sanitary Conferences, 1851–1938. *WHO Chronicle, 28*(Pt. 1), 159–171.

Huth, E. J., & Murray, T. J. (2000). *Medicine in quotations: Views of health and diseases through the ages* (p. 359). Philadelphia: American College of Physicians.

Institute of Medicine. (1997). *America's vital interest in global health: Protecting our people, enhancing our economy, and advancing our international interests.* Washington, DC: National Academy Press. Retrieved from http://books.nap.edu/openbook.php?record_id=5717&page=11

International Committee of the Red Cross. (n.d.). The mission. Retrieved from http://www.icrc.org/

International Labor Organization. (n.d.). About the ILO. Retrieved from http://www.ilo.org/global/About_the_ILO/lang—en/index.htm

Khoo, K. K. (1998). The Tao and the Logos: Lao Tzu and the Gospel of John. *International Review of Mission, 87*(344), 77–84.

Lee, S. (Ed.). (1898). *Dictionary of national biography*, Vol. 53. London: Smith, Elder, & Co.

Lemuel Shattuck (1793–1859): Prophet of American public health. (1959). *American Journal of Public Health and Nations Health, 49*(5), 676–677.

Low, G. (1999). Thomas Sydenham: The English Hippocrates. *Australian and New Zealand Journal of Surgery, 69*(4), 258–262.

Maharishi, Y. V. (1992). *Journey of consciousness* (pp. 2–50). New Delhi: Macmillan India Limited.

Maharishi, Y. V. (1998). *Logical solutions for the problems of humanity* (p. 4). Erode, India: Vethathiri Publications.

Major, R. H. (1954). *A history of medicine.* Springfield, IL: Charles Thomas Publishers.

Marshall, J. (1931). *Mohenjodaro and the Indus civilization* (3 vols.). London: Arthur Probsthain.

McDowell, I., & Newell, C. (1987). The theoretical and technical foundations of health measurement. In I. McDowell & C. Newell (Eds.), *Measuring health: A guide to rating scales and questionnaires* (pp. 10–42). New York: Oxford University Press.

Merson, M. H., Black, R. E., & Mills, A. J. (2006). Introduction. In M. H. Merson, R.E. Black, & A. J. Mills (Eds.), *International public health: Diseases, programs, systems, and policies* (2nd ed., pp. xiii–xxiv). Sudbury, MA: Jones and Bartlett Publishers.

Minkowski, W. L. (1992). Women healers of the middle ages: Selected aspects of their history. *American Journal of Public Health, 82*(2), 288–295.

Misra, V. N. (2001). Prehistoric human colonization of India. *Journal of Biosciences, 26*(4 Suppl.), 491–531.

Okasha, A. (2001). Egyptian contribution to the concept of mental health. *Eastern Mediterranean Health Journal, 7*(3), 377–380.

Park, J. E., & Park, K. (1986). *Textbook of preventive and social medicine* (11th ed.). Jabalpur, India: Banarasidas Bhanot Publishers.

Pena, J. C. (1999). Pre-Columbian medicine and the kidney. *American Journal of Nephrology, 19*(2), 148–154.

Perrin, K. M., & McDermott, R. J. (1997). The spiritual dimension of health: A review. *American Journal of Health Studies, 13*(2), 90–99.

Porter, R. (1997). *The greatest benefit to mankind.* London: Harper Collins Publishers.

Richman, S. (1991). The consequences of World War II. Retrieved from http://www.fff.org/freedom/1191c.asp

Romas, J. A., & Sharma, M. (2010). *Practical stress management: A comprehensive workbook for promoting health and managing change through stress reduction* (5th ed.). San Francisco, CA: Benjamin Cummings.

Rothschild, B. M. (2005). History of syphilis. *Clinical Infectious Diseases, 40*(10), 1454–1463.

Schmidt, N. (2007). Fifty years with Aesculapius. *Canadian Journal of Surgery, 50*(5), 347–348.

Scurlock, J. (2006). *Magico-medical means of treating ghost-induced illness in ancient Mesopotamia.* Leiden, The Netherlands: Brill Academic Publishers.

Shah, M. H. (1966). *The general principles of Avicenna's canon of medicine.* Karachi: Naveed Clinic.

Sharma, Y. D. (1956). Past patterns in living as unfolded by excavations at Rupar. *Lalit Kala, 1*(2), 121–129.

Shklar, G. (1998). Leeuwenhoek and Vermeer, an association of genius. *Journal of the History of Dentistry, 46*(2), 53–57.

Singh, K. (1983). *Religions of India* (pp. 76–78). New Delhi: Clarion Books.

Southgate, T. (n.d.). Public health in the 19th century. Why did central government accept increasing, but still limited, responsibility between 1800 and 1875? *Synthesis: A Journal by Du cercle de la rose noire.* Retrieved from: http://www.rosenoire.org/articles/hist22.php

Spiegel, A. D., & Springer, C. R. (1997). Babylonian medicine, managed care and Codex Hammurabi, circa 1700 B.C. *Journal of Community Health, 22*(1), 69–89.

Stempsey, W. E. (2001). Plato and holistic medicine. *Medicine, Health Care, and Philosophy, 4*(2), 201–209.

Stewart, A. J., & Devlin, P. M. (2006). The history of the smallpox vaccine. *Journal of Infection, 52*(5), 329–334.

Stiefel, M. (2006). The Edwin Smith papyrus: The birth of analytical thinking in medicine and otolaryngology. *The Laryngoscope, 116*(2), 182–188.

Subbarayappa, B. V. (2001). The roots of ancient medicine: An historical outline. *Journal of Biosciences, 26*(2), 135–143.

Sydenham, T. (1979). *Medical observations concerning the history and cure of acute diseases* (R. G. Latham, Trans.). Birmingham, AL: Classics of Medicine Library (Original work published 1666).

Tan, S. Y., & Rogers, L. (2007). Louis Pasteur (1822–1895): The germ theorist. *Singapore Medical Journal, 48*(1), 4–5.

Tan, S. Y., & Tasaki, A. (2007). Joseph Lister (1827–1912): Father of antisepsis. *Singapore Medical Journal, 48*(7), 605–606.

Todman, D. (2007). Childbirth in ancient Rome: From traditional folklore to obstetrics. *Australian & New Zealand Journal of Obstetrics & Gynaecology, 47*(2), 82–85.

United Nations. (n.d.). About the United Nations: History. Retrieved from http://www.un.org/aboutun/history.htm

United Nations Environment Program. (n.d.). About UNEP: The organization. Retrieved from http://www.unep.org/Documents/Multilingual/Default.asp?DocumentID=43

United Nations Population Fund. (n.d.). About UNFPA, the United Nations Population Fund. Retrieved from http://www.unfpa.org/about/index.htm

White, L. F., & Pagano, M. (2008). Transmissibility of the influenza virus in the 1918 pandemic. *PLoS ONE 3*(1), e1498. doi:10.1371/journal.pone.0001498

Winslow, C. E. A. (1920). The untilled fields of public health. *Modern Medicine, 2*(3), 183–191.

Winter, J. M. (1976). Some aspects of the demographic consequences of the First World War in Britain. *Population Studies, 30*(3), 539–552.

Winter, J. M. (1977). The impact of the First World War on civilian health in Britain. *The Economic History Review, 30,* 487–507.

Wolf, S. (1999). Early medicine in Mesopotamia. *Integrative Physiological and Behavioral Science, 34*(4), 217–218.

World Health Organization. (1974). Constitution of the World Health Organization. *Chronicle of the World Health Organization, 1,* 29–43.

World Health Organization. (1978). Declaration of Alma Ata. Retrieved from: http://www.who.int/hpr/NPH/docs/declaration_almaata.pdf

World Health Organization. (1986). *Ottawa charter for health promotion, 1986.* Geneva: Author.

World Health Organization. (2007). *Medium-term strategic plan 2008–2013 and proposed programme budget 2008–2009.* Geneva: Author.

World Health Organization. (n.d.). Archives of the League of Nations, health section files. Retrieved from http://www.who.int/archives/fonds_collections/bytitle/fonds_3/en/index.html

Wright, W. C. (1930). *Hieronymus Fracastorius. Contagion, contagious diseases, and their treatment.* New York: Putnam.

Yesilada, E. (2005). Past and future contributions to traditional medicine in the health care system of the Middle-East. *Journal of Ethnopharmacology, 100*(1–2), 135–137.

Zetterstrom, R. (2006). Robert Koch (1843–1910): Investigations and discoveries in relation to tuberculosis. *Acta Paediatrica, 95*(5), 514–516.

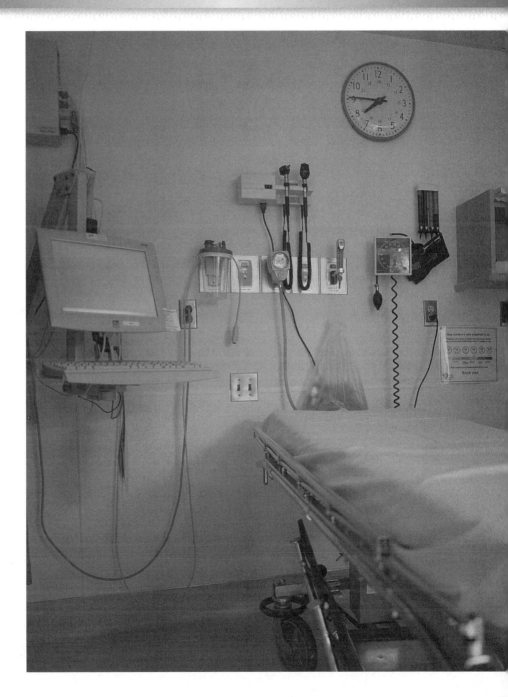

Health Indicators in International Health

AFTER READING THIS CHAPTER YOU SHOULD BE ABLE TO

- Differentiate between rates, ratios, and proportions
- Identify common indicators of mortality, morbidity, disability, fertility, and related health indicators
- Define descriptive and analytical epidemiology
- Explicate the criteria for cause-and-effect linkage

In international health we often make comparisons between different nations and different communities. In making such comparisons, we need indicators or markers that can discern changes from one place to another place and from one time to another time. The science that helps us with such comparisons is called **epidemiology**.

Epidemiology is the study of the distribution and determinants of health and health-related conditions and events in populations to prevent and control health problems (Last, 2000). There are two types: **descriptive epidemiology** deals with the time, place, and person distribution of health and health-related conditions and events; **analytical epidemiology** helps in identifying underlying causes of health and health-related conditions and events.

This chapter examines some of the indicators used in descriptive epidemiology to measure health, disease, and related dimensions. These indicators must be valid; that is, they must measure what they are purporting to measure. They should also be reliable or stable; that is, they should provide the same response each time. They should be objective; that is, the answer should be the same if measured by different people under similar circumstances. They should be specific, reflecting changes only in the situation concerned. Finally, these indicators should be sensitive; that is, they should be able to discern changes in environmental situations.

RATES, RATIOS AND PROPORTIONS

Three fundamental mathematical entities are needed to appreciate the various indicators used in international health and related fields. The first of these is a **rate**, which measures the occurrence of some particular event (development of disease, occurrence of birth, death, etc.) in a population during a given time period. It is a statement of the risk of developing a condition. The general mathematical formula by which a rate can be expressed is

$$[a/(a + b)t]c$$

where

a = number of persons experiencing a particular event during a given time period

$a + b$ = number of people who are at risk of experiencing the particular event during the same period

t = total time at risk

c = multiplier (usually 1,000 but can also be 100, 10,000, 100,000, etc., depending on how frequent the event is)

In a rate, time plays a very important role, and the quantity in the numerator is part of the denominator. Examples of rates are crude death rate and crude birth rate. Rates can be categorized as follows:

- *Crude rates*, which are based on actual observed data and are unadjusted, such as crude death rate

- *Specific rates*, which are based on actual observed data pertaining to a specific cause, such as death rate due to coronary heart disease
- *Adjusted rates* or *standardized rates*, which may use direct or indirect methods of adjustment to consider factors such as age, gender, social class, and so forth

The second mathematical entity of interest is a **ratio**, which is used to express a relation in size between two random quantities. It can be depicted by the expression

$$(a/d)c$$

where

a = number of persons experiencing a particular event during a given period

c = multiplier

d = number of persons experiencing some event different from event a but during the same period

It is important to note that the numerator and denominator are separate entities and that the numerator is not a part of the denominator, unlike rates. An example of a ratio used in international health is the sex ratio, which depicts the relative number of males to females in a given population.

The third entity is **proportion**, which depicts the relationship of a part to the whole. It is expressed as

$$[a/(a + b)]c$$

where

a = number of persons experiencing a particular event during a given period

$a + b$ = number of people who are at risk of experiencing the particular event during the same period

c = multiplier

In a proportion, the entity in the numerator is part of the denominator, but time is not involved. A proportion is usually expressed as a percentage, with the multiplier being 100. An example of a proportion is the proportion of children vaccinated with the DPT (diphtheria, pertussis, tetanus) vaccine in a community out of the total of children in that community.

MORTALITY INDICATORS

Information about mortality, or death, is routinely collected in all countries and provides readily available indicators of health (Lilienfeld & Stolley, 1994). To classify deaths, the International Classification of Diseases (ICD) is used. Currently, the

ICD-10, which came into use in 1994, is being used (World Health Organization [WHO], 2007). The cause of death is recorded on the International Death Certificate, which is routinely used to collect data.

Crude Death Rate

Crude death rate (CDR) is the most fundamental measure of mortality. It is calculated by taking the total number of deaths in a given calendar year and dividing that number by the midyear population of the community being studied. It is expressed per 1,000 population.

$$\text{Crude death rate (CDR)} = \frac{\text{No. of deaths in a given year}}{\text{Midyear population}} \times 1,000$$

Table 2.1 provides a comparison of crude death rates in selected countries. The table shows that this is not a very good measure for making comparisons between countries. For example, India, a developing country, has a crude death rate of 6.58 per 1,000 population, whereas the United States, a developed country, has a crude death rate of 8.26 per 1,000 population. This is because of the age structure in the two countries. If we adjusted for age, then the rates would be higher in India.

Crude death rate is the most fundamental measure of mortality, but it does not adjust for age, sex, and so forth.

Specific Death Rates

The crude death rate is affected by differences in age, sex, race, and so forth. Therefore, specific death rates are used. They may be cause specific, such as the number of deaths due to tuberculosis, or they may be group specific, such as the number of deaths in a certain age group. Examples of specific rates are as follows:

Specific death rate due to coronary heart disease

$$= \frac{\text{No. of deaths due to coronary heart disease in a given year}}{\text{Midyear population}} \times 1,000$$

Specific death rate in the age group 15 to 45 years $= \dfrac{\text{No. of deaths in the age group 15 to 45 years}}{\text{Midyear population}} \times 1,000$

TABLE 2.1   Comparison of Crude Death Rates in Selected Countries in 2007

Country	Crude Death Rate (deaths per 1,000 population)	Country	Crude Death Rate (deaths per 1,000 population)
Afghanistan	19.96	Haiti	10.40
Argentina	7.55	India	6.58
Australia	7.56	Iran	5.65
Austria	9.84	Iraq	5.26
Azerbaijan	8.35	Japan	8.98
Belgium	10.32	Kenya	10.95
Brazil	6.19	Libya	3.47
Bulgaria	14.28	Mexico	4.76
Cambodia	8.24	Moldova	10.85
Cameroon	12.66	Mongolia	6.21
China	7.00	Nigeria	16.68
Congo, Democratic Republic of the	10.34	Pakistan	8.00
		Peru	6.21
Congo, Republic of the	12.59	Philippines	5.36
Cuba	7.14	Russia	16.04
Denmark	10.30	Rwanda	14.91
Ecuador	4.21	Somalia	16.28
Egypt	5.11	United Kingdom	10.09
Ethiopia	14.67	United States	8.26
France	8.55	Zambia	21.46
Guinea-Bissau	16.29		

Source: Data compiled from Central Intelligence Agency. (2008). *The world fact book.* Retrieved from https://www.cia.gov/library/publications/the-world-factbook/geos/us.html

Infant Mortality Rate

Infant mortality refers to the death of an infant who is younger than 1 year. **Infant mortality rates (IMRs)** are calculated by dividing the total number of infant deaths in a given calendar year by the total number of live births in that same year. The results are shown per 1,000 live births:

$$\text{Infant mortality rate (IMR)} = \frac{\text{No. of deaths} < 12 \text{ months old}}{\text{No. of live births in that same year}} \times 1,000$$

Infant mortality rate is a useful index for comparing health status between and within countries. It is the single most sensitive index of health and standard of living. There has been a substantial decline in infant mortality rates over the last hundred years all over the world. Some of the reasons for this are improvements in the standards of living, better control of communicable diseases, better nutrition, better obstetric care, and the discovery of antibiotics and other drugs (Park & Park, 1986).

Table 2.2 provides a comparison of infant mortality rate in selected countries. It is evident from this table that there is a significant difference between the rates in developed nations such as Australia, which has a rate of 4.57 per 1,000 live births, and developing nations such as Zambia, which has a rate of 100.71 per 1,000 live births. The highest infant mortality rate is found in Angola, where it is 184.44 per 1,000 live births, and the lowest in Singapore, where it is 2.30 per 1,000 live births (Central Intelligence Agency, 2008). Most infant mortality in developing countries is due to pneumonia (Mulholland, 2007). Dehydration and diarrhea used to be the most common causes of infant mortality, but thanks to the worldwide campaign for oral rehydration solution (a mixture of water, salt, and sugar), their contribution to infant mortality has decreased; they are now in second position. Infant mortality rate is a useful and comparatively inexpensive indicator of population health (Reidpath & Allotey, 2003).

A study by Schell and colleagues (2007) assessed the strength of association between infant mortality rate and five major socioeconomic determinants (gross national income per capita, young female illiteracy, income equality using the Gini index, public spending on health, and poverty rate) in 152 countries. The results of the study showed that at the global level, gross national income per capita, young female illiteracy, and income equality predicted 92% of the variation in national infant mortality rates. Further, it was found that public spending on health and poverty rate after

TABLE 2.2   Comparison of Infant Mortality Rates in Selected Countries in 2007

Country	Infant Mortality Rate (deaths per 1,000 live births)	Country	Infant Mortality Rate (deaths per 1,000 live births)
Afghanistan	157.43	Haiti	63.83
Argentina	14.29	India	34.61
Australia	4.57	Iran	38.12
Austria	4.54	Iraq	47.04
Azerbaijan	58.31	Japan	2.80
Belgium	4.56	Kenya	57.44
Brazil	27.62	Libya	22.82
Bulgaria	19.16	Mexico	19.63
Cambodia	58.45	Moldova	13.88
Cameroon	65.84	Mongolia	42.65
China	22.12	Nigeria	95.52
Congo, Democratic Republic of the	65.52	Pakistan	68.84
		Peru	29.96
Congo, Republic of the	83.26	Philippines	22.12
Cuba	6.04	Russia	11.06
Denmark	4.45	Rwanda	85.27
Ecuador	22.10	Somalia	113.08
Egypt	29.5	United Kingdom	5.01
Ethiopia	91.92	United States	6.37
France	3.41	Zambia	100.71
Guinea-Bissau	103.5		

Source: Data compiled from Central Intelligence Agency. (2008). *The world fact book.* Retrieved from https://www.cia.gov/library/publications/the-world-factbook/geos/us.html

adjustment for confounders were nonsignificant variables. In stratified analyses, young female illiteracy was found to be the most important independent predictor for low-income countries—even more than gross national income per capita. Young female illiteracy was also an important predictor in middle-income countries. Along with young female literacy, income equality (Gini index) was also an

> *Infant mortality rate is a useful and comparatively inexpensive indicator of population health.*
>
> —Reidpath & Allotey (2003)

independent predictor of infant mortality in middle-income countries. In high-income countries, no significant associations between socioeconomic predictors and infant mortality rate were found. The study showed that the same policies cannot be applied in high-income and low-income nations. Efforts to raise gross national income per capita, young female literacy, and income equality would go a long way in reducing infant mortality in low-income countries.

Neonatal Mortality Rate

Neonatal mortality refers to the death of an infant between 0 and 28 days of age. Neonatal deaths can be further categorized as early neonatal deaths, which occur in the first 7 days, and late neonatal deaths, which occur from 7 days to 28 days. **Neonatal mortality rates (NMRs)** are calculated by dividing the neonatal deaths in a given calendar year by the total number of live births in that same year. The results are shown per 1,000 live births:

$$\text{Neonatal mortality rate (NMR)} = \frac{\text{No. of deaths at 0 to 28 days}}{\text{No. of live births in that same year}} \times 1,000$$

Neonatal mortality rate is considered a good indicator of both maternal and newborn health and care. Neonatal mortality rates are calculated from birth and death data obtained from either vital registration data or from household surveys. When neither survey nor vital registration data is available, the neonatal mortality rate can be estimated from the under-5 mortality using a regression adjusted for AIDS (WHO, n.d.-a).

Postneonatal Mortality Rate

Postneonatal mortality refers to the death of an infant between 28 days and 1 year of age. **Postneonatal mortality rates (PNMRs)** are calculated by dividing postneonatal deaths in a given calendar year by the total number of live births in that same year. The results are shown per 1,000 live births:

$$\text{Postneonatal mortality rate (PNMR)} = \frac{\text{No. of deaths between 28 days and 1 year old}}{\text{No. of live births in that same year}} \times 1{,}000$$

Perinatal Mortality Rate

Perinatal mortality refers to deaths that occur at greater than or equal to 28 weeks of gestation and 7 days of birth. **Perinatal mortality rates (PMRs)** are calculated by dividing perinatal deaths in a given calendar year by the total number of live births plus fetal deaths in that same year. The results are shown per 1,000 live births plus fetal deaths:

$$\text{Perinatal mortality rate (PMR)} = \frac{\text{No. of deaths at} \geq 28 \text{ wks gestation and 7 days of birth}}{\text{No. of live births} + \text{No. of fetal deaths}} \times 1{,}000$$

As an example, the PMR in 2003 for the United States was 6.74 per 1,000 live births and fetal deaths (Hamilton et al., 2007).

Fetal Mortality Rate

Fetal mortality refers to fetal deaths that occur at greater than or equal to 20 weeks of gestation. **Fetal mortality rates (FMRs)** are calculated by dividing fetal deaths in a given calendar year by the total number of live births plus fetal deaths in that same year. The results are shown per 1,000 live births plus fetal deaths:

$$\text{Fetal mortality rate (FMR)} = \frac{\text{No. of deaths at} \geq 20 \text{ wks gestation}}{\text{No. of live births} + \text{No. of fetal deaths}} \times 1{,}000$$

As an example, the FMR in the United States in 2003 was 6.23 per 1,000 live births plus fetal deaths (Hamilton et al., 2007).

Maternal Mortality Rate

Maternal mortality rate (MMR) is usually defined as the number of maternal deaths per 100,000 live births. In the ICD-10, *maternal death* is defined as "the death of a woman while pregnant or within 42 days of termination of pregnancy, irrespective of the duration and site of the pregnancy, from any cause related to or aggravated by the pregnancy or its management but not from accidental or incidental causes" (WHO, 2004a). In the ICD-10, unlike in previous editions, late maternal death has also been included, defined as "the death of a woman from direct or indirect obstetric causes more than 42 days but less than one year after termination of pregnancy" (WHO, 2004a).

$$\text{Maternal mortality rate (MMR)} = \frac{\text{No. of maternal deaths}}{\text{Total live births}} \times 100,000$$

Maternal mortality rate used to be denoted per 1,000 live births, but because of medical advancements maternal deaths are becoming rarer; therefore, it is now expressed per 100,000 live births. The number of live births used in the denominator is a proxy measure for the total population of pregnant women who may be at risk for a maternal death. By convention the measure is called a rate, but actually it is a ratio, so in the literature some authors refer it to as maternal mortality ratio. The maternal mortality rate is a good measure of the likelihood that a pregnant woman will die from maternal causes (National Center for Health Statistics, 2007). As an example, the maternal mortality rate for the world as a whole was 400 maternal deaths per 100,000 live births in 2000 (WHO, 2004b). At the lower end was Iceland, reporting 0 maternal deaths per 100,000 live births; at the upper end was Sierra Leone, with 2,000 maternal deaths per 100,000 live births.

Life Expectancy at Birth

Another very useful mortality indicator is **life expectancy at birth,** which is the average number of years of life a newborn can be expected to live if current mortality trends continue. It is calculated from life tables using statistical abstraction (Kahn & Sempos, 1989). Vital registration, census, and survey data along with age-specific mortality rates are required to compute life expectancy at birth. It is calculated differently for each of the sexes. To eliminate the influence of infant mortality, life expectancy at age 1 is also sometimes calculated. Life expectancy can be calculated for any age. **Table 2.3** summarizes life expectancy at birth for selected countries.

TABLE 2.3 Comparison of Life Expectancy at Birth in Selected Countries in 2007			
Country	Life Expectancy at Birth: Overall	Life Expectancy at Birth: Males	Life Expectancy at Birth: Females
Afghanistan	43.77	43.60	43.96
Argentina	76.32	72.60	80.24
Australia	80.62	77.75	83.63
Austria	79.21	76.32	82.26
Azerbaijan	65.96	61.86	70.66
Belgium	78.92	75.75	82.24
Brazil	72.24	68.30	76.38
Bulgaria	72.57	68.95	76.40
Cambodia	61.29	59.27	63.40
Cameroon	52.86	52.15	53.59
China	72.88	71.13	74.82
Congo, Democratic Republic of the	57.2	54.97	59.5
Congo, Republic of the	53.29	52.10	54.52
Cuba	77.08	74.85	79.43
Denmark	77.96	75.65	80.41
Ecuador	76.62	73.74	79.63
Egypt	71.57	69.04	74.22
Ethiopia	49.23	48.06	50.44
France	80.59	77.35	84.00
Guinea-Bissau	47.18	45.37	49.04
Haiti	57.03	55.35	58.75
India	68.59	66.28	71.17
Iran	70.56	69.12	72.07
Iraq	69.31	68.04	70.65

TABLE 2.3 (Continued)			
Country	Life Expectancy at Birth: Overall	Life Expectancy at Birth: Males	Life Expectancy at Birth: Females
Japan	82.02	78.67	85.56
Kenya	55.31	55.24	55.37
Libya	76.88	74.64	79.23
Mexico	75.63	72.84	78.56
Moldova	70.20	66.51	74.11
Mongolia	66.99	64.61	69.48
Nigeria	47.44	46.83	48.07
Pakistan	63.75	62.73	64.83
Peru	70.14	68.33	72.04
Philippines	70.51	67.61	73.55
Russia	65.87	59.12	73.03
Rwanda	48.99	47.87	50.16
Somalia	48.84	47.06	50.69
United Kingdom	78.70	76.23	81.30
United States	78.00	75.15	80.97
Zambia	38.44	38.34	38.54

Source: Data compiled from Central Intelligence Agency. (2008). *The world fact book.* Retrieved from https://www.cia.gov/library/publications/the-world-factbook/geos/us.html

MORBIDITY INDICATORS

Mortality indicators alone are insufficient in describing any population's health status. Many causes of ill health do not necessarily result in death (e.g., mental illnesses), but they affect the health status of a population. Therefore we need morbidity indicators. Morbidity indicators are useful in preventing and controlling diseases, planning and evaluating health services, maintaining surveillance of the quality of medical care, and measuring the utilization of health care facilities and services (Lilienfeld & Stolley, 1994). Data about morbidity can be obtained from registries of notifiable diseases.

Diseases such as plague, cholera, yellow fever, and typhus are notifiable by international convention (Tulchinsky & Varavikova, 2000). Special registries also exist for cancers, birth defects, and so on from which morbidity data can be collected. Morbidity data is also available from records of industrial and school absenteeism, insurance companies, tax-financed public assistance programs, special research programs, and morbidity surveys (Lilienfeld & Stolley, 1994). Morbidity indicators are of two types: incidence rates and prevalence rates.

Incidence Rates

Incidence rate is defined as the number of *new* cases of a disease occurring in a population during a given time period divided by the number of people exposed to the risk of developing that disease in that time period. It is expressed per 1,000 or per 10,000 or 100,000 population. The mathematical expression of incidence rate is as follows:

Incidence rate (I)

$$= \frac{\text{No. of new cases of a disease occurring in a population during a given time period}}{\text{No. of people exposed to the risk of developing that disease in that time period}} \times 1,000$$

Epidemiologically speaking, incidence rate is a direct estimate of the probability or risk of developing a disease during a given time period (Lilienfeld & Stolley, 1994). Incidence rates are used when determining whether a relationship exists between a potential etiologic factor and a disease. **Table 2.4** shows the number of new cases of tuberculosis and incidence rates of tuberculosis in the six WHO regions and globally in 2005. It is evident from this table that the incidence rate for tuberculosis is highest in Africa.

Prevalence Rates

Prevalence pertains to the total number of cases of a disease, both old and new. It is a useful measure for chronic diseases. **Prevalence rate** is calculated by taking the total number of cases of a disease present in a population during a given time period and dividing that by the number of people exposed to the risk of having that disease in that time period. It is expressed per 1,000 or per 10,000 or 100,000 population. The mathematical expression of prevalence rate is as follows:

Prevalence rate (P)

$$= \frac{\text{No. of total cases of a disease present in a population during a given time period}}{\text{No. of people exposed to the risk of having that disease in that time period}} \times 1,000$$

TABLE 2.4   Number of New Cases of All Forms of Tuberculosis and Incidence Rates, 2005

WHO Region	Number of New Cases of All Forms of Tuberculosis	Incidence Rate per 100,000 Population
Africa	2,528,915	343
Americas	351,703	39
Eastern Mediterranean	564,551	104
Europe	445,025	50
South East Asia	2,993,252	181
Western Pacific	1,927,359	110
World	8,810,805	136

Source: Taken from World Health Organization. (2007b). Global tuberculosis control. Annex 2. The Stop TB strategy, case reports, treatment outcomes and estimates of TB burden (pp. 167). Geneva: Author. Retrieved from http://www.who.int/tb/publications/global_report/2007/pdf/annex2.pdf

There are two types of prevalence rates: *point prevalence*, which measures the occurrence of disease at any given single point in time, and *period prevalence*, which measures the occurrence of disease in any given time period. Prevalence is expressed as a function of the incidence and duration of the disease (Lilienfeld & Stolley, 1994):

$$P = I \times D$$

where

P = the prevalence rate

I = the incidence rate

D = the duration of the disease measured from time of diagnosis to death

Prevalence rates are used in planning health services and allocating resources for disease prevention. **Table 2.5** shows the total number of cases of tuberculosis and prevalence rates of tuberculosis in the six WHO regions and globally in 2005. It is evident from this table that the prevalence rate for tuberculosis is highest in Africa.

TABLE 2.5 Total Number of Cases of All Forms of Tuberculosis and Prevalence Rates, 2005		
WHO Region	**Total Number of Cases of All Forms of Tuberculosis**	**Prevalence Rate per 100,000 Population**
Africa	3,772,508	511
Americas	447,815	50
Eastern Mediterranean	881,476	163
Europe	525,043	60
South East Asia	4,809,232	290
Western Pacific	3,616,138	206
World	14,052,212	217

Source: Taken from World Health Organization. (2007b). Global tuberculosis control. Annex 2. The Stop TB strategy, case reports, treatment outcomes and estimates of TB burden (pp. 167). Geneva: Author. Retrieved from http://www.who.int/tb/publications/global_report/2007/pdf/annex2.pdf

COMPOSITE MEASURES

Some indices have been developed that combine both mortality and morbidity—particularly disability resulting from morbidity—in a single number. These are called *composite measures* of population health and are used frequently in international health (Hyder & Morrow, 2006). These measures are useful when making allocations of resources either between different communities or between different programs. They are also useful for evidence-based decision making in international health policy.

Healthy Life Year

Healthy life year (HeaLY) is a composite measure that combines the amount of healthy life lost due to morbidity and that attributable to premature mortality (Hyder, Rotllant, & Morrow, 1998). This measure was first developed by the Ghana Health Assessment Project Team in 1981 (Ghana Health Assessment Project Team, 1981). The calculation of this measure is quite complex (Hyder & Morrow, 2006) and takes into consideration the following factors:

- Incidence rate per 1,000 population per year (I)
- Average age at onset (A_o)

- Average age at death (A_f)
- Expectation of life at age of onset $[E(A_o)]$
- Expectation of life at death $[E(A_f)]$
- Case fatality ratio (CFR), which is the proportion of total number of deaths due to a disease divided by the total number of cases and ranges from 0 to 1
- Case disability ratio (CDR), which is the proportion of total number of disabilities due to a disease divided by the total number of cases and ranges from 0 to 1
- Extent of disability (D_e), which is subjectively determined on a scale of 0 (none) to 1 (complete disability, equivalent to death)
- Duration of disability (D_t), expressed in years (if disability is temporary, then D_t = duration of that disability; if permanent and disease does not affect life expectation, then $D_t = E(A_o)$; if permanent and the disease does reduce life expectation, then $D_t = A_f - A_o$)

$$HeaLY = I \times (\{CFR \times [E(A_o) - (A_f - A_o)]\} + [CDR \times D_e \times D_t])$$

As an example, the burden of premature mortality for Pakistan in 2005 was 367 HeaLYs lost per 1,000 population (Hyder, Wali, Ghaffar, Masud, & Hill, 2005). More than half of the HeaLYs in Pakistan were lost due to infection, maternal and perinatal conditions, and malnutrition.

Disability-Adjusted Life Year

The **disability-adjusted life year**, or **DALY**, is a health gap measure that combines in a single measure the time lived with disability and the time lost due to premature mortality (Murray, Salomon, Mathers, & Lopez, 2002). It first appeared in the World Development Report of 1993 (World Bank, 1993) and is based on principles of ethics and economics (Murray & Acharya, 1997). It is used in cost-effectiveness analyses and epidemiologic studies (Jelsma, De Weerdt, & De Cock, 2002).

DALYs for a disease or a health condition are calculated as the sum of (1) the years of life lost (YLL) due to premature mortality in the population and (2) the years of healthy life lost due to disability (YLD) based on the incident cases of the health condition (WHO, n.d.-b).

$$DALY = YLL + YLD$$

The years of life lost can be computed as a function of the number of deaths multiplied by the standard life expectancy at the age at which death occurs. Thus, YLL is expressed as follows:

$$YLL = N \times L$$

where

N = number of deaths

L = standard life expectancy at age of death in years

To estimate years of healthy life lost due to disability (YLD) for a specific cause in a specific time period, the number of incident (new) cases in that period (I) is multiplied by the average duration of the disease (L) and a weight factor (DW) that reflects the severity of the disease on a scale from 0 (perfect health) to 1 (complete disability, equivalent to death). The mathematical expression for YLD is

$$YLD = I \times L \times DW$$

The DALY measure has been criticized for its use of weighting and inaccuracy (Anand & Hanson, 1997), but it is still used in international health. As an example of the calculation of DALYs, a Dutch study looked at the burden of disease due to 48 major causes in the Netherlands in 1994 (Melse, Essink-Bot, Kramers, & Hoeymans, 2000). The DALYs calculated for ischemic heart disease were highest (265,400), followed by anxiety disorders (218,900), cerebrovascular disease (169,600), and visual impairment (165,900).

Quality-Adjusted Life Year

Outcomes from medical treatment and public health efforts add to the quantity of life years and also to quality of life, but life expectancy measures only the quantity of life. To measure both quantity and quality of life, an indicator called **quality-adjusted life year (QALY)** was developed. It is the mathematical product of life expectancy and a measure of the quality of the remaining life years (Phillips & Thompson, 2001). It places a weight on the time spent in different health states. For example, a perfect health state is given a score of 1, and less than perfect health is given a score less than 1. Death is given a score of 0, and some health states that are worse than death are given negative points. Cost utility ratios are calculated when the costs of providing interventions are combined with QALYs.

Cost utility ratio

$$= \frac{(\text{Cost of intervention A} - \text{Cost of intervention B})}{(\text{No. of QALYs produced by intervention A} - \text{No. of QALYs produced by intervention B}}$$

An application of QALY can be found in a case study from India in which a cost-effectiveness analysis of the universal childhood hepatitis B immunization program was done (Aggarwal, Ghoshal, & Naik, 2003). The study showed that universal immunization reduced the hepatitis B carrier rate by 71% and increased the number of years lived by 0.173 years (61.072 vs. 60.899 years) and QALY lived by a birth cohort by 0.213 years (61.056 vs. 60.843 years). The costs were US$16.27 per life-year gained and US$13.22 per QALY gained, much lower than the annual per capita income. Thus the study recommended universal hepatitis B immunization as highly cost-effective in low-income countries with intermediate endemicity rates.

Disability-Free Life Expectancy

Disability-free life expectancy (DFLE) extends the concept of life expectancy to include an individual's ability to function in society. This index was created in 1971 by Sullivan and thus is also known as Sullivan's index (Sullivan, 1971). It is computed by subtracting from the life expectancy the probable duration of bed disability and inability to perform major activities at work, home, or school. Major activity limitations are those caused by a long-term physical or mental condition or a long-term health problem that has lasted or is expected to last six months or more. Minor activity limitations or nondisabling impairments are excluded. Disability-free life expectancy establishes a threshold based on the nature of the disabling limitations. Years of life lived in conditions above the threshold are counted in full. Those lived in conditions below the threshold are not counted.

Data for calculating DFLE are collected through censuses in some countries, whereas in others collection is through cross-sectional population surveys. As an example, a study looked at DFLE in different regions of Canada (Mayer, 2002) and found that the disability-free life expectancy in 1996 for Canada was 68.6 (95% CI [confidence interval]: 68.5, 68.6), as opposed to a life expectancy of 78.3 (95% CI: 78.3, 78.4).

Disability-Adjusted Life Expectancy

Disability-adjusted life expectancy (DALE) is a composite indicator that, along with life expectancy, introduces the concept of quality of life. It is little more sophisticated than disability-free life expectancy. DFLE is the anticipated period of life lived without a given disability, whereas DALE depicts the equivalent number of years of life expected to be lived in full health, taking into account the degree of disability (Kurimori, 2006). DALE combines data on mortality, long-term institutionalization, and activity limitations in the population and represents a comprehensive index of population health status (Statistics Canada, 2007). To calculate DALE, a set of weights (relative values) are assigned to four states of health: no activity limitations (greatest weight), activity limitations in leisure activities or transportation (second-highest weight), activity limitations at work, home, and/or school (second-lowest weight), and institutionalization in a health care facility (lowest weight). These units are summed to yield disability-adjusted life expectancy. As an example, Murray and Lopez (1997) have calculated the DALE for different regions of the world.

Health-Adjusted Life Expectancy or Healthy Life Expectancy

Health-adjusted life expectancy (HALE), also known as **healthy life expectancy**, summarizes the expected number of years to be lived in terms equivalent to complete health (Rosenberg, Fryback, & Lawrence, 1999). In calculating HALE, years of life are weighted by health status (Wolfson, 1996). The details of the exact calculation of this indicator are beyond the scope of this book. It is often considered to be the best available composite measure for measuring the overall health of a community (Mathers et al., 2001). **Table 2.6** summarizes the health-adjusted life expectancy for selected countries.

Health-adjusted life expectancy (HALE), or healthy life expectancy, is the best available composite measure for measuring the overall health of a community.

TABLE 2.6 Summary of Health-Adjusted Life Expectancy (HALE) for Selected Countries, 2002			
Country	**HALE at Birth: Overall**	**HALE at Birth: Males**	**HALE at Birth: Females**
Afghanistan	35.5	35.3	35.8
Argentina	65.3	62.5	68.1
Australia	72.6	70.9	74.3
Austria	71.4	69.3	73.5
Azerbaijan	57.2	55.8	58.7
Belgium	71.1	68.9	73.3
Brazil	59.8	57.2	62.4
Bulgaria	64.8	62.6	67.1
Cambodia	47.5	45.6	49.5
Cameroon	41.5	41.1	41.8
China	64.1	63.1	65.2
Congo, Democratic Republic of the	37.1	35.0	39.1
Congo, Republic of the	46.3	45.3	47.3

TABLE 2.6   *(Continued)*

Country	HALE at Birth: Overall	HALE at Birth: Males	HALE at Birth: Females
Cuba	68.3	67.1	69.5
Denmark	69.8	68.6	71.1
Ecuador	61.9	59.8	64.1
Egypt	59.0	57.8	60.2
Ethiopia	41.2	40.7	41.7
France	72.0	69.3	74.7
Guinea-Bissau	40.5	39.6	41.5
Haiti	43.8	43.5	44.1
India	53.5	53.3	53.6
Iran	57.6	56.1	59.1
Iraq	50.1	48.8	51.5
Japan	75.0	72.3	77.7
Kenya	44.4	44.1	44.8
Libya	63.7	62.3	65.0
Mexico	65.4	63.3	67.6
Moldova	59.8	57.2	62.4
Mongolia	55.6	53.3	58.0
Nigeria	41.5	41.3	41.8
Pakistan	53.3	54.2	52.3
Peru	61.0	59.6	64.2
Philippines	59.3	57.1	61.5
Russia	58.4	52.8	64.1
Rwanda	38.3	36.4	40.2
Somalia	36.8	36.1	37.5
United Kingdom	70.6	69.1	72.1
United States	69.3	67.2	71.3
Zambia	34.9	34.8	35.0

Source: World Health Organization (WHO). (2004c). World Health Report: Annex Table 4. Geneva: Author. Retrieved from http://www.who.int/whr/2004/en/09_annexes_en.pdf.

FERTILITY INDICATORS

A number of indicators exist to measure the fertility of a population. *Fertility* refers to the actual bearing of children. Sometimes the term *natality* is used instead of fertility. These indicators are helpful in international health and are used in making predictions and comparisons about the growth of populations.

Crude Birth Rate

Crude birth rate (CBR) is the simplest measure of fertility and is calculated by taking the total number of live births in a given year and dividing it by the midyear population of that community. It is usually expressed per 1,000:

$$\text{Crude birth rate (CBR)} = \frac{\text{No. of live births in a given year}}{\text{Midyear population}} \times 1{,}000$$

It is clear from looking at this indicator that the selected denominator is not the best choice because the entire population is not likely to bear children. Other indicators adjust for this limitation, which is why this measure is called the crude birth rate. **Table 2.7** depicts the crude birth rate for selected countries in the world.

General Fertility Rate

General fertility rate (GFR) is defined as the number of live births per 1,000 women in the childbearing age group, which is those aged 15 to 44 years in a given year. Sometimes, the age group that is considered is 15 to 49 years or 10 to 49 years. General fertility rate significantly controls for age and sex structure by relating the births mainly to the women at risk of having births. However, it still does not present an accurate picture because not all women in the denominator are exposed to the risk of childbirth.

$$\text{General fertility rate (GFR)} = \frac{\text{No. of live births}}{\text{No. of women of childbearing age}} \times 1{,}000$$

Sometimes GFR is restricted to only married women of childbearing age; it is then called the general marital fertility rate (GMFR).

TABLE 2.7   Crude Birth Rate for Selected Countries in the World, 2007

Country	Crude Birth Rate (births per 1,000 population)	Country	Crude Birth Rate (births per 1,000 population)
Afghanistan	46.21	Haiti	35.87
Argentina	16.53	India	22.69
Australia	12.02	Iran	16.57
Austria	8.69	Iraq	31.44
Azerbaijan	17.47	Japan	8.10
Belgium	10.29	Kenya	38.94
Brazil	16.30	Libya	26.09
Bulgaria	9.62	Mexico	20.36
Cambodia	25.53	Moldova	10.88
Cameroon	35.07	Mongolia	21.07
China	13.45	Nigeria	40.20
Congo, Democratic Republic of the	42.96	Pakistan	27.52
		Peru	20.09
Congo, Republic of the	42.16	Philippines	24.48
Cuba	11.44	Russia	10.92
Denmark	10.91	Rwanda	40.16
Ecuador	21.91	Somalia	44.60
Egypt	22.53	United Kingdom	10.67
Ethiopia	37.39	United States	14.16
France	12.91	Zambia	40.78
Guinea-Bissau	36.81		

Source: Data compiled from Central Intelligence Agency. (2008). *The world fact book.* Retrieved from https://www.cia.gov/library/publications/the-world-factbook/geos/us.html

Age-Specific Fertility Rate

Age-specific fertility rate is defined as the number of live births per 1,000 women in a specific age group. It can be calculated for any age.

$$\text{Age-specific fertility rate for 20-year-olds} = \frac{\text{No. of live births to 20-year-olds}}{\text{No. of women who are 20 years old}} \times 1{,}000$$

Total Fertility Rate

Total fertility rate (TFR) is defined as the average number of children a woman would bear if she were to live to the end of her childbearing age and bear children at each age in accordance with the age-specific fertility rate. In 2007, Mali had the highest TFR (7.38 children born per woman) and Hong Kong had the lowest TFR (0.98 children born per woman). **Table 2.8** shows total fertility rate for selected countries in 2007.

Gross Reproduction Rate

Gross reproduction rate (GRR) is defined as the average number of daughters who would be born to a woman if she experienced the age-specific birth rates observed in a given year throughout her childbearing years and if she did not die during her childbearing years. It is different from total fertility rate because it only takes into consideration daughters and does not adjust for mortality. Sometimes it is expressed per 1,000 women. As an example, the gross reproduction rate in 2002 for United States was 983 female births per 1,000 women (Hamilton, 2004).

Net Reproduction Rate

Net reproduction rate (NRR) is defined as the average number of daughters who would be born to a woman if she passed through her lifetime conforming to the age-specific fertility and mortality rates. This index takes into consideration both fertility and mortality. An NRR of 1.0 indicates that each mother is being replaced by exactly one daughter (Park & Park, 1986). Sometimes it is expressed per 1,000 women. As an example, in 2001, the NRR in the United States was 979 female births per 1,000 women (Hamilton, 2004).

TABLE 2.8   Total Fertility Rate for Selected Countries in 2007

Country	Total Fertility Rate (children born/woman)	Country	Total Fertility Rate (children born/woman)
Afghanistan	6.64	Haiti	4.86
Argentina	2.13	India	2.81
Australia	1.76	Iran	1.71
Austria	1.37	Iraq	4.07
Azerbaijan	2.05	Japan	1.23
Belgium	1.64	Kenya	4.82
Brazil	1.88	Libya	3.21
Bulgaria	1.39	Mexico	2.39
Cambodia	3.12	Moldova	1.25
Cameroon	4.49	Mongolia	2.25
China	1.75	Nigeria	5.45
Congo, Democratic Republic of the	6.37	Pakistan	3.71
		Peru	2.46
Congo, Republic of the	5.99	Philippines	3.05
Cuba	1.6	Russia	1.39
Denmark	1.74	Rwanda	5.37
Ecuador	2.63	Somalia	6.68
Egypt	2.77	United Kingdom	1.66
Ethiopia	5.1	United States	2.09
France	1.98	Zambia	5.31
Guinea-Bissau	4.79		

Source: Data compiled from Central Intelligence Agency. (2008). *The world fact book.* Retrieved from https://www.cia.gov/library/publications/the-world-factbook/geos/us.html

OTHER HEALTH INDICATORS

Other health indicators also exist. The list that follows is for illustrative purposes only and is not exhaustive.

- Indicators of health care delivery, such as physician/population ratio, physician/nurse ratio, hospital bed/population ratio, and so on
- Indicators of utilization, such as bed occupancy rates (average daily inpatients/ average beds), bed turnover ratio (average discharges/average beds), immunization coverage among 1-year-olds (percentage covered with one dose of measles, percentage covered with three doses of DPT, percentage covered with three doses of hepatitis B), percentage of antenatal coverage (percentage of women who received skilled care at least once during pregnancy as a percentage of live births), percentage of live births attended by skilled health personnel, percentage of children younger than 5 years in malaria-endemic areas who slept under an insecticide-treated net the previous night, percentage of antiretroviral therapy coverage among people with advanced HIV infection, percentage of children younger than 5 years with diarrhea receiving oral rehydration therapy, and so on
- Indicators of nutritional status, such as percentage of children with low birth weight, percentage of children younger than 6 months who are exclusively breastfed, percentage of children aged 6 to 9 months who are breastfed with complementary food, percentage of children younger than 5 years suffering from underweight, vitamin A supplementation coverage rate, and so on
- Educational indicators, such as adult literacy rate, number of phones per 100 population, number of Internet users per 100 population, gross primary school enrollment ratio, net primary enrollment ratio, net primary school attendance ratio, percentage of primary school entrants reaching grade 5, gross secondary school enrollment ratio, net secondary enrollment ratio, and so on
- Economic indicators, such as gross national income (GNI) per capita, total expenditure on health as a percentage of gross domestic product (GDP), percentage of government expenditure on health, percentage of government expenditure on education, percentage of government expenditure on defense, and so on

ANALYTICAL EPIDEMIOLOGY

In making comparisons with indicators, one cannot discern what caused the changes in the indicators. To understand the determinants or causes that underlie health conditions, we need analytical epidemiology. In analytical epidemiology, studies are conducted to determine whether or not the risk of a health condition is different for individuals exposed or not exposed to a factor of interest (Hennekens & Buring, 1987). There are two broad kinds of analytic studies: observational studies and intervention studies. Observational studies are again of two types: (1) *case control studies*, in which a set of patients who have the health condition and a control or comparison group of individuals who do not have the health condition are compared for the exposure of interest; and (2) *cohort studies*, in which participants are selected on the basis of either an exposure to an agent or no exposure to the agent and then are followed over time to see which group develops the health condition. In intervention studies, the researchers provide the exposure and watch the development of the health condition.

On the basis of these studies, a determination of the cause-and-effect relationship can be made. To do so, first and foremost a statistical association must be established (Hennekens & Buring, 1987). The role of chance must be ruled out, for which statistical tests such as the t-test, ANOVA, and chi-square are carried out and the p value calculated, which is the probability of obtaining, when the null is true (i.e., there is no relationship between exposure and health condition), a value of the test statistic as extreme or more extreme (in the appropriate direction) than the one actually computed. For statistical association to be present, bias must be ruled out. Bias is any systematic error that may arise as a result of the way participants are selected, questions are asked, and data are interpreted. Most good studies try their best to reduce bias, which cannot be completely eliminated. For statistical association, confounding (inextricable linkage of a third factor with the exposure and the health condition) must also be ruled out. As an example, for many years it was believed that coffee drinking was linked with heart disease, whereas it was the link of coffee drinking with cigarette smoking that was confounding the relation.

After establishing statistical association, one can begin to look at cause-and-effect relationship. Sir Austin Bradford Hill developed a set of nine criteria for establishing causality (Hill, 1965):

1. *Consistency:* There must be several studies that show similar results before one can conclude causality. One study is never sufficient.
2. *Temporality:* The putative cause must precede the effect.
3. *Strength of association:* Statistics such as R^2 or eta squared or other such indicators are indicative of how strong the association is. For the relationship to be causal, this association should be strong.
4. *Dose response relationship:* There must be a direct relationship between the risk factor (the independent variable) and the health condition (the dependent variable).
5. *Biological plausibility:* There must be a reasonable biological or theoretical basis or explanation for the association.

6. *Specificity:* The exposure alone can induce the outcome.
7. *Coherence:* There is no conflict with what is known about the variables under study and there are no other competing theories or rival hypotheses.
8. *Experimental evidence:* When experimental evidence is available, it strengthens the causality.
9. *Analogy:* When evidence is available in similar areas, comparisons can be made.

Focus Feature 2.1 shows how these criteria have been used to link smoking and lung cancer.

FOCUS FEATURE 2.1   Smoking and Lung Cancer

In 1950, two independent studies, one by Doll and Hill (1950) and another by Wynder and Graham (1950), empirically showed the linkage between smoking and lung cancer. Prior to these studies it had been suggested that smoking might be linked to lung cancer, but the unique feature of these studies was their methodologic rigor (Schlesselman, 2006). Both of these studies were case control studies; Wynder and Graham's study was conducted in the United States, whereas Doll and Hill's study was conducted in the United Kingdom. Let us examine the criteria of causality as they pertain to smoking and lung cancer.

1. *Consistency:* After these classic studies, several studies were published that have linked smoking and lung cancer.
2. *Temporality:* Smoking preceded lung cancer in a majority of cases.
3. *Strength of association:* The study by Doll and Hill (1950) found that the risk of developing lung cancer was approximately 50 times greater for those who smoke 25 or more cigarettes per day as for nonsmokers. Subsequent studies have also shown a strong association.
4. *Dose response relationship:* In the study by Doll and Hill (1950), for patients aged 45 to 74, the relative risk of the disease in men and women combined was estimated to be 6, 19, 26, 49, and 65 when the number of cigarettes smoked per day was 3, 10, 20, 35, and 60, respectively. Subsequent studies have also shown a dose response relationship.
5. *Biological plausibility:* There are various chemicals in tobacco smoke such as tar, acetone, hexamine, hydrogen cyanide, butane, and so forth. Many of these are linked with causing cancer in animals. So, biologically it is possible that smoking can cause lung cancer.
6. *Specificity:* Lung cancer is best predicted from the incidence of smoking.
7. *Coherence:* Prior to these studies it had been suggested that smoking might be linked to lung cancer; there are no other competing theories or rival hypotheses.
8. *Experimental evidence:* Experiments have been conducted that painted rabbits' ears with tar (derived from cigarette smoking) and have found that the ear tissue developed cancer (Rubin, 2001).
9. *Analogy:* Induced smoking in animal models also produces lung cancer.

SKILL-BUILDING ACTIVITY

Make a list of all the health indicators that you have learned about in this chapter. Then select any five countries of your choice. Using the Internet, try to locate the current data with regard to each of the indicators in your list and make a comparative table for the five countries. You may not be able to find the data for all the indicators, but this exercise will help sharpen your acumen for searching for such data, which would be helpful in writing research papers or doing other projects for your classes.

SUMMARY

Epidemiology is the study of the distribution and determinants of health and health-related conditions and events in populations to prevent and control health problems. It is of two types: descriptive epidemiology, which deals with the time, place, and person distribution of health and health-related conditions and events, and analytical epidemiology, which helps in identifying the underlying causes of health and health-related conditions and events.

Understanding the health indicators used in descriptive epidemiology is vital for international health. The first category of these indicators is mortality rates, which include crude death rate, specific death rates, infant mortality rate, neonatal mortality rate, postneonatal mortality rate, perinatal mortality rate, fetal mortality rate, maternal mortality rate (ratio), and life expectancy at birth. The second category is morbidity indicators, which comprise incidence and prevalence rates. The third category is the composite measures that combine mortality, morbidity, and disability in a single measure. These are healthy life year (HeaLY), disability-adjusted life year (DALY), quality-adjusted life year (QALY), disability-free life expectancy (DFLE), disability-adjusted life expectancy (DALE), and health-adjusted life expectancy or healthy life expectancy (HALE). The fourth category of measures is fertility indicators, which consist of crude birth rate, general fertility rate, age-specific fertility rate, total fertility rate, gross reproduction rate, and net reproduction rate. Finally, other health-related indicators include indicators of health care delivery and utilization, nutritional status, educational status, and economic indicators.

The purpose of analytical epidemiology is to establish cause-and-effect relationships in health. The nine criteria for establishing a cause-and-effect relationship are as follows: consistency, temporality, strength of association, dose response relationship, biological plausibility, specificity, coherence, experimental evidence, and analogy.

IMPORTANT TERMS

age-specific fertility rate
analytical epidemiology
crude birth rate (CBR)
crude death rate (CDR)
descriptive epidemiology
disability-adjusted life expectancy
   (DALE)
disability-adjusted life year (DALY)
disability-free life expectancy (DFLE)
epidemiology
fetal mortality rate (FMR)
general fertility rate (GFR)
gross reproduction rate (GRR)
health-adjusted life expectancy or
   healthy life expectancy (HALE)

healthy life year (HeaLY)
incidence rate
infant mortality rate (IMR)
life expectancy at birth
maternal mortality rate (or ratio) (MMR)
neonatal mortality rate (NMR)
net reproduction rate (NRR)
prevalence rate
perinatal mortality rate (PMR)
postneonatal mortality rate (PNMR)
proportion
quality-adjusted life year (QALY)
rate
ratio
total fertility rate (TFR)

REVIEW QUESTIONS

1. Define epidemiology. Differentiate between descriptive and analytical epidemiology.
2. Describe common mortality indicators. Discuss the limitations of mortality indicators.
3. Differentiate between incidence rate and prevalence rate.
4. Define any one composite indicator of population health.
5. Differentiate between HeALY and HALE.
6. Summarize key fertility indicators.
7. What are the criteria for establishing a cause-and-effect relationship?

WEB SITES TO EXPLORE

Central Intelligence Agency: The World Fact Book

https://www.cia.gov/library/publications/the-world-factbook/indcx.html

The *World Fact Book*, compiled by the Central Intelligence Agency, provides country-specific data for several of the indicators discussed in this chapter. Also included on the Web site are pages that rank countries with regard to area, population, birth rate, death rate, infant mortality rate, life expectancy, total fertility rate, HIV/AIDS prevalence rate, people living with HIV/AIDS, deaths due to HIV/AIDS, economy indicators, communication indicators, transportation indicators, and percentage of GDP spent on military. *Visit this Web site and identify countries that rank the highest and lowest in each of these indicators.*

Summary Measures of Population Health

http://www.intermed.med.uottawa.ca/Curriculum/IPH/data/Images/Summary%20Measures%20of%20Population%20Health.ppt

A PowerPoint slide presentation on summary measures of population health by Ian McDowell, developed in 2002. The presentation describes the rationale for summary measures, mortality-based measures, and measures that combine mortality and disability. *Review the PowerPoint slides. Which measures have been discussed in this textbook but were not discussed in the presentation, and vice versa?*

UNICEF: State of the World's Children 2008

http://www.unicef.org/sowc08/statistics/tables.php

The Web site of the State of the World's Children Report for 2008 has statistical tables for basic indicators, nutrition indicators, health indicators, HIV/AIDS indicators, education, demographic indicators, economic indicators, women, child protection, and rate of progress. *Explore the latest State of the World's Children Report and compare data for any one country with data from the World Health Organization. Which indicators did WHO collect data for that UNICEF did not, and vice versa?*

World Health Organization Indicator Definitions and Metadata

http://www.who.int/whosis/indicators/2007compendium/en/index.html

This Web site lists common indicators used by the World Health Organization. It provides definition and data from different countries regarding mortality, morbidity, health service coverage, risk factors, and health systems. *Visit this Web site and collect data for any one country of your choice.*

REFERENCES

Aggarwal, R., Ghoshal, U. C., & Naik, S. R. (2003). Assessment of cost-effectiveness of universal hepatitis B immunization in a low-income country with intermediate endemicity using a Markov model. *Journal of Hepatology, 38*(2), 215–222.

Anand, S., & Hanson, K. (1997). Disability-adjusted life years: A critical review. *Journal of Health Economics, 16*(6), 685–702.

Central Intelligence Agency. (2008). *The world fact book.* Retrieved from https://www.cia.gov/library/publications/the-world-factbook/index.html

Doll, R., & Hill, A. B. (1950). Smoking and carcinoma of the lung: Preliminary report. *British Medical Journal, 2,* 739–748.

Ghana Health Assessment Project Team. (1981). A quantitative method of assessing the health impact of different diseases in less developed countries. *International Journal of Epidemiology, 10,* 73–80.

Hamilton, B. E. (2004). Reproduction rates for 1990–2002 and intrinsic rates for 2000–2001: United States. *National Vital Statistics Report, 52*(17), 1–12. Retrieved from http://www.cdc.gov/NCHS/data/nvsr/nvsr52/nvsr52_17.pdf

Hamilton, B. E., Miniño, A. M., Martin, J. A., Kochanek, K. D., Strobino, D. M., & Guyer, B. (2007). Annual summary of vital statistics: 2005. *Pediatrics, 119*(2), 345–360.

Hennekens, C. H., & Buring, J. E. (1987). *Epidemiology in medicine.* Boston: Little, Brown and Company.

Hill, B. A. (1965). The environment and disease: Association or causation? *Proceedings of the Royal Society of Medicine, 58,* 295–300.

Hyder, A. A., & Morrow, R. H. (2006). Measures of health and disease in populations. In M. H. Merson, R. E. Black, & A. J. Mills (Eds.), *International public health: Diseases, programs, systems, and policies* (pp. 1–42). Sudbury, MA: Jones and Bartlett Publishers.

Hyder, A. A., Rotllant, G., & Morrow, R. H. (1998). Measuring the burden of disease: Healthy life-years. *American Journal of Public Health, 88*(2), 196–202.

Hyder, A. A., Wali, S. A., Ghaffar, A., Masud, T. I., & Hill, K. (2005). Measuring the burden of premature mortality in Pakistan: Use of sentinel surveillance systems. *Public Health, 119*(6), 459–465.

Jelsma, J., De Weerdt, W., & De Cock, P. (2002). Disability adjusted life years (DALYs) and rehabilitation. *Disability and Rehabilitation, 24*(7), 378–382.

Kahn, H. A., & Sempos, C. T. (1989). *Statistical methods in epidemiology.* Oxford: Oxford University Press.

Kurimori, S. (2006). Calculation of prefectural disability-adjusted life expectancy (DALE) using long-term care prevalence and its socioeconomic correlates in Japan. *Health Policy, 76*(3), 346–358.

Last, J. M. (Ed.). (2000). *A dictionary of epidemiology* (4th ed.). New York: Oxford University Press.

Lilienfeld, D. E., & Stolley, P.D. (1994). *Foundations of epidemiology* (3rd ed.). Oxford: Oxford University Press.

Mathers, C., Vos, T., Lopez, A., Salomon, J., Lozano, R., & Ezzati, M. (Eds.). (2001). *National burden of disease studies: A practical guide* (Edition 2.0). Geneva: World Health Organization.

Mayer, F. (2002). Disability-free life expectancy by health region. *Health Reports, 13*(4), 49–60.

Melse, J. M., Essink-Bot, M. L., Kramers, P. G., & Hoeymans, N. (2000). A national burden of disease calculation: Dutch disability-adjusted life-years. *American Journal of Public Health, 90*(8), 1241–1247.

Mulholland, K. (2007). Perspectives on the burden of pneumonia in children. *Vaccine, 25*(13), 2394–2397.

Murray, C. J. L., & Acharya, A. K. (1997). Understanding DALYs (disability-adjusted life years). *Journal of Health Economics, 16*(6), 703–730.

Murray, C. J. L., & Lopez, A. D. (1997). Regional patterns of disability-free life expectancy and disability-adjusted life expectancy: Global Burden of Disease Study. *The Lancet, 349*(9062), 1347–1352.

Murray, C. J. L., Salomon, J. A., Mathers, C. D., & Lopez, A. D. (Eds.) (2002). *Summary measures of population health: Concepts, ethics, measurement and applications.* Geneva: World Health Organization.

National Center for Health Statistics. (2007). NCHS definitions. Retrieved from http://www.cdc.gov/NCHS/datawh/nchsdefs/rates.htm

Park, J. E., & Park, K. (1986). *Textbook of preventive and social medicine* (11th ed.). Jabalpur, India: Banarasidas Bhanot Publishers.

Phillips, C., & Thompson, G. (2001). What is a QALY? Retrieved from http://www.evidence-based-medicine.co.uk/ebmfiles/WhatisaQALY.pdf

Reidpath, D. D., & Allotey, P. (2003). Infant mortality rate as an indicator of population health. *Journal of Epidemiology and Community Health, 57*(5), 344–346.

Rosenberg, M. A., Fryback, D. G., & Lawrence, W. F. (1999). Computing population-based estimates of health-adjusted life expectancy. *Medical Decision Making, 19*(1), 90–97.

Rubin, H. (2001). Synergistic mechanisms in carcinogenesis by polycyclic aromatic hydrocarbons and by tobacco smoke: A bio-historical perspective with updates. *Carcinogenesis, 22*(12), 1903–1930.

Schell, C. O., Reilly, M., Rosling, H., Peterson, S., & Ekstrom, A. M. (2007). Socioeconomic determinants of infant mortality: A worldwide study of 152 low, middle, and high-income countries. *Scandinavian Journal of Public Health, 35*(3), 288–297.

Schlesselman, J. J. (2006). The emerging case-control study: Lung cancer in relation to tobacco smoking. *Preventive Medicine, 43*(4), 251–255.

Statistics Canada. (2007). Definitions, data sources, and methods. Retrieved from http://www.statcan.ca/english/freepub/82-221- XIE/2007001/defin/defin1.htm#hf1dal

Sullivan, D. F. (1971). A single index of mortality and morbidity. *HSMSA Health Reports, 86,* 347–354.

Tulchinsky, T. H., & Varavikova, E. A. (2000). *The new public health: An introduction for the 21st century.* Burlington, MA: Academic Press.

Wolfson, M. C. (1996). Health-adjusted life expectancy. *Health Reports, 8*(1), 41–46.

World Bank. (1993). *World development report 1993: Investing in health.* New York: Oxford University Press.

World Health Organization. (2004a). *International statistical classification of diseases and related health problems* (10th revision): *Vol. 2. Instruction manual* (2nd ed.). Geneva: Author. Retrieved from http://www.who.int/classifications/icd/ICD-10_2nd_ed_volume2.pdf

World Health Organization. (2004b). *Maternal mortality in 2000: Estimates developed by WHO, UNICEF and UNFPA.* Geneva: Author.

World Health Organization. (2007). *International statistical classification of diseases and related health problems* (10th revision, version for 2007). Retrieved from http://www.who.int/classifications/apps/icd/icd10online/

World Health Organization. (n.d.-a). Neonatal mortality rate (per 1,000 live births). Retrieved March 2, 2008, from http://www.who.int/healthinfo/statistics/indneonatalmortality/en/

World Health Organization. (n.d.-b). Disability adjusted life years (DALY). Retrieved March 2, 2008, from http://www.who.int/healthinfo/boddaly/en/

Wynder, E. L., & Graham, E. A. (1950). Tobacco smoking as a possible etiologic factor in bronchiogenic carcinoma. A study of six hundred and eighty-four proved cases. *JAMA, 143,* 329–336.

The Role of Culture
and Behavior in Health

AFTER READING THIS CHAPTER YOU SHOULD BE ABLE TO

- Define culture and acculturation
- Discuss the role of culture in health
- Describe the role of behavior in health
- Explain some common theories of health behavior and behavior change
- Identify the main components of the PRECEDE-PROCEED model
- Elaborate the PEN-3 model

THE ROLE OF CULTURE

Understanding the role of **culture** in international health is of vital importance. With growing globalization, people from almost all countries are constantly coming in touch with people from different cultures; therefore, understanding culture and its role is essential. The word *culture* means different things to different people. Kluckhohn and

Kroeber (1952) noted 150 different definitions of culture in a review article. According to Merriam-Webster's online dictionary, *culture* has several meanings, but the one that we are interested in is as follows: "the integrated pattern of human knowledge, belief, and behavior that depends upon the capacity for learning and transmitting knowledge to succeeding generations." Another definition of culture, popular in **anthropology**, was given by E. B. Taylor in 1871 as "that complex whole which includes knowledge, belief, art, morals, law, custom, and any other capabilities and habits acquired by man as a member of society" (Leach, 1982).

Culture includes shared customs of communication and familiar experiences of living in the world (MacLachlan, 1997). Spector (1996) presents an analogy of culture as luggage that we carry around for our lifetime. The luggage consists of all our beliefs, practices, ways of life, likes, dislikes, customs, rituals, norms, and so on that we have learned from our families. Culture can also be seen a set of guidelines—implicit and explicit—that are inherited and tell a person how to view the world, how to experience it, and how to behave (Helman, 2007). An important aspect of culture is that it must always be examined in a given context (Helman, 1994). The context is composed of economic, historical, social, political, and geographic elements. Therefore, culture is always influenced by different factors; it is never possible to extract culture as an independent variable.

Culture is sometimes confused with race and ethnicity. Race is a biological term that includes inherited physical characteristics, whereas *ethnicity* refers to common physical features that are linked to psychological similarities (MacLachlan, 1997). One community differs from another community in its culture. Different cultures interpret the same phenomena differently and often they share the belief that their interpretation is the correct one. In many cultures (such as South Asia and the Middle East), religion is a dominant force and influences diet, days of work, dress, and gender roles (Fleming, Bennett, & Rao, 1998).

The interplay between culture and health is very complex and includes the social context in which majority and minority groups operate, the race and ethnicity of different groups, and different social variations (MacLachlan, 1997). The field that studies the relationships between culture and disease and culture and health is **medical anthropology** (Bailey, 2000). Medical anthropology embodies a biopsychosociocultural perspective that acknowledges the role of biological, psychological, social, and cultural factors in the causation of health and illness (Engel, 1977). The field of medical anthropology has evolved from three sources: (1) interest in "indigenous" or "native" medicine, (2) the culture and personality movement within anthropology in the 1930s and 1940s, and (3) the growing international public health movement following

World War II (Bailey, 2000). The field of medical anthropology tries to answer "why" questions such as the following: Why are certain types of behaviors considered mental illness in one society but normal in another? Why are certain diseases more common in certain cultures? Why do certain religions permit the use of certain drugs whereas others prohibit them?

Sometimes a culture is associated with certain diseases. There are several culture-bound syndromes, or diseases prevalent in certain cultures. These are a group of psychosocial conditions, each of which is unique to a particular group of people sharing a culture (see Chapter 10). It is very important to understand different cultures so as not to mistakenly misclassify a person as having a personality disorder because of behaviors that might be culturally acceptable in one culture, but not in another.

Culture not only affects mental health, but also physical health. For example, Seventh Day Adventists appear to live longer and have fewer health problems than other groups (Ilola, 1990; MacLachlan, 1997). This may be related to their belief that the human body is the temple of the Holy Spirit and must be treated with respect. Sometimes different cultures may interpret a health condition differently. For example, a person may be diagnosed as suffering from depression in the United States and be prescribed antidepressants, whereas in India he or she might be told that the condition is a result of a bad astrological period and be prescribed some astrological rings, and in Sudan the condition might be attributed to demons and some ceremonies performed to banish them.

In an international study done with IBM employees in 50 countries, Hofstede (1980, 1991) identified five dimensions of culture:

1. *Power/distance*, which is defined as the degree to which less influential members of an organization believe that power is unequally distributed. This dimension is about how inequality is experienced in the society. In low power/distance cultures (such as Austria, Israel, Denmark), there was interdependence between bosses and subordinates, whereas in high power/distance societies (such as Malaysia, Guatemala, and Panama), subordinates were dependent on their bosses and would not act independently (Hofstede, 1980).

2. *Individualism versus collectivism*, which means whether one thinks or acts individually or as a group. In an individualistic society each person thinks for himself or herself and acts accordingly, as in the United States, Australia, or the United Kingdom, whereas in a collective society people are integrated into groups and think of their group first, as in Panama, Ecuador, and Guatemala.

3. *Masculinity versus femininity*. In masculine cultures, men are supposed to be assertive, competitive, and striving for material success and women are expected to

care for children. In feminine cultures, men need not be competitive and women have broader roles. Countries that demonstrated a masculine culture were Japan, Austria, and Venezuela, whereas a feminine culture was found in Sweden, Norway, and the Netherlands.

4. *Uncertainty avoidance*, or the extent to which people in a culture feel threatened by unpredictable events. Greece, Portugal, and Guatemala were high on the uncertainty avoidance rating, whereas countries such as Singapore, Jamaica, and Denmark had a low uncertainty avoidance rating.

5. *Short-term orientation versus long-term orientation.* A short-term orientation refers to respect for tradition, fulfilling social obligations, and maintaining a position of respect, whereas a long-term orientation refers to focusing on future rewards. Countries with a short-term orientation were Pakistan, Nigeria, and the Philippines, whereas countries with a long-term orientation were China, Hong Kong, Taiwan, and Japan.

These dimensions have been applied in teaching, counseling, and psychotherapy (MacLachlan, 1997).

Mensah (1993) describes three different variations in providing health care in the context of culture: transcultural care, cross-cultural care, and multicultural care. In *transcultural care* a comparison is done between cultures in terms of their care, and the caregiver provides care to the cultural group after understanding what is the best way to deliver it. In transcultural care the onus of care is primarily on the caregiver. In *cross-cultural care* the receiver and the provider of care are from different groups and the approach is to establish a cross-cultural bridge between the two. Cross-cultural care is a joint effort. In *multicultural care* the concept extends to the entire system and attempts are made to provide overall culturally appropriate and culturally sensitive care through changes in policies and environments.

> *The belief that culture, community, and health are related is not simply a reflection of modern practice, it was also a belief in ancient times.*
>
> —MacLachlan (1997), p. 32

ACCULTURATION

Acculturation is the psychosocial adjustment and adaptation to a new culture of a person from another culture. Traditionally, acculturation has been defined as the behavioral and psychological changes in an individual that occur as a result of contact between people belonging to different cultural groups (Berry, 1997). Other researchers have approached acculturation in a slightly broader manner, calling it the social and psychological exchanges that take place when there is continuous contact and interaction between individuals from different cultures (Berry, 1997; Redfield, Linton, & Herskovits, 1936; Ryder, Alden, & Paulhus, 2000). Irrespective of how we define it, acculturation is often visualized as the individual's psychosocial adjustment and adaptation to a new culture. The specific set of difficulties that an individual immigrant has to face could be physical (new climatic conditions and a search for an abode), biological (changes in diet and diseases), social (dislocation of friends and formation of new relationships), cultural (sudden changes in political, economic, and religious contexts), and psychological (a need to change attitudes, values, and mental health connotations).

Berry's (1997) fourfold classification of acculturation has gained widespread acceptance despite limited research-based evidence. The four modes of acculturation he proposed are integration, assimilation, separation, and marginalization. *Integration* is the identification and involvement of an immigrant with both cultures, the mode that is linked with the most optimal mental health outcome. *Assimilation* is the state in which the immigrant identifies solely with the new culture. *Separation* is the situation in which the individual is involved only in his native culture, and *marginalization* is lack of involvement in either cultures and rejection of both of them.

The phenomenon of acculturation has assumed immense importance in contemporary times because more and more people are migrating from their native countries to others. A simple way of defining migration is to picture it as a phenomenon of individuals moving from one country, place, or locality to another. It can include the entire gamut of situations, from individuals who move to study, to seek better employment, to better their future, to avoid political and religious harassment, and to marry as well as family units that move to better their lives or join their preestablished family members elsewhere. Avoidance of persecution is a relatively uncommon but nonetheless important reason for migration. Needless to say, once having been through the process of migration, the individuals who migrated undergo the closely related process of acculturation.

Programs are often developed to facilitate the process of acculturation. In this context two terms need to be understood: cultural sensitivity and cultural competence. Resnicow and colleagues (2000) have defined **cultural sensitivity** as "the extent to which ethnic/cultural characteristics, experiences, norms, values, behavioral patterns, and beliefs of a target population as well as relevant historical, environmental, and social forces are incorporated in the design, delivery, and evaluation of targeted health promotion materials and programs." There are two structures of cultural sensitivity, which can be thought of in terms of two primary dimensions (Resnicow, Baranowski, Ahluwalia, & Braithwaite, 1999): surface structure and deep structure. The former involves matching intervention materials and messages to the visible social and behavioral characteristics of a target population. It also includes an identification of the channels of communication and settings that would work best for a target group. For audiovisual materials, surface structure may involve using brand names and languages familiar to, and chosen by, the target audience. For example, a health program attempting to reach out to inner-city African American women might best be executed in a church setting.

Deep structure is the second dimension of cultural sensitivity and takes into account the manner in which cultural, social, environmental, psychological, and historical factors influence health behaviors across different racial/ethnic populations. Comprehension of how the target population perceives the cause and effect of an intervention is included in the deep structure. For example, some ethnic groups ascribe certain diseases to paranormal phenomena, and a health intervention targeting one of those conditions is bound to fail if it does not consider how that ethnic group will perceive the individual elements of the program. To sum up, the surface structure of an intervention can increase the receptivity, understanding, or acceptance of messages, whereas deep structure conveys salience and consequently determines the program's impact (Simons-Morton, Donohew, & Crump, 1997).

The other important term is **cultural competence**. As it applies to health care, the term alludes to the notion that the health care industry has to be flexible enough to be able to meet the needs of an increasingly diverse population and discard the idea of one-size-fits-all health care. Cultural competence goes beyond either cultural awareness or cultural sensitivity. A more generic approach is to define it as the possession of cultural knowledge and respect for different cultural perspectives, or having skills and being able to use those skills effectively in cross-cultural situations (Cross, Bazron, Dennis, & Isaacs 1989; Orlandi, 1995). Andrulis and colleagues (1999) have presented the concept as a continuum, recognizing the fact that individuals and institutions can differ in the effectiveness of their responses to cultural diversity.

THE ROLE OF BEHAVIOR

Another important basic concept for international health is that of **behavior**, especially **health behavior**. *Merriam-Webster's Dictionary* defines behavior as anything that an organism does involving action and response to stimulation. The key word is *action*. A behavior is any overt action, conscious or unconscious, with a measurable frequency, intensity, and duration. *Frequency* refers to how many times the behavior occurs in a given time period. For example, for the behavior of physical activity, we might classify someone as being active who participates in some sort of physical activity five days a week. *Intensity* refers to how intense or how hard the behavior is performed. For example, for physical activity behavior, we might say that a behavior is mildly intense, moderately intense, or vigorous, depending on the effect it has on the heart rate or the number of calories it burns. *Duration* refers to the amount of time spent on each session. For example, physical activity may last for so many minutes on any given day. Behaviors shape health. There are positive behaviors that augment health and there are negative behaviors that are deleterious to health.

Any behavior is influenced by factors at five levels. The first level pertains to individual factors. For example, a person's attitude helps determine his or her behavior. A person who is partaking in physical activity behavior may believe that physical activity is refreshing. The second level pertains to interpersonal factors. For example, the person may be exercising because his or her spouse requested it. The third level pertains to institutional or organizational factors. For example, there may be a policy at the workplace that requires every person to work out for an hour, which may be the reason the person is performing the physical activity behavior. The fourth level pertains to community factors. For example, the person may be living or working in a community where the only available parking is 10 minutes away from the destination building; this may be the main reason that the person is physically active. The final level in determining one's behavior is the role of public policy factors. For example, laws and policies requiring the use of seat belts while driving may make a person perform that particular behavior.

Now let us focus our attention on defining health behavior. The World Health Organization (WHO) (1998) defines health behavior as "any activity undertaken by an individual regardless of actual or perceived health status, for the purpose of promoting, protecting, or maintaining health, whether or not such behavior is objectively effective toward that end." David Gochman (1982, 1997) defines health behavior as "those personal attributes such as beliefs, expectations, motives, values, perceptions, and other cognitive elements; personality characteristics, including affective and emotional states and traits; and behavioral patterns, actions, and habits that relate to health maintenance, to health restoration, and to health improvement." Three key foci of health behavior are clear in these definitions: maintenance of health, restoration of health, and improvement of health.

These foci can also be seen as corresponding to the three levels of prevention, namely, primary, secondary, and tertiary prevention (Modeste & Tamayose, 2004; Pickett & Hanlon, 1998). **Primary prevention** refers to those preventive actions that are taken prior to the onset of a disease or injury with the intention of removing the possibility of their ever occurring. **Secondary prevention** refers to actions that block the progression of an injury or disease at its incipient stage. **Tertiary prevention** refers to those actions taken after the onset of disease or an injury with the intention of assisting diseased or disabled people. Actions for primary, secondary, and tertiary level care are taken at individual, interpersonal, organizational, community, and public policy levels. Thus, health behavior can be defined as all actions with a potentially measurable frequency, intensity, and duration performed at the individual, interpersonal, organizational, community, or public policy level for primary, secondary, or tertiary prevention.

Health behaviors can be about positive attributes, such as promoting physical activity or eating five or more servings of fruits and vegetables. Health behaviors can also be about extinguishing negative attributes, such as smoking or binge drinking. A similar categorization of behaviors is as risk behaviors and protective behaviors. The World Health Organization (1998) defines risk behaviors as "specific forms of behavior which are proven to be associated with increased susceptibility to a specific disease or ill-health." For example, indiscriminate sexual behavior is a risk behavior for sexually transmitted diseases, including HIV/AIDS. Protective behaviors are those behaviors that protect a person from developing ill health or specific disease. For example, a person may get immunized against tetanus and thus prevent the disease.

Another categorization of behaviors is into what Green and Kreuter (2005) have defined as health-directed and health-related behaviors. *Health-directed behaviors* are those behaviors that a person consciously pursues for health improvement or health protection, such as immunizations, physical examinations, eating low-fat food, or using condoms. *Health-related behaviors* are those actions that are performed for reasons other than health, but which have health effects. An example is an individual trying to lose weight in order to improve his or her appearance.

THEORIES OF HEALTH BEHAVIOR AND BEHAVIOR CHANGE

In international health, one major category of intervention is that which pertains to health education and health promotion. Health education and health promotion interventions have multiple influences from several disciplines. The primary influence on health education is derived from

> *There is nothing so practical as a good theory*
>
> —Kurt Lewin

behavioral sciences, however, and health promotion is deeply embedded in social sciences. It is from the behavioral and social sciences that the practice of health education and health promotion borrows the strategic planning of its methods.

The core concepts in behavioral and social sciences are organized in the form of theories. Kerlinger and Lee (2000) have defined **theory** as "a set of interrelated concepts, definitions, and predispositions that present a systematic view of events or situations by specifying relations among variables in order to explain and predict the events or situations." In health education and health promotion, we are primarily interested in predicting or explaining changes in behaviors or environments. Use of theory is becoming almost mandatory for practitioners of health education and health promotion. Theories help us articulate assumptions and hypotheses regarding the strategies and targets of interventions (National Cancer Institute, 2005).

Polit and Hungler (1999) have classified theories into three types. The first are the *macro theories* or *grand theories* that purport to explain and describe large segments of the environment or human experience—for example, Talcott Parsons's (1951) theory on social functioning. Second are *middle-range theories* that describe or explain phenomena such as specific behaviors—for example, Albert Bandura's (1986, 2004) social cognitive theory. Finally, there are *descriptive theories* that describe or explain a single discrete phenomenon—for example, Hans Selye's (1974) general adaptation syndrome.

Glanz, Rimer, and Lewis (2002) have classified theories as *explanatory theories*, or *theories of the problem*, and *change theories*, or *theories of action*. Explanatory theories help describe and identify why a problem exists and search for modifiable constructs. Change theories guide the development of interventions and form the basis of evaluation.

Theories start by discussing concepts or ideas that are abstract entities. These are not measurable or observable. The concepts are adopted into theories and become known as *constructs*. For example, in social cognitive theory (Bandura, 1986, 2004), self-efficacy is a construct. When specific properties are assigned to the construct, it becomes an *indicator*. For example, ten items might be written in the form of a questionnaire for the construct of self-efficacy for physical activity, constituting the meaning of the construct. From this indicator a variable or quantitative score is derived, which varies from one individual to other. For example, in the ten-item questionnaire each item might be ranked from 1 to 5 and the summation might yield a score of 10 to 50. The constructs of a theory are constantly refined from empirical testing. Ideally, a theory must be able to demonstrate predictive power. Behavioral theories must be able to make significant changes on affect (feelings or conation), thought (cognition), and action (volition). Ideally, a theory must be able to provide practical guidance on what, why, and how. An ideal theory must be testable and must be generalizable. The constructs of the theory must be able to explain phenomena, which for health education and health promotion are behaviors or environmental conditions.

The use of theory derived from behavioral or social science helps the practice of health education and health promotion in several ways. First, it helps in developing program objectives that are measurable. For example, if the health education program uses social cognitive theory (Bandura, 1986, 2004) to change physical activity behavior in elementary school students, then the objectives can be based on selected constructs derived from the theory.

Second, theory helps in identifying the method to use in health education or health promotion. Continuing with the previous example, social cognitive theory prescribes that in order to change self-efficacy the behavior must be taught in small steps, so demonstration could be used as a method. Third, the theory helps in deciding the timing of the intervention. For example, theoretically it would make sense to design interventions that prevent use of tobacco at the middle school level because that is when the behavior often begins. Fourth, the theory helps in choosing the right mix of strategies and methods. In the earlier example, we were able to choose three constructs of the social cognitive theory because the theory suggests that those three are important for early-stage adolescents.

Fifth, theory aids communication between professionals. The constructs of each theory remain the same in different applications, and thus readers can understand what was done across studies. Sixth, the use of theory helps in replication of the program because the same constructs can be used from one intervention to the other. Finally, behavioral and social science theories help in making programs more effective (greater impact) and efficient (less time). For a detailed account of the theories used in health education and health promotion, please see *Theoretical Foundations of Health Education and Health Promotion* (Sharma & Romas, 2008). The following sections present a summarized discussion of the common theories in health education and health promotion applied in international interventions.

Health Belief Model

The **health belief model** (HBM) is the first theory that was developed exclusively for health-related behaviors (Rosenstock, 1974). It had its start in an exploration of the reasons people were not accessing free screening for tuberculosis in the United States. The HBM predicts behavior based on the constructs of perceived susceptibility, perceived severity, perceived benefits, perceived costs, cues to action, and self-efficacy. *Perceived susceptibility* refers to the subjective belief a person has regarding the likelihood of acquiring a disease or harmful state as a result of indulging in a particular behavior. *Perceived severity* refers to the subjective belief in the extent of harm that can result from the acquired disease or harmful state as a result of a particular behavior. Perceived susceptibility and perceived severity are together called *perceived threat*. *Perceived benefits* are beliefs in the advantages of the methods suggested for reducing the risk or seriousness

The Health Belief Model (HBM) hypothesizes that health related action depends upon the simultaneous occurrence of three classes of factors:

1. The existence of sufficient motivation (or health concern) to make health issues salient or relevant.

2. The belief that one is susceptible (vulnerable) to a serious health problem or to the sequelae of that illness or condition. This is often termed perceived threat.

3. The belief that following a particular health recommendation would be beneficial in reducing the perceived threat, and at a subjectively acceptable cost.

—Rosenstock, Strecher, & Becker (1988), p. 177

of the disease or harmful state resulting from a particular behavior. *Perceived barriers* are beliefs concerning the actual and imagined costs of following the new behavior. *Cues to action* are the precipitating forces that make a person feel the need to take action. *Self-efficacy* is the confidence that a person has in his or her ability to pursue a behavior.

The HBM has been widely used in international settings. Examples of its application in international settings are for breast cancer screening in Turkey (Canbulat & Uzun, 2008), changing attitudes of hospital personnel toward influenza vaccination in the Netherlands (Van den Dool et al., 2008), mammography screening in Iran (Abbaszadeh, Haghdoost, Taebi, & Kohan, 2007), colorectal cancer screening in Hong Kong (Sung et al., 2007), cervical cancer screening in Thailand (Boonpongmanee & Jittanoon, 2007), treatment of depression in Brazil (Antunes & Campos, 2007), condom usage in Zimbabwe (Cort & Modeste, 2006–2007), osteoporosis prevention in Iran (Hazavehei, Taghdisi, & Saidi, 2007), and breast cancer screening in Lithuania (Zelviene & Bogusevicius, 2007).

The Transtheoretical Model

The **transtheoretical model** (TTM), or stages of change (SOC) model, which originated in the field of psychotherapy (Prochaska, 1979), is at present the most popular model in research and practice related to health education. The TTM is a model of behavior change that posits that people move through five stages of change, from precontemplation (not thinking about change) to contemplation (thinking about change over the next 6 months) to preparation (thinking about change in the next month) to action (having made meaningful change, but not having completed 6 months) and finally to maintenance (acquisition of the healthy behavior for 6 or more months).

The TTM identifies ten processes of change and the constructs of decisional balance, self-efficacy, and overcoming temptations, which aid the behavior change. *Decisional balance* is the construct of TTM that addresses the relative importance placed by an individual on the advantages (pros) of behavior change as opposed to the disadvantages (cons). *Self-efficacy* is the confidence that a person has in his or her ability to pursue a given behavior. *Temptation* refers to the urge to engage in unhealthy behavior when confronted with a difficult situation.

The processes of change are categorized as either experiential or behavioral in nature. Experiential processes include consciousness raising, dramatic relief, environmental reevaluation, social liberation, and self-reevaluation. Behavioral processes include stimulus control, counterconditioning, helping relationships, reinforcement management, and self-liberation. These are summarized in **Table 3.1**.

TABLE 3.1 Key Processes of the Transtheoretical Model	
Process	**Definition**
Consciousness raising	Experiential process that entails raising awareness about causes, consequences, and cures for a particular problem
Dramatic relief	Experiential process that enhances emotional arousal about one's behavior and the relief that can come from changing it
Environmental reevaluation	Experiential process that involves both affective and cognitive components of how the behavior affects one's environment and how changing the behavior would influence the environment
Self-reevaluation	Experiential process that involves both affective and cognitive components and includes one's assessment of self-image with the new behavior
Self-liberation	Behavioral process that entails belief that one can change and a commitment and recommitment to act on that change
Counterconditioning	Behavioral process that requires learning of new, healthier behavior instead of old, unhealthy behavior
Reinforcement management	Behavioral process that utilizes reinforcements and punishments for taking steps in a particular direction
Stimulus control	Behavioral process that involves modifying the environment to increase cues for healthy behavior and decrease cues for unhealthy behavior
Helping relationships	Behavioral process that entails developing caring, open, trusting, and accepting relationships to adhere to the healthy behavior
Social liberation	Experiential process that refers to an increase in social opportunities or alternatives

The TTM has been widely used in international health. Some of its applications in international settings include mammography screening in South Korea (Kang, Thomas, Kwon, Hyun, & Jun, 2008), prevention of risky sexual behavior among HIV-positive youth in Thailand (Naar-King et al., 2008), smoking cessation intervention in Germany (Schumann et al., 2008), weight management in Malaysia (Chang, 2007), smoking cessation in South Korea (Ham & Lee, 2007), increasing calcium intake among women in Japan (Zhang, Ojima, & Murata, 2007), smoking prevention in Bulgaria (Anatchkova, Redding, & Rossi, 2007), breast self-examination in South Korea (Park, Hur, Kim, & Song, 2007), exercise behavior in South Korea (Kim, Cardinal, & Lee, 2006), an exercise counseling program in Switzerland (Märki, Bauer, Nigg, Conca-Zeller, & Gehring, 2006), sex education in England (Wallace et al., 2007), changing behaviors and attitudes in relation to tinnitus in Sweden (Kaldo, Richards, & Andersson, 2006), and prevention of osteoporosis among women in Iran (Shirazi et al., 2007).

Theory of Reasoned Action and Theory of Planned Behavior

In the late 1960s and early 1970s, Martin Fishbein and Icek Ajzen propounded the **theory of reasoned action** (TRA) (Fishbein & Ajzen, 1975). The theory claims that behavioral intention precedes behavior and is determined by an individual's attitude toward the behavior and subjective norms. *Attitude* toward the behavior is the individual's overall like or dislike of any given behavior and is determined by behavioral beliefs (beliefs that performing a given behavior lead to certain outcomes) and outcome evaluations (the value a person places on each outcome resulting from performance of a given behavior). A *subjective norm* is one's belief that most of the significant others in one's life think one should or should not perform the behavior and is determined by normative beliefs (a person's beliefs about how other people who are significant in his or her life would like him or her to behave) and motivation to comply (the degree to which a person wants to act in accordance with the perceived wishes of those significant in his or her life).

In the late 1980s and early 1990s, Ajzen added the construct of *perceived behavioral control* (how much a person feels that he or she is in command of enacting the given behavior) and created the **theory of planned behavior** (TPB) (Ajzen, 1991). The construct of perceived behavioral control is dependent on control beliefs (beliefs about internal and external factors that may inhibit or facilitate the performance of the behavior) and perceived power (perception about how easy or difficult it is to perform the behavior in each condition identified in the control beliefs).

Both the TRA and TPB have been used in health education and health promotion in international settings. Some of the applications in international settings have been for physical activity behavior in Australia (Caperchione, Duncan, Mummery, Steele, & Schofield, 2008), changing eating behaviors in Spanish women (Barberia, Attree, & Todd, 2008), influencing the intentions of hospital nurses to work with computers in Israel (Shoham & Gonen, 2008), understanding intention to dispense antibiotics for upper respiratory infections among community pharmacists in Thailand (Saengcharoen, Chongsuvivatwong, Lerkiatbundit, & Wongpoowarak, 2008), physical activity intervention in the United Kingdom (Kinmonth et al., 2008), condom use behavior in Spain (Muñoz-Silva, Sánchez-García, Nunes, & Martins, 2007), condom use in South Korea (Cha, Kim, & Doswell, 2007), and healthy eating behavior among children in New Zealand (Hewitt & Stephens, 2007).

Social Cognitive Theory

Albert Bandura, a professor of psychology at Stanford University, is the originator of **social cognitive theory** (previously called social learning theory) (Bandura, 1986, 2004). This theory explains human behavior as a triadic reciprocal causation among behavior, environment, and personal factors (such as cognitions, affect, and biological events). Five basic human capabilities describe human beings according to this theory: symbolizing capability (use of symbols in attributing meaning to experiences), vicarious capability (learning from observing other people's behavior and the consequences they face), forethought capability (most behavior is purposive and regulated by prior thoughts), self-regulatory capability (setting of internal standards and self-evaluative reactions for one's behavior), and self-reflective capability (analysis of experiences and thinking about one's own thought processes).

The constructs of the theory include knowledge (learning of facts and gaining insights related to an action, idea, object, person, or situation), outcome expectations (the anticipation of the probable outcomes that would ensue as a result of engaging in the behavior), outcome expectancies (the value a person places on the probable outcomes that result from performing a behavior), situational perception (how a person perceives and interprets the environment around himself or herself), environment (the physical or social circumstances or conditions that surround a person), self-efficacy (the confidence that a person has in his or her ability to pursue a behavior), self-efficacy in overcoming impediments (the confidence that a person has in overcoming barriers while performing a given behavior), goal setting or self-control (setting goals and developing plans to accomplish chosen behaviors), and emotional coping (techniques employed by the person to control the emotional and physiologic states associated with acquisition of a new behavior). The constructs are amenable to modification by different educational methods.

Social cognitive theory has been applied over the past 30 years in a variety of ways within health promotion and education. In international settings the theory has been applied for an HIV risk reduction program in China (Li et al., 2008), self-care behaviors to reduce depression in kidney transplant patients in Taiwan (Weng, Dai, Wang, Huang, & Chiang, 2008), bettering walking performance in older adults with knee osteoarthritis in Canada (Maly, Costigan, & Olney, 2007), smoking cessation in China (Zheng et al., 2007), childhood obesity prevention in China (Murnan, Sharma, & Lin, 2006–2007), understanding sexual behavior in Poland (Kopacz, 2006), studying lottery gamblers in Thailand (Ariyabuddhiphongs & Chanchalermporn, 2007), studying children's eating behavior in Norway (Bere & Klepp, 2005), and changing physical activity behavior after knee replacement in Thailand (Harnirattisai & Johnson, 2005).

> *Self-efficacy is the belief in one's capabilities to organize and execute the sources of action required to manage prospective situations.*
>
> —Bandura (1986)

Social Marketing

Social marketing is the use of commercial marketing techniques to help a target population acquire a beneficial health behavior. Social marketing had its origins in India in the 1960s for promoting the family planning program by marketing condoms (Harvey, 1999). In the United States the approach began to be used in the 1970s; it is at present a useful technique for behavior change all over the world (Andreasen & Kotler, 2003).

Social marketing differs from commercial marketing in that social marketing is more demanding, the scrutiny is done from a variety of sources, the idea that is sold is often totally new, and the educational level of the target audience is usually low. Also, social marketing often has to address what people do not want to change, has high involvement between the marketer and the public, and often has invisible benefits or benefits that go to third parties. The rewards offered for making the recommended change are self-rewards, and budgets and the choices of products are limited. A salient concept in social marketing is that of exchange theory, which implies the voluntary transfer or transaction of something valuable between two parties (Thackeray & Brown, 2005). The benefits to the consumer must be underscored.

Social marketing goes through five steps: (1) planning, (2) message and material development, (3) pretesting, (4) implementation, and (5) evaluation. In planning, audience segmentation and marketing mix are important. In audience segmentation, distinct groups of people who are similar to each other in particular characteristics and are thus likely to respond to messages in a similar way are identified. In marketing mix, the product (behavior), price (costs and barriers), place, and promotion are considered. Social marketing adds a further four Ps: publics, partnership, policy, and purse strings.

The social marketing model has been widely applied in health education and health promotion programs. Some examples of its applications in international settings are for blood donation in Spain (Martín-Santana & Beerli-Palacio, 2008), a brucellosis public health information and awareness campaign in Iraq (Maxwell & Bill, 2008), physical activity promotion in Canada (Brawley & Latimer, 2007), controlling HIV among injecting drug users in China (Wu et al., 2007), promoting healthy food choices and eating behaviors in New Zealand (Signal et al., 2008), reproductive health communication campaigns in Zambia (Van Rossem & Meekers, 2007), an alcohol campaign in Australia (Ricciardelli & McCabe, 2008), improving consumption of iron-fortified soy sauce among women in China (Sun, Guo, Wang, & Sun, 2007), promoting awareness of HIV risk and testing in Latinos living on the California-Mexico border (Olshefsky, Zive, Scolari, & Zuñiga, 2007), and promoting the use of insecticide-treated bed nets in Nigeria (Ordinioha, 2007) and Kenya (Fegan, Noor, Akhwale, Cousens, & Snow, 2007).

Diffusion of Innovations

The **diffusion of innovations** theory deals with the adoption of a new idea, practice, or object over a period of time (Rogers, 2003). The origins of this theory are almost 100 years old, but the first empirical study was done in the 1940s by Bryce Ryan and Neal Gross at Iowa State University, who studied the adoption process and the characteristics of farmers who adopted hybrid corn seed (Ryan & Gross, 1943). Their work had implications not only in agriculture, but also for a variety of disciplines, including health promotion and health education.

The four main constructs of the diffusion of innovations theory are innovation, communication channels, time, and social system. Several attributes of innovation are as follows: perceived relative advantage (perception about how much better the new product, idea, or practice is than the one it will replace); compatibility (perception regarding the innovation's consistency with the values, past experiences, and needs of potential adopters); complexity (perception of the degree of difficulty in understanding and using the new idea, practice, or product); demonstrability (the degree to which an innovation may be experimented with on a limited basis); clarity of results (the degree to which the outcomes of an innovation are clearly visible); costs (the tangible and intangible expenses incurred in the adoption of a new idea, practice, or product); reversibility (the ability and degree to which the status quo can be rein-stated by ceasing to use the innovation); pervasiveness (the degree to which an inno-vation requires changes or adjustments by other elements in the social system); and reinvention (the degree to which a potential adopter can adapt, refine, or modify the innovation to suit his or her needs).

The communication channels are of three kinds: (1) mass-media channels, such as television, radio, and newspapers; (2) interpersonal channels, which require face-to-face interaction between two or more individuals; and (3) interactive communica-tion channels, such as the Internet.

The time construct is involved with the diffusion of innovations in three ways: (1) the innovation-decision process, (2) adopter categories, and (3) rate of adoption. The social system construct comprises homophily (similarity among group mem-bers), social networks (person-centered webs of social relationships), change agents (people who influence a potential adopter's decision about innovation in a favorable way), and opinion leaders (influential individuals in a community who sway the beliefs and actions of their colleagues in either a positive or negative direction).

The diffusion of innovations theory has been widely applied in public health. Some examples of its applications in international settings include diffusion of elec-tronic medical records in Japan (Ochieng & Hosoi, 2006), diffusion of magnetic resonance imaging in Iran (Palesh, Fredrikson, Jamshidi, Jonsson, & Tomson, 2007), offering postabortion contraceptive counseling and methods in Bolivia and Mexico (Billings, Crane, Benson, Solo, & Fetters, 2007), innovations in dental education in China (Huang, Bian, Tai, Fan, & Kwan, 2007), diffusion of health technologies in Australia, Canada, Denmark, France, the Netherlands, Norway, Spain, Sweden, Switzerland, and the United Kingdom (Packer, Simpson, Stevens, & EuroScan, 2006), diffusion of advanced diagnostic devices in India (Mahal, Varshney, & Taman, 2006), and diffusion of new surgical techniques in Australia (Maddern, Middleton, Tooher, & Babidge, 2006).

FOCUS FEATURE 3.1   The World Health Organization's MONICA Project

The World Health Organization established the MONICA (Multinational MONItoring of Trends and Determinants in CArdiovascular Disease) Project in the early 1980s at several centers around the world (WHO MONICA Project, 2006). The purpose of this project was to monitor trends in coronary heart disease and cerebrovascular disease and to relate them to risk factors, daily living habits, health care, and socioeconomic factors in the population over a 10-year period. The centers were located in Australia, Belgium, Canada, China, the Czech Republic, Denmark, Finland, France, Germany, Iceland,

Italy, Lithuania, New Zealand, Poland, Russia, Spain, Sweden, Switzerland, the United Kingdom, the United States, and Yugoslavia. Forty-one MONICA collaborating centers used a standardized protocol and studied 118 reporting units (subpopulations) with a total population aged 25 to 64 (both sexes) of about 15 million (WHO, 1988).

Data collection included standardized coronary and stroke event registration; data on medical care of patients before, during, and after the attack; risk factor measurements through sample surveys of the study population; and data on population size and mortality in the study populations. The risk factors that were assessed included smoking, blood pressure, total and HDL cholesterol, height, weight, marital status, and education.

Some results of the study have been analyzed, whereas some are still being analyzed. One of the results indicated that there was a wide difference between populations in nonfatal as well as fatal coronary event rates (Tunstall-Pedoe et al., 1994). The coronary heart disease event rates in men ranged from 915 per 100,000 in North Karelia, Finland, to 76 per 100,000 in Beijing, China. The coronary heart disease event rates in women ranged from 256 per 100,000 in Glasgow, United Kingdom, to 30 per 100,000 in Catalonia, Spain. Likewise there was a wide range in 28-day case-fatality rates, from 37% to 81% for men (mean 49%) and from 31% to 91% for women (mean 54%) (Tunstall-Pedoe et al., 1994).

The MONICA Project is among the very few projects that have been conducted at such a large scale with such a large population across different cultures. It provides an excellent example of multicountry collaboration on an issue and shows how risk factors vary from one community to another with regard to cardiovascular diseases.

THE PRECEDE-PROCEED MODEL

Several models for planning health education programs exist. For a detailed account of these models, please see *Theoretical Foundations of Health Education and Health Promotion* (Sharma & Romas, 2008). In the international context, two models have been used: PRECEDE-PROCEED and PEN-3. As of the mid-2000s, there were close to 1,000 published applications of the **PRECEDE-PROCEED model** in the health field (Green & Kreuter, 2005). The acronym PRECEDE stands for predisposing, reinforcing, and enabling constructs in educational/environmental diagnosis and evaluation. The acronym PROCEED stands for policy, regulatory, and organizational constructs in educational and environmental development.

The model originated in the 1970s from applications in hypertension trials (Green, Levine, & Deeds, 1975; Green, Levine, Wolle, & Deeds, 1979), cost-benefit evaluations (the ratio of benefits accrued in dollar amounts to the dollars spent on the program) of health education (Green, 1974), family planning studies (Green, 1970), and immunization campaigns (Rosenstock, Derryberry, & Carriger, 1959). The model was initially called PRECEDE (predisposing, reinforcing, and enabling constructs in educational diagnosis and evaluation) and remained popular under that name throughout the 1980s (Green, Kreuter, Deeds, & Partridge, 1980). In the 1980s the movement for health promotion grew very strong. In response, the model evolved and came to be known in its present-day form as PRECEDE-PROCEED, in which a number of health promotion functions were added. In the 1990s the role of socioenvironmental approaches was strengthened even further, and the model emphasized the ecological approach. The latest edition of this model was published in 2005 (Green & Kreuter, 2005). For detailed discussion of this model, see *Health Program Planning: An Educational and Ecological Approach* (Green & Kreuter, 2005).

The PRECEDE-PROCEED model has eight phases that provide guidance in planning any health program (**Figure 3.1**). The first phase is the *social assessment and situational analysis phase*. In this phase an assessment of community perceptions is done

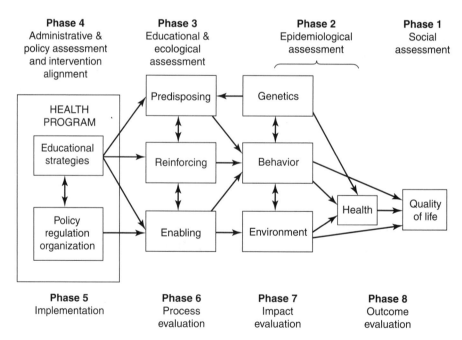

FIGURE 3.1 Generic representation of the PRECEDE-PROCEED model for health program planning and evaluation that shows the main lines of causation from program inputs and determinants of health to outcomes by the direction of the arrows.

Note: From Green, L. W., & Kreuter, M.W. (2005). Health program planning: An educational and ecological approach (4th ed., p. 10). Boston, MA: Mc Graw Hill. Reproduced with permission.

as a starting point for identifying quality of life concerns, using such methods as asset mapping, social reconnaissance, nominal group process, the Delphi method, focus groups, central location intercept interviews, and surveys. Asset mapping is an assessment of the strengths, capacities, and skills of individuals and the existing resources in a community. In social reconnaissance, a point of entry into the community is chosen and local players are identified; this is followed by preparation of research and briefing materials and identification of leaders and representatives, followed in turn by field interviews and then analysis, reporting, and follow-up. In the nominal group process, community participants are recruited and are given a single question on which to reflect. The responses are collected and then ranked in importance by the participants to establish a priority list. In the Delphi method, a panel of experts is recruited and sent a questionnaire. Subsequent mailings of the questionnaire aim at deriving consensus and narrow the choices with each iteration. Focus group discussions are small group discussions on a given topic that are moderated by a facilitator. Central location intercept interviews are conducted at shopping malls, churches, and other such places where target population members can be found. These interviews typically include structured, close-ended questions. Surveys also consist of asking questions of the target population and can be done by mail, e-mail, online, or other means.

The second phase is *epidemiologic assessment* and includes identifying what specific health problems are contributing to or interacting with the quality of life concerns identified in the social assessment. This phase also identifies the causative factors in the three categories of genetics, behaviors, and environments. Epidemiology consists of two parts: descriptive and analytic. This phase attempts to gather information on both these aspects. In descriptive epidemiology, facts regarding the time, place, and population attributes of the health problem are collected through mortality (death), morbidity (illness), and disability rates. Analytic epidemiology examines the determinants of health. In this model, analytic work translates into identifying behaviors and environments. Behaviors are of three types: proximal, or direct, actions affecting health; actions influencing the health of others; and distal actions affecting the organizational or policy environment. To diagnose behaviors that need targeting, a listing of all behavioral factors is made and the factors are rated in terms of importance and changeability, focusing on those behaviors that are more changeable and more important; behavioral objectives are then developed for those selected. To diagnose environments, the environmental factors are listed and then rated in terms of importance and changeability, again focusing on the more changeable and more important ones; environmental objectives are then determined.

The third phase is *educational and ecological assessment*. In this phase, factors are classified into the hallmark categories of this model as predisposing, enabling, or reinforcing factors. Predisposing factors are those factors that are antecedents to behavioral change and that provide motivation for the behavior (e.g., knowledge, beliefs, attitudes, values, perceptions). Enabling factors are antecedents to behavioral or environmental change that allow a motivation or environmental policy to be realized (e.g., availability of resources, accessibility, laws, legislations, skills). Reinforcing factors are those factors that follow a behavior and provide continuing reward for sustenance of the behavior (e.g., family, peers, teachers, employers, health providers, community leaders, decision makers). In this phase the factors are identified and sorted, priorities are determined, and once again priorities within categories are identified using the criteria of changeability and importance.

The fourth phase is the *administrative and policy assessment and intervention alignment phase*. In this phase the program components are aligned with priorities, the resources needed to run the program are identified, the barriers that can influence the program are identified, and the policies needed to run the program are developed. In aligning priority determinants with program components, matching of ecological levels with program components is done, followed by mapping of specific interventions, and finally by pooling of previous interventions to patch any gaps. This phase assesses aspects such as time, personnel, and budget.

The fifth phase is the *implementation phase*. In this phase several factors play a role that may hinder or augment the impact of the program. These pertain to the program (such as resources and goals), implementing organization (such as employee attributes, organizational goals, and organizational climate), political milieu, and environment (such as timing and other organizations).

The sixth phase is the *process evaluation*. In this phase, it is first determined whether the intervention is being done in the manner in which it has been planned. For example, if ten activities were planned, have all of these been implemented, and to what extent have they been implemented? Second, the reception of the program at the site where it has been implemented is determined. Third, the attitudes of the recipients of the program are considered. How satisfied have they been with the program? What are things they liked and what are things they disliked about the program? Fourth, the response of the person implementing the program is determined. What difficulties did he or she face while implementing the program? What things were easy to do? Finally, the competencies of the personnel involved are assessed. For example, if health education work was done, was it done by a certified health education specialist or someone else?

The seventh phase is the *impact evaluation*. Impact evaluation assesses the immediate effect of the program on its target behaviors or environments and their predisposing, enabling, and reinforcing antecedents. For example, a program designed to combat obesity in a community would measure physical activity behavior and consumption of fruits and vegetables.

The final phase is *outcome evaluation*. In this phase, changes in health status (such as mortality, morbidity, and disability indicators) and quality of life concerns (such as perceived quality of life and unemployment) are measured.

The PRECEDE-PROCEED model has been used in a variety of international settings. Some applications of the PRECEDE-PROCEED model in international settings are for control of foodborne parasitic zoonoses in Nepal (Jimba & Joshi, 2001), hypertension care and control among hypertensive blacks in South Africa (Dennison, Peer, Steyn, Levitt, & Hill, 2007), development of an early psychosis public education program in Canada (Yeo, Berzins, & Addington, 2007), a youth mental health community awareness campaign in Australia (Wright, McGorry, Harris, Jorm, & Pennell, 2006), training of health care professionals in the Democratic Republic of the Congo (Parent et al., 2004), a self-management asthma educational program in Taiwan (Chiang, Huang, Yeh, & Lu, 2004), promoting contraceptive use behavior in China (Wu, Wang, Rauyajin, & Good, 2002), and organizing a health fair in Mexico (Hecker, 2000).

The developers of this model, Larry Green and Marshall Kreuter, teamed up with Robert Gold to develop a computerized software program designed to help health educators in academia who teach community health courses and assist practitioners in the field to plan and implement community health programs. The software is called *EMPOWER (Enabling Methods of Planning and Organizing Within Everyone's Reach)* (Gold, Green, & Kreuter, 1998). The program provides a specific example in the area of breast cancer prevention and control and walks the user through the various steps of the PRECEDE-PROCEED model.

The PRECEDE-PROCEED model is by far the most popular and most researched model in the field of health promotion and health education. It has been in existence for four decades, and professionally trained health educators are familiar with this model. It is very comprehensive and covers all areas of planning. The initiation of the model relies on community inputs and participation, which is a big plus. The phase-wise evaluation is also a strong feature of the model.

However, the model does have a few limitations. First, it is too comprehensive to be implemented in its totality in all situations. Often, health promotion and education

> *The hallmarks of the PRECEDE-PROCEED model are: (1) flexibility and scalability, (2) evidence-based process and evaluability, (3) its commitment to the principle of participation, and (4) its provision of a process for appropriate adaptation of evidence-based "best practices."*
>
> —Green and Kreuter (2005), p. 18

funding is allocated for working in a specific area, and there is no provision for social assessment or epidemiologic assessment. In such cases the model is implemented in a piecemeal fashion. Second, health promotion and education programs are often implemented on a limited basis. These programs often do not account for changes in health outcomes, and thus outcome evaluation is often not possible. Third, the model is a mixture of several theories, and thus it is not possible to discern which component of the model is working and to what extent. Finally, comparative studies of this model with other models have not been done. Therefore, the relative utility of this model in relation to other models cannot be commented upon.

THE PEN-3 MODEL

The **PEN-3 model** originated in child survival programs in African countries (Airhihenbuwa, 1993, 1995). Later its use was extended to several other applications with minority populations, such as breast and cervical cancer screening in Latina women (Erwin, Johnson, Feliciano-Libid, Zamora, & Jandorf, 2005), cancer screening in African American men (Abernethy et al., 2005), dietary behaviors in African Americans (James, 2004), health factors in Latina immigrants (Garces, Scarinci, & Harrison, 2006), and smoking practices in African Americans (Beech & Scarinci, 2003).

The model consists of three dimensions, each of which contains the acronym PEN. The three dimensions are interrelated and interdependent. The first dimension, *health education*, has the following PEN:

P   *Person*. Health education should be committed to improving the health of every person.

E   *Extended family*. Health education should be directed toward not just the immediate family, but also the extended family or kinships of the person.

N   *Neighborhood*. Health education should be directed toward improving health in neighborhoods and communities. Involvement of community leaders is vital for culturally appropriate health programming.

The second dimension of the PEN-3 model is *educational diagnosis of health behavior*. This dimension evolved from the health belief model (Hochbaum, 1958), the theory of reasoned action (Fishbein & Ajzen, 1975), and the PRECEDE-PROCEED model (Green & Kreuter, 2005). In this dimension the PEN acronym is as follows:

P   *Perceptions*. These pertain to knowledge, beliefs, attitudes, and values that may facilitate or hinder motivation for changing a given behavior. Here the health programs must start with the perceived perceptions of the person rather than the real needs identified by the planners for the latter to be meaningful and acceptable.

E *Enablers.* These are societal or systemic forces that may augment the health behavior or hinder it by creating barriers. These include available resources, accessibility, referrals, and types of service.

N *Nurturers.* These are reinforcing factors that an individual may receive from significant others. These significant others could be members of the extended family, peers, employers, health personnel, religious leaders, or government officials.

The third dimension of the PEN-3 model is the *cultural appropriateness of health beliefs.* Thus, this model is particularly useful for work with minority populations and yields a culturally appropriate program. The PEN acronym in this dimension is as follows:

P *Positive.* These are the positive perceptions, enablers, and nurturers that help the person, family, or community to engage in positive healthy practices. These positive health practices lead to empowerment at the individual level, family level, and community level.

E *Exotic.* These consist of practices that are neither good nor bad and thus do not need to be changed.

N *Negative.* These are the negative perceptions, enablers, and nurturers that help the person, family, or community to engage in negative practices that impair health.

In planning, this model goes through several phases. The first phase is health education, in which the planners must decide whether the health education effort is directed toward individuals, extended families, or communities. In the second phase, the planners collect data by surveys or interviews or both and identify the beliefs and practices related to perceptions, enablers, and nurturers. The third phase entails classifying these beliefs into three categories: positive, exotic, or negative. In the final phase, the planners classify beliefs into those which are rooted in cultural patterns and those which are newly formed and select culturally appropriate health education strategies.

SKILL-BUILDING ACTIVITY

Let us take the most popular model for planning health education and health promotion programs, the PRECEDE-PROCEED model, and see how we can apply it to a practical situation. Let us assume we are interested in developing a smoking cessation program for smokers in a small city in India. **Figure 3.2** depicts each phase of the model and how it can be applied.

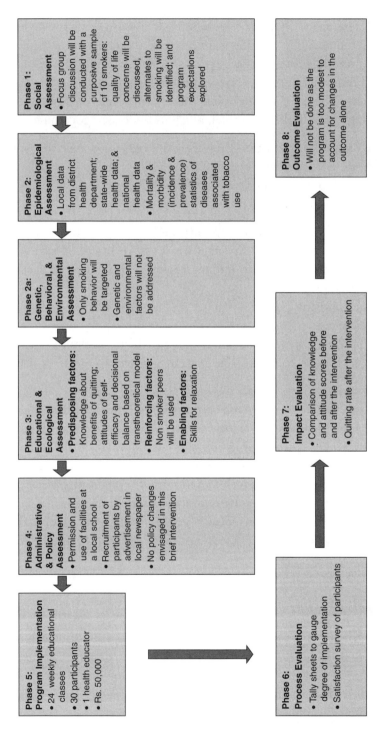

FIGURE 3.2   Application of PRECEDE-PROCEED Model for changing smoking behavior in a small group of smokers in a small city in India through a brief first-time educational intervention.

In the first phase, you could choose focus group discussion with the target audience for social assessment. The focus group discussion would identify the target audience's quality of life concerns, alternatives to smoking, and program expectations. In the first part of the second phase, epidemiologic assessment, you could collect local data from the district health department, statewide health data, and national health data about the adverse effects of tobacco and compile mortality and morbidity (incidence and prevalence) statistics of diseases associated with tobacco. In the second part of the second phase, only the behavioral factor of smoking can be chosen from the genetic, behavioral, and environmental factors.

In the third phase, educational and ecological assessment, you could select predisposing factors of knowledge about the benefits of quitting, attitudes of self-efficacy, and decisional balance based on the transtheoretical model (Prochaska & DiClemente, 1983). Nonsmoking peers can be used as reinforcing factors to deliver the message. In the enabling factors category, the program can build skills for relaxation as alternatives to smoking.

In the fourth phase of administrative and policy assessment, permission to use facilities at a local school can be obtained, and participants can be recruited by advertisement in the local newspaper. In the fifth phase, program implementation, one health educator could conduct 24 weekly educational sessions with 30 participants at a total cost of 50,000 rupees.

In the sixth phase, process evaluation, you could use tally sheets to gauge the degree of implementation, and perform a satisfaction survey of participants. In the seventh phase, impact evaluation, you could compare participants' knowledge and attitude scores before and after the intervention. Because the program is modest and of short duration, the eighth phase of outcome evaluation cannot be done.

Using this approach, you can also plan to work on a health issue of your choice with a target population of your choice. You can apply the PRECEDE-PROCEED model or another theory or model of your choice to plan your program.

SUMMARY

Culture refers to a shared set of knowledge, beliefs, customs, mores, traditions, practices, and values that are passed on from one generation to another. The field that studies the relationship between culture and disease and culture and health is medical anthropology. There are five dimensions of culture: power/distance, individualism versus collectivism, masculinity versus femininity, uncertainty avoidance, and short-term orientation versus long-term orientation. *Acculturation* is the psychosocial adjustment and adaptation to a new culture of people from another culture. The four modes of acculturation are integration, assimilation, separation, and marginalization.

In international health, one major category of intervention is that which pertains to health education and health promotion. The practice of health education and health promotion borrows theories from the behavioral and social sciences for the strategic planning of its methods. Some of the common theories of health education and health promotion are (1) the *health belief model*, which predicts behavior based on the constructs of perceived susceptibility, perceived severity, perceived benefits, perceived costs, cues to action, and self-efficacy; (2) the *transtheoretical model*, which posits that people move through five stages of change, from precontemplation to contemplation, preparation, action, and finally to maintenance; (3) the *theory of reasoned action*, which posits that behavioral intention precedes behavior and is determined by a person's attitude toward the behavior and subjective norms; (4) the *theory of planned behavior*, which posits that behavioral intention precedes behavior and is determined by an individual's attitude toward the behavior, subjective norms, and perceived behavioral control; (5) *social cognitive theory*, which explains human behavior as a triadic reciprocal causation among behavior, environment, and personal factors (expectations, expectancies, self-efficacy, and self control); (6) *social marketing*, which is the use of commercial marketing techniques to help a target population acquire a beneficial health behavior; and (7) *diffusion of innovations*, which explains the adoption of a new idea, practice, or object over a period of time. In addition, two planning models that have been used in international settings are the PRECEDE-PROCEED model and PEN-3 model.

IMPORTANT TERMS

acculturation

anthropology

behavior

culture

cultural competence

cultural sensitivity

diffusion of innovations

health behavior

health belief model

medical anthropology

PEN-3 model

PRECEDE-PROCEED model

primary prevention

secondary prevention

social cognitive theory

social marketing

tertiary prevention

theory

theory of planned behavior

theory of reasoned action

transtheoretical model

REVIEW QUESTIONS

1. What is culture? What are the dimensions of culture?
2. What is health behavior? Differentiate between health-directed and health-related behaviors.
3. Describe the constructs of the health belief model.
4. Discuss the five stages of behavior change in the transtheoretical model.
5. List and define the constructs of the theory of reasoned action.
6. List and define the constructs of the theory of planned behavior.
7. Describe the constructs of social cognitive theory.
8. Differentiate between social marketing and commercial marketing.
9. Discuss any five attributes of innovations.
10. Describe the PRECEDE-PROCEED model. How would you design a program to promote oral rehydration solution use in children in a developing country?
11. Describe the PEN-3 model.

WEB SITES TO EXPLORE

CORE Diffusion of Innovations Initiative

http://www.coregroup.org/diffusion/start.cfm

Part of the Web site of the CORE Group, a membership association of international nongovernmental organizations (NGOs). CORE promotes and improves the health of children and women in developing countries through collaborative NGO action and learning. In 2003–2004, CORE disbursed six awards to its members for the diffusion of promising child health innovations to a larger audience. The winning innovations were a practical guide for Africa on vitamin A supplementation, a guide for community-based volunteer health educators, a partnership defined quality (PDQ) approach, a barrier analysis manual, a census-based, impact-oriented (CBIO) approach, and a safe motherhood program. *Review this Web site and read more about each of these six interventions. Which one did you like most and why?*

Idea: Social Cognitive Theory Compared with Constructivism and Cooperative Learning

http://i-d-e-a.org/page109.html

This Web site presents an overview of social cognitive theory and compares it with the theory of constructivism and with cooperative learning. Social cognitive theory, as we have seen, underscores the role of self-efficacy, self-control, outcome expectations, and outcome expectancies in relation to behavior development. In constructivism, the learner actively constructs new ideas and interprets concepts based on his or her current and past knowledge. In cooperative learning, the learner is actively engaged in the learning process. *Review this Web site and compare and contrast the three theoretical approaches.*

PRECEDE-PROCEED Model

http://www.lgreen.net/precede.htm

The PRECEDE-PROCEED model has evolved since the1970s using inputs from professionals around the country. This Web site includes a brief history of the genesis and evolution of the model. *Explore this Web site to find out about the new features in the current edition of the book that describes this model.*

Professor Icek Aizen (Ajzen)

http://www.people.umass.edu/aizen/

The Web site of Professor Icek Aizen contains links to his contact information, professional background information, teaching interests, research interests, publications, and information on the theory of planned behavior. The link to the theory of planned behavior provides a depiction of the model, bibliography of the model, tips on constructing a questionnaire based on TPB, tips on designing an intervention based on TPB, a research manual on TPB developed by researchers at the University of New Castle, and frequently asked questions. *Read the frequently asked questions. Summarize what new things you learned.*

Resource Center for Adolescent Pregnancy Prevention (RECAPP)

http://www.etr.org/recapp/theories/hbm/index.htm

This Web site defines the health belief model and explains its components with examples. It discusses the application of HBM to sexuality education and presents a case study of its application to adolescent fertility control. *Review the case study and identify its strengths and weaknesses.*

Social Marketing Institute

http://www.social-marketing.org/index.html

In 1999, based on a funding grant from the Robert Wood Johnson Foundation, the Social Marketing Institute was formed with a mission to advance the science and practice of social marketing. The institute provides on-site team-based strategic guidance to programs, organizations, businesses, and foundations to apply social marketing approaches; carry out and disseminate research on social marketing best practices; train and educate in social marketing; sponsor academic research; and provide connections and leadership to social change professionals, commercial marketers, academics, and funders. *Navigate this Web site and read the social marketing success stories, such as the Click It or Ticket campaign, Florida's ant-smoking campaign, the oral rehydration campaign in Honduras, and many other such stories. Which story did you like most and why?*

Transtheoretical Model: Webcast

http://nursing.buffalo.edu/research/TTM.asp

This Web site from the School of Nursing at the State University of New York, Buffalo, presents a series of video clips from 2003 that show Dr. James Prochaska speaking about the TTM and its applications. *Visit this Web site, download the clips, and write your reaction to the presentation.*

REFERENCES

Abbaszadeh, A., Haghdoost, A., Taebi, M., & Kohan, S. (2007). The relationship between women's health beliefs and their participation in screening mammography. *Asian Pacific Journal of Cancer Prevention, 8*(4), 471–475.

Abernethy, A. D., Magat, M. M., Houston, T. R., Arnold, H. L., Jr., Bjorck, J. P., & Gorsuch, R. L. (2005). Recruiting African American men for cancer screening studies: Applying a culturally based model. *Health Education and Behavior, 32*(4), 441–451.

Airhihenbuwa, C. O. (1993). Health promotion for child survival in Africa: Implications for cultural appropriateness. *Hygie, 12*(3), 10–15.

Airhihenbuwa, C. O. (1995). *Health and culture: Beyond the Western paradigm.* Thousand Oaks, CA: Sage Publications.

Ajzen, I. (1991). The theory of planned behavior. *Organizational Behavior and Human Decision Process, 50,* 179–211.

Anatchkova, M. D., Redding, C. A., & Rossi, J. S. (2007). Development and validation of transtheoretical model measures for Bulgarian adolescent non-smokers. *Substance Use and Misuse, 42*(1), 23–41.

Andreasen, A. R., & Kotler, P. (2003). *Strategic marketing for nonprofit organizations* (6th ed.). Upper Saddle River, NJ: Prentice Hall.

Andrulis, D. P., Delbanco, T. L, & Shaw-Taylor, Y. (1999). *Cross cultural competence in health care survey.* Washington, DC: National Public Health and Hospital Institute.

Antunes, H. M., & Campos, C. J. (2007). Parents and caregivers of depressed adolescents: Learning about experiences that led to the search for specialized care [in Portuguese]. *Revista da Escola Enfermagem da USP, 41*(2), 205–212.

Ariyabuddhiphongs, V., & Chanchalermporn, N. (2007). A test of social cognitive theory reciprocal and sequential effects: Hope, superstitious belief and environmental factors among lottery gamblers in Thailand. *Journal of Gambling Studies, 23*(2), 201–214.

Bailey, E. J. (2000). Medical anthropology and African American health. Westport, Connecticut: Bergin & Garvey.

Bandura, A. (1986). *Social foundations of thought and action.* Englewood Cliffs, NJ: Prentice Hall.

Bandura, A. (2004). Health promotion by social cognitive means. *Health Education and Behavior, 31,* 143–164.

Barberia, A. M., Attree, M., & Todd, C. (2008). Understanding eating behaviours in Spanish women enrolled in a weight-loss treatment. *Journal of Clinical Nursing, 17*(7), 957–966.

Beech, B. M., & Scarinci, I. C. (2003). Smoking attitudes and practices among low-income African-Americans: Qualitative assessment of contributing factors. *American Journal of Health Promotion, 17*(4), 240–248.

Bere, E., & Klepp, K. I. (2005). Changes in accessibility and preferences predict children's future fruit and vegetable intake. *International Journal of Behavioral Nutrition and Physical Activity, 2,* 15.

Berry, J. W. (1997). Immigration, acculturation, and adaptation. *Applied Psychology: An International Review, 46*(1), 5–33.

Billings, D. L., Crane, B. B., Benson, J., Solo, J., & Fetters, T. (2007). Scaling-up a public health innovation: A comparative study of post-abortion care in Bolivia and Mexico. *Social Science and Medicine, 64*(11), 2210–2222.

Boonpongmanee, C., & Jittanoon, P. (2007). Predictors of Papanicolaou testing in working women in Bangkok, Thailand. *Cancer Nursing, 30*(5), 384–389.

Brawley, L. R., & Latimer, A. E. (2007). Physical activity guides for Canadians: Messaging strategies, realistic expectations for change, and evaluation. *Canadian Journal of Public Health, 98*(Suppl. 2), S170–184.

Canbulat, N., & Uzun, O. (2008). Health beliefs and breast cancer screening behaviors among female health workers in Turkey. *European Journal of Oncology Nursing,* PMID: 18314391 [Epub ahead of print].

Caperchione, C. M., Duncan, M. J., Mummery, K., Steele, R., & Schofield, G. (2008). Mediating relationship between body mass index and the direct measures of the theory of planned behaviour on physical activity intention. *Psychology, Health and Medicine, 13*(2), 168–179.

Cha, E. S., Kim, K. H., & Doswell, W. M. (2007). Influence of the parent-adolescent relationship on condom use among South Korean male college students. *Nursing and Health Sciences, 9*(4), 277–283.

Chang, C. T. (2007). Applicability of the stages of change and Weight Efficacy Lifestyle Questionnaire with natives of Sarawak, Malaysia. *Rural and Remote Health, 7*(4), 864.

Chiang, L. C., Huang, J. L., Yeh, K. W., & Lu, C. M. (2004). Effects of a self-management asthma educational program in Taiwan based on PRECEDE-PROCEED model for parents with asthmatic children. *The Journal of Asthma, 41*(2), 205–215.

Cort, M. A., & Modeste, N. N. (2006–2007). Attitudes toward condom use among high school and university students in Zimbabwe. *International Quarterly of Community Health Education, 26*(1), 61–72.

Cross, T. L., Bazron, B. J., Dennis, K. W, & Isaacs, M. R. (1989). *Towards a culturally competent system of care: A monograph on effective services for minority children who are severely emotionally disturbed.*

Washington, DC: CASSP Technical Assistance Center, Georgetown University Child Development Center.

Dennison, C. R., Peer, N., Steyn, K., Levitt, N. S., & Hill, M. N. (2007). Determinants of hypertension care and control among peri-urban black South Africans: The HiHi study. *Ethnicity & Disease, 17*(3), 484–491.

Engel, G. (1977). The need for a new medical model: A challenge for biomedicine. *Science, 196,* 129–136.

Erwin, D. O., Johnson, V. A., Feliciano-Libid, L., Zamora, D., & Jandorf, L. (2005). Incorporating cultural constructs and demographic diversity in the research and development of a Latina breast and cervical cancer education program. *Journal of Cancer Education, 20*(1), 39–44.

Fegan, G. W., Noor, A. M., Akhwale, W. S., Cousens, S., Snow, R. W. (2007). Effect of expanded insecticide-treated bednet coverage on child survival in rural Kenya: A longitudinal study. *Lancet, 370*(9592), 1035–1039.

Fishbein, M., & Ajzen, I. (1975). *Belief, attitude, intention, and behavior: An introduction to theory and research.* Reading, MA: Addison Wesley.

Fleming, L. E., Bennett, M. F., & Rao, N. (1998). Culture and health. In J. A. Herzstein, W. B. Bunn III, L. E. Fleming, J. M. Harrington, J. Jeyaratnam, & I. R. Gardner (Eds.), *International occupational and environmental medicine* (pp. 77–85). St. Louis, MO: Mosby.

Garces, I. C., Scarinci, I. C., & Harrison, L. (2006). An examination of sociocultural factors associated with health and health care seeking among Latina immigrants. *Journal of Immigrant and Minority Health, 8*(4), 377–385.

Glanz, K., Rimer, B. K., & Lewis, F. M. (2002). *Health behavior and health education: Theory, research, and practice* (3rd ed.). San Francisco, CA: Jossey-Bass.

Gochman, D. S. (1982). Labels, systems, and motives: Some perspectives on future research. *Health Education Quarterly, 9,* 167–174.

Gochman, D. S. (1997). Health behavior research: Definitions and diversity. In D. S. Gochman (Ed.), *Handbook of health behavior research: Vol. 1. Personal and social determinants.* New York: Plenum Press.

Gold, R. S., Green, L. W., & Kreuter, M. W. (1998). *EMPOWER: Enabling methods of planning and organizing within everyone's reach.* Sudbury, MA: Jones and Bartlett.

Green, L. W. (1970). Identifying and overcoming barriers to the diffusion of knowledge about family planning. *Advances in Fertility Control, 5,* 21–29.

Green, L. W. (1974). Toward cost-benefit evaluations of health education: Some concepts, methods and examples. *Health Education Monographs, 2*(Suppl. 1), 34–64.

Green, L. W., & Kreuter, M. W. (2005). *Health program planning: An educational and ecological approach* (4th ed.). Boston, MA: McGraw Hill.

Green, L. W., Kreuter, M. W., Deeds, S. G., & Partridge, K. B. (1980). *Health education planning: A diagnostic approach.* Palo Alto, CA: Mayfield.

Green, L. W., Levine, D. M., & Deeds, S. G. (1975). Clinical trials of health education for hypertensive outpatients: Design and baseline data. *Preventive Medicine, 4,* 417–425.

Green, L. W., Levine, D. M., Wolle, J., & Deeds, S. G. (1979). Development of randomized patient education experiments with urban poor hypertensives. *Patient Counseling and Health Education, 1,* 106–111.

Ham, O. K., & Lee, Y. J. (2007). Use of the transtheoretical model to predict stages of smoking cessation in Korean adolescents. *Journal of School Health*, *77*(6), 319–326.

Harnirattisai, T., & Johnson, R. A. (2005). Effectiveness of a behavioral change intervention in Thai elders after knee replacement. *Nursing Research*, *54*(2), 97–107.

Harvey, P. D. (1999). *Let every child be wanted: How social marketing is revolutionizing contraceptive use around the world.* Westport, CT: Auburn House.

Hazavehei, S. M., Taghdisi, M. H., & Saidi, M. (2007). Application of the health belief model for osteoporosis prevention among middle school girl students, Garmsar, Iran. *Education for Health*, *20*(1), 23.

Hecker, E. J. (2000). Feria de Salud: Implementation and evaluation of a communitywide health fair. *Public Health Nursing*, *17*(4), 247–256.

Helman, C. G. (1994). Culture, health and illness (3rd ed.). Oxford: Butterworth-Heinemann.

Helman, C. G. (2007). Anthropology and its contributions. In K. Bhui & D. Bhugra (Eds.), *Culture and mental health: A comprehensive textbook* (pp. 11–15). London: Hodder Arnold.

Hewitt, A. M., & Stephens, C. (2007). Healthy eating among 10- to 13-year-old New Zealand children: Understanding choice using the theory of planned behaviour and the role of parental influence. *Psychology, Health, and Medicine*, *12*(5), 526–535.

Hochbaum, G. M. (1958). *Public participation in medical screening programs: A sociopsychological study* (PHS Publication No. 572). Washington, DC: U.S. Government Printing Office.

Hofstede, G. (1980). *Culture's consequences: International differences in work-related values.* Beverly Hills, CA: Sage.

Hofstede, G. (1991). *Cultures and organizations.* London: Harper Collins Publishers.

Huang, C., Bian, Z., Tai, B., Fan, M., & Kwan, C. Y. (2007). Dental education in Wuhan, China: Challenges and changes. *Journal of Dental Education*, *71*(2), 304–311.

Ilola, L. M. (1990). Culture and health. In R. W. Brislin (Ed.), *Applied cross cultural psychology.* Newbury Park, CA: Sage.

James, D. C. (2004). Factors influencing food choices, dietary intake, and nutrition-related attitudes among African Americans: Application of a culturally sensitive model. *Ethnicity and Health*, *9*(4), 349–367.

Jimba, M., & Joshi, D. D. (2001). Health promotion approach for the control of food-borne parasitic zoonoses in Nepal: Emphasis on an environmental assessment. *Southeast Asian Journal of Tropical Medicine and Public Health*, *32*(Suppl. 2), 229–235.

Kaldo, V., Richards, J., & Andersson, G. (2006). Tinnitus Stages of Change Questionnaire: Psychometric development and validation. *Psychology, Health, and Medicine*, *11*(4), 483–497.

Kang, H. S., Thomas, E., Kwon, B. E., Hyun, M. S., & Jun, E. M. (2008). Stages of change: Korean women's attitudes and barriers toward mammography screening. *Health Care for Women International*, *29*(2), 151–164.

Kerlinger, F. N., & Lee, H. B. (2000). *Foundations of behavioral research* (4th ed.). Fort Worth, TX: Harcourt College Publishers.

Kim, Y., Cardinal, B. J., & Lee, J. (2006). Understanding exercise behavior among Korean adults: A test of the transtheoretical model. *International Journal of Behavioral Medicine*, *13*(4), 295–303.

Kinmonth, A. L., Wareham, N. J., Hardeman, W., Sutton, S., Prevost, A. T., Fanshawe, T., et al. (2008). Efficacy of a theory-based behavioural intervention to increase physical activity in an at-risk group in primary care (ProActive UK): A randomised trial. *Lancet*, *371*(9606), 41–48.

Kluckhohn, C., & Kroeber, A. (1952). Culture. *Peabody Museum Papers (Harvard University)*, *67*(1).

Kopacz, M. S. (2006). Sexual development and behaviour issues in Polish teenage magazines. *Central European Journal of Public Health*, *14*(4), 193–199.

Leach, E. (1982). Social anthropology (pp. 38–39). Glasgow: Fontana.

Li, X., Stanton, B., Wang, B., Mao, R., Zhang, H., Qu, M., et al. (2008). Cultural adaptation of the focus on kids program for college students in China. *AIDS Education and Prevention*, *20*(1), 1–14.

MacLachlan, M. (1997). *Culture and health*. New York: John Wiley & Sons.

Maddern, G. J., Middleton, P. F., Tooher, R., & Babidge, W. J. (2006). Evaluating new surgical techniques in Australia: The Australian Safety and Efficacy Register of New Interventional Procedures-Surgical experience. *Surgical Clinics of North America*, *86*(1), 115–28, ix–x.

Mahal, A., Varshney, A., & Taman, S. (2006). Diffusion of diagnostic medical devices and policy implications for India. *International Journal of Technology Assessment in Health Care*, *22*(2), 184–190.

Märki, A., Bauer, G. F., Nigg, C. R., Conca-Zeller, A., & Gehring, T. M. (2006). Transtheoretical model-based exercise counseling for older adults in Switzerland: Quantitative results over a 1-year period. *Sozial und Praventivmedizin*, *51*(5), 273–280.

Maly, M. R., Costigan, P. A., & Olney, S. J. (2007). Self-efficacy mediates walking performance in older adults with knee osteoarthritis. *Journals of Gerontology Series A Biological Sciences and Medical Sciences*, *62*(10), 1142–1146.

Martín-Santana, J. D., & Beerli-Palacio, A. (2008). Potential donor segregation to promote blood donation. *Transfusion and Apheresis Science*, PMID: 18343199 [Epub ahead of print].

Maxwell, J. R., & Bill, D. E. (2008). Developing a brucellosis public health information and awareness campaign in Iraq. *Military Medicine*, *173*(1), 79–84.

Mensah, L. (1993). Transcultural, cross-cultural and multicultural health perspectives in focus. In R. Masi, L. Mensah, & K. A. McLeod (Eds.), *Health and cultures I: Policies, professional practice and education*. London: Mosaic Press.

Modeste, N. M., & Tamayose, T. (Eds.). (2004). *Dictionary of public health promotion and education: Terms and concepts* (2nd ed.). San Francisco, CA: Jossey Bass.

Muñoz-Silva, A., Sánchez-García, M., Nunes, C., & Martins, A. (2007). Gender differences in condom use prediction with theory of reasoned action and planned behaviour: The role of self-efficacy and control. *AIDS Care*, *19*(9), 1177–1181.

Murnan, J., Sharma, M., & Lin, D. (2006–2007). Predicting childhood obesity prevention behaviors using social cognitive theory: Children in China. *International Quarterly of Community Health Education*, *26*(1), 73–84.

Naar-King, S., Rongkavilit, C., Wang, B., Wright, K., Chuenyam, T., Lam, P., et al. (2008). Transtheoretical model and risky sexual behaviour in HIV+ youth in Thailand. *AIDS Care*, *20*(2), 205–211.

National Cancer Institute. (2005). *Theory at a glance: A guide for health promotion practice* (2nd ed.). Washington, DC: U.S. Department of Health and Human Services. Retrieved from http://www.nci.nih.gov/theory/pdf

Ochieng, O. G., & Hosoi, R. (2006). Factors influencing diffusion of electronic medical records: A case study in three healthcare institutions in Japan. *The HIM Journal*, *34*(4), 120–129.

Olshefsky, A. M., Zive, M. M., Scolari, R., & Zuñiga, M. (2007). Promoting HIV risk awareness and testing in Latinos living on the U.S.-Mexico border: The Tú No Me Conoces social marketing campaign. *AIDS Education and Prevention*, *19*(5), 422–435.

Ordinioha, B. (2007). The use of insecticide-treated bed net in a semi-urban community in south-south, Nigeria. *Nigerian Journal of Medicine, 16*(3), 223–226.

Orlandi, M. A. (Ed.). (1995). *Cultural competence for evaluators: A guide for alcohol and other drug abuse prevention practitioners working with ethnic/racial communities. Vol. 1* (2nd ed.). OSAP Cultural Competence Series. Rockville, MD: U.S. Department of Health and Human Services.

Packer, C., Simpson, S., Stevens, A., & EuroScan. (2006). International diffusion of new health technologies: A ten-country analysis of six health technologies. *International Journal of Technology Assessment in Health Care, 22*(4), 419–428.

Palesh, M., & Fredrikson, S., Jamshidi, H., Jonsson, P. M., & Tomson, G. (2007). Diffusion of magnetic resonance imaging in Iran. *International Journal of Technology Assessment in Health Care, 23*(2), 278–285.

Parent, F., Kahombo, G., Bapitani, J., Garant, M., Coppieters, Y., Levêque, A., et al. (2004). A model for analysis, systemic planning and strategic synthesis for health science teaching in the Democratic Republic of the Congo: A vision for action. *Human Resources for Health, 2*(1), 16.

Park, S., Hur, H. K., Kim, G., & Song, H. (2007). Knowledge, barriers, and facilitators of Korean women and their spouses in the contemplation stage of breast self-examination. *Cancer Nursing, 30*(1), 78–84.

Parsons, T. (1951). *The social system.* New York: Free Press.

Pickett, G., & Hanlon, J. J. (1998). *Public health: Administration and practice* (10th ed.). St. Louis, MO: Mosby.

Polit, D. F., & Hungler, B. P. (1999). *Nursing research: Principles and methods* (6th ed.). Philadelphia, PA: Lippincott.

Prochaska, J. O. (1979). *Systems of psychotherapy: A transtheoretical analysis.* Homewood, IL: Dorsey Press.

Prochaska, J. O., & DiClemente, C. C. (1983). Stages and processes of self change in smoking: Toward an integrative model of change. *Journal of Consulting and Clinical Psychology, 5*, 390–395.

Redfield, R., Linton, R., & Herskovits, M. J. (1936). Memorandum for the study of acculturation. *American Anthropologist, 38*, 149–152.

Resnicow, K., Baranowski, T., Ahluwalia, J. S., & Braithwaite, R. L. (1999). Cultural sensitivity in public health: Defined and demystified. *Ethnicity and Disease, 9*(1), 10–21.

Resnicow, K., Soler, R., Braithwaite, R. L., Ahluwalia, J. S., & Butler, J. (2000). Cultural sensitivity in substance use prevention. *Journal of Community Psychology, 28*, 271–292.

Ricciardelli, L. A., & McCabe, M. P. (2008). University students' perceptions of the alcohol campaign: "Is Getting Pissed Getting Pathetic? (Just Ask Your Friends)." *Addictive Behaviors, 33*(2), 366–372.

Rogers, E. M. (2003). *Diffusion of innovations* (5th ed.). New York: Free Press.

Rosenstock, I. M. (1974). Historical origins of the health belief model. In M. H. Becker (Ed.), *The health belief model and personal health behavior* (pp. 1–8). Thorofare, NJ: Charles B. Slack.

Rosenstock, I. M., Derryberry, M., & Carriger, B. (1959). Why people fail to seek poliomyelitis vaccination. *Public Health Reports, 74*, 98–103.

Rosenstock, I. M., Strecher, V. J., & Becker, M. H. (1988). Social learning theory and the health belief model. *Health Education Quarterly, 15*, 175–183.

Ryan, B., & Gross, N. C. (1943). The diffusion of hybrid seed corn in two Iowa communities. *Rural Sociology, 8*, 15–24.

Ryder, A. G., Alden, L. E., & Paulhus, D. L. (2000). Is acculturation unidimensional or bidimensional? A head to head comparison in the prediction of personality, self-identity, and adjustment. *Journal of Personality and Social Psychology, 79*(1), 77–88.

Saengcharoen, W., Chongsuvivatwong, V., Lerkiatbundit, S., & Wongpoowarak, P. (2008). Factors influencing dispensing of antibiotics for upper respiratory infections among Southern Thai community pharmacists. *Journal of Clinical Pharmacy and Therapeutics, 33*(2), 123–129.

Schumann, A., John, U., Baumeister, S. E., Ulbricht, S., Rumpf, H. J., & Meyer, C. (2008). Computer-tailored smoking cessation intervention in a general population setting in Germany: Outcome of a randomized controlled trial. *Nicotine and Tobacco Research, 10*(2), 371–379.

Selye, H. (1974). *The stress of life.* New York: McGraw Hill.

Sharma, M., & Romas, J. A. (2008). *Theoretical foundations of health education and health promotion.* Sudbury, MA: Jones & Bartlett.

Shirazi, K. K., Wallace, L. M., Niknami, S., Hidarnia, A., Torkaman, G., Gilchrist, M., et al. (2007). A home-based, transtheoretical change model designed strength training intervention to increase exercise to prevent osteoporosis in Iranian women aged 40–65 years: A randomized controlled trial. *Health Education Research, 22*(3), 305–317.

Shoham, S., & Gonen, A. (2008). Intentions of hospital nurses to work with computers: Based on the theory of planned behavior. *Computers, Informatics, Nursing, 26*(2), 106–116.

Signal, L., Lanumata, T., Robinson, J. A., Tavila, A., Wilton, J., & Mhurchu, C. N. (2008). Perceptions of New Zealand nutrition labels by Māori, Pacific and low-income shoppers. *Public Health Nutrition,* PMID: 18167165 [Epub ahead of print].

Simons-Morton, B. G., Donohew, L., & Crump, A. D. (1997). Health communication in the prevention of alcohol, tobacco, and drug use. *Health Education & Behavior, 24*(5), 544–554.

Spector, R. E. (1996). *Cultural diversity in health and illness* (4th ed.) Stamford, CT: Appleton & Lange.

Sun, X., Guo, Y., Wang, S., & Sun, J. (2007). Social marketing improved the consumption of iron-fortified soy sauce among women in China. *Journal of Nutrition Education & Behavior, 39*(6), 302–310.

Sung, J. J., Choi, S. Y., Chan, F. K., Ching, J. Y., Lau, J. T., & Griffiths, S. (2007). Obstacles to colorectal cancer screening in Chinese: A study based on the health belief model. *American Journal of Gastroenterology,* PMID: 18047545 [Epub ahead of print].

Thackeray, R., & Brown, K. M. (2005). Social marketing's unique contributions to health promotion practice. *Health Promotion Practice, 6,* 365–368.

The WHO MONICA Project. (2006). Retrieved from http://www.ktl.fi/monica/.

Tunstall-Pedoe, H., Kuulasmaa, K., Amouyel, P., Arveiler, D., Rajakangas, A. M., & Pajak, A. (1994). Myocardial infarction and coronary deaths in the World Health Organization MONICA Project. Registration procedures, event rates, and case-fatality rates in 38 populations from 21 countries in four continents. *Circulation, 90*(1), 583–612.

Van den Dool, C., Van Strien, A. M., Akker, I. L., Bonten, M. J., Sanders, E. A., & Hak, E. (2008). Attitude of Dutch hospital personnel towards influenza vaccination. *Vaccine, 26*(10), 1297–1302.

Van Rossem, R., & Meekers, D. (2007). The reach and impact of social marketing and reproductive health communication campaigns in Zambia. *BMC Public Health, 7,* 352.

Wallace, L. M., Evers, K. E., Wareing, H., Dunn, O. M., Newby, K., Paiva, A., et al. (2007). Informing school sex education using the stages of change construct: Sexual behaviour and attitudes towards sexual activity and condom use of children aged 13–16 in England. *Journal of Health Psychology, 12*(1), 179–183.

Weng, L. C., Dai, Y. T., Wang, Y. W., Huang, H. L., & Chiang, Y. J. (2008). Effects of self-efficacy, self-care behaviours on depressive symptom of Taiwanese kidney transplant recipients. *Journal of Clinical Nursing*, PMID: 18266845 [Epub ahead of print].

World Health Organization. (1988). The World Health Organization MONICA Project (monitoring trends and determinants in cardiovascular disease): A major international collaboration. *Journal of Clinical Epidemiology, 41*(2), 105–114.

World Health Organization. (1998). *Health promotion glossary.* Retrieved from http://www.who.int/hpr/NPH/docs/hp_glossary_en.pdf

Wright, A., McGorry, P. D., Harris, M. G., Jorm, A. F., & Pennell, K. (2006). Development and evaluation of a youth mental health community awareness campaign—The Compass Strategy. *BMC Public Health*, 6, 215.

Wu, J., Wang, L., Rauyajin, O., & Good, S. (2002). Contraceptive use behavior among never married young women who are seeking pregnancy termination in Beijing. *Chinese Medical Journal, 115*(6), 851–855.

Wu, Z., Luo, W., Sullivan, S. G., Rou, K., Lin, P., Liu, W., et al. (2007). Evaluation of a needle social marketing strategy to control HIV among injecting drug users in China. *AIDS, 21*(Suppl. 8), S115–S122.

Yeo, M., Berzins, S., & Addington, D. (2007). Development of an early psychosis public education program using the PRECEDE PROCEED model. *Health Education Research, 22*(5), 639–647.

Zelviene, A., & Bogusevicius, A. (2007). Reliability and validity of the Champion's Health Belief Model Scale among Lithuanian women. *Cancer Nursing, 30*(3), E20–E28.

Zhang, Y., Ojima, T., & Murata, C. (2007). Calcium intake pattern among Japanese women across five stages of health behavior change. *Journal of Epidemiology, 17*(2), 45–53.

Zheng, P., Guo, F., Chen, Y., Fu, Y., Ye, T., & Fu, H. (2007). A randomized controlled trial of group intervention based on social cognitive theory for smoking cessation in China. *Journal of Epidemiology, 17*(5), 147–155.

CHAPTER 4

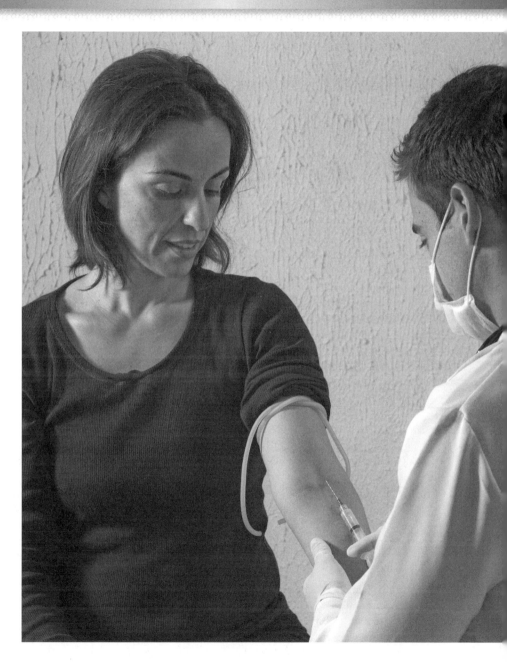

Infectious and Communicable Diseases

AFTER READING THIS CHAPTER YOU SHOULD BE ABLE TO

- Describe the epidemiology of and prevention and control measures for childhood vaccine-preventable diseases
- Explain the epidemiology of and prevention and control measures for malaria
- Discuss the epidemiology of and prevention and control measures for sexually transmitted diseases, including HIV/AIDS
- Describe the epidemiology of and prevention and control measures for tuberculosis
- Illustrate the epidemiology of and prevention and control measures for acute respiratory infections
- Explain the epidemiology of and prevention and control measures for acute gastrointestinal infections
- Describe the epidemiology of and prevention and control measures for meningococcal meningitis
- Explicate the epidemiology of and prevention and control measures for leprosy
- Discuss the epidemiology of and prevention and control measures for emerging infections

We are surrounded by microorganisms in our daily life. A large majority of these microorganisms are harmless and aid in various vital processes of life, such as photosynthesis, nitrogen fixation, production of vitamins in the human intestine, and decomposition of organic matter (Kok & Pechere, 2004). However, some of these microorganisms are not good for human beings and cause diseases. These are called *virulent* or *pathogenic* microorganisms. This chapter discusses some of the common ailments caused by these microorganisms. These diseases are called *infectious* or *communicable diseases*. It is beyond the scope of this text to discuss all infectious and communicable diseases, but some of the common ones are discussed, including the causative agent for each disease, aspects of transmission, clinical features, epidemiology, and aspects of prevention and control.

Infectious and communicable diseases are more common in low- and middle-income countries than in high-income countries. Eight diseases and health conditions account for 29% of all deaths (17.6 million deaths) in low-income and middle-income countries: tuberculosis, HIV/AIDS, diarrheal diseases, vaccine-preventable diseases of childhood, malaria, respiratory infections, maternal conditions, and neonatal deaths (Jamison et al., 2006).

CHILDHOOD VACCINE-PREVENTABLE DISEASES

Several communicable diseases are common in childhood, but are preventable by vaccinations: diphtheria, pertussis (whooping cough), tetanus, poliomyelitis, measles, mumps, rubella, *Haemophilus influenzae* infections, and varicella.

Diphtheria

Diphtheria is an acute communicable disease caused by the gram-positive bacterium *Corynebacterium diphtheriae* that affects the respiratory system. Sometimes it may involve skin wounds or other mucous membranes of the body. The disease typically spreads by respiratory secretions. Humans are the only known reservoir for *C. diphtheriae*. Diphtheria accounts for substantial morbidity and mortality in developing countries in situations where there is not effective vaccine coverage.

Clinical Features

The incubation period for diphtheria is 1 to 5 days, and it presents as sore throat, difficulty in swallowing, nasal discharge, hoarseness, malaise, and fever (Chambers, 2000).

The hallmark feature of this disease is formation of a tenacious gray membrane in the pharynx. Attempts to remove the membrane can lead to bleeding. *C. diphtheriae* produces an exotoxin that is responsible for two complications, namely, myocarditis (inflammation of the heart muscle) and neuropathy (damage of nerves). Myocarditis begins in the first to fourth week of illness and causes arrhythmias (irregular beating) of the heart, blockage of the heart, and heart failure, whereas neuropathy develops in the first through eighth week of illness and typically involves cranial nerves and can lead to double vision, slurred speech, and difficulty in swallowing. The disease can be fatal, with between 5 and 10% of diphtheria patients dying even with proper treatment. Without treatment the fatality rate is even greater. Without treatment, patients remain infective for 2 to 3 weeks. The disease is diagnosed clinically, and confirmation can be done by culturing the bacteria. Treatment is done by giving antitoxin that is prepared from horse serum along with antibiotics (penicillin or erythromycin).

Epidemiology

Mass immunization with diphtheria toxoid in the 1940s and 1950s resulted in virtual elimination of this disease in many developed countries by the 1970s (Efstratiou, 2004). However, the disease has been endemic in developing countries, and in the 1990s there was a major resurgence in the newly independent states of the former Soviet Union, where more than 125,000 cases and 4,000 deaths were reported, mainly among adults, between 1990 and 1995 (Hardy, Dittmann, & Sutter, 1996). A gap in adult immunity, lowered childhood immunization rates, increased population movement, and socioeconomic hardships were some of the reasons for this epidemic (Tiwari, 2008). Except for this resurgence, cases of diphtheria have been on a decline. With the introduction of the World Health Organization's Expanded Program on Immunization (EPI), cases of diphtheria worldwide have been reduced from close to 100,000 in 1980 to 3,978 in 2006 (World Health Organization [WHO], 2008a).

Prevention and Control

For prevention of diphtheria, active immunization with diphtheria toxoid is available and is part of the childhood immunization routine in most countries. After completion of the routine, the average duration of protection from diphtheria is about 10 years. The specific recommended routine for administration of diphtheria vaccine (which is administered along with tetanus and pertussis—DTP) varies from country to country. In the United States, a DTP vaccination is recommended at 4- to 8-week intervals beginning at 2 months of age. A fourth dose is recommended at 15 to 18 months of age, and a fifth dose at 4 to 6 years of age. An adolescent booster for tetanus is recommended at 11 to 12 years and should be repeated every 10 years (Tiwari, 2008). A three-dose application of diphtheria toxoid provides effective immunity in children. Effective and regular immunization against this disease is the best form of prevention and eventual eradication.

> *Due to World Health Organization's Expanded Program on Immunization (EPI) the cases of diphtheria worldwide have reduced from close to 100,000 in 1980 to 3,978 in 2006.*
>
> —World Health Organization (2008a)

Pertussis (Whooping Cough)

Pertussis, or whooping cough, is an acute communicable disease affecting the respiratory tract and is caused by the gram-negative coccobacillus *Bordetella pertussis*. It is transmitted from one human to another by droplet infection.

Clinical Features

Whooping cough occurs predominantly in children younger than 2 years and is characterized by a paroxysmal cough with a high-pitched whoop on inspiration that is often followed by vomiting (Chambers, 2000). The incubation period is 7 to 10 days (range 4 to 21 days), and the onset of illness is insidious (Cortese & Bisgard, 2008). Leukocytosis and lymphocytosis (increased white blood corpuscles) are often present in the disease. Complications are bronchopneumonia, which affects about 5% of patients, and encephalopathy, which is relatively rarer. Diagnosis is confirmed by culture; treatment entails giving erythromycin. Very few children in industrialized countries die of pertussis, but in developing countries the death rates may be as high as 3.9% in infants and 1% in children aged 1 to 4 years (WHO, 2005a).

Epidemiology

Attack rates range from 50% for school contacts to 80 to 90% for family contacts (Slack, 2004). Before the advent of vaccines, pertussis was among one of the most common childhood diseases. In industrialized nations the average annual incidence was 150 to 200 per 100,000, but extensive large-scale vaccination campaigns during the 1950s and 1960s led to a more than 90% reduction in the incidence and mortality of pertussis (WHO, 2005a). With the introduction of WHO's EPI in 1974, cases of pertussis worldwide have been reduced from close to 2,000,000 in 1980 to 115,924 in 2006 (WHO, 2008b).

Prevention and Control

The World Health Organization (2005a) recommends at least 90% coverage of the population with three doses of the diphtheria-tetanus-pertussis (DTP) vaccine in infants worldwide, particularly in places where pertussis is still a serious health problem in infants and young children. The dosage schedule of the vaccine varies from country to country. However, WHO recommends that the basic series be administered at the ages of 6, 10, and 14 weeks. It also recommends a booster 1 to 6 years after the initial series is complete (WHO, 2005a). Booster doses after 6 years of age have not been recommended except to control epidemics; in some countries, however, these boosters are being given to adolescents and adults (Heininger, 2008). Only Australia, Austria, Canada, France, and Germany have incorporated an adolescent booster dose into their current immunization schedules (Tan, Trindade, & Skowronski, 2005). There are two types of pertussis vaccines: whole-cell pertussis vaccine (wP) and acellular pertussis vaccine (aP). Whole-cell pertussis vaccine is cheaper and must often be used in low-resources situations, although acellular pertussis vaccine provokes fewer reactions.

> *The World Health Organization recommends at least 90% coverage of population with three doses of the diphtheria-tetanus-pertussis (DTP) vaccine in infants worldwide.*
>
> —World Health Organization (2005a)

Tetanus

Tetanus is the only vaccine-preventable disease that is not communicable from person to person (Kretsinger, Moran, & Roper, 2008). It is caused by the neurotoxin (tetanospasmin) produced by the anaerobic, gram-positive bacterium *Clostridium tetani*. These bacteria are present everywhere in soil; when introduced into a wound, their spores germinate and produce the toxin, causing the disease.

Clinical Features

The incubation period is 5 days to 15 weeks, with an average of 8 to 12 days (Chambers, 2000). The initial symptoms may consist of pain and tingling at the site where the bacteria entered the body. This could progress to localized spasticity of the muscles around the wound. The hallmark features of the disease are stiffness of the jaw (lockjaw) and neck. This is followed by spasms of the jaw muscles (trismus) and other muscles of the body. Ultimately, painful convulsions occur that are precipitated by minimal stimuli. Respiratory muscle spasms may result in death. Treatment consists of tetanus immunoglobulin, wound care, symptomatic treatment, and penicillin. Mortality as a result of tetanus can be as high as 40%.

Epidemiology

With the use of vaccination, the disease is rare in developed countries; however, it is still present in developing countries, especially among newborns. There were about 12,500 cases of neonatal tetanus in 1980, which rose to 30,000 in 1988 and decreased to 8,376 in 2006 (WHO, 2008c). In some cultures the practice of applying animal dung to the umbilical cord stump of the newborn is responsible for the disease (Wood, 2004a). Aseptic obstetric and postnatal umbilical-cord care practices account for maternal and neonatal tetanus in 48 countries, mainly in Asia and Africa (Roper, Vandelaer, & Gasse, 2007).

Prevention and Control

Tetanus is preventable by active immunization with tetanus toxoid. In children, the tetanus vaccine is administered with diphtheria and pertussis vaccines (DTaP). The World Health Organization recommends that to be protected against tetanus for life, an individual should receive three doses of DTP in infancy, followed by a tetanus toxoid-containing booster at school-entry age (4–7 years), in adolescence (12–15 years), and in early adulthood. Some countries, such as the United States, recommend a tetanus booster every 10 years for adults (Centers for Disease Control and Prevention [CDC], 2007a). Generally, concentrations of antibody to tetanospasmin of 0.01 IU/mL are protective against tetanus (Wood, 2004a). Passive immunization is also available for tetanus and is used in nonimmunized people with contaminated wounds. The World Health Organization has an initiative to eliminate maternal and neonatal tetanus, with one goal being the reduction of the incidence of neonatal tetanus to less than 1 case/1,000 live births/year in every district around the world.

Poliomyelitis

Poliomyelitis (also called infantile paralysis) is a viral disease caused by an enterovirus that has three serotypes. The most common route of infection is the fecal-oral route. Use of vaccines in the 1950s and 1960s rapidly eliminated poliomyelitis in industrialized countries; however, it is still endemic in developing countries (Sutter & Cochi, 2008).

Clinical Features

The incubation period is 5 to 35 days (typically 7 to 14 days) (Bouckenooghe & Shandera, 2000). A large majority of cases remain asymptomatic, but in some instances it manifests as abortive poliomyelitis, nonparalytic poliomyelitis, or paralytic poliomyelitis. Abortive poliomyelitis is characterized by symptoms of fever, headache, vomiting, diarrhea, and sore throat. Nonparalytic poliomyelitis may include meningeal irritation and muscle spasm in addition to the previously listed symptoms. Paralytic poliomyelitis, which includes 0.1% of all poliomyelitis cases, has two forms: spinal poliomyelitis, in which there is involvement of the muscles supplied by the spinal nerves, often causing flaccid paralysis of the lower limbs with muscle wasting; and bulbar poliomyelitis, in which the cranial nerves are involved and sometimes respiratory paralysis may occur. Bulbar poliomyelitis is associated with a death rate of up to 50%.

Epidemiology

There were about 52,000 reported cases of poliomyelitis all over the world in 1980, a number that was reduced to 2,001 cases in 2006 (WHO, 2008d). Implementation of the poliomyelitis eradication campaign worldwide since the 1980s has resulted in a decrease in the number of polio-endemic countries from more than 125 in 1988 to 7 at the end of 2002 (WHO, 2003a). The American and Western Pacific regions of the World Health Organization have been declared free of wild poliovirus, but Afghanistan, India, Pakistan, and Nigeria still have problems with the wild poliovirus (Wood, 2004b).

Prevention and Control

Two vaccines exist for poliomyelitis. Initially, Salk developed an inactivated poliovirus vaccine (IPV), which was found to be successful in the 1950s (Sutter & Cochi, 2008). Later, Sabin developed a live attenuated trivalent vaccine that could be administered orally. The oral polio vaccine (OPV) is administered at birth and at 6, 10, and 14 weeks. In the 1980s, the World Health Organization (2003a) developed a four-pronged poliomyelitis eradication campaign consisting of (1) attaining and sustaining high routine infant vaccination coverage with OPV; (2) setting up surveillance for poliomyelitis and poliovirus through acute flaccid paralysis notifications and laboratory investigation; (3) carrying out mass OPV campaigns (such as national immunization days) to eliminate widespread circulation of wild poliovirus; and (4) carrying out house-to-house OPV "mop-up" campaigns (localized campaigns targeted at high-risk areas) to interrupt any remaining chains of transmission.

Many countries use the OPV, but it is sometimes linked with vaccine-associated paralytic poliomyelitis. Therefore, some countries, such as the United States, use only the IPV. Four countries—Afghanistan, India, Nigeria, and Pakistan—have never been able to successfully interrupt wild polio virus transmission and use OPV, which has advantages in such situations (CDC, 2007b). Once wild poliovirus transmission is eliminated, it is recommended that OPV use be completely stopped.

> *Implementation of the poliomyelitis eradication campaign worldwide since the 1980s has resulted in a decrease in the number of polio-endemic countries from more than 125 in 1988 to 7 at the end of 2002.*
>
> —World Health Organization (2003a)

Measles

Measles, or rubeola, is an acute viral infection caused by a paramyxovirus. Transmission takes place by airborne droplet infection or by direct contact with the nasal or throat secretions of infected persons. Measles is among the most easily transmitted communicable diseases and the most deadly of all childhood rash/fever illnesses. Once infected by it, an individual develops permanent immunity.

Clinical Features

The incubation period is 9 to 11 days, and the disease begins abruptly with high-grade fever and coryza (nasal obstruction, sneezing, and sore throat). Koplik spots are the hallmark of this disease—they are white and irregular and appear in the buccal mucosa, usually opposite the upper premolars, but they may fill the entire inner cheek (Bouckenooghe & Shandera, 2000). At around the third to fifth day of the fever, a red rash appears on the body, which begins on the face and proceeds downward and outward, affecting the palms and soles last. Patients are contagious from 2 to 3 days before the onset of the rash to 1 to 2 days after the rash. Complications include secondary bacterial infections leading to otitis media (middle ear infection) and pneumonia (infection of the lungs), encephalitis, and gastroenteritis. In developed countries, death occurs in 1 in 4,000 cases, whereas in developing countries the mortality rate may be as high as 10 to 15% (Bannister, 2004). There is no specific treatment; symptomatic treatment that includes vitamin A supplementation is used.

Epidemiology

In most populations, more than 95% of adults are seropositive (Bannister, 2004). Epidemics in nonimmune communities typically occur in the spring and early summer of alternate years. The peak age of infection is around 4 years. There were around 4.2 million cases of measles worldwide in 1980, which had decreased to 373,421 in 2006 (WHO, 2008e). Between 2000 and 2006, mortality due to measles was reduced by 68%, from approximately 757,000 deaths in 2000 to 242,000 deaths in 2006 (WHO, 2007a). Measles was declared to be eliminated in the United States (Katz & Hinman, 2004).

Prevention and Control

There is no cure for measles; however, a highly effective, safe, and relatively inexpensive vaccine has been available since the 1960s (WHO, 2004). This is a live attenuated viral measles vaccine conferring active immunity. It is usually combined with mumps and rubella vaccine and given as MMR. One dose of the vaccine is given by the subcutaneous (usual) or intramuscular route, usually between 12 and 15 months of age in developed countries where the incidence of measles is low. The World Health Organization (2004) recommends early vaccination, usually at 9 months, in most developing countries where there are high attack rates among infants. However, early vaccination is associated with low (80 to 85%) seroconversion rates following vaccination. A second dose of MMR is recommended in the age group of 4 to 6 years (although it can be given any time after 1 month of the first dose), and sometimes a third dose at 11 to 12 years (Orenstein, Papania, & Strebel, 2008).

The World Health Organization and UNICEF developed a comprehensive strategy for measles mortality reduction, called the Measles Initiative, in 2001 (WHO, 2007a). Other partners in this initiative include the Centers for Disease Control and Prevention in the United States, the UN Foundation, the American Red Cross, the Global Alliance for Vaccines and Immunization, the Canadian International Development Agency, and the International Federation of Red Cross and Red Crescent Societies. The initiative focuses on 47 priority countries, mainly in Africa and Southeast Asia. The components of the strategy include the following: (1) achievement and maintenance of high coverage (> 90%), with the first dose of measles vaccine given to all children by the age of 12 months in every district and coverage delivered through routine immunization services; (2) making sure that all children receive a second opportunity for measles immunization (often through periodic supplementary immunization activities); (3) implementation of effective laboratory-backed surveillance and monitoring of immunization coverage; and (4) provision of appropriate clinical management.

Mumps

Mumps is an infectious disease caused by a paramyxovirus. The disease is transmitted by droplet infection or by coming in contact with an infected person. Natural infection with mumps is limited to humans. Most patients are children.

Clinical Features

The incubation period is between 14 and 21 days, with an average of 18 days. The infectious period ranges from 7 days prior to onset of the disease to 9 days after onset (Averhoff & Wharton, 2008). The disease is characterized by painful, swollen salivary glands, especially parotid glands (Bouckenooghe & Shandera, 2000). Fever and malaise are generally present. Sometime meningitis, characterized by neck stiffness, headache, and vomiting, may occur. In males, there may be testicular swelling and tenderness (orchitis). In females, there may be ovarian enlargement or oophoritis, characterized by lower abdominal pain. In some cases pancreatitis (involvement of the pancreas), characterized by abdominal pain, nausea, and vomiting, may be present. Rarely, encephalitis may also occur. Treatment for mumps is symptomatic. The entire course of mumps is a maximum of 2 weeks, and deaths are very rare.

Epidemiology

Mumps is endemic worldwide, with epidemics occurring every 2 to 3 years in populations not covered by vaccinations (Morgan-Capner, 2004). In 2006, China had the highest number of reported mumps cases, which totaled 273,242 (WHO, 2007b). Finland introduced a two-dose MMR schedule in 1982 and became the first country to declare elimination of mumps (Averhoff & Wharton, 2008).

Prevention and Control

Since 1960s a live attenuated vaccine has been available to prevent mumps. It is usually administered along with measles and rubella as MMR. One dose of the vaccine is given by the subcutaneous (usual) or intramuscular route, usually between 12 and 15 months of age. A second dose of MMR is recommended in the age group of 4 to 6 years. The protective efficacy of the vaccine is 75 to 85% (Morgan-Capner, 2004).

Rubella

Rubella (German or 3-day measles) is an infectious disease caused by a togavirus. It is transmitted from one person to another by inhalation of infective droplets. Humans are the only known reservoir for the disease. One attack usually confers permanent immunity.

Clinical Features

The incubation period is 14 to 21 days (average 16 days) (Bouckenooghe & Shandera, 2000). The sickness starts with fever and malaise, which may be accompanied by arthralgia (pain in the joints). A pink rash appears on the face, followed by the trunk and then the extremities, and usually lasts for one day in each area (for a total 3 days' duration). The disease can be transmitted from 1 week before the rash to 2 weeks after the rash. Encephalitis is a rare complication. Exposure to rubella during the first trimester of pregnancy can lead to congenital rubella syndrome (CRS), characterized by hearing deficits, congenital heart defects, large organs, cataracts, and other anomalies in the newborn. Rubella is a mild illness, but congenital rubella has a high mortality rate and is associated with permanent congenital defects.

Epidemiology

Rubella is present worldwide, and outbreaks appear in spring and early summer, with epidemics occurring every 8 to 10 years (Morgan-Capner, 2004). In 2006, the highest numbers of rubella cases were reported from the Russian Federation (133,289) and China (37,137) (WHO, 2007c). It is estimated that roughly 100,000 cases of CRS occur every year in developing countries (WHO, 2000). A well-documented epidemic of rubella occurred in the United States in 1964 and 1965 that resulted in an estimated 12.5 million cases, of which over 2,000 cases were complicated with encephalitis. The epidemic resulted in 11,250 abortions, over 20,000 cases of CRS, over 11,000 cases of deafness, 3,580 cases of blindness, and 1,800 children with mental retardation (WHO, 2000).

Prevention and Control

A potent live attenuated rubella virus vaccine is available for prevention of this disease. It is usually administered along with measles and mumps vaccines as MMR. Vaccine-induced immunity is generally assumed to be lifelong. Rubella vaccine is usually given between the ages of 12 and 15 months, but it can also be given to children as young as 9 months. Two approaches for prevention are recommended: (1) prevention of CRS through immunization of adolescent girls and/or women of childbearing age; or (2) elimination of rubella as well as CRS through universal vaccination of infants and young children and ensuring immunity in women of childbearing age (WHO, 2000). Adoption of universal vaccination has eliminated rubella from many developed and some developing countries.

> *Exposure to rubella during the first trimester of pregnancy can lead to congenital rubella syndrome, characterized by hearing deficits, congenital heart defects, large organs, cataracts, and other anomalies in the newborn.*

Haemophilus Influenzae Type B Infections

Haemophilus influenzae type b, or Hib, is a nonmotile, gram-negative bacterium that causes meningitis and pneumonia, especially in children younger than 5 years.

H. influenzae causes disease only in humans, and the human nasopharynx is its only reservoir (Chang, Flannery, & Rosenstein, 2008). Resistance to penicillin and ampicillin antibiotics is quite common with this bacteria; therefore, prevention is becoming even more important.

Clinical Features

Haemophilus influenzae **type b infections** are of two types: invasive and noninvasive (Slack, 2004). Invasive infections include meningitis, pneumonia, epiglottitis (inflammation and edema of the epiglottis), septic arthritis, osteomyelitis, cellulitis, and bacteremia. Noninvasive infections include otitis media (middle ear infection), sinusitis, acute exacerbation of chronic bronchitis, and conjunctivitis. Treatment requires antibiotics, usually vancomycin and a third-generation cephalosporin, such as ceftriaxone or cefotaxime (Chang, Flannery, & Rosenstein, 2008).

Epidemiology

Routine immunization in infancy in most developed countries and developing countries has eliminated this disease from a large part of the world. However, it is still endemic in many developing countries. *H. influenzae* is responsible for around 3 million serious illnesses and an estimated 386,000 deaths per year (WHO, 2008f). Higher incidence rates are found in certain racial groups, such as Apache and Navajo Native Americans, Alaskan Inuit, and Australian Aborigines (Slack, 2004).

Prevention and Control

Immunization is the most potent means of prevention of Hib infection. A vaccine in the form of a protein-polysaccharide conjugate is available. Complete vaccination requires three doses within the first six months of life, followed by a booster in the second year of life. The two major barriers to prevention of Hib infection are lack of information and lack of money (WHO, 2008f). Lack of information stems from the difficulty of diagnosing Hib disease. Most cases of Hib are never diagnosed because diagnosis requires taking blood or spinal fluid specimens and isolating the bacteria from the specimens, which may not always be feasible, especially in developing countries. Lack of money is a factor because Hib vaccine is more expensive than other childhood vaccines. It costs roughly seven times the total cost of the vaccines against measles, polio, tuberculosis, diphtheria, tetanus, and pertussis (WHO, 2008f). Therefore, WHO recommends Hib vaccine "where resources permit its use and the burden of disease is established." As of 2004, 89 countries offered infant immunization against Hib infection. Ninety-two percent of the children in developed countries, 42% in developing countries, and 8% in the least developed countries were vaccinated against Hib infection (WHO, 2008f).

Varicella

Varicella-zoster virus is a herpesvirus that causes **varicella** (chickenpox) or shingles (herpes zoster, a reactivation of varicella). Varicella (chickenpox) is a highly contagious disease that primarily affects children. It is transmitted by inhalation of infected droplets or by contact with skin lesions. There is no animal reservoir.

Clinical Features

The incubation period for varicella ranges from 10 to 21 days, with a typical period between 14 and 16 days (Guris, Marin, & Seward, 2008). The disease is characterized by fever, malaise, and a rash that looks like dew drops on a rose petal; the rash becomes pustular and eventually crusts. The crusts slough in 7 to 14 days (Bouckenooghe & Shandera, 2000). Complications include pneumonia, secondary bacterial infections, and Reye syndrome. It can be fatal, especially in neonates and in immunocompromised persons. Herpes zoster is a reactivation in adulthood of the virus that remains latent in the neural ganglia. It occurs in 10 to 20% of the cases. It is characterized by pain and a rash along the nerve roots. The most commonly involved nerve roots are the thoracic and lumbar. Antiviral agents (acyclovir and its derivatives) are used in treatment.

Epidemiology

Varicella is a highly communicable disease with worldwide distribution (WHO, 2003b). In temperate climates varicella occurs primarily during late winter to early spring. Secondary attack rates reach close to 90% in susceptible household contacts. Most cases of varicella occur before age 10. Both primary varicella and reactivation as herpes zoster are infectious (Bannister, 2004).

Prevention and Control

Varicella vaccines have been developed that are based on the attenuated Oka strain of the varicella-zoster virus. These are generally safe, efficacious, and cost-effective and have been introduced in the childhood immunization programs of several industrialized countries. The ideal age for varicella vaccination is 12 to 24 months. In Japan and many other countries, a single dose of the vaccine is considered sufficient. In the United States, two doses are recommended. It is found that 78% of recipients seroconvert after the first dose, and 99% after the second dose of the vaccine (WHO, 2003b).

Other Vaccine-Preventable Diseases

Besides the conditions discussed previously, vaccines are available for certain other diseases, namely, tuberculosis, hepatitis A, hepatitis B, human papillomavirus, influenza, meningococcal meningitis, pneumococcus, and rotavirus. Different countries have different recommendations regarding administration of these vaccines. **Table 4.1** presents the complete immunization schedule from the United States as an example.

TABLE 4.1	Complete Immunization Schedule: United States	
Vaccine	**Full Name**	**Schedule**
DTaP	Diphtheria and tetanus toxoid with acellular pertussis vaccine	2, 4, 6, 15–18 months; 4–6 years
HepA	Hepatitis A vaccine	12–23 months
HepB	Hepatitis B vaccine	Birth; 1–2, 6–18 months
Hib	*Haemophilus influenzae* type b vaccine	2, 4, 6, 12–15 months
HPV	Human papillomavirus vaccine	11–12 years
Influenza	Influenza	6–59 months
IPV	Inactivated polio vaccine	2, 4, 6–18 months; 4–6 years
MenC_conj	Meningococcal C conjugate vaccine	11–12 years
MMR	Measles, mumps, and rubella vaccine	12–15 months; 4–6 years
Pneumo_conj	Pneumococcal conjugate vaccine	2, 4, 6, 12–15 months
Pneumo_ps	Pneumococcal polysaccharide vaccine	≥ 2 years
Rotavirus	Rotavirus vaccine	2, 4, 6 months
Tdap	Tetanus and diphtheria toxoids and acellular pertussis vaccine	11–12 years
Varicella	Varicella vaccine	12–18 months; 4–6 years

Source: World Health Organization. (2008). Vaccine schedule by country. Retrieved from http://www.who.int/immunization_monitoring/en/globalsummary/ScheduleSelect.cfm

Focus Feature 4.1   Eradication of Smallpox

Smallpox is an ancient disease; descriptions of it are found in early Indian and Egyptian civilizations. It was once responsible for a large proportion of morbidity and mortality all over the world, particularly in children from all walks of life. It killed Queen Mary II of England, Emperor Joseph I of Austria, King Luis I of Spain, Tsar Peter II of Russia, Queen Ulrika Elenora of Sweden, and King Louis XV of France (WHO, 2008g). Smallpox is an acute infectious disease caused by the variola virus. It is characterized by fever, headache, backache, vomiting, and sometimes convulsions. Typical of smallpox is a rash that appears on the third day of the sickness and is centrifugal in distribution. The rash progresses from macular lesions to papules to vesicles to pustules and finishes with scabs that scar. There is no treatment for this disease. However, a vaccine is available for prevention.

Based on the efficacy of this vaccine and a myriad of other factors, this disease was eradicated in 1979, a conclusion that was endorsed by the World Health Assembly in 1980 (WHO, 2008g). Eradication means permanent and worldwide reduction of the incidence of the disease to zero. This eradication was a historic milestone and an accomplishment of science and technology. Besides the availability of an efficacious vaccine, several other factors were responsible for the eradication of smallpox. One such factor was the massive campaign launched by the World Health Organization in 1967 that led to international collaboration regarding the issue. Other factors were some of the characteristics of the disease itself, such as the absence of a human carrier state, the absence of an animal reservoir, the absence of subclinical cases, and the rarity of second attacks of the disease.

Further factors were the advances in vaccine development and delivery: a heat-stable, freeze-dried vaccine was developed that could be administered by a bifurcated needle that was easy to use and could be inserted into a jet injector gun that could facilitate vaccinating up to 1,000 people in 1 hour (Reingold & Phares, 2006). A final factor was the strategy of identifying cases through the introduction of financial incentives and then intensely vaccinating all the contacts surrounding the cases—the surveillance containment strategy (Reingold & Phares, 2006). This strategy was aided by the fact that the disease is easy to recognize even by laypersons and that it has a relatively slow transmission, which allows time to contain an outbreak.

Following eradication, routine smallpox vaccination was discontinued in all countries. Only two laboratories in the world—one in the United States and another in Russia—keep smallpox virus. However, there is constant fear of the potential use of smallpox virus by terrorist groups or as an agent for biological warfare. Because the population has not been exposed to smallpox virus for years, the likelihood is that it would cause havoc.

MALARIA

It was once thought that malaria originated in fetid marshes, which led to its name: *mal* (bad) *aria* (air). **Malaria** is a vector-borne disease that is transmitted through the bite of the female *Anopheles* mosquito and caused by protozoa. The protozoa belong to the genus *Plasmodium*, which has four species: *P. vivax*, *P. malariae*, *P. ovale*, and *P. falciparum*. *P. vivax* is found in Central and South America, North Africa, the Middle East, and within the Indian subcontinent. *P. malariae* occurs primarily in Africa. *P. ovale* is found primarily in West Africa. *P. falciparum* is most common in sub-Saharan Africa and Melanesia (Papua New Guinea and the Solomon Islands) (Pasvol, 2004).

Clinical Features

The incubation period for *P. vivax* is 12 to 17 days; *P. malariae*, 18 to 40 days; *P. ovale*, 16 to 18 days; and *P. falciparum*, 9 to 14 days (Kachur, deOliveira, & Bloland, 2008). The typical malarial attack consists of chills (cold stage) followed by high-grade fever (hot stage) and sweating (sweating stage). There may be accompanying fatigue, headache, muscle pains, joint pains, and backache. *P. falciparum* can lead to severe disease and death, whereas other varieties are generally not fatal. Complications can include rupture of the spleen, renal failure, disseminated intravascular coagulation, brain damage, and pulmonary edema (Kachur, deOliveira, & Bloland, 2008). Diagnosis can usually be made by detecting the protozoa in the blood smear. Treatment is done with chloroquine in areas with chloroquine-sensitive *Plasmodium*; artemisinin-based combination therapies (ACTs) are used for chloroquine-resistant *Plasmodium*.

Epidemiology

According to the World Health Organization's Global Health Atlas, in 2003 more than 51 million cases of malaria were reported, with over 63,000 deaths from all over the world. The highest number of cases were in Uganda (12,343,411), followed by Tanzania (10,712,526). Malaria is present in parts of Mexico, Haiti, the Dominican Republic, Central and South America, Africa, the Middle East, the Indian subcontinent, Southeast Asia, China, and Oceania (Goldsmith, 2000).

Prevention and Control

Case management is the most important aspect of malaria control—that is, early and accurate diagnosis followed by treatment with the correct medicines. Artemisinin-based combination therapies have been found to be highly effective, especially against multidrug-resistant protozoa. Artemisinin drugs (such as artesunate, artemether, artemotil, and dihydroartemisinin) have a short half-life, and therefore a multiple-dose regimen is required to achieve an acceptable cure rate. Furthermore, artemisinin drugs need to be combined with partner drugs that have a longer half-life and thus improve the efficacy of the combination. Combination reduces treatment duration from 7 days to 3 days and reduces the likelihood of development of resistance to the partner drug. Examples of some combination drugs are artesunate plus sulfadoxine/pyrimethamine, artesunate plus amodiaquine, artesunate plus mefloquine, and artemether plus lumefantrine (WHO, 2006a).

The second important aspect in malaria control is vector control, or controlling mosquitoes. Vector control measures include spraying insecticides to kill adult mosquitoes and using pesticides and environmental measures to reduce the numbers of mosquito larvae. Most malaria-carrying mosquitoes bite at night. Use of mosquito nets or insecticide-treated nets is also an effective means of creating a barrier between mosquitoes and humans, thereby reducing transmission.

Vaccines have also been experimented with for prevention of malaria, but no effective vaccine has yet been identified. For example, a trial of SFf66, a malaria vaccine, showed that although it was safe it was not efficacious (Nosten et al., 1996).

The World Health Organization (2006b) has developed a five-pronged Global Malaria Program (GMP) that includes research; case management; supply-chain management; vector control and prevention; and surveillance, monitoring and evaluation. In the research area, GMP recommends more work related to malaria case management, vector control, surveillance, monitoring, and evaluation, epidemics, and malaria in complex emergency situations. For case management, GMP recommends ACTs. In the realm of supply-chain management, GMP works to improve the supply of core malaria commodities and facilitate supply-chain management for countries. The Global Malaria Program is also working to increase the availability of these drugs at an affordable cost. For vector control and prevention, GMP recommends insecticide-treated nets and indoor residual spraying. In the area of surveillance, monitoring, and evaluation, GMP aims to accurately estimate the burden of disease and measure trends in malaria.

SEXUALLY TRANSMITTED INFECTIONS

Sexually transmitted infections (STIs) are diseases that are spread primarily through person-to-person sexual contact. Most of the agents that cause STIs are killed when exposed to a harsh environment and only survive in mucous membranes. Over 30 different sexually transmissible bacteria, viruses, and protozoa exist (WHO, 2007d). Some can also be transmitted from mother to child during pregnancy and childbirth and via blood products and tissue transfer. Except for HIV/AIDS, these diseases will be discussed as a single group in this chapter. Some of the common STIs are as follows.

Caused by Bacteria

- Chlamydia (caused by *Chlamydia trachomatis*)
- Gonorrhea (caused by *Neisseria gonorrhoeae*)
- Syphilis (caused by *Treponema pallidum*)
- Chancroid (caused by *Haemophilus ducreyi*)
- Granuloma inguinale (caused by *Klebsiella granulomatis*)

Caused by Viruses

- HIV/AIDS (caused by human immunodeficiency virus)
- Genital herpes (caused by herpes simplex virus type 2)
- Hepatitis (caused by hepatitis B virus)
- Genital warts and cervical cancer (caused by human papillomavirus)
- Cytomegalovirus disease (caused by cytomegalovirus)

Caused by Other Agents

- Vaginal trichomoniasis (caused by *Trichomonas vaginalis*)
- Vulvovaginitis in women and balanoposthitis in men (caused by *Candida albicans*)

Clinical Features

Each sexually transmitted infection has its own unique features, but in general, sexually transmitted infections are characterized by manifestations such as urethral discharge, genital ulcers, inguinal swellings, scrotal swelling, vaginal discharge, and lower abdominal pain (WHO, 2007d). Some of the complications of STIs are pelvic inflammatory disease, ectopic pregnancy, infertility, chronic pelvic pain, and STI-related neoplasia such as cervical cancer, anal cancer, and liver cancer (Friedel & Lavoie, 2008).

Epidemiology

According to 1999 WHO estimates, 340 million new cases of curable STIs occur every year throughout the world (WHO, 2001). The incidence of STIs is increasing in many countries, including the United States (Friedel & Lavoie, 2008). In the United States, approximately 18.9 million new cases of STIs were found in 2000, of which 9.1 million (48%) were among persons aged 15 to 24 years. Three STIs (human papillomavirus, trichomoniasis, and chlamydia) accounted for 88% of all new cases of STIs among 15- to 24-year-olds (Weinstock, Berman, & Cates,

2004). In developing countries, STIs along with their complications rank in the top five disease categories for which adults seek health care (WHO, 2007d).

Prevention and Control

Promoting abstinence and safer sex practices is the cornerstone of prevention and control of STIs. Latex condoms provide a mechanical barrier and serve a useful purpose in reducing transmission of STIs. Thus, ensuring the availability and accessibility of quality condoms at affordable prices must be a part of safer sex interventions. Behaviors such as a higher number of sex partners, variety in types of sex practiced, not using condoms, and selecting risky partners make a person more susceptible to contracting an STI (Friedel & Lavoie, 2008). Behavioral interventions that minimize these risky behaviors are also helpful in the prevention and control of STIs.

The World Health Organization (2007d) developed a global strategy in 2006 for prevention and control of STIs. Some of the elements of this strategy are as follows:

- Promotion of safer sexual behaviors
- Improved access to quality condoms at affordable prices
- Early diagnosis and treatment of patients suffering from STIs and their partners
- Inclusion of STI treatment in basic health services
- Concerted programs for high-risk populations such as sex workers, adolescents, long-distance truck drivers, military personnel, substance users, and prisoners
- Effective treatment of STIs, namely, use of correct and effective medicines, treatment of sexual partners, education, and advice

> *According to 1999 WHO estimates, 340 million new cases of curable sexually transmitted infections occur every year throughout the world.*
>
> —World Health Organization (2001)

- Screening of clinically asymptomatic patients, where feasible
- Provision for counseling and voluntary testing for HIV infection
- Prevention and care of congenital syphilis and neonatal conjunctivitis
- Involvement of the private sector and the community in the prevention and care of STIs

HUMAN IMMUNODEFICIENCY VIRUS AND ACQUIRED IMMUNODEFICIENCY SYNDROME

Prior to the 1980s, **human immunodeficiency virus/acquired immunodeficiency syndrome (HIV/AIDS)** was an unknown entity. In 1981 it was found that some young adults had a higher incidence of opportunistic infections, which led to identification of

HIV, a retrovirus. The three main modes of transmission of HIV are sexual transmission through rectal, vaginal, and even oral contact; parenteral transmission through injection, transfusion, or accidental exposure to blood or its components; and perinatal transmission from infected mothers to children before, during, or after childbirth (Greenberg, Drotman, Curran, & Janssen, 2008).

Clinical Features

Many people infected with HIV remain asymptomatic for many years even without any treatment. The mean time between exposure to HIV and development of AIDS is 10 years (Katz & Hollander, 2000). When symptoms occur, they can affect almost all organs of the body. Some general symptoms of AIDS are fever, night sweats, weight loss, wasting, and opportunistic infections due to lowered immunity. AIDS patients also suffer from nausea, vomiting, and anorexia, which are often secondary to other infections. The opportunistic infections include *Pneumocystis* pneumonia, tuberculosis, cryptococcal meningitis, sinusitis, esophageal candidiasis, and bacillary angiomatosis, among others. AIDS patient may also manifest noninfectious diseases such as Kaposi's sarcoma, non-Hodgkin's lymphoma, and interstitial pneumonitis.

The screening test for HIV is done by enzyme-linked immunosorbent assay (ELISA); positive specimens are then confirmed by a Western blot test. The sensitivity of the screening test is greater than 99.5%, and the specificity of positive results by these two methods is close to 100%. Treatment for HIV infection can be divided into four categories: treatment of opportunistic infections, antiretroviral drugs, hematopoietic stimulating factors, and prevention of opportunistic infections (Katz & Hollander, 2000).

Epidemiology

According to the World Health Organization and the United Nations Program on HIV/AIDS (2008), in 2006 there were 39.5 million (34.1–47.1 million) persons living with HIV all over the world, of whom 17.7 million (15.1–20.9 million) were women and 2.3 million (1.7–3.5 million) were children younger than 15 years. There were 4.3 million (3.6–6.6 million) people newly infected with HIV in 2006, of whom 530,000 (410,000–660,000) were children younger than 15 years. The number of deaths due to AIDS in 2006 was 2.9 million (2.5–3.5 million), of which 380,000 (290,000–500,000) were children younger than 15 years.

Prevention and Control

Promoting abstinence, monogamy, and safer sex practices, including condom use, is important in the prevention of HIV/AIDS caused through sexual intercourse. Targeting high-risk populations such as sex workers or men who have sex with men is a useful approach for safer sex interventions. Examples of such interventions were peer-based prevention programs for sex workers in Maharashtra, India, in the 1990s; a campaign in Zimbabwe that increased condom use from 5 to 50% in the 1990s; a mass media and social marketing campaign in Zaire that boosted condom sales from less than half a million in 1987 to over 20 million in 1991; and the "100% condom campaign" in Thailand in the 1990s (Moodie & Aboagye-Kwarteng, 1993; Ungphakorn & Sittitrai, 1994). Newer behavioral interventions such as one-on-one counseling, group skill-building interventions, interventions to delay sexual debut, interventions that promote consistent use of condoms, and environmental interventions such as providing housing to homeless persons living with HIV are current prevention research issues (Greenberg, Drotman, Curran, & Janssen, 2008).

In 2006 there were 39.5 million (34.1–47.1 million) persons living with HIV all over the world, of which 17.7 million (15.1–20.9 million) were women and 2.3 million (1.7–3.5 million) were children under 15 years of age.

—WHO and UNAIDS (2008)

HIV transmission through injecting drug use is addressed through referral to drug treatment programs and, for those who continue to inject, facilitation of consistent use of sterile injection equipment (Greenberg, Drotman, Curran, & Janssen, 2008). For reducing perinatal transmission, antiretroviral therapy administered to mothers and infants has been found to be effective.

Focus Feature 4.2   HIV/AIDS Prevention Efforts in Red-Light Areas of India

HIV poses a grave public health risk to the health and welfare of India. The World Health Organization estimates the number of people in India living with HIV/AIDS as over 4 million (United Nations Program on HIV/AIDS [UNAIDS], 2002); the prevalence estimates among newborns in at least four of the country's major cities have been pegged at an astounding 2 to 3% (UNAIDS, 2002). Among sex workers, HIV prevalence rates as high as 50 to 90% have been reported in Mumbai, Delhi, and Chennai (UNAIDS, 2002). Surprisingly, though, in the city of Kolkata (Calcutta), HIV infection rates among sex workers are a modest 11%, despite the fact that the city is one of the most impoverished urban centers in the world (UNAIDS, 2002). Also, condom use has consistently risen among the sex workers in Kolkata, from 3% in 1992 to 90% in 1999 (Jana, Basu, Rotheram-Borus, & Newman, 2004), a figure that stands in stark contrast to the otherwise steady rates of low condom use among sex workers in other Indian cities. The Sonagachi Project, a sustainable community intervention project, can be credited with most, if not all, of this success.

Sonagachi, literally meaning "a golden tree," is the biggest red-light district in Kolkata. The region it-self employs several thousand sex workers and houses several hundred multistory brothels. His-torically, Sonagachi was used by rich natives for maintaining concubines and mistresses in the 18th and 19th centuries, and numerous manors in this region trace their historical backgrounds to the early days of the British empire. Legends maintain that the "golden district of Kolkata" was famous as far as Paris. Today, several nonprofit and nongovernmental and government organiza-tions operate public health interventions here for the prevention of sexually transmitted diseases, including AIDS.

The Sonagachi Project is essentially a prostitute's cooperative that operates in the Sonagachi re-gion and empowers sex workers to insist on condom use during sexual encounters and to stand up against abuse. The program has defined HIV as an occupational health problem and includes multifaceted, multilevel interventions addressing community (having a high-status advocate; ad-dressing environmental barriers and resources), group (changing social relationships), and individ-ual factors (improving skills and competencies related to HIV prevention and treatment). The pro-ject is credited with keeping the HIV infection rate among the prostitutes at 5%, a remarkable achievement given the fact that the prevalence rates in other Indian red-light regions are much higher.

The Sonagachi model has been credited as a "best practices model" by the UNAIDS program and has been studied by public health agencies around the world (Jana, Basu, Rotheram-Borus, & Newman, 2004). The project is overseen by the Durbar Mahila Samanwaya Committee (DMSC), which lobbies for the recognition of sex workers' rights and full legalization, runs literacy and vocational programs, and provides micro loans (Jana, Basu, Rotheram-Borus, & Newman, 2004). *Durbar* is a word from the Bengali language that means "unstoppable." On November 14, 1997, DMSC hosted India's first national convention of sex workers in Kolkata. The theme of the convention was Sex Work Is Real Work: We Demand Workers Rights (Network of Sex Work Projects, 1997).

TUBERCULOSIS

Tuberculosis (TB) is an infectious disease caused by the bacterium *Mycobacterium tuberculosis* that primarily affects the lungs. Transmission takes place from person to person by inhalation of droplets containing the bacteria.

Clinical Features

Upon entry of the bacteria in a human host, three consequences follow (Hornick, 2008). The first is that the bacteria are walled off by the host's immune system. This stage is asymptomatic and is called *primary tuberculosis*. This is followed by *latent tu-berculosis infection*, which persists throughout the life of the host. The third outcome, which affects 5% of all infected individuals, occurs when the immune system of the host is weakened and the tuberculosis infection is activated, which can occur several months or years after the initial infection and is called *reactivation tuberculosis*. People with HIV are more likely to get reactivation TB as their immune status is lowered. Exposure to tuberculosis can be detected by the tuberculin skin test, but the test does not distinguish between current disease or past disease.

The general symptoms of reactivation tuberculosis are fatigue, weight loss, anorexia, low-grade fever, and night sweats (Chestnutt & Prendergast, 2000). Symptoms pertaining to the lung are a cough that is productive, with purulent sputum and blood, and chest pain. In open cases of tuberculosis, sputum contains the bacteria, which can be seen under the microscope and cultured. Standard treatment of tuberculosis requires a four-drug regimen consisting of isoniazid, rifampin, pyrazinamide, and either ethambutol or streptomycin. Therapy is given daily or two or three times weekly if directly observed for at least six months. Directly observed therapy, short course (DOTS), in which a health worker administers and monitors the therapy, is often used to ensure compliance, especially in developing countries. Because of noncompliance with treatment, strains of drug-resistant bacteria are becoming common; these require more extensive treatment (for up to two years) with several other drugs.

Epidemiology

Overall, one-third of the world's population is infected with tuberculosis (WHO, 2008h). It is very common in parts of Asia and Africa. In 2005, 8.8 million new cases of tuberculosis were reported worldwide, or 136 per 100,000 population (WHO, 2008h). Of these cases, 3.9 million (or 60 per 100,000 population) were smear positive, or infectious. The prevalence of TB was 14 million, or 217 per 100,000. An estimated 1.6 million people, or 24 per 100,000, died due to tuberculosis in 2005.

Prevention and Control

Improvements in quality of life such as improved nutrition and removal of overcrowding have been shown to be important factors in elimination of tuberculosis from developed countries. These factors are important in the prevention of tuberculosis. For control of tuberculosis, early detection and the completion of chemotherapy are vital components. Sputum examination, radiography, and the tuberculin test are all helpful in the detection of cases. The chemotherapy has already been discussed (see "Clinical Features"). There is a vaccine for tuberculosis, called Bacille

Calmette-Guérin, or BCG. It is made from a live attenuated bovine strain of tubercle bacilli. In countries where it is used, it is given at birth or at three months of age. It confers a protective effect against meningitis and disseminated TB in children (WHO, 2008i). However, it does not prevent primary infection or prevent reactivation of latent pulmonary infection. Therefore, the impact of BCG vaccination on transmission of TB is rather limited.

The World Health Organization initiated a new Stop TB Strategy in 2006. The cornerstone of this strategy is DOTS. The strategy contains six components:

1. Expanding and enhancing DOTS to remote and far-flung areas
2. Focusing on the issues of HIV with tuberculosis, multidrug-resistant tuberculosis, and other challenges
3. Strengthening health systems through national TB control programs that advance financing, planning, management, information, supply systems, and innovative service delivery
4. Connecting private, corporate, and voluntary health care providers so that high-quality care reaches all patients
5. Empowering people with TB and their communities so that they can undertake some essential TB control tasks
6. Facilitating and promoting research regarding TB

> *In 2005, 8.8 million new cases of tuberculosis were reported worldwide or 136 per 100,000 population.*
>
> —World Health Organization (2008h)

ACUTE RESPIRATORY INFECTIONS

Acute respiratory infections are infections of the respiratory tract caused primarily by bacteria and viruses. It is not possible to differentiate between viral and bacterial origin on the basis of signs and symptoms or radiological evidence. Therefore, these conditions are clubbed together as acute respiratory infections. Common bacterial pathogens responsible for acute respiratory infections are *Streptococcus pneumoniae*, *Staphylococcus aureus*, *Haemophilus influenzae* (discussed in detail earlier in the section on vaccine-preventable diseases), *Klebsiella pneumoniae*, and *Bordetella pertussis* and *Corynebacterium diphtheriae* (also discussed in detail earlier in the section on vaccine-preventable diseases) (Ena, 2008; A. W. Johnson, Osinusi, Aderele, & Adeyemi-Doro, 1993). Common viruses responsible for acute respiratory infections are rhinovirus, influenza virus, parainfluenza virus, respiratory syncytial virus, and adenovirus (B. R. Johnson, Osinusi, Aderele, & Tomori, 1993).

Clinical Features

Acute respiratory infections can be divided into upper respiratory tract infections, which include rhinitis, sinusitis, ear infections, acute pharyngitis, tonsillopharyngitis, epiglottitis, and laryngitis; and lower respiratory tract infections, which include bronchitis, pneumonia, and bronchiolitis. Rhinitis is characterized by nasal discharge and sore throat. Sinusitis is characterized by pain and pressure over different parts of the cheek and forehead. Ear infections manifest as pain in the ear, fever, and discharge from the ear. Pharyngitis, tonsillopharyngitis, epiglottitis, and laryngitis manifest as sore throat, fever, malaise, and difficulty in swallowing and speaking. Bronchitis is characterized by fever, wheezing, and cough that is usually productive with sputum. Pneumonia is characterized by fever, cough with or without sputum, difficulty in breathing, chest discomfort, and sweats or rigors. Radiograph of the chest is usually diagnostic. Bronchiolitis mainly affects infants and children. Symptoms are cough, tachypnea, hyperinflation, chest retraction, and widespread wheezes, crackles, or both (Ena, 2008). Treatment is usually antibiotics. All patients must be checked for malnutrition because it is a predictor of mortality. Supportive therapy includes giving oral fluids to prevent dehydration, continued feeding to reduce malnutrition, and antipyretics to reduce high fever.

Epidemiology

About 20% of children and 5% of adults develop influenza A or B every year (Ena, 2008). About 20% of all deaths in children younger than five years are due to acute lower respiratory tract infections (pneumonia, bronchiolitis, and bronchitis) (WHO, 2008j). Ninety percent of these deaths are due to pneumonia. Malnutrition is a strong predictor of acute lower respiratory tract infection-related deaths in preschool children (W. B. Johnson, Aderele, & Gbadero, 1992).

Prevention and Control

Prevention and control of acute respiratory infections requires minimization of exposure, specific protection by vaccines, and early diagnosis and treatment. To minimize exposure, airborne transmission should be curtailed by the use of masks by patients and those in contact with them, and contact transmission should be prevented through hand washing. Available vaccines should be used for specific protection. Vaccines for *H. influenzae*, *B. pertussis*, and *C. diphtheriae* are available and have been discussed earlier. Vaccines are also available for influenza A and B and *S. pneumonia*.

There are two types of vaccines against influenza: inactivated intramuscular vaccine, which is approved for use among children older than 6 months, and live attenuated intranasal vaccine, which is indicated for healthy persons aged 5 to 49 years (Zangwill & Belshe, 2004). Pneumococcal conjugate vaccine is recommended at 2, 4, and 6 months and then at 12 to 15 months, and pneumococcal polysaccharide vaccine is recommended for children older than 2 years. Finally, secondary prevention in the form of early diagnosis and treatment is vital.

ACUTE GASTROINTESTINAL INFECTIONS

Acute gastrointestinal infections are very common and cause a great deal of morbidity and mortality, especially in developing countries. These infections are caused by bacteria, viruses, and parasites (Valls, 2008). Some of the microorganisms responsible for gastrointestinal infections are as follows.

Bacteria

- *Bacillus cereus, B. subtilis*
- *Campylobacter jejuni*
- *Clostridium difficile*
- *Clostridium perfringens*
- *Escherichia coli*
- *Salmonella typhi, S. paratyphi, S. enteritidis, S. typhimurium* (causes typhoid fever)
- *Shigella sonnei, S. boydii, S. dysenteriae, S. flexneri*
- *Vibrio cholerae* (causes cholera)

Viruses

- Norovirus
- Rotavirus

Protozoa

- Cyclosporidium
- Cryptosporidium
- *Entamoeba histolytica*
- *Giardia duodenalis*

Clinical Features

Most gastrointestinal illnesses are characterized by diarrhea, often accompanied by nausea, vomiting, fever, and abdominal pain. Incubation periods for different agents vary from a few hours to a few days. Typhoid fever (enteric fever) is characterized by a fever that rises in a stepwise fashion. Typhoid is complicated by intestinal hemorrhage, intestinal perforation, urinary retention, pneumonia, myocarditis, and other organ involvement (Chambers, 2000). Cholera is characterized by rice-water stools (i.e., liquid, gray, and turbid stools without fecal odor, blood, or pus). Treatment of gastrointestinal illness is by replacement of fluids. In mild or moderate cases, oral rehydration is sufficient, but in severe cases of dehydration, intravenous fluids may be needed. For bacterial infections, antibiotics are used.

Epidemiology

According to a secondary analysis by Kosek, Bern, and Guerrant (2003), the median incidence for diarrhea in children younger than 5 years in developing countries was 3.2 episodes per child-year. The study further found that diarrhea-specific mortality rates for children younger than 5 years steadily fell from 13.6 per 1,000 per year in studies published between 1955 and 1979 to 5.6 per 1,000 per year in 1980 to 1989 and to 4.9 per 1,000 per year in studies published between 1992 and 2000. Despite the trends that demonstrated a decrease in mortality rates, diarrhea was still responsible for a median of 21% of all deaths of children younger than 5 years in developing countries. This amounted to a total of 2.5 million deaths per year.

Prevention and Control

Several general and specific measures exist for prevention of gastrointestinal infections (Valls, 2008). One of the general measures is promotion of exclusive breast-feeding to infants. Breast milk protects the child because it has antimicrobial factors and reduces the risk of exposure to contaminated water and food items. Another general measure is improving water supply and sanitation in areas where they are not safe. The habit of hand washing is also very important in prevention of gastrointestinal infections. Regarding specific measures, vaccines are available for rotavirus that should be administered at 2, 4, and 6 months. Vaccines are also available for salmonellosis and cholera, but these are only recommended for travelers under special circumstances. Treatment of diarrhea by oral rehydration therapy (ORT) in developing countries is a very important control method and has been responsible for saving many lives. The World Health Organization and UNICEF have been carrying out campaigns promoting oral rehydration in developing countries, but there is still more need for such campaigns.

MENINGOCOCCAL MENINGITIS

Meningococcal meningitis is caused by the bacterium *Neisseria meningitides*. Infection is usually found in the nasopharynx or oropharynx and remains asymptomatic. Infection is transmitted from person to person by droplets of respiratory or throat secretions. There is no animal reservoir.

Clinical Features

The incubation period is 4 days, with a range of 2 to 10 days. The clinical illness may take three forms: heavy infection of the blood, known as meningococcemia; meningococcemia with meningitis; and meningitis (Chambers, 2000). Meningococcemia occurs in 5% to 20% of patients and can cause death within 2 to 8 hours. It is associated with skin eruption and enlargement of both adrenal glands (Waterhouse-Friderichsen syndrome) (Soriano-Gabarro & Rosenstein, 2008). Meningitis is an infection of the meninges, the membranous lining that covers the brain and the spinal cord. Meningitis is characterized by high fever, chills, headache, and nausea and vomiting. Neck rigidity is typical of meningitis. Diagnosis is confirmed by examination and culture of cerebrospinal fluid from lumbar puncture. Treatment consists of giving antibiotics, including penicillin. During epidemics in developing countries, chloramphenicol is used because it can be administered in a single intramuscular injection.

Epidemiology

There are 12 subtypes or serogroups of *N. meningitidis*, four of which (A, B, C, and W-135) are recognized to cause epidemics (WHO, 2008k). The incidence of meningococcal meningitis ranges from 1 to 1,000 per 100,000 population in different parts of the world (Caugant, 2008). In temperate regions, more cases are seen during the winter and spring seasons. In Europe and the Americas, serogroups B and C account for a large proportion of cases of meningitis, whereas in Africa, serogroups A and C are more prevalent, and in Asia, serogroup A (WHO, 2008j). The greatest burden of meningococcal meningitis occurs in sub-Saharan Africa, which is known as the "Meningitis Belt." This belt begins from Senegal in the west to Ethiopia in the east and has an estimated total population of 300 million people. In recent years serogroup

W-135 has been found in epidemics in Saudi Arabia in 2000–2001 (Karima et al., 2003) and in Burkina Faso in 2003 (Zombré et al., 2007).

Prevention and Control

Purified polysaccharide vaccines are available against meningococcal meningitis. In the United States a licensed vaccine for subgroups A, C, Y, and W-135 (tetravalent) is available (Soriano-Gabarro & Rosenstein, 2008). In Africa a vaccine for serogroups A and C (bivalent) and, more recently, one for A, C, and W-135 (trivalent) are available. These vaccines provide only a short duration of protection and are, therefore, not recommended for routine vaccination in childhood but are useful in times of epidemics. Avoiding overcrowding is an important primary prevention measure. Finally, during epidemics, early diagnosis and treatment of cases must be done to control the sequelae of meningitis.

> *The greatest burden of meningococcal meningitis occurs in sub-Saharan Africa, which is known as the "Meningitis Belt." This belt begins from Senegal in the west to Ethiopia in the east and has an estimated total population of 300 million people.*

LEPROSY

Leprosy (also called Hansen disease) is a chronic infectious disease caused by the bacterium *Mycobacterium leprae*. It affects the skin, peripheral nervous system, eyes, and mucous membranes. The disease has existed for thousands of years and has been responsible for much suffering as a result of disfigurement and disabilities. It has been reported in ancient civilizations of China, India, and Egypt. The mode of transmission is through the respiratory route and requires long exposure during childhood (Nelson, 2008). The bacteria grow very slowly, and the onset of the disease is slow. It can take up to 20 years for symptoms to appear.

Clinical Features

The disease is characterized by pale, anesthetic, macular (flat) or nodular, red-colored skin lesions (Chambers, 2000). Peripheral nerves are also involved, which are thickened and associated with loss of sensation. Based on clinical and immunologic features, Ridley and Jopling (1966) classified leprosy into the following types: lepromatous (LL), borderline lepromatous (BL), midborderline (BB), borderline tuberculoid (BT), tuberculoid (TT), and indeterminate (I) leprosy. Currently, leprosy is classified into two types: multibacillary leprosy, consisting of LL, BL, and BB leprosy; and paucibacillary leprosy, consisting of BT and TT (Nelson, 2008). Patients with multibacillary leprosy have defective cellular immunity and their skin lesions contain an abundance of bacteria, whereas patients with paucibacillary leprosy have intact cell-mediated immunity and few bacilli in their lesions. It is important to ensure that patients with multibacillary disease are not treated with the regimen for the paucibacillary form of the disease. Treatment is by a multidrug regimen known as multidrug therapy (MDT). Usually dapsone, clofazimine, and rifampicin are used for 12 months in treating multibacillary leprosy, whereas dapsone and rifampicin are used for 6 months in treating paucibacillary leprosy.

Epidemiology

According to the World Health Organization (2008l), the global prevalence of leprosy at the beginning of 2007 was 224,717 cases, and the number of new cases detected during 2006 was 259,017. The number of new cases has been showing a downward trend over the past 5 years. Leprosy is still endemic in some areas of Angola, Brazil, the Central African Republic, the Democratic Republic of Congo, India, Madagascar, Mozambique, Nepal, and the United Republic of Tanzania.

Prevention and Control

According to the World Health Organization (2008l), the most effective way of preventing disabilities associated with leprosy and preventing its further transmission is through early diagnosis and treatment with multidrug therapy. In 1991 the World Health Assembly established a target of eliminating leprosy as a public health problem by the year 2000. Elimination was defined as reaching a prevalence (total cases) of less than 1 case per 10,000 people. Although this goal of reducing prevalence has been reached, the elimination efforts have not been completely successful (Lockwood & Suneetha, 2005). The efforts have been successful in delivering effective antibiotic therapy worldwide, however. Since 1995, WHO (2008l) has supplied MDT free of cost to leprosy patients in all endemic countries, initially through the Nippon Foundation and, since 2000, through Novartis and the Novartis Foundation for Sustainable Development. However, incidence rates (new cases) of leprosy have remained stable in many countries, such as Brazil and India. This is suggestive of the fact that infection has not been adequately controlled by antibiotics alone.

> *The most effective way of preventing disabilities associated with leprosy and preventing its further transmission is through early diagnosis and treatment with multidrug therapy.*

EMERGING INFECTIOUS DISEASES

Emerging infectious diseases are those infections in humans that have been seen in recent years or are threatening to increase in the near future. Also included are those infections that appear in new geographic areas or are reemerging after a period of low activity. During the past 30 years, 30 infectious agents have been identified as emerging (WHO, 2005b). Jones and colleagues (2008) have analyzed emerging infectious diseases and found that the majority are zoonoses originating in wildlife (e.g., severe acute respiratory virus, Ebola virus). It is not within the scope of this book to discuss each one of these emerging diseases, but some common ones are discussed in this section, namely, avian influenza (bird flu), severe acute respiratory syndrome (SARS), and Ebola hemorrhagic fever.

Avian Influenza (Bird Flu)

Since 1997, human infections from a bird influenza virus have been reported from different parts of the world, particularly Asia. The first known human case of **avian influenza (bird flu)** was in May 1997; a 3-year-old boy in Hong Kong died as a result of infection with avian influenza A (H5N1) virus (Mounts et al., 1999). An additional 17 cases occurred in this Hong Kong epidemic, and a case control study was carried out that revealed that exposure to live poultry in the week prior to the illness was significantly associated with infection with H5N1 (64% of cases vs. 29% of controls, odds ratio [OR] 4.5, $p = 0.045$) (Mounts et al., 1999). In a subsequent study in Vietnam, risk factors that were independently associated with H5N1 infection were (1) preparing sick or dead poultry for consumption (matched OR 8.99, 95% confidence interval [CI] 0.98–81.99, $p = 0.05$), (2) having sick or dead poultry in the household (matched OR 4.94, 95% CI 1.21–20.20, $p = 0.03$), and (3) lack of an indoor water source (matched OR 6.46, 95% CI 1.20–34.81, $p = 0.03$) (Dinh et al., 2006). The most common risk factor for human infection by avian influenza A (H5N1) is direct contact with infected birds or surfaces contaminated with their excretions (Katz, 2008).

The disease starts with typical influenza-like symptoms (fever, sore throat, cough, myalgia, etc.) and can very soon lead to severe respiratory illness and death. Some cases manifest as conjunctivitis (eye infection). For treatment, the Centers for Disease Control and Prevention (CDC) (2008) and WHO recommend oseltamivir, a prescription antiviral medication.

To prevent avian flu, people who are exposed to poultry must follow infection control practices, including hand washing. In the event of outbreaks, exposed persons are carefully monitored and prophylactic antiviral medication is given to those who have been exposed.

Severe Acute Respiratory Syndrome

Severe acute respiratory syndrome (SARS) is a respiratory disease caused by a coronavirus called SARS-associated coronavirus (SARS-CoV). In the first epidemic of the 21st century, in 2003, SARS affected 8,422 people in 29 countries, causing 916 deaths with a case fatality ratio of 11% (WHO, 2003c). The virus is spread from person to person by droplet infection. Health care workers account for 21% of the infections (WHO, 2003c). Other risk factors include household contact with a probable case of SARS, increasing age, male sex, and the presence of comorbidities. Transmission is also associated with air travel.

The incubation period ranges from 2 to 10 days (Ena, 2008). The symptoms of SARS include high fever, headache, body ache, and dry cough (Lam, Chan, & Wong, 2004). SARS starts as a mild illness, but can lead to pneumonia. Death occurs in about 10% of cases. Diagnosis can be established by a reverse transcription polymerase chain reaction (RT-PCR) test in clinical specimens such as blood, stool, and nasal secretions.

For treatment, the antiviral agent ribavirin is given intravenously in combination with high-dose corticosteroids. Antibiotics are given to prevent superadded infections. For prevention, basic infection control measures such as the wearing of masks by patients, close contacts, and those in health care are effective. Early detection and isolation of patients who may be infected with SARS virus is also a useful measure.

Ebola Hemorrhagic Fever

Ebola hemorrhagic fever was first discovered in 1976. It is a viral disease that affects humans and primates (monkeys, gorillas, and chimpanzees). The virus belongs to a family of RNA viruses called the Filoviridae that has four subtypes. Three of these four subtypes have caused disease in humans: Ebola-Zaire, Ebola-Sudan, and Ebola-Ivory Coast. The fourth subtype, Ebola-Reston, causes disease in primates, but not humans. Cases have been reported from the Democratic Republic of the Congo (formerly Zaire), Gabon, Sudan, Uganda, South Africa, and Côte d'Ivoire (Ivory Coast). As of 2008, approximately 1,850 cases with over 1,200 deaths had been reported due to Ebola virus since its discovery (WHO, 2007e). Transmission is by direct contact with blood, secretions, organs, or other bodily fluids of infected persons or animals.

The incubation period is 2 to 21 days. Ebola hemorrhagic fever is characterized by fever, intense weakness, muscular pain, headache, and sore throat. These symptoms are followed by vomiting, diarrhea, rash, impaired kidney and liver function, and internal and external bleeding. Diagnosis can be confirmed by detecting antibodies against the virus or by isolating the virus in cell culture. No specific treatment or vaccine is yet available for Ebola hemorrhagic fever.

The prevention of Ebola hemorrhagic fever is very difficult because the location of the natural reservoir of Ebola is not known (CDC, 2005). Early diagnosis and isolation of patients is important in curtailing spread of the disease. The aim of isolation should be to prevent contact with the blood and secretions of patients.

SKILL-BUILDING ACTIVITY

Lymphatic filariasis, also known as elephantiasis, is a disease that is prevalent in 80 countries around the world. Conduct a search for information about this disease on the Internet. Be sure to visit the Web sites of the Centers for Disease Control and Prevention and the World Health Organization. Collect the following information: (a) causative agent, (b) mode of transmission, (c) epidemiology, (d) clinical features, and (e) measures for prevention and control. Prepare a fact sheet with this information.

SUMMARY

Diseases caused by microorganisms are known as infectious or communicable diseases. They are more prevalent in developing countries. A first category consists of the vaccine-preventable diseases. Diphtheria is an acute communicable disease caused by the bacterium *Corynebacterium diphtheriae* that affects the respiratory system. Pertussis, or whooping cough, is an acute communicable disease affecting the respiratory tract and is caused by *Bordetella pertussis*. Tetanus is caused by infection of a wound with *Clostridium tetani*. For prevention of diphtheria, pertussis, and tetanus, a vaccine is given that is part of the childhood immunization routine in most countries. The other common vaccine-preventable diseases are poliomyelitis (caused by an enterovirus that leads to paralysis), measles and mumps (caused by a paramyxovirus), rubella (caused by a togavirus), *Haemophilus influenzae* type b (Hib) infection, which causes meningitis and pneumonia, and varicella. Vaccines provide specific protection against these diseases.

Malaria is a vector-borne disease that is transmitted through the bite of female *Anopheles* mosquitoes and is caused by protozoa of the genus *Plasmodium*. Case management consisting of early and accurate diagnosis followed by treatment with artemisinin-based combination therapies is the most important aspect of malaria control. Vector control (controlling mosquitoes) is another important part of malaria control.

Sexually transmitted infections, including HIV/AIDS, are diseases that are spread primarily through person-to-person sexual contact. Promoting abstinence, monogamy, and safer sex practices is the cornerstone of the prevention and control of sexually transmitted infections. Tuberculosis is an infectious disease caused by the bacterium *Mycobacterium tuberculosis* that primarily affects the lungs. For control of tuberculosis, early detection and completion of chemotherapy are vital components. In chemotherapy the emphasis is on supervised treatment called DOTS.

Acute respiratory infections are infections of the respiratory tract caused primarily by bacteria and viruses. Prevention and control of acute respiratory infections require minimization of exposure, specific protection by vaccines, and early diagnosis and treatment. Infections of the gastrointestinal tract are very common and cause a great deal of morbidity and mortality, especially in developing countries. Treatment of diarrhea by oral rehydration therapy in developing countries is a very important control method and has been responsible for saving many lives.

Meningococcal meningitis is caused by the bacterium *Neisseria meningitides*. Purified polysaccharide vaccines are available against meningococcal meningitis. Leprosy (also called Hansen disease) is a chronic infectious disease caused by the bacterium *Mycobacterium leprae*. The most effective way of preventing disabilities associated with leprosy and preventing its further transmission is through early diagnosis and treatment with multidrug therapy.

Emerging infectious diseases are those infections in humans that have been seen in recent years or are threatening to increase in the near future. Some of the common emerging infectious diseases are avian influenza (bird flu), severe acute respiratory syndrome (SARS), and Ebola hemorrhagic fever.

IMPORTANT TERMS

acute gastrointestinal infections
acute respiratory infections
avian influenza (bird flu)
diphtheria
Ebola hemorrhagic fever
Haemophilus influenzae type b infections
human immunodeficiency virus/acquired
   immunodeficiency syndrome
   (HIV/AIDS)
leprosy
malaria

measles
meningococcal meningitis
mumps
pertussis
poliomyelitis
rubella
severe acute respiratory syndrome (SARS)
sexually transmitted infections (STIs)
tetanus
tuberculosis (TB)
varicella

REVIEW QUESTIONS

1. Name the vaccine-preventable diseases. Discuss the prevention and control measures for these diseases.
2. How is malaria caused? What can be done for the prevention and control of malaria?
3. Name the sexually transmitted diseases. Discuss prevention and control measures for HIV/AIDS.
4. How is tuberculosis caused and transmitted? Discuss measures for the prevention and control of tuberculosis.
5. Name the causative agents for acute respiratory infections. What measures can be taken for prevention and control of acute respiratory infections?
6. Explain the prevention and control measures for acute gastrointestinal infections.
7. Describe the clinical features, epidemiology, and prevention and control measures for meningococcal meningitis.
8. How is leprosy caused? Discuss the prevention and control measures for leprosy.
9. What are emerging infections? Give examples of emerging infections. Discuss the prevention and control measures for any one emerging infection.

WEB SITES TO EXPLORE

Division of Tuberculosis Elimination, Centers for Disease Control and Prevention

http:// www.cdc.gov/TB/default.htm

This Web site was developed by the U.S. Centers for Disease Control and Prevention and provides links to questions and answers about TB, TB guidelines, fact sheets, education/training materials, slide sets, TB-related *Morbidity and Mortality Weekly Report* articles, surveillance reports, World TB Day, TB in African Americans, and TB-related links. Also provided are TB resources and a search engine for the Web site. *Review this Web site and prepare a set of prevention and control strategies for tuberculosis.*

Emerging Infectious Diseases

http://www.cdc.gov/ncidod/diseases/eid/disease_sites.htm

This Web site was developed by the U.S. Centers for Disease Control and Prevention. It provides a list of emerging infections, including bovine spongiform encephalopathy (mad cow disease) and variant Creutzfeldt-Jakob disease (vCJD), campylobacteriosis, dengue fever, Ebola hemorrhagic fever, *Escherichia coli* infection, group B streptococcal infection, hantavirus pulmonary syndrome, Lassa fever, MRSA (methicillin-resistant *Staphylococcus aureus*), Nipah virus infection, plague, Rift Valley fever, salmonellosis, trypanosomiasis (sleeping sickness), valley fever (coccidioidomycosis), West Nile virus infection, and yellow fever. *Review information about one or more of the emerging infections discussed on this site and prepare a fact sheet that includes clinical features, epidemiology, and prevention and control measures.*

Leprosy

http://www.who.int/lep/en/

This Web site about leprosy was developed by the World Health Organization. It contains links to prevention and control strategies, the global situation, multidrug therapy (MDT), monitoring and evaluation, partners, and research. Links to news, leprosy facts, and WHO publications are also presented. *Explore this Web site and find the latest cases of leprosy. Should leprosy elimination focus on just reduction of prevalence or should it also consider incidence?*

UNAIDS: The Joint United Nations Program on HIV/AIDS

http://www.unaids.org/en/

This is the Web site of the Joint United Nations Program on HIV/AIDS, which has its headquarters in Geneva and works in 80 countries around the world. UNAIDS has five focus areas: mobilizing leadership and advocacy for effective action on the HIV/AIDS epidemic; providing strategic information and policies to guide efforts in the AIDS response worldwide; tracking, monitoring and evaluation of the HIV/AIDS epidemic; engaging civil society and developing partnerships; and mobilizing financial, human, and technical resources to support an effective response. *Explore this Web site and read about UNAIDS policies, country responses, cosponsors, and partnerships. From the Knowledge Centre, find out the latest data about HIV/AIDS.*

World Health Organization's Global Health Atlas

http://www.who.int/globalatlas/default.asp

This Web site, developed by the World Health Organization, presents an atlas of global health. One can make data queries about many communicable diseases, human resources for health, noncommunicable diseases, and world health statistics. An analysis and comparison of data and statistics for infectious diseases at the country, regional, and global levels can be obtained. *Select Communicable Diseases, and then select a topic such as malaria, along with indicators, the geographic region (country or countries), and the time period. Compare the number of cases and deaths from malaria all over the world.*

REFERENCES

Averhoff, F., & Wharton, M. (2008). Mumps. In R. B. Wallace, N. Kohatsu, & J. M. Last (Eds.), *Wallace/Maxcy-Rosenau-Last public health and preventive medicine* (15th ed., pp. 105–107). New York: McGraw Hill Medical.

Bannister, B. A. (2004). Viral exanthems. In J. Cohen & W. G. Powderly (Eds.), *Infectious diseases* (2nd ed., Vol. 1, pp. 119–131). New York: Mosby.

Bouckenooghe, A., & Shandera, W. X. (2000). Infectious diseases: Viral and rickettsial. In L. M. Tierney, Jr., S. J. McPhee, & M. A. Papadakis (Eds.), *Current medical diagnosis and treatment* (39th ed., pp. 1295–1333). New York: Lange Medical Books/McGraw-Hill.

Caugant, D. A. (2008). Genetics and evolution of *Neisseria meningitidis*: Importance for the epidemiology of meningococcal disease. *Infection, Genetics and Evolution*, PMID 18479979 [Epub ahead of publication].

Centers for Disease Control and Prevention. (2005). Questions and answers about Ebola hemorrhagic fever. Retrieved from http://www.cdc.gov/ncidod/dvrd/Spb/mnpages/dispages/ebola/qa.htm

Centers for Disease Control and Prevention. (2007a). Recommended adult immunization schedule—United States, October 2007–September 2008. *Morbidity and Mortality Weekly Report, 56*(41), Q1–Q4. Retrieved from http://www.cdc.gov/mmwr/preview/mmwrhtml/mm5641a7. htm?s_cid= mm5641a 7_e

Centers for Disease Control and Prevention. (2007b). Update on vaccine-derived polioviruses—worldwide, January 2006–August 2007. *Morbidity and Mortality Weekly Report, 56*(38), 996–1001.

Centers for Disease Control and Prevention. (2008). Avian influenza A virus infections of humans. Retrieved from http://www.cdc.gov/flu/avian/gen-info/avian-flu-humans.htm

Chambers, H. F. (2000). Infectious diseases: Bacterial and chlamydial. In L. M. Tierney, Jr., S. J. McPhee, & M. A. Papadakis (Eds.), *Current medical diagnosis and treatment* (39th ed., pp. 1334–1375). New York: Lange Medical Books/McGraw-Hill.

Chang, M., Flannery, B., & Rosenstein, N. (2008). *Haemophilus influenzae* infections. In R. B. Wallace, N. Kohatsu, & J. M. Last (Eds.), *Wallace/Maxcy-Rosenau-Last public health and preventive medicine* (15th ed., pp. 124–127). New York: McGraw Hill Medical.

Chestnutt, M. S., & Prendergast, T. J. (2000). Lung. In L. M. Tierney, Jr., S. J. McPhee, & M. A. Papadakis (Eds.), Current medical diagnosis and treatment (39th ed., pp. 264–350). New York: Lange Medical Books/McGraw-Hill.

Cortese, M. M., & Bisgard, K. M. (2008). Pertussis. In R. B. Wallace, N. Kohatsu, & J. M. Last (Eds.), *Wallace/Maxcy-Rosenau-Last public health and preventive medicine* (15th ed., pp. 111–114). New York: McGraw Hill Medical.

Dinh, P. N., Long, H. T., Tien, N. T., Hien, N. T., Mai le, T. Q., Phong le, H., et al. (2006). Risk factors for human infection with avian influenza A H5N1, Vietnam, 2004. *Emerging Infectious Diseases, 12*(12), 1841–1847.

Efstratiou, A. (2004). Diphtheria. In J. Cohen & W. G. Powderly (Eds.), *Infectious diseases* (2nd ed., Vol. 2, pp. 1655–1688). New York: Mosby.

Ena, J. (2008). Infections spread by close personal contact: Acute respiratory infections. In R. B. Wallace, N. Kohatsu, & J. M. Last (Eds.), *Wallace/Maxcy-Rosenau-Last public health and preventive medicine* (15th ed., pp. 201–211). New York: McGraw Hill Medical.

Friedel, D., & Lavoie, S. (2008). Epidemiology and trends in sexually transmitted infections. In R. B. Wallace, N. Kohatsu, & J. M. Last (Eds.), *Wallace/Maxcy-Rosenau-Last public health and preventive medicine* (15th ed., pp. 155–188). New York: McGraw Hill Medical.

Goldsmith, R. S. (2000). Infectious diseases: Protozoal and helminthic. In L. M. Tierney, Jr., S. J. McPhee, & M. A. Papadakis (Eds.), *Current medical diagnosis and treatment* (39th ed., pp. 1396–1462). New York: Lange Medical Books/McGraw-Hill.

Greenberg, A. E., Drotman, D. P., Curran, J. W., & Janssen, R. S. (2008). The epidemiology and prevention of human immunodeficiency virus (HIV) infection and acquired immunodeficiency syndrome (AIDS). In R. B. Wallace, N. Kohatsu, & J. M. Last (Eds.), *Wallace/Maxcy-Rosenau-Last public health and preventive medicine* (15th ed., pp. 189–199). New York: McGraw Hill Medical.

Guris, D., Marin, M., & Seward, J. F. (2008). Varicella and herpes zoster. In R. B. Wallace, N. Kohatsu, & J. M. Last (Eds.), *Wallace/Maxcy-Rosenau-Last public health and preventive medicine* (15th ed., pp. 127–133). New York: McGraw Hill Medical.

Hardy, I. R., Dittmann, S., & Sutter, R. W. (1996). Current situation and control strategies for resurgence of diphtheria in newly independent states of the former Soviet Union. *Lancet, 347,* 1739–1744.

Heininger, U. (2008). Pertussis immunisation in adolescents and adults. *Advances in Experimental Medicine and Biology, 609,* 72–97.

Hornick, D. B. (2008). Tuberculosis. In R. B. Wallace, N. Kohatsu, & J. M. Last (Eds.), *Wallace/Maxcy-Rosenau-Last public health and preventive medicine* (15th ed., pp. 248–257). New York: McGraw Hill Medical.

Jamison, D. T., Breman, J. G., Measham, A. R., Alleyne, G., Claeson, M., Evans, D. B., et al. (Eds.). (2006). *Priorities in health.* Washington, DC: The World Bank.

Jana, S., Basu, I., Rotheram-Borus, M. J., & Newman, P. A. (2004). The Sonagachi Project: A sustainable community intervention program. *AIDS Education and Prevention, 16*(5), 405–414.

Johnson, A. W., Osinusi, K., Aderele, W. I., & Adeyemi-Doro, F. A. (1993). Bacterial aetiology of acute lower respiratory infections in pre-school Nigerian children and comparative predictive features of bacteraemic and non-bacteraemic illnesses. *Journal of Tropical Pediatrics, 39*(2), 97–106.

Johnson, B. R., Osinusi, K., Aderele, W. I., & Tomori, O. (1993). Viral pathogens of acute lower respiratory infections in pre-school Nigerian children and clinical implications of multiple microbial identifications. *West African Journal of Medicine, 12*(1), 11–20.

Johnson, W. B., Aderele, W. I., & Gbadero, D. A. (1992). Host factors and acute lower respiratory infections in pre-school children. *Journal of Tropical Pediatrics, 38*(3), 132–136.

Jones, K. E., Patel, N. G., Levy, M. A., Storeygard, A., Balk, D., Gittleman, J. L., et al. (2008). Global trends in emerging infectious diseases. *Nature, 451*(7181), 990–993.

Kachur, S. P., deOliveira, A. M., & Bloland, P. B. (2008). Malaria. In R. B. Wallace, N. Kohatsu, & J. M. Last (Eds.), *Wallace/Maxcy-Rosenau-Last public health and preventive medicine* (15th ed., pp. 373–386). New York: McGraw Hill Medical.

Karima, T. M., Bukhari, S. Z., Fatani, M. I., Yasin, K. A., Al-Afif, K. A., & Hafiz, F. H. (2003). Clinical and microbiological spectrum of meningococcal disease in adults during Hajj 2000: An implication of quadrivalent vaccination policy. *Journal of Pakistan Medical Association, 53*(1), 3–7.

Katz, M. (2008). Influenza. In R. B. Wallace, N. Kohatsu, & J. M. Last (Eds.), *Wallace/Maxcy-Rosenau-Last public health and preventive medicine* (15th ed., pp. 120–124). New York: McGraw Hill Medical.

Katz, M. H., & Hollander, H. (2000). HIV infection. In L. M. Tierney, Jr., S. J. McPhee, & M. A. Papadakis (Eds.), *Current medical diagnosis and treatment* (39th ed., pp. 1266–1294). New York: Lange Medical Books/McGraw-Hill.

Katz, S. L., & Hinman, A. R. (2004). Summary and conclusions: Measles elimination meeting, 16–17 March 2000. *Journal of Infectious Diseases, 189*(Suppl. 1), S43–S47.

Kok, M., & Pechere, J. (2004). Nature and pathogenicity of micro-organisms. In J. Cohen & W. G. Powderly (Eds.), *Infectious diseases* (2nd ed., Vol. 1, pp. 3–29). New York: Mosby.

Kosek, M., Bern, C., & Guerrant, R. L. (2003). The global burden of diarrhoeal disease, as estimated from studies published between 1992 and 2000. *Bulletin of the World Health Organization, 81*, 197–204.

Kretsinger, K., Moran, J. S., & Roper, M. H. (2008). Tetanus. In R. B. Wallace, N. Kohatsu, & J. M. Last (Eds.), *Wallace/Maxcy-Rosenau-Last public health and preventive medicine* (15th ed., pp. 115–117). New York: McGraw Hill Medical.

Lam, C. W., Chan, M. H., & Wong, C. K. (2004). Severe acute respiratory syndrome: Clinical and laboratory manifestations. *The Clinical Biochemist Reviews, 25*(2), 121–132.

Lockwood, D. N., & Suneetha, S. (2005). Leprosy: Too complex a disease for a simple elimination paradigm. *Bulletin of World Health Organization, 83*(3), 230–235.

Moodie, R., & Aboagye-Kwarteng, T. (1993). Confronting the HIV epidemic in Asia and the Pacific: Developing successful strategies to minimize the spread of HIV infection. *AIDS, 7*(12), 1543–1551.

Morgan-Capner, P. (2004). Measles, mumps, and rubella viruses. In J. Cohen & W. G. Powderly (Eds.), *Infectious diseases* (2nd ed., Vol. 2, pp. 1983–1991). New York: Mosby.

Mounts, A. W., Kwong, H., Izurieta, H. S., Ho, Y., Au, T., Lee, M., et al. (1999). Case-control study of risk factors for avian influenza A (H5N1) disease, Hong Kong, 1997. *Journal of Infectious Diseases, 180*(2), 505–508.

Nelson, K. E. (2008). Leprosy. In R. B. Wallace, N. Kohatsu, & J. M. Last (Eds.), *Wallace/Maxcy-Rosenau-Last public health and preventive medicine* (15th ed., pp. 258–263). New York: McGraw Hill Medical.

Network of Sex Work Projects. (1997). *Sex work is real work: We demand workers rights.* Retrieved from http://www.nswp.org/rights/dmsc/indiaconf.html

Nosten, F., Luxemburger, C., Kyle, D. E., Ballou, W. R., Wittes, J., Wah, E., et al. (1996). Randomised double-blind placebo-controlled trial of SPf66 malaria vaccine in children in northwestern Thailand. Shoklo SPf66 Malaria Vaccine Trial Group. *Lancet, 348*(9029), 701–707.

Orenstein, W. A., Papania, M., & Strebel, P. (2008). Measles. In R. B. Wallace, N. Kohatsu, & J. M. Last (Eds.), *Wallace/Maxcy-Rosenau-Last public health and preventive medicine* (15th ed., pp. 101–105). New York: McGraw Hill Medical.

Pasvol, G. (2004). Malaria. In J. Cohen & W. G. Powderly (Eds.), *Infectious diseases* (2nd ed., Vol. 2, pp. 1579–1591). New York: Mosby.

Reingold, A. L., & Phares, C. R. (2006). Infectious diseases. In M. H. Merson, R. E. Black, & A. J. Mills (Eds.), *International public health: Diseases, programs, systems, and policies* (2nd ed., pp. 127–186). Sudbury, MA: Jones and Bartlett.

Ridley, D. S., & Jopling, W. H. (1966). Classification of leprosy according to immunity. A five-group system. *International Journal of Leprosy and Other Mycobacterial Diseases, 34*(3), 255–273.

Roper, M. H., Vandelaer, J. H., & Gasse, F. L. (2007). Maternal and neonatal tetanus. *Lancet, 370*(9603), 1947–1959.

Slack, M. P. E. (2004). Gram negative coccobacilli. In J. Cohen & W. G. Powderly (Eds.), *Infectious diseases* (2nd ed., Vol. 2, pp. 2243–2264). New York: Mosby.

Soriano-Gabarro, M., & Rosenstein, N. (2008). Meningococcal disease. In R. B. Wallace, N. Kohatsu, & J. M. Last (Eds.), *Wallace/Maxcy-Rosenau-Last public health and preventive medicine* (15th ed., pp. 245–248). New York: McGraw Hill Medical.

Sutter, R. W., & Cochi, S. L. (2008). Poliomyelitis. In R. B. Wallace, N. Kohatsu, & J. M. Last (Eds.), *Wallace/Maxcy-Rosenau-Last public health and preventive medicine* (15th ed., pp. 133–137). New York: McGraw Hill Medical.

Tan, T., Trindade, E., & Skowronski, D. (2005). Epidemiology of pertussis. *Pediatric Infectious Disease Journal, 24*(5 Suppl.), S10–S18.

Tiwari, T. S. P. (2008). Diphtheria. In R. B. Wallace, N. Kohatsu, & J. M. Last (Eds.), *Wallace/Maxcy-Rosenau-Last public health and preventive medicine* (15th ed., pp. 117–120). New York: McGraw Hill Medical.

Ungphakorn, J., & Sittitrai, W. (1994). The Thai response to the HIV/AIDS epidemic. *AIDS, 8*(Suppl. 2), S155–S163.

United Nations Program on HIV/AIDS. (2002). Epidemiological fact sheets on HIV/AIDS and sexually transmitted infections: India. Retrieved from http://www.unaids.org/hivaidsinfo/statistics/fact_sheets/pdfs/India_en.pdf

Valls, V. (2008). Acute gastrointestinal infections. In R. B. Wallace, N. Kohatsu, & J. M. Last (Eds.), *Wallace/Maxcy-Rosenau-Last public health and preventive medicine* (15th ed., pp. 263–274). New York: McGraw Hill Medical.

Weinstock, H., Berman, S., & Cates, W. (2004). Sexually transmitted diseases among American youth: Incidence and prevalence estimates, 2000. *Perspectives on Sexual and Reproductive Health, 36*(1), 6–10.

Wood, M. J. (2004a). Toxin mediated disorders: Tetanus, botulism and diphtheria. In J. Cohen & W. G. Powderly (Eds.), *Infectious diseases* (2nd ed., Vol. 1, pp. 289–292). New York: Mosby.

Wood, M. J. (2004b). Neurotropic virus disorders. In J. Cohen & W. G. Powderly (Eds.), *Infectious diseases* (2nd ed., Vol. 1, pp. 321–327). New York: Mosby.

World Health Organization. (2000). Rubella vaccines. *Weekly Epidemiological Record, 75*(20), 161–169. Retrieved from http://www.who.int/immunization/wer7520rubella%20_May00_position_paper.pdf

World Health Organization. (2001). *Global prevalence and incidence of selected curable sexually transmitted infections: Overview and estimates.* Geneva: Author.

World Health Organization. (2003a). Introduction of inactivated poliovirus vaccine into oral poliovirus vaccine-using countries. *Weekly Epidemiological Record, 78*(28), 241–252. Retrieved from http://www.who.int/immunization/wer7828polio_Jul03_position_paper.pdf

World Health Organization. (2003b). Varicella vaccine. Retrieved from http://www.who.int/vaccines/en/ varicella.shtml

World Health Organization. (2003c). *Consensus document on the epidemiology of severe acute respiratory syndrome (SARS)*. Geneva: Author. Retrieved from http://www.who.int/csr/sars/en/WHO consensus.pdf

World Health Organization. (2004). Measles vaccines. *Weekly Epidemiological Record, 79*(14), 130–142. Retrieved from http://www.who.int/immunization_delivery/adc/measles/wer7914.pdf

World Health Organization. (2005a). Pertussis vaccines—WHO position paper. *Weekly Epidemiological Record, 80*(4), 31–39. Retrieved from http://www.who.int/immunization/topics/wer8004pertussis_ Jan_2005.pdf

World Health Organization. (2005b). *Combating emerging infectious diseases in the South East Asia region*. New Delhi: Author.

World Health Organization. (2006a). *Guidelines for the treatment of malaria*. Geneva: Author.

World Health Organization. (2006b). *Global malaria programme* [Brochure]. Retrieved from http://www.who.int/malaria/docs/GMPbrochure.pdf

World Health Organization. (2007a). Progress in global measles control and mortality reduction, 2000–2006. *Weekly Epidemiological Record, 82*(48), 418–424. Retrieved from http://www.who.int/ wer/2007/wer8248.pdf

World Health Organization. (2007b). Mumps reported cases. Retrieved from http://www. who.int/ immunization_monitoring/en/globalsummary/timeseries/tsinc idencemum.htm

World Health Organization. (2007c). Rubella reported cases. Retrieved from http://www.who.int/ immunization_monitoring/en/globalsummary/timeseries/tsinc idencerub.htm

World Health Organization. (2007d). Sexually transmitted infections. Retrieved from http://www.who.int/ mediacentre/factsheets/fs110/en/

World Health Organization. (2007e). Ebola haemorrhagic fever. Retrieved from http://www.who.int/ mediacentre/factsheets/fs103/en/

World Health Organization. (2008a). Immunization, surveillance, assessment, and monitoring: Diphtheria. Retrieved from http://www.who.int/immunization_monitoring/diseases/diphteria/en/ index.html

World Health Organization. (2008b). Immunization, surveillance, assessment, and monitoring: Pertussis. Retrieved from http://www.who.int/immunization_monitoring/diseases/pertussis/en/

World Health Organization. (2008c). Immunization, surveillance, assessment, and monitoring: Neonatal tetanus. Retrieved from http://www.who.int/immunization_monitoring/diseases/ neonatal_tetanus/en/index.html

World Health Organization. (2008d). Immunization, surveillance, assessment, and monitoring: Poliomyelitis. Retrieved from http://www.who.int/immunization_monitoring/diseases/poliomyelitis/ en/index.html

World Health Organization. (2008e). Immunization, surveillance, assessment, and monitoring: Measles. Retrieved from http://www.who.int/immunization_monitoring/diseases/measles/en/

World Health Organization. (2008f). *Haemophilus influenzae* type B (HiB). Retrieved from http:// www.who.int/mediacentre/factsheets/fs294/en/

World Health Organization. (2008g). Small pox. Retrieved from http://www.who.int/mediacentre/ factsheets/smallpox/en/

World Health Organization. (2008h). Tuberculosis. Retrieved from http://www.who.int/mediacentre/factsheets/fs104/en/index.html

World Health Organization. (2008i). BCG vaccine. Retrieved from http://www.who.int/biologicals/areas/ vaccines/bcg/en/

World Health Organization. (2008j). Acute respiratory infections in children. Retrieved from http://www.who.int/fch/depts/cah/resp_infections/en/

World Health Organization. (2008k). Meningococcal meningitis. Retrieved from http://www.who.int/mediacentre/factsheets/fs141/en/

World Health Organization. (2008l). Leprosy today. Retrieved from http://www.who.int/lep/en/

World Health Organization and United Nations Progam on HIV/AIDS. (2008). *Global summary of the HIV and AIDS epidemic, 2006.* Retrieved from http://www.searo.who.int/LinkFiles/News_and_Events_Epicore2006_02Oct06_en.ppt#262,1,Slide 1

Zangwill, K. M., & Belshe, R. B. (2004). Safety and efficacy of trivalent inactivated influenza vaccine in young children: A summary for the new era of routine vaccination. *Pediatric Infectious Disease Journal, 23*(3), 189–197.

Zombré, S., Hacen, M. M., Ouango, G., Sanou, S., Adamou, Y., Koumaré, B., et al. (2007). The outbreak of meningitis due to *Neisseria meningitidis* W135 in 2003 in Burkina Faso and the national response: Main lessons learnt. *Vaccine, 25*(Suppl. 1), A69–71.

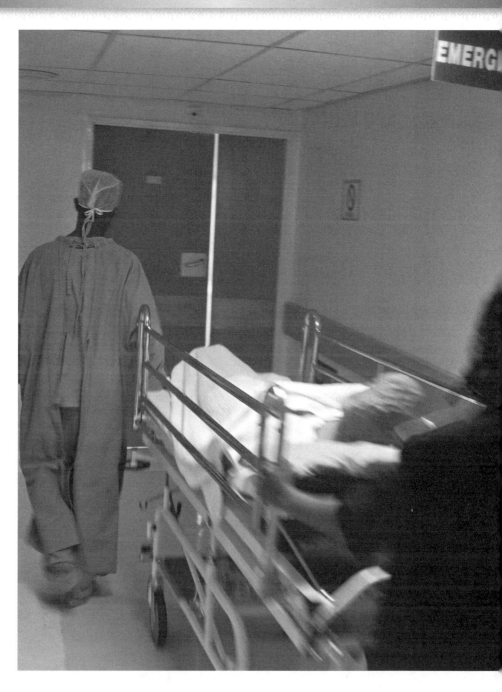

Noncommunicable Chronic Diseases

- alcohol use
- cancers
- cardiovascular diseases (CVD)
- cerebrovascular disease
- chronic obstructive pulmonary disease (COPD)
- coronary heart disease (CHD)

- diabetes
- osteoarthritis
- osteoporosis
- physical inactivity
- rheumatic heart disease (RHD)
- tobacco use
- unhealthy eating

AFTER READING THIS CHAPTER YOU SHOULD BE ABLE TO

- Describe the epidemiology of and prevention and control measures for lifestyle factors of tobacco use, alcohol use, physical inactivity, and unhealthy eating
- Discuss the epidemiology of and prevention and control measures for common cardiovascular diseases
- Explain the epidemiology of and prevention and control measures for cerebrovascular disease
- Describe the epidemiology of and prevention and control measures for cancers
- Discuss the epidemiology of and prevention and control measures for diabetes
- Describe the epidemiology of and prevention and control measures for chronic obstructive pulmonary disease

Noncommunicable chronic diseases are diseases of slow progression and long duration. Characteristic features of noncommunicable chronic diseases are uncertain causation, association with multiple risk factors, a long latency period, a long course of illness, noncontagious origin, associated functional impairment or disability, and incurability (McKenna, Taylor, Marks, & Koplan, 1998). Examples of noncommunicable chronic diseases include cardiovascular diseases, stroke, cancers, chronic lung diseases, and diabetes. Noncommunicable chronic diseases constitute the leading cause of mortality in the world and account for 60% of all deaths (World Health Organization [WHO], 2008a).

These diseases have surpassed infectious and communicable diseases in terms of burden on morbidity and mortality. They account for twice the number of deaths of all infectious diseases (including HIV/AIDS, tuberculosis, and malaria), maternal and perinatal conditions, and nutritional deficiencies combined (WHO, 2005a). Furthermore, 80% of all deaths due to chronic diseases occur in low- and middle-income countries, and half are in women.

Several risk factors are responsible for the causation of chronic diseases. At the first level are underlying socioeconomic, cultural, political, and environmental risk factors. Examples of these are low socioeconomic status, globalization, urbanization, and an aging population. At the second level are modifiable behavioral risk factors. Examples of these include tobacco use, alcohol abuse, physical inactivity, and unhealthy diet. At the third level are nonmodifiable risk factors. Examples include heredity and age. At the fourth level are intermediary risk factors such as high blood pressure, high cholesterol, and overweight or obesity.

> *Noncommunicable chronic diseases constitute the leading cause of mortality in the world and account for 60% of all deaths.*
>
> —World Health Organization (2008a)

As discussed in Chapter 3, there are three levels of prevention, and each of these applies to the prevention and control of chronic noncommunicable diseases. *Primary prevention* refers to those preventive actions that are taken prior to the onset of a disease or injury with the intention of removing the possibility of their ever occurring. Examples of measures in this category include physical activity promotion programs, smoking prevention programs, alcohol prevention programs, and healthy nutrition programs. *Secondary prevention* refers to actions that block the progression of an injury or disease at its incipient stage. Examples of measures in this category include screening programs for cancers or cardiovascular disease. *Tertiary prevention* refers to those actions taken after the onset of disease or an injury with the intention of assisting diseased or disabled people. Examples include eye examinations in diabetic patients.

This chapter first discusses some of the modifiable behavioral lifestyle risk factors for chronic noncommunicable diseases. It then discusses some common chronic noncommunicable diseases in terms of their clinical features, epidemiology, and prevention and control measures.

BEHAVIORAL LIFESTYLE RISK FACTORS

Some common behavioral lifestyle risk factors for chronic diseases are tobacco use, alcohol use, physical inactivity, and unhealthy eating. Each of these factors contributes to more than one disease.

Tobacco Use

Tobacco use entails smoking cigarettes, cigars, pipes, bidis or kreteks (clove cigarettes), or hookahs or using smokeless tobacco (snuff and chewing tobacco). Use of tobacco is associated with several chronic diseases. It has been implicated as a causative factor in coronary heart disease (CHD), peripheral vascular disease, cerebrovascular disease (CVD), lung cancer, oral cancer, laryngeal cancer, esophageal cancer, bladder cancer, renal cancer, pancreatic cancer, stomach cancer, cervical cancer, endometrial cancer, acute myeloid leukemia, chronic obstructive pulmonary disease (COPD), gastroesophageal reflux disease, and periodontitis (Doll, Peto, Boreham, & Sutherland, 2004; Giovino, 2007; Husten & Thorne, 2008). In addition, smoking by pregnant women has deleterious effects on the fetus. Smoking leads to low birth weight in infants. Infants born to women who smoke during pregnancy are an average 200 to 250 g lighter than infants born to nonsmokers (U.S. Department of Health and Human Services, 2001). Maternal smoking is also associated with preterm delivery and higher fetal, neonatal, and infant mortality.

Passive smoking, or exposure to secondhand smoke (SHS) or environmental tobacco smoke (ETS), occurs when a person is in close proximity to a smoker and is associated with some of the same hazards that are associated with smoking. Passive smokers inhale mainstream smoke exhaled by smokers as well as sidestream smoke from the burning end of cigarettes (Kalucka, 2007); the smoke is very similar to the smoke inhaled by smokers and contains 4,000 chemicals, including 50 carcinogens. It is responsible for coronary heart disease (Law, Morris, & Wald, 1997) and lung cancer (Hackshaw, Law, & Wald, 1997).

Epidemiology

Tobacco companies manufacture about 5.5 trillion cigarettes a year, or about 1,000 cigarettes per person/year (Mackay & Eriksen, 2002). China consumes the most cigarettes (1,542 billion), followed by the United States (431 billion), Japan (328 billion), Russia (258 billion), and Indonesia (215 billion). Over 15 billion cigarettes are smoked every day worldwide.

> *Over 15 billion cigarettes are smoked every day worldwide. There are approximately one billion men and 250 million women in the world who smoke.*
>
> —Mackay & Eriksen (2002)

Approximately 1 billion men and 250 million women in the world smoke (Mackay & Eriksen, 2002). Approximately 35% of men and 22% of women in developed countries and 50% of men and 9% of women in developing countries are smokers. The largest number of smokers is in China, where 300 million men smoke. With regard to smoking in men, trends in both developed and developing countries show that the rates have peaked and there is a slow decline; however, smoking is nowhere near elimination. With regard to smoking in women, declining trends are seen in some developed countries, such as Australia, Canada, the United Kingdom, and the United States, but in several European countries these rates are increasing; in developing countries these rates have been stable (Mackay & Eriksen, 2002). The tobacco industry has especially marketed cigarettes to women in recent years.

Another group to whom the tobacco industry has marketed cigarettes is youth. A large majority of smokers who begin smoking do so in their youth. If a person does not begin smoking by the end of his or her teens, the likelihood of that person starting smoking is very low. The highest rate of smoking in youth is found in central and eastern Europe, sections of India, and some of the western Pacific islands (Mackay & Eriksen, 2002). Besides marketing by the tobacco industry, some of the factors influencing tobacco use among youth are: accessibility to tobacco products at low price, peer pressure, lower self-image, the perception that tobacco use is "cool," and parental smoking. Because of the growing number of new smokers, the absolute number of smokers is likely to increase over the next couple decades even if the number of current smokers declines.

It is estimated that 0.1 billion people died from tobacco use in the 20th century and it is estimated that 1 billion people will die in the 21st century (Mackay & Eriksen, 2002). These deaths caused by tobacco are more than those caused by HIV/AIDS, drugs, road accidents, murder, and suicide combined.

Prevention and Control

School-based education is an essential component of primary prevention, or preventing smoking initiation. Such programs should build refusal skills in youth and must be theory based, as explained in Chapter 3. These programs should be targeted to grades 6 through 8, the time at which children are experimenting with smoking behavior. School-based educational programs should be combined with other strategies, such as legislation that bans advertisements that promote tobacco smoking. Comprehensive bans on all forms of tobacco promotion are an effective means to reduce tobacco use. This includes decreasing television and movie imagery supporting tobacco use, prohibiting the distribution of free tobacco products, and eliminating the promotion of sports and cultural events by tobacco companies (Novotny & Giovino, 1998). Cigarette packaging is also a tool for marketing, and many countries are advocating packaging cigarettes in plain packets (Mackay & Eriksen, 2002).

Likewise, the marketing of cigarettes as "light" or "mild" is objectionable because it conveys a false impression that the cigarettes so labeled are less harmful.

A measure that has been implemented by the majority of countries around the world is to print health warnings on cigarette packs. Many countries still do not carry such health warnings, however, and in many countries the warnings are inconspicuous or not in the local language. Canada has some quite vivid warnings, which can be emulated by other countries. Legislation that restricts the sale of tobacco products to minors is also helpful in preventing the initiation of tobacco use. Countries such as the United States have implemented such laws. Increasing the price of tobacco products is also helpful in reducing tobacco use by youth (National Cancer Institute, 1993).

An example of a measure to reduce environmental tobacco smoke is legislation to ban smoking in public places. Banning smoking in workplaces is an effective means to reduce exposure to passive smoking as well as to reduce smoking by smokers, who consume fewer cigarettes per day. All major airlines are smoke free, and there are laws in most countries to make public buildings, hospitals, and other institutions smoke free.

Smokers should be detected early by routine questioning at the health care provider's office and should be directed to smoking cessation programs. Smoking cessation approaches include nicotine replacement therapy, Bupropion therapy, social support, relaxation training, and problem-solving skills training. **Table 5.1** summarizes various prevention and control approaches to tobacco use.

Alcohol Use

Alcohol has been used by humankind for thousands of years. **Alcohol use** commonly involves the drinking of beer, wine, or spirits. In some parts of the world local home-brewed alcoholic beverages are also drunk, such as *burukutu* in Nigeria or *desi sharab* in India. Alcohol use ranges from mild use to abuse to dependence and is associated with a myriad of adverse health consequences. Besides the development of diseases, chronic use of alcohol is also responsible for injuries and deaths due to motor vehicle accidents and homicides. According to the 2002 World Health Report (WHO, 2002a), hazardous and harmful use of alcohol was ranked as the leading risk factor for morbidity in developing countries and as the third leading risk factor in developed countries.

The negative consequences of alcohol use can be categorized as follows (Dufour, 1998):

- *Acute effects of drinking large amounts of alcohol:* Unintentional and intentional injuries are a major group of consequences resulting from the acute effects of alcohol; these include accidents and alcohol poisoning.

TABLE 5.1   Prevention and Control Measures for Tobacco Use

Prevention

School-based education

Legislation that bans advertisements that promote tobacco smoking
- Decreasing television and movie imagery
- Prohibiting distribution of free tobacco products
- Eliminating promotion of sports and cultural events by tobacco companies
- Using plain packaging

Cigarette packs that carry vivid health warnings

Legislation that restricts sales of tobacco products to minors

Increasing the price of tobacco products

Banning smoking in public places

Smoking Cessation

Nicotine replacement therapy

Bupropion therapy

Social support

Relaxation training

Problem-solving skills training

- *Risk factor in causation of chronic diseases:* Alcohol is a causative factor in alcoholic hepatitis and cirrhosis of the liver (Reuben, 2008). It is also a risk factor for liver cancer (hepatocellular carcinoma) (Raoul, 2008) and has been associated with cancers of the oral cavity, larynx, and esophagus (Corrao, Bagnardi, Zambon, & La Vecchia, 2005). A study from China showed that after adjusting for tobacco use and other potential confounders, regular alcohol drinkers had a twofold greater risk than nondrinkers of developing esophageal cancer (hazards ratio = 2.02; 95% confidence interval = 1.31–3.12) (Fan, Yuan, Wang, Gao, & Yu, 2008). In terms of effects of alcohol on cardiovascular diseases, it has been found that moderate alcohol consumption (two or fewer drinks per day) is not associated with any significant morbidity and may confer some protection from acute heart attacks through antithrombotic properties and elevation of high-density lipoproteins; however, three or more drinks per day is associated with hypertriglyceridemia, cardiomyopathy, hypertension, and stroke (Saremi & Arora, 2008). Alcohol use disorders are found in comorbidity with other psychiatric disorders (Cook & Liesveld, 2008). Alcohol use is also associated with central nervous system degenerative processes such as Wernicke encephalopathy and dementia. Alcohol use is associated with obstructive sleep apnea (Remmers, 1984) and with diseases such as epilepsy (Leone et al., 1997), acute and chronic pancreatitis (Ammann, Heitz, & Klöppel, 1996; Pelli, Lappalainen-Lehto, Piironen, Sand, & Nordback, 2008), and psoriasis (Kirby et al., 2008). Alcohol consumption during pregnancy is associated with a number of risks to the fetus, including fetal alcohol syndrome (FAS). The characteristic features of FAS are pre- and postnatal growth retardation, dysfunction of the central nervous system, and facial dysmorphology (Applebaum, 1995). Fetal alcohol syndrome can also affect the cardiac, skeletal, and muscular systems and lead to inability to function as an independent adult.

- *Habitual alcohol use:* Can lead to alcoholism or becoming dependent on alcohol, which is characterized by compulsive drinking and disruption of an individual's social or occupational life. The *Diagnostic and Statistical Manual of Mental Disorders* (DSM-IV-TR) defines alcohol dependence as a "maladaptive pattern of alcohol use, leading to clinically significant impairment or distress as manifested by three (or more) of the following occurring at any time in the same 12-month period: (a) tolerance; (b) withdrawal; (c) alcohol use in greater quantity or for longer period than intended; (d) persistent desire or unsuccessful efforts to cut down or control alcohol use; (e) a great deal of time is spent acquiring, using, or recovering from alcohol's effects; (f) important social, occupational, or recreational activities are given up or reduced because of alcohol use; (g) alcohol use is continued despite knowledge of having a persistent or recurrent physical or psychological problem that is likely to have been caused by or exacerbated by alcohol use" (American Psychiatric Association, 2000).

Epidemiology

About 2 billion people all over the world consume alcoholic beverages, and 76.3 million have diagnosable alcohol-related disorders (WHO, 2004a). The global per capita consumption of alcohol in 2001 was 5.1 liters, of which beer accounts for 1.9 liters; wine, 1.3 liters; and spirits, 1.7 liters (WHO, 2004a). Worldwide, alcohol was responsible for 1.8 million deaths (or 3.2% of total deaths) and 58.3 million (4% of total) disability-adjusted life years (DALYs) (WHO, 2008b). Neuropsychiatric conditions account for close to 40% of the DALYs. Unintentional injuries account for 32.0% of the total number of alcohol-attributable deaths; intentional injuries account for 13.7% (WHO, 2007a). Thus, injuries account for roughly half of all alcohol-related deaths. Between 10 and 18% of all emergency department visits are related to alcohol (WHO, 2007a). On a global level, alcohol consumption has shown an increase in recent decades, with a large majority of that increase occurring in developing countries. In terms of global gender distribution, men are more likely than women to drink, to consume a greater amount of alcohol, and to cause more problems associated with alcohol (Wilsnack, Wilsnack, & Obot, 2005).

> *There are about 2 billion people all over the world who consume alcoholic beverages and there are 76.3 million with diagnosable alcohol use related disorders.*
>
> —World Health Organization (2004a)

Prevention and Control

Primary prevention strategies for combating the alcohol problem are based on policy and educational measures. The primary policy measure is reduction of the availability of alcohol (WHO, 2007b). This entails a wide range of governmental controls on the production, distribution, and sales of alcoholic beverages by either government monopolization of these activities or by issuing licenses that restrict the number of outlets for alcohol and their hours of operation. A related policy measure is restricting sales of alcohol. Moslem countries have a total ban on alcohol. Other countries ban sales to minors and have a minimum drinking age. The United States, for example, has a minimum drinking age of 21 years. Such measures are helpful in restricting the number of alcohol users. Another policy measure is increasing taxes on alcohol, thereby deterring its use by a large number of people. A further policy measure pertains to restricting alcohol advertisements, especially those that influence young people. This includes decreasing television and movie imagery supporting alcohol use and eliminating the promotion of sports and cultural events by alcohol companies.

Another policy measure is the use of blood alcohol concentration (BAC) laws regarding drinking and driving. Many countries, such as Hungary, Romania, and the Czech Republic, have instituted a zero-tolerance policy for drinking and driving (0.0 mg/mL of BAC). The most liberal policy is found in some states in the United States that allow up to 1.0 mg/mL of BAC as the permissible limit (International Center for Alcohol Policies [ICAP], 2002). In Finland, the BAC limit is 0.5 mg/mL, whereas in the United States it varies from 0.8 mg/mL to 1.0 mg/mL (ICAP, 2002).

Borkenstein (1976) found that alcohol was involved in 50% of highway deaths in the United States, whereas the comparable figure in Finland was only 27%. Similar comparisons can be made with other countries, and it will generally be found that the more rigorous the BAC limits, the less deadly the consequences. Furthermore, it is well documented in scientific literature that even a minimal trace of blood alcohol can influence driving ability (Heifer, 1991).

Educational measures for primary prevention of alcohol start with school-based educational programs. Such programs should be delivered in middle and high school. Along with school-based educational programs, involvement of the mass media and educational community-based interventions are essential. All educational programs should be theory based, as elaborated in Chapter 3. Another educational intervention is that of posting health warning signs on alcohol products. However, the WHO expert committee on problems related to alcohol consumption found that posting warning signs on alcohol products was not as effective as in the case of tobacco (WHO, 2007b).

Secondary prevention of alcohol abuse is done through early diagnosis and treatment. Several instruments are available for screening for alcohol problems. One such simple instrument is the four-item CAGE questionnaire (Mayfield, McLeod, & Hall, 1974), which asks the following questions: (1) Have you ever felt you should cut down on your drinking? (2) Have people annoyed you by criticizing your drinking? (3) Have you ever felt bad or guilty about your drinking? (4) Have you ever taken a drink first thing in the morning (eye opener) to steady your nerves or get rid of a hangover? A cut-off score of two positive answers identifies an alcohol problem.

Pregnant women should be screened for alcohol use and warned of potential harms to the fetus. Interventions for alcohol-related problems should be available both in primary care settings and in specialized settings where more intensive treatment can be offered. Finally, tertiary prevention in the form of rehabilitation services for those recovering from severe alcohol dependence should be available. **Table 5.2** summarizes the measures for the prevention and control of alcohol abuse.

Physical Inactivity

Physical inactivity is defined as not meeting the minimum requirements with regard to physical activity. Physical activity is any bodily movement that increases energy expenditure. A special type of physical activity is exercise that is planned, structured, and repetitive and is done with an objective of improving physical fitness, including

TABLE 5.2 Measures for the Prevention and Control of Alcohol Abuse		
Level of Prevention	**Approach**	**Measure**
Primary	Policy	Reduction of availability of alcohol • Governmental control • Licensing
		Restricting sales of alcohol • Total ban • Restricting sales to minors
		Increasing taxes on alcohol
		Restricting alcohol advertisements • Decreasing television and movie imagery supporting alcohol use • Eliminating promotion of sports and cultural events by alcohol companies
		Zero-tolerance and maximum blood alcohol concentration laws
	Educational	School-based educational programs
		Mass media
		Community-based educational programs
		Posting health warning signs on alcohol products
Secondary	Early diagnosis and treatment	Screening
		Primary care interventions
		Intensive interventions in specialized settings
Tertiary	Rehabilitation	Rehabilitation centers

cardiorespiratory functioning, muscular conditioning, metabolic balance, morphologic structure, and motor performance (Ainsworth & Macera, 1998).

The American College of Sports Medicine (ACSM, 2007) and the American Heart Association (AHA) have promulgated the following guidelines regarding the minimum requirements for physical activity for adults younger than 65: Doing moderately intense cardiorespiratory or aerobic activity (such as brisk walking) 30 minutes a day for 5 days a week *or* doing vigorously intense cardiorespiratory or aerobic activity (such as jogging or running) 20 minutes a day for 3 days a week *and* doing eight to ten strength-training exercises (such as weight lifting), with 8 to 12 repetitions of each exercise, twice a week. Moderate-intensity physical activity means working hard enough to raise one's heart rate and break a sweat, yet still being able to carry on a conversation. This minimum corresponds to a daily expenditure of 150 kilocalories (Ainsworth & Macera, 1998). For young people (5–18 years), the recommendations are for 60 minutes of moderate to vigorous physical activity each day that is developmentally appropriate and involves a variety of activities.

Physical inactivity has several adverse health consequences. It is a risk factor for coronary heart disease; the risk is almost twofold for those who are physically inactive compared with those who are physically active (Powell, Thompson, Caspersen, & Kendrick, 1987; Sofi, Capalbo, Cesari, Abbate, & Gensini, 2008). Physical inactivity is also associated with developing diabetes mellitus, stroke, breast cancer, and colon cancer (Allender, Foster, Scarborough, & Rayner, 2007). Regular physical activity has beneficial effects on improving the outcomes associated with depression (Kerse et al., 2008) and promotes psychological well-being (U.S. Department of Health and Human Services, 1996).

Epidemiology

Approximately 60% of the world's population does not meet the minimum recommendation of 30 minutes of moderate-intensity physical activity every day (WHO, 2008c). According to the 2002 World Health Report, approximately 17% of the world's population is completely inactive, and 31 to 51% are active at insufficient levels (WHO, 2002a). Physical activity has been shown to decline with age and is higher among girls and women.

> *Approximately 60% of the world's population does not meet the minimum recommendation of 30 minutes moderate intensity physical activity every day.*
>
> —World Health Organization (2008c)

Physical inactivity is estimated to be responsible for causing two million deaths annually worldwide. In studies from all over the world, physical inactivity has been found to be a factor in approximately 10 to 16% of the cases of breast cancer, colon cancer, and diabetes, and about 22% of cases of coronary heart disease (WHO, 2008c).

Multiple factors, both individual and environmental, are responsible for physical inactivity. Among the individual factors are lack of time, low motivation, the costs outweighing the benefits from the individual's perspective, and laziness. Among the environmental factors are population overcrowding, increased poverty, increased levels of crime, high-density traffic, low air quality, and lack of parks, sidewalks, and sports/recreation facilities (WHO, 2008d).

Prevention and Control

Physical activity interventions can be designed to either change individuals or change environments and policies. Physical activity interventions can be targeted at a variety of levels: schools, worksites, community, and patient care. School-based interventions generally utilize physical education classes. One study that shows the importance of physical education classes was done at the kindergarten level by Datar and Strum (2004) in the United States and examined the effect of physical education instruction time on body mass index (BMI). They looked at the data from a national sample of 9,751 kindergartners to compare the effect of an increase in physical education instruction time between kindergarten and first grade on the difference in BMI. It was found that an increase of one hour of physical education time in first grade compared with the time in kindergarten reduced BMI among girls who were overweight or at risk for overweight in kindergarten (coefficient = −0.31, $p < 0.001$). Sequential physical education should be provided in schools, with adequate amounts of time allocated for it. In many parts of the world not enough time is given for physical education. Policies that ensure enough time and funding for physical education in schools should be a priority.

Interventions designed for worksite, community, or patient care settings should be based on behavioral theories as explained in Chapter 3. Social cognitive theory and the transtheoretical model in particular have been used for the promotion of physical activity. Because physical activity and nutrition are closely linked, interventions often tackle both these issues at the same time. Such interventions are especially popular when designed to reduce childhood or adult obesity or prevent cardiovascular diseases. Worksite, community, and patient care interventions generally use activities such as walking, aerobic dancing, and physical education classes, among others. The use of a buddy system for social support is also a popular approach. Various professionals are involved in facilitating these interventions. These include health educators, counselors, exercise professionals, physical trainers, lay health advisors, physicians, nurse practitioners, and nurses.

Besides advocating for greater physical education time in schools, there are several other environmental and policy measures that can be implemented for promoting physical activity and preventing and controlling physical inactivity. Examples of such measures include removing environmental barriers, de-emphasizing automation, building more accessible facilities to promote movement, subsidizing parks and recreational facilities, and installing bicycle trails, walking trails, and sidewalks in developments (Ainsworth & Macera, 1998).

Beginning in 2002, WHO initiated a Move for Health day. On February 17, 2003, Move for Health was officially started as an annual global initiative to promote physical activity as essential for health. In 2004 the theme was "Active Youth"; in 2005, "Supportive Environments"; in 2006, "Active Communities"; and in 2007, "Active Workplaces." The objectives of Move for Health day are as follows (WHO, 2008e):

- Facilitating the development of sustained national and local physical activity initiatives, policies, and programs
- Increasing population-wide physical activity participation in all areas (leisure time, transport, work) and settings (school, community, home, workplace)
- Increasing participation in physical activity through sport organizations, events, and other sociocultural forums
- Promoting healthy behaviors and lifestyles and addressing health-related issues such as tobacco use, healthy diet, and reduction of violence, stress, and social isolation through sports and physical activity

Unhealthy Eating

Some dietary behaviors constitute **unhealthy eating** and are risk factors for several chronic diseases. One such behavior is not consuming enough fruits and vegetables. There is an inverse relationship between fruit and vegetable consumption and cancers of the stomach, lung, esophagus, oral cavity, pharynx, larynx, rectum, bladder, cervix, and endometrium (Kushi & Foerester, 1998). Consumption of fruits and vegetables also decreases the risk for cardiovascular diseases (WHO, 2003). Fruits and vegetables are rich in antioxidants and fiber, which offer protection against chronic diseases. The World Health Organization (2003) recommends consumption of at least 400 g of fruits and vegetables per day to prevent diet-related chronic diseases. In the United States this recommendation has been translated as consuming five or more servings of fruits and vegetables a day.

A second unhealthy behavior is consuming saturated fat, dietary cholesterol, and red meat. It is generally accepted that consumption of high saturated fat and dietary cholesterol is associated with coronary heart disease (Kushi & Foerester, 1998). Particularly harmful are *trans* fatty acids, which are formed through hydrogenation, because they result in an increase in low-density lipoproteins (LDL), or "bad" cholesterol, and a decrease in high-density lipoproteins (HDL), or "good" cholesterol. Consumption of unsaturated fatty acids from vegetable sources and polyunsaturated fatty acids is associated with a lower risk for type 2 diabetes (Salmerón et al., 2001). Polyunsaturated fatty acids also decrease the risk for coronary heart disease (Erkkilä, de Mello, Risérus, & Laaksonen, 2008). In addition, it has been shown that red meat consumption has a positive association with cardiac disease risk (Kontogianni, Panagiotakos, Pitsavos, Chrysohoou, & Stefanadis, 2008). Fat intake has also been associated with breast cancer (Di Pietro, Medeiros, Vieira, Fausto, & Belló-Klein, 2007), colon cancer (Hu et al., 2007), and prostate cancer (Fleshner, & Zlotta, 2007).

A third unhealthy eating behavior is consuming large quantities of salt. High salt intake is linked to hypertension (Cook, 2008). Hypertensive patients, particularly those older than 44 years, are recommended to restrict the intake of dietary sodium to a target range of 90 to 130 mmol per day (or 3 to 7 g of salt per day) (Fodor, Whitmore, Leenen, & Larochelle, 1999). High salt intake has adverse cardiovascular effects in normotensive individuals as well (Tzemos, Lim, Wong, Struthers, & MacDonald, 2008).

Epidemiology

It has been estimated that 2.7 million lives could potentially be saved each year worldwide if fruit and vegetable consumption were increased (WHO, 2005b). According to the 2002 World Health Report, 26.7 million (1.8%) DALYs worldwide are attributable to low fruit and vegetable intake (WHO, 2002a). Likewise, a diet high in saturated fats is responsible for a large proportion of mortality worldwide.

> *It has been estimated that 2.7 million lives could potentially be saved each year worldwide if fruit and vegetable consumption were increased.*
>
> —World Health Organization (2005b)

Prevention and Control

The World Health Organization (2008f) has the following recommendations for individuals and populations regarding diet:

- Achieve energy balance and a healthy weight
- Limit energy intake from total fats and move fat consumption away from saturated fats to unsaturated fats with elimination of *trans* fatty acids

- Increase consumption of fruits and vegetables, including legumes, whole grains, and nuts
- Limit the intake of free sugars
- Limit salt (sodium) consumption from all sources and ensure that salt is iodized

Educational programs implemented in schools, communities, worksites, and patient care settings are the cornerstone of prevention and control efforts in the area of diet and nutrition. Policies to make fruits and vegetables available to and affordable by the masses are also important. The labeling of food products to disclose ingredients is a useful strategy. Public health authorities in different countries also need to explore whether restrictions can be placed on the advertising, sponsorship, and promotion of unhealthy food products.

In May 2004, WHO adopted a global strategy on diet, physical activity, and health. The strategy has four main objectives (WHO, 2008g):

- Reduce risk factors for chronic diseases that originate from unhealthy diets and physical inactivity through public health actions
- Increase awareness and understanding of the role of diet and physical activity on health and the positive impact of preventive interventions
- Develop, strengthen, and implement global, regional, and national policies and action plans to improve diets and increase physical activity that are sustainable, comprehensive, and actively engage all sectors
- Monitor science and promote research on diet and physical activity.

Besides WHO, a number of other stakeholders have been involved in developing this strategy. These stakeholders include member states, international partners, nongovernmental organizations, and organizations from the private sector.

CARDIOVASCULAR DISEASES

There has been a gradual decline in **cardiovascular diseases (CVD)** in developed countries in the last few decades, yet these continue to be the leading cause of death in such countries and are likely to remain so in coming decades. In developed countries, cardiovascular diseases were responsible for 48.6% of the deaths in 2000 and are projected to be responsible for 46.4% in 2020 (Aboderin et al., 2002). In developing countries, 33.8% of all deaths will also occur from CVD by 2020. Mortality figures capture only a portion of the total burden imposed by CVD, because CVD also accounts for a large proportion of hospitalizations. Cardiovascular disease is responsible for 10% of DALYs lost in low- and middle-income countries, and 18% in high-income countries (WHO, 2008h).

Cardiovascular diseases can be classified in several ways. This book is not interested in a comprehensive classification and coverage of all cardiovascular diseases; thus, it only discusses two conditions that are common and of public health importance in an international context: coronary heart disease and rheumatic heart disease.

Coronary Heart Disease

Coronary heart disease (CHD), also known as ischemic heart disease (IHD) or arteriosclerotic coronary artery disease, is the most common cause of cardiovascular disability and death. It is characterized by the narrowing of the coronary arteries that supply blood to the heart. There are a number of risk factors for CHD, including family history, age, male gender, abnormal blood lipid profile (higher ratio of LDL cholesterol versus HDL cholesterol), hypertension, physical inactivity, smoking, environmental tobacco smoke exposure, diabetes mellitus, obesity, high blood homocysteine levels, and lower estrogen levels in women. **Table 5.3** shows the levels of total, LDL, and HDL cholesterol that are healthy and that pose risk for CHD.

Coronary heart disease can manifest as sudden death, angina pectoris, or acute myocardial infarction. Angina pectoris is characterized by chest pain that is usually precipitated by exertion or stress; on angiography, obstruction of coronary vessels is

TABLE 5.3   Levels of Total, LDL, and HDL Cholesterol and the Associated Risk for Coronary Heart Disease (CHD)

Variable	Level	Risk
Total cholesterol	< 200 mg/dL	Healthy
	200–239 mg/dL	Borderline high risk for CHD
	> 240 mg/dL	High risk for CHD
LDL cholesterol	< 100 mg/dL	Healthy
	100–129 mg/dL	Near healthy
	130–159 mg/dL	Borderline high risk for CHD
	160–189 mg/dL	High risk for CHD
	> 190 mg/dL	Very high risk for CHD
HDL cholesterol	< 40 mg/dL	High risk for CHD
	40–59 mg/dL	Borderline high risk for CHD
	> 60 mg/dL	Healthy

revealed. In myocardial infarction, there is sudden pain in the chest along with elevation of cardiac enzymes, and an electrocardiograph shows ST segment elevation or depression.

Epidemiology

Coronary heart disease represents 51% of cardiovascular deaths and 21% of deaths from all causes (Anderson, Kochonck, & Murphy, 1997). It affects men more than women by an overall ratio of 4:1, but before age 40 this ratio is 8:1, and after age 70 the ratio is 1:1 (Massie & Amidon, 2000). The incidence of CHD after 40 years of age is 40% for men and 32% for women, and 1 of 5 deaths are due to CHD (American Heart Association, 2003). Migration can change the risk of CHD. For example, Japan has a low rate of CHD, but when Japanese migrate to the United States, their rates become equal to those of Americans (WHO, 2008h).

Prevention and Control

Some of the risk factors for CHD are not modifiable, but some are modifiable. Primary prevention efforts must aim at reducing the modifiable factors, namely, tobacco use, physical inactivity, unhealthy eating, hypertension, and abnormal blood lipid profile (higher ratio of LDL cholesterol versus HDL cholesterol). Strategies for prevention and control of tobacco use, physical inactivity, and unhealthy eating were discussed earlier in this chapter.

Hypertension itself has several risk factors, which include high sodium intake, excessive caloric intake, physical inactivity, excessive alcohol consumption, and deficient intake of potassium (Labarthe & Roccella, 1998). Primary prevention of hypertension can be done either through interventions with the general population (population strategy) or through efforts with high-risk populations (targeted strategy). Screening, early detection, and drug therapy are also important measures for the secondary prevention of hypertension.

> *The incidence of coronary heart disease (CHD) after 40 years of age is 40% for men and 32% for women and 1 out of 5 deaths are due to CHD.*
>
> —American Heart Association (2003)

Abnormal blood lipid profiles can be controlled by diet or drug therapy, or both. Several clinical trials have demonstrated the effectiveness of cholesterol-lowering medications (McBride & Anda, 1998). Efforts to change dietary patterns at the population level are helpful for the primary prevention of abnormal lipid profiles.

FOCUS FEATURE 5.1   North Karelia Project in Finland for Prevention of Coronary Heart Disease

The North Karelia Project in Finland was started in 1972 in response to a local petition to reduce the high rates of CHD in the area. The project was implemented in cooperation with the World Health Organization and local and national experts. Involvement of the people and ongoing evaluations were strong components of the project. The North Karelia Project is often viewed as a model program for achieving community-wide reductions in the risk factors and mortality associated with CHD.

The primary goals of the North Karelia Project were to (Puska & Uutela, 2001):

* Disseminate information and enhance awareness about coronary heart disease
* Improve preventive services to identify risk factors for coronary heart disease and provide services
* Assist people to make changes in their behaviors
* Conduct training for skills in self-management, environmental control, and performing healthful activities
* Provide social support to develop healthy lifestyles
* Make changes in the environment to improve opportunities for healthy actions and eliminate unhealthy actions
* Actively utilize community organizations

Eight different kinds of activities were conducted in the North Karelia Project (Puska & Uutela, 2001). The first was the involvement of 800 opinion leaders who were trained to promote healthy lifestyles. The second activity entailed extensive programming on television channels about smoking cessation and other healthy lifestyles. The third activity used "quit and win" contests to provide rewards for people who quit smoking. The fourth activity consisted of youth projects that involved children and adolescents and developed healthy behaviors. The fifth activity entailed several worksite interventions. The sixth activity involved collaboration with a housewives' organization, Martta, in rural and semirural areas that led to adoption of new cooking habits. The seventh activity required collaboration with food industry and supermarkets to promote low-fat dairy products, low-fat sausage, and reducing salt in food items. The final activity was with produce growers to promote consumption of local berries and to support their farming.

According to the National Public Health Institute in Finland (2008), the project has favorably affected most of the risk factors and, most important, mortality rates due to cardiovascular diseases. The mean serum cholesterol in men was 6.9 mmol/L in 1972, which decreased to 5.4 mmol/L in 2007. Likewise, for women, the mean cholesterol level was 6.8 mmol/L in 1972, which was down to 5.2 mmol/L in 2007. In 1972, the mean blood pressure for men was 149/92, and for women, 153/92; these decreased to 138/83 and 134/78, respectively, in 2007. Smoking rates decreased for men from 52% in 1972 to 31% in 2007, but increased for women from 10% in 1972 to 22% in 2007. The rate of deaths in North Karelia among men aged 35 to 64 years from all cardiovascular diseases in 1969 to 1971 was 855 per 100,000, which decreased to 182 per 100,000 (79% decrease) in 2007; CHD in particular declined from 672 per 100,000 in 1969 to 1971 to 103 per 100,000 (85% decrease) in 2007.

Rheumatic Heart Disease

Rheumatic fever (RF) and **rheumatic heart disease (RHD)** are important public health problems in many developing countries. Rheumatic fever is a delayed immune response to group A beta-hemolytic streptococcal infection of the pharynx. Signs of RF usually start 2 to 3 weeks after infection and affect mainly children aged 5 to 15 years. Rheumatic fever can lead to RHD. The diagnosis of RF is based on the Jones criteria, which specify the presence of two major criteria or one major and one minor criterion (Massie & Amidon, 2000). The major criteria are carditis (inflammation of the heart muscle), erythema marginatum (skin rash) and subcutaneous nodules, Sydenham chorea (uncoordinated movements and muscular weakness), and migratory multiple joint arthritis. The minor criteria are fever, changes on the electrocardiogram, elevated erythrocyte sedimentation rate, and evidence of streptococcal infection. Treatment of RF entails giving antibiotic therapy to remove streptococcal infection, and salicylates and corticosteroids to suppress the inflammatory process. Valvular defects of the heart occur in RHD; surgery is often the answer for rectifying those defects.

Epidemiology

According to the World Health Organization (2004b), in 1994 an estimated 12 million people suffered from RF and RHD globally. Of these, approximately 3 million developed congestive heart failure that required repeated hospitalization. The estimated number of deaths from RHD was 332,000 in 2000, with an estimated 6.6 million DALYs being lost per year all over the world. The prevalence of RHD estimated from surveys of school-aged children varies from 0.2 per 1,000 schoolchildren in Cuba to 77.8 per 1,000 in Samoa (WHO, 2004b). Poverty, overcrowding, malnutrition, and inadequate medical care increase the risk for RF and RHD (Luepker, 2008).

Prevention and Control

Primary prevention of RF entails giving antibiotic therapy for group A streptococcal upper respiratory infections. Laboratory diagnosis of streptococcal infections by detecting antigen or by culture is available and routinely practiced in developed countries, but detection is often not available in developing countries. For antibiotics to be effective, they must be started within nine days of streptococcal infection. Penicillin and erythromycin are the antibiotics of choice.

Secondary prevention of RF involves patients with a previous attack of RF or with well-documented RHD and entails continuous administration of specific antibiotics

(WHO, 2004b). The purpose of continuous antibiotic therapy is to prevent colonization with group A streptococci and the development of recurrent attacks of RF. Antibiotic administration in secondary prophylaxis can range in duration from five years to lifelong.

CEREBROVASCULAR DISEASE

Cerebrovascular disease entails ischemic (clogging by thrombus or embolus) or hemorrhagic (rupture) disturbances of the blood vessels of the brain. The most severe form of cerebrovascular disease is known as *stroke*; a less severe condition is known as *transient ischemic attack* (TIA). The World Health Organization defines stroke as "rapidly developing clinical signs of focal (or global) disturbance of cerebral function, with symptoms lasting 24 hours or longer or leading to death, with no apparent cause other than of vascular origin" (WHO MONICA Project Investigators, 1988).

The incidence of cerebrovascular disease is strongly linked with age. In developed countries, the average age at which stroke occurs is 73 years (Truelsen, Begg, & Mathers, 2006). Mortality from stroke is high. Between 20 and 50% of stroke patients die within the first month of the stroke. Approximately 80% of strokes in Caucasian populations are ischemic, whereas 15 to 20% are hemorrhagic (Truelsen, Begg, & Mathers, 2006). In Asian populations, the rate of hemorrhagic strokes is higher (20 to 30%).

Hypertension and smoking are two of the most important modifiable risk factors for cerebrovascular disease. Some other risk factors are high serum cholesterol, dietary factors, alcohol consumption, physical inactivity, lower socioeconomic status, diabetes mellitus, and coronary heart disease.

Epidemiology

Globally, stroke is the second most common cause of death and a major cause of disability (Donnan, Fisher, Macleod, & Davis, 2008). It is estimated that cerebrovascular disease or stroke accounts for 5.5 million deaths worldwide, or 9.6% of all deaths (WHO, 2002a). Approximately two-thirds of these deaths are in developing countries, and 40% are in people younger than 70 years. Because the world's population is aging, the burden from stroke is projected to increase significantly during the next 20 years, especially in developing countries (Donnan, Fisher, Macleod, & Davis, 2008).

> *It is estimated that cerebrovascular disease or stroke accounts for 5.5 million deaths or 9.6% of all deaths all over the world.*
>
> —World Health Organization (2002a)

Prevention and Control

Primary prevention of stroke entails reducing risk factors such as hypertension, smoking, physical inactivity, and unhealthy eating. The prevention and control of smoking, physical inactivity, and unhealthy eating have already been discussed in detail. As discussed earlier, primary prevention of hypertension can be done either through interventions with the general population (population strategy) or through efforts with high-risk populations (targeted strategy). Screening, early detection, and drug therapy are important measures for the secondary prevention of hypertension.

There are no definitive tests that can detect stroke early. Therefore, screening for hypertension and other risk factors by clinicians is the only important measure for secondary prevention. For tertiary prevention, advanced imaging techniques such as computerized axial tomography (CAT) scans, magnetic resonance imaging (MRI), and radionuclide angiography (nuclear brain scans) are useful diagnostic tests. Rehabilitation of stroke patients requires medical treatment, physiotherapy, occupational therapy, and speech therapy.

CANCERS

Cancers are a diverse group of diseases that have in common an uncontrolled growth of cells and the spread of these cells. Cell growth can be either benign (not harmful) or malignant, which denotes uncontrolled growth of cells. The tendency of these abnormal cells to spread is known as metastasis. Cancers are classified according to their organ or tissue of origin, and according to their histologic features. Given that there are 22 major sites and 88 major histologic types, there are hundreds of cancers (Brownson, Reif, Alavanja, & Bal, 1998).

The Harvard Center for Cancer Prevention (1996) has identified several risk factors for cancers. The proportion of cancer deaths attributed to these various factors are as follows: tobacco, 30%; diet, 30%; infective processes, 5%; occupation, 5%; family history, 5%; reproductive and sexual history, 3%; sedentary lifestyle, 5%; perinatal factors (larger birth weight), 5%; geophysical location (exposure to radiation and sunlight), 2%; alcohol intake, 3%; socioeconomic status, 3%; pollution, 2%; medication and medical procedures, 1%; and food additives, salt, and other contaminants, 1%.

Epidemiology

According to the World Health Organization (2008i), from a total of 58 million deaths all over the world in 2005, 7.6 million deaths (13%) were due to cancers.

A large majority of these deaths (> 70%) occurred in low- and middle-income countries. Deaths due to cancers are predicted to continue to increase, with an estimated 9 million people dying from cancers in 2015 and 11.4 million in 2030. In the United States alone the direct costs of cancer are $72 billion annually, or about 5% of the total health care costs (Dennis, Lynch, & Smith, 2008). In the United

> *In 2005, from a total of 58 million deaths all over the world 7.6 million deaths (13%) were due to cancers.*
>
> —World Health Organization (2008i)

States, the most common cancers in men are those of the prostate, lung, colon, and rectum, whereas in women the most common cancers are of the breast, lung, colon, and rectum (Dennis, Lynch, & Smith, 2008).

Prevention and Control

At least one-third of all cancers are preventable (WHO, 2008j). Prevention is the most cost-effective strategy currently available for the control of cancer. Primary prevention of cancers entails modification of lifestyle risk factors. The most effective way to prevent cancer is preventing tobacco use and exposure to environmental tobacco smoke, because tobacco causes 80 to 90% of lung cancer deaths. Strategies for the prevention and control of tobacco use were discussed earlier in this chapter. Dietary modification is another important measure for cancer prevention. Consuming fruits and vegetables offers protection against cancers. Likewise, avoiding saturated fats (particularly red meat) protects against colorectal cancer. Regular physical activity is also helpful in preventing cancer. Avoiding heavy drinking of alcohol is important in the prevention of cancers of the liver, oral cavity, esophagus, and breast (Dennis, Lynch, & Smith, 2008).

Prevention and treatment of infectious agents that produce cancers are also effective means for preventing cancers. Liver cancer is caused by viral hepatitis B and C. Cervical cancer is caused by human papillomavirus (HPV). The chances of stomach cancer are increased by infection with the bacterium *Helicobacter pylori*. Bladder cancer risk is increased by the parasitic flat worm infection schistosomiasis. Cancer of the bile ducts is related to infestation by liver flukes. Vaccines are available for some of these maladies, such as HPV, whereas general preventive measures need to be instituted for other infections.

Prevention of occupational exposure to possible carcinogens is also important. Examples of some occupational carcinogens include asbestos, which can lead to lung cancer; coal tar, which can lead to skin cancers; aniline dyes, which can cause bladder cancer; and benzene, which can lead to leukemia. Specific protection against carcinogens is a useful prevention measure.

Excessive exposure to ultraviolet (UV) radiation in sunlight is responsible for skin cancers (squamous and basal cell carcinomas). Avoiding excessive exposure to the sun and wearing sun screens and protective clothing are some measures to prevent such cancers from occurring.

Secondary prevention of cancers requires effective screening programs. Some early warning signs of cancers are lumps, abnormal bleeding, sores that fail to heal, persistent indigestion, and chronic hoarseness. Regular breast self-examination and mammography are helpful in detecting breast cancers. Likewise, having regular Papanicolaou (Pap) tests for screening of cervical cancer is another example of secondary prevention. Another screening test is the prostate specific antigen (PSA) blood test for detecting prostate cancer. To screen for colorectal cancer, a combination of the fecal occult blood test, flexible sigmoidoscopy, double-contrast barium enema, and colonoscopy is recommended. However, it is to be noted that in many developing countries facilities for such tests are nonexistent or are too expensive to be afforded by the masses.

Treatment measures for tertiary prevention include chemotherapy, surgery, radiation therapy, and hormonal therapy, or some combination of these. Some of these treatments are expensive and only available in developed countries.

DIABETES

Diabetes (full name diabetes mellitus) is a chronic disease in which either the pancreas does not produce enough insulin or the body develops resistance to insulin's action. In uncontrolled diabetes, elevated blood sugar (hyperglycemia) can lead to damage to various body parts such as the eyes, kidneys, and nerves. There are two types of diabetes: type 1 (formerly called insulin-dependent or juvenile diabetes) constitutes 10% of all cases, and type 2 (formerly called non-insulin-dependent or adult-onset diabetes) constitutes 90% of all cases. Type 1 diabetes is caused by autoimmune destruction of the beta cells of the pancreas; there is no way to prevent this type of diabetes, and life-long insulin therapy is the only treatment. Type 2 diabetes may be secondary to diseases such as acromegaly, Cushing syndrome, and hemochromatosis or may be drug-induced as a result of drugs such as thiazide diuretics or oral contraceptives (Zgibor, Dorman, & Orchard, 2008). Symptoms of diabetes include excessive excretion of urine (polyuria), thirst (polydipsia), constant hunger, weight loss, vision changes, and fatigue.

Among the risk factors for type 2 diabetes is a condition called metabolic syndrome or cardiometabolic syndrome, Cardiometabolic syndrome is associated with cardiovascular disease and diabetes, and includes a constellation of risk factors such as central obesity, elevated blood pressure, insulin resistance, dyslipidemia, microalbuminuria, and hypercoagulability (Govindarajan, Whaley-Connell, Mugo, Stump, & Sowers, 2005). Usually, cardiometabolic syndrome is defined as the presence of three or more of the following: waist circumference of 35 inches or more (women) or 40 inches or more (men); fasting blood glucose level of 100 mg/dL or higher; serum triglyceride levels of 150 mg/dL or higher; blood pressure 135/85 mm Hg or higher; and HDL cholesterol of less than 40 mg/dL (men) or less than 50 mg/dL (women) (Dhingra et al., 2007). Physical inactivity and cigarette smoking are other risk factors for type 2 diabetes (Bishop, Zimmerman, & Roesler, 1998).

Complications of diabetes include diabetic retinopathy (damage to the small blood vessels in the retina of the eye), which can lead to blindness; diabetic neuropathy (damage to nerves), which can lead to foot ulcers and eventual limb amputation; and kidney failure. Diabetes is a risk factor for heart disease and stroke.

Epidemiology

In 2000, there were 171 million diabetic individuals worldwide; this number is expected to increase to 366 million by 2030 (Zgibor, Dorman, & Orchard, 2008). According to the World Health Organization (2008k), diabetes is responsible for 5% of deaths annually worldwide. These deaths are likely to increase by 50% in the next 10 years. Eighty percent of people with diabetes are in low- and middle-income countries and are middle-aged (45 to 64 years). Type 2 diabetes occurs in all races, but its prevalence is higher in American Indians, Micronesians, Polynesians, African Americans, and Mexican Americans (Zgibor, Dorman, & Orchard, 2008). The prevalence of diabetes is higher in developed countries than in developing countries, but the incidence of diabetes is increasing in developing countries because of urbanization and the adoption of Western lifestyles.

> *In 2000, all over the world there were 171 million diabetics and this number is expected to increase to 366 million by 2030.*
>
> —Zgibor, Dorman, & Orchard (2008)

Prevention and Control

Type 1 diabetes is unpreventable, and life-long insulin injection is the only treatment. For primary prevention of type 2 diabetes, physical activity and dietary changes are useful approaches. Measures to reduce obesity greatly help in reducing the onset of diabetes. The Da Qing study in China (Pan et al., 1997) demonstrated that diet and/or exercise interventions led to a significant decrease in the incidence of diabetes. Likewise, the Diabetes Prevention Study in Finland (Tuomilehto et al., 2001) showed that type 2 diabetes can be prevented by changes in lifestyle.

Secondary prevention of diabetes is very important because many people who have diabetes do not know that they suffer from it. Early diagnosis and treatment of diabetes is essential. Mass screening for diabetes is not cost-effective; however, screening should be done with high-risk groups, such as people who have a family history of diabetes (Bishop, Zimmerman, & Roesler, 1998). Upon diagnosis, people with type 2 diabetes can be treated with oral medications, but some may require insulin. Oral medications include sulfonylurea, which stimulates endogenous insulin release from the pancreas; metformin, which increases insulin action in the liver; and acarbose, which blocks intestinal starch and sucrose digestion. Tertiary prevention of diabetes is also quite important and includes screening for retinopathy, kidney disease, and foot ulcers.

The World Health Organization's diabetes prevention program has the goal of improving health through invigorating and sustaining the adoption of effective measures for the surveillance, prevention, and control of diabetes and its complications, especially in low- and middle-income countries (WHO, 2008l). The specific functions of this program are to

- Supervise the development and acceptance of internationally agreed standards and norms for the diagnosis and treatment of diabetes, its complications, and risk factors
- Foster surveillance of diabetes, its complications and mortality, and its risk factors
- Build capacity for the prevention and control of diabetes
- Enhance awareness about the importance of diabetes as a global public health problem
- Conduct advocacy for the prevention and control of diabetes in vulnerable populations

CHRONIC OBSTRUCTIVE PULMONARY DISEASE

Chronic obstructive pulmonary disease (COPD), or chronic obstructive lung disease (COLD), is not a single disease, but rather an umbrella term that is used to describe chronic lung diseases that cause limitations in airflow to the lungs. Common symptoms of COPD include breathlessness (or a need for air), increased sputum production, and an accompanying chronic cough. Confirmation of diagnosis of COPD can be done by spirometry, which measures how deeply a person can breathe and how rapidly air moves in and out of the lungs. Included in the term COPD are three conditions: chronic bronchitis, bronchial asthma, and emphysema. The primary risk factors for COPD are tobacco smoke (direct and environmental), indoor and outdoor air pollution, and occupational dusts and chemicals. In developed countries tobacco smoke is the prime risk factor, whereas in developing countries use of biomass fuels for cooking and heating is most often responsible for COPD. According to the World Health Organization (2008m), approximately three billion people worldwide use biomass and coal as their main source of energy for cooking, heating, and other household needs. Chronic obstructive pulmonary disease is not curable, but treatment can slow the progression of disease.

Epidemiology

According to the World Health Organization (2008m), in 2005 COPD affected 210 million people worldwide and caused 3 million deaths, which corresponds to 5% of all deaths globally. Chronic obstructive pulmonary disease is often underdiagnosed and not listed either as a primary or contributory cause of death (WHO, 2002b). It is estimated that it will become the third leading cause of death by 2030. Almost 90% of COPD deaths occur in low- and middle-income countries (WHO, 2008m). A few decades ago, COPD was more common in men, but because of increased tobacco use among women in developed countries and the higher risk

> *Chronic obstructive pulmonary disease affected 210 million people worldwide in 2005, and 3 million people died, which corresponds to 5% of all deaths globally.*
>
> —WHO (2008m)

of exposure to indoor air pollution (such as biomass fuel used for cooking and heating) in developing countries, COPD now affects men and women almost equally.

Prevention and Control

Primary prevention of COPD entails reduction of risk factors, particularly tobacco smoke and indoor air pollution. Alternative sources of cooking and heating need to be made available to people in the developing world. For secondary and tertiary prevention of COPD, health care systems need to be strengthened, particularly in developing countries.

The Global Alliance against Chronic Respiratory Diseases (GARD) is a coalition of national and international organizations, institutions, and agencies (led by the World Health Organization) working toward a common goal of improving global lung health. The Global Initiative for Chronic Obstructive Lung Disease (GOLD) is part of GARD.

OTHER CHRONIC CONDITIONS

Osteoarthritis

Osteoarthritis is a degenerative joint disease in which there are biomechanical alterations in the cartilage and the underlying bone in a joint. The incidence of osteoarthritis increases with age. It can commonly affect the knees, hands, feet, hips, and spine. The major modifiable risk factors for osteoarthritis are joint trauma, obesity, and repetitive occupational usage of the joint (Scott & Hochberg, 1998). Osteoarthritis is related to occupation; higher prevalence is found in the elbows and knees of miners, the fingers of cotton pickers, the hips of farmers, and in the fingers, elbows, and knees of dock workers (Kelsey & Sowers, 2008). Important measures for the prevention of osteoarthritis are maintaining a healthy weight, avoiding joint trauma, and modifying occupation-related joint stress. There are no screening tests for osteoarthritis. Treatment is nonsteroidal anti-inflammatory drugs, with surgical joint replacement in severe cases.

Osteoporosis

Osteoporosis is a bone disorder characterized by low bone mass that leads to fractures with minimal trauma. Osteoporosis is a significant public health problem in countries that have aging populations. The common fractures that occur are of the hip, vertebrae, and distal radius. Women are affected more than men. Common risk factors for osteoporosis include prolonged periods of immobility, thin body build, heavy alcohol use, chronic use of corticosteroids, lack of use of estrogen replacement hormones, cigarette smoking, physical inactivity, and low calcium intake (Scott & Hochberg, 1998). Efforts for primary prevention of osteoporosis must begin in childhood and adolescence with a diet rich in calcium and an emphasis on weight-bearing physical activities. For secondary prevention, drugs such as estrogen, calcitonin, and alendronate are used.

SKILL-BUILDING ACTIVITY

Alzheimer disease is a chronic degenerative disease of the brain. As of 2008 there were about 18 million people worldwide suffering from Alzheimer disease, which will increase to an estimated 34 million by 2025. Conduct a search for information about this disease on the Internet. Be sure to visit the Web sites of the Centers for Disease Control and Prevention and the World Health Organization. Collect the following information: epidemiology, clinical features, and measures for prevention and control. Prepare a fact sheet with this information.

SUMMARY

Noncommunicable chronic diseases are diseases of slow progression and long duration. Characteristic features of noncommunicable chronic diseases are uncertain causation, association with multiple risk factors, long latency periods, a long course of illness, noncontagious origin, associated functional impairment or disability, and incurability. Some of the modifiable behavioral risk factors for chronic diseases include tobacco use, alcohol abuse, physical inactivity, and unhealthy diet.

Tobacco use is causally linked to coronary heart disease, peripheral vascular disease, cerebrovascular disease, lung cancer, oral cancer, laryngeal cancer, esophageal cancer, bladder cancer, renal cancer, pancreatic cancer, stomach cancer, cervical cancer, endometrial cancer, acute myeloid leukemia, chronic obstructive pulmonary disease, gastroesophageal reflux disease, and periodontitis. Strategies for prevention and control of tobacco use include school-based education, legislation that bans advertisements that promote tobacco use, legislation that restricts sales of tobacco products to minors, the printing of vivid health warnings on cigarette packs, increasing the price of tobacco products, banning smoking in public places, and facilitating smoking cessation.

Alcohol abuse is a causative factor in accidents, poisoning, alcoholic hepatitis, cirrhosis of the liver, liver cancer, cancers of the oral cavity, larynx, and esophagus, hypertriglyceridemia, cardiomyopathy, hypertension, stroke, Wernicke encephalopathy, dementia, obstructive sleep apnea, epilepsy, acute and chronic pancreatitis, and psoriasis. Alcohol consumption during pregnancy is associated with a number of risks to the fetus, including fetal alcohol syndrome. Habitual alcohol use can lead to alcoholism or becoming dependent on alcohol. Measures for the prevention and control of alcohol abuse include reduction of the availability of alcohol, restricting sales of alcohol, increasing taxes on alcohol, restricting alcohol advertisements, passing zero-tolerance and blood alcohol concentration laws, school-based educational programs, mass media, community-based educational programs, posting health warning signs on alcohol products, screening, primary care interventions, and rehabilitation centers.

Physical inactivity is a risk factor for coronary heart disease, diabetes mellitus, stroke, breast cancer, colon cancer, and depression. Physical activity interventions can be designed to change individuals or to change environments and policies. Unhealthy eating involves dietary behaviors that are risk factors for several chronic diseases, such as consuming less than 400 g of fruits and vegetables per day; consuming saturated fat, dietary cholesterol, and/or red meat; and consuming large quantities of salt. Interventions for changing unhealthy eating behaviors can be designed to change individuals or to change environments and policies.

Examples of noncommunicable chronic diseases include cardiovascular diseases, stroke, cancers, diabetes, and chronic obstructive pulmonary disease. Two cardiovascular diseases are particularly important in the international context: coronary heart disease and rheumatic heart disease. Coronary heart disease is characterized by narrowing and/or blockage of the coronary arteries that supply blood to the heart. Cerebrovascular disease entails ischemic (clogging by thrombus or embolus) or hemorrhagic (rupture) disturbances of the blood vessels of the brain. The most severe form of cerebrovascular disease is stroke; a less severe condition is transient ischemic attack.

Cancers are a diverse group of diseases that have in common an uncontrolled growth of cells and spread of these cells. Cancers are classified according to their organ or tissue of origin and according to their histologic features. Diabetes is a chronic disease in which either the pancreas does not produce enough insulin or the body develops resistance to insulin's action. In uncontrolled diabetes, elevated blood sugar (hyperglycemia) can lead to damage to various body parts such as the eyes, kidneys, and nerves. Chronic obstructive pulmonary disease is not a single disease but rather an umbrella term that is used to describe chronic lung diseases that cause limitations in airflow to the lungs. Prevention and control of chronic diseases entails modification of modifiable risk factors, early diagnosis and treatment, and rehabilitation.

IMPORTANT TERMS

alcohol use	diabetes
cancers	osteoarthritis
cardiovascular diseases (CVD)	osteoporosis
cerebrovascular disease	physical inactivity
chronic obstructive pulmonary disease (COPD)	rheumatic heart disease (RHD)
	tobacco use
coronary heart disease (CHD)	unhealthy eating

REVIEW QUESTIONS

1. Discuss strategies for the prevention and control of tobacco use.
2. Describe measures for the prevention and control of alcohol abuse.
3. What are the recommendations for physical activity for adults? How can physical activity levels be increased in a given population?
4. Name three behaviors that constitute unhealthy eating. Discuss measures for the prevention and control of unhealthy eating behaviors.
5. Discuss the epidemiology of and prevention and control measures for coronary heart disease.
6. What can be done to prevent and control rheumatic heart disease?
7. Discuss the epidemiology of and prevention and control measures for cerebrovascular disease.
8. Define cancer. What can be done to prevent and control cancer?
9. What is diabetes? How can type 2 diabetes be prevented and controlled?
10. Describe chronic obstructive pulmonary disease. What can be done to prevent and control it?

WEB SITES TO EXPLORE

American Heart Association: Risk Factors and Coronary Heart Disease

http://www.americanheart.org/presenter.jhtml?identifier=4726

This Web site discusses the risk factors for coronary heart disease. It divides risk factors into those that can and cannot be changed. The Web site provides links to the American Heart Association's scientific statements on prevention of coronary heart disease and stroke. *Follow the links and read any one report. Summarize what you learned.*

eMedicine Health: Coronary Heart Disease

http://www.emedicinehealth.com/coronary_heart_disease/article_em.htm

This Web site presents an overview of coronary heart disease, its causes and symptoms, information on when to seek medical care, exams and tests for detecting coronary heart disease, treatment, self-care, follow-up, and prevention. *Read the information presented. What can be done to prevent coronary heart disease?*

International Agency for Research on Cancer

http://www.iarc.fr/

The International Agency for Research on Cancer (IARC) is part of the World Health Organization. Its Web site contains information about the agency, including its scientific structure, opportunities for fellowships, postdoctoral positions, training courses, vacancies, publications, scientific papers, press releases, seminars, and other links. *Explore this Web site and learn about various activities of the IARC. Follow the link to training courses and see whether anything interests you.*

International Center for Alcohol Policies

http://www.icap.org/

The International Center for Alcohol Policies (ICAP) is an alcohol policy think tank involving governments, the alcohol industry, and public health professionals. The Web site provides information about ICAP, policy issues, building partnerships, research, education, and publications. *Explore the policy issues link. Choose any one policy issue and summarize it in a one-page paper.*

International Diabetes Federation

http://www.idf.org/

The International Diabetes Federation (IDF) is a worldwide coalition of over 200 diabetes associations from 160 countries that works to enhance the lives of people with diabetes all over the world. The Web site has links for information about IDF, news, facts and figures, care and education, the IDF shop, regions, and diabetes events. *Explore the links. Go to the news room and then click on the diabetes prevention fact sheet. What did you learn?*

International Society for the Prevention of Tobacco Induced Diseases

http://isptid.globalink.org/index.html

This Web site of a not-for-profit, academic, scientific, and humanitarian organization of health professionals and scientists called the International Society for the Prevention of Tobacco Induced Diseases (ISPTID) has information about the organization, news items related to tobacco, and information on meetings and publications. *Visit the links to Facts and News. What new information did you learn?*

REFERENCES

Aboderin, I., Kalache, A., Ben-Shlomo, Y., Lynch, J. W., Yajnik, C. S., Kuh, D., et al. (2002). *Life course perspectives on coronary heart disease, stroke and diabetes: Key issues and implications for policy and research*. Geneva: World Health Organization. Retrieved from http://whqlibdoc.who.int/hq/2002/WHO_NMH_NPH_02.1.pdf

Ainsworth, B. E., & Macera, C. A. (1998). Physical inactivity. In R. C. Brownson, P. L. Remington, & J. R. Davis (Eds.), *Chronic disease epidemiology and control* (2nd ed., pp. 191–213). Washington, DC: American Public Health Association.

Allender, S., Foster, C., Scarborough, P., & Rayner, M. (2007). The burden of physical activity-related ill health in the UK. *Journal of Epidemiology and Community Health, 61*(4), 344–348.

American College of Sports Medicine. (2007). *Physical activity and public health guidelines*. Retrieved from http://www.acsm.org/AM/Template.cfm?Section=Home_Page&TEMPLATE=/CM/HTMLDisplay.cfm&CONTENTID=7764

American Heart Association. (2003). *Heart disease and stroke statistics—2003 update*. Dallas, TX: Author.

American Psychiatric Association. (2000). *Diagnostic and statistical manual of mental disorders* (4th ed., text revision). Washington, DC: Author.

Ammann, R. W., Heitz, P. U., & Klöppel, G. (1996). Course of alcoholic chronic pancreatitis: A prospective clinicomorphological long-term study. *Gastroenterology, 111*(1), 224–231.

Anderson, R. N., Kochonck, K. D., & Murphy, S. L. (1997). A report of final mortality statistics, 1995. *Monthly Vital Statistics Report, 45*(11, Suppl. 2). Hyattsville, MD: National Center for Health Statistics.

Applebaum, M. G. (1995). Fetal alcohol syndrome: Diagnosis, management, and prevention. *Nurse Practitioner, 20*(10), 24, 27–28, 31–33.

Bishop, D. B., Zimmerman, B. R., & Roesler, J. S. (1998). Diabetes. In R. C. Brownson, P. L. Remington, & J. R. Davis (Eds.), *Chronic disease epidemiology and control* (2nd ed., pp. 421–464). Washington, DC: American Public Health Association.

Borkenstein, R. F. (1976). Efficacy of law enforcement procedures concerning alcohol, drugs, and driving. *Modern Problems in Pharmacopsychiatry, 11*, 1–10.

Brownson, R. C., Reif, J. S., Alavanja, M. C. R., & Bal, D. G. (1998). Cancer. In R. C. Brownson, P. L. Remington, & J. R. Davis (Eds.), *Chronic disease epidemiology and control* (2nd ed., pp. 335–373). Washington, DC: American Public Health Association.

Cook, B. L., & Liesveld, J. (2008). Alcohol-related health problems. In R. B. Wallace, N. Kohatsu, & J. M. Last (Eds.), *Wallace/Maxcy-Rosenau-Last public health and preventive medicine* (15th ed., pp. 999–1012). New York: McGraw Hill Medical.

Cook, N. R. (2008). Salt intake, blood pressure and clinical outcomes. *Current Opinion in Nephrology and Hypertension, 17*(3), 310–314.

Corrao, G., Bagnardi, V., Zambon, A., & La Vecchia, C. (2005). A meta-analysis of alcohol consumption and the risk of 15 diseases. *Preventive Medicine, 38*(5), 613–619.

Datar, A., & Strum, R. (2004). Physical education in elementary school and body mass index: Evidence from the early childhood longitudinal study. *American Journal of Public Health, 94*, 1501–1506.

Dennis, L. K., Lynch, C. F., & Smith, E. M. (2008). Cancer. In R. B. Wallace, N. Kohatsu, & J. M. Last (Eds.), *Wallace/Maxcy-Rosenau-Last public health and preventive medicine* (15th ed., pp. 1047–1070). New York: McGraw Hill Medical.

Dhingra, R., Sullivan, L., Jacques, P. F., Wang, T. J., Fox, C. S., Meigs, J. B., et al. (2007). Soft drink consumption and risk of developing cardiometabolic risk factors and the metabolic syndrome in middle aged adults in the community. *Circulation, 116*(5), 480–488.

Di Pietro, P. F., Medeiros, N. I., Vieira, F. G., Fausto, M. A., & Belló-Klein, A. (2007). Breast cancer in southern Brazil: Association with past dietary intake. *Nutricion Hospitalaria, 22*(5), 565–572.

Doll, R., Peto, R., Boreham, J., & Sutherland, I. (2004). Mortality in relation to smoking: 50 years' observations on male British doctors. *British Medical Journal, 328*(7455), 1519.

Donnan, G. A., Fisher, M., Macleod, M., & Davis, S. M. (2008). Stroke. *Lancet, 371*(9624), 1612–1623.

Dufour, M. C. (1998). Alcohol use. In R. C. Brownson, P. L. Remington, & J. R. Davis (Eds.), *Chronic disease epidemiology and control* (2nd ed., pp. 149–190). Washington, DC: American Public Health Association.

Erkkilä, A., de Mello, V. D., Risérus, U., & Laaksonen, D. E. (2008). Dietary fatty acids and cardiovascular disease: An epidemiological approach. *Progress in Lipid Research, 47*(3), 172–187.

Fan, Y., Yuan, J. M., Wang, R., Gao, Y. T., & Yu, M. C. (2008). Alcohol, tobacco, and diet in relation to esophageal cancer: The Shanghai cohort study. *Nutrition and Cancer, 60*(3), 354–363.

Fleshner, N., & Zlotta, A. R. (2007). Prostate cancer prevention: Past, present, and future. *Cancer, 110*(9), 1889–1899.

Fodor, J. G., Whitmore, B., Leenen, F., & Larochelle, P. (1999). Lifestyle modifications to prevent and control hypertension. Recommendations on dietary salt. Canadian Hypertension Society, Canadian Coalition for High Blood Pressure Prevention and Control, Laboratory Centre for Disease Control at Health Canada, Heart and Stroke Foundation of Canada. *Canadian Medical Association Journal, 160*(9 Suppl.), S29–S34.

Giovino, G. A. (2007). The tobacco epidemic in the United States. *American Journal of Preventive Medicine, 33*(6 Suppl.), S318–S326.

Govindarajan, G., Whaley-Connell, A., Mugo, M., Stump, C., & Sowers, J. R. (2005). The cardiometabolic syndrome as a cardiovascular risk factor. *American Journal of Medical Science, 330*, 311–318.

Hackshaw, A. K., Law, M. R., & Wald, N. J. (1997). The accumulated evidence on lung cancer and environmental tobacco smoke. *British Medical Journal, 315,* 980–988.

Harvard Center for Cancer Prevention. (1996). Harvard report on cancer prevention. Vol. 1: Causes of human cancer. *Cancer Causes Control, 7*(Suppl. 1), S3–S59.

Heifer, U. (1991). Blood alcohol concentration and effect, traffic medicine characteristics and legal traffic relevance of alcohol limit values in road traffic [In German]. *Butalkohol, 28,* 121–145.

Hu, J., Morrison, H., Mery, L., DesMeules, M., Macleod, M., & Canadian Cancer Registries Epidemiology Research Group. (2007). Diet and vitamin or mineral supplementation and risk of colon cancer by subsite in Canada. *European Journal of Cancer Prevention, 16*(4), 275–291.

Husten, C. G., & Thorne, S. L. (2008). Tobacco: Health effects and control. In R. B. Wallace, N. Kohatsu, & J. M. Last (Eds.), *Wallace/Maxcy-Rosenau-Last public health and preventive medicine* (15th ed., pp. 953–998). New York: McGraw Hill Medical.

International Center for Alcohol Policies. (2002). *Blood alcohol concentration limits worldwide* (ICAP Report No. 11). Washington, DC: Author.

Kalucka, S. (2007). Consequences of passive smoking in home environment. *Przeglad Lekarski, 64*(10), 632–641.

Kelsey, J. L., & Sowers, M. (2008). Musculoskeletal disorders. In R. B. Wallace, N. Kohatsu, & J. M. Last (Eds.), *Wallace/Maxcy-Rosenau-Last public health and preventive medicine* (15th ed., pp. 1125–1138). New York: McGraw Hill Medical.

Kerse, N., Falloon, K., Moyes, S. A., Hayman, K. J., Dowell, T., Kolt, G. S., et al. (2008). DeL-LITE depression in late life: An intervention trial of exercise. Design and recruitment of a randomised controlled trial. *BMC Geriatrics, 8,12.*

Kirby, B., Richards, H. L., Mason, D. L., Fortune, D. G., Main, C. J., & Griffiths, C. E. (2008). Alcohol consumption and psychological distress in patients with psoriasis. *British Journal of Dermatology, 158*(1), 138–140.

Kontogianni, M. D., Panagiotakos, D. B., Pitsavos, C., Chrysohoou, C., & Stefanadis, C. (2008). Relationship between meat intake and the development of acute coronary syndromes: The CARDIO2000 case-control study. *European Journal of Clinical Nutrition, 62*(2), 171–177.

Kushi, L. H., & Foerester, S. B. (1998). Diet and nutrition. In R. C. Brownson, P. L. Remington, & J. R. Davis (Eds.), *Chronic disease epidemiology and control* (2nd ed., pp. 215–259). Washington, DC: American Public Health Association.

Labarthe, D. R., & Roccella, E. J. (1998). High blood pressure. In R. C. Brownson, P. L. Remington, & J. R. Davis (Eds.), *Chronic disease epidemiology and control* (2nd ed., pp. 261–277). Washington, DC: American Public Health Association.

Law, M. R., Morris, J. K., & Wald, N. J. (1997). Environmental tobacco smoke exposure and ischaemic heart disease: An evaluation of the evidence. *British Medical Journal, 314,* 973–980.

Leone, M., Bottacchi, E., Beghi, E., Morgando, E., Mutani, R., Amedeo, G., et al. (1997). Alcohol use is a risk factor for a first generalized tonic-clonic seizure. The ALC.E. (Alcohol and Epilepsy) Study Group. *Neurology, 48*(3), 614–620.

Luepker, R. V. (2008). Heart disease. In R. B. Wallace, N. Kohatsu, & J. M. Last (Eds.), *Wallace/Maxcy-Rosenau-Last public health and preventive medicine* (15th ed., pp. 1071–1088). New York: McGraw Hill Medical.

Mackay, J., & Eriksen, M. (2002). *The tobacco atlas.* Geneva: World Health Organization.

Massie, B. M., & Amidon, T. M. (2000). Heart. In L. M. Tierney, Jr., S. J. McPhee, & M. A. Papadakis (Eds.), *Current medical diagnosis and treatment 2000* (39th ed., pp. 351–443). New York: Lange Medical Books/McGraw-Hill.

Mayfield, D., McLeod, G., & Hall, P. (1974). The CAGE questionnaire: Validation of a new alcoholism instrument. *American Journal of Psychiatry, 131,* 1121–1123.

McBride, P. E., & Anda, R. F. (1998). Cholesterol. In R. C. Brownson, P. L. Remington, & J. R. Davis (Eds.), *Chronic disease epidemiology and control* (2nd ed., pp. 279–295). Washington, DC: American Public Health Association.

McKenna, M. T., Taylor, W. R., Marks, J. S., & Koplan, J. P. (1998). Current issues and challenges in chronic disease control. In R. C. Brownson, P. L. Remington, & J. R. Davis (Eds.), *Chronic disease epidemiology and control* (2nd ed., pp. 1–26). Washington, DC: American Public Health Association.

National Cancer Institute. (1993). *The impact of cigarette excise taxes on smoking among children and adults: Summary report of a National Cancer Institute expert panel.* Washington, DC: Author.

National Public Health Institute in Finland. (2008). North Karelia Project. Retrieved from http://www.ktl.fi/portal/11694

Novotny, T. E., & Giovino, G. A. (1998). Tobacco use. In R. C. Brownson, P. L. Remington, & J. R. Davis (Eds.), *Chronic disease epidemiology and control* (2nd ed., pp. 117–148). Washington, DC: American Public Health Association.

Pan, X. R., Li, G. W., Hu, Y. H., Wang, J. X., Yang, W. Y., An, Z. X., et al. (1997). Effects of diet and exercise in preventing NIDDM in people with impaired glucose tolerance. The Da Qing IGT and Diabetes Study. *Diabetes Care, 20(4),* 537–544.

Pelli, H., Lappalainen-Lehto, R., Piironen, A., Sand, J., & Nordback, I. (2008). Risk factors for recurrent acute alcohol-associated pancreatitis: A prospective analysis. *Scandinavian Journal of Gastroenterology, 43(5),* 614–621.

Powell, K. E., Thompson, P. D., Caspersen, C. J., & Kendrick, J. S. (1987). Physical activity and the incidence of coronary heart disease. *Annual Review of Public Health, 8,* 253–287.

Puska, P., & Uutela, A. (2001). Community intervention in cardiovascular health promotion: North Karelia, 1972–1999. In N. Scheiderman, M. A. Speers, J. M. Silvia, H. Tomes, & J. H. Gentry (Eds.), *Integrating behavioral and social sciences with public health* (pp. 73–96). Washington, DC: American Psychological Association.

Raoul, J. L. (2008). Natural history of hepatocellular carcinoma and current treatment options. *Seminars in Nuclear Medicine, 38(2),* S13–S18.

Remmers, J. E. (1984). Obstructive sleep apnea: A common disorder exacerbated by alcohol. *American Review of Respiratory Disease, 130,* 153–155.

Reuben, A. (2008). Alcohol and the liver. *Current Opinion in Gastroenterology, 24(3),* 328–338.

Salmerón, J., Hu, F. B., Manson, J. E., Stampfer, M. J., Colditz, G. A., Rimm, E. B., et al. (2001). Dietary fat intake and risk of type 2 diabetes in women. *American Journal of Clinical Nutrition, 73(6),* 1019–1026.

Saremi, A., & Arora, R. (2008). The cardiovascular implications of alcohol and red wine. *American Journal of Therapeutics, 15(3),* 265–277.

Scott, J. C., & Hochberg, M. C. (1998). Arthritis and other musculoskeletal diseases. In R. C. Brownson, P. L. Remington, & J. R. Davis (Eds.), *Chronic disease epidemiology and control* (2nd ed., pp. 465–489). Washington, DC: American Public Health Association.

Sofi, F., Capalbo, A., Cesari, F., Abbate, R., & Gensini, G. F. (2008). Physical activity during leisure time and primary prevention of coronary heart disease: An updated meta-analysis of cohort studies. *European Journal of Cardiovascular Prevention and Rehabilitation, 15*(3), 247–257.

Truelsen, T., Begg, S., & Mathers, C. (2006). The global burden of cerebrovascular disease. Retrieved from http://www.who.int/healthinfo/statistics/bod_cerebrovasculardiseasestroke.pdf

Tuomilehto, J., Lindström, J., Eriksson, J. G., Valle, T. T., Hämäläinen, H., Ilanne-Parikka, P., et al. (2001). Prevention of type 2 diabetes mellitus by changes in lifestyle among subjects with impaired glucose tolerance. *New England Journal of Medicine, 344*(18), 1343–1350.

Tzemos, N., Lim, P. O., Wong, S., Struthers, A. D., & MacDonald, T. M. (2008). Adverse cardiovascular effects of acute salt loading in young normotensive individuals. *Hypertension, 51*(6), 1525–1530.

U.S. Department of Health and Human Services. (1996). *Physical activity and health: A report of the surgeon general.* Atlanta, GA: U.S. Department of Health and Human Services, Centers for Disease Control and Prevention, and National Center for Chronic Disease Prevention and Health Promotion.

U.S. Department of Health and Human Services. (2001). *Women and smoking: A report of the surgeon general.* Rockville, MD: U.S. Public Health Service, Office of the Surgeon General.

Wilsnack, R. W., Wilsnack, S. C., & Obot, I. S. (2005). Why study gender, alcohol and culture? In I. S. Obot & R. Room (Eds.), *Alcohol, gender and drinking problems:. Perspectives from low and middle income countries* (pp. 1–24). Geneva: World Health Organization. Retrieved from http://www.who.int/substance_abuse/publications/alcohol_gender_drinking_problems.pdf

World Health Organization. (2002a). *The world health report 2002: Reducing risks, promoting healthy life.* Geneva: Author.

World Health Organization. (2002b). *WHO strategy for prevention and control of chronic respiratory diseases.* Geneva: Author. Retrieved from http://www.who.int/respiratory/publications/WHO_MNC_CRA_02.1.pdf

World Health Organization. (2003). *Diet, nutrition and the prevention of chronic diseases: Report of a joint WHO/FAO expert consultation.* Geneva: Author.

World Health Organization. (2004a). *Global status report on alcohol 2004.* Geneva: Author. Retrieved from http://www.who.int/substance_abuse/publications/global_status_report_2004_overview.pdf

World Health Organization. (2004b). *Rheumatic fever and rheumatic heart disease: Report of a WHO expert consultation, Geneva, 29 October–1 November 2001* (WHO Technical Report Series 923). Geneva: Author. Retrieved from http://www.who.int/cardiovascular_diseases/resources/en/ cvd_trs923.pdf

World Health Organization. (2005a). Chronic diseases and their common risk factors. Retrieved from http://www.who.int/chp/chronic_disease_report/media/Factsheet1.pdf

World Health Organization. (2005b). *Preventing chronic diseases: A vital investment.* Geneva: Author.

World Health Organization. (2007a). *Alcohol and injury in emergency departments: Summary of the report from the WHO Collaborative Study on Alcohol and Injuries.* Geneva: Author. Retrieved from http://www.who.int/substance_abuse/publications/alcohol_injury_summary.pdf

World Health Organization. (2007b). *WHO Expert Committee on Problems Related to Alcohol Consumption: Second report* (WHO Technical Report Series 944). Geneva: Author. Retrieved from http://www.who.int/substance_abuse/expert_committee_alcohol_trs944.pdf

World Health Organization. (2008a). Chronic diseases. Retrieved from http://www.who.int/topics/chronic_diseases/en/

World Health Organization. (2008b). Alcohol drinking. Retrieved from http://www.who.int/topics/alcohol_drinking/en/

World Health Organization. (2008c). Physical activity. Retrieved from http://www.who.int/dietphysicalactivity/publications/facts/pa/en/index.html

World Health Organization. (2008d). Physical inactivity: A global public health problem. Retrieved from http://www.who.int/dietphysicalactivity/factsheet_inactivity/en/index.html

World Health Organization. (2008e). "Move for health" day. Retrieved from http://www.who.int/moveforhealth/countries/en/

World Health Organization. (2008f). Diet. Retrieved from http://www.who.int/dietphysicalactivity/diet/en/index.html

World Health Organization. (2008g). Global strategy on diet, physical activity, and health. Retrieved from http://www.who.int/dietphysicalactivity/goals/en/index.html

World Health Organization. (2008h). Global burden of coronary heart disease. Retrieved from http://www.who.int/cardiovascular_diseases/en/cvd_atlas_13_coronaryHD.pdf

World Health Organization. (2008i). Cancer. Retrieved from http://www.who.int/cancer/en/

World Health Organization. (2008j). Cancer prevention. Retrieved from http://www.who.int/cancer/prevention/en/

World Health Organization. (2008k). Diabetes. Retrieved from http://www.who.int/diabetes/en/

World Health Organization. (2008l). Goal of the diabetes programme. Retrieved from http://www.who.int/diabetes/goal/en/index.html

World Health Organization. (2008m). Living with chronic lung diseases. Retrieved from http://www.who.int/features/2007/copd/en/index.html

World Health Organization MONICA Project Investigators. (1988). The World Health Organization MONICA Project (Monitoring trends and determinants in cardiovascular disease). *Journal of Clinical Epidemiology, 41*, 105–114.

Zgibor, J. C., Dorman, J. S., & Orchard, T. J. (2008). Diabetes. In R. B. Wallace, N. Kohatsu, & J. M. Last (Eds.), *Wallace/Maxcy-Rosenau-Last public health and preventive medicine* (15th ed., pp. 1101–1112). New York: McGraw Hill Medical.

CHAPTER 6

Malnutrition, Nutritional Deficiencies, and Obesity

AFTER READING THIS CHAPTER YOU SHOULD BE ABLE TO

- Describe the causes, types, epidemiology, and prevention and control measures of protein-energy malnutrition
- Discuss common vitamin deficiency disorders, including deficiencies of vitamin A, vitamin D, vitamin E, vitamin K, thiamin, riboflavin, niacin, vitamin B_6, pantothenic acid, folic acid, vitamin B_{12}, and vitamin C
- Explain the causes of and measures for the prevention and control of iron deficiency
- Describe the epidemiology of and prevention and control measures for iodine deficiency disorders
- Discuss the epidemiology of and prevention and control measures for overweight and obesity

Both undernutrition and overnutrition are problems in the world today. Common forms of undernutrition are protein-energy malnutrition, vitamin deficiency disorders, iron deficiency, and iodine deficiency disorders. Undernutrition is typically manifested in the form of wasting, stunting, and micronutrient deficiency and is often linked with poverty, hunger, and deprivation. Extreme forms of undernutrition are present in large pockets of south Asia and most of sub-Saharan Africa. Less extreme forms of undernutrition can be seen in Latin America, north Africa, the Middle East, and central and east Asia. Certain sections of populations are at greater risk for undernutrition, namely, growing fetuses, infants, preschoolers, women of reproductive age, and the elderly (West, Caballero, & Black, 2006).

Overnutrition often manifests itself as overweight and obesity. Obesity is occurring in societies that have moved away from traditional staple diets to processed foods that are rich in refined sugars and fats and contain less dietary fiber. Physical inactivity also contributes to the causation of obesity. The World Health Organization (2008a) projects that by 2015, there will be approximately 2.3 billion overweight adults worldwide and more than 700 million who are obese. The problem is more prevalent in middle- and high-income countries.

An understanding of nutritional issues is derived from multiple disciplines, including agriculture, animal sciences, biochemistry, clinical medicine, dietetics, epidemiology, and public health. The focus of this chapter is on the epidemiologic and public health aspects of nutritional issues in the international context.

PROTEIN-ENERGY MALNUTRITION

The terms **protein-energy malnutrition (PEM)** and *protein-energy deficiency* are used to denote a general lack of food as opposed to deficiency of any one type of vitamin or mineral. More specifically, PEM occurs when the body's needs for proteins or energy or both cannot be met through diet. Protein-energy malnutrition occurs in three situations: in young children in poor communities, mainly in developing countries; in adults as a result of severe illness (hospital malnutrition), which occurs even in developed countries; and in people of all ages during a famine (Truswell, 2002). Protein-energy malnutrition can thus be primary, as a result of inadequate food intake, or secondary, as a result of other diseases. It is an important disease for developing countries because of its high prevalence, association with child mortality, impaired physical growth, and impact on economic and social development.

Causes of Protein-Energy Malnutrition

The causes of PEM can be classified as socioeconomic, biological, and environmental (Torun & Chew, 1999). The most important socioeconomic factor is poverty, which often leads to lack of access to enough food, lack of resources, overcrowding, unhygienic conditions, and inadequate means for child care. A second socioeconomic factor is lack of knowledge, which may be about such things as child rearing practices, types of foods, feeding practices during illnesses, and food distribution in the family. Improper weaning practices, including inadequate breastfeeding, delayed supplementary feeding, and overdilution of milk are also socioeconomic factors in PEM, as are social problems such as child abuse or maternal maltreatment. A final socioeconomic factor is cultural practices, such as restrictions regarding some food items because of cultural reasons.

TABLE 6.1 Causes of Protein-Energy Malnutrition	
Type of Factor	**Factor**
Socioeconomic	Poverty
	Lack of knowledge
	Improper weaning practices
	Social problems such as child abuse or maternal maltreatment
	Cultural practices
Biological	Maternal malnutrition
	Infectious and parasitic diseases
Environmental	Natural disasters such as famines or floods
	Human-made catastrophes such as wars
	Overcrowding and unsanitary living conditions
	Large family size

The most important biological factor for PEM is maternal malnutrition either before or during pregnancy. Lack of food for the pregnant mother means lack of food for the growing fetus. Likewise, if a lactating mother is malnourished, this translates into poor nutrition for the child. The second category of biological factors comprises infectious and parasitic diseases. The presence of diarrheal diseases, measles, HIV/AIDS, and tuberculosis often leads to protein-energy malnutrition.

Environmental factors for PEM include natural disasters such as famines or floods and human-made catastrophes such as wars. Also included are conditions such as overcrowding and unsanitary living conditions. Large family size also contributes to PEM. **Table 6.1** summarizes all these factors.

Types

Protein-energy malnutrition is generally classified into two types on the basis of clinical signs and the relative intake of protein to energy: **marasmus** (mainly energy deficiency with no edema) and **kwashiorkor** (mainly protein deficiency with edema). A third variant, **marasmic kwashiorkor**, is also described, in which there is a combination of

TABLE 6.2	The Wellcome Classification of Protein-Energy Malnutrition in Children		
Weight (% of standard for age)		**Edema Present**	**Edema Absent**
80–60		Kwashiorkor	Undernutrition
< 60		Marasmic kwashiorkor	Marasmus

chronic energy deficiency and chronic or acute protein deficiency with edema. The Wellcome classification of PEM in children (Walker, 1970) is summarized in **Table 6.2**.

In adult men and women, mild protein-energy malnutrition is characterized by a body mass index (BMI) of 17.0 to 18.4 kg/m^2. Moderate protein-energy malnutrition corresponds to a BMI of 16.0 to 16.9 kg/m^2, and severe malnutrition to a BMI less than 16.0 kg/m^2.

Marasmus

The term *marasmus* is derived from the Greek word *marasmos*, which means wasting. It is characterized by generalized muscle wasting and lack of subcutaneous fat, giving an affected child a typical skin-and-bones appearance. The child is very thin and there is no edema or swelling. The weight of a marasmic child is usually less than 60% of the median reference weight for his or her age. The hair is sparse, thin, and dry, and the skin is dry and thin and wrinkles easily. The child has an anxious look; along with sunken cheeks as a result of subcutaneous fat, this gives the face an appearance of that of a monkey or old person. The visceral organs are small, and, in advanced cases, the heart becomes atrophied and brain weight is reduced. Complications include gastroenteritis, dehydration, respiratory infections, and eye lesions as a result of deficiency of vitamin A.

Kwashiorkor

Although marasmus has been known for centuries, kwashiorkor was first described in Ghana, west Africa, in 1935 by Cecily Williams, who used the name for this syndrome that local mothers used in the Ga language. The hallmark of kwashiorkor is painless, pitting edema that is typically present in the feet and legs, but also extends to the perineum, upper extremities, and face in severe cases. The child is miserable and withdrawn and does not eat. Most patients have skin lesions because the epidermis peels off very easily, leading to infections. The hair is dry, brittle, and often depigmented.

Sometimes alternating bands of depigmented and normal hair may correspond with alternating periods of poor and good protein intake, leading to what is known as the flag sign. Complications include gastroenteritis, skin infections, respiratory infections, pulmonary edema with bronchopneumonia, and septicemia.

Marasmic Kwashiorkor

Marasmic kwashiorkor combines the clinical characteristics of marasmus (namely, muscle wasting and loss of subcutaneous fat) and kwashiorkor (namely, edema). When marasmic kwashiorkor is treated in its early stages, the edema disappears and the patient looks like he or she has marasmus. The complications are similar to those described with marasmus and kwashiorkor.

Epidemiology

The World Health Organization (WHO) has made an attempt to provide a global overview of protein-energy malnutrition (DeOnis, Monteiro, Akre, & Clugston, 1993). In 1986, WHO started a global database on child growth. The primary purposes of the database were to describe the worldwide distribution of child growth failure, make intercountry and interregional comparisons, and monitor national, regional, and global trends. Data on prevalence of wasting (low weight-for-height), stunting (low height-for-age), and underweight (low weight-for-age) were collected. The database covered 87% of the total population of those younger than 5 years, or about 468 million children. The results showed that more than a third of the world's children were affected with malnutrition. For all the indicators (wasting, stunting, and underweight), low or moderate prevalence was found in Latin America, high or very high prevalence was found in Asia, and an intermediate situation was found in Africa.

According to Torun and Chew (1999), there are about 800 million undernourished people in the world. Of these, 30% are in south Asia, 30% in eastern Asia, 25% in sub-Saharan Africa, and 8% in Latin America and the Caribbean. Furthermore, 193 million children younger than 5 years (36%) in developing countries are underweight, 230 million (43%) are stunted, and 50 million (9%) are wasted.

Prevention and Control

Primary prevention of PEM requires overall socioeconomic development. Political will is needed to remove the underlying causes of malnutrition, such as poverty. Education is also important to promote breastfeeding, introduce correct weaning techniques, correct misperceptions, and provide knowledge. Children should eat food rich in protein sources. Animal foods are rich sources of proteins, but in cultures where animal foods are not eaten or in situations where they are expensive, legumes and beans are equally good. After six months of age, or earlier if weight gain is not satisfactory, all children should receive supplementary foods. Measures to prevent infections and parasitic infestations, such as immunizations, the practice of good hygiene, and proper sanitation, are also helpful in reducing PEM. In cases of diarrhea, oral rehydration solution and continued feeding should be practiced. UNICEF has developed a seven-pronged strategy called GOBI-FFF to combat malnutrition: **g**rowth monitoring, **o**ral rehydration, **b**reastfeeding, **i**mmunization, **f**emale education, **f**amily planning, and **f**ood supplementation.

For secondary and tertiary prevention, early diagnosis and treatment is essential, and the child should be treated at home as long as possible. Hospitalization introduces the possibility of acquiring infections, so it should be avoided unless the case is severe. Treatment corrects fluid and electrolyte disturbances, eradicates infections, and corrects vitamin A deficiency. Malnourishment is slowly treated by a diet of 125 to 150 kcal and 3 to 4 g of good-quality protein per kilogram of body weight per day, which may have to be provided as a liquid in severe cases. With proper treatment, recovery can occur in a few weeks.

> *There are about 800 million undernourished people in the world.*
>
> —Torun & Chew (1999)

FOCUS FEATURE 6.1   The Hunger Project

The Hunger Project is a global organization working toward the sustainable end of world hunger (Hunger Project, n.d.). It was founded in 1977 after the debate on world hunger that began at the first World Food Conference in Rome. It formed itself as a strategic organization rather than a relief organization. The organization's vision is to eradicate hunger from the world without aiming for everyone to attain a Western-style, high-consumption lifestyle, which it believes is environmentally unsustainable. The approach that the Hunger Project has developed is called "strategic planning in action" and entails an eight-step process: (1) mobilizing and building village-level (grassroots) leadership; (2) bringing together all sectors (business, academia, media, nongovernmental organizations, and government agencies); (3) building a shared understanding; (4) developing a well-articulated, unifying, and achievable vision that aims to solve the problem of hunger society-wide; (5) taking catalytic, high-leverage action that can affect the situation; (6) identifying what is missing; (7) taking immediate action; and (8) creating a momentum of accomplishment.

The Hunger Project uses a bottom-up empowerment approach as opposed to a top-down service delivery approach. The programs of the Project build on three elements: mobilization, gender equality, and democracy. Mobilization is getting local people involved and performing self-reliant action.

(continued)

Because a gender inequality that favors men is a factor in the hunger problem, the Project aims to empower women. Developing and strengthening local democratic structures are often helpful in addressing the problem of hunger.

The Hunger Project has worked in eight areas: ending hunger and abject poverty, improving education, ensuring gender equality, reducing child mortality, improving maternal health, halting the spread of HIV/AIDS, protecting the environment, and fostering partnership. The Project raises money for these activities from people it terms investors rather than donors.

Jill Lester is the president and chief executive officer of the organization. Some of the prominent members on the board include Joaquim Alberto Chissano (former president of Mozambique), Queen Noor of Jordan, Javier Pérez de Cuéllar (former secretary-general of the United Nations), Amartya Sen (1998 Nobel laureate in economics), and M. S. Swaminathan (nutrition scientist from India).

VITAMIN DEFICIENCY DISORDERS

Vitamin deficiency disorders are common in international settings. The following sections present an overview of these disorders.

Vitamin A Deficiency

Vitamin A, also known as retinol, is either ingested preformed or is synthesized from plant caroteinoids, especially beta-carotene, found in pigmented vegetables. It is a fat-soluble vitamin. Vitamin A is essential for normal functioning of the retina and also plays a role in cell growth and differentiation (Baron, 2000). Epidemiologic studies have shown that vitamin A is helpful in reducing the risk of cancers, particularly those of epithelial origin. Nutritional deficiency of vitamin A is one of the most common vitamin deficiencies and is still common in many parts of the world.

Night blindness is the earliest symptom of vitamin A deficiency. Dryness of the conjunctiva (xerophthalmia) and development of white patches on the conjunctiva (Bitot spots) are hallmarks of the disease. With progression of the disease, the cornea becomes ulcerated, which can lead to blindness. An estimated 3 to 10 million children suffer from xerophthalmia each year, and between 250,000 and 500,000 go blind (Ross, 1999). International public health programs provide supplements of vitamin A (50,000 to 200,000 IU) to high-risk children in developing countries. Improved dietary intake is the long-term solution to

It is estimated that each year 3 to 10 million children suffer from xerophthalmia and between 250,000 and 500,000 go blind.

—Ross (1999)

prevention of vitamin A deficiency. Excess vitamin A is also harmful because it can lead to hypervitaminosis A, but it is relatively rare in the context of international health.

Vitamin D Deficiency

Vitamin D is synthesized in the skin by the action of ultraviolet rays in sunlight. Because it is synthesized by the body, it is also called a prohormone. In some countries, such as the United States, milk is fortified with vitamin D to provide a dietary source of this vitamin. Vitamin D is a fat-soluble vitamin that is required to maintain normal blood levels of calcium and phosphate, which are necessary for the healthy mineralization of bone, muscular contractions, nerve conduction, and the general functioning of cells all over the body.

Vitamin D deficiency is common. Infants are a high-risk group for vitamin D deficiency because they have relatively large vitamin D needs as a result of a high rate of skeletal growth. The other high-risk group is adolescents, who also require large amounts of vitamin D because of skeletal growth at puberty. The elderly, pregnant women, and lactating mothers also have higher needs of vitamin D. Deficiency of vitamin D leads to rickets in children and osteomalacia in adults. Rickets is a severe bone-deforming disease characterized by enlargement of the epiphyses of long bones, bowing of the legs, bending of the spine, and weak and toneless muscles. Osteomalacia is characterized by painful proximal muscle weakness, especially of the pelvic girdle, bone pain, and tenderness (Fitzgerald, 2000). Prevention entails adequate exposure to sunlight; in countries where there is less sunlight, fortification in the diet is a useful measure.

Vitamin E Deficiency

Vitamin E, or alpha-tocopherol, is an antioxidant and may play a role in the prevention of cancer, coronary heart disease, and cataracts (Baron, 2000). Vitamin E is a fat-soluble vitamin. Deficiency can occur in certain genetic conditions and fat malabsorption syndromes. Some manifestations of vitamin E deficiency include absence of neurologic reflexes, abnormal gait, and paralysis or weakness of one or more of the muscles that control eye movement. The major food source for vitamin E is vegetable seed oil. If the diet is lacking vitamin E, it can be supplemented.

Vitamin K Deficiency

Vitamin K plays an important role in blood coagulation. It is found in both plant and animal sources. Some of the food sources are citrus fruits, spinach, turnip greens, and cow's milk (Olson, 1999). It is also synthesized endogenously in the body by intestinal bacteria. Vitamin K is a fat-soluble vitamin. Vitamin K deficiency can occur as a result of poor diet, malabsorption, and intake of antibiotics. Prolonged bleeding time is the primary manifestation of its deficiency. Deficiency can be completely corrected with replacement.

Thiamin Deficiency

Thiamin, also known as vitamin B_1, is a water-soluble vitamin that is required for carbohydrate oxidation and nerve conduction. Some excellent sources of thiamin are yeast, lean pork, and legumes. Thiamin deficiency leads to beriberi, which is common in breastfed infants whose mothers are deficient in thiamin, in adults who have a diet derived mainly from milled rice, and in chronic alcoholics (Tanphaichitr, 1999). Beriberi is classified into two types: infantile and adult. In infantile beriberi, which occurs usually between 2 and 3 months, the infant usually presents with a loud piercing cry, difficulty in breathing, vomiting, faster heart rate, and enlargement of the heart. Adult beriberi is of three types: (1) dry beriberi, which is characterized by peripheral neuropathy that involves symmetric impairment of sensory, motor, and reflex functions of the distal segments of limbs; (2) wet beriberi, which includes edema, a faster heart rate, heart enlargement, and heart failure; (3) and Wernicke-Korsakoff syndrome, which is mainly caused by alcoholism and is characterized by incoordination of muscle movements, paralysis or weakness of eye muscles, and derangement of mental functions. These conditions usually respond well to treatment.

Riboflavin Deficiency

Riboflavin, or vitamin B_2, is a water-soluble vitamin. It is an important ingredient in many oxidation-reduction reactions in the body. Milk is an excellent source of riboflavin. Bread and pasta in many countries are enriched with riboflavin. Riboflavin deficiency occurs in combination with other deficiencies, including protein-energy malnutrition (Baron, 2000). Riboflavin deficiency is characterized by inflammatory lesions at the corners of mouth, inflammation of the tongue, seborrheic dermatitis, anemia, and weakness. These problems can be corrected by supplementation.

Niacin Deficiency

Niacin, or nicotinic acid, is a water-soluble vitamin. It can be synthesized from the amino acid tryptophan and is an essential component in many oxidation-reduction reactions in the body. Major food sources are protein foods containing tryptophan and several cereals, vegetables, and dairy products. Deficiency of niacin causes pellagra, which frequently occurs in populations where corn is the major element in the diet. It can also occur as a result of alcoholism. The hallmark of pellagra is the triad of dermatitis, diarrhea, and dementia. The dermatitis is symmetrical and involves sun-exposed areas. Diarrhea is usually severe and can be accompanied by atrophy of intestinal villi. Dementia begins with insomnia, irritability, and apathy and progresses to confusion, memory loss, hallucinations, and psychosis (Baron, 2000). Pellagra can be effectively treated.

Vitamin B_6 Deficiency

Vitamin B_6, or pyridoxine, is involved in several essential metabolic functions in the body. It is a water-soluble vitamin that is found in vegetables, legumes, animal products, nuts, fruits, and cereals. Vitamin B_6 deficiency can occur as a result of interaction with medications or as a result of alcoholism or protein-energy malnutrition. The manifestations of deficiency include mouth soreness, inflammation of the tongue, weakness, and irritability (Baron, 2000). Severe deficiency can lead to peripheral neuropathy, anemia, and seizures. Vitamin B_6 deficiency can be effectively treated with oral vitamin B_6 supplements.

Pantothenic Acid Deficiency

Pantothenic acid is a water-soluble vitamin that is needed in cell metabolism and protein modification. Some of the rich sources of pantothenic acid are liver, kidney, yeast, egg yolk, milk, and broccoli. Pantothenic acid deficiency is rare, but occurs with severe malnutrition. Some of the manifestations of its deficiency are numbness in the toes and painful burning sensations in the feet. Deficiency can be corrected with supplementation in diet.

Folic Acid Deficiency

Folic acid, or folate, is a water-soluble vitamin present in most fruits and vegetables. It is especially found in citrus fruits and green leafy vegetables. The most common cause of folic acid deficiency is inadequate dietary intake (Linker, 2000). Clinical manifestations of folic acid deficiency include megaloblastic anemia and megaloblastic changes in the mucosa. Deficiency responds well to oral folic acid, and improvement occurs in 2 to 3 months.

Vitamin B$_{12}$ Deficiency

Vitamin B$_{12}$ belongs to the family of cobalamins and is a water-soluble vitamin. It serves as a cofactor for several important metabolic reactions in the body. It is present in food items of animal origin. The liver stores large amounts of vitamin B$_{12}$, and therefore, deficiency of this vitamin manifests 2 to 3 years after cessation of its absorption. Dietary deficiency of vitamin B$_{12}$ is rare and usually occurs in vegans (people who are strict vegetarians and avoid even dairy products) (Linker, 2000). Deficiency can also occur due to poor absorption as a result of several diseases or gastrectomy. Clinical manifestations of vitamin B$_{12}$ deficiency include megaloblastic anemia, peripheral neuropathy, and dementia. With treatment, prognosis is good.

Vitamin C Deficiency

Vitamin C, or ascorbic acid, is a water-soluble vitamin that is involved in many oxidation-reduction reactions and is a potent antioxidant. It is also required for synthesis of collagen. It is found in fresh fruits and vegetables, especially citrus fruits. Its deficiency leads to a condition called scurvy, which is a problem in poor people, the elderly, and alcoholics (Baron, 2000). Clinical manifestations include hemorrhage around hair follicles, bleeding gums, hemarthroses (bleeding in the joints), anemia, and impaired wound healing. In late stages it can lead to neuropathy, intracerebral hemorrhage, and death. It can be treated with oral administration of vitamin C, and improvement can be seen within days.

Table 6.3 summarizes all the vitamin deficiency disorders.

IRON DEFICIENCY

Iron is a key element involved in the metabolism of all living organisms. Iron is part of heme, which is the site of oxygen uptake by hemoglobin. Total body iron ranges from 2 g to 4 g, or approximately 50 mg/kg in men and 35 mg/kg in women (Linker, 2000). A large proportion of iron is present in hemoglobin in circulating red blood cells. A small proportion is present in myoglobin and nonheme enzymes. A third site of iron is in storage as ferritin or hemosiderin in macrophages. Dietary sources of iron include meat products, legumes, and green leafy vegetables.

Iron deficiency is the most common cause of anemia around the world. Most preschool children and pregnant women in developing countries and at least 30 to 40% in industrialized countries manifest iron deficiency (WHO, 2001a). Iron deficiency can happen as a result of deficiency in diet, decreased absorption, blood loss, or infestation

TABLE 6.3 Vitamin Deficiency Disorders	
Vitamin	**Deficiency**
Vitamin A	Night blindness and xerophthalmia
Vitamin D	Rickets and osteomalacia
Vitamin E	Absence of neurologic reflexes, abnormal gait, and paralysis or weakness of one or more of the muscles that control eye movement
Vitamin K	Prolonged bleeding time
Thiamin	Beriberi
Riboflavin	Inflammatory lesions at the corners of mouth, inflammation of the tongue, seborrheic dermatitis, anemia, and weakness
Niacin	Pellagra
Vitamin B_6	Mouth soreness, inflammation of the tongue, weakness, irritability, peripheral neuropathy, anemia, and seizures
Pantothenic acid	Numbness in the toes and painful burning sensations in the feet
Folic acid	Megaloblastic anemia and megaloblastic changes in mucosa
Vitamin B_{12}	Megaloblastic anemia, peripheral neuropathy, and dementia
Vitamin C	Scurvy

by hookworms. Pregnancy and lactation also impose a greater demand on iron and, if iron is not supplemented, can lead to iron deficiency. The clinical manifestations of iron deficiency anemia are easy fatigability, increased heart rate, palpitations, and breathlessness on exertion. Treatment is by giving oral or parenteral iron.

Most preschool children and pregnant women in developing countries and at least 30 to 40% in industrialized countries manifest iron deficiency.

—World Health Organization (2001a)

Prevention of iron deficiency anemia, like other deficiency disorders, involves reducing poverty. Both in developing and developed countries, iron deficiency anemia affects mainly those who are poor. Along with poverty reduction, improved access to diversified diets, improved health services and sanitation, and the promotion of better care and feeding practices are important measures in reducing iron deficiency anemia (WHO, 2001a). In some countries food products are fortified with iron. For example, in the Philippines, rice is fortified with ferrous sulfate.

IODINE DEFICIENCY DISORDERS

Iodine is an essential constituent of the hormones of the thyroid gland, namely, triiodothyronine (T_3) and thyroxine (T_4). The World Health Organization (2001b) recommends that the daily intake of iodine should be 90 µg for preschool children (0 to 59 months), 120 µg for schoolchildren (6 to 12 years), 150 µg for adults (those older than 12 years), and 200 µg for pregnant and lactating women.

Iodine is found in the ocean and in deep wells. It gets leached away from the soil surface by snow, water, and heavy rainfall. As a result of leaching, some of the most deficient areas are the mountainous areas of the world, such as the Himalayas, the Andes, and the European Alps, and flooded river valleys, such as those in India and Bangladesh. A 2003 WHO survey found the total prevalence of goiter (an iodine deficiency disorder) worldwide to be 15.8%, which was an increase of 31.7% from 1993 (WHO, 2004). The prevalence was highest for the eastern Mediterranean region (37.3%), followed by Africa (28.3%). The Americas had the lowest prevalence (4.7%). The worldwide prevalence of goiter of 15.8% is an indication of a serious public health problem. The survey also measured urinary iodine, which is a measure of dietary iodine, and found that 36.5% of school-aged children (6 to 12 years) and 35.2% of the general population had insufficient iodine intake.

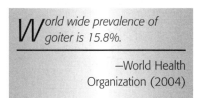

World wide prevalence of goiter is 15.8%.

—World Health Organization (2004)

Signs and Symptoms

Iodine deficiency is one of the world's most prevalent and readily preventable causes of brain damage. Iodine deficiency results in a wide variety of physical, neurologic, and intellectual deficits and is associated with higher rates of spontaneous abortions, stillbirths, neonatal and infant mortality, and learning disabilities (McArthur, 1995). All these disorders are called **iodine deficiency disorders (IDD)** and result from deficiency of iodine and deficient synthesis of T_3 and T_4 by the thyroid gland. The spectrum of IDD ranges from fetal abnormalities to aberrations in neonates and children to deviations in adults. The most visible manifestation of iodine deficiency is goiter. In the absence of sufficient iodine, thyroid-stimulating hormone stimulates the thyroid and causes its enlargement in the neck region. The most severe damage due to iodine deficiency occurs from the fetal period to the third month after birth, during which iodine deficiency can produce cretinism, an irreversible form of mental retardation. A meta-analysis of 19 studies conducted in iodine-deficient areas demonstrated that iodine deficiency resulted in a mean IQ loss of 13.5 points in the population

(Bleichrodt & Born, 1994). In endemic areas cretinism can affect as much as 5 to 15% of the population (WHO, 2004).

In epidemiologic studies, urinary iodine is measured to determine iodine deficiency. Levels below 20 µg/L indicate severe iodine deficiency, of 20 to 49 µg/L indicate moderate iodine deficiency, and of 50 to 99 µg/L indicate mild deficiency. Levels of 100 to 199 µg/L indicate optimal level of iodine; levels over 300 µg/L indicate excessive iodine, which can lead to hyperthyroidism and other autoimmune thyroid diseases.

Prevention and Control

In 1922, Marine and Kimball demonstrated in a study in schoolchildren in Akron, Ohio, that endemic goiter could be prevented and reduced by the administration of small amounts of iodine (Hetzel & Clugston, 1999). Around the same time, mass prophylaxis of goiter using iodized salt was introduced in Switzerland and the United States and was found to reduce goiter and prevent cretinism. Another major effort was launched in Papua New Guinea between 1959 and 1972 for people living in remote mountain villages, who were given iodized oil injections that led to reduction of goiter and cretinism (Hetzel & Clugston, 1999).

There are four main strategies to prevent and control IDD: correction of iodine deficiency; surveillance, including monitoring and evaluation; intersectoral collaboration and advocacy; and communication to mobilize public health authorities and educate the public (WHO, 2004). Iodine deficiency can be corrected by oral administration of iodine or iodized oil in endemic areas. As mentioned earlier, this approach was used in Papua New Guinea; it was also used in China, Africa, and Latin America. Iodized salt is a better and more economical method, however. Since the 1990s, the World Health Organization has advocated for universal salt iodization. Salt iodization is helpful because salt is consumed by everyone, it is easy to implement, it costs less (2 to 9 cents per person per year), and iodization does not alter any properties of salt such as taste, color, or odor. It is recommended to add 20 to 40 ppm of iodine to salt. Usually, potassium iodate is used for tropical climates, whereas potassium iodide is used in temperate areas.

OVERWEIGHT AND OBESITY

Overweight and **obesity** are characterized by excessive deposition of fat, which is a detriment to good health. To determine overweight and obesity, a measure called body mass index (BMI) is used, which is calculated by taking an individual's weight in kilograms and dividing it by the square of his or her height in meters (kg/m^2). A BMI between 18.5 kg/m² and 24.9 kg/m² is considered normal. A BMI between 25 kg/m² and 29.9 kg/m² is considered overweight, and a BMI more than 30 kg/m² is considered obese.

Epidemiology

Overweight and obesity are major causes of morbidity and mortality in most industrialized countries of the world. In 2005, according to the World Health Organization (2008a), there were 1.6 million adults who were overweight and 400 million who were obese. Overall, 10% of the school-aged children in the world are overweight (Lobstein, Baur, Uauy, & IASO International Obesity Task Force, 2004).

In the United States, the prevalence of obesity has been increasing since the 1980s (Flegal, Carroll, Kuczmarski, & Jonson, 1998). According to the National Health and Nutrition Examination Survey (NHANES) the prevalence of overweight in U.S. adults in 2003 to 2004 was 66.3%, of whom 32.2% were found to be obese (Ogden et al., 2006). This was an increase from 1999 and 2000, when the prevalence of overweight was 64.5% and that of obesity was 30.5% (Flegal, Carroll, Ogden, & Johnson, 2002). According to the Behavioral Risk Factor Surveillance System (BRFSS), a random-digit telephone survey conducted in all states in 2000, the prevalence of obesity among 184,450 adults older than 18 years was 19.8% (Mokdad et al., 2001).

Similarly, in the United Kingdom in 2003, 60% of women and 68% of men were overweight or obese (Fisher, 2005). In Germany, 70% of men and 50% of women were found to be obese (Mensink, Lampert, & Bergmann, 2005). In Spain, the prevalence of obesity was found to be 14.5% in one study (Carraro & Garcia Cebrian, 2003) and 13% in another study (Martinez, Moreno, & Martinez-Gonzalez, 2004). A 1994 analysis in Denmark showed the prevalence of obesity in that country to be 12% in men and 11% in women (Heitmann, Stroger, Mikkelsen, Holst, & Sorensen, 2004). In a study in Iceland, the prevalence of obesity was found to be 19% (Thogeirsdottir, Steingrimsdottir, Olafsson, & Gudnason, 2005). In a study in Poland in 2003, it was found that 15% of women and 6.5% of men were obese (Milewicz et al., 2005). In Canada in 2003, 15.2% of individuals were found be obese (Vanasse, Demers, Hemiari, & Courteau, 2006). A study in south Australia found that obesity rates increased significantly in that region, from 8.7% in 1991 to 14.1% in 2003; severe obesity also increased significantly, from 2.6% in 1991 to 5.3% in 2003 (Dal Grande, Gill, Taylor, Chittleborough, & Carter, 2005). In a study in Turkey, the prevalence of obesity was found to be 35% (Sanisoglu, Oktenli, Hasimi, Yokusoglu, & Ugurlu, 2006). A study done in Saudi Arabia found the prevalence of overweight to be 36.9% and that of obesity to be 35.5% (Al-Nozha et al., 2005).

In the United States, it is estimated that approximately 300,000 deaths annually are attributable to obesity-related conditions (Allison, Fontaine, Manson, Stevens, & Vanitallie, 1999). The economic burden of adult obesity is estimated to be as high as $100 billion per year (Wolf, 1998). In 1995, about 5% of the national health care budget was spent on the direct costs of obesity and its consequent diseases (Dietz, 2002).

> *Worldwide, there are 1.6 million adults who are overweight and 400 million who are obese.*
>
> —(World Health Organization, 2008a)

Determinants of Overweight and Obesity

Overweight and obesity are caused by various factors. Body weight is shaped by a combination of genetic, metabolic, behavioral, environmental, cultural, and socioeconomic influences. The Human Obesity Gene Map Consortium has counted over 240 genes that are able to modulate body weight and adiposity through the regulation of food intake, energy expenditure, lipid and glucose metabolism, adipose tissue development, and inflammation processes (Rankinen, Zuberi, & Changnon, 2006). Numerous studies have indicated additional genetically related determinants. For instance, the presence of overweight in one or both parents represents a higher risk of obesity for their children (Ness, 2004). Another genetically related factor is sex, with a predisposition in females to be overweight, independent of age (Rapp, Schick, Bode, & Weiland, 2005). Race also seems to determine some differences in weight status. For example, black and Hispanic populations have a higher risk of obesity compared with white populations (Strauss & Pollack, 2001).

Gluckman and Hanson (2004) have indicated that the risk of developing obesity starts very early in life, even as early as fetal development. Kramer and colleagues (1985) conducted a study to evaluate potential determinants of weight and adiposity in the first year of life. The study found that birth weight, sex, age at introduction of solids, and duration of breastfeeding were all significant predictors of weight at 12 months.

A study by Harvey and colleagues (2007) examined maternal influences on neonatal body composition using assessment of fat and lean body mass by dual x-ray absorptiometry within two weeks of birth. The study found that bigger maternal size, higher parity, smoking history, mothers who walked slower, and mothers who had greater fat stores were important determinants of greater fat in neonatal body composition.

High consumption of unhealthy foods, including fast foods and sweetened beverages, has been found to contribute to obesity. When children consume fast food, their energy and fat intake is more likely to be higher and their fruit and vegetable intake lower than the recommended servings (Bowman, Gortmaker, Ebbeling, Pereira, & Ludwig, 2004). Ludwig, Peterson, and Gortmaker (2001) found that the consumption of soft drinks was positively associated with obesity in children older than 19 months. As the incidence of overweight and obesity has escalated, a corresponding increase in the portion size of foods served in restaurants and fast food establishments has occurred. Huang, Howarth, and Lin (2004) reported that portion size was positively associated with BMI percentile in boys aged 6 to 11 years and in adolescents aged 12 to 19 years.

Snacking has also been noted as a risk factor for obesity. Individuals have become less inclined to eat three meals a day, preferring more frequent, irregular intervals of eating. Snacking has been associated with more energy-dense foods and more total food consumed, which contributes to the positive energy balance known to lead to weight gain (Procter, 2007). Family environment is probably one of the most important factors that influences the food choices and eating behaviors of children. Parents influence food behaviors of their own children through the availability and accessibility of food, meal structure, food socialization practices, their own body weight, socio–economic status, cultural beliefs, food preferences, family structure, and attitudes toward their children (Tabacchi, Giammanco, La Guardia, & Giammanco, 2007).

Goran, Reynolds, and Lindquist (1999) concluded that physical activity protects individuals from development of obesity by increasing energy expenditure and increasing resting metabolic rate. In a sample of children, Lioret, Maire, Volatier, and Charles (2007) found that 15.2% of the children were overweight (of whom 3.5% were obese) and that those children who engaged in leisure-time physical activity were significantly less likely to be overweight than children who performed no leisure-time physical activity. Duration of television watching for more than two hours per day was positively associated with overweight in children (Rapp, Schick, Bode, & Weiland, 2005).

Table 6.4 summarizes the various determinants of overweight and obesity.

Prevention and Control

Prevention and control of overweight and obesity utilize educational and policy-level approaches to promote physical activity and healthy nutrition. Physical activity and nutrition interventions are targeted at a variety of levels, including schools, worksites, community, and patient care. Interventions designed for school, worksite, community, or patient care settings must be based on behavioral theories, as explained in Chapter 3. Social cognitive theory and the transtheoretical model have particularly been used for the promotion of physical activity and healthy nutrition. In worksite, community, and patient care interventions, activities such as walking, aerobic dancing, and physical education classes are generally used. Use of a buddy system for social

TABLE 6.4 Determinants of Overweight and Obesity	
Category	**Examples**
Genetic	Genes
	Parental body mass index (BMI)
	Sex
	Race
Influences in first years of life	Fetal development
	Birth weight
	Growth in infancy
Maternal behaviors	Maternal BMI
	Smoking during pregnancy
	Breastfeeding
Family food environment and dietary behaviors	Nutritional preferences
	Dietary fat and fat types
	Consumption of unhealthy foods
	Portion sizes and snacking
	Family environment
Physical activity and inactivity	Physical activity levels
	Screen time
Environmental factors	Sociodemographic status

support is also a popular approach. Various professionals are involved in facilitating these interventions, including health educators, counselors, exercise professionals, physical trainers, lay health advisors, physicians, nurse practitioners, and nurses.

Besides advocating for greater physical education time in schools, there are several other environmental and policy measures that can be implemented to promote physical activity and prevent and control physical inactivity. Examples of such measures include removing environmental barriers, de-emphasizing automation, building more accessible facilities to promote movement, subsidizing parks and recreational facilities, and installing bicycle trails, walking trails, and sidewalks in developments (Ainsworth & Macera, 1998).

In May 2004, the World Health Organization adopted a global strategy on diet, physical activity, and health. The strategy has four main objectives (WHO, 2008b):

- Reduce risk factors for chronic diseases that originate from unhealthy diets and physical inactivity through public health actions
- Increase awareness and understanding of the role of diet and physical activity on health and the positive impact of preventive interventions
- Develop, strengthen, and implement global, regional, and national policies and action plans to improve diets and increase physical activity that are sustainable, comprehensive, and actively engage all sectors
- Monitor science and promote research on diet and physical activity

EATING DISORDERS

Eating disorders include abnormal eating behaviors, marked by compulsive eating or behaviors targeted toward avoiding eating, that negatively affect both one's physical and mental health. They are of two types—anorexia nervosa and bulimia nervosa—and are discussed in detail in Chapter 10.

SKILL-BUILDING ACTIVITY

Calcium is an important element required by the human body. It is involved in the development of bones and teeth as well as the functioning of parathyroid hormone, calcitonin, and vitamin D. Conduct a search regarding the role of this mineral on the Internet and in your library. Collect the following information: dietary sources, deficiency diseases, and strategy for ensuring adequate calcium for all people of the world. Prepare a fact sheet with this information.

SUMMARY

Both undernutrition and overnutrition are problems in the world today. Common forms of undernutrition are protein-energy malnutrition, vitamin deficiency disorders, iron deficiency, and iodine deficiency disorders. Protein-energy malnutrition denotes a general lack of food and occurs in three situations: in young children in poor communities, mainly in developing countries; in adults as a result of severe illness (hospital malnutrition), which occurs even in developed countries; and in people of all ages during a famine. Protein-energy malnutrition is generally classified into two forms on the basis of clinical signs and relative intake of protein and energy: marasmus (mainly energy deficiency and no edema) and kwashiorkor (mainly protein deficiency and with edema). A third variant, marasmic kwashiorkor, combines chronic energy deficiency and chronic or acute protein deficiency with edema.

Vitamin deficiency disorders are common in international settings. Vitamin A deficiency leads to night blindness and xerophthalmia. Vitamin D deficiency causes rickets in children and osteomalacia in adults. Vitamin E deficiency leads to absence of neurologic reflexes, abnormal gait, and paralysis or weakness of one or more of the muscles that control eye movement. Vitamin K deficiency leads to prolonged bleeding time. Thiamin deficiency leads to beriberi. Riboflavin deficiency causes inflammatory lesions at the corners of mouth, inflammation of the tongue, seborrheic dermatitis, anemia, and weakness. Niacin deficiency causes pellagra. Vitamin B_6 deficiency leads to mouth soreness, inflammation of the tongue, weakness, irritability, peripheral neuropathy, anemia, and seizures. Folic acid deficiency causes megaloblastic anemia. Vitamin B_{12} deficiency causes megaloblastic anemia, peripheral neuropathy, and dementia. Vitamin C deficiency leads to scurvy.

Deficiency of iron is the most common cause of anemia around the world. Iodine deficiency disorders result from deficiency of iodine and deficient synthesis of triiodothyronine (T_3) and thyroxine (T_4) by the thyroid gland. Iodine deficiency disorders include fetal abnormalities, goiter, and cretinism.

Overweight and obesity are characterized by excessive deposition of fat, which is a detriment to good health. A body mass index (BMI) between 25 kg/m^2 and 29.9 kg/m^2 is considered overweight, and a BMI more than 30 kg/m^2 is considered obese. Prevention and control of overweight and obesity utilize educational and policy-level approaches to promote physical activity and healthy nutrition.

IMPORTANT TERMS

iodine deficiency disorders (IDD)
iron deficiency
kwashiorkor
marasmic kwashiorkor
marasmus

obesity
overweight
protein-energy malnutrition (PEM)
vitamin deficiency disorders

REVIEW QUESTIONS

1. Define protein-energy malnutrition (PEM). Discuss the causes of PEM.
2. Describe the strategies for prevention and control of protein-energy malnutrition.
3. What are the consequences of vitamin A deficiency? How can its deficiency be prevented?
4. Name some water-soluble vitamins and describe the consequences of their deficiency.
5. What are the causes of iron deficiency anemia? What can be done for prevention and control of iron deficiency anemia?
6. What are the consequences of iodine deficiency? What can be done to prevent and control iodine deficiency disorders?
7. Define overweight and obesity. Discuss strategies for the prevention and control of overweight and obesity in populations.

WEB SITES TO EXPLORE

Doctors Without Borders

http://www.doctorswithoutborders.org/

Doctors Without Borders, or Médecins Sans Frontières (MSF), is an international medical humanitarian organization working in approximately 60 countries to help people whose survival is affected by violence, neglect, or disaster. In keeping this mandate it often works in the area of combating malnutrition. *Visit this Web site and search for information on this organization's work related to malnutrition. You can also see how you can work for this organization.*

International Council for the Control of Iodine Deficiency Disorders

http://www.iccidd.org/

The International Council for the Control of Iodine Deficiency Disorders (ICCIDD) is an international organization of over 600 specialists from more than 100 countries that is formed to promote optimal iodine nutrition and the elimination of iodine deficiency disorders all over the world. The Web site has links to a book by Basil Hetzel, frequently asked questions and other information about iodine, a global scorecard, and technical resources, among other links. *Go to the Global Scorecard link and locate the data regarding total goiter prevalence and percentage of households consuming iodized salt for any five countries of your choice.*

Iron Deficiency Anemia

http://www.mayoclinic.com/health/iron-deficiency-anemia/DS00323
This Web site from the Mayo Clinic in the United States describes iron deficiency anemia, including its definition, symptoms, causes, risk factors, when to seek medical advice, tests and diagnosis, complications, treatments and drugs, and prevention. The Web site also links to the Iron Disorders Institute, National Anemia Action Council, and National Women's Health Information Center: Anemia. *Explore this Web site and write down five new things you learned about iron deficiency anemia.*

Malnutrition Matters

http://www.malnutrition.org/
Malnutrition Matters is a Canadian not-for-profit organization that works toward providing sustainable low-cost food technology solutions for malnutrition. It uses mainly soya products and cereals, grains, fruits, and vegetables. It supports programs through nongovernmental organizations in developing countries. *The Web site has links to projects in India, Africa, and North Korea. Read about these projects and identify key aspects.*

The Obesity Society

http://www.obesity.org/
The Obesity Society is a U.S.-based scientific society dedicated to the study of obesity, established in 1982. The Obesity Society works toward encouraging research on the causes, treatment, and prevention of obesity as well as keeping the scientific community and public informed of new advances in the field. *Review the fact sheets and position statements posted by this society. Summarize the findings from one position statement.*

Vitamin A Deficiency

http://www.who.int/nutrition/topics/vad/en/index.html
This Web site of the World Health Organization summarizes salient aspects of vitamin A deficiency. Links are provided to the WHO global database on vitamin A deficiency and to relevant publications. *Review the information on this Web site and then explore the publications in the area of vitamin A deficiency. Download, read, and summarize the key findings from one publication.*

REFERENCES

Ainsworth, B. E., & Macera, C. A. (1998). Physical inactivity. In R. C. Brownson, P. L. Remington, & J. R. Davis (Eds.), *Chronic disease epidemiology and control* (2nd ed., pp. 191–213). Washington, DC: American Public Health Association.

Allison, D. B., Fontaine, K. R., Manson, J. E., Stevens, J., & Vanitallie, T. B. (1999). Annual deaths attributed to obesity in the United States. *Journal of the American Medical Association, 282,* 1530–1538.

Al-Nozha, M. M., Al-Mazrou, Y. Y., Al-Maatouq, M. A., Arafah, M. R., Khalil, M. Z., Khan, N. B., et al. (2005). Obesity in Saudi Arabia. *Saudi Medical Journal, 26*(5), 824–829.

Baron, R. B. (2000). Nutrition. In L. M. Tierney, Jr., S. J. McPhee, & M. A. Papadakis (Eds.), *Current medical diagnosis and treatment* (39th ed., pp. 1211–1240). New York: Lange Medical Books/McGraw-Hill.

Bleichrodt, N., & Born, M. P. (1994). A meta-analysis of research on iodine and its relationship to cognitive development. In J. B. Stanbury (Ed.), *The damaged brain of iodine deficiency* (pp. 195–200). New York: Cognizant Communication.

Bowman, S. A., Gortmaker, S. L., Ebbeling, C. B., Pereira, M. A., & Ludwig, D. S. (2004). Effects of fast-food consumption on energy intake and diet quality among children in a national household survey. *Pediatrics, 113,* 112–118.

Carraro, R., & Garcia Cebrian, M. (2003). Role of prevention in the contention of the obesity epidemic. *European Journal of Clinical Nutrition, 57*(Suppl. 1), S94–S96.

Dal Grande, E., Gill, T., Taylor, A. W., Chittleborough, C., & Carter, P. (2005). Obesity in South Australian adults—prevalence, projections and generational assessment over 13 years. *Australia and New Zealand Journal of Public Health, 29*(4), 343–348.

DeOnis, M., Monteiro, C., Akre, J., & Clugston, G. (1993). The worldwide magnitude of protein energy malnutrition: An overview from the WHO global database on child growth. *Bulletin of the World Health Organization, 71*(5), 703–712.

Dietz, W. (2002). Current trends in obesity: Clinical impact and interventions that work. *Ethnicity and Disease, 12*(1 Suppl. 2), S17–S20.

Fisher, K. (2005). Government initiatives to tackle the obesity epidemic. *Nursing Times, 101*(39), 23–24.

Fitzgerald, P. A. (2000). Endocrinology. In L. M. Tierney, Jr., S. J. McPhee, & M. A. Papadakis (Eds.), *Current medical diagnosis and treatment* (39th ed., pp. 1079–1151). New York: Lange Medical Books/McGraw-Hill.

Flegal, K. M., Carroll, M. D., Kuczmarski, R. J., & Jonson, C. L. (1998). Overweight and obesity in the United States: Prevalence and trends, 1960–1994. *International Journal of Obesity and Related Metabolic Disorders, 22,* 39–47.

Flegal, K. M., Carroll, M. D., Ogden, C. L., & Johnson, C. L. (2002). Prevalence and trends in obesity among U.S. adults, 1999–2000. *Journal of the American Medical Association, 288*(14), 1723–1727.

Gluckman, P. D., & Hanson, M. A. (2004). The developmental origins of the metabolic syndrome. *Trends in Endocrinology Metabolism, 15,* 183–187.

Goran, M. I., Reynolds, K. D., & Lindquist, C. H. (1999). Role of physical activity in the prevention of obesity in children. *International Journal of Obesity and Related Metabolic Disorders, 23*(Suppl. 3), S18–S33.

Harvey, N. C., Poole, J. R., Javaid, M. K., Dennison, E. M., Robinson, S., Inskip, H. M., et al. (2007). Parental determinants of neonatal body composition. *Journal of Clinical Endocrinology and Metabolism, 92*, 523–526.

Heitmann, B. L., Stroger, U., Mikkelsen, K. L., Holst, C., & Sorensen, T. I. (2004). Large heterogeneity of the obesity epidemic in Danish adults. *Public Health Nutrition, 7*(3), 453–460.

Hetzel, B. S., & Clugston, G. A. (1999). Iodine. In M. E. Shils, J. A. Olson, M. Shike, & A. C. Ross (Eds.), *Modern nutrition in health and disease* (9th ed., pp. 253–264). Baltimore, MD: Williams & Wilkins.

Huang, T., Howarth, N., & Lin, B. (2004). Energy intake and meal portions: Associations with BMI percentile in U.S. children. *Obesity Reviews, 12*, 1875–1885.

Hunger Project. (n.d.). Empowering women and men to end their own hunger. Retrieved July 11, 2008, from http://www.thp.org/

Kramer, M. S., Barr, R. G., Leduc, D. G., Boisjoly, C., McVey-White, L., & Pless, I. B. (1985). Determinants of weight and adiposity in the first year of life. *Journal of Pediatrics, 106*, 10–14.

Linker, C. A. (2000). Blood. In L. M. Tierney, Jr., S. J. McPhee, & M. A. Papadakis (Eds.), *Current medical diagnosis and treatment* (39th ed., pp. 499–552). New York: Lange Medical Books/ McGraw-Hill.

Lioret, S., Maire, B., Volatier, J. L., & Charles, M. A. (2007). Child overweight in France and its relationship with physical activity, sedentary behaviour and socioeconomic status. *European Journal of Clinical Nutrition, 61*, 509–516.

Lobstein, T., Baur, L., Uauy, R., & IASO International Obesity Task Force. (2004). Obesity in children and young people: A crisis in public health. *Obesity Reviews, 5*(Suppl. 1), 4–104.

Ludwig, D. S., Peterson, K. E., & Gortmaker, S. L. (2001). Relation between consumption of sugar-sweetened drinks and childhood obesity: A prospective, observational analysis. *Lancet, 357*, 505–508.

Martinez, J. A., Moreno, B., & Martinez-Gonzalez, M. A. (2004). Prevalence of obesity in Spain. *Obesity Reviews, 5*(3), 171–172.

McArthur, L. H. (1995). Iodine deficiency disorders. In J. E. Craighead (Ed.), *Pathology of environmental and occupational disease* (pp. 149–152). St. Louis, MO: Mosby.

Mensink, G. B., Lampert, T., & Bergmann, E. (2005). Overweight and obesity in Germany 1984–2003 [In German]. *Bundesgesundheitsblatt Gesundheitsforschung Gesundheitsschutz, 48*(12), 1348–1356.

Milewicz, A., Jedrzejuk, D., Lwow, F., Bialynicka, A. S., Lopatynski, J., Mardarowicz, G., et al. (2005). Prevalence of obesity in Poland. *Obesity Reviews, 6*(2), 113–114.

Mokdad, A. H., Bowman, B. A., Ford, E. S., Vinicor, F., Marks, J. S., & Koplan, J. P. (2001). The continuing epidemics of obesity and diabetes in the United States. *Journal of the American Medical Association, 286*(10), 1195–2000.

Ness, A. R. (2004). The Avon Longitudinal Study of Parents and Children (ALSPAC): A resource for the study of the environmental determinants of childhood obesity. *European Journal of Endocrinology, 151*(Suppl. 3), U141–149.

Ogden, C. L., Carroll, M. D., Curtin, L. R., McDowell, M. A., Tabak, C. J., & Flegal, K. M. (2006). Prevalence of overweight and obesity in the United States, 1999–2004. *Journal of the American Medical Association, 295*(13), 1549–1555.

Olson, R. E. (1999). Vitamin K. In M. E. Shils, J. A. Olson, M. Shike, & A. C. Ross (Eds.), *Modern nutrition in health and disease* (9th ed., pp. 363–380). Baltimore, MD: Williams & Wilkins.

Procter, K. L. (2007). The aetiology of childhood obesity: A review. *Nutrition Research, 20,* 29–45.

Rankinen, T., Zuberi, A., & Changnon, Y. (2006). The human obesity gene map: The 2005 update. *Obesity, 14,* 529.

Rapp, K., Schick, K. H., Bode, H., & Weiland, S. K. (2005). Type of kindergarten and other potential determinants of overweight in pre-school children. *Public Health Nutrition, 8,* 642–649.

Ross, A. C. (1999). Vitamin A and retinoids. In M. E. Shils, J. A. Olson, M. Shike, & A. C. Ross (Eds.), *Modern nutrition in health and disease* (9th ed., pp. 305–327). Baltimore, MD: Williams & Wilkins.

Sanisoglu, S. Y., Oktenli, C., Hasimi, A., Yokusoglu, M., & Ugurlu, M. (2006). Prevalence of metabolic syndrome-related disorders in a large adult population in Turkey. *BMC Public Health, 6,* 92.

Strauss, R., & Pollack, H. (2001). Epidemic increases in childhood overweight. *Journal of the American Medical Association, 286,* 2845–2648.

Tabacchi, G., Giammanco, S., La Guardia, M., & Giammanco, M. (2007). A review of the literature and a new classification of the early determinants of childhood obesity: From pregnancy to the first years of life. *Nutrition Research, 27,* 587–604.

Tanphaichitr, V. (1999). Thiamin. In M. E. Shils, J. A. Olson, M. Shike, & A. C. Ross (Eds.), *Modern nutrition in health and disease* (9th ed., pp. 381–390). Baltimore, MD: Williams & Wilkins.

Thogeirsdottir, H., Steingrimsdottir, L., Olafsson, O., & Gudnason, V. (2005). Trends in overweight and obesity in 45–64 year old men and women in Reykjavik 1975–1994 [In Icelandic]. *Laeknabladid, 91*(1), 115–121.

Torun, B., & Chew, F. (1999). Protein-energy malnutrition. In M. E. Shils, J. A. Olson, M. Shike, & A. C. Ross (Eds.), *Modern nutrition in health and disease* (9th ed., pp. 963–988). Baltimore, MD: Williams & Wilkins.

Truswell, S. (2002). Protein-energy malnutrition. In J. Mann & A. S. Truswell (Eds.), *Essentials of human nutrition* (2nd ed., pp. 289–298). Oxford: Oxford University Press.

Vanasse, A., Demers, M., Hemiari, A., & Courteau, J. (2006). Obesity in Canada: Where and how many? *International Journal of Obesity, 30*(4), 677–683.

Walker, A. C. (1970). Classification of infantile malnutrition. *Lancet, 2*(7681), 1028.

West, K. P., Caballero, B., & Black, R. E. (2006). Nutrition. In M. H. Merson, R. E. Black, & A. J. Mills (Eds.), *International public health: Diseases, programs, systems, and policies* (2nd ed., pp. 187–272). Sudbury, MA: Jones and Bartlett.

Wolf, A. M. (1998). What is the economic case for treating obesity? *Obesity Research, 6,* 2S.

World Health Organization. (2001a). *Iron deficiency anaemia: Assessment, prevention and control. A guide for programme managers.* Geneva: Author.

World Health Organization. (2001b). *Assessment of iodine deficiency disorders and monitoring their elimination: A guide for programme managers* (2nd ed.). Geneva: Author.

World Health Organization. (2004). *Iodine status worldwide: WHO global database on iodine deficiency.* Geneva: Author. Retrieved from http://whqlibdoc.who.int/publications/2004/9241592001.pdf

World Health Organization (2008a). Obesity and overweight. Retrieved from http://www.who.int/mediacentre/ factsheets/fs311/en/index.html

World Health Organization. (2008b). Diet. Retrieved from http://www.who.int/dietphysicalactivity/diet/en/index.html

Environmental Health and Population Issues

AFTER READING THIS CHAPTER YOU SHOULD BE ABLE TO

- Describe the major demographic trends of the 21st century and their long-term impacts
- Describe the major family planning programs under way internationally
- Describe the different human actions that cause climate change
- Describe the impact of climate change
- Discuss the major international treaties on climate change
- Discuss the major kinds of pollution and how each of them affects the ecosystem, including human health
- Describe the major efforts under way to counter the different kinds of pollution

GLOBAL DEMOGRAPHIC TRENDS

Global Population Structure

According to a report by the Central Intelligence Agency (CIA, 2008), the total population of the world as of July 2008 was estimated to be 6,677,563,921. The age structure of this population is such that it is predominantly composed of individuals between the ages of 15 and 64 years (65%); the 0- to 14-years bracket contributes 27% to the total breakdown, and the 65-and-over bracket 8%. The median age of a male currently is estimated at 27.4 years, whereas females have an estimated median age of 28.7 years.

The population growth rate has been pegged at 1.159%. The global birth and death rates are estimated to be 19.97 births per 1,000 population and 8.32 deaths per 1,000 people, respectively (CIA, 2008). For most of the population subgroups, the sex ratio is tilted toward males. The ratio of males to females at birth is 1.07; from birth to ages younger than 15 years, 1.06; and for ages 15 to 64 years, 1.02. It then shifts favorably toward females (presumably because of higher female longevity), to 0.78 males per female for the group aged 65 years and older. The life expectancy at birth for a male is 64.18 years, whereas that for a female is 68.2 years (CIA, 2008).

Rapid Population Growth

The rate of population growth varies tremendously across different regions of the world, but the 20th century provided an unusual scenario. Globally, the largest increase in population in the annals of human history was seen. This increase may be attributed partially to medical advances and partially to massive increases in agricultural productivity.

The United Nations estimated in 2000 that the global human population was enlarging at a rate of 1.14% (or about 75 million people) annually (U.S. Census Bureau, 2008). In the last couple of centuries, the number of people living on Earth has increased multiple times. Human population has increased by estimates of 203,800 to 211,090 every day (CIA, 2008). Even though the global population growth rate has been continually declining from its peak of 2.19% in 1963, growth remains high in the Middle East and sub-Saharan African regions (Nielsen, 2006).

Despite the global rapid population growth, some countries have been faced with a negative population growth (i.e., a net decrease in the population over time), especially in central and eastern Europe (mainly as a result of low fertility rates) and southern Africa (as a result of the high number of HIV-related deaths). Japan and certain western European countries are expected to encounter negative population growth due to subreplacement fertility rates within the next few decades.

Population growth that exceeds the **carrying capacity** of an area or environment (the maximum capacity of the area or environment to be able to support population)

Once it was necessary that the people should multiply and be fruitful if the race was to survive. But now to preserve the race it is necessary that people hold back the power of propagation.

—Helen Keller

results in overpopulation. On the other hand, if the populations are not large enough to maintain an ecosystem, the regions may remain underpopulated. Even though population growth around the world is rapidly declining, the population dynamics still boil down to a net positive rate of growth. The world population is expected to peak at 9.2 billion in 2075 (CIA, 2008; Nielsen, 2006; U.S. Census Bureau, 2008).

Global Urbanization

Apart from the recent meteoric rise in the sheer size of human population, several other trends define the way the distribution of the human population has changed in the recent past. According to a report by the United Nations Population Fund (2007), the world population was expected to surpass a historic milestone in the year 2008; the first time in the annals of mankind when more than half of the entire human population would be residing in urban areas. A report by the Central Intelligence Agency (2001) puts the estimated time for reaching this milestone somewhat conservatively at the year 2015. The number of people living in urban areas, however, is expected to burgeon to almost 5 billion by the year 2030, which would account for more than two-thirds of the developing world. **Urbanization** has been defined as the process of transition from a predominantly rural to an urban society (United Nations Population Fund [UNFPA], 2007).

The CIA report (2001) offers several other interesting aspects to this projected urban boom. The population growth rates in many rapidly urbanizing cities will be around 2.3% per year, compared with the world average of 1.8% for urban areas and about 1% for the total world population between 2000 and 2030. There will be further sprawling of mega-urban regions—also referred to as extended metropolitan regions—that might reach 80 million. The phenomenon will be particularly remarkable in the African and Asian continents, where the urban population is expected to double between the three decades spanning 2000 to 2030 (CIA, 2001; UNFPA, 2007).

The phenomenon of urbanization can be attributed to a number of socioeconomic factors; some of the more important of these factors are as follows (CIA, 2001):

- Access to information and the accompanying resurgence in urban centers as hubs of economic development
- Gradual loss of economic strength in rural areas
- Record low infant mortality rates combined with high birth rates
- Migration (It is important to note that the phenomenon of migration is both a demographic trend in itself and a potential causative factor that shapes and influences some of the other trends.)

Aging and the Youth Bulge

Perhaps the principal paradox evident in current global demographics is the simultaneous existence of two completely contradictory trends: the **youth bulge** and the phenomenon of aging. Research estimates reveal several startling facts. Before discussing the phenomenon of aging, it is useful to introduce the concept of an **age cohort**, which is a group of people delimited by an age-based criterion. Most demographic research is organized in terms of different age cohorts.

For instance, by 2050, the global cohort of people aged 65 years or older will triple in size to about 1.5 billion, or 16% of the total population, and even the youngest of the regions (i.e., Latin America, Asia, and Africa) will have sizeable elderly populations (CIA, 2001). The brunt of the impact of aging, however, will be felt by the industrialized regions, especially Europe and Japan (Shaw, 2001). Some other interesting facts regarding the phenomenon of aging are as follows (CIA, 2001; Shaw, 2001):

- By the year 2003, Italy will have nearly 19% elderly, followed closely by Japan in 2005, Germany in 2006, and Spain in around 2012. France and Britain will cross that milestone around 2016, and Canada and the United States in 2021 and 2023, respectively.
- With the current rates of growth and migration, the ratio of taxpaying workers to nontaxpaying pensioners in the developed world will plunge from a present-day ratio of 4:1 to a low of 2:1.
- There will be a precipitous decline in the labor force in the developed world despite some of the aging population being replaced by an incoming migrant workforce.

Despite this universal trend toward aging, many developing countries will exhibit the phenomenon of a youth bulge. The theory of youth bulge was first proposed by Gunnar Heinsohn, a German sociologist, who argued that an excess young adult male population is predictably responsible for social unrest, war, and terrorism (Heinsohn, 2003). Heinsohn has successfully employed his theory of youth bulge to explain social phenomena such as European colonialism, 20th-century fascism, and ongoing conflicts such as that in Darfur and terrorism.

The phenomenon of youth bulge remains one of the most impressive demographic trends of the 21st century. The trend is mostly visible in developing nations, the magnitude being notably substantial in **slum** populations. It is estimated that more than 60% of all urban occupants will be younger than 18 years by 2030 (UNFPA, 2007). The largest of these youth bulges will be located in Pakistan, Afghanistan, Saudi Arabia, Yemen, and Iraq. Young populations have a huge potential that, if tapped, can provide a dynamic and virtually illimitable source of energy. However, without proper nurture and guidance, it is quite possible to have this source of energy turn to destructive ways. Heinsohn's prophecy can and will be proven the hard way if urgent steps are not taken to address the youth bulge right now.

Demographic Transition

The twin concepts of youth bulge and aging can be understood better through the phenomenon of **demographic transition**. Demographers describe the history of population growth through a process termed the demographic transition, a paradigm that charts three characteristics of population growth (UNFPA, 2007). The model divides the history of population growth into four stages (**Figure 7.1**), characterized mainly by changing patterns of birth and death rates.

Stage 1: The first stage, which characterized the world throughout most of human history, is typically marked by high death and birth rates. No steady growth is achieved despite fluctuating population levels.

Stage 2: In this stage, birth rates are maintained at steady levels but mortality rates begin to decline secondary to improvements that reduce the toll of infectious diseases—the big killer in countries with high death rates. As a consequence, population begins to grow. The Western world entered this stage somewhere around 1800.

Stage 3: The decrease in death rates achieved in the previous stage continues and is accompanied by a decline in birth rates. Population continues to grow for years even after the drop in fertility rates because of a disproportionate share of people in the childbearing years.

Stage 4: This stage is marked by a rough parity between births and deaths and is exemplified by the situation of the developed world today. Population grows very sluggishly, and immigration becomes the driving force for additional population growth.

During the next several decades, regions in the early stages of the demographic transition are expected to generate a disproportionate share of global population growth. Sub-Saharan Africa, for instance, despite its high death rates, is the world's fastest-growing area, and nearly 60% of the population there lives in countries that are either in stage 1 or stage 2 of the population curve (UNFPA, 2007). The Middle East, the second-fastest-growing region, is somewhat farther along in the transition than Africa. Asia presents a more bipolar picture: about half of its population lives in countries that have reached stage 4; the other half are in countries at earlier stages. Latin

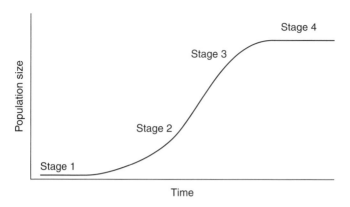

FIGURE 7.1   Sigmoid curve demonstrating the four stages of demographic transition.

America is largely in stage 3. Fertility rates there have dropped substantially, but the youthful age structure of the population still produces rapid growth. The region is expected to advance to the terminal stage in the coming years. North America and Europe, already in stage 4, are at or below replacement-fertility levels, but their demographic prospects differ because of their different policy approaches toward immigration (CIA, 2001; UNFPA, 2007).

Migration

Migration probably began with the birth of human civilization. Perhaps the simplest way of defining migration would be to picture it as a phenomenon of individuals moving from one country, place, or locality to another (International Organization for Migration, n.d.). The movement itself can be in groups or individually, unidirectional or bidirectional, and intermittent or continuous. The long-term trends of migration have been predicted in terms of the temporal profile of migration, the ethnic groups involved in the process, and the end destinations of the process. Human beings are known to have migrated extensively throughout the course of history.

In modern times, the phenomenon of migration of human populations has continued under both voluntary and involuntary forms—the former evidenced by movement within one's region, country, or beyond, and the latter illustrated by the slave trade, trafficking in human beings, and ethnic cleansing. Depending on the historical setting and perspective, individuals who migrate are called *migrants* or, more specifically, *emigrants*, *immigrants*, or *settlers*.

The forces of human migrations, whether as obvious invasions or by protracted cultural infiltration and resettlement, have affected major periods in human history (e.g., the fall of the Western Roman Empire); under the form of colonization, migration has transformed the world (e.g., the prehistoric and historic settlements of Australia and the Americas).

Different kinds of migration include the following:

- Daily human commuting
- Seasonal human migration (seen mostly in agriculturally based economies)
- Permanent migration, for the purposes of permanent or long-term stays
- Rural to urban (more common in developing countries secondary to urbanization)
- Urban to rural (more common in developed countries as a result of a higher cost of urban living)
- International migration (when persons cross state boundaries and stay in the host state for some minimum length of time)

Factors Governing Migration

The underlying factors governing migrations have changed over the centuries and continue to change. Some of these factors are constant; others are not. As an example, the trends of labor migration seen in the 21st century cannot be traced back to the 18th or 19th centuries. Most commonly, these factors can be divided into two broad categories: push and pull factors (**Table 7.1**). Both types of factors can be rooted in economics, politics, culture, and the environment (International Organization for Migration, n.d.; Kline, 2003).

Migration, like any other social trend, has the potential to influence multiple aspects of human life and has both advantages and disadvantages. Some figures regarding global migration are as follows (International Organization for Migration, n.d.):

- The total estimated number of migrants worldwide was approximately 191 million in 2005, up from 176 million in 2000. This number would potentially constitute the fifth most populous country in the world.
- Migrants make up roughly 3% of the global population.
- Females accounted for 49.6% of the total global migrants in 2005.
- Remittance flows in the year 2006 are estimated to have exceeded $276 billion worldwide, $206 billion of which went to developing countries.
- A total of 15 to 20% of the total global immigrant pool (roughly 30 to 40 million people) is composed of unauthorized migrants.

TABLE 7.1 Factors Governing Migration	
Push Factors	**Pull Factors**
Lack of job opportunities	Job opportunities
Primitive conditions	Better living conditions
Inadequate medical care	Advanced medical care
Political fear; religious intolerance	Political and/or religious freedom and persecution
Natural disasters; threats to life	Security
Slavery	Education
Poor housing/landlords	Family links
Poor chances of finding courtship	Better chances of finding courtship

- In 2006, the global number of refugees reached an estimated 9.9 million persons.

Some current global migration trends include the following (Omelaniuk, 2005):

- Migration flows have demonstrated significant shifts in recent years, with changing poles of attraction for labor migration.
- Some regions of the world have seen a total decrease of the migrant pool.
- Although the total number of Asian migrants increased from 28.1 million in 1970 to 43.8 million in 2000, Asia's share of the global migrant stock decreased from 34.5 to 25% during the same time frame.
- A similar trend was seen in Africa, with its share of international migrants dropping from 12% in 1970 to 9% in 2000.
- A sharp increase in the migrant stock was seen in North America between 1970 and 2000 (from 15.9 to 23.3%). A similar increase in the former Soviet Union during that time period (3.8 to 16.8%) is largely attributed to the redefinition of borders rather than the actual movement of people.
- The pool of international migrants continues to be concentrated in relatively select countries. For example, 75% of all international migrants are in 12% of all countries.

Some of the effects of migrations are as follows:

- Changes in population distribution
- Demographic consequences: Because migration is age selective, a crisis of aging can result in both the country of origin of the migrant populations and the destination country
- Economic results, which are of the greatest importance for the development of the countries

Ethnic Shifts

Globally, increased immigration and birth rates are skewed toward some ethnic groups but not others, causing profound **ethnic shifts**. Consequently, ethnic shifts are expected in the demographic distribution of countries with significant migrant stock. A 1996 report published by the U.S. Census Bureau (Campbell, 1996) projected that by the year 2050, immigration patterns and differences in birth rates, combined with an overall slowdown in growth of the country's population, will produce a United States in which 53% of the population will be non-Hispanic whites, down from 74% in 1996. The projections also maintain that Hispanic people will make up 24.5% of the population, up from 10.2% in 1996, and Asians will increase to 8.2% from 3.3%. A similar scenario is being forecasted for the United Kingdom; recent reports claim that a number of British towns and cities will have no single ethnic group in a majority within the next 30 years (Hill, 2007). Similar developments are expected in other countries with high migrant stocks.

Such ethnic shifts will change the overall structure and composition of the global human population. A cursory glance at Focus Feature 7.1 should be enough to make one ponder the gravity of such projections and how such trends will affect the overall structure of our society as a whole.

FOCUS FEATURE 7.1   Snapshot of the World Population in the Year 2020

If the total human population inhabiting earth in the year 2020 were scaled down to 100, the following would be the geographical distribution of people contributing to that figure:

- 56 of those individuals would hail from Asia, including 19 Chinese and 17 Indians.
- 13 would originate from the Northern hemisphere, including 4 from the United States.
- 16 of those people would come from Africa, including 13 from sub-Saharan Africa.
- 3 would be from the Middle East.
- 7 would be from eastern Europe and the former Soviet Union.
- 5 individuals would hail from western Europe.

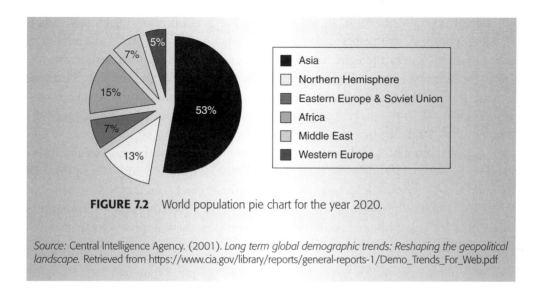

FIGURE 7.2   World population pie chart for the year 2020.

Source: Central Intelligence Agency. (2001). *Long term global demographic trends: Reshaping the geopolitical landscape.* Retrieved from https://www.cia.gov/library/reports/general-reports-1/Demo_Trends_For_Web.pdf

Implications of Current Demographic Trends

Humanitarian Crises

One of the many potential implications of the demographic trends just described is the genesis of multiple humanitarian crises around the globe. The widening youth bulge in developing nations could precipitate economic, political, and social turmoil and also boost external migration because of inadequate social mobility (CIA, 2001). In combination with high unemployment rates or state indifference, youth bulges have the potential to cause conflict and radical movements (Heinsohn, 2003). In some regions of the world, rapid population growth will intensify environmental degradation, the clash for limited resources, susceptibility to disease, and support for extremist political and religious movements, occasionally culminating in violent conflict. These issues will be particularly important for developing countries with high fertility rates and unstable or weak state institutions. Quite possibly, legal and illegal movement across national and international borders could evoke tensions, prejudice, and violence; strain health care delivery systems; and contribute to disease outbreaks, particularly in receiving areas.

Social Effects

Since the middle of the 20th century, the twin events of urbanization and migration have catalyzed cultural change both within countries and on a global scale. With the advancement of globalization, an unprecedented impact on ideas, values, and beliefs is being observed. Inequality becomes more manifest as the gap between social groups widens. Under such circumstances, cities can generate both creativity and solidarity on the one hand and acute conflicts on the other (Miranda, 2000). Growing cities, especially the metropolitans, harbor various generations of migrants, each with a different social and cultural background. A transition to an urban life exposes the newcomer to a medley of cultural stimuli, thereby providing opportunities for cultural enrichment. The social effects may also lead to a sense of marginalization, however, if the newcomer loses touch with his or her own norms and values; this can be followed by crises of identity, feelings of frustration, and aggressive behavior (UNFPA, 2007). The processes of modernization and globalization are sometimes met with a feeling of resentment by residents who view them as processes that are associated with an imposition of Western values on their own cultures (Massey, 1996; Roy, 2005).

Economic Effects

One of the most dramatic effects of the current demographic trends can be measured in economic terms. Increasing poverty in the increasing urban population has already been documented as a major socioeconomic problem in the developing world. With the phenomenon of urbanization expected to continue at least for several more decades, this problem is only expected to multiply.

The future economic effects of urbanization can be gauged from the following facts. More than 90% of slum dwellers today belong to the developing world. The rank order has south Asia with the largest share, followed by eastern Asia, sub-Saharan Africa, and Latin America. China and India together account for 37% of the world's slums. In sub-Saharan Africa, urbanization has become virtually synonymous with slum growth: 72% of the region's urban population live in slum conditions, compared with 56% in south Asia. The slum population of sub-Saharan Africa almost doubled in 15 years, reaching nearly 200 million in 2005, and is expected to further increase in the coming years at an alarming pace (UNFPA, 2007).

> A "slum household" is a group of individuals living under the same roof in an urban area who lack one or more of the following: durable housing, sufficient living area, access to improved water, access to sanitation and secure tenure.
>
> —United Nations (2006)

In certain cities of sub-Saharan Africa, sharing three toilets and one shower with 250 households in a community is not uncommon. Conditions like these are bound to increase stress on all the inhabitants, especially females. In Latin

America, only 33.6% of the urban poor have access to flush toilets, compared with 63.7% of their nonpoor urban counterparts (Montgomery, 2007; UNFPA, 2007).

Data regarding within-city differentials reveal striking differences in access to education and levels of literacy between slums and more affluent neighborhoods. In some countries, such as Bangladesh, Colombia, India, and Pakistan, the literacy of women living in slums is 30 to 50% lower than those in nonslum communities. Age at marriage, pregnancy, and household responsibilities greatly influence the ability of young people to continue school. Young women and men in low-income households are more likely to have children, be married, or head a household than their upper-income counterparts (United Nations, 2006; UNFPA, 2007).

Health Effects

Health concerns are likely to move to the forefront of our problems. Infectious diseases are expected to continue to be leading causes of death in developing nations. Of the seven biggest killers worldwide, tuberculosis, malaria, hepatitis, and, of note, HIV/AIDS continue to swell. HIV/AIDS and tuberculosis are expected to account for the majority of deaths from infectious disease in developing countries by 2020. The rapid spread of infectious conditions would likely result in changes in human behavior:

Whereas infections will continue to claim a large toll of lives in the developing world and consequently aggravate and occasionally even cause economic decay, social division, and political destabilization in the hardest-hit countries in the developing world, lifestyle-induced diseases are expected to continue being increasingly important factors in the number of aged population who need costly long-term care. Some of the more likely global threats divided in terms of the geographic regions are as follows (CIA, 2001):

- Sub-Saharan Africa will continue to be the region hardest hit by infectious diseases, with about half of the deaths by infectious diseases being claimed by the region. The health care capacity of sub-Saharan Africa is expected to continue to lag behind that of the Western world and even behind that of the developing world.
- The Asian continent and the Pacific, where multidrug-resistant tuberculosis, malaria, and cholera are epidemic, will probably experience an alarming increase in the number of deaths due to infectious diseases. The spread of HIV/AIDS in east Asia will further bolster this ominous trend.

- The part of the world that comprised the former Soviet Union and parts of eastern Europe will likely witness a sizeable surge in infectious disease incidence and death, the effect being more pronounced in the former Soviet Union than elsewhere. A precipitous decline in the quality of health care and related services in the erstwhile Soviet Union has ushered in a resurgence of diphtheria, cholera, hepatitis B and C, and tuberculosis.
- Latin American countries have shown good progress in the control of infectious diseases, but lopsided economic development has facilitated the resurgence of certain infectious diseases such as cholera, malaria, and tuberculosis and, in some regions, dengue.
- The Middle East and north African geographic zones have limited prevalence of HIV/AIDS and malaria despite a significant prevalence of tuberculosis and hepatitis B and C. Conservative customs, climate, and the high health care budget are factors that help to some extent. However, isolated epidemics (a prevalence of 5% or more in some subpopulations) have been reported among intravenous drug users in Iran and Libya, a disconcerting trend that may portend that a major epidemic is in the making (Obermeyer, 2006).
- In western Europe and North America (the developed world), lifestyle–related diseases remain the biggest threats, with cancer, diabetes, and heart diseases being some of the major players. However, in today's world of international travel and trade, the risk of importing exotic diseases such as tuberculosis, HIV/AIDS, and hepatitis B and C is increased.

Environmental Effects

Multiple environmental effects of population growth have already been observed, and these effects are expected to magnify and become more manifest with passing time. Freshwater scarcity, **deforestation** (the conversion of forests to agricultural land), soil deterioration, and environmental disasters are just some of the more important implications of population growth.

Freshwater Scarcity   The availability of water is likely to come to the forefront of all problems facing mankind in the 21st century. With global water consumption rising rapidly, scarcity of water will be a pressing global challenge (Vorosmarty, Green, Salisbury, & Lammers, 2000). This situation will be further compounded by population growth, leading to severe water scarcities, particularly in the Middle East, sub-Saharan Africa, south Asia, and China, a trend that may heighten regional tensions between different countries. Over 3 billion people in over 48 countries will be facing a freshwater shortage by the year 2025 (CIA, 2001).

Deforestation   Research has provided a convincing relationship between population growth and the phenomenon of deforestation (Ehrhardt-Martinez, 1998; Mather & Needle, 2000). A report by the United Nations Food and Agriculture Organization (2005) presented several important findings. Currently, forests cover 30% of the total land area, but the distribution between different countries is highly skewed. Whereas the ten most forest-rich countries account for two-thirds of the forest areas, there are ten countries with absolutely no forest cover. The report also notes that total forest area continues to decrease, although the rate of net loss had slowed down. Another important finding is that the data related to deforestation are severely underreported. Finally, although deforestation has been arrested and even reversed in regions of Europe and North America, a continuous demand for wood and wood products in developed countries will continue to put pressure on forests there (Food and Agriculture Organization, 2005). This demand will be much more acute in developing countries.

Soil Deterioration   Human activities have often led to degradation of the world's land resources, which are the basis for sustained food security. This phenomenon is called *soil deterioration*. A global assessment of human-induced soil degradation shows that 15% of the total world land has undergone some land damage (Bridges & Oldeman, 1999; Oldeman, Hakkeling, & Sombroek, 1990). Thirteen percent of this land damage has been graded as light and moderate, and 2% as severe and very severe. The factors responsible for deterioration have mainly been erosion, a decline in the nutrient levels, and **salinization** (accumulation of water-soluble salts in the soil secondary to human activities). Severely degraded soil is found in most parts of the world. However, the negative impact of soil degradation hits agriculturally based economies the hardest.

Natural or Human-Made Environmental Disasters   Environmental disasters, natural and human made, are expected to cause damaging effects on man and the material world due mainly to the thriving human populations in vulnerable areas. The developing countries have a poor infrastructure for dealing with disasters. According to the Centre for Research on the Epidemiology of Disasters (n.d.), there were a total of 1,312 disasters during the 25 years from 1966 to 1990, which killed 1.7 million people and affected more than 2 billion, in the top ten most disaster-prone countries of the Asia-Pacific region, namely, Australia, Bangladesh, China, India, Indonesia, Iran, Japan, New Zealand, the Philippines, and Vietnam. The number of accidents such as the Bhopal gas tragedy, in which an accidental release of the toxic gas methyl-isocyanate into the environment claimed more than 10,000 lives in India, and the Chernobyl disaster in Russia, which remains the worst nuclear power plant accident in history, is expected to rise.

World Population Day

World Population Day is an annual event, observed on July 11, that is designed to spread awareness of global population issues. The governing council of the United Nations Development Program established this event in 1989. Interest in this date was roused on July 11, 1987, the approximate date on which the world's population reached a count of 5 billion people.

The theme for the 2008 World Population Day as envisaged by the United Nations Population Fund (2008) was "Plan Your Future: Plan Your Family." The idea driving the theme is that when people plan their families they can plan their lives and devise ways and strategies to counter poverty because the socioeconomic status of a family depends on the number of children in that family to a large extent. Some of the recent themes of World Population Day have been closely linked to maternal and child and adolescent health, such as the 2007 theme of "Men as Partners in Maternal Health," the 2006 theme of "Young People," and the 2005 theme of "Equality Empowers."

FAMILY PLANNING

Despite the development of safer and more effective contraceptives and the provision of affordable and accessible **family planning** services in recent decades, millions of individuals and couples globally are unable to plan their families according to their desires. More than 120 million couples do not use contraceptives, despite an interest in spacing or limiting childbearing (World Health Organization [WHO], n.d.). Moreover, many females who do use contraceptives end up becoming pregnant, whereas some couples who want to bear children are unable to conceive.

Family planning implies the ability of individuals and couples to anticipate and attain their desired number of children and the spacing and timing of their births. It is achieved through use of contraceptive methods and the treatment of involuntary infertility.

—WHO Department of Reproductive Health and Research

Factors that can account for this huge unmet need for family planning services are as follows (WHO, n.d.):

- Deficiency of services or barriers to their access
- Poor quality of services, such as suboptimal interactions between clients and providers, substandard

technical competence of providers, inadequate information, and poor design and management of service delivery systems

- Issues pertaining to technology, for instance, limited or inappropriate choice of methods, fear, or the side effect profile of a particular contraceptive method
- Social issues, such as an individual's lack of knowledge, power struggles within couples and families, and sociocultural, religious, and gender barriers

Family planning is not simply controlling family size. It is a process through which couples can exercise control over the spacing and timing of their children. This section discusses some of the more noteworthy family planning policies from around the globe.

China

The **one-child policy** is the population control policy (or planned birth policy) of the People's Republic of China (PRC). It was introduced in 1979 by the Chinese government as a means to ease the social and environmental problems of China (Hesketh, Lu, & Xing, 2005). The policy remains controversial both inside and outside China because of the issues it raises, because of the manner in which the policy has been executed, and because of attendant concerns about negative economic and social consequences. The one-child policy is enforced at the provincial level through fines that are imposed based on the income of the family and other factors. The policy is expected to be in place for at least the next few years.

The effects of the one-child policy and the debate surrounding its basic premise (voluntary versus involuntary birth control) are controversial. The total fertility rate (defined as the average number of children born per woman) in China has fallen from 2.9 in 1979 to 1.7 in 2004, with a rate of 1.3 in urban areas and just under 2.0 in rural areas. A peculiar demographic pattern of urban families with predominantly one child and rural families with predominantly two children has resulted as a result of this trend (Hesketh, Lu, & Xing, 2005). It has been argued that the compulsory one-child approach may only be partially responsible for the reduction in the total fertility rate. The most striking decrease in the rate occurred before the one-child policy replaced the largely voluntary "late, long, few" policy (Hesketh, Lu, & Xing, 2005). That strategy recommended later childbearing, greater spacing between children, and fewer children and halved the total fertility from 5.9 to 2.9.

The one-child policy has been blamed for resulting in a skewed sex ratio. Since the onset of the one-child policy, there has been a steady increase in the reported sex ratio, from 1.06 in 1979 to 1.11 in 1988, and to 1.17 in 2001.

India

Currently, India's annual population growth rate is 1.74%. It is the second most populous country in the world, contributing about 20% of births worldwide (South-East Asia Regional Office [SEARO], n.d.). In 1952 the Indian government was one of the first governing bodies to formulate a national family planning program. Some of the more important features of the family planning initiatives adopted in India are as follows (SEARO, n.d.):

- From its inception in the early 1950s, the family planning initiatives have been completely voluntary.
- The planning initiatives have been largely decentralized, with the onus of responsibility lying with local governing bodies.
- Legislation has been passed to regulate and prevent the misuse of modern prenatal diagnostic techniques, largely for sex-selective abortion.
- In 2000, the National Population Policy advocated a holistic, multisectoral approach toward population stabilization. For the first time it was decided to set no targets for specific contraceptive methods except for achieving a national average total fertility rate of 2.1 by the year 2010. As a consequence, there was a major paradigm shift from centrally fixed targets to target-free dispensation through a decentralized, participatory approach.

Regardless of the definitive gains made, there still remains a large unmet need for contraception in India. A significant percentage of pregnancies (21% of all pregnancies that result in live births) are still untimed or unintentional. Although the family planning needs of the majority (86%) of women who wish to stop childbearing are being satisfied, the needs of women who wish to delay or space childbearing remain largely unsatisfied (only 30% of these women have their needs met). Consequently, the National Population Policy, the guiding framework for family planning efforts, has included the twin objectives of population stabilization and promoting reproductive health within the wider context of sustainable development (National Commission on Population, n.d.).

Iran

Between 1956 and 1986 Iran's population grew at a rate of more than 3% per year. After the government-led initiation of a major population control program in the mid-1980s, the rate began to decline. By 2007 the growth rate had declined to 0.7% per year, with a birth rate of 17 per 1,000 persons and a death rate of 6 per 1,000 (Roudi-Fahimi, 1999, 2002).

In December 1989, the revived family planning program was inaugurated with three major goals:

- Encourage spacing of three to four years between pregnancies
- Discourage pregnancies among women aged under 18 and over 35 years
- Limit family size to three children. In May 1993, a law was passed that included disincentive penalties for couples who had more than three children

According to the Iranian Ministry of Health and Medical Education, there was an increased use of contraceptives among married women, and the total fertility rate dropped from 5.2 to 2.6 children. Consequent to the precipitous drop in its growth rate from an all-time high of 3.2% in 1986 to just 1.2% in 2001, Iran has emerged as a model for other countries that want to lessen the risk of overpopulation (Roudi-Fahimi, 1999, 2002).

This rapid decline in growth is attributed to a combination of factors, chiefly the disincentive penalties for couples with more than three children, the wide availability and increased acceptance of contraceptives by couples, and the involvement of the religious clergy in the whole process. Interestingly, committed health professionals even obtained fatwas (religious proclamations concerning everyday life) from top-ranking clerics to the effect that "contraceptive use was not against Islamic principles as long as it was used with the informed consent of the husband and did not endanger the health of the couple" (Roudi-Fahimi, 1999, 2002).

United States of America

In the United States, Title X of the Public Health Service Act enacted in 1970 provides access to contraceptive services, supplies, and information to those requiring it (Friedman, 2007). People with low income receive priority for services. Title X is a vital source of funding for family planning clinics across the country. These clinics have a pivotal role in the provision of reproductive health care. The education and services supplied by the Title X–funded clinics support both young individuals and low-income families (Alan Guttmacher Institute, 1997; Friedman, 2007).

Title X has allowed millions of American women to receive necessary reproductive health care, plan their pregnancies, and prevent abortions. It is dedicated exclusively to funding family planning and reproductive health care services. The impact of Title X on the reproductive health of couples has been phenomenal. The following facts help exemplify the phenomenal impact of this program (Alan Guttmacher Institute, 1997):

- Each year, publicly funded contraceptive services help women avoid 1.3 million unintended pregnancies, which would end up in 534,000 births, 632,000 abortions, and 165,000 miscarriages.
- It is projected that the number of total abortions within the United States would be 40% higher than it is currently if the publicly funded family planning services were not available.
- Abortions in teenagers would increase by 58% of the current value in the absence of family planning programs.
- In the absence of publicly funded family planning services, an extra 356,000 unmarried women would give birth each year. This would swell the total out-of-wedlock births by one-quarter.

Africa

Despite the fact that in the developing world as a whole the average number of children born per woman has declined from 6.1 in the 1960s to 3.8 in 1990, a lot of ground still remains to be covered. This decline has not been uniform, and there is an immense variation among different regions (Bongaarts, 1994). The most impressive gains have been made in east Asia, where fertility has declined to 2.3 births per woman, a level that parallels the developed world. However, reproductive behavior has changed very little, if at all, in sub-Saharan African nations such as Botswana, Kenya, South Africa, and Zimbabwe (Bongaarts, 1994).

The only evidence of modern contraception in Africa in the 1970s was either in the form of pilot program activities (National Research Council, 1993) or the early efforts of International Planned Parenthood affiliates and other nongovernmental organizations, which operated mostly in urban areas. Mainly because they did not experience the high population density that characterized the Asian context, African policy makers expressed little encouragement for population control. This was the time when the first family planning programs were in their infancy in Asia and Latin America. The issue of family planning was controversial in the sociocultural setting in most of Africa, which was another disincentive for the policy makers (Miller, Miller, Askew, Marjorie, & Ndhlovu, 1998).

During the 1990s the vast majority of women in most African nations received modern family planning methods from governmental sources, rather than from nongovernmental agencies, pharmacies, or private practitioners. Among users of prevailing contraception methods, the proportions receiving them from governmental sources ranged from 95% in Botswana and 71% in Kenya (two of the most successful programs) to a low of 43% in Ghana (Ross, Mauldin, & Miller, 1993). One hallmark of African family planning efforts has been the delivery of family planning services mainly through governmental health facilities rather than community-based distribution systems. The latter have been implemented on a much more restricted scale in Africa than was the case in Asia in the 1970s and 1980s (Phillips & Greene, 1993).

In their analysis of the reasons why the family planning situation in parts of Africa remained grim despite significant gains in other parts of the continent, Miller and colleagues (1998) found that the clinic facilities that are the hallmark of the family planning efforts are plagued with problems. Their analysis revealed serious imperfections across the entire gamut of functioning, and most importantly in the availability of and access to services, the gap between family planning services offered in urban centers as opposed to rural centers, technical competence, and the availability and functioning of infrastructure.

Some of the recommendations that have been made to improve family planning endeavors in Africa are: more efficient use of existing resources; improved staff training on specific issues, particularly on broader reproductive health counseling; closing the gap between established protocols and provider behavior; strengthening supervisor training and widening the introduction of new supervisory tools; and more research for better comprehension of the factors supporting the present pattern of service delivery, as well as client perspectives on quality (Cleland et al., 2006; Miller et al., 1998).

CLIMATE CHANGE AND GLOBAL WARMING

The term **climate change** implies any significant alteration in the indices used to measure climate (such as temperature, precipitation, or wind) extending for a longer than usual duration. Usually, climate trends span decades or even longer (Environmental Protection Agency [EPA], n.d.). The factors that can lead to climate change can be natural factors such as changes in the intensity of the sun; other natural processes within our climate system (e.g., changes in ocean circulation); and human activities that change the basic composition of the atmosphere (e.g., consumption of fossil fuels) and the land surface (e.g., deforestation, reforestation, urbanization, soil erosion secondary to human-made structures such as dams, desertification) and consequently affect the climate.

Global warming, although included within the larger umbrella expression of climate change, is a separate entity that refers to an average increase in the temperature of the atmosphere near the Earth's surface and in the troposphere, which can contribute to changes in the patterns of climate globally (EPA, n.d.). Global warming can occur from a variety of causes, both natural and human induced. Usually, however, the phrase "global warming" describes the warming that accompanies increased emissions of greenhouse gases from human activities.

Greenhouse gases are heat-trapping gases that basically prevent heat from escaping to space, in a manner similar to the glass panels of a greenhouse. For over the past two centuries, the combustion of fossil fuels, mostly coal and oil, and deforestation have caused the concentrations of heat-trapping greenhouse gases to increase significantly in the atmosphere (EPA, n.d.). Even though greenhouse gases such as carbon dioxide and methane are indispensable to human life, they pose a grave threat to the environment because their concentrations continue to rise in the atmosphere. Evidence shows that the average surface temperature on Earth has risen by about 1.2° to 1.4°F in the last 100 years (Lindgren & Gustafson, 2001; Solomon et al., 2007a, 2007b). Since 1850, the top eight warmest years have been documented since 1998, and 2005 was the warmest year on record. The report by Solomon and colleagues (2007a, 2007b) argues that most of the warming in recent decades is very likely attributable to human activities. Other aspects of the climate that have been found to be changing are rainfall patterns, snow and ice cover, and sea level. Climate models project that if greenhouse gases continue to increase at their current rates, the average temperature at the Earth's surface could increase from 3.2° to 7.2°F above 1990 levels by the end of the 21st century.

Greenhouse Effect

The energy from the sun that powers Earth's climate is partly (one-third) reflected back in space and partly (two-thirds) absorbed by the surface and, to a lesser extent, by the atmosphere. To balance the absorbed incoming energy, the Earth radiates energy back to space; however, because Earth is much colder than the sun, it radiates at a different wavelength, and much of that radiation is absorbed by the atmosphere, including clouds, and reradiated back to Earth. This is called the **greenhouse effect**.

Analogous to the glass walls in a greenhouse that reduce airflow and increase the temperature of the air inside, the Earth's greenhouse effect warms the surface of the planet. The natural greenhouse effect is needed for the very sustenance of life—in its absence, the average temperature at Earth's surface would be below the freezing point of water. However, human activities, mainly the combustion of fossil fuels and deforestation, greatly intensify this natural greenhouse effect, setting the process of global warming into motion.

How Human Activities Bring About Climate Change

Some of the ways in which human activities have affected the climate are as follows:

- Carbon dioxide emissions have increased from fossil fuels used in transportation, heating and cooling systems in buildings, and the manufacture of cement and multiple other processes (Solomon et al., 2007a, 2007b). Furthermore, the process of deforestation releases carbon dioxide and minimizes its uptake by plants.
- Methane levels have increased as a result of human activities closely related to agriculture, natural gas distribution, and landfills. Methane, however, is not a potent contributor to climate change and the global warming phenomenon.
- Fossil fuel combustion and fertilizer use also emit nitrous oxide, a potent greenhouse gas.
- Halocarbon gases such as the chlorofluorocarbons (e.g., CFC-11 and CFC-12) were extensively used as refrigeration agents and in multiple other industrial processes until their atmospheric concentration was found to cause ozone depletion. Fortunately, their abundance is decreasing thanks to the adoption of international regulations such as the Montreal Protocol in 1987, designed to protect the ozone layer (Haas, 1992). Ozone is one of the many greenhouse gases that is continually manufactured and destroyed in the atmosphere by natural chemical reactions. However, this balance has been tipped in the troposphere, one of the many layers of the atmosphere, by human activities that cause release of gases such as carbon monoxide, hydrocarbons, and nitrogen oxide, chemicals that react to produce ozone. Halocarbons released by human activities destroy ozone in the stratosphere and have caused the ozone hole over Antarctica.
- Water vapor is the most plentiful and important of all the greenhouse gases. Human activities have only had a marginal influence in affecting water vapor levels, and the influence is essentially exerted indirectly. A warmer atmosphere is known to contain a higher percentage of water vapor. The rise of several other greenhouse gases has indirectly led to a small increase in the atmospheric levels of water vapor.
- Aerosols are tiny particles with widely differing sizes, concentration, and chemical structure present in the atmosphere abundantly. They contain both naturally occurring chemicals as well as those emitted as a result of human activities. Fossil fuel and biomass burning have increased the presence of aerosols containing sulphur and organic compounds (Solomon et al., 2007b).

- Wastes can be divided into two broad categories depending on the duration it takes for them to be dissipated. *Biodegradable waste* is a type of waste, typically originating from plant or animal sources, that can be broken down by other living organisms. Waste that cannot be broken down by other living organisms for prolonged periods of time is called *nonbiodegradable waste*. Styrofoam is a good example of the latter, whereas sewage and food wastes exemplify biodegradable wastes. Human activities have generated a large amount of nonbiodegradable waste.

Climate Change Effects

Research evidence from simulation models and projections based on existing environmental models have led environmentalists and scientists to propose some fairly damaging consequences of climate change if the current trends were to continue. The Intergovernmental Panel on Climate Change (IPCC) was established jointly by the World Meteorological Organization and the United Nations Environment Program to provide an authoritative international consensus of scientific understanding pertaining to climate change. The panel's regular assessments of the causes, effects, and possible response strategies to climate change provide a fairly exhaustive and reliable source of information pertaining to climate change. The possible effects of climate change are discussed in the 2001 IPCC report (McCarthy, Osvaldo, Leary, Dokken, & White, 2001) and include effects on ecosystems, human health, agriculture, the polar regions, precipitation, and the sea level.

Effects on Ecosystems

Ecosystem damage has already been seen as a direct consequence of climatic change (Brown, Valone, & Curting, 1997). As the climate continues to warm, major changes may occur in ecosystem structure and function, species' ecological interactions, and species' geographic ranges, with predominantly negative consequences for biodiversity. In addition, climate changes such as increased floods and droughts are predicted to increase the risk of extinction for some plant and animal species, many of which are already at risk as a result of other non-climate-related factors.

Effects on Human Health

The prevalence of some diseases and other threats to human health depends largely on local climate. Extremely hostile weather conditions always have the potential to disrupt human health. Excessively high temperatures can lead directly to loss of life or heat-related illnesses, whereas a reduction in the severity of winters can potentially decrease the number of cold-related deaths. Climate-related disturbances in ecological systems, such as changes in the range of some parasites, can indirectly affect the incidence of serious infectious diseases. An earlier onset of the spring pollen season in parts of Europe and North America has already been documented as a consequence of climate change (McCarthy et al., 2001). Moreover, higher temperatures can increase air and water pollution, which in turn harm human health.

Kovats and colleagues (1999) reviewed the existing state of knowledge regarding climate change and its impact on human health in the European region. They concluded that climate change, including changes in thermal stress and in the distribution and seasonality of vector-borne diseases, influence human health and recommended that monitoring of health indicators, including enhanced surveillance of diseases sensitive to climate, should be developed to detect and respond to the impacts of climate change on human health.

Changes Affecting Agriculture

Variations in climate and weather extremes hold enormous potential to affect agriculture. To a large extent, farm productivity depends on climatic factors. Although some characteristics of the forecasted climate change are expected to augment food production (e.g., higher rainfalls, longer growing season), other factors (e.g., floods and heat waves) will undoubtedly have adverse effects. The end result would depend on an interaction of the positive and negative factors and is fairly difficult to predict at this point.

Changes in the Polar Regions

It is expected that as a consequence of global warming the polar ice caps will warm to a greater magnitude than any other part of the world. Ice has a greater reflectivity than either ocean or land. As the highly reflective snow melts, darker land and ocean surface is exposed, which absorbs more of the heat than it reflects and further heats the planet, perpetuating a vicious cycle. Melting due to climate change is predicted to diminish the extent of the polar ice caps and further threaten the existence of several endangered Arctic plant and animal species (McCarthy et al., 2001).

Changes in Precipitation

Research estimates maintain that rising temperatures globally have caused a 5% increase in the concentration of atmospheric water vapor. This, in turn, has translated into an increased intensity of precipitation and the impending risk of heavy rains and snow. Higher temperatures are also associated with the risk of increased evaporation and consequently the risk of droughts in some areas. Climate change thus increases the risk of both floods and droughts.

Changes in Sea Level

Recently, sea levels have risen worldwide, the approximate rise being 4.8 to 8.8 inches during the last 100 years (McCarthy et al., 2001). Scientific predictions maintain that by the year 2100, the global average sea level will have risen by 7 to 24 inches. Melting ice sheets could further contribute to this sea level rise.

International Treaties and Protocols Related to Climate Change

Kyoto Protocol

The Kyoto Protocol is a multinational agreement linked to the United Nations Framework Convention on Climate Change (UNFCCC). The importance of the Kyoto Protocol lies in the fact that it lays down binding targets for 37 developed nations and the European community for reducing greenhouse gas emissions.

The major distinction between the protocol and the framework convention is that whereas the convention encouraged industrialized countries to stabilize greenhouse gas emissions, the protocol commits them to do so. Recognizing that developed countries are principally responsible for the current high levels of greenhouse gas emissions in the atmosphere as a result of more than 150 years of industrial activity, the protocol places a heavier burden on developed nations under the principle of "common but differentiated responsibilities" (UNFCCC, n.d.).

The Kyoto Protocol was adopted in Kyoto, Japan, on December 11, 1997, and implemented with full effect on February 16, 2005. To date, 180 nations have ratified the treaty. The comprehensive rules for the implementation of the Kyoto Protocol were adopted three years later, in 2001, and are called the Marrakesh Accords (UNFCCC, n.d.).

The Kyoto Mechanisms The means that the protocol lays down for successful attainment of target emission rates have come to be called the Kyoto mechanisms. The mechanisms are market-based approaches that can aid the individual measures implemented by the different countries. These mechanisms are as follows:

- *Emissions trading (also known as the carbon market):* Countries with obligations under the Kyoto Protocol have acknowledged targets for curbing or reducing emissions. The targets are defined as levels of allowed emissions from 2008 to 2012. Emissions trading, as the Kyoto Protocol defines it, allows nations with excess emission units to sell those excess units to countries that are over their targets. Hence, the protocol resulted in the creation of a new commodity in the form of emission reductions and removals. Carbon dioxide is the primary greenhouse gas. Therefore, this bargaining between member nations has come to be called *carbon trading*, and the institution is widely known as the carbon market.

- *The clean development mechanism (CDM):* The CDM allows a country with an emission-reduction or emission-limitation commitment some leeway in the manner by which the reduction or limitation is executed. Developed countries with such commitments can implement emission-reduction projects in the developing world and earn emission credits. A CDM project activity might, for instance, involve the implementation of a solar panel–based electrification program to replace conventional fossil fuel–based systems in the rural outreaches of a developing nation. This system stimulates emission reductions and provides the industrialized countries a degree of flexibility in meeting their emission targets.

- *Joint implementation:* Article 6 of the Kyoto Protocol defines joint implementation as a means by which one country with an emission reduction or limitation obligation under the Kyoto Protocol can earn emission reduction units (ERUs) that count toward its Kyoto targets by implementing emission-reduction or emission-removal projects in another country. Joint implementation offers the signatories an accommodating and cost-effective symbiotic means of fulfilling a part of their Kyoto commitments, which benefits the host party through the influx of investment and technology.

Montreal Protocol

The Montreal Protocol on ozone-depleting substances is an international treaty designed to protect the ozone layer by gradually phasing out the production of a number of human-made chemicals that when released into the atmosphere are believed to be responsible for ozone depletion (United Nations Environment Program [UNEP], 2000). The consequences of ozone depletion can be disastrous. Once the protective ozone shield is depleted, increased levels of ultraviolet radiation reaching the Earth's surface would result in elevated rates of skin cancers and cataracts and cause impairment of human immune systems. Agricultural productivity and levels of oceanic plankton would also be adversely affected as a consequence.

> *Perhaps the single most successful international agreement to date has been the Montreal Protocol.*
>
> —Kofi Annan,
> former secretary-general
> of the United Nations

The Montreal Protocol was opened for signatures on September 16, 1987, and entered into force on January 1, 1989. It has undergone seven revisions since its inception. The protocol has been acknowledged as an example of exceptional international solidarity.

The actual treaty focuses on halogenated hydrocarbons—human-made chemicals that have been proven to cause depletion of the ozone layer. The halogenated hydrocarbons, also called chlorofluorocarbons (CFCs), contain either chlorine or bromine and are capable of causing such depletion. The treaty sets down a timetable for each group of hydrocarbons, target deadlines by which those chemicals must be phased out and ultimately eliminated. The purpose of the treaty is for the signatory nations to accept a succession of stepped limits on the production and use of CFCs (UNEP, 2000). Some of these stipulations are as follows.

- *1991 to 1992:* Levels of consumption and production of the controlled substances in specified signatory countries (developed countries) do not exceed 150% of its calculated levels of production and consumption of those substances in 1986.
- *1994 to 1996:* Levels of production and consumption of those controlled substances in the signatory nations does not exceed, on a yearly basis, 25% of its calculated level of consumption and production in 1986.
- *1996 onward:* The production and consumption of the controlled substances should not exceed zero.

The protocol also specifies a slower phase-out of other substances, and certain chemical compounds (e.g., carbon tetrachloride) have been given special attention. The less active CFCs will be completely phased out over an extended time by a target deadline of 2030 (UNEP, 2000).

Antarctic Treaty System

The Antarctic Treaty and related agreements, collectively called the Antarctic Treaty System or ATS, regulate international relations among states with respect to Antarctica, the only continent on Earth without an indigenous population (Scientific Committee on Antarctic Research, 2008). For the purpose of the treaty, Antarctica has been defined as all land and ice shelves south of 60°S latitude parallel. Forty-six countries, including the United Kingdom, the United States, and the former Soviet Union, are signatories to this treaty.

The treaty establishes the Antarctic region as a scientific zone and preserve, thereby emphasizing freedom of scientific investigation in that region and holding all territorial claims in suspension. Military activity on the glacial continent is completely banned under the provisions of this treaty. This was the first arms control agreement established during the Cold War (Scientific Committee on Antarctic Research, 2008).

United Nations Framework Convention on Climate Change

The United Nations Framework Convention on Climate Change is an international environmental accord that was produced at the United Nations Conference on Environment and Development, also known as the Earth Summit, organized in Rio de Janeiro in 1992. The treaty was directed toward the stabilization of greenhouse gas concentrations in the atmosphere at a level that would prevent hazardous human interference with the climate system (UNFCCC, 1992).

In its original form, the treaty set no mandatory limits on greenhouse gas emissions for individual signatories, contained no enforcement provisions, and was nonbinding for all legal purposes. The treaty did have provisions for future updates that could mandate emission limits. The Kyoto Protocol was the main update to the UNFCCC. The Convention on Climate Change first set an overall framework for intergovernmental endeavors to engage with the climate challenges brought on as a result of human activities. The convention enjoys almost universal membership, with 192 countries having ratified.

The convention provides ways through which international signatories can collect and share information related to greenhouse emissions. It also includes provisions for financial and technological support to developing countries for adaptation to the impacts of climate change. Officially, the convention entered into force on March 21, 1994. The establishment of a national greenhouse inventory, as a count of greenhouse gas emissions and removals, was the first achievement of the convention. The convention mandates submission of these inventories by member countries on a regular basis.

Stockholm Convention

The Stockholm Convention is an international agreement, legally binding on signatory nations, pertaining to **persistent organic pollutants**, which are defined by the United Nations Environment Program as "chemical substances that persist in the environment, bio-accumulate through the food web, and pose a risk of causing adverse effects to human health and the environment" (UNEP, 2008a). In 1995 the agency called for international action to counter the threat posed by persistent organic pollutants.

The convention entered into force on May 17, 2004. An agreement was reached to outlaw several of the chemicals identified as persistent organic pollutants and limit the use of DDT (dichloro-diphenyl-trichloroethane, a synthetic pesticide) to malaria control and to curtail inadvertent production of more persistent organic pollutants. Currently, the convention is reviewing several other substances for inclusion in the agreement.

AIR POLLUTION

Air pollution refers to the deterioration of ambient air secondary to multiple sources such as factories, power plants, dry cleaners, cars, buses, trucks, and even windblown dust and wildfires. Air pollution can threaten the health of human beings, plants, and animals and can potentially damage the ozone layer and buildings (EPA, 2008a). It may also cause haze and reduce visibility in national parks and wilderness areas. Air pollution can be either indoor (within the confines of a building) or outdoor.

Some common indoor pollutants are radon, molds, asbestos fibers, volatile organic compounds, and carbon monoxide. One of the important indices of indoor air pollution is **indoor air quality** (IAQ), which deals mainly with the content of interior air that could adversely affect the health and comfort of the inhabitants of that building. The IAQ may be disrupted by microbial contaminants (mold, bacteria), chemicals (such as carbon monoxide or radon), allergens, or any mass or energy stressor that can generate health effects. In fact, indoor air is often a greater health hazard than the corresponding outdoor setting because of the protracted amount of exposure time and the relatively lesser dilution of the toxic contaminant. A key source of indoor air pollution in developing, but not developed, countries is the combustion of biomass (e.g., wood, charcoal, dung, or crop residue) for heating and cooking.

Air pollution is usually concentrated in heavily populated metropolitan regions, especially in developing countries where environmental regulations are more permissive than the developed world. However, unhealthy levels of pollution are frequently found even in densely populated areas of developed countries. **Table 7.2** lists some of the most polluted cities of the world according to a 2004 estimate that was based on the amount of particulate matter (tiny particles of solid or liquid suspended in a gas) in the atmosphere of these cities.

TABLE 7.2 Most Polluted World Cities by Particulate Matter in 2004	
Particulate Matter (μg/m³)	City
169	Cairo, Egypt
150	Delhi, India
128	Kolkata, India
125	Tianjin, China
123	Chongqing, China
109	Kanpur, India
109	Lucknow, India
104	Jakarta, Indonesia
101	Shenyang, China

Source: World Bank. (2007). *World development indicators 2007: Users guide.* Washington, DC: The International Bank for Reconstruction and Development/The World Bank.

Health Effects

Outdoor Pollution

Outdoor air pollution is by and large an outcome of the combustion of fossil fuels for transport, power generation, and other human activities (WHO, 2005; Lawrence Berkeley National Laboratory, n.d.). The process of combustion produces a complex blend of pollutants that includes both primary emissions (diesel soot, lead, etc.) and secondary products produced after atmospheric transformation (e.g., ozone and sulfate particles formed from the burning of sulfur-containing fuel). Outdoor air pollution remains a serious health concern in cities around the globe, particularly in the metro cities of developing countries, and it is estimated that a quarter of the world population is exposed to unhealthy concentrations of air pollutants. Children are particularly at risk because of the immaturity of their respiratory organ systems.

Two other phenomena that are inevitable consequences of outdoor air pollution and have effects on health are smog and acid rain (Lawrence Berkeley National Laboratory, n.d.).

- *Acid rain:* When a pollutant, such as sulfuric acid, combines with droplets of water in the air, the water (or snow) can become acidified. The effects of acid rain on the environment can be grave. It damages plants by destroying their leaves, it poisons the soil, and it alters the chemistry of lakes and streams. Acid rain can potentially destroy trees and endanger the health of animals, fish, and other wildlife.

- *Smog (smoke plus fog):* Smog is a dramatic manifestation of large-scale outdoor pollution caused by chemical reactions between pollutants derived from different sources, mainly automobile exhaust and industrial emissions. The Great London Smog of 1952 that is said to have claimed more than 4,000 lives directed the world's attention to the problems of air pollution for the first time (Met Office, n.d.).

Indoor Pollution

The World Health Organization (2005) estimated indoor air pollution as the eighth most important risk factor for the global burden of disease. Indoor air pollution claims 1.6 million lives annually, secondary to pneumonia, chronic respiratory disease, and lung cancer, and its health burden exceeds that caused by outdoor air pollution fivefold. In high-mortality developing countries, indoor smoke is responsible for an estimated 3.7% of the overall disease burden, making it the most deadly killer after malnutrition, unsafe sex, and lack of safe water and sanitation. Some of the health effects of indoor pollution are as follows:

- *Pneumonia and other acute lower respiratory infections:* Exposure to indoor air pollution more than doubles the risk of pneumonia.
- *Chronic obstructive pulmonary disease:* The incidence of chronic obstructive pulmonary disease (COPD), such as chronic bronchitis, in women exposed to indoor smoke is thrice that of women who cook and heat with electricity, gas, and other cleaner fuels. Among males, similar exposure nearly doubles the risk of chronic respiratory disease (WHO, 2005).
- *Lung cancer:* Exposure to smoke from coal fires (widespread in China and many other developed countries) doubles the risk of lung cancer, in particular among women, who tend to smoke less than men in most developing countries.
- *Disproportionate impacts on children and women:* In most societies, women are in charge of cooking and—depending on individual circumstances and social norms—spend between 3 and 7 hours per day near the stove, preparing food. Fifty-nine percent of all indoor air pollution–attributable deaths thus fall on women. Young children may often be carried on their mother's back or kept close to the warm fireplace. Consequently, infants spend many hours breathing indoor smoke during their first year of life when their developing airways

make them particularly vulnerable to hazardous pollutants (WHO, 2005). As a result, 56% of all indoor air pollution–attributable deaths occur in children younger than 5 years.

Interventions

The Partnership for Clean Indoor Air was launched at the World Summit on Sustainable Development in Johannesburg in September 2002 (Partnership for Clean Indoor Air, 2007). The guiding idea behind this voluntary collaboration was to tackle the increased environmental health risk faced by billions of people who burn traditional fossil fuels indoors for cooking and heating. This voluntary alliance brings together governments, public and private organizations, multilateral institutions, industry, and others to increase the use of affordable, reliable, clean, efficient, and safe home cooking and heating practices and thereby improve health, livelihood, and quality of life (Partnership for Clean Indoor Air, 2007). About 160 partner nations are collaborating to find long-term answers to the problem of smoke exposure secondary to cooking and heating practices in households around the globe.

The Montreal Protocol, discussed previously, has been one of the major success stories in the global endeavors directed against the detrimental health and environmental effects of pollution, including indoor air pollution.

A number of developed and developing countries have established strict legislative measures regarding air pollutants. Some of these standards (such as the U.S. National Ambient Air Quality Standards) set maximum permissible atmospheric concentrations for specific pollutants; attainment of these target levels is attempted through regulations enacted by local- and national-level environmental agencies. Another class of standards (such as the North American Air Quality Index) takes the form of a scale with various thresholds, which is used to communicate to the public the relative risk of outdoor activity. The latter sets of standards often do not focus on individual contaminants, but rather focus on the overall quality of the ambient air.

WATER POLLUTION

Scope of the Problem

Water pollution refers to the contamination of water bodies (e.g., lakes, rivers, oceans, and groundwater) secondary to human activities. Such contamination can be harmful to organisms and plants that live in those water bodies. It can also have other damaging consequences for the ecosystem.

The primary sources of water pollution are generally grouped into two categories based on their point of origin (EPA, 2008b). *Point-source pollution* refers to contaminants that enter a waterway through a discrete source (the point source). Examples of this category include discharges from a wastewater treatment plant, outfalls from a factory, and leaking underground tanks. *Non-point-source pollution*, as the name suggests, does not originate from a single discrete source. Non-point-source pollution is often a cumulative effect of small amounts of contaminants gathered from a large area. Examples of this category include nutrient runoff in storm water from sheet flow over an agricultural field, or metals and hydrocarbons from an area with high impervious surfaces and vehicular traffic.

The magnitude of water pollution is global in nature. However, because of the nature of such pollution it is extremely hard to quantify with one or even multiple variables, and cross-national comparisons often become difficult. Even within a country, statistics regarding purity of water between two regions can at best compare only those contaminants for which documented toxic effects and predetermined toxic levels are available. The guideline values for chemicals in water are established on available evidence, frequent presence of the contaminant in water, and international concern about particular substances. In many cases the values are much lower than those described in documented toxic effects, whereas in other cases the evidence is unclear and guidelines may not be available on substances not normally present in water or where the evidence of health effects is inadequate (WHO, 1993, 1996).

The Chernobyl nuclear power station accident in Ukraine in 1986 showed how quickly radioactive contaminants can spread into waters far away from the pollution source. Similarly, the 1984 Bhopal disaster in India included pollution of large volumes of water. These are examples of accidents whose impact is of such magnitude that they make the headlines. However, smaller accidents also occur that can pose an insidious threat to human health by causing a cumulative effect of released contaminants. Water supplies are also vulnerable to pollution from other sources related to human production systems, such as pesticide runoffs from agriculture or toxic waste from mining operations.

Exposure to contaminated water sources can cause serious health problems, and the risk of such a mischance is much greater if health is already compromised by malnutrition, poverty, and poor sanitation. Although the hazards from some elements, such as lead and mercury, are decreasing as a result of risk-based interventions, the rapid expansion and spread of industry also means that an increasing proportion of the world's population is exposed to new industrial processes and their discharges into environmental water sources.

New chemical compounds are constantly introduced into the marketplace, some safer than previous chemicals, and others with unknown effects on health. The commercial realm presently uses around 100,000 chemical substances, and about 2,000 new compounds are added to the market every year (International Program on Chemical Safety, 2000). Almost two-thirds of the 70,000 chemical products used in American industry have no reliable information regarding their health impacts (Pan American Health Organization, 2000).

Health Effects of Water Pollution

Health effects secondary to consumption of contaminated water depend primarily on the type of contaminant. The consumption can be direct (consumption of contaminated water) or indirect (consumption of fish with toxic levels of contaminant metals).

Lead, for instance, is a general toxicant that builds up in the skeleton, with the most serious effects visible in infants, young children up to the age of six years, and pregnant women. Lead is toxic mainly to the nervous system; its other effects include interference with vitamin D metabolism, anemia, and possible cancers from long-term exposure. Cyanide damages the thyroid gland, reducing the iodine uptake essential for hormone production; it can cause serious malformations in the fetus if a pregnant mother is exposed to it. Radioactive contamination as a consequence of nuclear fallout poses serious health risks. Even though water contamination usually accounts for only a small proportion of the risk following a nuclear accident, it may persist for some years because of wash-off from contaminated soil and the persistence of radioactive nuclides in sediment. The Chernobyl accident was a glaring demonstration of this problem.

A number of contaminants found in water do not cause any overt or covert health effects in low doses, but beyond a threshold level they manifest adverse health effects. A number of these contaminants are present in a higher amount in animals lower in the food chain, contributing to the phenomenon called *biomagnification*. Biomagnification, also known as bioamplification, bioaccumulation, or biological magnification, is the increase in concentration of a substance, such as the pesticide DDT, that occurs in a food chain as a consequence of food chain energetics and a low (or nonexistent) rate of excretion or degradation of the substance (see Focus Feature 7.2)

Regulations and Interventions

The Stockholm Convention, discussed earlier, remains one of the pivotal international agreements aimed at an overall reduction of environmental pollution secondary

FOCUS FEATURE 7.2   Minamata Disease

Minamata disease is a neurologic syndrome caused by severe mercury poisoning. Symptoms include ataxia (incoordination of muscles), numbness in the hands and feet, general muscular weakness, narrowing of the field of vision, and damage to hearing and speech. In extreme cases, insanity, paralysis, coma, and death follow within weeks of the onset of symptoms. A congenital form of the disease can also affect fetuses inside the womb.

The disease was first discovered in the city of Minamata in Kumamoto prefecture, Japan, in 1956. It was caused by the discharge of methyl mercury in industrial wastewater from the Chisso Corporation's chemical factory, which continued from 1932 to 1968. This highly lethal chemical bioaccumulated in shellfish and fish in Minamata Bay and the Shiranui Sea. Mercury poisoning resulted when high amounts of these fish were consumed by the local populace. Over several years, animal and human deaths secondary to the poisoning continued, and little was done to prevent them. The connection between the contamination and the deaths was publicly acknowledged by government officials in 1968.

As of March 2001, 2,955 persons had been certified as Minamata disease patients in the Yatsushiro Sea area and the Agano River basin, and a total of approximately 144.1 billion yen had been paid as compensation from the responsible companies. Lawsuits and claims for compensation continue to this day.

Source: Ministry of the Environment. (2002). Minamata disease: The history and measures. Retrieved from http://www.env.go.jp/en/chemi/hs/minamata2002/index.html

to persistent organic pollutants. Enforced in 2004, this convention remains a legally binding instrument regarding environmental pollution.

A number of countries have their own rules and regulations regarding water contamination levels. The Clean Water Act of 1977 established the basic mechanisms for regulating contaminant discharges in the United States and established the authority of the Environmental Protection Agency to implement wastewater standards for industry. In the United Kingdom, the Control of Pollution Act of 1984 deems any pollution of a lake, river, groundwater or sea, or the discharge of any liquid into such water bodies without proper authority a criminal act. In Australia, the Environment Protection (Water Quality) Policy of 2003 aims to improve the quality of water and water usage through legislated standards, guidelines, and practice codes.

A 2002 fact sheet from the water, sanitation, and health unit of the World Health Organization discusses some practical ways by which industrial water pollution can be minimized (Smith, 2002). These include the following:

- International and national agreements on safety precautions
- Public-private partnerships on environmental issues aiming to reduce water pollution

- "Think globally, act locally" by fostering community agreement on the causes of environmental water contamination
- Improved surveillance of health effects of contaminants
- Education at all levels to further an understanding of risk, the interactions of the ecosystem, and the importance of biodiversity in water sources.
- Improving the health and living conditions of disadvantaged groups (e.g., slum dwellers)
- Conservation activities, such as recycling; cleaning up refuse areas; reducing the risk of harmful substances reaching water sources; and voluntary restriction on use of chemicals
- Learning from past disasters (e.g., the Chernobyl accident)
- Developing risk and environmental impact assessment tools for industry and urban planning
- Developing and promoting the use of environmentally safe technologies in developing countries (e.g., integrated pest control)

NOISE POLLUTION

Noise pollution, sometimes simply referred to as environmental noise, is displeasing unwanted sound, whether human or machine produced, that can serve as an environmental stressor. The word *noise* itself comes from the Latin *nausea*, which means "seasickness." **Table 7.3** lists some of the more common noise levels produced by appliances typical of a household and at distances fairly typical of human use. Continuous exposures to sounds of 85 to 90 decibels can produce progressive loss of hearing, and exposures to levels as low as 50 decibels have been documented to have adverse health effects (Passchier-Vermeer & Passchier, 2000).

Human Health Effects

Health effects secondary to noise can be both physiologic and psychological in nature. Noise pollution can cause annoyance and aggression, hypertension, high stress levels, tinnitus, hearing loss, sleep disturbances, and other harmful effects (Kryter, 1994). Furthermore, stress and hypertension are the leading causes of health problems, and tinnitus can lead to forgetfulness, severe depression, and, at times, panic attacks (Kryter, 1994).

The World Health Organization (2007) identifies the following as some of the more important health risks posed by noise pollution:

TABLE 7.3 Typical Noise Levels	
Device or Situation	**Decibels (db)**
Quiet room	28–33
Computer	37–45
Radio playing in background	45–50
Normal conversation	55–65
Alarm clock	60–66
Dishwasher	63–66
Phone	66–75
Handheld electronic games	68–76
Inside car, windows open, at 30 mph	72–76
Lawn mower	88–94
Maximum output of stereo	100–110

Source: Noise Pollution Clearinghouse. (n.d.). Typical noise levels. Retrieved from http://www.nonoise.org/library/household/index.htm

- Pain and hearing fatigue
- Hearing impairment, including tinnitus
- Annoyance
- Interference with social behavior (e.g., aggressiveness, protest, and helplessness)
- Interference with speech communication
- Sleep disturbance and all its consequences on a long- and short-term basis
- Cardiovascular effects
- Hormonal responses (stress hormones) and their possible consequences on the human metabolism (nutrition) and immune system
- Performance at work or school

Hearing Loss

A progressive loss of hearing, along with an increased threshold of hearing sensitivity, can result from exposures to continuous noise of 85 to 90 decibels, common in industrial settings and in the developed world. The impact of sound energy on the inner ear results in hearing impairments. Levels of environmental noise, however, are much lower than the above-mentioned range, and effects on nonauditory health cannot be explained as a consequence of sound energy (Kryter, 1994). Even though some amount of hearing loss may come naturally with age, the cumulative effect of noise is enough to impair the hearing of a large segment of the population over the course of a lifetime in many developed nations (Rosenhall, Pedersen, & Svanborg, 1990).

Cardiovascular and Other Health Effects

Important cardiovascular health problems have been linked with noise (Ising, Babisch, & Kruppa, 1999). Studies have suggested that noise levels of 50 decibels at night may also increase the risk of myocardial infarction by chronically elevating certain hormones in the body (Passchier-Vermeer & Passchier, 2000). Research has also found that there was sufficient evidence to demonstrate a causal relationship between noise and hearing impairment, hypertension, ischemic heart disease, annoyance, school performance, and sleep disturbances (sleep patterns, awakening, sleep stages, subjective sleep quality, heart rate, and next-day mood), although evidence proving a relationship between noise and immune effects, psychiatric disorders, and biochemical effects was limited (Passchier-Vermeer & Passchier, 2000).

Legal Statutes and Regulations

Governments have traditionally visualized noise pollution as a nuisance rather than a true environmental problem. Within the United States, there are federal benchmarks for highway and aircraft noise; states and local governments typically have very specific statutes on building codes, urban planning, and roadway development.

As early as 1974, in a document entitled "Information on Levels of Environmental Noise Requisite to Protect Public Health and Welfare with an Adequate Margin of Safety," the U.S. Environmental Protection Agency published guidelines regarding permissible levels of noise (EPA, 2007). The document identified a 24-hour exposure level of 70 decibels as the level of environmental noise that would prevent any measurable hearing loss over a lifetime. Likewise, levels of 55 decibels outdoors and 45 decibels indoors were identified as preventing activity interference and annoyance. These levels of noise still permit spoken conversation and other activities, such as sleeping, working, and recreation, that are part of daily human activities.

The World Health Organization's guidelines recommend a nighttime average level of noise suitable for undisturbed sleep as being from 35 to 30 decibels, with a peak nighttime maximum of 45 decibels. However, according to an Organization for Economic

Cooperation and Development (OECD) survey of traffic noise, 16% of people in Europe suffer more than 40 decibels of noise in their bedrooms at night (Bond, 1996).

The Congressional intent behind the passage of the Noise Control Act (NCA) of 1972 was to encourage an environment for all Americans free from noise that endangered health or welfare. During the 1970s, the Office of Noise Abatement and Control (ONAC) issued reports identifying the key products responsible for noise pollution and providing information on ways to control the noise they generated, for instance, the regulation of noise emissions from aircraft. The EPA further assisted communities to conduct noise surveying, design local noise ordinances, and train noise enforcement officers. The Noise Control Act was superseded by the Quiet Communities Act of 1978 as a means to promote the development of effective state and local noise control programs, provide funds for noise research, and produce and disseminate educational materials to the public on the harmful effects of noise and ways to effectively control it. In the United States, a conservation initiative has been established with the goal of creating sites where human-caused noise pollution will not be tolerated (Geary, 1996).

In the European Union, every city with more than 250,000 inhabitants were required to draw up noise maps of their streets by 2002 (Bond, 1996). Building houses in areas with 24-hour average noise levels exceeding 50 decibels is illegal in the Netherlands (UNEP, 2008b). The Noise Act of Great Britain gives local authorities powers to confiscate noisy equipment and to penalize people who produce excessive nighttime noise. Several countries are also investing in porous asphalt, which can cut traffic noise by up to 5 decibels (UNEP, 2008b). In the African and Asian continents, noise pollution as an active environmental concern receives an indifferent treatment from governments.

Irrespective of whatever regulations and statutes might exist, the realm of noise laws and ordinances is highly patchy, and enforcement is very difficult. Conflicts over noise pollution are handled by negotiations between the emitter and the receiver. Escalation procedures vary by country, and may include action in conjunction with local authorities, in particular, the police. Noise pollution often persists because very few people affected by it ever lodge official complaints. There is a lack of general awareness regarding people's rights related to noise pollution and where infractions can be reported.

Mitigation

Noise mitigation, alternatively called *noise abatement*, refers to strategies designed to reduce unwelcome environmental sound. The main heads under which all noise mitigation strategies can be divided are transportation noise control, architectural design, and occupational noise control. Roadway noise and aircraft noise are the most invasive sources of environmental noise worldwide, and despite increasing concern, little change has been effected in source control in these areas since the original vehicles were invented. A noteworthy exception to this trend, however, is the development of the hybrid vehicle.

A variety of techniques have been developed to address interior sound intensities. In certain architectural projects, planners are encouraged to work with design engineers to examine trade-offs of roadway design and architectural design. Some of these techniques include design of exterior walls, party walls, and floor/ceiling assemblies; moreover, there exist a range of means and techniques by which to dampen reverberation from special-purpose rooms such as auditoria, concert halls, dining areas, and meeting rooms. A number of these techniques depend on materials science applications such as constructing sound baffles or using sound-absorbing liners for interior spaces. Industrial noise control is really a subset of the interior architectural control of noise, with emphasis on specific methods of sound isolation from industrial machinery and on protection of workers at their task stations.

PHOTOPOLLUTION

Photopollution, also known as light pollution or luminous pollution, is described as "artificial light having adverse effects on wildlife" (Verheijen, 1985). Like any other kind of pollution, photopollution has a distinct set of adverse health effects on humans and animals. Photopollution obscures the stars and in general diminishes the human experience of the night for city dwellers, as well as interferes with astronomical observatories.

An alternate term, *ecological light pollution*, is used to describe light pollution and its attendant effects on the ecosystem and includes chronic or periodically increased illumination, unexpected changes in illumination, and direct glare. For purposes of simplicity, this textbook simply uses the term *photopollution*. The attention given to photopollution is essentially nonexistent when compared with the other big players—namely, air and water pollution—but awareness is increasing.

Scope

Photopollution is of global extent (Cinzano, Falchi, & Elvidge, 2001). The first atlas of artificial night sky brightness documented that photopollution is existent in every inhabited continent (Cinzano, Falchi, & Elvidge, 2001). Only 40% of Americans live in a locality where it becomes sufficiently dark at night for the human eye to make a complete transition from cone to rod vision. It has also been found that almost 19% of the terrestrial surface of the Earth is exposed to night sky brightness that is polluted by astronomical standards. These levels of illumination can have significant ecological consequences. Even lights that do not effectively increase the sky glow (e.g., cruise ships, offshore oil drilling rigs) can have impacts on ecosystems.

The tropical regions may be unusually sensitive to changes in natural (24-hour) patterns of light and dark because of the year-long constancy of daily cycles (Gliwicz, 1999). A cropped or expanded night would be more likely to affect tropical species that are adapted to a lifetime with minimal seasonal variation, as opposed to other, extratropical, species that are fairly used to climatic variations.

The impacts of photopollution can be explored under two broad categories: effects on humans and effects on other species and the ecosystem.

Effects on Humans

Some of the documented effects of photopollution are psychological stress; disturbances in sleep/wake cycles, especially in children; and diminution of the effectiveness of the body's immune system (Campaign for Dark Skies, n.d.). That exposure to light has a definitive link with mood and the feeling of well-being has been supported by evidence for a medical condition called *seasonal affective disorder*, a condition in which people exhibit mood symptoms similar to depression. The symptoms are remediable with exposure to light, a process called *phototherapy*. The more precise effects of photopollution on human health remain to be researched further.

Effects on Other Species and the Ecosystem

Increased orientation and alertness or disorientation in animals can be a consequence of additional illumination. Also, animals can be attracted to or repulsed by glare, which in turn affects foraging, reproduction, communication, and other critical behaviors (Longcore & Rich, 2004). Artificial light disrupts interspecies interactions (predator/prey relationships, for instance) that evolved in natural patterns of light and dark, with serious implications for community ecology. (Longcore & Rich, 2004).

SKILL-BUILDING ACTIVITY

One of the many potential challenges any family planning initiative has to face is a clash with traditionally cherished values. The most controversial aspect of family planning is abortion. Both Iran and the United States have developed practical and rational family planning programs despite the controversies associated with some aspects of those programs. Compare and contrast family planning in these two countries under the following heads: (a) potential difficulties, (b) ways used to circumvent those difficulties, and (c) outcome. Compile your findings in a tabular format.

SUMMARY

The 21st century has seen some unique demographic trends. Some of the more important demographic trends are a generally rapid population growth, a shift toward urbanization, the twin phenomena of youth bulge and aging, the tremendous increase in the number of people migrating to foreign lands, and a changing ethnic picture in some of the economic hubs of the world. These trends will continue to be important for the coming decades. Likewise, the implications of these trends have to be prepared for. Humanitarian crises, social unrest, adverse health effects, and environmental degradation remain some of the concerns. World Population Day, established by the United Nations in 1989, is an annual event whose purpose is to spread awareness of global population issues.

Family planning, or attempts to manage and control the size of one's family, has become important given some of the current demographic trends. China, India, Iran, and the United States are all countries with well-developed family planning programs. Initiatives in Africa remain lacking. Given the high fertility rates in Africa, urgent interventions are needed. Some of the recommendations that have been made to improve family planning endeavors in Africa are more efficient use of existing resources; improving staff training on specific issues, particularly on broader reproductive health counseling; closing the gap between established protocols and provider behavior; strengthening supervisor training; and enhancing the focus on quality and research.

The term *climate change* implies any significant alteration in the indices used to measure climate (such as temperature, precipitation, or wind) extending for a longer than usual duration. The phenomenon has gained attention because it is associated with human activities. Global warming, the average increase in the temperature of the atmosphere near the Earth's surface and in the troposphere, has also gained fame recently. Global warming is mostly thought to be a consequence of the greenhouse gas effect. Both these phenomena have the potential to cause disastrous long-term effects, damaging ecosystems globally. As a response to the potential consequences of climate change, global accords have been negotiated. The Kyoto Protocol, which puts a ceiling on the amount of greenhouse gas emissions allowed to member nations, and the

Montreal Protocol, the planned phase-out of chemicals that pose a threat to the ozone layer, are two prime examples.

Air, water, and noise pollution and photopollution involve contamination of natural entities as a consequence of human activities. Each of these kinds of pollution has significant effects on human health and longevity. Interventions have been designed for countering each of these types of pollution, but interventions are still lacking in most of the world.

IMPORTANT TERMS

age cohort	noise mitigation
carrying capacity	one-child policy
climate change	persistent organic pollutants
deforestation	salinization
demographic transition	slum
ethnic shifts	soil deterioration
family planning	urbanization
global warming	World Population Day
greenhouse effect	youth bulge
indoor air quality	

REVIEW QUESTIONS

1. Define youth bulge. List two ways by which a youth bulge would have an impact on the health of the global human population.
2. What are some of the demographic trends of the 21st century?
3. How do human activities bring about climate change?
4. Define global warming. What are greenhouse gases and how do they contribute to global warming?
5. Describe the ways through which the Kyoto Protocol aimed to reduce emissions.
6. Enumerate five nonauditory health effects of noise pollution. What do you understand by the term *noise mitigation*?
7. Why do you think the World Population Day is important?
8. How does the phenomenon of migration affect global human population?

WEB SITES TO EXPLORE _____

CIA World Factbook

https://www.cia.gov/library/publications/the-world-factbook/

The World Factbook is an annual publication of the U.S. Central Intelligence Agency containing almanac-style information about the countries of the world. The *Factbook* provides a two- to three-page summary of the demographics, geography, communications, government, economy, and military of U.S.-recognized countries, dependencies, and other areas in the world. *Explore this Web site and prepare a health profile of a country you would like to know more about.*

International Atomic Energy Agency

http://www.iaea.org/

The International Atomic Energy Agency (IAEA) is an international organization that seeks to promote the peaceful use of nuclear energy and to inhibit its use for military purposes. Originally established as the world's "Atoms for Peace" organization in 1957 within the United Nations, this agency now works with its member states and multiple partners worldwide to promote safe, secure, and peaceful nuclear technologies. *Review the section entitled "About IAEA." Prepare a fact sheet on the organization.*

International Energy Agency

http://www.iea.org/

The International Energy Agency (IEA) is an intergovernmental organization, currently based in Paris, that was founded by the Organization for Economic Cooperation and Development (OECD) in 1974 in the wake of the oil crisis. Initially, the IEA concerned itself with prevention of oil disruptions and maintenance of statistics about the international oil market and other energy sectors. More recently, the IEA has included energy security, economic development, and environmental protection in its mandate. *Review the section entitled "About IEA." Prepare a short description of the agency.*

International Organization for Migration

http://www.iom.int/jahia/Jahia/lang/en/pid/2

The International Organization for Migration (IOM) is an intergovernmental organization that works in close collaboration with multiple governmental, intergovernmental, and nongovernmental partners and aims at promoting "humane and orderly migration for the benefit of all." With 125 member states, the IOM is one of the leading agencies in the field of migration. *Explore this Web site and read about the activities of the IOM. Summarize the salient activities undertaken by this agency in Africa.*

International Planned Parenthood Federation

http://www.ippf.org/en/

The International Planned Parenthood Federation (IPPF) is a global nongovernmental organization that serves as a leading advocate of sexual and reproductive health and rights for all. The organization was first established in 1952 in Bombay, India, and now consists of more than 149 member associations working in more than 189 countries. The IPPF has six regional offices, one each in Africa (Nairobi, Kenya); the Arab world (Tunis, Tunisia); Europe (Brussels, Belgium); south Asia (New Delhi, India); east and southeast Asia and Oceania (Kuala Lumpur, Malaysia); and the Western hemisphere (New York, USA). *Review this Web site and summarize the resources that this organization has to offer.*

Noise Pollution Clearinghouse

http://www.nonoise.org/

The Noise Pollution Clearinghouse (NPC) is a national nonprofit organization based in the United States of America that attempts to raise awareness about the phenomenon of noise pollution, to strengthen laws and government efforts to control the same, and to launch networks among multidisciplinary professionals working on noise pollution issues. *Make sure to browse through the NPC law library, which includes links to European laws and regulations regarding the domain of noise pollution.*

United Nations Environment Program

http://www.unep.org/

The United Nations Environment Program (UNEP) is the designated watchdog of the United Nations system regarding environmental issues at the national and international levels. The organization serves to coordinate international environmental policy consensus and helps facilitate focus on emerging environmental issues on an international scale. UNEP was founded as a result of the United Nations Conference on the Human Environment in June 1972 and has its headquarter in Nairobi, Kenya. It also has six regional offices and various country offices. *Check out the section on environmental short films, which offers some very interesting eco-friendly tips.*

United Nations Framework Convention on Climate Change

http://www.unfccc.int

The United Nations Framework Convention on Climate Change is an international environmental treaty created at the United Nations Conference on Environment and Development, organized in 1992 in Rio de Janeiro. This treaty aims to stabilize greenhouse gas concentrations in the atmosphere to safe levels. Because the treaty did not enforce emission standards, it was not legally binding. The treaty was superseded by its principal update, the Kyoto Protocol. *Explore this Web site and read about the Kyoto Protocol. What additional information did you find that was not mentioned in this book?*

United Nations Population Fund

http://www.unfpa.org/

The United Nations Population Fund (UNFPA) is an international development organization that promotes the right of every woman, man, and child to enjoy a life of health and equal opportunity. According to the UNFPA mission statement, it "supports countries in using population data for policies and programmes to reduce poverty and to ensure that every pregnancy is wanted, every birth is safe, every young person is free of HIV/AIDS, and every girl and woman is treated with dignity and respect." *Check out the population indicator section and select two to four countries of your interest to compare their population indicators. You may also review the population indicators of a single country.*

United States Environmental Protection Agency

http://www.epa.gov/epahome/aboutepa.htm

The U.S. Environmental Protection Agency (EPA) is a federal agency charged with protecting human health and with safeguarding the natural environment: air, water, and land. The EPA came into being in 1970 and has since then been mainly responsible for the environmental policy of the United States. *Explore this Web site and visit the EPA newsroom. Read at least five news items and summarize any one of them for your class.*

REFERENCES

Alan Guttmacher Institute. (1997). *Title X and the U.S. family planning effort.* Retrieved from http://www.guttmacher.org/pubs/ib16.html
Bond, M. (1996). Plagued by noise. *New Scientist, 152*(2056), 14–15.
Bongaarts, J. (1994). Population policy options in the developing world. *Science, 263*(5148), 771–776.

Bridges, E. M., & Oldeman, L. R. (1999). Global assessment of human-induced soil degradation. *Arid Soil Research and Rehabilitation, 13*(4), 319–325.

Brown, J. H., Valone, T. J., & Curtin, C. G. (1997). Reorganization of an arid ecosystem in response to recent climate change. *Proceedings of the National Academy of Sciences, 94*(18), 9729–9733.

Campaign for Dark Skies. (n.d.). Medical problems. Retrieved June 26, 2008, from http://www.britastro.org/dark-skies/health.html

Campbell, P. R. (1996). Population projections for states by age, sex, race, and Hispanic origin: 1995 to 2025. Retrieved from http://www.census.gov/population/www/projections/ppl47.html

Central Intelligence Agency. (2001). *Long term global demographic trends: Reshaping the geopolitical landscape.* Retrieved from https://www.cia.gov/library/reports/general-reports-/Demo_Trends_For_Web.pdf

Central Intelligence Agency. (2008). *The world factbook.* Retrieved from https://www.cia.gov/library/publications/the-world-factbook/geos/xx.html

Centre for Research on the Epidemiology of Disasters. (n.d.). *The bibliography database.* Retrieved June 19, 2008, from http://www.cred.be/embib/index.htm

Cinzano, P., Falchi, F., & Elvidge, C. D. (2001). The first world atlas of the artificial night sky brightness. *Monthly Notices of the Royal Astronomical Society, 328*(3), 689–707.

Cleland, J., Bernstein, S., Ezeh, A., Faundes, A., Glasier, A., & Innis, J. (2006). Family planning: The unfinished agenda. *Lancet, 368*(9549), 1810–1827.

Ehrhardt-Martinez, K. (1998). Social determinants of deforestation in developing countries: A cross-national study. *Social Forces, 77*(2), 567–586.

Environmental Protection Agency. (2007). Information on levels of environmental noise requisite to protect public health and welfare with an adequate margin of safety. Retrieved from http://www.nonoise.org/library/levels74/levels74.htm

Environmental Protection Agency. (2008a). Air pollution. Retrieved from http://www.epa.gov/ebtpages/airairpollution.html

Environmental Protection Agency. (2008b). Water pollution. Retrieved from http://www.epa.gov/ebtpages/watewaterpollution.html

Environmental Protection Agency. (n.d.). Climate change. Retrieved June 9, 2008, from http://www.epa.gov/climatechange/basicinfo.html

Food and Agriculture Organization. (2005). *Global forest resources assessment 2005.* Retrieved from http://www.fao.org/forestry/fra2005/en/

Friedman, D. (2007). *America's family planning program: Title X.* Retrieved from http://www.plannedparenthood.org/issues-action/birth-control/family-planning-6553.htm

Geary, J. (1996). Saving the sounds of silence. *New Scientist 2025*(1), 13.

Gliwicz, Z. M. (1999). Predictability of seasonal and diel events in tropical and temperate lakes and reservoirs. In J. G. Tundisi & M. Straskraba (Eds.), *Theoretical reservoir ecology and its applications* (pp. 99–124). São Carlos, Brazil: International Institute of Ecology.

Haas, P. M. (1992). Banning chlorofluorocarbons: Epistemic community efforts to protect stratospheric ozone. *International Organization, 46*(1), 187–224.

Heinsohn, G. (2003). *Söhne und weltmacht. Terror im aufstieg und fall der nationen.* Zürich: Orell Füssli.

Hesketh, T., Lu, L., & Xing, Z. W. (2005). The effect of China's one-child family policy after 25 years. *New England Journal of Medicine, 353*(11), 1171–1176.

Hill, A. (2007). *The changing face of British cities by 2020.* Retrieved from http://www.guardian.co.uk/society/2007/dec/23/communities.population

International Organization for Migration. (n.d.). About migration. Retrieved July 6, 2008, from http://www.iom.int/jahia/jsp/index.jsp

International Program on Chemical Safety. (2000). *Hazardous chemicals in human and environmental health: A resource book for school, college and university students.* Geneva: World Health Organization.

Ising, H., Babisch, W., & Kruppa, B. (1999). Noise-induced endocrine effects and cardiovascular risk. *Noise and Health, 1*(4), 37–48.

Kline, D. S. (2003). Push and pull factors in international nurse migration. *Journal of Nursing Scholarship, 35*(2), 107–111.

Kovats, R., Haines, A., Stanwell-Smith, R., Martens, P., Menne, B., & Bertollini, R. (1999). Climate change and human health in Europe. *British Medical Journal, 318*(7199), 1682–1685.

Kryter, K. D. (1994). *The handbook of hearing and the effects of noise: Physiology, psychology, and public health.* Boston: Academic Press.

Lawrence Berkeley National Laboratory. (n.d.). Outdoor air pollution. Retrieved July 4, 2008, from http://www.lbl.gov/Education/ELSI/Frames/pollution-outdoor-f.html

Lindgren, E., & Gustafson, R. (2001). Tick-borne encephalitis in Sweden and climate change. *Lancet, 358*(9275), 16–18.

Longcore, T., & Rich, C. (2004). Ecological light pollution. *Frontiers in Ecology and the Environment, 2*(4), 191–198.

Massey, D. S. (1996). The age of extremes: Concentrated affluence and poverty in the twenty-first century. *Demography, 33*(4), 395–412.

Mather, A. S., & Needle, C. L. (2000). The relationships of population and forest trends. *Geographical Journal, 166*(1), 2–13.

McCarthy, J. J., Osvaldo, F. C., Leary, N. A., Dokken, D. J., & White, K. S. (2001). *Climate change 2001: Impacts, adaptation, and vulnerability. Contribution of Working Group II to the Third Assessment Report of the Intergovernmental Panel on Climate Change.* Cambridge, England: Cambridge University Press.

Met Office. (n.d.). The great smog of 1952. Retrieved July 4, 2008, from http://www.metoffice.gov.uk/education/secondary/students/smog.html

Miller, K., Miller, R., Askew, I., Marjorie, C. H., & Ndhlovu, L. (Eds.). (1998). *Clinic-based family planning and reproductive health services in Africa: Findings from situation analysis studies.* New York: The Population Council.

Miranda, D. S. (2000). Reflexões sobre o papel da cultura na cidade de São Paulo. *Sao Paulo em Perspectiva, 14*(4), 105–110.

Montgomery, M. R. (Ed.). (2007). *Cities transformed: Demographic change and its implications in the developing world.* Washington, DC: National Academies Press.

National Commission on Population. (n.d.). *National population policy 2000.* Retrieved July 4, 2008, from http://populationcommission.nic.in/npp.htm

National Research Council. (1993). *Factors affecting contraceptive use in Sub-Saharan Africa.* Washington, DC: National Academy Press.

Nielsen, R. (2006). *The little green handbook: Seven trends shaping the future of our planet.* Picador, NY: Macmillan.

Obermeyer, C. M. (2006). HIV in the Middle East. *British Medical Journal, 333*(7573), 851–854.

Oldeman, L. R., Hakkeling, R. T. A., & Sombroek, W. G. (1990). *Global assessment of soil degradation.* Wageninen: International Soil Reference Information Centre.

Omelaniuk, I. (Ed.). (2005). *World migration: Costs and benefits of international migration 2005.* Geneva: International Organization for Migration.

Pan American Health Organization. (2000). *Environmental impact on child health.* Washington, DC: Author.

Partnership for Clean Indoor Air. (2007). Partnership for Clean Indoor Air. Retrieved from http://www.pciaonline.org/site/c.krLWJ7PIKqG/b.2660445/

Passchier-Vermeer, W., & Passchier, W. F. (2000). Noise exposure and public health. *Environmental Health Perspectives, 108*(Suppl. 1), 123–131.

Phillips, J., & Greene, W. (1993). *Community based distribution of family planning in Africa: Lessons from operations research.* New York: Population Council.

Rosenhall, U., Pedersen, K., & Svanborg, A. (1990). Presbycusis and noise-induced hearing loss. *Ear and Hearing, 11*(4), 257–263.

Ross, J., Mauldin, W. P., & Miller, V. (1993). *Family planning and population: A compendium of international statistics.* New York: United Nations Population Fund and Population Council.

Roudi-Fahimi, F. (1999). Iran's revolutionary approach to family planning. *Population Today, 27*(7), 4–5.

Roudi-Fahimi, F. (2002). *Iran's family planning program: Responding to a nation's needs.* Washington, DC: Population Reference Bureau.

Roy, S. K. (2005). Urban development: A critique. *Journal of the Indian Anthropological Society, 40*(2–3), 209–226.

Scientific Committee on Antarctic Research. (2008). The Antarctic treaty system: An introduction. Retrieved from http://www.scar.org/treaty/

Shaw, C. (2001). *United Kingdom population trends in the 21st century: Considering likely trends in the population over the next hundred years.* Retrieved from http://www.statistics.gov.uk/articles/population_trends/UKpoptrends_pt103.pdf

Smith, R. S. (2002). *World Water Day 2001: Pollution from industry, mining and agriculture.* Retrieved from http://www.worldwaterday.org/wwday/2001/thematic/pollution.html

Solomon, S., Qin, D., Manning, M., Melinda, M., Kristen, A., Tignor, M. M. B., et al. (2007a). *The physical science basis. Contribution of Working Group I to the Fourth Assessment Report of the Intergovernmental Panel on Climate Change.* Cambridge, England: Cambridge University Press.

Solomon, S., Qin, D., Manning, M., Melinda, M., Kristen, A., Tignor, M. M. B., et al. (2007b). *The physical science basis. Frequently asked questions and selected technical summary boxes.* Cambridge, England: Cambridge University Press.

South-East Asia Regional Office. (n.d.). India and family planning: An overview. Retrieved July 5, 2008, from www.searo.who.int/LinkFiles/Family_Planning_Fact_Sheets_india.pdf

United Nations. (2006). *Implementation of the outcome of the United Nations conference on human settlements (Habitat II) and strengthening of the United Nations human settlements programme (UN-Habitat): Report of the secretary general.* New York: Author.

United Nations Environment Program. (2000). *The Montreal Protocol on substances that deplete the ozone layer.* Retrieved on June 15, 2008, from http://www.unep.org/OZONE/pdfs/Montreal-Protocol2000.pdf

United Nations Environment Program. (2008a). Stockholm Convention on persistent organic pollutants. Retrieved from http://chm.pops.int/

United Nations Environment Program. (2008b). Noise pollution. Retrieved from http://earthwatch.unep.net/health/noisepollution.php

United Nations Framework Convention on Climate Change. (1992). *The United Nations Framework Convention on Climate Change.* Retrieved from http://unfccc.int/resource/docs/convkp/conveng.pdf

United Nations Framework Convention on Climate Change. (n.d.). Kyoto Protocol. Retrieved June 6, 2008, from http://unfccc.int/kyoto_protocol/items/2830.php

United Nations Population Fund. (2007). *State of world population 2007: Unleashing the potential of urban growth.* Retrieved from http://www.unfpa.org/swp/2007/presskit/pdf/sowp2007_eng.pdf

United Nations Population Fund. (n.d.). Plan your future: Plan your family. Retrieved June 26, 2008, from http://www.unfpa.org/wpd/

U.S. Census Bureau. (2008). International data base. Retrieved from http://www.census.gov/ipc/www/idb/

Verheijen, F. J. (1985). Photopollution: Artificial light optic spatial control systems fail to cope with incidents, causation, remedies. *Experimental Biology, 44*(1), 1–18.

Vorosmarty, C. J., Green, P., Salisbury, J., & Lammers, R. B. (2000). Global water resources: Vulnerability from climate change and population growth. *Science, 289*(5477), 284–288.

World Health Organization. (1993). *Guidelines for drinking water quality volume 1: Recommendations.* Geneva: Author.

World Health Organization. (1996). *Guidelines for drinking water quality volume 2: Health criteria and other supporting information.* Geneva: Author.

World Health Organization. (2005). Indoor air pollution and health. Retrieved from http://www.who.int/mediacentre/factsheets/fs292/en/

World Health Organization. (2007). Noise and health. Retrieved from http://www.euro.who.int/Noiamily planning. Retrieved July 6, 2008, from http://www.who.int/reproductive-health/family_planning/index.html

Women's Health

DEFINING WOMEN'S HEALTH

Women's health refers to health issues specific to the anatomic makeup of a human female. These often pertain to structures such as female genitalia and breasts and health-related conditions arising from those structures. The term may also refer to health conditions produced by hormones specific to, or most prominent in, females. Menstruation, contraception, maternal health, childbirth, and menopause are just some of the issues included in women's health. Medical situations in which women handle problems not directly related to their biology (e.g., gender-based differences in health care access) may also be included within the scope of women's health.

Some autonomous women's health bodies have advocated a broader approach to women's health. The Society for Women's Health Research in the United States, for instance, argues that women's health should go beyond issues specific to human female anatomy to include areas in which biological sex differences between males and females exist. This field has been called **gender-based biology** or **sex-based biology** and refers to scientific inquiry committed to identifying the biological and physiologic differences between men and women (Society for Women's Health Research, 2008).

The World Health Organization (WHO) upholds the importance of a **gender-based approach** to public health, stating that "[a] gender-based approach to public health begins from the recognition of the differences between women and men. It helps us to identify the ways in which the health risks, experiences, and outcomes are different for women and men, boys and girls, and to act accordingly" (WHO, 2007a).

Even today there continues to be an unequal power relation between the two sexes in most societies, with women continuing to occupy a lower social status than men. By virtue of this lower status in families, communities, and society, women have less access to and control over resources. Consequently, a systematic devaluing and neglect of women's health has followed. The twin implications of this chronic neglect are that women's health often needs advocates to bring it up to par with men's, and that any association devoted to investigating and rectifying such gender inequalities in health will, in practice, find itself acting as just such an advocate (WHO, 2008a).

In the past, work on women's health was limited to the health problems of women during pregnancy and childbirth. A gender-based approach has immensely improved our comprehension of women's health problems. This, in turn, has helped identify ways to address those problems in females of all ages. For example, cardiovascular disease is as important a cause of death in women as it is in men. Delays in seeking treatment and diagnosis among women often occur because this fact is not well known. Armed with this information regarding gender differences in cardiovascular diseases, many countries have been able to develop effective health promotion and prevention strategies that have improved women's health (Wizemann & Pardue, 2001; WHO, 2007a, 2008b).

THE WOMEN'S HEALTH MOVEMENT AS PART OF THE LARGER FEMINIST MOVEMENT

The **feminist movement** (alternatively known as the women's movement or women's liberation) is a sequence of campaigns on female-centric issues such as reproductive rights (often including abortion), domestic violence, maternity leave, equal pay, sexual harassment, and sexual violence. The goals of the movement have varied from one country to another, such as opposition to female genital cutting in Sudan and concern over the differential pay grades for men and women in similar jobs in developed countries. The movement has been intimately linked with the health concerns of women at multiple levels. Many of the contemporary aspects of the movement have a bearing on the health of women globally. The recent emphasis on a gender-based approach to public health owes much of its existence to the original feminist movement.

Convention on the Elimination of All Forms of Discrimination Against Women

The United Nations adopted the **Convention on the Elimination of All Forms of Discrimination Against Women (CEDAW)** on December 18, 1979. The treaty was a result of the First World Conference on Women in Mexico City in 1975. Prior to CEDAW, there was no international agreement that comprehensively addressed women's rights within political, cultural, economic, social, and family life (Vandenhole, 2005).

CEDAW is the most comprehensive and meticulous international agreement targeting the advancement of women. It establishes rights for women in areas not previously subject to international standards. The treaty provides a universal definition of discrimination against women so that those who would discriminate on the basis of sex can no longer claim that no clear definition exists. It also calls for action in nearly every field of human endeavor: politics, law, employment, education, health care, commercial transactions, and domestic relations. Moreover, CEDAW establishes a committee to review periodically the progress being made by its adherents. As of December 2003, 177 countries had ratified the convention, pledging to give women equal rights in all aspects of their lives (Vandenhole, 2005).

Increase in Global Awareness

Advocacy initiatives related to women's health and against gender-based discrimination in medical practice began to gain momentum globally during the mid-1970s, during the United Nations' Decade for Women. This social change could trace its roots to the feminist movement of the 1960s in many developed nations and to the women's movements emerging out of the progressive social movements in many developing countries during the 1970s. The biomedical model of health and illness was challenged by advocates of women's health. Gender-based inequalities (a woman's lack of control over her sexuality and reproduction, for instance) came to the forefront as significant determinants of the poor health of women.

Still later, during the 1970s and 1980s, health activists and advocates worldwide worked to demystify medical knowledge and set up alternative models of care for women, models that viewed women holistically and not just as reproducers or care providers for children. Domestic violence against women, women's occupational and mental health, sexual and reproductive health, and rights beyond maternal health were put on the national health policy and program agendas (WHO, 2006).

Important events that greatly influenced global thinking and shaped public opinion on gender issues in health included the International Conference on Population and Development in Cairo, Egypt, in 1994, closely followed by the Fourth World Conference on Women in Beijing, China, in 1995. Both of these conferences identified gender-based inequalities as critical factors that influenced health and called for the investigation of these inequalities.

These global changes have led to the emergence of initiatives to address women's health issues worldwide. There is increasing recognition of the need for sensitivity to diversity and cultural and social factors, including gender, that affect health and illness worldwide. Initiatives to address gender issues in health have included a number of attempts to build health professionals' capacity to identify and address sex- and gender-based differences in health care needs (WHO, 2006).

Focus Feature 8.1   Facts About Women's Health

- Smoking rates among men tend to be ten times higher than women. However, because of recent aggressive tobacco marketing campaigns aimed at women, tobacco use among younger females in developing countries is rising rapidly. Women generally have less success in quitting the habit and have more relapses than men, and nicotine replacement therapy may be less effective among women.
- Of all adults living with HIV in sub-Saharan Africa, 61% are women. In the Caribbean, the proportion of women living with the virus is 43%. The numbers of women living with HIV in Latin America, Asia, and eastern Europe are also growing.

(continued)

- Between 15 and 71% of women around the world have suffered physical or sexual violence committed by an intimate male partner at some point in their lives. Such abuse cuts across all social and economic backgrounds and has serious consequences for women's health.
- Even though early marriage is on the decline, an estimated 100 million girls will marry before their 18th birthday over the next 10 years. This is one-third of the adolescent girls in developing countries (excluding China). Young married girls often lack knowledge about sex and the risks of sexually transmitted infections and HIV/AIDS.
- Some studies show that up to one in five women report being sexually abused before the age of 15.
- About 14 million adolescent girls become mothers every year. More than 90% of these very young mothers live in developing countries.
- Every day, 1,600 women and more than 10,000 newborns die from preventable complications during pregnancy and childbirth. Almost 99% of maternal and 90% of neonatal mortalities occur in the developing world.
- Insecticide-treated nets reduce cases of malaria in pregnant women and their children. When women earn an income, they are more likely than men to buy the nets for their households. However, use of the nets is often linked to sleeping patterns that sometimes preclude their actual use by women.
- In most countries women tend to be in charge of cooking. When they cook over open fires or traditional stoves, they breathe in a mix of hundreds of pollutants on a daily basis. This indoor smoke is responsible for half a million of the 1.3 million annual deaths due to chronic obstructive pulmonary disease among women worldwide. During pregnancy, exposure of the developing embryo to such harmful pollutants may cause low birth weight or even stillbirth.
- Across the world and at all ages, women have a significantly higher risk of becoming visually impaired than men. Even so, women do not have equal access to health care to treat eye diseases, often because of their inability to travel unaccompanied to health facilities and because of cultural differences in the perceived value of surgery or treatment for women.

Source: World Health Organization (WHO). (2008a). *10 facts about women's health.* Geneva: Author. Retrieved from http://www.who.int/features/factfiles/women/en/index.html

COMMON HEALTH CONDITIONS OF WOMEN

This section discusses some of the common and epidemiologically important diseases affecting women. The focus remains on the public health perspective rather than clinical descriptions. Diseases specific to pregnancy and childbirth are discussed later in the chapter (see the section "Maternal Mortality and Morbidity").

Sexually Transmitted Infections

Sexually transmitted infections (STIs), also known as **sexually transmitted diseases (STDs)**, are infections that are spread mainly through sexual contact between two individuals. These are discussed in detail in Chapter 4. Here the information is presented in the context of its importance to women. Of the more than 30 known STIs, several can also be transmitted from a mother to her child during pregnancy and childbirth, as well as being transmitted through blood products and tissue transfer (WHO, 2007b). Depending on the type of organism causing the infection, STIs can be divided into bacterial and viral. Examples of bacterial STIs are syphilis, chlamydia, and gonorrhea, whereas examples of viral STIs are genital warts, hepatitis B, and genital herpes.

Public Health Importance

Sexually transmitted infections, along with their complications, rank in the top five disease categories for which adults seek health care in developing countries. Sexually transmitted infections can lead to acute symptoms, chronic infection, and severe delayed consequences such as infertility, **ectopic pregnancy** (a pregnancy in which the zygote or egg implants outside the uterus of the female into an unusual anatomic location), cervical cancer, and the untimely death of infants and adults (WHO, 2007b).

The public health importance of STIs in females is even higher than in males for the following reasons (WHO, 2000a):

- Women are much more vulnerable to STIs biologically, culturally, and socioeconomically.
- The majority of STIs are asymptomatic in women (e.g., 60 to 70% of gonococcal and chlamydial infections), and severe morbidity may result because of lack of recognition of early infection.
- As compared with males, the consequences of STIs are more severe in women and occasionally even fatal. Further, the consequences of STIs can extend to the newborns of an infected woman, leading to a much higher mortality and morbidity rate.
- Sexually transmitted infections are more stigmatizing in females. Women often tend to seek treatment less often than men because of the attached stigma as well as because of a lack of time and money.

Some consequences of STIs in women are as follows:

- *Infertility:* Sexually transmitted infections remain the major preventable cause of infertility in women. Between 10 and 40% of women with untreated chlamydial infection develop symptomatic pelvic inflammatory disease. Furthermore, women who have had pelvic inflammatory disease are six to ten times more likely to develop an ectopic pregnancy than those who have not; 40 to 50% of ectopic pregnancies can be attributed to previous pelvic inflammatory disease. Infection with certain strains of the human papillomavirus is associated with the development of cervical cancer in women (WHO, 2007b).

- *Pregnancy:* Left untreated, STIs are associated with congenital infections in newborns. For instance, because of the lack of effective prophylaxis, about one-third to one-half of all infants born to mothers with untreated gonorrhea will develop a severe eye infection that can cause blindness. Between 1,000 and 4,000 newborn babies become blind every year worldwide because of this condition (WHO, 2007b).
- *HIV:* The presence of an untreated STI increases the risk of both acquisition and transmission of HIV by ten times.

Detection and Management of Sexually Transmitted Infections

The signs (objective markers of a disease revealed during examination by a health care provider) and symptoms (subjective markers of a disease revealed by a patient, such as pain) for most of the STIs overlap significantly. Some of the most common signs and symptoms of an STI are urethral discharge, genital ulcers, vaginal discharge, and pain in the lower abdomen. The constellation of such signs and symptoms is often called a *syndrome*. Some of these signs and symptoms are easily recognizable and fairly consistent. For instance, a urethral discharge in men can be caused by gonorrhea alone, chlamydia alone, or both together. A **syndromic approach** would entail treating with antibiotics any men with a urethral discharge and other typical features consistent with an infectious picture.

The World Health Organization has advocated a syndromic approach to the detection and management of STIs since the early 1990s. The syndromic approach is a scientifically based method that uses common signs and symptoms as proxies for underlying infection and offers accessible and timely treatment. Flowcharts are used to guide diagnosis and treatment. The approach is more precise than diagnosis based on only clinical judgment and more cost-effective for some syndromes than use of laboratory tests. Overtreatment may be a flipside of the syndromic approach (Vuylsteke, 2004; WHO, 2007b).

Prevention and Control of Sexually Transmitted Infections

Given their significant mortality and morbidity and the consequent public health impact, the need for prevention and control of STIs is an urgent one. By far, abstinence from sexual intercourse remains the most effective means to avoid becoming infected with or transmitting an STI. In May 2006, a global strategy for the prevention and control of STIs was endorsed by the World Health Assembly. Some of the recommendations made in the strategy are as follows (WHO, 2007b):

- Prevention by means of safer sexual behaviors
- Easy access to quality condoms at reasonable prices
- Making treatment of STIs part of basic health services
- Specific interventions for high-risk populations, such as sex workers, adolescents, substance users, and prisoners
- Appropriate treatment of STIs
- Screening of clinically asymptomatic patients, where feasible (e.g., for syphilis, chlamydia)
- Providing counseling and voluntary testing for HIV infection
- Involving the private sector and the community in the prevention and care of STIs

Sexual Abuse and Violence

Violence against women and girls remains a major public health and human rights concern. Women can experience physical or mental abuse at any point during their lives: in infancy, childhood and adolescence, during adulthood, or even when elderly. Violence against women holds severe consequences for the affected individual and is a social ill that deserves a concerted effort from multiple sectors.

Definition of Violence Against Women

The Declaration on the Elimination of Violence Against Women was adopted in 1993 and defined **violence against women** as "any act of gender-based violence that results in, or is likely to result in, physical, sexual or mental harm or suffering to women, including threats of such acts, coercion or arbitrary deprivation of liberty, whether occurring in public or in private life." This definition is understood to include the following components (United Nations, 1994):

- Physical, sexual, and psychological violence occurring in the family and in the general community, including battering, sexual abuse of children, dowry-related violence, rape, and female genital mutilation and other traditional practices harmful to women
- Nonspousal violence
- Violence related to exploitation, sexual harassment, and intimidation at work, in educational institutions, and elsewhere

- Trafficking in women and forced prostitution
- Violence perpetrated or condoned by the state

Violence Against Women as a Public Health Concern

Research statistics reveal an ominous trend concerning violence against women in general. Some of the research done has also shed light on the characteristics of perpetrators of this violence.

- Reliable, large-scale self-report studies have consistently shown that between 10 and 50% of women have been physically abused by an intimate partner in their lifetime (Hamberger, Saunders, & Hovey, 1992; Mezey, Bacchus, Bewley, & White, 2005; White & Olson, 1996).
- According to population-based studies, approximately 12 to 25% of women have experienced attempted or completed forced sex by an intimate partner or ex-partner at some time in their lives.
- In 1998, interpersonal violence was the tenth leading cause of death for women aged 15 to 44 years (WHO, 2000b).
- **Trafficking** in women for the purpose of sexual exploitation is a multibillion dollar shadow market. Women are trafficked to, from, and through every region in the world using methods that have become new forms of slavery. The value of the global trade in women as commodities for sex industries is estimated to be between $7 and $12 billion annually (Hughes, 2000).

Most studies exploring violence against women suggest that the perpetrators are mostly men. Women are at the greatest risk of violence from men they know rather than from strangers; females of all ages are the most frequent victims of violence within the family and between intimate partners. Physical abuse in intimate relationships is almost always accompanied by severe psychological and verbal abuse. The social institutions put in place to protect citizens, however, too often blame or ignore battered women (WHO, 2000b, 2002).

Between 10 and 50% of women have been physically abused by an intimate partner in their lifetime.

Violence adversely affects both a woman's physical and mental health. Violence in the form of intentional homicide, severe injury, or suicide can be fatal. The likelihood of depression, anxiety, psychosomatic symptoms, eating problems, and sexual dysfunctions is much higher in abused women than in women who have not been abused. Violence may also adversely affect the reproductive health of a female by:

- Increasing sexual risk-taking behaviors among adolescent females
- Increasing the transmission of STIs, including HIV/AIDS
- Increasing the incidence of unplanned pregnancies
- Precipitating various gynecologic problems, including chronic pelvic pain and painful intercourse

Consequences such as HIV/AIDS or unplanned pregnancies may then themselves act as risk factors for further violence, forming a vicious cycle of abuse.

Violence presents an undue burden on the health system. Studies from the United States, Zimbabwe, and Nicaragua indicate that women who have been physically or sexually assaulted use health services more than women with no history of violence, thus increasing health care costs. Also, the use of health care services has been shown to increase with the severity of the assault sustained (Campbell, 2002). Studies elsewhere have found rape to be a strong predictor of utilization of health care services (WHO, 2000b).

Current Initiatives to Address Violence Against Women

The World Health Organization's *World Report on Violence and Health* divides possible interventions into five broad headings: individual approaches, developmental approaches, community-based efforts, and legal and policy responses (WHO, 2002).

Individual Approaches   Individual-based interventions are mostly designed for victims and occasionally for perpetrators. Counseling, therapy, and support group initiatives have been found to be fairly helpful following sexual assaults, particularly in the presence of complicating factors related to the violence itself or to the process of recovery. Programs targeting perpetrators of sexual violence are rare; they are generally aimed at men convicted of assault and are localized to industrialized countries. In the developed world, women's crisis centers and battered women's shelters have been the cornerstone of programs for victims of domestic violence. These shelters typically provide emergency shelter in addition to emotional, legal, and material support to women and their children. Many developing countries have seen an impressive growth of such shelters and crisis centers in recent years.

Developmental Approaches   Research has stressed the importance of encouraging nurturing, with better and more gender-balanced parenting, to prevent sexual violence. A prevention model by Schwartz (1991) adopts such a developmental approach, with interventions before birth, during childhood, and in adolescence and young adulthood. In this model, emphasis is placed on introducing children to the negatives of sexual abuse and violence early on during their childhood with an aim of developing health modeling behaviors in them. Currently, developmental approaches are rarely employed as interventions targeting abuse of women.

Health Care Response   An effective health care response can significantly limit the physical and psychological damage that may accompany a sexual or physical assault. Furthermore, timely and appropriate documentation can help intercept the perpetrator, perhaps preventing any further acts of abuse. In many countries, when sexual violence is reported the health sector has the duty to collect medical and legal evidence to corroborate the accounts of the victims or to help in identifying the perpetrator (WHO, 2002).

Issues concerning sexual violence need to be addressed in the training of all health service staff, including psychiatrists and counselors, in basic training as well as in specialized postgraduate courses. Such training should give health care workers greater knowledge and awareness of sexual violence and make them better able to detect and handle cases of abuse in a sensitive but effective manner. Existing interventions have focused on sensitizing health care providers, encouraging routine screening for abuse, and drawing up protocols for the proper management of abuse. Active screening for abuse—questioning patients about their possible histories of suffering violence by intimate partners—is generally considered good practice in this field (Olson et al., 1996).

Community-Based Efforts   Attempts to change public attitudes toward sexual and physical violence using the media have included advertising on billboards and in public transport, as well as on radio and television. Television has been used effectively in South Africa and Zimbabwe (Njovana & Watts, 1996). An important element in preventing sexual and physical violence against women is a collective initiative by men. Men's groups against domestic violence and rape can be found in Australia, Africa, Latin America and the Caribbean, Asia, and many parts of North America and Europe (Flood, 2001). Action in schools is vital for reducing sexual and other forms of violence. In many countries, a sexual relation between a teacher and a pupil is not a serious disciplinary offence and policies on sexual harassment in schools either do not exist or are not implemented.

Legal Reform   Legal reform remains one of the most effective interventions that can help limit the incidence of sexual and physical abuse against women. Several Asian nations, including the Philippines, have enacted legislation reforms drastically redefining rape and mandating state assistance to victims. The result has been a

Focus Feature 8.2   Female Genital Mutilation

Female genital mutilation (FGM) refers to the partial or total removal of the external female genitalia, or any other injury caused to the female genital organs for nonmedical reasons. Traditionally, the mutilation was practiced by traditional circumcisers, but it is increasingly being performed by medical personnel. Globally, the number of females living after having been subjected to this practice is around 100 to 140 million. In the African continent alone about 3 million girls are at risk for FGM each year. Mostly carried out on young girls, the procedures have no health benefits for females.

Female genital mutilation is internationally recognized as a violation of the human rights of girls and women. It can have short-term and long-term health consequences, none of which are beneficial. Severe pain, shock, bleeding, infection, and inability to urinate are some of the immediate complications. Recurrent bladder and urinary tract infections, infertility, and the need for repeat surgeries later on in life are some of the long-term health-related complications. Female genital mutilation also has an enormous psychological effect on the individual exposed to it.

Female genital mutilation is most commonly found in the western, eastern, and northeastern regions of Africa, in some countries in Asia and the Middle East, and among certain immigrant communities in North America and Europe. Multiple cultural, religious, and social factors within families and communities are responsible for the maintenance of this heinous practice as a tradition. Cultural ideals of femininity and modesty, an assumption that the practice has religious support, and the fact that the practice happens to be a cultural tradition make it hard to eradicate. Local structures of power and authority, such as community leaders, religious leaders, circumcisers, and even some medical personnel, can contribute to upholding the practice (WHO, 2008c).

The World Health Organization issued a joint statement with the United Nations Children's Fund (UNICEF) and the United Nations Population Fund (UNFPA) against the practice of FGM in 1997. A revised statement, with broader United Nations support, was issued in February 2008 to support increased advocacy for the abandonment of FGM. The revised statement included newer evidence collected over the past 10 years regarding the practice of female genital mutilation. It focuses on the increased recognition of the human rights and legal dimensions of the problem and provides current data on the frequency and scope of FGM. It also provides evidence-based research exploring the reasons why FGM continues, how to curb it, and its detrimental effects on the health of women, girls, and newborns.

substantial increase in the number of reported cases (WHO, 2002). International treaties and laws are especially useful for curbing international human trafficking.

MATERNAL MORTALITY AND MORBIDITY

Globally, roughly 1,500 women die from either pregnancy- or childbirth-related complications. In 2005 alone, the total number of maternal deaths worldwide was 536,000.

Most of the mortality occurs in developing countries and, sadly, most of it is preventable (WHO, 2008b, 2008d). The international community adopted a set of eight goals called the **Millennium Development Goals** (MDGs) at the UN Millennium Summit in 2000. Improving maternal health is one of those goals. Even though one target is to curtail the **maternal mortality ratio** (MMR, defined as the number of maternal deaths per 100,000 live births during a specified time period, usually 1 year) by three-fourths between 1990 and 2015, the progress made so far is only modest. Between 1990 and 2005, the global MMR declined by a mere 5%. Obviously, at the current rate the goal will not be met.

Distribution

The sheer difference in the maternal mortality indicators between different parts of the world is astounding. Maternal mortality is spread inequitably, and the trend closely mimics the economic differences between developed and developing countries. Whereas a woman's lifetime risk of maternal death is 1 in 75 in the developing regions, the risk falls to an amazing 1 in 7,300 in well-developed countries. Developing countries account for 99% of all maternal deaths worldwide. Sub-Saharan Africa alone accounts for more than half of all the deaths, while southern Asia accounts for another third. The countries with the highest MMRs (1,000 or greater) are, in rank order, Sierra Leone, Afghanistan, Malawi, Angola, Niger, the United Republic of Tanzania, Rwanda, Mali, Somalia, Zimbabwe, Chad, Central African Republic, Guinea Bissau, Kenya, Mozambique, Burkina Faso, Burundi, and Mauritania (AbouZahr, 2003; WHO, 2008b, 2008d). Even within a country, large disparities in the mortality and morbidity indices between the rich and the poor are often seen.

Reasons for Maternal Mortality and Morbidity

Women die of a wide range of direct or indirect causes in pregnancy, childbirth, or the postpartum period. Normally, a distinction is made between a direct and an indirect maternal death. Whereas *direct maternal death* refers to the result of a complication of the pregnancy, delivery, or its management, *indirect maternal death* refers to a pregnancy-related death in a patient with a preexisting or newly developed health problem.

Worldwide, approximately 80% of maternal deaths are due to direct causes. As illustrated in **Table 8.1**, the four major killers are severe bleeding (mostly postpartum hemorrhage, or after-birth bleeding), infections (mostly sepsis), hypertensive disorders in pregnancy (usually **eclampsia**—the onset of seizures in a pregnant female with

TABLE 8.1 Causes of Maternal Death	
Cause	Proportion of Maternal Deaths (%)
Severe bleeding	25
Indirect causes	20
Infections	15
Unsafe abortion	13
Eclampsia	12
Obstructed labor	8
Other direct causes	8

Source: World Health Organization. (2008). Making pregnancy safer: Maternal mortality. Retrieved from http://www.who.int/making_pregnancy_safer/topics/maternal_mortality/en/

pregnancy-induced hypertension), and **obstructed labor** (discrepancy in the size of the baby and the birth canal or an abnormally positioned baby that leads to a halt in the childbirth process). Complications after unsafe abortion cause 13% of maternal deaths. Among the indirect causes of maternal death are diseases that complicate pregnancy or are aggravated by pregnancy, such as malaria, anemia, HIV/AIDS, and cardiovascular diseases (WHO, 2005, 2008b).

The above-mentioned causes also bring about considerable morbidity. An estimated 12% of women survive maternal hemorrhage, but are left with severe anemia. Infertility resulting from tubal occlusion is estimated to affect some 450,000 women each year as a secondary consequence of sepsis during delivery. An estimated 73,000 women suffer the most serious and debilitating nonfatal health outcome of obstructed labor, namely, **obstetric fistula**, which refers to a hole in the vagina or rectum caused by childbirth that is prolonged and unattended by skilled nursing care (AbouZahr, 2003).

Reasons for Inadequate Maternal Care

Current antenatal (before birth), natal (during the process of childbirth), and post-natal (after-birth) care still leaves much to be desired in developing countries. Only about 60% of deliveries in developing countries were assisted by a skilled birth attendant in 2006. The coverage fluctuates from a low of 34% in eastern Africa to a more encouraging 93% in South America (WHO, 2008d). The coverage of antenatal care reflects similar trends. In Peru, 87% of pregnant women had at least four antenatal care visits, whereas in Ethiopia the coverage was only 12% (WHO, 2008e).

Some of the reasons why women may not receive optimal antenatal, natal, and postnatal care are as follows:

- Lack or minimal availability of qualified professional care
- Lack of access to health facilities, either because of lack of transportation or secondary to economic constraints
- Cultural beliefs or a woman's low social status

Prevention and Control of Maternal Mortality

Fortunately, with proper preventive measures and modern medical management, most maternal deaths are avoidable. Skilled nursing care at birth can make the difference between life and death. For instance, following simple aseptic techniques during delivery can greatly decrease the risk of maternal death due to sepsis. Pre-eclampsia, a common hypertensive disorder in pregnancy, can be monitored, and with appropriate medications the risk of developing fatal seizures can be minimized. Skilled birth attendants can prevent or manage another frequent cause of maternal death, namely, obstructed labor.

Safe Motherhood Initiative

In close collaboration, the World Health Organization, the World Bank and the United Nations Population Fund sponsored the Safe Motherhood Conference in Nairobi in 1987. Throughout the world this conference was seen as a major stepping stone toward reducing the burden of maternal mortality, particularly in developing countries. The conference issued a call to action to reduce maternal mortality and morbidity by one-half by the year 2000. The **Safe Motherhood Initiative** that arose from this conference essentially includes all events that make pregnancy unsafe, irrespective of the outcome. Subsequent work on safe motherhood has outlined clear strategies and specified interventions for the reduction of maternal morbidity and mortality, often referred to as the pillars of safe motherhood (Mahler, 1987; UNFPA, 2007)

Prompt availability of good-quality maternal health services by trained health workers is vital in the struggle to reduce life-threatening risks and mortality. Consequently, safe motherhood strategies have to be comprehensive in nature, going beyond quality health services and addressing social, economic, and cultural factors that may obstruct the proper use of those services by women.

Safe motherhood programs attempt to address all of these issues, as well as closely related health issues such as STIs, unplanned pregnancy, obstetric fistula, and female genital mutilation. The four-part strategy outlined in the Nairobi conference sought to provide the following (Mahler, 1987; UNFPA, 2007):

- Adequate primary health care and an adequate share of available food for females from infancy to adolescence, as well as universally available family planning
- Good prenatal care, including nutrition, with early detection and referral of those at high risk
- The assistance of a trained person at all births
- Access to the essential elements of obstetric care for women at higher risk

Some of the more important approaches advocated for these initiatives are contraceptive services, skilled attendance and midwives, and emergency obstetric care.

Risk Reduction via Contraceptive Services

Lack of knowledge about and lack of access to contraception are responsible for a large number of maternal deaths, especially in developing countries. Every pregnancy multiplies a woman's chance of dying from complications of pregnancy or childbirth. The mortality rates are exceptionally high for young and poor females, who have the least access to contraceptive services. More than one-fourth of all pregnancies worldwide culminate in abortion. A number of these abortions are performed under unsafe conditions. The high level of unmet need for quality contraceptive services—and the corresponding number of unwanted pregnancies—is a key reason why so many seek out abortions. There is an urgent need to address the gap between the number of individuals who use contraceptives and those who would like to delay or limit their families.

Skilled Attendance

Skilled attendance at all births is considered to be the single most critical intervention for ensuring safe motherhood because it hastens the timely delivery of emergency obstetric and newborn care when life-threatening complications arise. The term **skilled attendance** encompasses the presence of midwives and others with midwifery skills as well as an environment conducive to childbirth. Easy access to a more comprehensive,

higher level of care is also implied in the definition. The presence of a skilled attendant has been found to drastically curtail maternal and neonatal mortality. Consequently, the proportion of births attended by a skilled health provider is one of the
two indicators for measuring progress toward the fifth Millennium Development
Goal, that of improving maternal health.

Emergency Obstetric Care

Some of the components of **emergency obstetric care** are administration of intravenous antibiotics, manual removal of the placenta, assisted vaginal delivery, and, occasionally, blood transfusions. Making emergency obstetric and newborn care available to all women who develop complications is crucial in global efforts to reduce
maternal mortality. All five of the major causes of maternal mortality—hemorrhage,
sepsis, unsafe abortion, hypertensive disorders, and obstructed labor—can be treated
at a well-staffed, well-equipped health facility. In 1997 WHO, UNICEF, and
UNFPA issued joint guidelines that recommended the following standards (UNFPA,
2007):

- For every 500,000 people there should be four facilities offering basic and one
  facility offering comprehensive essential obstetric care.
- To manage obstetric complications—the life-saving component of maternity
  care—a facility must have at least two skilled attendants covering 24 hours a
  day and 7 days a week, assisted by trained support staff.
- To manage complications requiring surgery, the facilities must have a functional operating theater and support staff and must be able to administer blood
  transfusions and anesthesia.

The Three Delays Model

The **three delays model** portrays the roles of communities and health systems in the
use of emergency obstetric care (Maine, 1993). This model postulates that the result
of an obstetric emergency is influenced by factors that govern deciding to seek care,
reaching the medical facility, and receiving adequate care.

The first two "delays" (delays in deciding to seek care and in reaching an appropriate care facility) relate directly to the issue of health care access, influenced by
factors operating in the family and the community. The third "delay" (delay in
receiving care at health facilities) relates to factors in the health facility, including
quality of care.

Making Pregnancy Safer Initiative

The World Health Organization was part of the original Safe Motherhood Initiative. However, the need for another initiative was felt, and the **Making Pregnancy Safer** (MPS) initiative was launched by WHO in 2000. The 2005 creation of MPS as a separate department within WHO reflects the recognition of the need to accelerate the reduction of maternal and newborn mortality and to ensure access to skilled attendance and the highest attainable standards of health for all women and babies. The major aims of the department are reinforcing advocacy, technical support, monitoring and evaluation, and partnerships in countries to ensure the provision of the latest information and guidance on maternal and newborn health. The department has staff spread over 75 country offices (WHO, 2008f).

> *The "Three Delays" model proposes that pregnancy-related mortality is overwhelmingly due to delays in: (1) deciding to seek appropriate medical help for an obstetric emergency; (2) reaching an appropriate obstetric facility; and (3) receiving adequate care when a facility is reached. Any safe motherhood program should adequately address all three delays in order to be able to succeed.*
>
> —United Nations Population Fund (2007)

Integrated management of pregnancy and childbirth (IMPAC) functions as the center point of the technical assistance activities offered by the MPS department. IMPAC provides guidance and tools to improve pregnant women's access to high-quality health services. The integrated approach seeks to enhance maternal and newborn health by addressing diverse factors that are vital for the access to skilled care before, during, and after pregnancy and childbirth. It targets health systems and health workers as well as families and communities (WHO, 2008g). In addition to improving access to health care services, the integrated approach attempts to better the quality of essential and emergency care by developing the skills and abilities of health care workers. Clinical guidelines for care before, during, and after birth are available from the department. The integrated approach also addresses cultural beliefs and norms by providing education and logistic support for communities to help increase the use of health services by women.

HIV/AIDS IN WOMEN

According to recent global estimates, women make up 50% of the population living with HIV. In certain parts of the world, this figure is even higher, with women constituting 60% of all people with HIV. Because of multiple socioeconomic factors, the number of women with HIV has steadily grown in recent years (International Women's Health Coalition, 2008; WHO, 2008h).

Causes

Gender-based norms are responsible, to a large extent, for these skewed statistics. Males may be encouraged to have more sexual partners or to have sexual relations with females younger than them. This may, in some settings, contribute to higher infection rates among young women (aged 15 to 24 years). Because of the stigmatizing nature of sexually transmitted diseases in general and HIV in particular, access to HIV information and services may be restricted for young women.

Violence against women (physical, sexual, and emotional), which is experienced by 10 to 60% of women aged 15 to 49 years worldwide, increases their vulnerability to HIV. This can include forced sex. Women may also feel reluctant to request their partners to use condoms or may feel powerless to refuse unsafe sexual intercourse.

Women may face significant barriers to accurate and comprehensive HIV prevention, treatment, and care as a result of their lack of access to and control over resources, childcare responsibilities, restricted mobility, and limited decision-making power. Lack of education may further affect the future of thousands of females. Lack of information about HIV can naturally foster unsafe sexual behaviors, increasing the likelihood of acquiring HIV. Educating girls makes them more prepared to make safer and healthier sexual decisions. Eight of ten women aged 15 to 24 in developing (low and middle income) countries cannot correctly identify strategies for preventing HIV transmission.

In 2008, only 52% of countries that reported to the UN General Assembly included specific, budgeted support for women-focused HIV/AIDS programs (WHO, 2008h). This failure to address gender-based inequalities is endemic to virtually all HIV/AIDS initiatives and programs in developing countries.

Prevention and Control

All of the factors just discussed can be addressed and remedied by effectively structured programs. Gender norms can be tackled by working with males to challenge and modify long-held norms and customs pertaining to fatherhood, sexual responsibility, decision making, and violence. The instruction should be culturally relevant and age appropriate. Violence against women can be addressed by offering empowering programs that teach safer sex negotiation and life skills training, offering medicolegal services to sexual abuse victims, and working internationally with other countries to strengthen laws that help reduce violence against women. Health care access for women can be improved by removing financial barriers that limit access to services and designing programs that specifically target HIV-related stigma and discrimination.

The **HIV/AIDS Program of the World Health Organization** is conducted in close collaboration with multiple other United Nation agencies, nongovernmental organizations, health services providers, and health care institutions across the globe. The purpose of the program is to reinforce all aspects of the health sector to improve HIV-related services. The program is comprehensive in that it is spread out across six regional offices and 193 nations. The eventual aim is to help develop and popularize evidence-based standards that will help realize universal access to HIV services. The five core strategies employed by this program are as follows (WHO, 2008i):

- *Increase an individual's knowledge of his or her HIV status:* To increase the percentage of people who are aware of their HIV status, WHO has published guidelines that define the conditions under which health workers may routinely recommend HIV testing and counseling to patients in support of universal access.
- *Maximize the health sector's contribution to HIV prevention:* Research-based interventions should be targeted to at-risk populations such as sex workers and their clients, drug users, homosexual males, incarcerated populations, and so on. Guidelines have also been developed to prevent the forward transmission of HIV in those living with HIV.
- *Accelerate HIV treatment and care:* In collaboration with international partners, the World Health Organization is developing an all-inclusive package of services designed to guarantee efficacy and safety and to maximize health care access to all who need it, especially high-risk populations.
- *Fortify and expand health systems:* In many high-prevalence and resource-limited settings, health systems are weak, inequitable, and unresponsive. The World Health Organization helps countries to build health system capacity and fully mobilize the health workforce for the expansion of HIV treatment and care.
- *Invest in strategic information to better inform the HIV response:* The World Health Organization ensures the provision of technical support and guidance to countries that need it. It also guarantees that member nations have adequate surveillance and reporting programs in place.

TRAFFICKING OF WOMEN

The issue of human trafficking, especially in minors and young women with the intention of sexual exploitation, has, by virtue of its rapid growth, assumed global dimensions in recent years. The phenomenon has become transnational in scope. An ominous trend associated with this increase has been the increasing involvement of criminal organizations who exploit populations living in developing, relatively poorer nations.

Human trafficking is defined by the United Nations Protocol to Prevent, Suppress and Punish Trafficking in Persons, especially Women and Children (also called the **Palermo Convention and Protocol**) as follows (Betti, 2003):

> "Trafficking in persons" shall mean the recruitment, transportation, transfer, harboring or receipt of persons, by means of the threat or use of force or other forms of coercion, of abduction, of fraud, of deception, of the abuse of power or of a position of vulnerability, or of the giving or receiving of payments or benefits to achieve the consent of a person having control over another person, for the purpose of exploitation. Exploitation shall include, at a minimum, the exploitation of the prostitution of others or other forms of sexual exploitation, forced labor or services, slavery or practices similar to slavery, servitude or the removal of organs.

Scope

Trafficking in people, especially women and children, is one of the most rapidly growing areas of international criminal activity and consequently one of grave global concern. Trafficking is now considered the third-largest source of profits for organized crime, behind only drugs and guns, generating billions of dollars annually. The scope of this problem is staggering. Despite affecting virtually every nation on earth, trafficking draws most of its victims from Asia (Pan American Health Organization, 2001). An estimated 225,000 victims each year from southeast Asia and over 150,000 from south Asia are funneled into human trafficking each year.

The former Soviet Union has recently turned into a large supply center for prostitution and the sex industry, with more than 100,000 individuals trafficked each year from that region. An additional 75,000 or more are trafficked from central and eastern Europe. More than 100,000 individuals come from Latin America and the Caribbean, and over 50,000 victims are from Africa. Most of the victims are sent to Asia, the Middle East, western Europe, and North America (Library of Congress, 2002). Estimates put the total number of humans trafficked each year worldwide for forced labor, domestic servitude, or sexual exploitation at an astonishing 700,000.

Effects on Human Health

Human trafficking, especially that of women and children for sexual exploitation, potentially leads to chronic, permanent, or even life-threatening health consequences. A trafficked and sexually abused victim can never attain the highest possible level of physical, mental, and social well-being. Physical injuries such as bruises, broken bones, head wounds, stab wounds, and mouth and teeth injuries may occur. Long-term psychiatric consequences may occur in the form of depression, self-mutilating behavior, personality disorders, and so on. Sexual abuse is associated with a higher risk of sexually transmitted infections. The risk of acquiring HIV is of particular importance. Lack of access to health care may further accentuate the severity of such infections. Pregnancy and forced or unsafe abortions are yet other prime concerns.

Abused females may resort to using drugs or alcohol as a coping mechanism, and all too frequently addiction may result. Fear of detection and deportation can leave undocumented women reluctant to access social services and health care. Because of extremely restricted access to health care, trafficking victims are at high risk of complications arising from undiagnosed and untreated infections, such as pelvic inflammatory disease, chronic pelvic pain, ectopic pregnancy, and sterility (Pan American Health Organization, 2001).

Global and Regional Initiatives Against Human Trafficking

The definition of "trafficking in persons" in the Protocol to the UN Convention on Transnational Organized Crime, widely adopted in Palermo in 2000, was a major global step toward addressing the problem of human trafficking. Despite the fact that many nations have signed the protocol, the number of countries who have ratified it is lower (Betti, 2003). Multiple other international instruments seek to address various aspects of human trafficking. Several regional and hemispheric conventions or resolutions also exist that call on countries to fight human trafficking (e.g., the Inter-American Convention on the Prevention, Punishment and Eradication of Violence Against Women).

Many governments and regional and international entities are designing programs to ensure better cooperation between law enforcement agencies, nongovernmental organizations, and international organizations such as the United Nations Children's Fund (UNICEF), the International Labor Organization, and so on. Some of these programs include training in identification of victims, interview techniques, referrals, and protection and assistance (United Nations, 2005).

European Union programs and programs funded by the United States and other governments and international organizations are also helping nations across the globe in building capacity for dealing with the menace of trafficking. Such programs have shown promise in the number of new laws and training programs in place in a number of vulnerable regions.

Finally, assisted return and reintegration programs for victims who choose to return to their home countries play a crucial role in the success of these efforts. An estimated 5% of trafficked women returned to their home countries are retrafficked. With proper reintegration and assisted return programs, this figure can be reduced (United Nations, 2005).

BREAST CANCER

The term *cancer* refers to an uncontrolled proliferation or growth of normal human cells. **Breast cancer** is a special type of cancer that affects the breast tissue, mostly in females, but rarely also in males. Breast cancer is the most common cancer worldwide. It is an important public health concern because it affects a vast number of women and also because timely interventions can prevent significant mortality and morbidity (Susan G. Komen for the Cure, 2008a, 2008b).

Warning Signs

Breast tumors usually grow very slowly, so that by the time one is large enough to be felt as a lump, it may have been growing for as long as 10 years. Warning signs of breast cancer are early indications that something may be wrong and that a medical checkup may be needed. All of the warning signs can also occur because of conditions other than cancer, some entirely harmless. A woman may find out that she has breast cancer after a routine **mammogram** (an imaging study of the breasts done with the use of low-dose x-rays). Some women may not have any signs of breast cancer until very late in the disease, when not much can be offered in terms of prevention or even treatment.

Some warning signs of breast cancer are as follows (Centers for Disease Control and Prevention, 2006):

- New lump in the breast or underarm (armpit)
- Thickening or swelling of part of the breast
- Irritation or dimpling of breast skin
- Redness or flaky skin in the nipple area of the breast
- Pulling in of the nipple or pain in the nipple area
- Nipple discharge other than breast milk, including blood
- Any change in the size or the shape of the breast
- Pain in any area of the breast

Statistics

An estimated 182,460 new cases of breast cancer are expected to be diagnosed in American women in 2008 alone. In 1975 the incidence (the number of new cases) of breast cancer in the United States was 107 per 100,000 for white women and 94 per 100,000 for black women. Twenty-nine years later, in 2004, the number of new cases per year had risen to 128 per 100,000 for white women and 119 per 100,000 for black women.

Breast cancer rates vary greatly around the world, but industrialized countries generally have higher rates than nonindustrialized countries. China and the eastern African region, for instance, both have breast cancer incidences of approximately 20 per 100,000 females, whereas the incidence in Australia and New Zealand exceeds 80 per 100,000. This discriminatory trend is attributed, in part, to differences between such countries in lifestyle and reproductive factors (Susan G. Komen for the Cure, 2008b).

Risk Factors

Breast cancer has multiple risk factors. Some of those risk factors can be modified, whereas others cannot (Susan G. Komen for the Cure, 2008c).

- *Age:* The incidence of breast cancer increases with age. Assuming an average life expectancy of 90, the risk of acquiring breast cancer is about 1 in 7. But the risk constantly increases from birth onward, and although it is about 1 in 229 for a woman younger than 40, the risk goes up to 1 in 13 for a woman between the ages of 60 and 79.
- *Personal history of breast cancer:* A personal history of breast cancer increases the risk of recurrence of the disease. It also increases the chances of a breast cancer over that of someone who never had one.
- *Family history:* Breast cancer in one's family can have a major impact on an individual's risk. However, the risk depends on the proximity and age of the affected relative. For instance, a history of breast cancer in a maternal grandmother at the age of 80 confers significantly less risk than a similar history in one's mother at the age of 25.
- *Certain breast changes:* Certain biological changes in the breast tissue are associated with an elevated risk of developing breast cancer in the future. These changes are not themselves cancerous, though.
- *Genetic alterations:* Certain genetic abnormalities increase the risk of developing breast cancer. Often, families with such genetic abnormalities may have multiple female members who develop cancer of the breast. However, it's also vital to remember that most women with breast cancer have no significant family history of the disease.
- *Menstrual history:* Women who had their first period before they were 12 years old or who went through menopause after 55 have a higher risk of breast cancer than women with fewer years of exposure to hormones made by the ovaries.
- *Race:* In the United States, breast cancer occurs more often in white women than in Latina, Asian, or African American women. However, African American women have the highest risk for women younger than 40 years.

- *Breast density:* Females with dense breasts are more likely to be diagnosed with cancer of the breast than those who have less dense breasts.
- *Late pregnancy or no pregnancy:* Women who had their first full-term pregnancy after age 30 and women who never had a full-term pregnancy are at higher risk for breast cancer than those who gave birth earlier in life. A full-term pregnancy, which stops the menstrual cycle for 9 months, seems to offer protection against breast cancer.
- *Radiation therapy to the chest:* Such therapy before the age of 30 years can increase the risk of developing breast cancer. This has been seen in young women receiving radiation to treat Hodgkin's disease, a cancer of blood cells.

Screening and Early Detection

Breast cancer is the most common cancer among women worldwide, and there are several possible methods for screening. If facilities are available, screening by mammography alone, with or without physical examination of the breasts, plus follow-up of individuals with positive or suspicious findings, will reduce mortality from breast cancer by up to one-third among women aged 50 to 69 years. Much of the benefit is obtained by screening once every 2 to 3 years. There is limited evidence for its effectiveness for women aged 40 to 49 years. This suggests that a program to encourage breast self-examination alone would not reduce mortality from breast cancer. Women should, however, be encouraged to seek medical advice immediately if they detect any change in a breast that suggests breast cancer (Humphrey, Helfand, Chan, & Woolf, 2002; WHO, 2008j).

Unfortunately, mammography is an expensive test that requires great care and expertise both to perform and to interpret the results. It is, therefore, currently not a viable option for many countries. Also, mammography is not without its own drawbacks. The potential harms of mammography include anxiety as well as ensuing procedures and costs that result from mammograms that suggest cancer when there is none (Humphrey et al., 2002). Although there is inadequate evidence that physical examination of the breasts as a single screening modality reduces mortality from breast cancer, there are indications that good clinical breast examinations by specially trained health workers could have an important role.

SKILL-BUILDING ACTIVITY

Obstetric fistula is one of the most serious injuries associated with childbearing. Conduct an online search for information regarding this condition. Visit at least three to five different Web sites to collect information. Compile your material in the following format: (a) causative or predisposing factors, (b) clinical features, (c) treatment, and (d) prevention and control measures. Prepare a fact sheet with this information.

SUMMARY

Women's health refers to health issues specific to the anatomic makeup of a human female. These often pertain to structures such as the female genitalia and breasts and health-related conditions arising from those structures. The term may also refer to health conditions produced by hormones specific to, or most prominent in, females. Lately, the concept of a gender-based approach toward health has gained importance.

The feminist movement has been intimately linked with the health concerns of girls and women at multiple levels. The 1979 adoption of the Convention on the Elimination of All Forms of Discrimination Against Women (CEDAW) by the United Nations fortified the global commitment to women's health on December 18, 1979.

Sexually transmitted infections (STIs), also called sexually transmitted diseases (STDs), are infections that are spread mainly through sexual contact between two individuals. Sexually transmitted infections, along with their attendant complications, rank in the top five disease categories for which adults seek health care in developing countries. The consequences of STIs in women can be devastating, ranging from infertility and abortion to increasing the chances of acquiring HIV. The syndromic approach to STIs has been advocated by the World Health Organization in recent years.

Violence against women and girls remains a major public health and human rights concern. Women can experience physical or mental abuse at any point during their lives. The Declaration on the Elimination of Violence Against Women was adopted in 1993 and defined violence against women for the first time. The consequences of violence against women can be grave, such as increased sexual risk-taking behaviors among adolescent females, increased transmission of STIs, and increased incidence of unplanned pregnancies. Current interventions targeting violence against women can be grouped under four broad headings: individual approaches, developmental approaches, community-based efforts, and legal and policy responses.

Pregnancy and childbirth take an enormous toll on women in terms of morbidity and mortality, much of which is avoidable. Improving maternal health is one of the eight Millennium Development Goals adopted at the UN Millennium Summit in 2000. The four major causes of mortality are severe bleeding (mostly postpartum hemorrhage, or after-birth bleeding), infections (mostly sepsis), hypertensive disorders in pregnancy, and obstructed labor. These causes also bring about considerable morbidity.

Some of the reasons why women may not receive optimal antenatal, natal, and postnatal care are attributable to the limited availability of qualified professional care, lack of access to health facilities (either because of lack of transportation or secondary to economic constraints), and cultural beliefs or a woman's low social status. Initiatives for safe motherhood have been sponsored by international agencies, such as the Safe Motherhood Initiative and, more recently, the Making Pregnancy Safer (MPS) initiative. To improve maternal health, all the interventions focus on contraceptive services, skilled attendance and midwives, and emergency obstetric care.

HIV/AIDs is a public health issue of immense significance. According to recent global estimates, women make up 50% of the population living with HIV. Gender-based norms, violence against women, barriers to health care access, lack of education, and failure to address gender-based inequalities are some important reasons behind this trend. The HIV/AIDS Program of the World Health Organization is conducted in close collaboration with multiple other UN agencies, nongovernmental organizations, health services providers, and health care institutions across the globe. The purpose of the program is to reinforce all aspects of the health sector to improve HIV-related services.

Trafficking in people, especially women and children for sexual exploitation, is one of the most rapidly growing areas of international criminal activity and consequently one of grave global concern. Such trafficking can lead to chronic, permanent, or even life-threatening health consequences. The risk of acquiring HIV is of particular importance. Lack of access to health care access may further accentuate the severity of such infections. Many governments and regional and international entities are designing programs to ensure better cooperation between law enforcement agencies, nongovernmental organizations, and international organizations to address human trafficking. Some of these programs include training in identification of victims, interview techniques, referrals, and protection and assistance. Assisted return and reintegration programs for victims who choose to return to their home countries play a crucial role in the success of these efforts.

Breast cancer is an important public health concern because it affects a vast number of women and also because timely interventions can prevent significant mortality and morbidity. Age, personal or family history of breast cancer, certain breast changes, genetic alterations, menstrual history, race, breast density, late pregnancy or no pregnancy, and radiation therapy to the chest before the age of 30 years are risk factors for breast cancer. If facilities are available, screening by mammography alone, with or without physical examination of the breasts, plus follow-up of individuals with positive or suspicious findings, will reduce mortality from breast cancer by up to one-third among women aged 50 to 69 years. Much of the benefit is obtained by screening once every 2 to 3 years.

IMPORTANT TERMS

breast cancer
Convention on the Elimination of All
  Forms of Discrimination Against
  Women (CEDAW)
eclampsia
ectopic pregnancy
emergency obstetric care
female genital mutilation
feminist movement
gender-based approach
gender-based biology
HIV/AIDS Program of the World
  Health Organization
integrated management of pregnancy
  and childbirth (IMPAC)
Making Pregnancy Safer (MPS)
mammogram

maternal mortality ratio
Millennium Development Goals
obstetric fistula
obstructed labor
Palermo Convention and Protocol
Safe Motherhood Initiative
sex-based biology
sexually transmitted diseases
  (STDs)
sexually transmitted infections (STIs)
skilled attendance
syndromic approach
three delays model
trafficking
violence against women
women's health

REVIEW QUESTIONS

1. What do you understand by the term *gender-based biology*?
2. What are some of the consequences of sexually transmitted infections in women?
3. How can violence affect a woman's health status? Discuss some of the different approaches being employed to deal with violence against women.
4. Define maternal mortality ratio. Discuss some of the ways by which you can decrease this ratio in developing countries.
5. Enumerate the major causes of maternal death.
6. What is the three delays model with respect to utilization of emergency obstetric care?
7. Define trafficking in women. Discuss some of the public health interventions being implemented to counter the same.
8. Enumerate any two warning signs for breast cancer.

WEB SITES TO EXPLORE

Coalition to Abolish Slavery and Trafficking

http://www.castla.org/

The Coalition to Abolish Slavery and Trafficking (CAST) is a human rights organization, established in 1998, whose mission is to assist persons trafficked for the purpose of forced labor and slavery-like practices and to work toward ending all instances of such human rights violations. CAST is one of the leading American anti-trafficking organizations and is a grantee of the Department of Justice and the Department of Health and Human Services. *Search this Web site for the different kind of services the organization provides, including legal, social, and training and advocacy. Compile one instance of each of these services provided by the organization. Reflect on the multifaceted nature of trafficking and why an anti-trafficking organization needs to offer such an assortment of services.*

Coalition Against Trafficking in Women

http://www.catwinternational.org/

The Coalition Against Trafficking in Women-International (CATW) is a nongovernmental organization that seeks to promote the human rights of women by collaborating internationally to combat sexual exploitation in all its forms. CATW was founded in 1988 and has the distinction of being the first international nongovernmental organization to focus on human trafficking, especially sex trafficking of women and girls. *Visit the Fact Book section of the Web site and select any two countries, preferably a developed and a developing country, and compare and contrast the statistics on human trafficking from those two countries.*

Feminist Majority Foundation

http://www.feminist.org/

The Feminist Majority Foundation (FMF) is a feminist nonprofit organization in the United States dedicated to women's equality, reproductive health, and nonviolence. The organization was founded by Eleanor Smeal in 1987 and currently has offices in Washington, D.C., and Los Angeles, California. It carries out research and action programs focusing on advancing the legal, social, and political equality of women with men, countering the backlash to women's advancement, and recruiting and training young feminists to encourage future leadership for the feminist movement in the United States. *In the Global Feminism section, read about the global gag rule, a U.S. policy initiative that affects the reproductive health of females globally. After reading about the policy, make an informed decision about whether you support it or not and give reasons for your choice.*

International Planned Parenthood Federation

http://www.ippf.org/en

The International Planned Parenthood Federation is a global nongovernmental organization and a leading advocate for sexual and reproductive health and rights for all. It was first formed in 1952 in Bombay, India, and now consists of more than 149 member associations working in more than 189 countries. Member associations provide nonprofit family planning services, sexual health and abuse prevention training, and education. *Explore the "5 A's" on the organization Web site and select one of those A's. Which of these A's do you think is most important with respect to the health of a woman and why?*

The Society for Women's Health Research

http://www.womenshealthresearch.org/site/PageServer

The Society for Women's Health Research is a one-of-a-kind nonprofit American organization that seeks to improve the health of all females through research, education, and advocacy. The society has pushed the concept of gender-based research and, since its inception in 1990, has brought to national attention the need for the appropriate inclusion of women in major medical research studies and the need for more information about conditions affecting women exclusively, disproportionately, or differently than men. *Read any one of the fact sheets available on the Web site regarding women's health. Was any of the information new or unexpected to you?*

Susan G. Komen for the Cure

http://ww5.komen.org/AboutUs/AboutUs.html

Susan G. Komen for the Cure, previously known as the Susan G. Komen Breast Cancer Foundation, is an international organization supporting breast cancer research. Founded in 1982, the organization has raised more than $1 billion for research, education, and health services. Komen has more than 75,000 volunteers nationwide, with 122 affiliates in the United States (47 of the 50 states) and 3 in other countries. *Explore the section on complementary therapies for breast cancer. Select any one therapy and compare it with more standard therapies such as radiation therapy or surgical procedures for breast cancer. Do you think the complementary therapy you selected should be funded or researched? Explain the reasoning behind your answer.*

The White Ribbon Alliance for Safe Motherhood

http://www.whiteribbonalliance.org/

The White Ribbon Alliance for Safe Motherhood is an international coalition of individuals and organizations formed to promote increased public awareness of the need to make pregnancy and childbirth safe for all women and newborns in developing countries as well as developed countries. The alliance was launched in 1999 and today boasts of members in 107 countries. The organization recently launched a worldwide campaign—A Promise to Mothers Lost—to foster political will to invest in maternal health with an aim of reducing poverty and securing human dignity for people all over the world. *Explore the Web site in detail and come up with four unique ways by which you could contribute to improving maternal health on a local or international level. Compare your ideas with your colleagues.*

REFERENCES

AbouZahr, C. (2003). Global burden of maternal death and disability. *British Medical Bulletin, 67*(1), 1–11.

Betti, S. (2003). New prospects for inter-state co-operation in criminal matters: The Palermo Convention. *International Criminal Law Review, 3*(2), 151–167.

Campbell, J. C. (2002). Health consequences of intimate partner violence. *Lancet, 359*(9314), 1331–1336.

Centers for Disease Control and Prevention. (2006). Cancer: Symptoms of breast cancer. Retrieved from http://www.cdc.gov/cancer/breast/basic_info/symptoms.htm

Flood, M. (2001). Men's collective anti-violence activism and the struggle for gender justice. *Development, 44*(3), 42–47.

Hamberger, L. K., Saunders, D. G., & Hovey, M. (1992). Prevalence of domestic violence in community practice and rate of physician inquiry. *Family Medicine, 24*(4), 283–287.

Hughes, D. M. (2000). The "Natasha" trade: The transnational shadow market of trafficking in women. *Journal of International Affairs, 53*(2), 625–651.

Humphrey, L. L., Helfand, M., Chan, B. K. S., & Woolf, S. H. (2002). Breast cancer screening: A summary of the evidence for the US Preventive Services Task Force. *Annals of Internal Medicine, 137*(5 Pt. 1), 347–360.

International Women's Health Coalition. (2008). *Women and risk of HIV/AIDS infection.* Retrieved from http://iwhc.org/docUploads/Women%20and%20HIV%206.4.08%20final%20update.pdf

Library of Congress. (2002). *Trafficking in women and children: The U.S. and international response.* Retrieved from http://conventionagainsttorture.biz/crs_country/CRSReportTrafficking InWomenAndChildrenTheU.S.AndInternationalResponse(July22,2002)Updated.pdf

Mahler, H. (1987). The safe motherhood initiative: A call to action. *Lancet, 1*(8534), 668–670.

Maine, D. (1993). *Reduction of maternal mortality in Bangladesh during 1995–2000: Concept paper.* Dhaka: United Nations Children's Fund.

Mezey, G., Bacchus, L., Bewley, S., & White, S. (2005). Domestic violence, lifetime trauma and psychological health of childbearing women. *BJOG An International Journal of Obstetrics, 112*(2), 197–204.

Njovana, E., & Watts, C. (1996). Gender violence in Zimbabwe: A need for collaborative action. *Reproductive Health Matters, 7,* 46–55.

Olson, L., Anctil, C., Fullerton, L., Brillman, J., Arbuckle, J., & Sklar, D. (1996). Increasing emergency physician recognition of domestic violence. *Annals of Emergency Medicine, 27*(6), 741–746.

Pan American Health Organization. (2001). *Trafficking of women and children for sexual exploitation in the Americas.* Retrieved from http://www.paho.org/English/AD/GE/TraffickingPaper.pdf

Schwartz, I. L. (1991). Sexual violence against women: Prevalence, consequences, societal factors, and prevention. *American Journal of Preventive Medicine, 7*(6), 363–373.

Society for Women's Health Research. (2008). Just the facts! Retrieved October 16, 2008, from http://www.womenshealthresearch.org/site/PageServer?pagename=hs_healthfacts

Susan G. Komen for the Cure. (2008a). What is breast cancer? Retrieved October 15, 2008, from http://www.komen.org/BreastCancer/WhatisBreastCancer.html

Susan G. Komen for the Cure. (2008b). Statistics. Retrieved November 11, 2008, from http://www.komen.org/BreastCancer/Statistics.html

Susan G. Komen for the Cure. (2008c). Risk factors and prevention. Retrieved October 11, 2008, from http://www.komen.org/breastcancer/loweryourrisk.html

United Nations. (1994). Declaration on the elimination of violence against women. Retrieved from http://www.unhchr.ch/huridocda/huridoca.nsf/(Symbol)/A.RES.48.104.En?Opendocument

United Nations. (2005). *United Nations expert group meeting on international migration and development.* Retrieved from http://www.un.org/esa/population/meetings/ittmigdev2005/P15_IOmelaniuk.pdf

United Nations Population Fund. (2007). Stepping up efforts to save mothers' lives. Retrieved from http://www.unfpa.org/mothers/

Vandenhole, W. (2005). *Non-discrimination and equality in the view of the UN human rights treaty bodies.* Antwerp, Netherlands: Intersentia.

Vuylsteke, B. (2004). Current status of syndromic management of sexually transmitted infections in developing countries. *Sexually Transmitted Infections, 80*(5), 333–334.

Wilt, S., & Olson, S. (1996). Prevalence of domestic violence in the United States. *Journal of the American Medical Women's Association, 51*(3), 77–82.

Wizemann, T. M., & Pardue, M. L. (2001). *Exploring the biological contributions to human health. Does sex matter?* Washington, DC: National Academy Press.

World Health Organization. (2000a). Women and sexually transmitted infections. Retrieved from http://www.who.int/mediacentre/factsheets/fs249/en/

World Health Organization. (2000b). Violence against women. Retrieved from http://www.who.int/mediacentre/factsheets/fs239/en/

World Health Organization. (2002). *World report on violence and health.* Retrieved from http://libdoc.who.int/publications/2002/9241545615_eng.pdf.

World Health Organization. (2006). *Integrating gender into the curricula for health professionals: Meeting report.* Retrieved from http://www.who.int/gender/documents/GWH_curricula_web2.pdf

World Health Organization. (2007a). What is a gender-based approach to public health? Retrieved from http://www.who.int/features/qa/56/en/index.html

World Health Organization. (2007b). Sexually transmitted infections. Retrieved from http://www.who.int/mediacentre/factsheets/fs110/en/

World Health Organization. (2008a). Why gender and women's health? Retrieved from http://www.who.int/gender/genderandwomen/en/index.html

World Health Organization. (2008b). Making pregnancy safer: Maternal mortality. Retrieved from http://www.who.int/making_pregnancy_safer/topics/maternal_mortality/en/

World Health Organization. (2008c). Female genital mutilation. Retrieved from http://www.who.int/mediacentre/factsheets/fs241/en/

World Health Organization. (2008d). *Proportion of births attended by a skilled health worker—2008 updates.* Retrieved from http://www.who.int/reproductive-health/global_monitoring/skilled_attendant_at_birth2008.pdf.

World Health Organization. (2008e). *Tracking progress in maternal, newborn and child survival.* Retrieved from http://www.who.int/entity/pmnch/Countdownto2015FINALREPORT-apr7.pdf.

World Health Organization. (2008f). Making pregnancy safer. Retrieved from http://www.who.int/making_pregnancy_safer/about/department/en/index.html

World Health Organization. (2008g). IMPAC—a MPS cornerstone. Retrieved from http://www.who.int/making_pregnancy_safer/about/impac/en/index.html

World Health Organization. (2008h). *The world health report 1998. Life in the 21st century: A vision for all.* Retrieved November 7, 2008, from http://www.who.int/entity/whr/1998/en/whr98_en.pdf

World Health Organization. (2008i). *The HIV/AIDS program at WHO.* Available from http://www.who.int/hiv/mediacentre/Who_we_are_A4_en.pdf

World Health Organization. (2008j). Screening for breast cancer. Retrieved from http://www.who.int/cancer/detection/breastcancer/en/

Child Health

AFTER READING THIS CHAPTER YOU SHOULD BE ABLE TO

- Define abuse and be able to discuss the different kinds of abuse
- Enumerate major causes of mortality and morbidity in infancy and early and late childhood
- Discuss the World Health Organization's Global Strategy for Infant and Young Child Feeding and how it builds on the earlier Innocenti Declaration and the Baby-Friendly Hospital Initiative
- Describe the epidemiology and prevention of HIV/AIDS in children
- Explain the integrated management of childhood illness approach of the World Health Organization
- Discuss the importance of breastfeeding from a public health perspective
- Assess the importance of the Millennium Declaration and the Millennium Development Goals and define the three indicators used to assess progress in achieving those goals

MAJOR HEALTH ISSUES CONCERNING CHILDREN _____

Currently, approximately 10 million children younger than 5 years die annually. Most children could easily survive beyond this age if they were provided easy access to simple, affordable health interventions. The risk of dying is highest in the first month of life and decreases thereafter (World Health Organization [WHO], 1999a, 2008a). Significant overlap exists between the diseases claiming the maximum number of fatalities in children and the diseases responsible for their major morbidity, or **burden of disease** (the gap between current health status and an ideal situation in which everyone lives into old age free of disease and disability).

Tables **9.1** and **9.2** illustrate the major causes responsible for death and disability in children younger than 15 years, across both sexes and globally. Premature birth, birth asphyxia, and infections are responsible for most newborn deaths. Newborn deaths and other health risks can be effectively minimized by the provision of quality care during pregnancy, ensuring safe delivery by a skilled birth attendant, and **comprehensive neonatal care** (i.e., immediate attention to breathing and warmth, hygienic cord and skin care, and early initiation of exclusive breastfeeding).

TABLE 9.1 Top Five Leading Causes of Death in Children in 1998 (Both Sexes)	
Age Group	**Cause of Death (in decreasing order of lives claimed)**
0–4 years	Acute lower respiratory infections
	Diarrheal diseases
	Measles
	Malaria
	Congenital abnormalities
5–14 years	Acute lower respiratory infections
	Diarrheal diseases
	Measles
	Malaria
	Congenital abnormalities

Source: Taken from World Health Organization. (1999a). *Injury: A leading cause of the global burden of disease* (p. 11). Geneva: Author. Retrieved from http://whqlibdoc.who.int/hq/1999/WHO_HSC_PVI_99.11.pdf

TABLE 9.2	The Top Five Leading Causes of Burden of Disease in Children in 1998 (Both Sexes)
Age Group	**Underlying Cause (in decreasing order of importance)**
0–4 years	Perinatal conditions
	Acute lower respiratory infections
	Diarrheal diseases
	Malaria
	Measles
5–14 years	Falls
	Road traffic injuries
	Acute lower respiratory infections
	Malaria
	Drowning

Source: Taken from World Health Organization. (1999a). *Injury: A leading cause of the global burden of disease* (p. 12). Geneva: Author. Retrieved from http://whqlibdoc.who.int/hq/1999/WHO_HSC_PVI_99.11.pdf

From 1 month to 5 years of age, pneumonia, diarrhea, malaria, measles, and HIV infection account for the maximum number of deaths. Protein-energy malnutrition (or malnutrition) is estimated to contribute to one of every three deaths in this age group. As explained in Chapter 6, the terms *protein-energy malnutrition* (PEM) and *protein-energy deficiency* are used to denote a general lack of food as opposed to a deficiency of any one type of vitamin or mineral. In children younger than 5 years, pneumonia is the prime cause of death. Global statistics on pneumonia are highly skewed, with almost 75% of cases occurring in just 15 countries. Addressing issues such as malnutrition and indoor air pollution, enforcing vaccination, and encouraging breastfeeding can help prevent most, if not all, of these deaths. Antibiotics and oxygen treatment are also vital for effectively managing illnesses (WHO, 1999a).

In developing nations, diarrheal diseases are a leading cause of sickness and death among children. Breastfeeding can help prevent diarrhea among young children. Treatment of sick children with **oral rehydration solution or salts (ORS)** combined with zinc supplements is safe, cost-effective, and saves lives. Oral rehydration solution consists of a solution of salts and sugars that is administered orally as a simple, cheap, and effective treatment for the dehydration associated with diarrhea, particularly gastroenteritis such as that caused by cholera or rotavirus.

Pertussis, or whooping cough, is a vaccine-preventable bacterial disease of the respiratory tract acquired via droplet infection. Coughing spells that last 4 to 8 weeks are the major clinical feature of this disease. Whooping cough, rarely seen in the developed world, is responsible for significant mortality and morbidity in the 0-to-4-years age group globally (WHO, 2008a).

For the 5-to-14-years age group, the top five causes of death are acute lower respiratory infections, diarrheal diseases, measles, malaria, and congenital abnormalities (birth defects that are present at birth). Protein-energy malnutrition remains an important cause of mortality even for this age group. Surprisingly, the causes for maximum morbidity are somewhat different for this age group than the causes for mortality. Of the top ten causes of maximum morbidity, the first five causes are falls, road traffic injuries, acute lower respiratory infections, malaria, and drowning. HIV/AIDS, pertussis, tetanus, and malnutrition account for the remaining five causes.

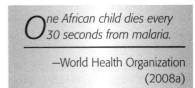

One African child dies every 30 seconds from malaria.

—World Health Organization (2008a)

Practical, low-cost interventions can prevent almost two-thirds of child deaths. Programs initiated by global agencies such as the World Health Organization are helping countries improve child health by providing instruction on how to deliver integrated, effective care in a continuum that starts with a healthy pregnancy for the mother and proceeds through birth and care of the child up to 5 years of age.

CHILD MORTALITY

The distribution of mortality in young populations is highly skewed. Even in the 0-to-5 age group, the distribution is quite uneven. The youngest children are the most at risk: 69% of under-5 deaths occur in infancy (the first year of life), particularly during the neonatal period (the first month of life), when nearly 37% of all child deaths occur.

The **Millennium Declaration** by the United Nations, adopted at the Millennium Summit in 2000, promoted the development of child epidemiology. The epidemiologic indicators employed to follow the progress made in achieving the Millennium Development Goals related to child mortality are as follows (WHO, 2008b):

- **Under-5 mortality rate:** The probability of a child born in a specific year or period dying before reaching the age of 5, if subject to age-specific mortality rates of that period
- **Infant mortality rate:** The probability of a child born in a specific year or period dying before reaching the age of 1, if subject to age-specific mortality rates of that period

- **Proportion of 1-year-old children immunized against measles:** The percentage of children younger than 1 year who have received at least one dose of a measles vaccine

Globally, striking disparities exist in the under-5 and infant mortality rates and the distribution of the causes of death contributing to those rates. For instance, the infant mortality rates across the globe vary from a low of 6.37 in the United States to a high of 157.43 in Afghanistan. However, some trends can be surmised from the available data. Middle- and low-income countries shoulder a disproportionately high burden of child death. Of the six world regions defined by the World Health Organization, the African region is the location of almost 50% of child deaths, and the South-East Asian region is the location of 25%. The progress toward achievement of the Millennium Development Goals is also highly uneven, with the African region lagging far behind the Americas and the European region (WHO, 2008b).

> *M*illennium Development Goal (MDG) 4 aims to reduce by two thirds the mortality rate of children under five between 1990 and 2015.
>
> —World Health Organization (2008b)

Table 9.3 lists the top nine causes of death in neonates and children younger than 5 years (WHO, 2008c). It should be borne in mind that the occurrence of each

TABLE 9.3 Major Causes of Death in Neonates and Children Younger Than 5 Years, 2004	
Cause of Death	**Frequency (%)**
Neonatal deaths	36
Acute respiratory infections	17
Diarrheal diseases	16
Malaria	7
Measles	4
HIV/AIDS	2
Other infectious and parasitic diseases	9
Noncommunicable diseases (postneonatal)	4
Injuries (postneonatal)	4

Source: Adapted from World Health Organization. (2008c). *The global burden of disease: 2004 update* (p. 14). Geneva: Author. Retrieved from http://www.who.int/entity/healthinfo/global_burden_disease/GBD_report_2004update_full.pdf

of these conditions varies enormously across different countries. For example, whereas measles was formally eradicated from the United States in 2002 (with only sporadic cases reported every now and then), it continues to be a public health issue of concern in Africa.

FOCUS FEATURE 9.1   Ten Facts on Child Health

1. A child's risk of dying is highest in the first month of life, when safe childbirth and effective neonatal care are essential. Preterm birth, birth asphyxia, and infections cause most newborn deaths. Once children have reached 1 month of age, and up until the age of 5 years, the main causes of loss of life are pneumonia, diarrhea, malaria, measles, and HIV. Malnutrition contributes to more than half of all child deaths.
2. Newborn life is fragile. Almost 4 million children die every year within a month of their birth.
3. Pneumonia is the largest single cause of death in children under 5 years of age. Addressing the major risk factors for the illness—malnutrition and indoor air pollution—is essential to prevention, along with vaccination. Antibiotics and oxygen are vital treatment tools.
4. Diarrheal diseases are a leading cause of sickness and death among children in developing countries. Exclusive breastfeeding helps prevent diarrhea among young children. Treatment of sick children with oral rehydration solution (ORS) and zinc supplements is safe, cost-effective, and saves lives. The lives of more than 50 million children have been saved in the last 25 years as a result of ORS.
5. Child survival rates differ significantly around the world—three-quarters of child deaths occur in Africa and South-East Asia. Within countries, child mortality is higher in rural areas, and among poorer and less educated families.
6. Over 90% of children with HIV are infected through mother-to-child transmission, which is preventable with the use of antiretrovirals, as well as safer delivery and feeding practices. An estimated 2.3 million children younger than 15 years are living with HIV, and every day more than 1,400 are newly infected. Without intervention, more than half of all HIV-infected children die before their second birthday.
7. About 20 million children under 5 worldwide are severely malnourished, which leaves them more vulnerable to illness and early death. Around three-quarters of these children can be treated with ready-to-use therapeutic foods. These highly fortified and energy-rich foods provide ample nutrients for malnourished children older than 6 months and allow them to be treated at home.
8. About two-thirds of child deaths are preventable through access to practical, low-cost interventions and effective primary care up to 5 years of age.
9. One of the eight Millennium Development Goals relates directly to child health and aims to reduce the under-5 mortality rate by two-thirds by 2015.
10. Every 30 seconds a child dies from malaria in Africa. It is the leading cause of death in that region among under-5s. Insecticide-treated nets prevent transmission and increase child survival. Early treatment with antimalarial medication saves lives.

Source: World Health Organization (WHO). (2007). *Ten facts on child health*. Geneva: Author. Retrieved from http://www.who.int/features/factfiles/child_health2/en/#

NUTRITION

Global Strategy for Infant and Young Child Feeding

As mentioned previously, malnutrition is an important cause of death and disability in children. Malnutrition can cause death by itself, but can also weaken the immune system enough for other infections and conditions to set in. Further, the growth and development of a child can be severely affected as a consequence. Good nutrition is important for survival, physical and mental development, performance, productivity, health, and well-being across the entire life span of a human being.

With this in mind, the **Global Strategy for Infant and Young Child Feeding** was endorsed by the member states of the World Health Organization and the executive board of the United Nations Children's Fund (UNICEF) in 2002. The strategy aimed to rekindle global efforts to guard, foster, and support appropriate infant and young child feeding. This global approach builds on previous initiatives such as the **Innocenti Declaration** and the **Baby-Friendly Hospital Initiative** and is employed by WHO to facilitate research and development in the field and provide technical support to countries. The purpose of this WHO strategy is to attend to the needs of children globally, especially children in difficult or high-risk circumstances, such as infants of mothers living with HIV, low-birth-weight infants, and infants in emergency situations (WHO, 2008d).

Breastfeeding

The profound health benefits of breast milk have been proven without doubt. For infants younger than 2 years, breastfeeding can be a powerful preventive intervention, with the potential to prevent 1.4 million under-5 deaths in the developing world. Being the natural first food, breast milk provides all the energy and nutrients that the infant needs for the first months of life, up to one-half the child's nutritional needs during the second half of the first year, and one-third of the needs for the second year. It helps promote sensory and cognitive development, and protects the infant against infectious and chronic diseases. Infant mortality due to common childhood illnesses such as diarrhea or pneumonia can be reduced with breastfeeding. Convalescence is also greatly shortened. For mothers, breastfeeding is a natural method of spacing children, reduces the risk of ovarian and breast cancer, and helps in bonding with the baby (UNICEF, 2008a; WHO, 2008e).

Evidence-based recommendations regarding breastfeeding have been compiled by the World Health Organization and UNICEF. These recommendations include the following: initiation of breastfeeding within the first hour after birth; exclusive breastfeeding for the first 6 months; and continued breastfeeding for 2 years or more, together with safe, nutritionally adequate, age-appropriate, responsive complementary feeding starting in the sixth month. These global health organizations also provide technical support to countries and carry out special educational programs for high-risk children and mothers.

Innocenti Declaration

The Innocenti Declaration on the Protection, Promotion and Support of Breastfeeding was prepared and adopted by participants at a meeting of policy makers jointly sponsored by WHO and UNICEF in Florence, Italy, in 1990 (UNICEF, 2008b). The declaration endorsed breast milk as the ideal nutrition for and a contributor to the healthy growth and development of infants. Working on an international agenda with ambitious targets for the protection, promotion, and support of breastfeeding, the declaration set a number of operational targets whereby all governments, by 1995, would have done the following:

- Appointed a national breastfeeding coordinator and a multisectoral national breastfeeding committee
- Ensured that every facility providing maternity services fully practices all of the **Ten Steps to Successful Breastfeeding** (Table 9.4)

TABLE 9.4   Ten Steps to Successful Breastfeeding
Every facility providing maternity services and care for newborn infants should:
1. Have a written breastfeeding policy that is routinely communicated to all health care staff
2. Train all health care staff in skills necessary to implement this policy
3. Inform all pregnant women about the benefits and management of breastfeeding
4. Help mothers initiate breastfeeding within a half-hour of birth
5. Show mothers how to breastfeed, and how to maintain lactation even if they should be separated from their infants
6. Give newborn infants no food or drink other than breast milk, unless medically indicated
7. Practice rooming-in (allowing mothers and infants to remain together) 24 hours a day
8. Encourage breastfeeding on demand
9. Give no artificial teats or pacifiers (also called dummies or soothers) to breastfeeding infants
10. Foster the establishment of breastfeeding support groups and refer mothers to them on discharge from the hospital or clinic

Source: Taken from World Health Organization and UNICEF. (1989). *Protecting, promoting and supporting breast feeding—The special role of maternity services.* Geneva: Author. Retrieved from http://www.who.int/bookorders/anglais/detart1.jsp?sesslan=1&codlan=1&codcol=15&codcch=326

- Taken action to give effect to the principles and aim of the international code of marketing of breast milk substitutes
- Enacted imaginative legislation protecting the breastfeeding rights of working women

Baby-Friendly Hospital Initiative

The Baby-Friendly Hospital Initiative (BFHI) aims to reduce infant morbidity and mortality across the globe by creating a health care environment where breastfeeding is the norm. The World Health Organization and the United Nations Children's Fund confer the title of "baby-friendly hospital" to institutions worldwide that promote evidence-based strategies concerning infant feeding. As a consequence of this initiative, the likelihood of informed decision making regarding infant feeding is increased and more and more mothers acquire the skills needed to initiate and continue breastfeeding. It is termed *baby friendly* because it is a worldwide strategy inclusive of and helpful to all mothers irrespective of how they choose to feed their infants. Health care institutions must fulfill stringent criteria to be able to earn the designation of "baby friendly" (WHO, 2008f). The prime objectives of the BFHI are to:

- Enable mothers to make an informed choice about how to feed their newborns
- Support early initiation of breastfeeding
- Promote exclusive breastfeeding for the first 6 months
- Ensure the cessation of free and low-cost infant formula supply to hospitals
- Incorporate at a more advanced stage other maternal and infant health care issues to the initiative

Complementary Feeding

When breast milk is not enough to meet the infant's nutritional demands, complementary foods should be added to the diet of the child. **Complementary feeding** is the transitional period from exclusive breastfeeding to family foods, which usually covers the ages from 6 months to 18 to 24 months. It is a very vulnerable period for the child, and it is around this time that malnutrition affects most infants. Poor complementary feeding practices contribute considerably to the high prevalence of malnutrition in children younger than 5 years worldwide (WHO, 2008g).

Certain important points should be borne in mind regarding complementary feeding in order to harness its full benefits. It is vital to start complementary feeding in a timely manner, usually around 6 months of age, for all infants. It should be adequate in amount so as to provide roughly the same nutritional value as would breast milk. All measures should be taken to minimize the risk of contamination with pathogens; hence, food preparation and handling should be done with caution. Finally, it is important to deliver the food in an appropriate manner, the texture should be baby friendly, and the quantity should be sufficient.

> *Active or responsive feeding* is an approach towards complementary feeding where the caregiver responds to the child's clues for hunger and which involves active care and stimulation of the child.
>
> —World Health Organization (2008g)

According to the World Health Organization's recommendations, all infants should start receiving complementary foods at 6 months of age in addition to breast milk. The frequency should initially be twice or thrice a day between 6 to 8 months, increasing to three or four times a day between 9 to 11 months and 12 to 24 months, with additional nutritious snacks offered one or two times per day, as needed.

Significant initiatives are being undertaken on a global scale to ensure that the prevalence of breastfeeding is maximized worldwide. As part of its larger integrated management of childhood illness strategy, WHO has developed a protocol for adapting feeding recommendations to better suit local feeding practices, dealing with common regional problems associated with feeding, and defining adequate complementary foods. Courses for health professionals are being developed that provide fairly detailed guidelines on how to support complementary feeding.

Feeding in Unusually Difficult Circumstances

There is a growing realization that despite the multiple advantages of breastfeeding, the current guidelines for breastfeeding may be harder to adhere to for certain vulnerable groups. Such families in challenging circumstances need special attention and practical support to be able to feed their children adequately. Some of these vulnerable groups are as follows:

- HIV-infected mothers and their infants
- Low-birth-weight or premature infants
- Infants and young children who are malnourished
- Adolescent mothers and their infants
- People suffering the consequences of natural or human-made tragedies such as floods, drought, earthquakes, war, civil unrest, and severe political and economic living conditions

- Children residing in special circumstances, such as foster care, or with mothers who have physical or mental disabilities, or children whose mothers are incarcerated or involved in substance abuse

Technical guidelines and materials for infant and young child feeding for vulnerable groups (in particular HIV-infected mothers and their infants), infant feeding in emergency situations, feeding of malnourished children, and feeding low-birth-weight and premature infants have been developed by the **Department of Child and Adolescent Health and Development**, a department created within WHO for preventing and managing the health problems of infants, children, and adolescents (WHO, 2008h).

Extra attention is often needed, both during initial rehabilitation and over a longer term, for malnourished children because, by virtue of natural and socioeconomic factors, such children often cluster in regions and environments where improving the quality and quantity of food intake is exceptionally difficult. For infants and young children, continued breastfeeding and even restarting lactation can have striking health benefits.

Ready-to-use therapeutic food (RUTF) has radically transformed the treatment of severe malnutrition. This recently developed home-based treatment for severe acute malnutrition is improving the lives of hundreds of thousands of children every year by providing foods that are safe to use at home and that ensure rapid weight gain in severely malnourished children.

HIV Infection and Infant Feeding

As discussed earlier, breastfeeding is the best food for an infant. However, a woman infected with HIV can transmit the virus to her child during pregnancy, labor or delivery, or even later through breastfeeding. It is a public health duty to prevent HIV infection in infants and young children, more so in countries with high rates of infection among pregnant women. On the other hand, supporting optimal breastfeeding to prevent childhood mortality and illness due to diarrhea and respiratory infections is also a public health responsibility. Consequently, the issue of breastfeeding by women infected with HIV creates a serious dilemma.

The general range of the risk of HIV transmission through breastfeeding of any kind without any interventions is 5 to 20% (WHO, UNICEF, UNFPA, & UNAIDS, 2004, 2007). Other estimates are more conservative. Exclusive breastfeeding from about 6 weeks to 6 months was found to carry a risk of about 4% in South Africa

(Coovadia et al., 2007). In Zimbabwe, the HIV transmission rate between 6 weeks and 6 months among infants exclusively breastfed for at least 3 months was estimated at about 1.3% (Iliff et al., 2005). The reason the period measured starts from about 6 weeks and not birth is because this is the time at which it is usually possible to differentiate HIV transmission during delivery from transmission during breastfeeding.

In October 2006, an interagency task team working on behalf of four global agencies involved in prevention and control interventions for HIV/AIDS (namely, the World Health Organization, the United Nations Population Fund [UNFPA], the United Nations Children's Fund, and the Joint United Nations Program on HIV/AIDS [UNAIDS]) endorsed a set of recommendations pertaining to HIV and infant feeding. Most of the endorsed recommendations were carried over from a similar endorsement in 2000, but certain clarifications and updates were made (WHO, UNICEF, UNFPA, & UNAIDS, 2004, 2007). Some of the recommendations are as follows:

- An HIV-infected mother is free to select the most suitable infant feeding option for herself depending on her individual circumstances (including her health status and the local situation) and the availability of health services, counseling, and support.
- HIV-infected mothers should engage in exclusive breastfeeding for the first 6 months of life unless replacement feeding is satisfactory, viable, affordable, sustainable, and safe for both the mothers and their infants before that time.
- When replacement feeding meets the criteria mentioned above, the guidelines recommend avoidance of all breastfeeding by HIV-infected mothers.
- If replacement feeding does not meet the aforementioned criteria, even at 6 months continuation of breastfeeding with additional complementary foods is recommended. Breastfeeding should be completely stopped once a nutritionally satisfactory and safe diet without breast milk can be made available.
- Mothers of HIV-positive infants and young children should be strongly encouraged to continue breastfeeding up to 2 years or beyond.

The remaining guidelines essentially discuss the provision of information and education on mother-to-child transmission of HIV, counseling and other HIV/AIDS-related services for the infected mother, and helping support national programs and primary interventions for HIV prevention, treatment, and care services.

Malnutrition

Even though it is seldom recorded as a direct cause of death, malnutrition is estimated to contribute to more than one-third of all child deaths. Multiple socioeconomic and geopolitical factors are responsible for the highly skewed global distribution of malnutrition. Lack of access to nourishing food, poor feeding practices (inadequate breastfeeding, offering the wrong foods, and a lack of enough quantity of food), and infections (especially diarrheal diseases, pneumonia, measles, and malaria) also damage a child's nutritional status.

The epidemiology, clinical features, and prevention of protein-energy malnutrition are discussed in depth in Chapter 6. This section discusses a public health innovation developed recently that may transform the treatment for malnutrition as we know it today.

Ready-to-Use Therapeutic Food

Ready-to-use therapeutic food, or RUTF, is palatable, soft and crushable nutrient- and energy-dense foods that can be eaten by children more than six months of age without adding water, thereby minimizing the risk of bacterial infection. The end product, which is composed of peanut butter mixed with dried skimmed milk and vitamins and minerals, taken orally, provides the nutrients needed for full recovery. It has an impressive shelf life and can be stored for greater than 15 weeks without any refrigeration, even at tropical temperatures (Manary, 2006; WHO, 2008i, 2008j). RUTF has an exceptionally high energy density of 5.5 kcal/gram. The consumption of just a few spoonfuls of RUTF five to seven times a day by a severely malnourished child can lead to sufficient nutrient intake for complete recovery.

If other medical complications and comorbidities have been ruled out, a malnourished child aged 6 months or older, with good appetite, can be given a standard dose of RUTF adjusted to his or her weight. The food can be consumed with minimal supervision, directly from a container, at any time of the day or night. However, because RUTF does not contain water, access to safe drinking water is essential.

The technology to manufacture RUTF is relatively straightforward and can be easily replicated by any country with a minimal industrial infrastructure. RUTF costs about US$3 per kilogram when locally produced. A child being treated for severe acute malnutrition will need approximately 10 to 15 kg of RUTF consumed over a period of 6 to 8 weeks. Local production of RUTF paste is already under way in several countries, including Congo, Ethiopia, Malawi, and Niger (WHO, 2008i, 2008j).

Focus Feature 9.2   The Integrated Child Development Services Project in India

The Integrated Child Development Services (ICDS) was launched on October 2, 1975, seeking to provide an integrated package of services in a convergent manner for the holistic development of the child. It is an intersectoral program that seeks to directly reach out to children younger than 6 years, especially from vulnerable and remote areas, and give them a head-start by providing an integrated program of early childhood education, health, and nutrition.

With the understanding that a program on early childhood care and education cannot function without the cooperation and participation of mothers, ICDS puts special emphasis on the capability of mothers to look after the health, nutritional, and developmental needs of the child.

The five objectives of the program are to:

1. Lay the foundation for proper psychological development of the child
2. Improve the nutritional and health status of children aged 0 to 6 years
3. Reduce the incidence of mortality, morbidity, malnutrition, and school dropout
4. Enhance the capability of the mother and family to look after the health, nutritional, and development needs of the child
5. Achieve effective coordination of policy and implementation among various departments to promote child development

The package of services provided under the ICDS scheme are supplementary nutrition, nonformal preschool education, immunization, health checkups, referral services, and nutrition and health education. The center point for provision of basic services with the help of community-based workers and helpers is a place called Anganwadi. The Anganwadi, literally meaning a courtyard play center, is a childcare center located within the community.

The strength of the ICDS experiment draws from its core of dedicated Anganwadi workers, community-based frontline female voluntary workers who serve as agents of social change, mobilizing community support for better care of young children, girls, and women. Currently, services under the scheme are being provided to about 56 million beneficiaries, comprising about 46 million children (0–6 years) and approximately 9.5 million pregnant and lactating mothers through a system of about 0.75 million Anganwadi centers.

One of the core objectives of the ICDS project is to reduce the incidence of child mortality and morbidity, malnutrition, and school dropout. Infant mortality in India has declined significantly, from 129 per 1,000 live births in 1970 to 57 per 1,000 live births in the year 2005–2006. Similarly, under-5 mortality has declined from 202 per 1,000 in 1970 to 85 per 1,000 in 2002. The project has been found to have an impact of significant magnitude.

Source: Ministry of Women and Child Development. (2008). *Integrated Child Development Services (ICDS) scheme*. Retrieved November 11, 2008, from http://wcd.nic.in/icds.htm

INTEGRATED MANAGEMENT OF CHILDHOOD ILLNESS _____

The provision of quality health care to a child in a developed country is difficult because of multiple reasons. Limited supplies and equipment severely limit the ability of a physician to practice complicated clinical procedures. The **integrated management of childhood illness (IMCI) strategy** is an integrated approach to child health that attempts to address these limitations of health care systems in developing countries. IMCI focuses on the well-being of the child as a whole and strives to reduce death, illness, and disability and to promote improved growth and development among children younger than 5 years of age. It blends both preventive and curative components of health care (WHO, 2008k).

IMCI is better than the traditional single-condition approach, which focuses on a single medical condition at a time and is more suited for developed countries. In a developing nation, children who seek medical care are often suffering from more than one condition, making a single diagnosis impossible and impractical. IMCI targets the myriad of factors that are responsible for diseases in children and ensures the combined treatment of the major childhood illnesses, emphasizing prevention of disease through immunization and improved nutrition. Seventy-five countries around the globe have already been introduced to IMCI.

IMCI incorporates three main components to help improve the diagnosis and management of diseases in children:

- Improving the case management skills of health care staff
- Improving overall health systems
- Improving family and community health practices

In health facilities, the IMCI approach fosters the precise identification of childhood illnesses in outpatient settings, guarantees optimal combined treatment of all major illnesses, strengthens the counseling of caretakers, and helps speed the referral of gravely ill children. In the home setting, it promotes appropriate care-seeking behaviors, improved nutrition and preventive care, and the correct implementation of prescribed care (WHO, 2008k).

The results of a multicountry evaluation to evaluate the impact, cost, and effectiveness of the IMCI strategy are reassuring. The evaluation has been conducted so far in Brazil, Bangladesh, Peru, Uganda, and the United Republic of Tanzania (Bryce, Victora, Habicht, Vaughan, & Black, 2004). The evaluation found the following results:

- Health workers' performance and quality of care has improved as a consequence of the IMCI approach.
- Under-5 mortality and nutritional status can improve with optimal implementation of IMCI.

- IMCI helps with cost containment since the IMCI approach costs almost six times less per child correctly managed than current care.
- A significant reduction in under-5 mortality can only be achieved if the intervention is implemented on a large scale.
- For best outcomes the intervention needs to be complemented by activities that strengthen system support.

PEDIATRIC HIV/AIDS

The epidemiology and prevention and control of HIV infection and the acquired immunodeficiency syndrome (AIDS) are discussed in Chapter 4. Issues concerning feeding and nutrition in infants and children, especially with regard to breastfeeding by HIV-positive mothers, have been dealt with earlier in this chapter. This section discusses the public health importance of pediatric HIV/AIDS and the measures being instituted to deal with it.

> *Over 90% of children with HIV are infected through mother-to-child transmission, which can be prevented with medications, as well as safer delivery and feeding practices.*
>
> —World Health Organization (2008b)

The significance of HIV as an important public health issue can be gauged from the fact that every day, around 1,500 children (younger than 15 years) are newly infected with HIV. Almost 90% of these children live in sub-Saharan Africa. Globally, AIDS currently accounts for 3% of deaths in children, and 1 of every 6 deaths attributed to HIV is of a child younger than 15 years. Without adequate HIV care, including antiretroviral therapy, the evolution of HIV infection in children is particularly aggressive. Countries such as Botswana and Zimbabwe provide dismal statistics, with HIV being the underlying reason for more than a third of all deaths among children under the age of 5. Pediatric HIV has been practically eliminated in developed countries. Unfortunately, simple preventive programs required for the effective prevention and control of pediatric HIV are essentially missing from the regions where they are most needed, such as sub-Saharan Africa and south Asia (WHO, 2008l).

Epidemiology

More than 95% of HIV-infected children living in sub-Saharan Africa acquire HIV from their mothers in utero (before being born), during delivery, or while being breastfed. Unsafe injections, transfusion of infected blood or blood products, sexual intercourse (more important in adolescents), and scarification are responsible for a small fraction of the number of HIV infections each. Without effective prevention, the risk of HIV transmission from an HIV-infected mother to her child before or during the child's birth is 15% to 25%. With breastfeeding by the mother to 18 to 24 months of age, the transmission risk increases to 30% to 45%. Because of their lack of a well-developed immune system, children, particularly newborns, who have acquired HIV before or during birth or during breastfeeding show a much faster progression of the disease than adults. It has been estimated that between 25% and 30% of children who acquire HIV from their mothers die before their first birthday (WHO, 2002, 2008l).

Prevention and Treatment

All pregnant women must have timely access to HIV testing and counseling to enable them to find out their HIV status and make educated decisions about pregnancy, delivery, and feeding options. Knowledge of their HIV status can also result in prevention of unintended pregnancies among HIV-infected women. Access should be provided to health care services for HIV-positive women that will ensure safe delivery and safe postnatal care and support for the child and the mother. Finally, the use of antiretroviral drugs for treating the mother and preventing infection in the baby could prevent an estimated 315,000 pediatric HIV infections annually with currently available technology (WHO, 2002, 2008l).

Antiretroviral therapy is now the standard of care and has proven to be highly effective in children. Rapid initiation of treatment restores and preserves immune functions, promotes normal growth and development, and prolongs life. Treatment with antiretroviral medications has been shown to reduce mortality by five times or more, resulting in survival rates of 80% and higher (Gibb et al., 2003).

CHILD ABUSE, INJURIES, AND VIOLENCE _____

Child Injuries and Violence

Child injuries and violence are a global public health issue. According to recent estimates, violence and injury claimed more than 5 million lives in the year 2002. An estimated 875,000 of those who lost their lives were children and adolescents under the age of 18 years (World Health Organization. (2008m). Injuries are the leading cause of death for children after their first birthday. Many thousands of children continue to live with varying degrees of disability or psychological scarring. A large share of these injuries (for example, falls, burns, and drowning) occur in either the home or in leisure environments. Traffic-related deaths are another important group of preventable deaths in children. An estimated 3,000 or more people are believed to die on the world's roads every day. Children, pedestrians, cyclists, and the elderly are among the most vulnerable of road users. Worldwide, road traffic injuries are the leading cause of death among young people aged 10 to 24 years.

Violence by young people also affects the health of children and adolescents. The global media is being overwhelmed with daily reports on violence by gangs, in schools, or by young people on the streets. The main victims and perpetrators of such violence are adolescents and young adults themselves. Homicide and nonfatal assaults involving young people contribute greatly to the global burden of premature death, injury, and disability (Reza, Krug, & Mercy, 2001). Childhood injuries and violence can influence a victim's health, social functioning, and general well-being years later in his or her life.

For all the main areas of risk discussed, there are proven ways of reducing both the likelihood and severity of child injury. Traffic-related deaths have declined by enforcing the use of child safety seats, reducing speed, lowering blood alcohol limits, and using graduated driver licensing schemes for novice drivers; burns have been reduced through the use of fire-resistant clothing; and drowning has been prevented by covering wells and fencing swimming pools. Prevention programs that use a multidisciplinary strategy have been shown to be effective in many countries (WHO, 2008m).

Most of the strategies and prevention efforts advocated by global organizations are multidisciplinary in nature. Involvement of policy makers, schools, health facilities, workplaces, the general public, and the media should be a part of any preventive effort that seeks to address child injuries and violence. Policy makers can help support preventive efforts by developing plans of actions, enacting safer

The global launch of the World Report on Child Injury Prevention was scheduled for December 10, 2008, in Hanoi, Vietnam. This report has been developed by WHO and UNICEF to increase awareness about the magnitude, risk factors, and impacts of child injuries globally, to draw attention to the preventability of the problem, and to present what is known about the effectiveness of intervention strategies.

laws, and holding high-level policy discussions. Schools can incorporate child injury prevention into the curriculum. Health facilities can help disseminate information pertaining to child injuries, and the media can complement the same.

Child Abuse

Child abuse has been a part of human civilization since its birth. Reports of infanticide, mutilation, abandonment, and other forms of violence against children have been chronicled in literature, art, and science around many parts of the world and are found in records dating back to early civilizations (Bensel, Rheinberger, & Radbill, 1997). The consequences of child abuse are profound, both in terms of the health of the abused child and the financial costs of the health care needed for the child. Because of the widely divergent rules regarding acceptable parenting practices between different cultures, arriving at a consensus on the definition of child abuse is challenging.

A working definition was drafted by the WHO Consultation on Child Abuse Prevention in 1999 (WHO 1999b):

> Child abuse or maltreatment constitutes all forms of physical and/or emotional ill-treatment, sexual abuse, neglect or negligent treatment or commercial or other exploitation, resulting in actual or potential harm to the child's health, survival, development or dignity in the context of a relationship of responsibility, trust or power.

Based on this definition, four kinds of abusive behaviors can be discussed. It should be borne in mind that these four kinds of abuses are not exclusive to child abuse and can be found across the age spectrum. Further, abuse can also be viewed as either an **act of omission**, in which a caretaker fails to do something he or she is morally, ethically, or legally expected to do, or an **act of commission**, in which a caretaker actively engages in an action detrimental to the health and development of the child.

- **Physical abuse:** Those acts of commission by a caregiver that either cause actual physical harm or have the potential for the same.
- **Sexual abuse:** The use of a child for sexual gratification by a caretaker.
- **Emotional abuse:** The failure of a caregiver to provide an appropriate and nurturing environment, including acts that have an unfavorable effect on the emotional health and development of a child. Restriction of movement, threats and intimidation, discrimination, and rejection can all qualify as emotional abuse.
- **Neglect:** The failure of a caretaker to provide for the development of the child (provided the caretaker has the capacities for doing so) in one or more of the following areas: health, education, nutrition, emotional development, shelter, and safe living conditions. Most forms of neglect are, in fact, acts of omission. Neglect should be distinguished from circumstances arising out of poverty in that neglect can occur only in cases where the family or caregiver has reasonable resources.

Risk Factors for Child Abuse

Risk factors for child abuse can be divided into four broad categories: characteristics specific to the child, caregiver and family characteristics, community factors, and societal factors.

Characteristics Specific to the Child   Certain characteristics (such as age and sex) of a child can increase the prospects of being abused. Vulnerability to child abuse (physical, sexual, and via neglect) is largely based on the child's age. Fatal cases of physical abuse are found mostly among young infants. The distribution of nonfatal abuse is also skewed toward young children. Rates of sexual abuse, on the other hand, peak after the onset of puberty, with the highest rates seen in adolescents (Finkelhor, 1994; Madu & Peltzer, 2000). Gender has also been found to be an important determinant of child abuse. Girls are at higher risk than boys for infanticide, sexual abuse, educational and nutritional neglect, and forced prostitution in most countries (National Research Council, 1993).

Cultural differences regarding the place of women in society and the differential values attached to male and female children can potentially explain many of these differences. Premature infants, twins, and handicapped children have also been shown to be at increased risk for physical abuse and neglect (National Research Council, 1993).

Caregiver and Family Characteristics   Certain traits of the caregiver, as well as elements of the family environment, are closely linked to child abuse and neglect. Whereas some of the factors, particularly geographic ones, modify the risk of abuse, others relate to the psychological and behavioral characteristics of the caregiver or to aspects of the family environment that may adversely affect parenting and lead to child maltreatment. Whether abusers are more likely to be male or female depends, in part, on the kind of abuse. Even though women report using more discipline, men are the most common perpetrators of life-threatening head injuries, abusive fractures, and other fatal injuries.

Perpetrators of sexual abuse of male and female victims are predominantly men (National Research Council, 1993). Physically abusive parents are usually young, single, poor, and unemployed and often have less education than their nonabusing counterparts. In both developing and developed nations, poor, young, single mothers are at the highest risk of using violence toward their children. The personality and behavioral traits associated with higher risk of child abuse and neglect are low self-esteem, poor impulse control, mental health problems, and antisocial behavior (National Research Council, 1993). Abusive parents often have a history of having been abused as children themselves. Domestic violence, stress, and social isolation of the parent have also been linked to child abuse and neglect.

The likelihood of abuse is increased by the size of the family, with overcrowding consistently increasing the potential of child abuse. Chronic neglect is often seen in unstable family environments in which the constitution of the household recurrently changes as family members and others move in and out (Dubowitz & Black, 2001).

Community Factors   A strong association has been found between poverty and child abuse. Higher levels of unemployment and concentrated poverty often predict a higher level of child abuse in a community. In such communities a deterioration of the physical and social infrastructures and scarcity of resources have been blamed as the motivating factors for child abuse. The degree of cohesion and solidarity existing within a community is called **social capital** and is inversely related to the risk of abuse. Higher amounts of social capital or cohesion can neutralize other risk factors favoring abuse (Runyan et al., 1998).

Societal Factors   Several societal factors are believed to have a bearing on the overall risk for child abuse, such as inequalities based on gender and income, cultural norms defining gender roles, the strength of the social welfare system, parent-child relationships, and larger social conflicts and war. However, most of these factors have not been formally examined.

The Consequences of Child Abuse

The consequences of child abuse are severe and often long lasting. Child abuse can have health consequences and financial implications.

Health Burden   A significant share of the global burden of disease is ascribed to poor health attributed directly or indirectly to child abuse. Chronic conditions such as ischemic heart disease, cancer, chronic lung disease, irritable bowel syndrome, and fibromyalgia have been found to be related to experiences of abuse during childhood. It is believed that the adoption of behavioral risk factors such as smoking, alcohol abuse, poor diet, and lack of exercise by the victim is the underlying mechanism.

Short- and long-term psychological damage in victims has also been documented. The physical, behavioral, and emotional symptoms of abuse differ widely between children depending on the child's developmental stage at the time of abuse, the severity of the abuse, the relationship of the perpetrator to the child, the length of time over which the abuse continues, and other environmental factors (National Research Council, 1993).

Financial Burden   The financial costs associated with child abuse are formidable. Both direct costs (costs associated with treatment, visits to the hospital and doctor, and other health services) and indirect costs (lost productivity, disability, decreased quality of life, and premature death) are responsible for the final financial burden.

Prevention

Different approaches have been employed for designing interventions against abuse. Most of the programs focus either on victims or perpetrators of child abuse and neglect. Primary prevention is rarely employed in such interventions. As discussed in the section on violence against women in Chapter 8, the different approaches that can be used to design interventions are family support approaches, health service approaches, therapeutic approaches, legal efforts, and community-based and societal efforts (WHO, 2008m).

Family Support Approaches Many interventions seek to develop parenting practices and provide family support by educating parents, especially in high-risk families, on child development and helping them better their skills in managing their child's behavior. Home visitation programs bring community resources to families in their homes and provide information, support, and other services to improve the functioning of the family. Intensive family preservation services attempt to keep the family together and to avoid children being placed in foster care.

Health Service Approaches Screening by health care professionals plays a key role in the timely identification, treatment, and referral of cases of abuse and neglect; hence, it is imperative that optimal screening guidelines are in place and are adhered to by all health care professionals. Formal education on the detection and reporting of early signs and symptoms of child abuse and neglect exist in the medical school curriculum in some countries (Alpert, 1998). Screening guidelines can only produce results if practitioners have adequate training on child abuse.

Therapeutic Approaches Responses to child abuse and neglect depend on many factors, including the age and developmental level of the child and the presence of environmental stress factors. Interventions can be designed for children who experience abuse directly or vicariously, and also for adults abused as children.

Legal Efforts Reporting of suspected child abuse is mandated by law in a number of countries. Several other countries make the reporting voluntary (Bross, Miyoshi, Miyoshi, & Krugman, 2000). Encouraging reporting is based on the premise that early detection of abuse can avert more serious abuse later on. Child protection service agencies have been established in many nations. They investigate and attempt to substantiate reports of suspected child abuse and, if verified, determine appropriate treatment and referral for the abused child. Court-mandated treatment for child abusers is another approach recommended in several countries.

Community-Based Efforts   Community-based interventions may either focus on a selected population group in a restricted setting, such as in schools, or may be conducted on an extensive scale involving multiple population groups. One of the most widely applied preventive strategies is the inclusion of programs to prevent child sexual abuse in the regular school curriculum in several countries (MacIntyre & Carr, 1999). Another approach to reduce child abuse and neglect is adoption of widespread prevention and educational campaigns, which are believed to cause an increased awareness and understanding of the phenomenon among the general population, consequently resulting in a lower level of abuse. Finally, concerted efforts to change certain community attitudes and behavior can go a long way toward reducing the incidence of child abuse and neglect.

Societal Efforts   National policies and programs can address the root cause of child abuse by successfully dealing with poverty, improving educational levels and job opportunities, and increasing the availability and quality of child care. International treaties can help create mass awareness of child abuse and a commitment to reducing it. The adoption of the **Convention on the Rights of the Child** by the United Nations General Assembly in 1989 is one example of such a treaty. The convention lays down the principle that the rights of children are equal to those of adults.

ADOLESCENT HEALTH

Adolescents (aged 10 to 19 years) constitute almost 20% of the current world population, and 85% of the current adolescent population lives in developing countries. The most pressing health concerns of adolescents are in the areas of mental health, substance abuse, violence, unintentional injuries, nutrition, sexual and reproductive health, and HIV/AIDS. Poverty, lack of access to health care services, and unsafe environments can further complicate the situation.

Almost two-thirds of premature deaths and one-third of the total disease burden in adults are associated with conditions or behaviors that began in youth, including tobacco use, a lack of physical activity, unprotected sex, or exposure to violence. Health promotion interventions during adolescence and programs that better safeguard this age group from risks will ensure longevity and improved productivity overall (WHO, 2008n).

Mental Health

Late childhood and early adolescence mark the emergence of many mental health problems. Interventions aimed at developing social skills, problem-solving skills, and self-confidence can help prevent many mental health problems such as conduct disorders, anxiety, and depression. A comprehensive package of mental health care that includes counseling, therapy, and psychotropic medications should be available for the best outcome.

Substance Use

Strengthening laws, reducing demand, and limiting the availability of illegal substances, tobacco, and alcohol can help promote the healthy development of adolescents. Interventions aimed at increasing the awareness of the dangers of substance use and the development of skills to resist peer pressure can help reduce motivation for substance use.

Violence

Life skills and social development programs for children and adolescents and skill-building initiatives for the child that involve teachers and parents can both be effective in reducing violence. Ongoing psychological and social support can help adolescents deal with the long-term psychological effects of violence and prevent untoward future repercussions.

Unintentional Injuries

Enforcing speed limits, promoting seat belt and helmet use, preventing drunk driving, and providing safer and inexpensive alternatives to driving can all assist in safeguarding adolescent health. Educating children and adolescents regarding how to prevent drowning, burns, and falls can help reduce the probability of their occurrence.

Nutrition

Chronic malnutrition is best intercepted and treated during early childhood, because any delay can lead to unfavorable long-term health and social consequences. Actions to improve access to food could benefit adolescents as well, however. Some ways in which optimal nutritional intake could be ensured among adolescents is by preventing frequent pregnancies, improving access to nutritious food, and using micronutrient supplementation. Promoting healthy eating and exercise habits is also critical to breaking the obesity epidemic.

Sexual and Reproductive Health

Females should be protected from sexual harassment and coercion in educational institutions, workplaces, and in other community settings. Sexual coercion in adolescence needs to be fought by reinforcement of existent laws and enactment of new laws, if needed. A full complement of reproductive health services should be provided to the pregnant adolescent. Effective care during childbearing is important for ensuring the survival of mothers and their babies and the prevention of problems such as fistulas (WHO, 2008p).

HIV/AIDS

The age of initiating sexual intercourse closely parallels the risk of acquiring HIV in young individuals. Abstinence from sexual intercourse and delayed initiation of sexual behavior should be at the heart of any HIV prevention efforts targeting young people (WHO, 2008n).

SCHOOL HEALTH PROMOTION

Even though school health programs have been part of schooling for most of this century, the development of health-promoting schools as a tool in the multifaceted approach to school health is relatively new. Research has shown the importance of well-designed educational programs in schools. For instance, worm infections are the biggest cause of disease among children aged 5 to 14 years worldwide, whereas injury is the leading cause of death and disability among school-aged youth. These and many other health problems can be prevented or their impact diminished through successful school-based health programs (Leger, 1999; WHO, 1951, 2008o).

The first school health promotion programs were based on the classic medical model and targeted specific diseases or health problems in isolation. The focus was on educating children about health and the determinants of disease. The significance of teaching skills pertaining to healthy lifestyles was soon accepted, and skill building is now a part of most health promotion programs.

Programs have been developed to address the major public health problems of contemporary times, such as drug and alcohol misuse, smoking, nutritional patterns, physical activity, mental illness, obesity, injuries, sexual health, and HIV/AIDS. Well-designed school-based health educational and promotional initiatives can be highly cost-effective in that they simultaneously benefit both a nation's education and health (Leger, 1999).

Developments in health promotion policy have greatly influenced the development of health promotion programs. In 1978, the World Health Organization organized an international conference on primary health care in Alma Ata, in what was then the Soviet Union. The end result of the conference was the Declaration of

Alma Ata. One of the ten clauses of this declaration defines the attributes of primary health care as being multisectoral and involving public participation in developing and providing health programs. Both these qualities are found in almost all health promotion programs today.

In 1995, WHO produced a set of guidelines targeted toward schools seeking the coveted designation of a **health-promoting school** (WHO, 1996). These guidelines revolved around six main themes:

- School health policies
- The physical environment of the school
- The social environment of the school
- School/community relationships
- Development of personal health skills
- School health services.

Based on these themes, a health-promoting school is one that constantly improves its capacity as a healthy setting for living, learning, and working by promoting health and scholarship with its entire capacity. Such a school employs health and education officials, teachers, teachers' unions, students, parents, health providers, and community leaders in endeavors to make the school a healthier place. It also encourages policies and practices that promote a healthy environment, school health education, and school health services. Finally, it attempts to improve the health of school employees, families, and community members as well as pupils, and works with community leaders to help them understand how the community affects health and education (Leger, 1999; WHO, 2008o).

SKILL-BUILDING ACTIVITY

The Baby-Friendly Hospital Initiative (BFHI) aims to reduce infant morbidity and mortality across the globe by creating a health care environment in which breastfeeding is the norm. The World Health Organization and the United Nations Children's Fund confer the title of "baby-friendly hospital" on institutions worldwide that promote evidence-based strategies concerning infant feeding. Locate a baby-friendly hospital in your city, state, or region. Find out how the hospital of your choice achieves each of the following five objectives of the BFHI and compile a one-page report on the topic.

1. Enables mothers to make an informed choice about how to feed their newborns
2. Supports early initiation of breastfeeding

3. Promotes exclusive breastfeeding for the first 6 months
4. Ensures the cessation of free and low-cost infant formula supply to hospitals
5. Incorporates at a more advanced stage other maternal and infant health care issues to the initiative

SUMMARY

Approximately 10 million children younger than 5 years die annually; most of these deaths are preventable. The risk of dying is highest in the first month of life and decreases thereafter. Premature birth, birth asphyxia, and infections are responsible for most newborn deaths. Newborn deaths and other health risks can be effectively minimized by provision of quality care during pregnancy, ensuring safe delivery by a skilled birth attendant, and comprehensive neonatal care. From 1 month to 5 years of age, pneumonia, diarrhea, malaria, measles, and HIV infection account for the maximum number of deaths. Protein-energy malnutrition is estimated to contribute to one of every three deaths in this age group. In children younger than 5 years, pneumonia is the prime cause of death. In developing nations, diarrheal diseases are a leading cause of sickness and death among children. Breastfeeding can help prevent diarrhea among young children. Treatment for dehydrated children with oral rehydration solution (ORS) combined with zinc supplements is safe, cost-effective, and saves lives.

For the 5-to-14-years age group, the top five causes of death are acute lower respiratory infections, diarrheal diseases, measles, malaria, and congenital abnormalities. Protein-energy malnutrition remains an important cause of mortality even for this age group. Surprisingly, the causes for maximum morbidity are somewhat different for this age group than the causes for mortality. Of the top ten causes of maximum morbidity, the first five causes are falls, road traffic injuries, acute lower respiratory infections, malaria, and drowning. HIV/AIDS, pertussis, tetanus, and malnutrition account for the remaining five causes.

Practical, low-cost interventions can prevent almost two-thirds of child deaths. Programs initiated by global agencies such as the World Health Organization are helping countries improve child health by providing instruction on how to deliver integrated, effective care in a continuum starting with a healthy pregnancy for the mother through birth and care up to 5 years of age.

The Millennium Declaration by the United Nations promoted the development of pediatric epidemiology. The under-5 mortality rate, infant mortality rate, and the proportion of 1-year-old children immunized against measles are the indicators used to gauge the progress made toward achieving the declaration's goals. Globally, striking disparities exist in the under-5 and infant mortality rates and in the distribution of the causes of death contributing to those rates.

Malnutrition is an important cause of death and disability in children. The Global Strategy for Infant and Young Child Feeding was endorsed by the member states of the World Health Organization and the executive board of the United Nations Children's Fund in 2002. Evidence-based recommendations regarding breast-feeding have been compiled by the World Health Organization and UNICEF. The Innocenti Declaration on the Protection, Promotion and Support of Breast-feeding endorsed breast milk as the ideal nutrition and a contributor to the healthy growth and development of infants. The Baby-Friendly Hospital Initiative aims to reduce infant morbidity and mortality across the globe by creating a health care environment in which breastfeeding is the norm. The World Health Organization and the United Nations Children's Fund confer the title of "baby-friendly hospital" on institutions worldwide that promote evidence-based strategies concerning infant feeding. When breast milk is not enough to meet the infant's nutritional needs, complementary foods should be added to the diet of the child. Technical guidelines and materials for infant and young child feeding for vulnerable groups have been developed by the World Health Organization. Ready-to-use therapeutic food has radically transformed the treatment of severe malnutrition.

A woman infected with HIV can transmit the virus to her child during pregnancy, labor or delivery, or even later through breastfeeding. It is a public health duty to prevent HIV infection in infants and young children, especially in countries with high rates of infection among pregnant women. A set of recommendations pertaining to HIV and infant feeding were endorsed by global agencies.

The integrated management of childhood illness (IMCI) strategy is an integrated approach to child health that attempts to address the limitations of health care systems in developing countries. IMCI focuses on the well-being of the child as a whole and strives to reduce death, illness, and disability and to promote improved growth and development among children younger than 5 years.

HIV has become an important public health issue for children. Modes of transmission can be in utero, during delivery, or while being breastfed or through unsafe injections, transfusion of infected blood or blood products, and sexual intercourse. Timely access to HIV testing and counseling, access to health care services, and the use of antiretroviral drugs for treating the mother and preventing infection in the baby can prevent a huge number of pediatric HIV infections.

Child injuries and violence and child abuse are important global public health issues. There are proven ways of reducing both the likelihood and severity of every kind of child injury. Four kinds of abusive behaviors can be identified: physical abuse, sexual abuse, emotional abuse, and neglect. Risk factors for child abuse can be divided into four broad categories: characteristics specific to the child, caregiver and family characteristics, community factors, and societal factors. Child abuse can have both health and financial consequences. Different preventive approaches that can be used to design interventions for child abuse are family support approaches, health service approaches, therapeutic approaches, legal efforts, and community-based and societal efforts.

Adolescents (aged 10 to 19 years) constitute almost 20% of the current world population, and 85% of the current adolescent population lives in developing countries. The most pressing health concerns of adolescents are in the areas of mental health, substance abuse, violence, unintentional injuries, nutrition, sexual and reproductive health, and HIV/AIDS.

Well-designed school-based health educational and promotional initiatives can be highly cost-effective in that they simultaneously benefit both a nation's education and health. One of the ten clauses of the Alma Ata Declaration defines the attributes of primary health care as being multisectoral and involving public participation in developing and providing health programs. Both these qualities are found in almost all health promotion programs today. A health-promoting school is one that constantly improves its capacity as a healthy setting for living, learning, and working by promoting health and scholarship with its entire capacity.

IMPORTANT TERMS

act of commission

act of omission

active or responsive feeding

Baby-Friendly Hospital Initiative

burden of disease

child abuse

complementary feeding

comprehensive neonatal care

Convention on the Rights of the Child

Department of Child and Adolescent
  Health and Development

emotional abuse

Global Strategy for Infant
  and Young Child Feeding

health-promoting school

infant mortality rate

Innocenti Declaration

integrated management of childhood
  illness (IMCI) strategy

Millennium Declaration

neglect

oral rehydration solution or salts (ORS)

physical abuse

proportion of 1-year-old children
  immunized against measles

ready-to-use therapeutic food (RUTF)

sexual abuse

social capital

Ten Steps to Successful Breastfeeding

under-5 mortality rate

REVIEW QUESTIONS

1. Enumerate the different kinds of child abuse. Define neglect and give an example.
2. Enumerate the top five causes of mortality for children younger than 4 years.
3. Cite four benefits of breastfeeding. What is the Innocenti Declaration?
4. List four situations in which breastfeeding an infant according to established guidelines might be difficult.
5. What are some of the benefits of using ready-to-use therapeutic food in the global fight against malnutrition?
6. How do children acquire HIV infection? Discuss the global efforts directed toward preventing pediatric HIV infections.
7. Describe possible risk factors for child abuse.
8. Define health-promoting school.

WEB SITES TO EXPLORE

American Academy of Pediatrics

http://www.aap.org/

The official Web site of the American Academy of Pediatrics (AAP), an institution composed of 60,000 pediatricians committed to the attainment of optimal physical, mental, and social health and well-being for all infants, children, adolescents, and young adults, contains general information on child health and specific guidelines pertaining to specific pediatric issues. The policies and guidelines of the AAP are also available here. *Select any pediatric condition or disease that interests you from the topics page and compile a one-page fact sheet with the following information: (a) risk factors for that condition, (b) symptoms, (c) treatment(s) available, and (d) prevention, if any.*

Child Rights and You

http://www.cry.org/index.html

Child Rights and You (formerly Child Relief and You), commonly abbreviated as CRY, is a nonprofit organization, established in 1979, that aims to restore children's rights in India. The organization partners with grassroots nongovernmental organizations within and outside India to uplift thousands of Indian children denied basic children's rights. The organization maintains that its role is mainly that of an enabler, that is, a catalyst between two groups of people: (1) the development organizations and individuals working at grassroots level with marginalized children, their families, and communities, and (2) individuals who believe in the rights of children and are willing to provide support or resources for those rights. *Explore the Web site and come up with three unique ways (other than monetary donation) in which you could get involved with CRY and contribute to its cause.*

International Road Federation

http://www.irfnet.org/index.php

An estimated 3,000 or more people are believed to die on the world's roads every day. Children, pedestrians, cyclists, and the elderly are among the most vulnerable of road users. The International Road Federation (IRF) is a nongovernmental, not-for-profit organization spanning 80 countries across six continents, with the mission to support and promote development and maintenance of better, safer, and more sustainable roads and road networks. It helps put in place technological solutions and management practices that provide maximum economic and social returns from national road investments. *Download and read the document "IRF Report 2006: Past and Future Challenges." What do you understand by the terms "contracting for maintenance" and "road financing"?*

International Society for Prevention of Child Abuse and Neglect

http://www.ispcan.org/

The International Society for the Prevention of Child Abuse and Neglect (ISPCAN) is a multidisciplinary international organization that was founded in 1977. ISPCAN's mission is to support individuals and organizations working to protect children from abuse and neglect worldwide. ISPCAN boasts of members from almost 180 different nations. The organization offers educational and training events geared toward child abuse prevention in many countries. The organization has a well-known publication, *Child Abuse and Neglect: The International Journal. Visit the ISPCAN Web site and go to the section titled "Presentation Materials and On-line Resources." Watch the PowerPoint presentation titled "Summary of Child Abuse and Neglect." Compare the definitions regarding child abuse and neglect provided in this chapter with the ones provided in the presentation.*

National Center for Children in Poverty

http://www.nccp.org/about.html

The National Center for Children in Poverty (NCCP) is an American nonpartisan public-interest research organization dedicated to promoting the economic security, health, and well-being of America's low-income families and children. NCCP was founded in 1989 as a division of the Mailman School of Public Health at Columbia University. NCCP uses research to inform policy and practice with the goal of ensuring positive outcomes for the next generation. *Visit the Web site's "50-State Demographics Wizard." Select a state and an area of interest (income level, parental education, marital status, or other options provided) and create a demographic table with the help of the wizard. Repeat the task but select a different state. Compare the data obtained for the two states.*

REFERENCES

Alpert, E. (1998). Family violence curricula in US medical schools. *American Journal of Preventive Medicine, 14*(4), 273–282.

Bensel, R. W. T., Rheinberger, M. M., & Radbill, S. X. (1997). Children in a world of violence: The roots of child maltreatment. In M. E. Helfer & R. S. Krugman (Eds.), *The battered child* (pp. 3–27). Chicago: University of Chicago Press.

Bross, D. C., Miyoshi, T. J., Miyoshi, P. K., & Krugman, R. D. (2000). *World perspectives on child abuse: The fourth international resource book.* Denver, CO: Kempe Children's Center.

Bryce, J., Victora, C. G., Habicht, J. P., Vaughan, P., & Black, R. E. (2004). The multi-country evaluation of the integrated management of childhood illness strategy: Lessons for the evaluation of public health interventions. *American Journal of Public Health and the Nations Health, 94*(3), 406–415.

Coovadia, H., Rollins, N., Bland, R., Little, K., Coutsoudis, A., Bennish, M., et al. (2007). Mother-to-child transmission of HIV-1 infection during exclusive breastfeeding in the first 6 months of life: An intervention cohort study. *Lancet, 369*(9567), 1107–1116.

Dubowitz, H., & Black, M. B. (2001). Child neglect. In R. M. Reece & S. Ludwig (Eds.), *Child abuse: Medical diagnosis and management* (pp. 339–362). Philadelphia: Lippincott Williams & Wilkins.

Finkelhor, D. (1994). The international epidemiology of child sexual abuse. *Child Abuse & Neglect, 18*(5), 409-417.

Gibb, D. M., Duong, T., Tookey, P. A., Sharland, M., Tudor-Williams, G., Butler, K., et al. (2003). Decline in mortality, AIDS, and hospital admissions in perinatally HIV-1 infected children in the United Kingdom and Ireland. *British Medical Journal, 327*(7422), 1019–1024.

Iliff, P. J., Piwoz, E. G., Tavengwa, N. V., Zunguza, C. D., Marinda, E. T., Nathoo, K. J., et al. (2005). Early exclusive breastfeeding reduces the risk of postnatal HIV-1 transmission and increases HIV-free survival. *Advanced Information Systems, 19*(7), 699–708.

Leger, L. H. S. (1999). The opportunities and effectiveness of the health promoting primary school in improving child health—a review of the claims and evidence. *Health Education Research, 14*(1), 51–69.

MacIntyre, D., & Carr, A. (1999). Evaluation of the effectiveness of the Stay Safe primary prevention programme for child sexual abuse. *Child Abuse and Neglect, 23*(12), 1307–1325.

Madu, S. N., & Peltzer, K. (2000). Risk factors and child sexual abuse among secondary school students in the Northern Province (South Africa). *Child Abuse & Neglect, 24*(2), 259–268.

Manary, M. J. (2006). Local production and provision of ready-to-use therapeutic food (RUTF) spread for the treatment of severe childhood malnutrition. *Food and Nutrition Bulletin, 27*(3 Suppl.), S83–S89.

National Research Council. (1993). *Understanding child abuse and neglect*. Washington, DC: National Academy of Sciences Press.

Reza, A., Mercy, J. A., Krug, E. (2001). Epidemiology of violent deaths in the world. *Quality and Safety in Health Care*, 7(2), 104–111.

Runyan, D. K., Hunter, W. M., Socolar, R. R. S., Amaya-Jackson, L., English, D., Landsverk, J., et al. (1998). Children who prosper in unfavorable environments: The relationship to social capital. *Pediatrics, 101*(1), 12–18.

United Nations Children's Fund. (2008a). Breastfeeding: Impact on child survival and global situation. Retrieved November 12, 2008, from http://www.unicef.org/nutrition/index_24824.html

United Nations Children's Fund. (2008b). Innocenti Declaration: On the protection, promotion and support of breastfeeding. Retrieved from http://www.unicef.org/programme/breastfeeding/innocenti.htm

World Health Organization. (1951). *Expert committee on health education of the public* (Technical Report Series 30). Geneva: Author.

World Health Organization. (1996). *School health promotion—Series 5: Regional guidelines. development of health promoting schools: A framework for action*. Manila: Author.

World Health Organization. (1999a). *Injury: A leading cause of the global burden of disease*. Retrieved from http://whqlibdoc.who.int/hq/1999/WHO_HSC_PVI_99.11.pdf

World Health Organization. (1999b). *Report of the consultation on child abuse prevention*. Geneva: Author.

World Health Organization. (2002). Prevention of HIV in infants and young children: Review of evidence and WHO's activities. Retrieved from http://www.who.int/entity/hiv/mtct/ReviewofEvidence.pdf

World Health Organization. (2008a). What are the key health dangers for children? Retrieved from http://www.who.int/features/qa/13/en/index.html

World Health Organization. (2008b). Measuring child mortality. Retrieved from http://www.who.int/child_adolescent_health/data/child/en/index.html

World Health Organization. (2008c). *The global burden of disease: 2004 update*. Retrieved from http://www.who.int/entity/healthinfo/global_burden_disease/GBD_report_2004update_full.pdf

World Health Organization. (2008d). Nutrition. Retrieved from http://www.who.int/child_adolescent_health/topics/prevention_care/child/nutrition/en/index.html

World Health Organization. (2008e). Breastfeeding. Retrieved from http://www.who.int/child_adolescent_health/topics/prevention_care/child/nutrition/breastfeeding/en/index.html

World Health Organization. (2008f). Baby-Friendly Hospital Initiative. Retrieved from http://www.who.int/nutrition/topics/bfhi/en/index.html

World Health Organization. (2008g). *Complementary feeding*. Retrieved from http://www.who.int/entity/nutrition/publications/guidingprin_nonbreastfed_child.pdf

World Health Organization. (2008h). Feeding in exceptionally difficult circumstances. Retrieved from http://www.who.int/child_adolescent_health/topics/prevention_care/child/nutrition/fiedc/en/index.html

World Health Organization. (2008i). Malnutrition. Retrieved from http://www.who.int/child_adolescent_health/topics/prevention_care/child/nutrition/malnutrition/en/index.html

World Health Organization. (2008j). *Community-based management of severe acute malnutrition*. Retrieved from http://www.who.int/entity/nutrition/topics/Statement_community_based_man_sev_acute_mal_eng.pdf

World Health Organization. (2008k). Integrated management of childhood illness (IMCI). Retrieved from http://www.who.int/child_adolescent_health/topics/prevention_care/child/imci/en/index.html

World Health Organization. (2008l). A call to action: Children the missing face of AIDS. Retrieved from http://www.afro.who.int/cah/documents/hiv/hiv_and_children_call_for_action.pdf

World Health Organization. (2008m). *World report on violence and health.* Retrieved from http://whqlibdoc.who.int/publications/2002/9241545615_eng.pdf

World Health Organization. (2008n). Which health problems affect adolescents and what can be done to prevent and respond to them? Retrieved from http://www.who.int/child_adolescent_health/topics/prevention_care/adolescent/dev/en/index.html

World Health Organization. (2008o). School health and youth health promotion: Facts. Retrieved from http://www.who.int/ school_youth_health/facts/en/index.html

World Health Organization. (2008p). What is a health promoting school? Retrieved from http://www.who.int/school_youth_health/gshi/hps/en/index.html

World Health Organization & United Nations Children's Fund. (1989). *Protecting, promoting and supporting breast feeding: The special role of maternity services.* Geneva: World Health Organization.

World Health Organization, UNICEF, UNFPA, & UNAIDS. (2004). *HIV transmission through breastfeeding: Review of available evidence.* Geneva: World Health Organization.

World Health Organization, UNICEF, UNFPA, & UNAIDS. (2007). *HIV and infant feeding: Update.* Retrieved from http://whqlibdoc.who.int/publications/2007/97AGE 7

Mental Health

AFTER READING THIS CHAPTER YOU SHOULD BE ABLE TO

- Describe the way mental health care has changed over the years
- Identify the most common features of the major mental health conditions
- Discuss the epidemiology of suicide, along with the risk and protective factors for it
- Describe culture-bound syndromes
- Discuss the public health impact of violence and aggression

HISTORY OF MENTAL HEALTH

The treatment of mental health disorders has undergone multiple changes over the years, including some major paradigm shifts. Before tracing the history of the mental health movement from primitive eras to contemporary times, we need to appreciate the concept of **mental health**. The World Health Organization (WHO) defines mental health as "a state of well-being in which every individual realizes his or her own potential, can cope with the normal stresses of life, can work productively and fruitfully, and is able to make a contribution to her or his community" (WHO, 2001, 2008a).

Over the course of history, mental illnesses and disorders have been approached essentially in three different ways: supernaturally, biologically, and psychologically. During most of history the supernatural model was used to explain and attempt to remedy mental illnesses.

Primitive Times

There is evidence to indicate that mental illnesses existed during primitive times and that attempts were made to treat them. The supernatural concept of disease in general and mental illnesses in particular held that mental illness was created by divinities, demons, spirits, or magnetic fields emanating from the stars and moon (hence the term *lunatics*). It was widely believed that mental illnesses were created by evil spirits entering into and taking over the body. These evil spirits were forced out of the body by medicine men through magic and reincarnation. Records indicate that as early as 300 BCE some primitive tribes even went as far as drilling holes in the skulls to let the evil spirits out, a technique called trephining (Horsley, 1888). Prayer and faith healing were also used, as was astrology. Exorcisms were widespread.

Ancient Civilizations

The mentally ill were treated humanely by the ancient Romans, Greeks, and Arabs, and there was a movement away from belief in the supernatural origins of mental illnesses toward more rational explanations. Music, sedation with opium, activity, nutrition, and hygiene were some means through which care was given (Alexander & Selesnick, 1966). Hippocrates (460–377 BCE), the Greek physician, and Plato (429–348 BCE) had concerns about how the mentally ill were treated. Hippocrates attempted to classify people by the way in which they behaved.

Middle Ages

With the fall of the Roman Empire in 476 CE, the rational and humanitarian approach to mental illnesses was forgotten and was eventually replaced with witchcraft, shamanism, superstition, and mysticism. Usually, the mentally ill were locked in asylums, where they were treated harshly—flogged, starved, and often tormented. Occasionally, however, families would hide the mentally ill, or they were left to roam the streets. During the later part of the Dark Ages (476 to 1000 CE), religious influences in Europe mainly dictated the treatment administered to the mentally ill. Burnings at the stake and the practice of witchcraft were fairly common during this period (Alexander & Selesnick, 1966).

The Renaissance

The Renaissance (derived from French *renaissance*, meaning "rebirth") was a cultural movement spanning the 14th to 17th centuries that encompassed a revival of learning based on classical sources, the development of linear perspective in painting, and educational reform (Shorter, 1997). Unfortunately, the approach to mental illnesses and the mentally ill changed little. The Middle Age belief that mental illnesses were caused by evil spirits carried on into this period. The mentally ill were frequently imprisoned or locked away in mental asylums and denied any professional care. Mental illnesses were mostly considered irreversible. The methods used to cure mental illnesses during this time were all rooted in ignorance and included purging, bleeding, and blistering. Viewed as demon-possessed or characterized as senseless animals, the mentally ill were subjected to appalling treatments. The widespread use of physical restraints—straitjackets and heavy arm and leg chains—often deprived patients of their self-respect and freedom (Shorter, 1997).

Paracelsus (1493–1541), a Swiss physician, did not believe that evil spirits caused mental illness. This, however, did not change the general treatment of the mentally ill. No real advancements in the care of the mentally ill were made before the 18th century (Alexander & Selesnick, 1966; Shorter, 1997; Trimble, 1996).

The Eighteenth Century

Frank Mesmer (1733–1815), an Austrian physician, initiated a therapeutic approach to behavior. Mesmer suggested that the mentally ill could be cured by holding rods filled with iron filings in water. He based his treatment on the idea that it would give people a balance in the universe. Even though Mesmer's technique proved to be wrong, it heralded a major paradigm shift in the perception and treatment of mental illnesses.

In 1793, **Phillip Pinel** (1745–1826), a French physician, challenged the traditional wisdom of keeping the mentally ill restrained when he removed the chains from patients at the Asylum de Bicetre in Paris (Shorter, 1997). He divided the patients and categorized them according to different disorders, replacing purging, bleeding, and blistering with simple and humane psychological treatments, along with observing and talking to the patients. Pinel divided all mental illnesses into four categories—mania, melancholia, dementia, and idiocy—which was a revolutionary stride for those times. His theories on mental illness were the first to span both physiologic and psychological explanations. He suggested that mental illnesses were either the result of having sustained excessive social or psychological stress or the consequence of hereditary causes or damage to the body. Pinel is credited as the first person to maintain written case studies on patients, which focused on their long-term treatment (Alexander & Selesnick, 1966; Shorter, 1997).

Pinel saw asylums as places for treatment and not places to hide the mentally ill. They were to be places where patients were seen as sick human beings deserving of dignity, compassion, and medical treatment. It was Pinel who first thought that those suffering from mental illness could be rehabilitated and returned to society. He oversaw the conversion of a residence for the mentally ill from a mad house into a hospital during his lifetime. Soon, Pinel's reforms were being imitated throughout the rest of Europe.

> *Phillip Pinel was the first to think that those suffering from mental illness could be rehabilitated and returned to society.*

The Nineteenth Century

Jean-Martin Charcot (1825–1893) was a French neurologist and professor of anatomic pathology, nicknamed "the Napoleon of the neuroses" (Jay, 2000). His work greatly influenced the mental health movement. Charcot's most impressive work was on hypnosis and hysteria. Charcot maintained that hysteria was a neurologic disorder caused by hereditary problems in the nervous system. He used hypnosis to induce hysterical states in patients and scrutinized the results. Charcot was responsible for changing the French medical community's outlook regarding the validity of hypnosis (the practice had been previously rejected as Mesmerism).

Dorothea Lynde Dix (1802–1887) was an American activist on behalf of the indigent insane who is credited with the creation of the first generation of American mental asylums. During the Civil War, she served as superintendent of army nurses. Dix traveled throughout the country and, through a vigorous program of lobbying state legislatures and the U.S. Congress, was able to effect legislation for better care of the mentally ill.

Among other important happenings during this time period were the establishment of the first psychiatric training program in the United States at McLean Hospital in Waverly, Massachusetts; research on the effects of the venereal disease syphilis on the mind; and a general humane approach toward the mentally ill.

The Twentieth Century

Clifford Beers, a Yale graduate and young businessman, was largely responsible for ushering in 20th century reforms in psychiatric care. After having suffered an acute breakdown brought on by the death of his brother, Beers was hospitalized in a private mental institution (Alexander & Selesnick, 1966; Shorter, 1997). He was subjected to the degrading treatment and mental and physical abuses typical of those times. The deplorable treatment he received over the next couple of years in multiple mental health institutions led Beers to publish his autobiography, *A Mind That Found Itself.* The need for better care of the mentally ill was thus made public. The book had an immediate impact, spreading his vision of a massive mental health reform movement across the land and oceans. The execution of the movement began soon thereafter when Beers founded the Connecticut Society for Mental Hygiene. The society expanded the following year, forming the National Committee for Mental Hygiene. The society, both in Connecticut and eventually nationally, set forth the following goals:

- Improving attitudes toward mental illness and the mentally ill
- Improving services for the mentally ill
- Working for the prevention of mental illness and promoting mental health

The mental health movement was fairly well established by the time Beers died in 1943.

Sigmund Freud (1856–1939) was an Austrian neurologist and psychiatrist who founded the psychoanalytic school of psychology (Shorter, 1997). Freud is best known for his theories of the unconscious mind, which probe deeply into the psychological side of the individual. He is also well known for his redefinition of sexual desire as the primary motivational energy of human life that is directed toward a wide variety of objects. Because of his seminal work on psychoanalysis, Freud is commonly referred to as the father of psychoanalysis. Freud's work has been highly influential, popularizing such notions as the unconscious, the id, superego, and ego, the Oedipus complex, defense mechanisms, Freudian slips, and dream symbolism.

> *Every normal person, in fact, is only normal on the average. His ego approximates to that of the psychotic in some part or other and to a greater or lesser extent.*
>
> —Sigmund Freud

Among other pivotal incidents of the 20th century that helped shape the path of mental health care were three unrelated discoveries: the discovery of psychosurgery as a treatment for certain mental health disorders; the introduction of neuroleptic drugs, which included antipsychotics and tranquilizers; and the introduction of **electroconvulsive therapy** as a treatment for certain mental illnesses.

Psychosurgery was completely revolutionized in the 20th century by Antonio Egas Moniz (Micale & Porter, 1994; Shorter, 1997), a Portuguese neurologist who introduced the psychosurgical technique of lobotomy (the removal or severing of certain connections in the brain). Lobotomies were used in the past to treat a wide range of severe mental illnesses, including schizophrenia, clinical depression, and various **anxiety disorders**. They fell out of use after neuroleptics were introduced.

The introduction of neuroleptic drugs, including antipsychotics and major tranquilizers, in the 1950s marked the beginning of a new chapter in the annals of mental health. The use of these drugs led to a markedly reduced need for physical restraints. Over the past decades, substantial interest in the research and development of novel neuroleptic drugs has led to the introduction of newer, relatively safer alternatives to the original medications.

Finally, one of the most important events pertaining to mental health that happened during the 20th century was the discovery of electroconvulsive therapy (ECT). In 1938, Ugo Cerletti, an Italian psychiatrist, first tested ECT on human patients (Alexander & Selesnick, 1966; Shorter, 1997). In the years after, Cerletti and others experimented with ECT on a much broader scale and were able to establish its utility and safety in clinical practice. Today, even though arguments regarding whether ECT is therapy or cruelty persist, it is established as a therapeutic option for mental conditions such as acute schizophrenia, manic-depressive illness, and episodes of major depression.

FOCUS FEATURE 10.1 Facts You Should Know About Mental Illness

1. About half of mental disorders begin before the age of 14. Around 20% of the world's children and adolescents are estimated to have mental disorders or problems, with similar types of disorders being reported across cultures. Yet, the regions of the world with the highest percentage of population under the age of 19 have the poorest level of mental health resources. Most low- and middle-income countries have only one child psychiatrist for every 1 to 4 million people.
2. Depression is ranked as the seventh most important cause of disease burden in low- and middle-income countries. Depression is the leading cause of disease burden in Brazil and the second leading cause among women in Chile.
3. About 800,000 people commit suicide every year, 86% of them in low- and middle-income countries. More than half of the people who kill themselves are aged between 15 and 44. The highest suicide rates are found among men in eastern European countries.
4. In emergencies, the number of people with mental disorders is estimated to increase by 6% to 11%. People in emergency situations also often experience psychosocial problems that cannot be quantified.

(continued)

5. Mental disorders are among the risk factors for communicable and noncommunicable diseases. They can also contribute to unintentional and intentional injury. At the same time, many health conditions increase the risk for mental disorder and complicate diagnosis and treatment. For instance, obesity has been associated with significant increases in depression, bipolar disorder, and panic disorder.

6. Stigma about mental disorders and discrimination against patients and families prevent people from seeking mental health care. In South Africa, a public survey showed that most people thought mental illnesses were related to either stress or a lack of willpower rather than to medical disorders. Contrary to expectations, levels of stigma were higher in urban areas and among people with higher levels of education.

7. Human rights violations (including physical restraint, seclusion, and denial of basic rights) of psychiatric patients are routinely reported in most countries. Few countries have a legal framework that adequately protects the rights of people with mental disorders.

8. Shortages of psychiatrists, psychiatric nurses, psychologists, and social workers are among the main barriers to providing treatment and care in low- and middle-income countries. Low-income countries have 0.05 psychiatrists and 0.16 psychiatric nurses per 100,000 people, compared with 200 times more in high-income countries.

9. To increase the availability of mental health services, five key barriers need to be overcome: the absence of mental health from the public health agenda and its implications for funding; the current organization of mental health services; lack of integration within primary care; inadequate human resources for mental health; and lack of public mental health leadership.

10. To increase mental health services, especially in low- and middle-income countries, the financial resources needed are relatively modest: $2 per person per year in low-income countries and $3 to $4 in middle-income ones.

Source: World Health Organization (WHO). (2008b). *WHO fact file.* Geneva: Author. Retrieved from http://www.who.int/features/factfiles/mental_health/en/index.html

THE TREATMENT GAP FOR MENTAL HEALTH

The care of people with mental and brain disorders is a growing public health concern. These disorders are highly prevalent and exact a high emotional toll on individuals, families, and society. Across the globe, community-based epidemiologic studies have estimated the rates of lifetime prevalence of mental disorders among adults as ranging from 12.2 to 48.6% and the 12-month prevalence rates as ranging from 8.4 to 29.1% (Andrews, Hall, Teesson, & Henderson, 1999). Apart from being highly prevalent, mental disorders are also highly disabling. When measured by years lived with disability and by premature death in disability-adjusted life years (DALYs, a concept that is discussed in Chapter 2), psychiatric along with neurologic conditions accounted for almost 13% of the global disease burden in the year 2001.

Among individuals aged 15 to 44, unipolar depression is the second leading contributor of DALYs, with alcohol-related disorders, schizophrenia, and bipolar disorder among the top ten disorders. Approximately 33% of all years lived with disability (YLD) are imputed to neuropsychiatric conditions. Of the ten leading causes of YLD in the world among individuals of all ages, four are psychiatric conditions, with unipolar depression being the leading cause (Henderson, Andrews, & Hall, 2000). Among individuals between the ages of 15 and 44, panic disorder, drug use disorders, and obsessive-compulsive disorder (OCD) were included in the top 20 disorders.

> *Among individuals aged 15 to 44, unipolar depression is the second leading contributor of DALYs, with alcohol-related disorders, schizophrenia, and bipolar disorder among the top ten disorders.*

Despite the unusually high morbidity attributable to mental health disorders, there has been a global discordance between mental health needs and the available health resources, a trend called the **treatment gap**. The treatment gap represents the absolute difference between the true prevalence of a disorder and the treated proportion of individuals affected by the disorder. Alternatively, the treatment gap may be visualized as the percentage of individuals who require care but do not receive treatment.

Some of the reasons behind the excess disability due to mental disorders are as follows (Kohn, Saxena, Itzhak, & Benedetto, 2004). In part, the excess morbidity is attributable to the early age of onset of these disorders. This burden is further multiplied as a consequence of the fact that very few individuals with these disorders ever receive treatment in the specialized mental health care system or in the general health care system. Initial treatment is often delayed for long periods secondary to lack of acknowledgement of the problem, a perception on the part of the patient that the problem will recede on its own, or a desire to deal with the problem without external assistance. Last but not least, a lack of knowledge about mental disorders and the stigma associated with mental disorders remain other major impediments to care. Issues of accessibility, as well as limited availability or lack of availability, of services in many countries or for some populations also remain potent barriers to mental health care.

A review study conducted under the auspices of the World Health Organization by Kohn and colleagues (2004) explored the global trends and the treatment gap in mental health care and delivery. For schizophrenia and other **psychotic disorders**, the treatment gap was found to be 32.2%. For other disorders, the treatment gap was as follows: major depression, 56.3%; dysthymia, 56.0%; bipolar disorder, 50.2%; panic disorder, 55.9%; general anxiety disorder, 57.5%; and OCD, 59.5%. Alcohol abuse and dependence had the largest treatment gap at 78.1%.

Huge variation existed in the treatment gap between different countries. For instance, for schizophrenia the gap among young adult Jews in Israel was only 5.9%, whereas the rate in New Zealand in a population of 21-year-olds was 61.5%. For major depression, the treatment gap in Italy was close to 16%, whereas studies conducted in United Kingdom gave a comparable estimate of 84%. Alcohol abuse and dependence had a universally high treatment gap across all studies: Jewish Israeli young adults had the lowest gap (49.4%), but in the general adult population in Mexico City few were in treatment (96.0%). The treatment gap for major depression in the WHO European region and the Americas was 45.4%, and 56.9%, respectively.

To address the treatment gap, the 2001 World Health Report (WHO, 2001) laid out ten recommendations, presented in **Table 10.1**.

CONTEMPORARY TRENDS IN MENTAL HEALTH CARE

Deinstitutionalization

Deinstitutionalization is the process of transferring formerly committed individuals to sheltered community environments or community homes with a view to facilitating an easy transition to the best possible social functioning for those individuals (Braun et al., 1981). Some of the causes that ushered in the phenomenon of deinstitutionalization were as follows:

- Scientific research on psychiatric disorders that demonstrated that socioenvironmental factors were strong determinants in the development of mental illnesses

TABLE 10.1   Recommendations to Address the Mental Health Treatment Gap

1. Mental health treatment should be accessible in primary care.
2. Psychotropic drugs need to be readily available.
3. Care should be shifted away from institutions and toward community facilities.
4. The public should be educated about mental health.
5. Families, communities, and consumers should be involved in advocacy, policy making, and forming self-help groups.
6. National mental health programs should be established.
7. The training of mental health professionals should be increased and improved.
8. Links with other governmental and nongovernmental institutions should be increased.
9. Mental health systems should be monitored using quality indicators.
10. More support should be provided for research.

Source: Taken from World Health Organization. (2001). *The world health report 2001. Mental health: New understanding, new hope.* Geneva: Author. Retrieved from http://www.who.int/entity/whr/2001/en/ whr01_en.pdf

- The introduction of psychotropic medications (first the phenothiazines, then the second- and third-generation medications that effectively reduced the symptoms of active psychosis) in the United States and elsewhere in the mid-1950s
- An increasing realization that the clients in state mental institutions lived in poor conditions

Selection of the Appropriate Care Site

Triage is the process of prioritizing patients based on the severity of their condition so as to treat as many as possible when resources are insufficient for all to be treated immediately. The term originates from the French verb *trier*, meaning "to sort, sift, or select." The most important factors that guide decision making in mental health care are the state of the person with the disorder and the place where the most effective care can be provided for that person.

Some of the questions that should be answered before the decision is made regarding whether to commit a person to an inpatient setting or to treat him or her as an outpatient are as follows:

- Is there any immediate danger to the life of the patient or others around him or her as a result of the disorder?
- Is there a life-threatening comorbid medical disorder that needs to be addressed?
- What forms of support does the individual have and are they reliable enough or not?
- Who will pay for the services (patient or insurance)?

Some of these questions, especially the last one, are more appropriate in health care settings with a third-party payer system, such as the United States. In countries with universal health coverage (Canada, for instance), the last question is often not a factor in the decision-making process.

Biological Psychiatry

In recent years there has been a return to **biological psychiatry** as the primary means of approaching and treating mental health disorders. Biological psychiatry, also called biopsychiatry, is an interdisciplinary approach to psychiatry that aims to understand mental disorder in terms of the biological functioning of the nervous system (Trimble, 1996). It is interdisciplinary in that it draws from diverse sciences such as neuroscience, psychopharmacology, biochemistry, genetics, and physiology to form theories about the biological basis of human behavior and psychopathology. The return to biological psychiatry has been facilitated by a more comprehensive understanding of the nervous system and the development of psychotropic medications.

The development of a variety of mental health disciplines that train individuals to work with different facets of a mental health client's psychological and social functioning in both inpatient and community care settings is another recent trend that has influenced the field of mental health care and delivery.

MAJOR TYPES OF MENTAL DISORDERS

A classification and description of all mental disorders currently recognized would take an entire book, so the focus here is on the statistically more important disorders and their global impact. The classification and descriptions in this section borrow heavily from the fourth edition (text revision) of the American Psychiatric Association's *Diagnostic and Statistical Manual of Mental Disorders* (**DSM-IV-TR**) (American Psychiatric Association [APA], 2000). The DSM-IV-TR is an American instruction manual for mental health professionals that lists different categories of mental disorders along with the criteria for diagnosing them; it is used worldwide by physicians, researchers, insurance companies, pharmaceutical companies, and policy makers.

Mood Disorders

Mood disorders, also known as *affective disorders*, are responsible for most of the morbidity and mortality associated with mental illnesses. A mood disorder is a state in which the existing emotional mood is unsuitable to the circumstances. Depression (unipolar depression) and bipolar disorder are the two main types of mood disorders.

Depression

The World Health Organization expects depression to be the second leading cause of disability, after heart disease, by 2020 (Holden, 2000). Major depressive disorder (unipolar depression) is a common mental disorder that includes, among other features, a pervasive low mood, a loss of interest in usual activities, and reduced ability to feel pleasure.

Even though people often describe common temporary states of feeling blue as "depression," major depression by definition is a severe and often debilitating condition that can adversely affect an individual's work, social life, sleep-wake cycles, and general health.

The temporal course of depression may vary from individual to individual. Depression can be a single event with no recurrences or may have multiple recurrences; it can appear either slowly or suddenly, and may either last for a few months or be a condition lasting throughout one's life. Depression is known to be a risk factor for suicide; it also increases mortality from other causes.

The most important symptoms that typify clinical depression are a marked change in mood, a pervasive feeling of sadness, and a conspicuous loss of interest or pleasure in favorite activities. Other symptoms include the following:

- Persistently anxious mood
- Loss of appetite and weight loss, or occasionally an increase in appetite and weight gain
- Restlessness and/or irritability
- Insomnia, early-morning awakenings, or oversleeping
- Feelings of worthlessness, inappropriate guilt, hopelessness, pessimism
- Trouble thinking, concentrating, remembering, or making decisions
- Thoughts of death or suicide or attempts at suicide
- Loss of interest or pleasure in hobbies and activities that were once enjoyed, including sex
- Decreased energy, lethargy, feeling slowed down or sluggish
- Persistent physical symptoms that do not respond to treatment, such as headaches, digestive disorders, and chronic pain

There is considerable variation in the presentation of individual patients, and the number and severity of the above-mentioned symptoms vary among individuals. According to the DSM-IV-TR criteria, the symptoms must last for at least two weeks before being considered major depression.

The diagnosis of depression in children is more difficult than it is in adults. Children often present with irritability, a noticeable change in social activities and life, a loss of interest in school and poor academic performance, and possibly extreme changes in appearance. Abuse of drugs and alcohol may also be linked to depression in younger populations.

Bipolar Disorder

Bipolar disorder, also known as manic-depressive illness, is a brain disorder that causes extraordinary shifts in a person's mood, energy, and ability to function. These shifts are quite different (and more severe) than the normal mood fluctuations that everyone goes through. They can result in damaged interpersonal relationships, poor job or school performance, and even suicide. Severe changes in energy and behavior go along with these changes in mood. The periods of highs and lows are called episodes of mania and depression. Furthermore, bipolar disorder is typically a chronic disease with periods of remission and relapse.

In 1990, bipolar disorder was estimated to be the seventh leading cause of nonfatal burden in the world in 1990, accounting for 3% of YLDs, which is around the same percentage as chronic obstructive lung conditions (Ayuso-Mateos, 2006). Bipolar disorder also had the distinction of being in the top ten causes of YLDs at a global level, accounting for 2.5% of all global years lived with a disability. These figures underscore the global impact of bipolar disorder.

> *In 1990, bipolar disorder was estimated to be the seventh leading cause of nonfatal burden in the world in 1990, accounting for 3% of total years lived with a disability, which is around the same percentage as chronic obstructive lung conditions.*
>
> —Ayuso-Mateos (2006)

Figure 10.1 illustrates the spectrum of mood disorders and indicates how the two poles of mania and depression lie far removed from the median zone of relatively normal mood (euthymia). A manic episode is diagnosed if elevated mood occurs with three or more of the other symptoms most of the day, nearly every day, for 1 week or longer. If the mood is irritable, four of the following additional symptoms must be present:

- Increased energy, activity, and restlessness
- Excessively "high," overly good, euphoric mood

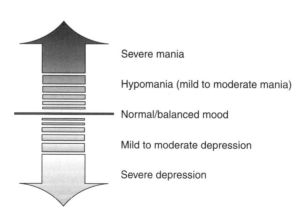

Severe mania

Hypomania (mild to moderate mania)

Normal/balanced mood

Mild to moderate depression

Severe depression

FIGURE 10.1   The spectrum of mood disorders.

Note: National Institute of Mental Health (2008). Bipolar disorder. Available from http://www.nimh.nih.gov/health/publications/bipolar-disorder/nimhbipolar.pdf

- Extreme irritability
- Racing thoughts and talking very fast, jumping from one idea to another
- Distractibility, can't concentrate well
- Reduced need for sleep
- Unrealistic beliefs in one's abilities and powers
- Poor judgment
- Spending sprees
- A lasting period of behavior that is different from usual
- Increased sexual drive or high-risk sexual behavior
- Abuse of drugs, particularly cocaine, alcohol, and sleeping medications
- Provocative, intrusive, or aggressive behavior
- Denial that anything is wrong

Psychotic Disorders

Psychosis is a generic psychiatric term for a mental state or condition often described as involving a loss of contact with reality. Someone suffering from psychosis is said to be *psychotic*. People experiencing psychosis may report hallucinations or delusions and may exhibit personality changes and disorganized thinking. This may be accompanied by unusual or bizarre behavior, as well as difficulty with social interaction and impairment in carrying out the activities of daily living. The DSM-IV-TR lists nine formal psychotic disorders, but psychosis may accompany a number of other mental health conditions as well. The nine formal disorders are as follows:

- Schizophrenia
- Schizoaffective disorder
- Schizophreniform disorder
- Brief psychotic disorder
- Delusional disorder
- Shared psychotic disorder (folie à deux)
- Substance-induced psychosis
- Psychosis due to a general medical condition
- Psychosis—not otherwise specified

The hallmarks of most psychotic conditions are **hallucinations**, **delusions**, lack of insight, and thought disorder.

- *Hallucinations:* Sensory perceptions in the absence of sensory stimuli. Hallucinations can be classified depending on the kind of sensory perception. They may occur in any of the five senses and take on almost any form, from simple sensations (such as lights, colors, tastes, and smells) to more complex and meaningful experiences such as seeing and interacting with fully formed people, hearing elaborate commentaries and voices, and perceiving complex tactile sensations.

- *Delusions:* Fixed false beliefs; in everyday language the term is used to describe a belief that is either false or deceptive. The belief is fixed because, in most cases, it persists even if evidence refuting the basis of that delusion is offered.
- *Thought disorder:* An underlying disturbance in conscious thinking. A thought disorder is classified largely by its effects on speech and writing. Affected persons may show pressure of speech (speaking incessantly and quickly), derailment or flight of ideas (switching topic midsentence or inappropriately), thought blocking, and rhyming or punning.
- *Lack of insight:* One significant and perplexing feature of psychosis is usually an accompanying lack of insight into the bizarre nature of the person's experience or behavior. Even in the case of the most florid psychosis, the person manifesting the symptoms may be completely unaware that his or her colorful hallucinations and impractical delusions are in any way unrealistic.

Epidemiology

Global data about psychotic disorders are deficient because there are few psychiatrists in developing countries. Within the United States, the lifetime prevalence of schizophrenia is roughly 1%, with a reported range of 0.6 to 1.9% (Kaplan & Sadock, 1998). According to the DSM-IV-TR, the annual incidence of schizophrenia ranges from 0.5 to 5.0 per 100,000, with the incidence being higher for individuals born in urban regions of industrialized countries. Schizophrenia is found in all societies, and its incidence and prevalence are roughly the same worldwide. The prevalence of delusional disorder is much rarer, with an estimate of 0.025 to 0.03% within the United States. The exact incidence and prevalence rates of brief psychotic disorder are unavailable, but the disorder is thought to be uncommon and related to major psychosocial stressors (Kaplan & Sadock, 1998). Psychosis due to a general medical condition is most often encountered in the context of chronic alcohol or other substance abuse (Kaplan & Sadock, 1998). Reliable epidemiologic estimates for most of the psychotic disorders other than schizophrenia have been harder to gauge.

Eating Disorders

Eating disorders are abnormal eating behaviors, marked by compulsive eating or behaviors targeted toward avoiding eating, that negatively affect both one's physical and mental health. Cumulative evidence from well-designed surveys has established the point prevalence of anorexia nervosa and bulimia nervosa in young Western women to be less than 1% and around 1%, respectively (Hay, 1998). It is generally accepted that these two disorders are most common in young women (Hoek, 1995). Eating disorders have also been reported in other affluent Western countries, such as Britain, with similar incidence and prevalence. In Australia, for instance, it is generally estimated that 2 to 3% of adolescent and adult females satisfy the DSM-IV-TR diagnostic criteria for anorexia and bulimia nervosa. The incidence of bulimia nervosa and of binge eating disorder in the general Australian population is 5 in 100 and 4%, respectively.

In recent years, there has been some debate as to whether eating disorders represent culture-bound syndromes. Eating disorders are more frequent in industrialized societies, where there is an abundance of food and being thin, especially for females, is considered attractive. Eating disorders are most common in the United States, Canada, Europe, Australia, New Zealand, and South Africa. The rates are increasing, especially in non-Western countries such as Japan and China, where women are exposed to cultural change and modernization (Davis & Katzmann, 1999; Nadaoka et al., 1996). In the United States, eating disorders are common in young Hispanic, Native American, and African American women, but these rates are still lower than in white women (Crago, Shisslak, & Estes, 1996). African American women are more likely to develop bulimia and more likely to purge. Female athletes involved in running and gymnastics, ballet dancers, male body builders, and wrestlers are also at increased risk (Garner, Rosen, & Barry, 1998).

The two main eating disorders that have been widely discussed are anorexia nervosa and bulimia nervosa. A diagnostic category has recently emerged called binge eating disorder that has some overlap of symptoms with these two disorders.

> *Eating disorders are more frequent in industrialized societies, where there is an abundance of food and being thin, especially for females, is considered attractive. Eating disorders are most common in the United States, Canada, Europe, Australia, New Zealand, and South Africa.*

Anorexia Nervosa

The three quintessential features of anorexia nervosa are (1) refusal to maintain a minimally normal body weight, (2) intense fear of gaining weight, and (3) significant disturbance in the perception of the shape or size of one's body. Individuals frequently lack insight into the problem and are brought to professional attention by a family member after marked weight loss.

The DSM-IV-TR identifies two types of anorexia nervosa: restricting type and binge eating/purging type. Comorbid psychiatric symptoms include depressive symptoms such as depressed mood, social withdrawal, irritability, insomnia, and decreased sexual interest. Many depressive features may be secondary to the physiologic sequelae of semistarvation. Symptoms of mood disturbances need to be reassessed after partial or complete weight restoration. Obsessive-compulsive features such as thoughts of food, hoarding food, picking or pulling apart small portions of food, or collecting recipes are common. Anxiety symptoms and concerns about eating in public are also frequent.

Bulimia Nervosa

The essential features of bulimia nervosa are binge eating and inappropriate compensatory behaviors such as fasting, vomiting, laxative use, or exercising to prevent weight gain. Binge eating is classically triggered by abnormal mood states, interpersonal stressors, and intense hunger following dietary restraints or negative feelings related to body weight, body shape, and food. Individuals are typically ashamed of their eating problems, and binge eating usually occurs in secrecy. Unlike those with anorexia, individuals with bulimia are typically within normal weight range and restrict their total caloric consumption between binges.

A comorbid condition, or comorbidity, refers to the presence of one or more disorders (or diseases) in addition to a primary disease or disorder. Common conditions comorbid with eating disorders include the following (Halmi et al., 1991):

- Major depressive disorder (50 to 75%)
- Bipolar disorder (4 to 13%)
- Obsessive-compulsive disorder (25% with anorexia)
- Sexual abuse (20 to 50%),
- Substance abuse (12 to 18% with anorexia and 30 to 37% with bulimia)

Anxiety Disorders

Anxiety disorder is an umbrella term for multiple different forms of abnormal anxiety-based conditions. All of these conditions are, however, marked by some degree of pathologic anxiety, abnormal fears, or phobias. The anxiety in anxiety disorders is almost always illogical and not based on facts. Some of the common anxiety disorders are discussed in this section.

Generalized Anxiety Disorder

Generalized anxiety disorder (GAD) is a common chronic disorder characterized by pervasive and long-lasting anxiety that is not focused on any particular person or situation. Because of their constant and all-pervasive worrying, people with this disorder may manifest physical symptoms such as headaches, dizziness, chest pain, or insomnia. Statistically, GAD is known to affect twice as many females as males and causes significant functional impairment.

Panic Disorder

Panic disorder is characterized by abbreviated attacks of intense terror and apprehension that lead to trembling and shaking, confusion, dizziness, nausea, difficulty breathing, and, typically, feelings of impending doom. The American Psychiatric Association (2000) defines a panic attack as fear or discomfort that arises abruptly and peaks in 10 minutes or less, and can occasionally last hours.

Phobias

A strong and irrational fear of an object or situation is called a *phobia*. The sufferer tries to actively avoid any reference or association with the object causing the phobia. A person suffering from a phobia of spiders might feel so frightened by a spider that he or she would try to jump out of a speeding car to get away from one.

Agoraphobia

Agoraphobia is anxiety about being in a place or situation where escape is difficult or embarrassing. It holds a special place in the spectrum of anxiety disorders.

Social Anxiety Disorder (Social Phobia)

Social phobia is marked by an intense fear of being negatively evaluated by others or of being publicly embarrassed and humiliated because of impulsive acts. The fear of public scrutiny and potential humiliation becomes so pervasive that normal life can become impossible (Margolis & Rabins, 2001).

Obsessive-Compulsive Disorder

Obsessive compulsive disorder is a type of anxiety disorder primarily characterized by obsessions and/or compulsions. Obsessions are distressing, repetitive, intrusive thoughts or images that the individual often realizes are senseless. Compulsions are repetitive behaviors that the person feels forced or compelled into doing in order to relieve anxiety. For example, the compulsion of walking in a certain pattern may be employed to alleviate the obsession that something bad is about to happen. More often, though, the compulsion is inexplicable, simply an urge to complete a ritual triggered by nervousness. Light switches and other household items are common objects of obsession.

Post-traumatic Stress Disorder

Post-traumatic stress disorder (PTSD) is an anxiety disorder that results from a traumatic experience. Post-traumatic stress can result from an extreme situation, such as being involved in warfare, rape, hostage situations, or a serious accident. The sufferer may experience flashbacks, avoidant behavior, and other symptoms. In a recent report, the World Health Organization (2008b) noted that the estimated burden of PTSD has increased to 0.6% of total global YLDs.

The DSM-IV-TR defines PTSD as necessarily stemming from an event in which one is exposed to serious threat of injury or death and then experiences extreme fear, helplessness, or horror. After World Wars I and II, research studies exploring psychological distress among combatants and concentration camp survivors ushered in the recognition of the chronic negative effects of exposure to trauma. The exploration of the impact of rape on women by Ann Burgess helped acknowledge the psychological impact of trauma (Burgess & Holmstrom, 1974). Scholars who studied rape survivors and Vietnam veterans helped formulate the diagnosis of PTSD.

Epidemiology   When first recognized as a separate entity, PTSD was thought to be a relatively rare disorder. Lately, epidemiologic studies have verified high prevalence rates of exposure to traumatic events in the general population and confirmed that PTSD occurs as a consequence of a wide range of extreme life events. However, in comparison with the frequent exposure to potentially devastating events, the outcome of PTSD still remains rare.

In the United States, the National Comorbidity Survey Replication (a nationally representative sample of 5,692 individuals), found an overall lifetime PTSD prevalence rate of 6.8% (Kessler, Berglund, Demler, Jin, & Walters, 2005). Among U.S.

combatants, the rates are even higher than the general population. Among soldiers deployed during Operation Iraqi Freedom and Operation Enduring Freedom, the percentage of soldiers who met the screening criteria for PTSD after deployment to Afghanistan and Iraq was 6.2% and 12.9%, respectively (Hoge et al., 2004).

In developed nations, a wide range of PTSD prevalence rates are often reported, perhaps attributable to differences in culture, languages, and experiences and, of course, study methodologies. Iceland claims the credit for the lowest rates of PTSD, with a lifetime rate of 0.6% and no men meeting the criteria (Lindal & Stefansson, 1993). In Australia, prevalence was estimated at 1.5%, with similar rates documented for either sex.

PTSD prevalence rates in less economically developed countries tend to be higher than in more developed countries. A study of Mexican adults pegged the PTSD lifetime prevalence at 19% (Norris, Murphy, Baker, & Perilla, 2003). Among adult Israeli residents, a prevalence of 9.4% was found (Bleich, Gelkopf, & Solomon, 2003), with higher rates for women than men (16.2% vs. 2.4%). In a study of a Palestinian sample, PTSD prevalence rates of 21.5% and 13.2% for men and women, respectively, were found (Punamaki, Komproe, Qouta, Elmasri, & de Jong, 2005). Non-Western and developing nations often have higher rates of PTSD. Many of these estimates have been derived following periods of war and political turmoil, a fact that could potentially skew the results. Large samples of individuals aged 16 years or older residing in Algeria, Cambodia, Ethiopia, and Gaza were found to have high rates of PTSD: 37.4%, 28.4%, 15.8%, and 17.8%, respectively (Keane, Marshall, & Taft, 2006).

The statistics from these international research studies come with a caveat. The limitation of PTSD-based research is that most of it is based in the developed world despite the fact that people living in developing countries appear to be at elevated risk for experiencing trauma in comparison with the populations based in the developed world. An estimated 6% of PTSD prevalence studies were conducted in developing countries (De Giralomo & McFarlane, 1996). It is highly unlikely that research done in the United States and other developed countries can be generalized to the developing world. Differences in violence, disasters, cultures, social structures, and coping behaviors are bound to alter the prevalence and course of PTSD among people of different countries (De Giralomo & McFarlane, 1996).

Risk Factors   Potential PTSD risk factors can be divided into three major categories (Keane, Marshall, & Taft, 2006):

- Factors related to the traumatic event, such as the severity of the trauma and also the immediate response to the traumatic events (detachment from the trauma vs. prolonged exposure)

- Preexisting factors specific to the individual, such as familial psychopathology, demographic factors such as sex (PTSD is more common in females than males), race, socioeconomic status, and marital status
- Events that occur following the trauma, such as perceived social support

Public Health Importance   The interpersonal, psychosocial, physical health, and social impacts of PTSD are enormous (Keane, Marshall, & Taft, 2006). Research evidence shows that individuals diagnosed with PTSD are more likely to divorce their partners, encounter troubles during child rearing, indulge in intimate partner aggression, develop depression and other psychological challenges, report lesser satisfaction with their lives, develop physical health problems, and become involved with the legal system (Jordan et al., 1992; Koss, Koss, & Woodruff, 1991; Kulka et al., 1990; Schnurr & Green, 2004; Walker et al., 2003). These studies imply that PTSD is a major public health problem of global proportions and underscore the need for prevention and intervention efforts.

SUICIDE

According to the World Health Organization (2008c), on average around 800,000 individuals commit suicide annually, with 86% of those being in low- and middle-income countries. More than half of these individuals are between the ages of 15 and 44. Men in eastern European countries have the highest suicide rates. Mental disorders remain one of the most important and potentially treatable causes of suicide. WHO's suicide prevention report (2008d) outlines some very disturbing statistical trends pertaining to suicide:

- In the year 2000, approximately one million people died from suicide: a global mortality rate of 16 per 100,000, or 1 death every 40 seconds.
- In the last 45 years suicide rates have increased by 60% worldwide. Suicide is now among the three leading causes of death among those aged 15 to 44 years (both sexes); these figures do not include suicide attempts, which are up to 20 times more frequent than completed suicide.
- Suicide worldwide was estimated to represent 1.8% of the total global burden of disease in 1998, and is projected to be 2.4% in countries with market and former socialist economies in 2020.
- Although traditionally suicide rates have been highest among the male elderly, rates among young people have been increasing to such an extent that they are now the group at highest risk in a third of countries, in both developed and developing countries.

- Mental disorders (particularly depression and substance abuse) are associated with more than 90% of all cases of suicide; however, suicide results from many complex sociocultural factors and is more likely to occur during periods of socioeconomic, family, and individual crisis situations (e.g., after loss of a loved one, employment, or honor).

> *On average about 800,000 individuals commit suicide annually, 86% of them in low- and middle-income countries.*
>
> —World Health Organization (2008c)

Effective Interventions

Strategies involving restriction of access to common methods of suicide have proved to be effective in reducing suicide rates; however, there is a need to adopt multisectoral approaches involving other levels of intervention and activities, such as crisis centers. There is compelling evidence indicating that adequate prevention and treatment of depression, alcohol abuse, and substance abuse can reduce suicide rates. School-based interventions involving crisis management, self-esteem enhancement, and the development of coping skills and healthy decision making have been demonstrated to reduce the risk of suicide among youth (Gould, Greenberg, Velting, & Shaffer, 2003).

Challenges and Obstacles

Some of the prime challenges to addressing the prevention of suicide worldwide are a basic lack of awareness of suicide as a major problem and the taboo in many societies about openly discussing suicide. Reliability of suicide certification and reporting is also an issue that needs a great amount of improvement. It is clear that suicide prevention requires intervention from outside the health sector as well and calls for an innovative, comprehensive multisectoral approach, including education, labor, police, justice, religion, law, politics, and the media.

Risk Factors

Some of the risk factors that correlate with higher suicide rates have been explored in contemporary research. A brief description of each of these factors follows.

Personal Characteristics

Psychopathology   Research on youth suicides has found that more than 90% of youth suicides have had at least one major psychiatric disorder antecedent to the suicide attempt. However, younger adolescent suicide victims have lower rates of psychopathology—somewhere in the vicinity of 60% (Shaffer et al., 1996). Although depressive disorders are unfailingly the most prevalent disorders among adolescent suicide victims (estimates range from 49% to 64%), the increased risk of suicide (odds ratios) for those with an affective disorder ranges from 11 to 27 (Shaffer et al., 1996). Female victims are more likely than males to have had an affective disorder (Brent et al., 1994; Shaffer et al., 1996).

Substance abuse, especially among older adolescent male suicide victims, a high prevalence of comorbidity between affective and substance abuse disorder, and the commonality of disruptive disorders in male suicide victims are some of the other trends in the epidemiology of suicide that have been unraveled by research (Shaffer et al., 1996). Approximately one-third of male suicides have had a conduct disorder, often comorbid with a mood, anxiety, or substance abuse disorder.

Prior Suicide Attempts   A history of a prior suicide attempt is one of the strongest predictors of completed suicide, conferring higher risk for males (30-fold increase) and a relatively less elevated risk for females (3-fold increase) (Shaffer et al., 1996). Robust associations between a history of suicidal behavior and future attempts have been reported in general population surveys as well as longitudinal studies (Lewinsohn, Rohde, & Seeley, 1994; McKeown et al., 1998). The risk for a future attempt increases somewhere between 3 and 17 times for those with prior suicidal behavior.

Cognitive and Personality Factors   Even though hopelessness has been often linked with suicidality, once depression is taken into account the predictive value is not consistent. Poor interpersonal problem-solving ability and aggressive impulsive behavior have also been linked with an increased risk of suicidal behavior (Gould, Greenberg, Velting, & Shaffer, 2003; Sourander, Helstela, Haavisto, & Bergroth, 2001). In a school-based study in Finland (Sourander et al., 2001), aggressive 8-year-olds were more than twice as likely to think about or attempt suicide at age 16.

Sexual Orientation   A significant two- to sixfold increased risk of nonlethal suicidal behavior for homosexual and bisexual youth was revealed in cross-sectional and longitudinal epidemiologic studies (Russell & Joyner, 2001). Among a nationally representative sample of almost 12,000 adolescents, those who reported same-sex sexual orientation also exhibited significantly higher rates of other risk factors for suicidal behavior (Russell & Joyner, 2001). Even after adjusting for these risks, the effect of same-sex sexual orientation on suicidal behavior remained, but was extensively mediated by victimization, depression, family history of attempts, and alcohol abuse.

Biological Factors   Over the past 30 years, an extensive body of research-based evidence has accumulated indicating that aberrations in serotonin function play an important role in suicidal and impulsive, aggressive behavior in individuals, irrespective of their psychiatric diagnosis. Serotonin is a neurotransmitter synthesized in the central nervous system and the gastrointestinal tract of animals, including humans. In the central nervous system, serotonin is believed to play an important role in the modulation of anger, aggression, body temperature, mood, sleep, sexuality, and appetite as well as stimulating vomiting. It has been suggested that the dysequilibrium of serotonin may be a biological trait that predisposes to suicide (Mann, Waternaux, Haas, & Malone, 1999). Thus, a mentally ill person with this biological predilection is much more likely to respond to a stressful experience in an impulsive fashion that may include a decision to commit suicide. Even though research in the field of suicidality is still limited, there remains the promise that further research on the genetics of suicide may help steer suicide prevention programs to newer and more precise levels.

Family Characteristics

Family History of Suicidal Behavior   A family history of suicidal behavior immensely increases the risk of both attempted and completed suicide (Gould, Greenberg, Velting, & Shaffer, 2003). Because of the close association of suicidal behaviors and psychiatric illnesses, it is imperative to take into account whether apparent familial risk of suicide reflects suicide specifically or instead an association with parental psychiatric illness. Research by Agerbo, Nordentoft, and Mortensen (2002) has pointed out that even after adjusting for parental psychiatric history, youth suicide is nearly five times more likely in the offspring of mothers who have completed suicide and twice as common in the offspring of fathers who have completed suicide.

Parental Psychopathology   High rates of mental illnesses in parents, notably substance abuse and depression, have been found to be associated with suicidal ideation, attempts, and completed suicides in adolescents (Brent et al., 1994; Gould, Greenberg, Velting, & Shaffer, 2003). Brent and colleagues (1994) reported that a family history of depression and substance abuse significantly increased the risk of completed suicide. The exact mechanism through which a family background of psychopathology increases the risk for completed suicide is still unknown.

Parental Divorce   Even though it appears that the victims of suicide are more likely to originate from disjointed families, this apparent association between separation or divorce and suicide markedly decreases after parental psychopathology is accounted for (Brent et al., 1994).

Parent-Child Relationships   Damaged relationships between parents and children have been traditionally associated with increased risk of suicide and suicide attempts among youths. However, parent-child conflict is no longer associated with completed suicide or suicide attempts if a youth's psychopathology is controlled for (Brent et al., 1994; Lewinsohn, Rohde, & Seeley, 1994).

Adverse Life Circumstances

Stressful Life Events   Life stressors, such as interpersonal losses (e.g., breaking up with a significant other) and legal or disciplinary problems, are associated with a higher risk of suicide attempts and completed suicide (Gould, Greenberg, Velting, & Shaffer, 2003). However, the specific stressors that are associated with this enhanced risk for suicide (both attempt and completion) vary depending on the victim's age. For younger adolescents, parent-child conflict may be a more common precipitant, whereas romantic issues might underlie suicide in older adolescents and adults. Research has also demonstrated that bullying, both as the victim and as the perpetrator, is likely to increase the risk for suicidal ideation (Kaltiala-Heino, Rimpela, Marttunen, Rimpela, & Rantanen, 1999).

Physical Abuse   Physical abuse endured during childhood is associated with an elevated risk of suicide attempts in late adolescence or even early adulthood. This association holds true even after adjusting for demographic characteristics, psychiatric symptoms during childhood and early adolescence, and parental psychiatric disorders (Johnson et al., 2002). Johnson and colleagues have suggested a probable mechanism through which abuse might increase suicidal behavior. They propose that physically abused children may have problems in honing the social skills necessary for healthy relationships. This lack of social skills may lead to social isolation and even antagonistic interactions with others, which can endanger these children in their later years.

Sexual Abuse   Sexual abuse is another factor associated with suicide. Even though sexual abuse has been found to be associated with subsequent suicidality, the association is greatly reduced but not entirely eliminated once other confounding risk factors such as parental substance abuse and so forth are controlled for (Fergusson, Horwood, & Lynskey, 1996).

Socioenvironmental and Contextual Factors

Socioeconomic Status   Typically, research studies have found no or minimal association between completed suicides and socioeconomic disadvantage of the victim (Agerbo, Nordentoft, & Mortensen, 2002). However, suicide attempters, compared with community controls, have been consistently found to have higher rates of socioeconomic disadvantage. The reason for this discrepancy is not entirely known.

School and Work Problems   Problems while enrolled in school, not enrolled in school and not working, and not going to college pose significant risks for completed suicide (Gould, Fisher, Parides, Flory, & Shaffer, 1996).

Contagion or Imitation   Typically, the term *contagion* refers to the transmission of a disease by direct or indirect contact and is usually applied to communicable diseases such as tuberculosis. However, research evidence is accumulating to attribute suicide clusters and contagions to media influence. The effect of media on suicide rates has been documented since the early 1990s in the United States as well as in multiple other countries, including Australia, Germany, Hungary, and Japan. For further exploration of the role of media in suicide, see the review study by Gould and colleagues (2003), which cites multiple research leads from all the countries mentioned earlier. The magnitude of the increase in suicide rates is proportional to the amount, duration, and prominence of media coverage, and the impact of suicide stories on subsequent completed suicides appears to be greatest for teenagers (Gould, 2001).

Protective Factors

Regrettably, contemporary research has not focused as much on the protective factors against suicidal behavior. The two factors that have been hypothesized as being protective are family cohesion and religiosity.

Family Cohesion

Family cohesion, or the degree of emotional involvement that family members have toward one another, has been reported to be a protective factor for suicidal behavior among adolescents in multiple studies. Students who described family life in terms of a high degree of mutual involvement, shared interests, and emotional support were 3.5 to 5.5 times less likely to be suicidal than were adolescents from less cohesive families who had the same levels of depression or life stress (Gould, Greenberg, Velting, & Shaffer, 2003).

Religiosity

Gould and colleagues (2003), in their review of the risk of suicide and preventive interventions in youth, found that the protective value of religiosity against suicidal behavior had been documented in adolescents and young adults.

Table 10.2 summarizes the risk factors and protective factors for suicidal behaviors, which include both attempted and completed suicide.

VIOLENCE AND AGGRESSION

According to the *World Report on Violence and Health* (Krug, Dahlberg, Mercy, Zwi, & Lozano, 2002), conservative estimates put the annual toll of people losing their lives to violence at 1.6 million. Violence remains one of the leading causes of death for

TABLE 10.2 Risk Factors and Protective Factors Related to Suicidal Behavior		
	Risk Factors	**Protective Factors**
Personal attributes	Psychopathology/mental illness Prior suicide attempts Cognitive and personality factors Sexual orientation Biological factors	Coping mechanisms
Family characteristics	Family history of suicide Parental psychopathology Parental divorce Parent-child relationships	Family cohesion
Life circumstances	Stressful life events Physical abuse Sexual abuse	
Socioenvironmental and contextual factors	Socioeconomic status School and work problems Contagion/imitation	Social support Religiosity Resources

individuals aged 15 to 44 years globally; it accounts for 14% of male and 7% of female deaths. Moreover, violence also results in a range of physical, sexual, reproductive and mental health problems, as well as burdening national economies by costing them billions of U.S. dollars each year in health care, law enforcement, and reduced or lost productivity.

> *An estimated 1.6 million people worldwide lose their lives to violence every year.*
>
> —Krug, Dahlberg, Mercy, Zwi, & Lozano (2002)

The World Health Organization (Krug et al., 2002) has defined violence as "[t]he intentional use of physical force or power, threatened or actual, against oneself, another person, or against a group or community, that either results in or has a high likelihood of resulting in injury, death, psychological harm, mal-development or deprivation." Broadly speaking, violence can be visualized as falling into three major categories, with the division based on the attributes of those perpetrating the violent act:

- *Self-directed violence.* Self-directed violence can be subclassified into suicidal behavior (suicidal ideation, attempted suicides, and completed suicides) and self-abuse, which includes acts such as self-mutilation.
- *Interpersonal violence.* Interpersonal violence refers to violence within the family or between intimate partners, most often taking place within the confines of a home.
- *Collective violence.* Collective violence refers to violence perpetrated by larger groups of individuals or by entire states. Violence purporting to further a particular kind of agenda (such as the extermination of Jews at the hands of the Nazi regime) would fall into this category.

The extent of lethal violence in a specific community or geographic region can be gauged through data on fatalities, such as statistics regarding homicides and suicides in that community or region. Mortality figures only provide one facet of the larger problem, however. For a proper and more realistic appraisal of the problems related to violence and aggression, nonlethal outcomes of violence also have to be accounted for because such outcomes heavily outnumber lethal outcomes. Also, including both categories provides a more holistic picture regarding the conditions accompanying specific incidents and is a more complete description of the full impact of violence on the health of individuals and communities. Such data may include the following:

- Data on prevalent diseases, injuries, and other health conditions caused as a result of exposure to violence
- Self-reported data on attitudes, beliefs, behaviors, cultural practices, victimization, and exposure to violence

- Community-based figures on population characteristics and levels of income, education, and unemployment and how the latter affect the levels of lethal and nonlethal outcomes of violence
- Crime data on the characteristics and circumstances of violent events and perpetrators of violence
- Economic data related to treatment costs
- Description of the economic burden on health care systems and the possible impact of prevention programs in preventing lethal or nonlethal outcomes
- Policy and legislation-based data

The World Report (Krug et al., 2002) discusses the many problems related to the collection and compilation of violence-related data. Some of these problems are as follows:

- *Availability of data.* Even though most countries maintain registries of mortality data and keep at least a basic count of homicides and suicides, the calculation of rates from these basic statistics is often difficult because the data are either not complete or are of questionable quality. This factor is most important for dynamic populations, for instance, populations in certain African countries torn with civil unrest, where frequent migration may distort the statistics from the mortality registries.
- *Quality of data.* Even if data are available, the quality may be suboptimal. Data may vary in quality and comprehensiveness depending on the kind of agency or institution maintaining them.
- *Other obstacles.* Some of the other barriers that affect the compilation of violence-related data are the difficulty of developing instruments that are relevant and specific to population subgroups and across different cultural contexts, ethical considerations regarding research into violence, and the designing of proper protocols for protection of the confidentiality of victims to ensure their safety.

Despite physical and sexual assaults being fairly commonplace, precise national and international estimates of each remain lacking. Surveillance systems for compiling and reporting these injuries are in many countries either totally lacking or still in the stages of infancy. Surveys and special studies of different population groups remain the major source of knowledge regarding nonfatal violence. For instance, national surveys place the percentage of women who reported ever being physically assaulted by an intimate partner at 10% in Paraguay and the Philippines, 22.1% in the United States, 29.0% in Canada, and 34.4% in Egypt (Krug et al., 2002).

Costs of Violence

Violence exacts both a human and an economic toll on nations, and costs economies many billions of U.S. dollars each year in health care, legal costs, absenteeism from work, and lost productivity. A study by Miller and Cohen (1992) estimated the direct and indirect annual costs of gunshot wounds in the United States at $126 billion. Cutting or stab wounds cost an additional $51 billion. In the Canadian province of New Brunswick, the total direct and indirect costs of violence, including costs for health care services, autopsies, police investigations, and lost productivity resulting from premature death, amounted to nearly US$80 million in a 1996 study (Clayton & Barcel, 1996).

Studies sponsored by the Inter-American Development Bank on the magnitude and economic impact of violence in six Latin American countries between 1996 and 1997 explored the expenditures, as a result of violence, for health care services and law enforcement and judicial services, as well as intangible losses and losses from the transfer of assets (Buvinic & Morrison, 1999). Expressed as a percentage of the gross domestic product (GDP) of these nations in 1997, the cost of health care expenditures arising from violence was 1.9% of the GDP in Brazil, 5.0% in Colombia, 4.3% in El Salvador, 1.3% in Mexico, 1.5% in Peru, and 0.3% in Venezuela (Krug et al., 2002).

Violence Prevention

It is quite important to gather information regarding the need for and effectiveness of preventive interventions, as well as on the risk and protective factors that need addressing in different populations prone to violence. Designing effective prevention programs around that data set of knowledge is the ultimate goal.

Public health interventions are traditionally characterized in terms of three levels of prevention. In the case of violence, these levels are as follows:

- *Primary prevention:* Approaches that aim to prevent violence before it occurs. School-based interventions for skill building in young students can be visualized as a kind of primary prevention of violence.
- *Secondary prevention:* Tactics that focus on the more immediate responses to violence, such as prehospital care, emergency services, or acute psychiatric care following a devastating experience such as rape.
- *Tertiary prevention:* Approaches that focus on long-term care resulting from the aftermath of violence. Rehabilitation aimed toward lessening the trauma or reducing the long-term disability associated with violence is one such example.

These three levels of prevention are defined by their temporal expression—whether prevention takes place before exposure to violence occurs, immediately after it happens, or over the longer term. Although the secondary and tertiary levels of prevention conventionally refer to the victims of violence in a health care setting, they have also come to have relevance for the perpetrators of violence, and are applied in judicial settings in response to violence.

Research in the field of violence prevention has focused on defining prevention from a standpoint of the target group of interest. Tolan and Guerra (1994) have classified interventions targeting violence as follows:

- *Universal interventions:* Generic approaches aimed at the general population without regard to individual risk; examples include school-based violence prevention curricula delivered to all students in a school or all children of a particular age in a community.
- *Selected interventions:* Approaches targeting those considered at increased risk for violence (having one or more risk factors for violence); an example of such an intervention is training in parenting provided to low-income single parents.
- *Indicated interventions:* Approaches aimed at those who have already demonstrated violent behavior, such as treatment for individuals incarcerated for perpetrating violent acts.

CULTURE-BOUND SYNDROMES AND PHENOMENA

Culture-bound syndromes and phenomena have been an increased focus of clinical and research attention. The inclusion of such syndromes in the DSM-IV-TR, the gold-standard reference book for all mental health conditions, underscores the need to study such syndromes (APA, 2000). The DSM-IV-TR contains symptomatic descriptions of around 25 culture-bound syndromes, such as amok, latah, and koro, to name just a few. The definition of culture-bound syndrome written by the APA's Group on Culture and Diagnosis and appearing in the DSM-IV-TR is as follows:

> The term culture-bound syndrome denotes recurrent, locality-specific patterns of aberrant behavior and troubling experience that may or may not be linked to a particular DSM-IV diagnostic category. Many of these patterns are indigenously considered to be "illnesses," or at least afflictions, and most have local names . . . . [C]ulture-bound syndromes are generally limited to specific societies or culture areas and are localized, folk, diagnostic categories that frame coherent meanings for certain repetitive, patterned, and troubling sets of experiences and observations.

A culture-bound syndrome is typically characterized by the following:

- Categorization as a disease in the culture (i.e., not as a voluntary behavior or false claim)
- Widespread familiarity in the culture of origin
- Complete lack of familiarity of that condition for people in other cultures
- No objectively demonstrable biochemical or tissue abnormalities (symptoms)
- Usually recognized and treated by the folk medicine of the culture

The idea that some psychiatric disorders may be restricted to a single culture or group of cultures is not new. In the 18th century, George Cheyne published his famous *English Malady* (1733) about a collection of nervous symptoms, including "spleen, vapours, lowness of spirits, hypochondriacal and hysterical distempers, etc.," that he believed were much more common in England than elsewhere. Cheyne attributed these to local climatic and dietary features and to certain English cultural characteristics such as "the inactivity and sedentary occupations of the better sort [of people] among which this evil most rages" and "the humour of living in great, populace and consequently unhealthy towns." Cheyne's descriptions remain one of the earliest allusions to the possibility of a culture-bound syndrome.

This section describes some of the more familiar of the culture-bound syndromes. In line with the international focus of this book, we have included culture-bound syndromes from across the world.

Dhat

Dhat derives from the Sanskrit word *dhatu* meaning "metal" and also "elixir" or "constituent part of the body." Dhat has been described as early as 1960 (Wig, 1960) as comprising vague somatic symptoms of fatigue, weakness, anxiety, loss of appetite, guilt, and sexual dysfunction attributed by the patient to a loss of semen through urine, nocturnal emissions, or masturbation. Anxiety-related symptoms regarding semen loss are common in Indian historical writing. In Ayurvedic texts (dated between the 5th millennium BCE and the 7th century CE), the production of semen has been described as follows: food converts to blood, which converts to flesh, which changes to marrow, and the marrow is finally changed into semen. Traditional texts maintain that it typically takes 40 days for 40 drops of food to be converted to 1 drop of blood, 40 drops of blood to 1 drop of flesh, and so on (Bhugra & Buchanan, 1989). In the individual collective psyche of these regions, therefore, semen starts to take on an overwhelming importance. These ideas panic the individual into developing a sense of impending doom with the smallest amount of semen loss, thereby precipitating a series of somatic symptoms (Chadha & Ahuja, 1990).

Koro

The classic full-blown koro syndrome is most commonly seen in China and the southeastern regions of Asia. The word *koro* literally means "head of the turtle" in Malay. In Cantonese the entity is known as "Suk yeong," which translates to "shrinking penis." The condition is known by similar names in other local Chinese and south Asian languages. This culture-bound syndrome is characterized by the belief that the penis is shrinking and will disappear into the abdomen, causing death (Tseng et al., 1988).

An intense fear of death accompanies these beliefs, and maneuvers such as tying, clamping, or grasping the penis aimed at preventing the imagined outcome are attempted by the victim. Koro occurs both in sporadic and epidemic forms and has also been described in females. Most commonly, it is a relatively short-lived condition. Local cultural beliefs maintain that disguised ghosts of the dead, who are deprived of genitals, will take away the victims' genitals so as to come back to life again, which induces great fear and panic in someone displaying the symptoms.

Susto

Susto is a "fright sickness" with strong psychological overtones thought to be caused by a frightening event involving another person, an animal, or a situation. The word *susto* has its roots in Portuguese and Spanish terms for fright (i.e., sudden intense fear, as of something urgently threatening). In the areas of the world where the condition is familiar, it is a common belief that if a person is suffering from susto, his or her soul is separated from the body. The distress caused by the event is believed to dislodge "an immaterial substance, an essence" from the body and cause the victim to become ill at some point in the future—days, months, or even years later (Rubel, O'Nell, & Rolando, 1984). Symptoms may include nervousness, malaise, difficulty sleeping, poor appetite, involuntary muscle tics, and sometimes gastrointestinal complaints (stomach ache, diarrhea, vomiting). Rituals aimed at restoring the equilibrium between the body and the "essence," also referred to in the literature as the *espiritu* (spirit or soul), and returning the *espiritu* to the body are considered the treatment for susto. Such rituals often involve praying, a discussion of the event or events that caused the sickness, a "drawing out" of the sickness, and return of the "essential part of the self" (Rubel, 1960, 1964).

Hwa-Byung

Hwa-Byung (HB) has been categorized as a Korean culture-bound syndrome that refers to an insidious, chronic, serious dissatisfaction that is projected into the body and is manifested by multiple symptoms such as insomnia, fatigue, panic, palpitations, dyspnea, and so on (Park, Kim, Kang, & Kim, 2001). In oriental medicine, HB has been visualized as follows:

- A neurotic fire or anger that develops due to repression of emotions in reaction to suffering extreme injustice (Cho, 1991)
- A dissonance between vital energy (Ki) and fire (Koo & Lee, 1993)
- An illness with the patterns of Hwa or an illness related to the Hwa concept in Chinese medicine in terms of neurosis and psychosomatism (Lin, 1983)
- The state with a sense of heat in the body due to emotional stress and an illness caused by a disequilibrium in the balance between yin (negative force) and yang (positive force)

Usually, the factors that precipitate HB are marital or family conflicts, financial losses, poverty and hardship, separation from loved ones, and other chronic psychological stresses of daily life (Park et al., 2001).

Taijin Kyofusho

Taijin kyofusho is a Japanese culture-bound syndrome. *Taijin* is the Japanese word for "interpersonal," and *kyofusho* means "phobia" or "fear"; by derivation, the name of the condition thus literally means "the disorder of fears of interpersonal relations." Patients with this disorder often complain that particular parts of their bodies displease others, and they have specific fears related to those parts (Tanaka-Matsumi, 1979). Morita Masatake (also known as Morita Shoma) described the condition as a vicious cycle of self-examination and reproach that can occur in people of hypochondriacal temperament. By Western standards of medicine, the disorder closely resembles a form of social anxiety. In the official Japanese diagnostic system, taijin kyofusho is subdivided into the following categories:

- *Sekimen-kyofu*, the phobia of blushing
- *Shubo-kyofu*, the phobia of a deformed body, similar to body dysmorphic disorder
- *Ikoshisen-kyofu*, the phobia of eye contact
- *Jikoshu-kyofu*, the phobia of having foul body odor

Latah

Latah is a culture-bound syndrome endemic to Malaysia and Indonesia and is typically characterized by hypersensitivity to sudden fright, often with echopraxia (an involuntary repetition or imitation of the observed movements of another), echolalia (repetition of vocalizations made by another person), and trancelike behavior. The Malaysian syndrome is more frequent in middle-aged women.

Brain Fag or Brain Fog

Fairly common in parts of West Africa, brain fag is a condition experienced primarily by male high school or university students. Symptoms include difficulties in concentrating, remembering, and thinking. Those affected will often state that their brains are "fatigued." Additional symptoms focus on the head and neck regions of the body and include pain, pressure, tightness, blurring of vision, heat, or burning.

SKILL-BUILDING ACTIVITY

Select any one mental health disorder and at least one other common medical condition (e.g., infectious diseases such as tuberculosis or malaria or noncommunicable chronic diseases such as diabetes or coronary heart disease).

1. In what ways is the diagnosis of the mental disorder different from that of the common medical condition that you selected?
2. Using the Internet, find out what treatments are available for each of the two conditions and how much time, on average, those treatments would take.
3. What factors would govern whether or not a person with either of those two conditions receives the right treatment? Are those factors different or do they overlap?
4. Would it be more likely or easier for an individual to seek help for one but not the other condition? Why or why not?

SUMMARY

The treatment of mental health disorders has undergone multiple changes over the years, including some major paradigm shifts. Psychotropic medications are a major achievement of the 20th century and have revolutionized the manner in which mental illnesses are treated. Two other recent developments include a move toward deinstitutionalization (the process of transferring formerly committed individuals to sheltered community environments or community homes) and a return to biological psychiatry (the approach that aims to understand mental illnesses in terms of the biological functioning of the nervous system).

Globally, the lifetime prevalence of mental disorders among adults ranges from 12.2 to 48.6%, and the 12-month prevalence rate ranges from 8.4 to 29.1%. Despite the unusually high morbidity attributable to mental health disorders, there has been a global discordance between mental health needs and the available health resources, a trend called the treatment gap. The treatment gap represents the absolute difference between the true prevalence of a disorder and the treated proportion of individuals affected by the disorder.

The major kinds of mental health disorders are mood disorders, anxiety disorders, psychotic disorders, personality disorders, and eating disorders. Risk and protective factors for suicide can be divided into personal attributes, family characteristics, life circumstances, and socioenvironmental and contextual factors.

Violence remains one of the leading causes of death for individuals aged 15 to 44 years globally; it accounts for 14% of male and 7% of female deaths. It also claims enormous socioeconomic costs globally. Primary, secondary, and tertiary levels of prevention can be employed to design effective interventions targeting violence.

Culture-bound syndromes are recurrent, locality-specific patterns of aberrant behavior and troubling experience that may or may not be linked to a particular DSM-IV-TR diagnostic category. Dhat, koro, and susto are a few examples of culture-bound syndromes.

IMPORTANT TERMS

anxiety disorders

biological psychiatry

culture-bound syndromes

Clifford Beers

deinstitutionalization

delusions

DSM-IV-TR

eating disorders

electroconvulsive therapy

hallucinations

mental health

mood disorders

Phillip Pinel

psychotic disorders

Sigmund Freud

treatment gap

triage

REVIEW QUESTIONS

1. Define the treatment gap. List five ways by which the treatment gap can be addressed.
2. What are some of the trends in contemporary mental health care?
3. What are the hallmark features of psychotic conditions?
4. What are the main risk factors for suicide?
5. Enumerate some of the recent trends regarding suicide.
6. What are the three different kinds of violence?
7. What do you understand by the term *culture-bound syndrome*? Describe any one culture-bound syndrome.

WEB SITES TO EXPLORE

National Institute of Mental Health

http://www.nimh.nih.gov/index.shtml

The U.S. National Institute of Mental Health (NIMH) is one of the largest scientific organizations in the world dedicated to research focused on the understanding, treatment, and prevention of mental disorders and the promotion of mental health. *Review this Web site and check the Science News section, which offers the latest cutting-edge research in the field of mental health.*

Substance Abuse and Mental Health Services Administration

http://mentalhealth.samhsa.gov/

The Substance Abuse and Mental Health Services Administration (SAMHSA), an agency of the U.S. Department of Health and Human Services, was established by an act of Congress in 1992 under Public Law 102-321. SAMHSA was created as a services agency to focus attention, programs, and funding on improving the lives of people with or at risk for mental and substance abuse disorders. *Use the mental health services locator on this Web site to find out what resources for mental health are available in your proximity.*

Suicide and Mental Health Association International

http://suicideandmentalhealthassociationinternational.org/

Suicide and Mental Health Association International (SMHAI) is an organization founded by survivors left behind after suicide. This not-for-profit organization is dedicated to suicide and mental health–related issues; its main goal is the prevention of suicidal behavior and relieving its effects on all who may be affected by it. *Check out the online support groups section and try to join and actively participate in any one of those groups.*

World Federation for Mental Health

http://www.wfmh.org/00about.htm

The World Federation for Mental Health (WFMH) is an international membership organization (spread over 100 countries and 6 continents) founded in 1948 to advance, among all peoples and nations, the prevention of mental and emotional disorders, the proper treatment and care of those with such disorders, and the promotion of mental health. *Explore this Web site. Browse its global advocacy directory and see if you can come across a site that you would join for advocacy initiatives.*

World Health Organization: Mental Health

http://www.who.int/mental_health/en/

This Web site contains global statistics on different mental health disorders. It is part of the larger World Health Organization site and offers comparisons and insights into the differences in prevalence, therapeutic approach, and overall management among different sections of the world. *Explore this Web site and check the fact file for some interesting facts on mental disorders around the globe.*

REFERENCES

Agerbo, E., Nordentoft, M., & Mortensen, P. B. (2002). Familial, psychiatric, and socioeconomic risk factors for suicide in young people: Nested case-control study. *British Medical Journal, 325*(7355), 74–85.

Alexander, F., & Selesnick, S. T. (1966). *The history of psychiatry: An evaluation of psychiatric thought and practice from prehistoric times.* New York: Harper & Row.

American Psychiatric Association. (2000). *Diagnostic and statistical manual of mental disorders: DSM-IV-TR.* (Rev. 4th ed.). Arlington, VA: Author.

Andrews, G., Hall, W., Teesson, M., & Henderson, S. (1999). *The mental health of Australians.* Australia: Mental Health Branch, Commonwealth Department of Health and Aged Care.

Ayuso-Mateos, J. L. (2006). *Global burden of bipolar disorder in the year 2000.* Retrieved from http://www.who.int/healthinfo/statistics/bod_bipolar.pdf

Bhugra, D., & Buchanan, A. (1989). Impotence in ancient Indian texts: Implications for modern diagnosis. *Sexual and Marital Therapy, 4*(1), 87–92.

Bleich, A., Gelkopf, M., & Solomon, Z. (2003). Exposure to terrorism, stress-related mental health symptoms, and coping behaviors among a nationally representative sample in Israel. *Journal of the American Medical Association, 290*, 612–620.

Braun, P., Kochansky, G., Shapiro, R., Greenberg, S., Gudeman, J. E., Johnson, S., et al. (1981). Overview: Deinstitutionalization of psychiatric patients, a critical review of outcome studies. *American Journal of Psychiatry, 138*(6), 736–749.

Brent, D. A., Perper, J. A., Moritz, G., Liotus, L., Schweers, J., Balach, L., et al. (1994). Familial risk factors for adolescent suicide: A case-control study. *Acta Psychiatrica Scandinavica, 89*(1), 52–58.

Burgess, A. W., & Holmstrom, L. (1974). Rape trauma syndrome. *American Journal of Psychiatry, 131*(9), 981–986.

Buvinic, M., & Morrison, A. (1999). *Violence as an obstacle to development.* Washington, DC: Inter-American Development Bank.

Chadha, C., & Ahuja, N. (1990). Dhat syndrome: A sex neurosis of the Indian subcontinent. *British Journal of Psychiatry, 156*, 577–579.

Cheyne, G. (1733). *The English malady: Or, a treatise of nervous diseases of all kinds, as spleen, vapors, lowness of spirits, hypochondriacal, and hysterical distempers, &c.* London: G. Strahan.

Cho, H. G. (1991). *The treatment methods of stress and Hwa-Byung in oriental medicine.* Seoul, Korea: Open Books.

Clayton, D., & Barcel, A. (1999). The cost of suicide mortality in New Brunswick, 1996. *Chronic Diseases in Canada, 20*(2), 89–95.

Crago, M., Shisslak, C. M., & Estes, L. S. (1996). Eating disturbances among American minority groups: A review. *International Journal of Eating Disorders, 19*(3), 239–248.

Davis, C., & Katzman, M. A. (1999). Perfection as acculturation: Psychological correlates of eating problems in Chinese male and female students living in the United States. *International Journal of Eating Disorders, 25*(1), 65–70.

De Giralomo, G., & McFarlane, A. (1996). The epidemiology of PTSD: A comprehensive review of the international literature. In A. Marsella, M. Friedman, E. Gerrity, & R. Surfield (Eds.), *Ethnocultural aspects of posttraumatic stress disorder: Issues, research, and clinical applications.* Washington, DC: American Psychological Association.

Fergusson, D. M., Horwood, L. J., & Lynskey, M. T. (1996). Childhood sexual abuse and psychiatric disorder in young adulthood: II. Psychiatric outcomes of childhood sexual abuse. *Journal of the American Academy of Child and Adolescent Psychiatry, 35*(10), 1365–1374.

Garner, D. M., Rosen, L. W., & Barry, D. (1998). Eating disorders among athletes: Research and recommendations. *Child and Adolescent Psychiatric Clinics of North America, 7*(4), 839–857.

Gould, M. S. (2001). Suicide and the media. In H. Hendin & J. J. Mann (Eds.), *Suicide prevention: Clinical and scientific aspects.* New York: New York Academy of Sciences.

Gould, M. S., Fisher, P., Parides, M., Flory, M., & Shaffer, D. (1996). Psychosocial risk factors of child and adolescent completed suicide. *Archives of General Psychiatry, 53*(12), 1155–1162.

Gould, M. S., Greenberg, T., Velting, D. M., & Shaffer, D. (2003). Youth suicide risk and preventive interventions: A review of the past 10 years. *Journal of the American Academy of Child and Adolescent Psychiatry, 42*(4), 386–405.

Halmi, K. A., Eckert, E., Marchi, P., Sampugnaro, V., Apple, R., & Cohen, J. (1991). Comorbidity of psychiatric diagnoses in anorexia nervosa. *Archives of General Psychiatry, 48*(8), 712–718.

Hay, P. (1998). The epidemiology of eating disorder behaviors: An Australian community-based survey. *International Journal of Eating Disorders, 23*(4), 371–382.

Henderson, S., Andrews, G., & Hall, W. (2000). Australia's mental health: An overview of the general population survey. *Australian and New Zealand Journal of Psychiatry, 34*(2), 197–205.

Hoek, H. W. (1995). Distribution of eating disorders. In K. D. Brownell & C. G. Fairburn (Eds.), *Eating disorders and obesity: A comprehensive handbook* (pp. 207–211). New York: Guilford Press.

Hoge, C. W., Castro, C. A., Messer, S. C., McGurk, D., Cotting, D. I., & Koffman, R. L. (2004). Combat duty in Iraq and Afghanistan, mental health problems, and barriers to care. *New England Journal of Medicine, 351*(1), 13–22.

Holden, C. (2000). Global survey examines impact of depression. *Science, 288*(7), 39–40.

Horsley, V. (1888). Trephining in the Neolithic period. *The Journal of the Anthropological Institute of Great Britain and Ireland, 17*(1888), 100–106.

Jay, V. (2000). The legacy of Jean-Martin Charcot. *Archives of Pathology and Laboratory Medicine, 124*(1), 10–11.

Johnson, J. G., Cohen, P., Gould, M. S., Kasen, S., Brown, J., & Brook, J. S. (2002). Childhood adversities, interpersonal difficulties, and risk for suicide attempts during late adolescence and early adulthood. *Archives of General Psychiatry, 59*(8), 741–749.

Jordan, B. K., Marmar, C. R., Fairbank, J. A., Schlenger, W. E., Kulka, R. A., Hough, R. L., et al. (1992). Problems in families of male Vietnam veterans with posttraumatic stress disorder. *Journal of Consulting and Clinical Psychology, 60*(3), 916–926.

Kaltiala-Heino, R., Rimpela, M., Marttunen, M., Rimpela, A., & Rantanen, P. (1999). Bullying, depression, and suicidal ideation in Finnish adolescents: School survey. *British Medical Journal, 319*(7206), 348–351.

Kaplan, H. I., & Sadock, B. J. (1998). *Kaplan and Sadock's synopsis of psychiatry: Behavioural sciences, clinical psychiatry* (8th ed.). Baltimore, MD: Williams and Wilkins.

Keane, T., Marshall, A., & Taft, C. (2006). Posttraumatic stress disorder: Etiology, epidemiology, and treatment outcome. *Annual Review of Clinical Psychology, 2*(3), 161–197.

Kessler, R. C., Berglund, P., Demler, O., Jin, R., & Walters, E. E. (2005). Lifetime prevalence and age-of-onset distributions of DSM-IV disorders in the National Comorbidity Survey Replication. *Archives of General Psychiatry, 62*(4), 593–602.

Kohn, R., Saxena, S., Itzhak, L., & Benedetto, S. (2004). The treatment gap in mental health care. *Bulletin of the World Health Organization, 82*(11), 858–866.

Koo, B. S., & Lee, J. S. (1993). The literature review of Hwa-Byung in Oriental medicine. *Journal of Oriental Neuropsychiatry, 4*(1), 1–18.

Koss, M. P., Koss, P. G., & Woodruff, W. F. (1991). Deleterious effects of criminal victimization on women's health and medical utilization. *Archives of Internal Medicine, 151*(2), 342–347.

Krug, E. G., Dahlberg, T. T., Mercy, J. A., Zwi, A. B., & Lozano, R. (2002). *World report on violence and health*. Retrieved from http://www.who.int/violence_injury_prevention/violence/world_report/en/

Kulka, R. A., Schlenger, W. E., Fairbank, J. A., Hough, R. L., Jordan, B. K., Marmar, C. R., et al. (1990). *Trauma and the Vietnam war generation*. New York: Brunner/Mazel.

Lewinsohn, P. M., Rohde, P., & Seeley, J. R. (1994). Psychosocial risk factors for future adolescent suicide attempts. *Journal of Consulting and Clinical Psychology, 62*(2), 297–305.

Lin, K. M. (1983). Hwa-Byung: A Korean culture-bound syndrome? *American Journal of Psychiatry, 140*(1), 105–107.

Lindal, E., & Stefansson, J. G. (1993). The lifetime prevalence of anxiety disorders in Iceland as estimated by the US National Institute of Mental Health Diagnostic Interview Schedule. *Acta Psychiatrica Scandinavica, 88*(4), 29–34.

Mann, J. J., Waternaux, C., Haas, G. L., & Malone, K. M. (1999). Toward a clinical model of suicidal behavior in psychiatric patients. *American Journal of Psychiatry, 156*(2), 181–189.

Margolis, S., & Rabins, P. (2001). *The Johns Hopkins white papers: Memory.* New York: Medletter Associates.

McKeown, R. E., Garrison, C. Z., Cuffe, S. P., Waller, J. L., Jackson, K. L., & Addy, C. L. (1998). Incidence and predictors of suicidal behaviors in a longitudinal sample of young adolescents. *Journal of the American Academy of Child and Adolescent Psychiatry, 37*(6), 612–619.

Micale, M. S., & Porter, R. (1994). *Discovering the history of psychiatry.* New York: Oxford University Press.

Miller, T. R., & Cohen, M. A. (1997). Costs of gunshot and cut/stab wounds in the United States, with some Canadian comparisons. *Accident Analysis and Prevention, 29*(3), 329–341.

Nadaoka, T., Oiji, A., Takahashi, S., Morioka, Y., Kashiwakura, M., & Totsuka, S. (1996). An epidemiological study of eating disorders in a northern area of Japan. *Acta Psychiatrica Scandinavica, 93*(4), 305–310.

Norris, F. H., Murphy, A. D., Baker, C. K., & Perilla, J. L. (2003). Severity, timing, and duration of reactions to trauma in the population: An example from Mexico. *Biological Psychiatry, 53*(9), 769–778.

Park, Y., Kim, H., Kang, H., & Kim, J. (2001). A survey of Hwa-Byung in middle-age Korean women. *Journal of Transcultural Nursing, 12*(2), 115–122.

Punamaki, R. L., Komproe, I. H., Qouta, S., Elmasri, M., & de Jong, J. T. (2005). The role of peritraumatic dissociation and gender in the association between trauma and mental health in a Palestinian community sample. *American Journal of Psychiatry, 162*(3), 545–551.

Rubel, A. J. (1960). Concepts of disease in Mexican-American culture. *American Anthropologist, 62*(5), 795–814.

Rubel, A. J. (1964). The epidemiology of a folk illness: Susto in Hispanic America. *Ethnology, 3*(3), 268–283.

Rubel, A. J., O'Nell, C. W., & Rolando C. (1984). *Susto, a folk illness.* Berkeley: University of California Press.

Russell, S. T., & Joyner, K. (2001). Adolescent sexual orientation and suicide risk: Evidence from a national study. *American Journal of Public Health, 91*(8), 1276–1281.

Schnurr, P. P., & Green, B. L. (2004). Understanding relationships among trauma, post-traumatic stress disorder, and health outcomes. *Advances in Mind-Body Medicine, 20*(1), 18–29.

Shaffer, D., Gould, M. S., Fisher, P., Trautman, P., Moreau, D., Kleinman, M., et al. (1996). Psychiatric diagnosis in child and adolescent suicide. *Archives of General Psychiatry, 53*(4), 339–348.

Shorter, E. (1997). *A history of psychiatry: From the era of the asylum to the age of Prozac.* New York: John Wiley & Sons.

Sourander, A., Helstela, L., Haavisto, A., & Bergroth, L. (2001). Suicidal thoughts and attempts among adolescents: A longitudinal 8-year follow-up study. *Journal of Affective Disorders, 63*(1), 59–66.

Tanaka-Matsumi, J. (1979). Taijin kyofusho: Diagnostic and cultural issues in Japanese psychiatry. *Culture, Medicine and Psychiatry, 3*(3), 231–245.

Tolan, P. H., & Guerra, N. G. (1994). Prevention of juvenile delinquency: Current status and issues. *Journal of Applied and Preventive Psychology, 3*, 251–273.

Trimble, M. R. (1996). *Biological psychiatry.* New York: Wiley.

Tseng, W., Mo, K., Hsu, J., Li, L., Ou, L., Chen, G., et al. (1988). A sociocultural study of koro epidemics in Guangdong, China. *American Journal of Psychiatry, 145*(12), 1538–1543.

Walker, E. A., Katon, W., Russo, J., Ciechanowski, P., Newman, E., & Wagner, A. W. (2003). Health care costs associated with posttraumatic stress disorder symptoms in women. *Archives of General Psychiatry, 60*(4), 369–374.

Wig, N. N. (1960). Problems of mental health in India. *Journal of Clinical and Social Psychiatry (India), 17,* 48–53.

World Health Organization. (2001). *The World Health Report 2001. Mental health: New understanding, new hope.* Retrieved from http://www.who.int/whr2001/

World Health Organization. (2008a). *Mental health.* Retrieved from http://www.who.int/mental_health/en/

World Health Organization. (2008b). Global burden of post-traumatic stress disorder in the year 2000: Version 1 estimates. Retrieved from http://www.who.int/healthinfo/statistics/bod_posttraumaticstressdisorder.pdf

World Health Organization. (2008c). WHO fact file: 10 facts on mental health. Retrieved from http://www.who.int/features/factfiles/mental_health/en/index.html

World Health Organization. (2008d). Suicide prevention (SUPRE). Retrieved from http://www.who.int/mental_health/prevention/suicide/suicideprevent/en/

CHAPTER 11

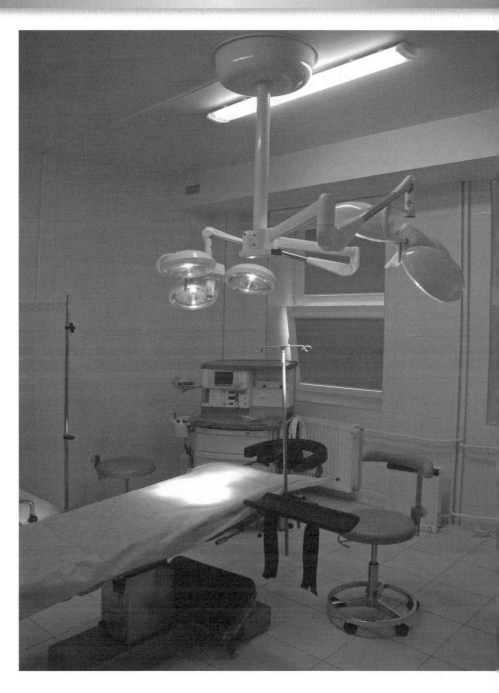

World Health Systems

AFTER READING THIS CHAPTER YOU SHOULD BE ABLE TO

- Define a health system and be able to discuss the importance of and functions served by a health system
- Describe the four basic models of health care systems, along with important features and examples of each
- Compare and contrast the American health care system with systems across the globe
- Describe the basic mechanisms by which health care systems are financed
- Discuss the salient features of health care systems in the United States, Canada, France, Argentina, Germany, Japan, the United Kingdom, Russia, China, India, and Nigeria

DEFINITION OF A HEALTH SYSTEM

The definition of a **health system** is a somewhat daunting task. According to the World Health Organization (WHO, 2008a), a health system includes "[a]ll the activities whose primary purpose is to promote, restore or maintain health." Another way of defining a health system is as follows: "A health system comprises all organizations, institutions and resources devoted to producing actions whose primary intent is to improve health" (WHO, 2008b).

Recognized health services (including the professional delivery of individual medical attention), traditional medicine, any medications that can potentially affect the health of an individual, and home care of the sick are all included under the umbrella of a health system. Other activities of a public health focus, such as health education and promotion, disease prevention, and even social and ecological interventions such as road and environmental safety improvement are also within the definition of a health system. The WHO report specifically excludes from the definition of a health system any and all such activities that have their prime focus in an area other than health irrespective of any secondary health-related effects that such an activity might have on individual and community health. For example, increasing cross-border patrols to counter drug trafficking primarily helps control crime; thus, even though a reduction in access to drugs of abuse might have long-time health impacts on a society, the activity would be excluded from the umbrella of a health system.

FUNCTIONS OF A HEALTH SYSTEM

The concept of a health system can be better understood if one envisions the basic functions a health system performs. A health system is expected to meet three broad objectives (WHO, 2008a):

- *Improving the health of people served by that health system.* This objective envisions preventive and restorative health care services with a view to improving the health of the population served. It could include primary intervention efforts that improve overall health by reducing the chances of acquiring a disease. It could also include secondary and tertiary preventions and limiting the morbidity consequent to a medical condition.
- *Responding to people's expectations.* Timely provision of information and services in a manner that is compatible with people's expectations goes a long way toward ensuring the success of a health system. Aggressive treatment of a disease against the wishes of a competent patient is usually avoided in most health systems. Expectations also raise some delicate ethical questions regarding what is and is not acceptable. Euthanasia for terminally ill patients, especially if desired by them, remains an ethical dilemma for health systems around the world.

- *Providing financial protection against the costs of ill-health.* The burden of illness can be catastrophic if a huge financial element is associated with it. This burden hits the poor harder than it does the rich.

All of these objectives matter irrespective of how a health system is funded or organized.

The importance of health care systems can be comprehended if one tries to envision a world without them. The mere process of establishing norms and guidelines to guide the entire caregiving process, from primary prevention efforts directed toward healthy children to palliative care for terminally ill elders, helps streamline costs and improve standards. Most of the recent global reduction in mortality and morbidity secondary to infectious diseases has been attributed to the fact that countries around the globe have built effective health systems that streamline the care delivery process. Antibiotics were the actual cure for many diseases, but without an organization in place, little concerted effort toward reaching and optimizing the availability of that cure would have been made. A proactive approach to potential epidemics has often controlled or even reversed potential disaster. For example, in the Brazilian Amazon, a more intense focus on early detection and management of malaria cases combined with targeted mosquito control helped slash the cost of saving a life from approximately $13,000 to about $2,000 (Akhavan, Musgrove, Abrantes, & Gusmao, 1999).

FINANCING HEALTH CARE SYSTEMS

One of the most important differences between the health care systems of different nations is the manner in which those systems are funded. Funding, or *health financing*, as it is often called, serves multiple purposes. It makes available the basic funds that will help procure both the services of health care providers and the equipment needed to efficiently deliver those services. It also helps set the right financial incentives for health care providers, to make certain that all individuals have easy access to effective public health and personal health care. This implies a reduction or elimination of the possibility that an individual would be unable to pay for such care, or would be impoverished as a result of trying to do so (WHO, 2008a).

To guarantee that every individual has access to optimal health services, three interdependent functions of health system financing have to be addressed: revenue collection, pooling of resources, and purchasing of interventions. As alluded to previously, the revenue collection step forms an important means of differentiating different health care systems. Likewise, we can also segregate these systems based on how resources are pooled and how interventions are procured.

These three interventions do not function in a vacuum but rather have an intimate interrelationship. The eventual challenge of any health care system is to arrange, in the most optimum fashion, the needed technical, organizational, and institutional arrangements so that such interactions will look after people financially the fairest way possible and set incentives for providers that will motivate them to increase health and improve the responsiveness of the system. The three functions are often integrated in a single organization, which is the case for most of the health systems in the world. Each of these three steps is briefly discussed here.

Revenue Collection

Revenue collection is the process by which the health system generates the capital needed to run its operations. It may do so by receiving money from households and organizations or companies, as well as from donors. The percentages of each of these sources may vary depending on how the health care system is structured. There can be many different approaches to collecting revenue, such as the following (WHO, 2008a):

- General taxation
- Mandated social health insurance contributions (usually salary related and almost never risk related)
- Voluntary private health insurance contributions (usually risk related)
- **Out-of-pocket payment** (whereby the individual pays the entire costs for any health care services procured from his or her own financial resources)
- Donations

These approaches do not have to be exclusive; indeed, most health care systems differ primarily in the percentage of revenue generated from one or more of these approaches. For instance, most high-income developed countries rely heavily on either general taxation or mandated social health insurance contributions (e.g., the United Kingdom). Low-income countries, on the other hand, depend a lot more on out-of-pocket financing: in 60% of countries with incomes below $1,000 per capita, out-of-pocket spending is 40% or more of the total (WHO, 2008a).

Pooling

Pooling, the second crucial element in the financing of a health care system, is defined as "the accumulation and management of revenues in such a way as to ensure that the risk of having to pay for health care is borne by all the members of the pool and not by each contributor individually" (WHO, 2008a). Pooling has also been called the "insurance function" within the health system, irrespective of whether the insurance is explicit (e.g., voluntary subscription to a health insurance scheme) or implicit (e.g., tax revenues). The primary purpose of pooling is to share among large numbers the financial risk inherently associated with health interventions with an uncertain need. For instance, not everyone subscribing to a health insurance plan that covers two weeks of hospitalization for a valve replacement will actually need that procedure. In fact, the chances are that only a small minority of the subscribers would need it. It is important to remember that when a system is based entirely on an out-of-pocket system, no pooling is involved.

For public health activities and even for aspects of personal health care—such as health checkups—for which the need is fairly certain or highly probable or the cost is low, funds can be directed straight from the collection stage to purchasing, and pooling can be bypassed. This is important because consumers prefer insurance programs that focus on interventions of high probability and low cost (relative to the household capacity to pay). A family of four is more likely to opt for an insurance plan that offers unlimited free health checkups (high probability) for the entire family than for one that offers only five free annual checkups but also offers free hospital stays for surgical procedures. Pooling reduces uncertainty for both citizens and providers. Pooling is essential because by enhancing and stabilizing demand and the flow of funds, it can increase the likelihood that patients will be able to afford services and that a higher volume of services will justify new provider investments.

Purchasing

Purchasing is the last step in the functioning of a health care system that ensures the provision of services. It is the process through which pooled funds are remunerated to providers in order to deliver a prespecified or unspecified set of health interventions.

Purchasing can be classified as passive or strategic. **Passive purchasing** refers to adherence to a preset budget and simply paying bills when presented. **Strategic purchasing** is a more dynamic process involving an uninterrupted search for the best ways to maximize health system performance by deciding which interventions should be purchased, how the purchase should be done, and from whom those services should be procured. Strategic purchasing can deliver superior results, at least in theory, because the pursuit for the best interventions is ongoing and is not evaluated depending on the budgetary cycle. Strategic purchasing can be thought of as a more performance-based system, with better performance being rewarded by renewed contracts, and inferior performance being punished.

Lately, many nations, including Hungary (Adeyi, Chellaraj, Goldestein, Preker, & Ringold, 1997), New Zealand (Hornblow, 1997), and the United Kingdom (Robinson

& Julian, 1994), have attempted to reform their health care systems by introducing an active purchasing role within their public health systems.

THE FOUR MODELS OF HEALTH CARE SYSTEMS

Reid (2008a) has described four major models of health care systems. The fact that most countries follow one or the other of these models should be tempered with the knowledge that there are many subtle variations in the way each country executes its health care system, depending on local customs, norms, expectations, and government structure.

The Beveridge Model

The **Beveridge model** is named for William Beveridge, a social reformer who structured Great Britain's National Health Service (Reid, 2008a). In this system, health care is provided and financed by the government through tax payments, just like the security forces. This feature of complete reliance on tax revenues for financing is what separates the Beveridge model from other social insurance systems of health care (Matcha, 2003).

This model or a variation of it is adhered to by countries such as Great Britain, Sweden, Norway, Cuba, and Spain among many others. Most, if not all, hospitals and clinics are owned by the government; most physicians are government employees, but there are also private physicians who collect their remunerations from the government. In Britain, you never get a doctor bill. On the whole, the Beveridge model tends to have low costs per capita, because the government, as the single payer, controls what health care providers can do and what they can charge. Interestingly, Cuba, a communist nation, represents the extreme application of the Beveridge method; it is probably the world's purest example of absolute government control over health care.

The Bismarck Model, or Social Insurance Model

The **Bismarck model** (also called the **social insurance model**) is named after Prussian Chancellor Otto von Bismarck, who invented the approach during the unification of Germany in the 19th century. Although government is involved in financing, the Bismarck model is a partnership between the public and private sectors of the economy for the main motive of ensuring provision of universal health coverage for all citizens (Matcha, 2003). On a superficial basis, it is somewhat similar to the American system. It uses an insurance system—the insurers are called "sickness funds"—usually financed jointly by employers and employees through payroll deductions. However, unlike the

American insurance industry, the Bismarck-type health insurance plans have to provide coverage for everybody, and they are not expected to make a profit. The Bismarck model is followed by nations such as France, Germany, Belgium, the Netherlands, Japan, Austria, Switzerland, and, to a certain extent, by some nations in Latin America. One of the major problems with Bismarck-based health systems has been lack of financial reserves for long-term care, an issue that is now being addressed in many of these countries.

National Health Insurance Model

The **national health insurance model** combines elements of both the Beveridge and Bismarck models. Even though it uses private-sector providers, the payment comes from a government-run insurance program that every citizen pays into. The classic national health insurance system is found in Canada; Taiwan and South Korea have also adopted this model. The lack of need for marketing, denial of claims, and profits makes these universal programs considerably cheaper than their American counterparts. The single payer, which happens to be the government, tends to have sizeable market power to negotiate for lower prices. National health insurance plans also control costs by limiting the medical services for which they will pay, or by making patients wait to be treated. The long waiting times are often cited as one of the pertinent negatives of this model.

The Out-of-Pocket Model

Unfortunately, the concept of a formally organized health care system is limited to the developed world. Approximately 40 of the world's 200 countries have formally established health care systems. Developing nations simply do not have the means to provide any kind of mass medical care. The **out-of-pocket model** simply refers to a model in which patients pay at the time of treatment. Thus, the rich get health care and the poor are left behind. Rural regions of Africa, India, China, and South America exemplify this model (Reid, 2008a).

HEALTH SYSTEMS AROUND THE GLOBE

The Health System in the United States

The United States is alone among developed nations in that it lacks a universal health care system (Institute of Medicine, 2004). Health care in the United States does, however, have significant publicly funded components. **Medicare** is a social insurance program administered by the U.S. government that provides health insurance coverage to people aged 65 and over and to people with a historical work record who are disabled. **Medicaid** is the U.S. health program for eligible individuals and families with low incomes and resources. It is a means-tested program that is jointly funded by the states and federal government and is managed by the states. Among the groups of people served by Medicaid are eligible low-income parents, children, seniors, and people with disabilities (Centers for Medicare and Medicaid Services, 2006a). The **State Children's Health Insurance Program (SCHIP)** covers children of low-income families. The Veterans Health Administration directly provides health care to U.S. military veterans through a nationwide network of government hospitals; active-duty service members, retired service members, and their dependents are eligible for benefits through Tricare. Together, these tax-financed programs cover 27.8% of the population (Institute of Medicine, 2004) and make the government the largest health insurer in the nation. Per capita spending on health care by the U.S. government placed it among the top ten highest spenders among United Nations member countries in 2004.

Care is generally provided by privately owned hospitals or physicians in private practice, but public hospitals are common in older cities. Just over 59% of Americans receive health insurance through an employer, although this number is declining. Employees' expected contributions to these plans vary widely and are increasing as costs escalate. A significant number of people cannot obtain health insurance through their employer and are unable to afford individual coverage. The U.S. Census Bureau estimated that 15.3% of the U.S. population, or 45.7 million people, were uninsured in 2007. More than one-third of the uninsured are in households earning $50,000 or more per year.

The United States essentially follows a fragmented approach to national health care, drawing from elements of each of the health models discussed earlier. Traditionally, health insurance in the United States has been delivered in one of the following ways:

- As a benefit of employment, either directly or through a union, with continued benefits available to retirees. Health insurance benefits available to retirees are subsidized, thus making this component of American health care similar to the Bismarck model, in which private and public coalitions ensure universal health coverage.
- Through government-funded programs, such as Medicaid and Medicare, for eligible sections of the population. This component of the American health care system uses private-sector providers and closely resembles the national health insurance system of Canada.

*T*he State Children's Health Insurance Program (SCHIP) was created in 1997 to help states provide insurance for children of the working poor, for people with full-time jobs which didn't offer employment based insurance, and for those who earned too much for Medicaid, but not enough to afford private insurance. Because eligibility is at the discretion of the states, different rules apply, and several have tightened eligibility or capped the program.

—Centers for Medicare and Medicaid Services (2006b)

- Through the Veterans Administration, which follows the Beveridge model of government-financed and government-provided health care.
- Through private purchase of health insurance (generally for self-employed individuals).
- For the increasing number of Americans with no insurance coverage, health costs are mostly paid out of pocket if possible, which resembles the scenario in developing countries.

Pros and Cons of the System

Pros

- For people with good insurance or other financial resources, the United States offers unarguably the best care in the world.
- There is some insurance afforded to the most vulnerable sections of the population (children, the elderly, the destitute, and the emergently sick).

Cons

- *Delays in seeking care and increased use of emergency care.* Uninsured Americans are less likely to have regular health care and to use preventive services. Consequently, delay in seeking care is expected, which results in more medical crises, which are more costly than ongoing treatment for such conditions as diabetes and high blood pressure. This has been thought to cause overcrowding in emergency rooms (Derlet & Richards, 2000), although research both questions, and even disproves, this long-held notion (Schull, 2005).
- *Health disparities in minority populations.* Disparities are well documented in minority populations such as African Americans, Native Americans, Asian Americans, and Hispanics (Frist, 2005; Williams & Collins, 1995). When compared with whites, these minority groups have a higher incidence of chronic diseases, higher mortality, and poorer health outcomes. Among the disease-specific examples of racial and ethnic disparities in the United States is the cancer incidence rate among African Americans, which is 25% higher than among whites (U.S. Department of Health and Human Services, 2004).
- *Administrative costs.* The administrative costs in a health care system like the one in America are considerably higher than a single-payer system such as

Canada, mainly because of the multitude of players involved. A joint study done by Harvard Medical School and the Canadian Institute for Health Information determined that some 31% of U.S. health care dollars, or more than $1,000 per person per year, went to health care administrative costs, almost double the administrative overhead in Canada on a percentage basis (Woolhandler, Campbell, & Himmelstein, 2003).

- *Lack of mental health parity.* The lack of mental health coverage for Americans bears significant ramifications for the U.S. economy and social system. It is estimated that fewer than 50% of all people with mental illnesses receive treatment because of factors such as stigma and lack of access to care. Most people with mental disorders in the United States remain either untreated or inadequately treated. Interventions are needed to enhance treatment initiation and quality (Wang et al., 2005).

FOCUS FEATURE 11.1 The Emergency Medical Treatment and Active Labor Act (EMTALA)

The Emergency Medical Treatment and Active Labor Act (**EMTALA**) was passed by the U.S. Congress in 1986 as part of the Consolidated Omnibus Budget Reconciliation Act. It requires hospitals and ambulance services to provide care to anyone in need of emergency treatment regardless of citizenship, legal status, or ability to pay. There are no reimbursement provisions (American College of Emergency Physicians, 2008). As a result of the act, patients needing emergency treatment can be discharged only under their own informed consent or when their condition requires transfer to a hospital better equipped to administer the treatment.

Hospitals have three obligations under EMTALA:

1. Individuals requesting emergency care must receive a medical screening examination to determine whether an emergency medical condition exists. Examination and treatment cannot be delayed to inquire about methods of payment or insurance coverage.
2. The emergency room must treat an individual with an emergency medical condition until the condition is resolved or stabilized. If the hospital does not have the capability to treat the condition, the hospital must make an appropriate transfer of the patient to another hospital with such capability.
3. Hospitals with specialized capabilities must accept such transfers.

Because the cost of emergency care required by EMTALA is not covered by the federal government, this law has been criticized as an unfunded mandate forcing charity care on hospitals that is leading to the closure of many emergency departments and threatening the ability of emergency departments to care for all patients (American College of Emergency Physicians, 2008).

The Health System in Canada

As mentioned previously, Canada follows a national health insurance model. Canadians receive health care coverage through 13 different government-provided plans, with each plan being administered by a provincial or territorial authority. Financing is provided by the government through tax payments. The onus of responsibility for administering the plans is distributed between the federal government and the provinces, with each having well-defined roles.

In the Canadian system, the federal government delineates and administers health care standards, helps secure funds for provincial health systems, and provides health care to specified groups such as Native Canadians, veterans, military recruits, inmates, inmates housed in federal penitentiaries, and the Royal Canadian Mounted Police (National Coalition on Health Care, 2008a). Health care for all individuals other than these specified groups is managed by the provincial governments. The planning, financing, and evaluation of care provided by nonfederal health care institutions is also arranged by the provincial governments.

The thread that unifies the functioning of all 13 provinces and their territorial plans is the Canada Health Act of 1984, which lays down the principles each province should adhere to while designing and implementing its health care plans in order to receive its full share of federal funding:

- The plan should be publicly administered.
- It should be comprehensive, which means it should cover all medically essential services provided by hospitals and doctors.
- The terms, conditions, and care offered to every individual in the plan should be uniform.
- There must be **portability**; that is, coverage for insured services must be preserved when an insured person travels within or outside of Canada.
- There must be **accessibility**; that is, reasonable access of insured individuals to medically necessary care cannot be obstructed by financial barriers.

Primary care physicians (about 51% of all Canadian doctors) provide most of the health care. Referral to specialists and hospitals and prescription of tests and drugs is also done by primary care physicians. Most doctors are private practitioners, who are generally paid on a fee-for-service basis and submit claims to the provincial health plan. A small minority of physicians who work in settings such as community health centers receive government salaries. Also, most hospitals (>95%) in Canada are private nonprofit organizations (National Coalition on Health Care, 2008a).

Pros and Cons of the System

Pros

- Minimal administrative costs remain one of the best achievements of the Canadian health care system. As an example, the per capita gap between U.S. and Canadian spending on health care administration has grown to US$752 (Woolhandler, Campbell, & Himmelstein, 2003).

Cons

- Health costs are high and are shouldered mostly by the budgets of provincial governments, a source of constant discord between the provinces and the federal government (Woolhandler, Campbell, & Himmelstein, 2003).
- Many Canadian people are unhappy with the health care system, especially concerning the waits for specialists, emergency room services, and diagnostic tests.
- Scarcity of resources: Canada has on an average 2.1 doctors per 1,000 persons, which is significantly lower than other developed nations (National Coalition on Health Care, 2008a).

The Health System in France

The French health care system is quite similar to some of the other national health insurance plans discussed earlier. Any salaried employee in France is covered by the national health insurance plan, which is called **Securite sociale** (National Coalition on Health Care, 2008b). Spouses and children of salaried employees draw insurance benefits without having employee status. Special coverage is made compulsory for people who are not entitled to the national insurance plan. Additional insurance plans can be purchased to complement the national plan.

Some of the salient features regarding the functioning of the French insurance system are as follows (Docteur & Oxley, 2003; National Coalition on Health Care, 2008b; Rodwin & Sandier, 1993):

- The national insurance program decides the fees for seeing different kinds of doctors; it is more expensive to see a specialist than it is to see a general practitioner. Referrals are not needed to see a specialist.
- Home visits, night visits, or Sunday visits cost more than visits on regular days and times.

- Prescription drugs are sold only through pharmacies, and only prescription drugs may be reimbursed through the national insurance. The reimbursement rate for prescription drugs varies depending on the utility of the drug. For "comfort" drugs (drugs with no established therapeutic advantage), patients may be responsible for up to 65% of the cost.
- Inpatient treatment is reimbursed for 80% for the first month and 100% afterward.

Pros and Cons of the System

Pros

- Patient satisfaction with the health care system is fairly high. Approximately 79% of French citizens were very or fairly satisfied with their health care system according to a 1999 survey (Docteur & Oxley, 2003).
- The waiting period for elective care is minimal in the French system, especially in comparison with other health care systems that follow a national health insurance approach.

Cons

- Because of its high levels of reimbursement and coverage, French health care is among the most expensive in the world. Without the institution of urgent health care reforms to limit spending, this cost is only expected to grow.
- The lack of a gatekeeper practitioner means that patients are free to change doctors as frequently as they desire and to visit multiple specialists, further adding to the cost.

The Health System in Argentina

Argentina's health care system is composed of three segments:

- The public sector, financed through taxes
- The private sector, financed through voluntary insurance schemes
- The social security sector, financed through obligatory insurance schemes

The Ministry of Health and Social Action (MSAS) oversees all three segments of the health care system and is responsible for the setting of regulations, evaluation, and collecting statistics. In essence, the Argentinean system is close to the

American health care system, with different sectors catering to different segments of the population.

The Social Security Sector

The public sector is funded and managed by **Obras Sociales**, umbrella organizations for Argentine worker's unions. There are over 300 Obras Sociales in Argentina, with each chapter organized according to the occupation of the beneficiary. These organizations vary greatly in quality and effectiveness. The top 30 chapters hold 73% of the beneficiaries and 75% of resources for all Obras Sociales schemes; the monthly average that a beneficiary receives varies from $5 to $80 (Belmartino, 2000). Only workers employed in the formal sector are covered under Obras Sociales insurance schemes. After Argentina's economic crisis of 2001, the number of those covered under these schemes fell slightly (as unemployment increased and employment in the informal sector rose). In 1999, there were 8.9 million beneficiaries covered by Obras Sociales (Belmartino, 2000).

The Private Sector

Great heterogeneity characterizes the private health care sector in Argentina, which is composed of a great number of fragmented facilities and small networks. It consists of over 200 organizations and covers roughly 2 million Argentines (Belmartino, 2000). Private insurance often overlaps with other forms of health care coverage, making it hard to accurately estimate the degree to which individual beneficiaries are dependent on the private and public sectors. Foreign competition has increased in Argentina's private health care sector, with Swiss, American, and other Latin American health care providers entering the market. The entry of foreign players has not been formally regulated (Belmartino, 2000).

The Public Sector

The public system serves those not covered by Obras Sociales or private insurance schemes. It also provides emergency services. The public system is highly decentralized to the provincial level; often primary care is under the purview of local townships. The total number of Argentines relying on the public sector has increased since 2001. According to 2000 figures, 37.4% of Argentines had no health insurance, 48.8% were covered under Obras Sociales, 8.6% had private insurance, and 3.8% were covered by both Obras Sociales and private insurance schemes (Barrientos & Lloyd-Sherlock, 2000).

Drawbacks of the System

Argentina's public system exhibits many problems, as detailed below.

Cons

- Serious structural deterioration and managerial inefficiency
- A high degree of administrative centralization at the provincial level
- Rigidity in its staffing structure and labor relationships
- No adequate system of incentives
- Inadequate information systems on which to base decision making and control
- Serious deficits in facilities and equipment maintenance
- A system of management ill-suited to its size
- Inequities (A Solidarity Redistribution Fund has been created by the MSAS to attempt to address beneficiary inequities.)

The Health System in Japan

Japan has universal health coverage in the form of a social insurance system, but individuals often receive coverage in quite different ways. Broadly speaking, individuals can obtain coverage either via the national health insurance, which is a not-for-profit community-based plan, or through the Employee Health Insurance scheme (National Coalition on Health Care, 2008c; Reid, 2008a).

Employee Health Insurance covers people who are working for medium to large companies, national or local government, or private schools. The government also has a program within this program for employees of small businesses. Premiums are based on monthly salary (excluding bonuses); half this cost is paid by the employer, and half by the employee. Twenty percent of the medical costs associated with a hospitalization and 30% of outpatient costs have to be borne by the patient under this scheme. Prescription drugs may also require copayments. Patients share costs to a certain level and then receive full coverage. For chronic illnesses, the employee or the employee's spouse is provided an allowance based on salary (National Coalition on Health Care, 2008c).

The second component of the Japanese health care system—the national health insurance—protects the health of self-employed workers or those working in agriculture, forestry, or fisheries, as well as the unemployed (including expectant mothers, students, retirees, etc.). Under this plan, the insured pay 30% of inpatient or outpatient costs, as well as copayments for prescription drugs. Similar to the Employee Health Insurance program, patients share costs up to a certain ceiling, after which point they receive full coverage. Finally, there is also a national health program for the elderly. People older than 70 qualify for this program, which is funded by contributions from the two main plans.

Pros and Cons of the System

Pros

- Unlike in the British system, there are no gatekeeper general practitioners in Japan; patients can seek any specialists they want, whenever they want.
- The Japanese Ministry of Health negotiates with physicians every two years to set the price for every health care procedure. This negotiation helps keep the costs down (Reid, 2008a).

Cons

- The absence of gatekeeper physicians means that there's often little or no check on how often the Japanese use health care and what factors control the utilization of specialist care (Reid, 2008a).
- The social system in Japan is expected to grapple with demographic issues in the near future, as its elderly population will greatly outnumber that of its young working citizens. This is expected to have long-term repercussions on the health care system.

The Health System in Germany

Like Japan, Germany also employs a social insurance model. As mentioned previously, the Bismarck model, which is the prototype of social insurance models, was created in Germany. One feature that differentiates the German approach from that of the Japanese is that Germans are free to buy their insurance from an entire range of private, nonprofit "sickness funds," unlike the Japanese, who have to get insurance either from work or through a community fund (Reid, 2008a). The poor receive public assistance to pay their premiums.

Most German citizens obtain health care coverage through the state health insurance plans, which are funded from contributions. Below a set income limit, an employee pays half the insurance contributions while the employer bears the other half. The poor, the unemployed, and the elderly get additional subsidies. The compulsory state insurance program covers over 90% of the population. Above a specified income limit, a salaried employee has the freedom to either enroll in the state program or purchase private health insurance. Approximately a quarter of the German population opt for private insurance. It is commendable that only 0.2% of the population remains uninsured (National Coalition on Health Care, 2008d).

Sickness funds are not for profit and cannot refuse coverage based on preexisting conditions. These funds compete with each other for members and are paid based on the size of their recruitments. Like in Japan (another single-payer system), the insured can go straight to a specialist, bypassing a gatekeeper primary practitioner; however, they may have to pay a higher copayment if they choose to do so (National Coalition on Health Care, 2008d; Reid, 2008a).

Anyone subscribing to the constitutional health care plan has to contribute toward the cost of prescription drugs, wound dressings, and bandages; a share of the cost of inpatient preventive treatment and rehabilitation; outpatient rehabilitation; and inpatient hospital care and costs pertaining to travel. Children (anyone younger than 18 years) and people receiving social assistance, war victims' benefits, unemployment or education assistance, or assistance for the disabled are all exempt from this requirement to contribute. The fee for general practitioners is negotiated centrally, and they are paid on a fee-for-service basis.

Pros and Cons of the System

Pros

- Because of the single-payer system, only 0.2% of the German population is uninsured.
- Despite being a Bismarck-type model, there still are provisions for private insurance, which increases the choices available to at least a segment of the population.

Cons

- German physicians often report feeling underpaid despite having to pay much less for medical school expenses and malpractice insurance premiums than their American counterparts.
- The richest 10% of the German population have chosen to opt out of the sickness funds in favor of American-style for-profit insurance. Needless to say, these patients get quicker and easier access to health care because the for-profit insurers pay doctors more than the sickness funds (Reid, 2008a).

The Health System in the United Kingdom

The United Kingdom uses the Beveridge model of health care. There are no annual costs borne by a family other than taxes imposed by the government on all citizens.

Most services do not require copayments; however, some dental care procedures, eyeglasses, and about 5% of services require a copayment. The young and elderly populations are exempted from all copayment requirements (Reid, 2008b).

The system followed by Britain is essentially a form of **socialized medicine** because the government is responsible for both providing and paying for health care. The taxes paid by British citizens for health care are funneled to the government-run National Health Service (NHS), which then distributes those funds to health care providers. Whereas physicians working in hospitals get fixed salaries, practitioners running private practices are paid by the NHS based on the number of patients they see. A small minority of specialists opt to work outside this system and see private-pay patients.

Pros and Cons of the System

Pros

- Administrative costs are minimal. The British system is essentially funded through taxes, which keeps administrative costs low. Unlike a health system based on insurance companies and copayments, there are no bills to collect or claims to review in this system.
- The primary physician serves as a gatekeeper to the entire health care system and for referrals to specialists.
- General practitioners are remunerated based on how effective they are at providing preventive care. Consequently, Britain is a leader in the field of preventive medicine.

Cons

- Long waiting times
- A very limited choice offered to patients regarding who they want to be treated by and where they want to be treated

Attempts have been made by the British government to address these discrepancies by having hospitals compete for NHS funds in order to make care somewhat more competitive. Also, patients are increasingly being given some choice as to where they want to be treated (Reid, 2008b).

The Health System in the Russian Federation

After the dissolution of the Soviet Union, the health care system in the Russian Federation was decentralized. The health care system closely follows the administrative structure of the country and is divided into federal, regional, and municipal administrative levels. According to the constitution of the Russian Federation, the state is responsible for the regulation and protection of human and citizen rights and freedoms, and the federal and regional levels are jointly responsible for the coordination of health care issues (WHO Regional Office for Europe, 2008).

The parallel system (otherwise known as "departmental" or "ministerial") consists of ministries other than the Ministry of Health as well as public enterprises that traditionally have provided health care services exclusively for their respective employees and their families. The parallel system accounts for about 15% of all outpatient facilities and about 6% of inpatient facilities.

After the independence of the Russian Federation in 1991, the former Academy of Medical Sciences of the USSR became the Academy of Medical Sciences of the Russian Federation, and continued to be responsible for medical research. It continues to assert its independence from the Federal Ministry of Health. Financed through the federal budget, the Academy of Medical Sciences receives its research allocation from the Ministry of Finance in agreement with the Ministry of Science, and its allocation for clinical activity from the Ministry of Health (WHO Regional Office for Europe, 2008).

The Ministry of Finance continues to formulate national budgets and to recommend spending levels for local government. It has a department dealing with all issues of health care financing, including the level of health insurance contributions. In addition, surveillance programs for particular disease groups and certain types of capital expenditure are financed from federal sources.

The Ministry for Social Protection, established to protect the interests of the most vulnerable, was reabsorbed into the Ministry of Labor, forming the Ministry of Labor and Social Protection, which works closely with the Ministry of Health. It has now taken on responsibility for social care and (in conjunction with the ministries of trade and industry) for health and safety practices.

Health Care Reform Legislation

In 1991, legislation established an obligatory health insurance system intended to remediate the critical underfunding of health care and facilitate the transition to a market-based economy. In theory, this was to be consummated by a purchaser/provider split that would augment efficiency, quality, and equity in the health care system through the operation of market forces (Chernichovsky & Potapchik, 1997; WHO Regional Office for Europe, 2008). A second key feature of the health care reform legislation was the establishment of independent third-party payers to purchase health care on behalf of subscribers.

Under the Soviet system, state budgetary resources at multiple levels exclusively financed health care. As Soviet authority began to diminish in the 1980s, liberalization of central planning allowed for experimentation in health care organization. New organizational and financing methods were investigated with an aim of improving efficiency and quality in health care services.

The new financing system envisaged by the health insurance legislation was expected to include the following salient elements:

- A fundamental change in health care financing through the establishment of a nonbudgetary source of revenues in order to increase the total amount of funds available for health without displacing any existing sources of funds
- Establishment of a federal mandatory health insurance fund (MHIF)
- Payroll contribution rates of 3.4% of wages, paid only by the employer, to be transferred to the territorial funds and 0.2% of wages to the federal fund for equalization purposes
- Local government payment for the nonworking population (in an unspecified amount)
- An undefined scope of insurance benefits left to subsequent regulations at the federal level, with regions free to define benefits above the minimum
- Voluntary insurance permitted to cover services outside the basic compulsory insurance package
- Purchasing of care on behalf of citizens to be carried out by private insurance companies
- Insurers to pay providers on the basis of performance-related methods, according to annually renegotiated tariffs agreed by the territorial fund, regional health authorities, local governments, medical associations, and others at the discretion of the region

Employers can opt to purchase voluntary health insurance for their employees for coverage of services not included in statutory provisions. Purchase of voluntary health insurance is to be subsidized by the government through tax relief. Finally, citizens also have the choice of purchasing voluntary health insurance if they so desire, or of paying out of pocket for health care (WHO Regional Office for Europe, 2008).

This system of reforms envisioned a combination of public and private health coverage initiatives. However, more than a decade after the passage of the original health insurance legislation, the health care financing system in the Russian Federation is still in a state of turmoil and transition.

Drawbacks of the System
Cons

- *Limited freedom of choice for consumers.* The law makes consumers free to choose their insurers, consequently allowing the freedom of selecting from among the insurer's contracted providers. This is important in terms of consumer satisfaction and as an encouragement to insurer and provider competition. However, the restricted availability of insurers in many parts of the country limits the actual freedom of choice.
- *Regulatory weakness.* Extremely rapid decentralization of health care administration has precipitated an absolute loss of the state's regulatory capacity. After the introduction of the health insurance legislation, no efforts were made to oversee the interactions between the various components of the system. This resulted in a lack of development of a legal and regulatory basis for mandatory health insurance.

The Health System in China

The health care system in China has traditionally been run by the government with three primary means of revenue generation. Recently, there has been growth in private-sector initiatives in the health field.

Typically, in the Chinese health care system dual control exists: horizontal control by the government unit and line management by the professional health unit. Each tier, down to the county level, has a Department of Public Health. The Ministry of Public Health is at the apex of the pyramid and is accountable to the State Council. The ministry holds a central budget and directly controls and finances medical schools, some hospitals, and specialized research institutions. Through special agencies it coordinates task forces concerned with the eradication of infectious and parasitic disease and the support of maternal and child health; these agencies are, however, usually administered locally. Health institutions at provincial, municipal, and city prefecture level are usually called "urban" in China, and those at county level or below are referred to as "rural," even though they may be located in a county town or local township (Hillier & Shen, 1996).

Institutions other than the government run health structures too. The People's Liberation Army runs its own medical schools and hospitals. Some large state-managed industries, such as the railways, possess their own hospitals and in some cases even medical schools. These hospitals and schools are not under the control of the Ministry of Public Health.

Almost one-third of hospitals are in the private sector, with many businesses in the larger urban centers owning their own hospitals. There are also a growing number of privately owned and financed hospitals and clinics, which are run as profit-making enterprises. This trend has been made possible by the relative economic deregulatory approach that has been the hallmark of Chinese domestic policy in recent years. In comparison with the fixed, bureaucratically organized, and relatively easy to describe Chinese health care system of the 1970s, the current system is composed of multiple ever-evolving entities, and responds more to the dynamics of the market than to the urgency of health needs or planning (Hillier & Shen, 1996).

The three traditional types of health care financing schemes in China are the labor insurance medical care scheme, the public service medical care scheme, and the cooperative medical care scheme. Those individuals not covered by these schemes have to pay out of pocket for medical care they seek on a fee-for-service basis (Gu & Tang, 1995).

Labor Insurance Medical Care

As per a 1951 government stipulation, all enterprises with more than 100 employees are obliged to institute labor insurance. This meant that the health expenses of workers and staff should be paid by their enterprises, with employees' dependents entitled to a 50% reimbursement of their medical care costs as well. In general, expenses incurred by businesses due to the labor insurance medical care scheme are managed and paid for by that individual business. Initially, 5.5% of an enterprise's total wages was budgeted toward health care costs. This figure has been revised recently, and a business is free to allocate an amount of money equivalent to 15% of an employee's wages as a public welfare fund to cover expenditures of medical care and other welfare for employees. The population coverage of labor insurance has increased gradually with economic development during the 1980s. The total number of employees covered in 1990 was 203.16 million (roughly 17.9% of the total Chinese population), of whom state employees accounted for 47%, collective employees 20%, and dependents of employees 33% (Gu & Tang, 1995; Henderson et al., 2000).

Public Service Medical Care

The Regulation of Public Service Medical Scheme, issued by the Chinese government in 1952, made medical care free for all government staff, including retired staff, as well as students in colleges and universities. Expenses for public service medical care are covered by government funds. Management of the medical scheme can be done by the local health authority, by state-owned institutions, or by the appointed hospital. Expenditure due to the public service medical scheme is paid out of the government budget, specifically, from funds appropriated to the health sector from the Ministry of Finance. The public service medical care scheme covered 26.84 million people in 1990, accounting for roughly 2.4% of the total Chinese population (Henderson et al., 2000).

The Cooperative Medical Scheme

The cooperative medical scheme is an arrangement whereby one or two health workers (traditionally called barefoot doctors) are made responsible for the provision of primary health care for a rural population at low cost. These health workers are paid by the collectives based on the work points they have earned. This system also receives financial contribution from the rural population served through a prepayment mechanism. During the 1960s this scheme was extended to most of rural China, and by the mid-1970s the cooperative medical scheme had been implemented in about 90% of Chinese villages and became the primary means of financing rural health services. Currently, only 7% of the total Chinese population is served by this scheme (Gu & Tang, 1995).

Fee-for-Service Model (Out of Pocket)

Even though not a traditional part of Chinese health care, the fee-for-service model has made a significant increase in the Chinese market in recent years. Presently, 14% of urban residents and 93% of rural residents have to pay for medical care out of their pockets. The ability to pay is a strong determinant of utilization of medical care. Financial constraints remain the main reason for people's unmet medical care needs. A national household health survey in 1988 showed that 20% of rural patients did not seek outpatient services. Among those in poor counties, half of the patients not treated were not treated as a result of the burden of health care costs.

Pros and Cons of the System

The introduction of a largely private market in health care has led to only sporadic improvement in health care delivery. For the vast majority the outcome has been disappointing (Hillier & Shen, 1996). The only two silver linings have been that the quality and supply of curative hospital services to urban or richer rural dwellers have been improved, and the government has been able to rid itself of the increasing costs associated with unprofitable hospitals.

Because of a lack of health insurance for a sizeable population and a lack of planning regarding the burgeoning private sector, the Chinese health care system is in need of significant reforms. Perhaps the most pressing need is to modify the health care system in such a way that it can adequately respond to the challenges of the epidemiologic transition. This mainly means reducing premature death and disability in economically productive adults, because heart disease, chronic obstructive lung disease, cancers, stroke, industrial injuries, and suicide now account for a staggering 72% of all deaths in China (Shi, 1993). At the same time, the minimum structure needed to maintain child health and fight endemic infectious diseases has to be maintained. These twin requirements mandate a thorough planning of preventive services (Wu et al., 2001).

The other inadequacy inherent in the health care system of China is the lack of a proper health care financing method. This issue, of course, is not limited to China but is being seen more or less across the globe in developing and developed nations. Recent attempts to reduce government and labor insurance costs by systems with up to 50% copayments may be effective in controlling costs and the wasteful use of resources.

The Health System in India

As mentioned earlier, the health care system in India is essentially an out-of-pocket payment type. Those who can afford health care purchase it while a significant percentage is left behind. Health care is essentially the responsibility of the individual states.

The national health policy was endorsed by the parliament in 1983. It laid down a phased, time-bound program for setting up a well-dispersed network of comprehensive primary health care services, linked with extension and health education, and designed in the context of the ground reality that elementary health problems can be resolved by the people themselves (Ministry of Health and Family Welfare, 2008). The salient features of this policy are as follows:

- Intermediation through "health volunteers" having appropriate knowledge, simple skills, and requisite technologies
- Institution of an efficient referral system to ensure that patient load at the higher levels of the hierarchy is not needlessly burdened by those who can be treated at the decentralized level
- An integrated network of evenly spread specialty and superspecialty services, and encouragement of such facilities through private investments for patients who can pay, so that the draw on the government's facilities is limited to those entitled to free use

However, more than two decades after the institution of the national health policy, there still remains a huge gap between the realities on the ground and the policy goals.

The national health policy in its latest form focuses on the eradication of multiple infectious diseases such as polio, leprosy, filariasis, and so on. It also aims to reduce mortality secondary to tuberculosis, increase utilization of public health facilities from less than 20% to more than 75% by 2010, and establish an integrated system of surveillance (WHO Regional Office for South-East Asia, 2008).

The division of health care between central and state governments is not as clear-cut as in some of the developed nations discussed earlier. Central government initiatives for influencing public health have focused on five-year plans, on coordinated planning with the states, and on sponsoring major health programs. Government expenditures are jointly shared by the central and state governments. Goals and strategies are set through central-state government consultations of the Central Council of Health and Family Welfare. Central government efforts are administered by the Ministry of Health and Family Welfare, which provides both administrative and technical services and manages medical education. States provide public services and health education (Library of Congress, 2005).

Indigenous or traditional medical practitioners continue to practice throughout the country. The two main forms of traditional medicine practiced are the Ayurvedic system, which deals with mental and spiritual as well as physical well-being, and the Unani herbal medical practice. These professions are frequently hereditary. A variety of institutions offer training in indigenous medical practice. Only in the late 1970s did official health policy refer to any form of integration between Western-oriented medical personnel and indigenous medical practitioners (Banerji, 1981).

Pros and Cons of the System

Pros

- India has been successfully able to eradicate multiple communicable diseases and significantly retard the progress of many other infections.
- Lately, there has been an increased recognition that in a few decades, the focus of health care policies may have to be changed to chronic conditions. As a result, the government has adopted an integrated effort to control and manage chronic noncommunicable conditions (WHO, 2002).

Cons

- The government of India has been making a concerted effort to maximize the benefits of decentralization. The national health policy and its successive revisions have attempted to streamline efforts needed to achieve optimal health care in rural India based on health indicators and research outcomes. However, despite serial five-year plans rooted in common sense, the chasm between those who can pay for health care and those who cannot continues to widen.
- It has been argued by critics that the national policy lacks specific measures to achieve broad stated goals. Particular problems that have been cited include the failure to integrate health services with wider economic and social development, the lack of nutritional support and sanitation, and the poor participatory involvement at the local level.
- A failure to effectively control the burgeoning population has essentially negated most, if not all, of the positive outcomes of the health care initiatives undertaken by the national and state governments.

The Health System in Nigeria

Health care provision in Nigeria is a concurrent responsibility of the three tiers of government in the country (Akhtar, 1991). By virtue of being a mixed economy (an economy that contains both privately owned and state-owned enterprises or that combines elements of capitalism and socialism), private providers of health care have an increasingly important role to play in health care delivery. The federal government coordinates the functioning of the university teaching hospitals, the state government manages the various general hospitals, and the local government bodies are responsible for the dispensaries. The National Agency for Food and Drug Administration and Control (NAFDAC) is the Nigerian government agency responsible for regulating and controlling the manufacture, importation, exportation, advertisement, distribution, sale, and use of food, drugs, cosmetics, medical devices, chemicals, and prepackaged water (Iwu & Wooton, 2002).

Salient Functions of the NAFDAC

1. Regulation and control of the importation, exportation, manufacture, advertisement, distribution, sale and use of drugs, cosmetics, medical devices, bottled water, and chemicals (Iwu & Wooton, 2002)

2. Conduct appropriate tests and ensure compliance with standard specifications designated and approved by the council for the effective control of quality of food, drugs, cosmetics, medical devices, bottled water, and chemicals

3. Undertake appropriate investigation into the production premises and raw materials for food, drugs, cosmetics, medical devices, bottled water, and chemicals and establish a relevant quality assurance system, including certification of the production sites and of the regulated products (Iwu & Wooton, 2002)

4. Undertake inspection of imported foods, drugs, cosmetics, medical devices, bottled water, and chemicals and establish a relevant quality assurance system, including certification of the production sites and of the regulated products.

5. Compile standard specifications, regulations, and guidelines for the production, importation, exportation, sale and distribution of food, drugs, cosmetics, medical devices, bottled water, and chemicals (Iwu & Wooton, 2002)

6. Control the exportation and issue quality certification of food, drugs, medical devices, bottled water, and chemicals intended for export

7. Establish and maintain relevant laboratories or other institutions in strategic areas of Nigeria as may be necessary for the performance of its functions

Health Insurance

Historically, health insurance in Nigeria has been delivered to a minority of the population and has been fragmented in structure (Vogel, 1993). The three ways by which health insurance is currently delivered, at least in theory, are as follows:

- Free health care provided and financed for all citizens
- Health care provided by the government through a special health insurance scheme for government employees
- Private firms entering contracts with private health care providers

In May 1999, the Nigerian government created the National Health Insurance Scheme, which encompasses government employees, the organized private sector, and the informal sector. According to the legislation as written, the scheme also covered children younger than 5, permanently disabled persons, and prison inmates (Okonkwo, 2001; Vogel, 1993). However, the scheme has not been completely implemented and has run into multiple obstacles.

Pros and Cons of the System

Pros

- The National Agency for Food and Drug Administration and Control has regulatory authority over the manufacture, importation, exportation, advertisement, distribution, sale, and use of food, drugs, cosmetics, medical devices, chemicals, and prepackaged water. This is a welcome feature of the health care system because Nigeria has been plagued with multiple instances of food, drug, and water adulteration in recent years.

- The passage of the National Health Insurance Scheme by the Nigerian government is an important step in the right direction. By making health coverage a federal mandate, many challenges have sprung up and many other deficiencies of the health care system have been unraveled. However, it remains to be seen how well and how soon the idea of national health insurance is implemented.

Cons

- *Inequity of health care.* Different regional factors influence the quality or quantity of health care delivery. Largely, this is a consequence of the varying level of state and local government involvement and investment in health care programs and education. Approximately 70% of the budget of the Nigerian Ministry of Health is spent in urban areas, where only 30% of the population resides (Akhtar, 1991).
- *Brain drain.* **Brain drain** refers to a large emigration of individuals with technical skills or knowledge, normally due to conflict, lack of opportunity, political instability, or health risks. Migration of health care personnel to the developed world is an important issue in the Nigerian health care system (Clark, Stewart, & Clark, 2006).

SKILL-BUILDING ACTIVITY

Medical underwriting is an insurance term referring to the use of medical or health status information in the evaluation of an applicant for coverage (typically for life or health insurance). As part of the underwriting process, health information may be used in making two related decisions: whether to offer or deny coverage, and what premium rate to set for the policy. Select any health insurance provider that operates in your city and find out the following:

1. What medical conditions would increase the cost of coverage for a potential applicant offered by the provider of your choice?
2. Are there any demographic factors (sex, age, race, etc.) that affect the coverage cost?
3. Are there any medical conditions that disqualify an applicant for health coverage by this provider?

4. What are the coverage benefits pertaining to mental health care offered by this provider?

5. Is there a discrepancy between the coverage extended for mental health disorders (such as depression) and that provided for other medical conditions (e.g., hypertension)?

Compile your findings in a fact sheet format.

SUMMARY

According to the World Health Organization (2008a), a health system includes "all the activities whose primary purpose is to promote, restore or maintain health." Recognized health services, including the professional delivery of individual medical attention; traditional medicine; any medication that can potentially affect the health of an individual; and home care of the sick are all included under the umbrella of a health system. Other activities with a public health focus, such as health education and promotion, disease prevention, and even social and environmental interventions such as the organization of local neighborhood watches, are also within the system.

The basic functions of a health system are improving the health of people served by that health system, responding to people's expectations, and providing financial protection against the costs of ill-health. The ways in which health care systems are financed account for most of the differences among health care systems across the globe. The three interdependent functions of a health care system that guarantee its optimal functioning are revenue collection, pooling of resources, and purchasing.

There are four basic models of health care delivery. Most of the countries follow one or the other of these models, and some follow a mixed approach. In the Beveridge model (followed by Britain), health care is provided and financed by the government through tax payments, just like the security forces. In the Bismarck model (followed in France and Germany), although the government is involved in financing, there is a partnership between the public and private sectors of the economy for the main motive of ensuring provision of universal health coverage for all citizens. The national health insurance model combines elements of both the Beveridge and Bismarck models. It uses private-sector providers, but the payment comes from a government-run insurance program that every citizen pays into. The classic national health insurance system is found in Canada. Taiwan and South Korea have also adopted this model. The final model is the out-of-pocket model, in which an individual is expected to pay all costs for any health care service that he or she may need.

Most developing nations simply do not have the means to provide any kind of mass medical care. In the out-of-pocket model, the rich preferentially get health care and the poor are left behind. Rural regions of Africa, India, China, and South America exemplify this model.

IMPORTANT TERMS

accessibility
Beveridge model
Bismarck model
brain drain
EMTALA
health system
Medicaid
Medicare
national health insurance model
Obras Sociales
out-of-pocket model
out-of-pocket payment

passive purchasing
pooling
portability
purchasing
revenue collection
State Children's Health Insurance
    Program (SCHIP)
Securite sociale
social insurance model
socialized medicine
strategic purchasing

REVIEW QUESTIONS

1. Define a health system. Discuss any two functions of a health care system.
2. Enumerate the four models of health care systems. Describe the salient features of each.
3. Give an example of one country that follows each of the four models of health care system discussed in the text.
4. What are the pros and cons of the American health care system?
5. What is the primary difference between the health care system followed in the United Kingdom and the one followed in America?
6. What kind of a health care system is universally found in developing countries? Discuss the salient features of such a system.
7. In the context of a health care system, what do you understand by the terms *pooling* and *purchasing*?
8. What is the importance of pooling in a health care system?

WEB SITES TO EXPLORE

Country Health Profiles: WHO Regional Office for Africa

http://www.afro.who.int/home/countryprofiles.html

This site includes the World Health Organization's compilation of health system indicators for the 46 countries that make up the African continent. Some of the important statistics included are mortality and morbidity indicators arranged by age and specific population groups, health services coverage statistics, and health system statistics (density of physicians, nurses, and other medical and allied personnel). Each fact sheet also includes a pie chart comparing how that country does with respect to the rest of Africa. *Pick any two countries from the list and compare some of their health system statistics (particularly the density of physicians and nurses). Then compare it with similar data from a developed country.*

National Health Service (England)

http://www.nhs.uk/aboutnhs/pages/about.aspx

The National Health Service (NHS) is the publicly funded health care system in the United Kingdom. The NHS provides health care to anyone normally resident in the United Kingdom, with most services free at the point of use for the patient, although there are charges associated with eye tests, dental care, prescriptions, and many aspects of personal care. It covers everything from antenatal screening and routine treatments for coughs and colds to open heart surgery, accident and emergency treatment, and end-of-life care. *Select a medical condition of your choice. Then thoroughly explore the NHS Web site and gather information regarding what kind of support the NHS system provides to a patient seeking help for your condition of choice. How would this differ from the scenario in the United States?*

Practicing Physicians per 1000 Population, OECD Countries

http://www.oecd.org/dataoecd/53/12/38976551.pdf

The Organization for Economic Cooperation and Development (OECD) is a group of 30 member countries committed to democracy and the market economy. It is concerned with researching social changes and evolving patterns in trade, environment, agriculture, technology, fiscal policy, and more. *Compare the number of practicing physicians in developed and developing countries and discuss why you think there is a discrepancy between the two.*

Sick Around the World: Five Capitalist Democracies and How They Do It

http://www.pbs.org/wgbh/pages/frontline/sickaroundtheworld/countries/

This Web site does a commendable job of comparing the health care systems of five capitalist democracies from the developed world, namely, Japan, Germany, the United Kingdom, Switzerland, and Taiwan. Comparisons are drawn between these five health care systems based on their functioning, revenue generation, and costs. The site also discusses the relative merits and demerits of each system. *Compile the indicators discussed on this site for any country of your choice and see how those indicators compare with any one of the five health care systems discussed on the Web site.*

The World Health Report 2000

http://www.who.int/whr/2000/media_centre/press_release/en/

The 2000 World Health Report is WHO's analysis of world health systems, which produced some interesting findings. The report compares world health systems in 191 member states using five performance indicators. One of the conclusions was that France provided the best overall health care, followed among major countries by Italy, Spain, Oman, Austria, and Japan. The Web site includes a press release detailing the most important findings of the report. *Compile a list of ten interesting findings from the World Health Report and share your findings with another colleague. Discuss further any findings that may strike you as odd or counterintuitive.*

REFERENCES

Adeyi, O., Chellaraj, G., Goldestein, E., Preker, A., & Ringold, D. (1997). Health status during the transition in Central and Eastern Europe: Development in reverse? *Health Policy and Planning, 12*(2), 132–145.

Akhavan, D., Musgrove, P., Abrantes, A., & Gusmao, R. D. (1999). Cost-effective malaria control in Brazil: Cost-effectiveness of a malaria control program in the Amazon Basin of Brazil, 1988–1996. *Social Science and Medicine, 49*(10), 1385–1399.

Akhtar, R. (1991). *Health care patterns and planning in developing countries.* London: Greenwood Press.

American College of Emergency Physicians. (2008). Patient center: EMTALA. Retrieved November 3, 2008, from http://www.acep.org/patients.aspx?id=25936

Banerji, D. (1981). The place of indigenous and Western systems of medicine in the health services of India. *Social Science and Medicine, 15*(2), 109–114.

Barrientos, A., & Lloyd-Sherlock, P. (2000). Reforming health insurance in Argentina and Chile. *Health Policy and Planning, 15*(4), 417–423.

Belmartino, S. (2000). The context and process of health care reform in Argentina. In S. Fleury, S. Belmartino, & E. Baris (Eds.), *Reshaping health care in Latin America: A comparative analysis of health care reform in Argentina, Brazil, and Mexico.* Retrieved November 11, 2008, from http://www.idrc.ca/en/ev-35159-201-1-DO_TOPIC.html

Centers for Medicare and Medicaid Services. (2006a). Medicaid program: General information. Retrieved November 11, 2008, from http://www.cms.hhs.gov/MedicaidGenInfo/

Centers for Medicare and Medicaid Services. (2006b). Low cost health insurance for families and children. Retrieved November 11, 2008, from http://www.cms.hhs.gov/LowCostHealthIns-FamChild/

Chernichovsky, D., & Potapchik, E. (1997). Health system reform under the Russian health insurance legislation. *International Journal of Health Planning and Management, 12*(4), 279–295.

Clark, P. F., Stewart, J. B., & Clark, D. A. (2006). The globalization of the labour market for health-care professionals. *International Labour Review, 145*(1–2), 37–64.

Derlet, R. W., & Richards, J. R. (2000). Overcrowding in the nation's emergency departments: Complex causes and disturbing effects. *Annals of Emergency Medicine, 35*(1), 63–68.

Docteur, E., & Oxley, H. (2003). *Health-care systems: Lessons from the reform experience* (OECD Health Working Paper). Paris: OECD.

Frist, W. H. (2005). Overcoming disparities in US health care. *Health Affairs, 24*(2), 445–451.

Gu, X. Y., & Tang, S. L. (1995). Reform of the Chinese health care financing system. *Health Policy, 32*(1–3), 181–191.

Henderson, G., Shuigao, J., Zhiming, L., Jianmin, M., Yunan, H., Xiping, Z., et al. (2000). Distribution of medical insurance in China. *Social Science and Medicine, 41*(8), 1119–1130.

Hillier, S., & Shen, J. (1996). Health care systems in transition: People's Republic of China. Part I: An overview of China's health care system. *Journal of Public Health, 18*(3), 258–265.

Hornblow, A. (1997). New Zealand's health reforms: A clash of cultures. *British Medical Journal, 314*(7098), 1892–1894.

Institute of Medicine. (2004). *Insuring America's health: Principles and recommendations.* Washington, DC: The National Academies Press.

Iwu, M. M., & Wooton, J. C. (Eds.). (2002). *Ethnomedicine and drug discovery.* Amsterdam: Elsevier.

Library of Congress. (2005). *A country study: India.* Retrieved October 20, 2008, from http://lcweb2.loc.gov/frd/cs/intoc.html

Matcha, D. A. (2003). *Health care systems of the developed world: How the United States' system remains an outlier.* Westport, CT: Greenwood Publishing Group.

Ministry of Health and Family Welfare. (2008). National health policy—2002. Retrieved October 20, 2008, from http://mohfw.nic.in/np2002.htm

National Coalition on Health Care. (2008a). Health care in Canada. Retrieved October 17, 2008, from http://www.nchc.org/documents/Canada.pdf

National Coalition on Health Care. (2008b). Health care in France. Retrieved October 17, 2008, http://www.nchc.org/documents/France.pdf

National Coalition on Health Care. (2008c). Health care in Japan. Retrieved October 17, 2008, from http://www.nchc.org/documents/Japan.pdf

National Coalition on Health Care. (2008d). Health care in Germany. Retrieved October 17, 2008, from http://www.nchc.org/documents/Germany.pdf

Okonkwo, A. (2001). Nigeria set to launch health insurance scheme. *Lancet, 358*(9276), 131.

Reid, T. R. (2008a). Frontline: Sick around the world. Health care systems: The four basic models. Retrieved October 17, 2008, from http://www.pbs.org/wgbh/pages/frontline/sickaroundtheworld/countries/models.html

Reid, T. R. (2008b). Frontline: Sick around the world. Five capitalist democracies and how they do it. Retrieved October 17, 2008, from http://www.pbs.org/wgbh/pages/frontline/sickaroundtheworld/countries/

Robinson, R., & Julian, L. G. (1994). *Evaluating the NHS reforms*. London: King's Fund.

Rodwin, V. G., & Sandier, S. (1993). Health care under French national health insurance. *Health Affairs, 12*(3), 111–131.

Schull, M. J. (2005). Rising utilization of US emergency departments: Maybe it is time to stop blaming the patients. *Annals of Emergency Medicine, 45*(1), 13–14.

Shi, L. (1993). Health care in China: A rural-urban comparison after the socioeconomic reforms. *Bulletin of the World Health Organization, 71*(6), 723–736.

U.S. Department of Health and Human Services. (2004). *Progress review: Cancer*. Retrieved November 11, 2008, from www.healthypeople.gov/data/2010prog/focus03

Vogel, R. J. (1993). *Financing health care in sub-Saharan Africa*. London: Greenwood Press.

Wang, P. S., Lane, M., Olfson, M., Pincus, H. A., Wells, K. B., & Kessler, R. C. (2005). Twelve-month use of mental health services in the United States: Results from the National Comorbidity Survey Replication. *Archives of General Psychiatry, 62*(6), 629–640.

Williams, D. R., & Collins, C. (1995). US socioeconomic and racial differences in health: Patterns and explanations. *Annual Review of Sociology, 21*(1), 349–386.

Woolhandler, S., Campbell, T., & Himmelstein, D. U. (2003). Costs of health care administration in the United States and Canada. *New England Journal of Medicine, 349*(8), 768–775.

World Health Organization. (2002). *Integrating prevention into health care*. Retrieved from http://www.who.int/topics/health_systems/en/

World Health Organization. (2008a). *The world health report 2000. Health systems: Improving performance*. Retrieved from http://www.who.int/whr/2000/en/

World Health Organization. (2008b). Health systems. Retrieved October 20, 2008, from http://www.who.int/topics/health_systems/en/

World Health Organization Regional Office for Europe. (2008). *Health care systems in transition: Russian Federation*. Retrieved November 11, 2008, from http://www.euro.who.int/document/e81966.pdf

World Health Organization Regional Office for South-East Asia. (2008). *Country health system profile: India*. Retrieved October 20, 2008, from http://www.searo.who.int/en/Section313/Section1519_10853.htm

Wu, Z., Yao, C., Zhao, D., Guixian, W., Wang, W., Liu, J., et al. (2001). Sino-MONICA Project: A collaborative study on trends and determinants in cardiovascular diseases in China. Part I: Morbidity and mortality monitoring. *Circulation, 103*(3), 462–468.

CHAPTER 12

Future Issues in International Health

AFTER READING THIS CHAPTER YOU SHOULD BE ABLE TO

- Discuss the public health threats that have arisen as a consequence of globalization
- Elaborate on biological and chemical warfare
- Discuss the characteristics of biological and chemical agents
- Describe the Global Outbreak Alert and Response Network
- Explain disaster preparedness
- Discuss stem cell research and the ethical issues surrounding it

GLOBALIZATION

Globalization refers to the increased interconnectedness and interdependence of people and countries. The phenomenon is understood to include two interrelated elements: the opening of international borders to an increasingly fast flows of goods, services, finance, people, and ideas; and the changes in institutional and state policies at the international and national levels that assist or promote such flows (World Health Organization [WHO], n.d.). The integration of national economies into the international economy through trade, foreign direct investment, capital flows, migration, and the spread of technology is an integral component of globalization (Bhawati, 2004; WHO, n.d.).

Globalization, although not new, has increased tremendously in recent years. It has been driven by technological advances and the reduced cost of making transactions (exchanges) across borders and distances, as well as the increased mobility of capital. These forces mean that globalization not only consists of economic activity, but also extends to political, cultural, environmental, and security issues, and relates to the increasing interconnectivity of countries and communities. Globalization has resulted in significant social, economic, and political changes across the face of the globe (WHO, n.d.), among them being the following:

- *Economic change:* Liberalization of international trade regulations, deregulation, and expansion of the global marketplace
- *Political change:* Redistribution of power from states to interstate bodies and the growth of global civil society
- *Technological change:* Improved global telecommunications and transport links, among other changes

In the contemporary world, only through coordinated action and collaboration between governments, societies, the media, and individuals can health security be provided. No single establishment or state can boast of all the capacities required to respond to public health emergencies of a global magnitude caused by epidemics, natural disasters or environmental emergencies, or emerging infectious diseases (WHO, 2007). These emergencies can be prevented or immobilized only through a rapid concerted effort in the earliest hours and at an international level.

Some of the major public health threats existent or anticipated as a consequence of globalization are as follows:

- Emerging diseases
- Economic instability and poverty
- International crises and humanitarian emergencies
- Environmental change
- Chemical, radioactive, and biological terror threats

EMERGING DISEASES

Emerging diseases of global magnitude are a very serious threat posed as an undesired consequence of globalization. The subject is discussed in detail in Chapter 4. This section briefly recapitulates some aspects of this public health threat.

Surveillance in Hanoi, Vietnam, detected the first cluster of young children with H5N1 avian influenza virus outside of China and the Hong Kong Special Administrative Region in January 2004 (WHO, 2004a). Ever since, international health organizations and state departments have been on a high alert for an influenza pandemic. Such a pandemic would have the potential to spread to every corner of the world within a matter of weeks or months, thereby extending the devastating consequences seen with severe acute respiratory syndrome (SARS) (WHO, 2007).

Because new diseases often originate as a by-product of the manner in which humanity inhabits this planet, the emergence of new diseases is only expected to increase. Between the approximately three decades from 1973 to 2000, almost 40 infectious agents capable of producing human disease were newly identified (Heymann, 2003). An increase in the development of microbial resistance, which has outpaced scientific discovery of replacement drugs, has further magnified the threat.

The possibility is a very real one that new diseases to which all world states are universally susceptible will arise. Perhaps one of the most important impediments to international health security is the expectation that in case of a pandemic, any affected country would be unable to effectively mount surveillance and emergency response system over long time periods (WHO, 2007).

ECONOMIC INSTABILITY AND POVERTY

Although increasing global economic assimilation has reduced poverty significantly in many lower-income countries of the world, in its wake globalization has also increased the exposure of those countries to "global public bads" (WHO, 2007). International transport of contaminated food products, black markets, and the spread of disease are just a few instances of these "global public bads." Despite the fortunate fact that SARS did not become a global pandemic, it still caused considerable economic losses and insecurity in markets across the globe. Although the total case count did not exceed 10,000, Asian countries had to bear an astounding $60 billion in gross expenditure and business losses in the second quarter of 2003 alone (Rossi & Walker, 2005). An actual pandemic could compound such economic impacts. Because the current manufacture rates and stocks of vaccines and medications are inadequate in every country, the potential magnitude of mortality and morbidity could paralyze markets and economies globally (WHO, n.d.).

INTERNATIONAL CRISES AND HUMANITARIAN EMERGENCIES

Natural disasters, food and water shortages, and armed conflict can each give birth to humanitarian emergencies. Such emergencies can cripple not just individuals but entire health care systems that people far removed from the site of the actual emergency might rely on.

Indirect effects of such crises can include malnutrition, population displacement, and exacerbation of chronic disease and the threat of infectious disease. To deal with each one of these effects, strong health systems are needed. Coordinated early warning and response systems along with concerted cooperation between public health professionals and volunteers and the strategic and focused availability of vaccines, supplies, and money can provide optimal relief to those worst affected (WHO, 2007).

> *In 2006, 134.6 million people were affected and 21,342 were killed by natural disasters.*
>
> —Centre for Research on the Epidemiology of Disasters (2006)

With a judicious mix of the right policies and preparation, natural disasters are survivable. Much of the damage following emergencies is often rooted in the management of land, infrastructure, and development policies. For example, proper preparation and anticipation could have prevented the loss of many lives in coastal Sri Lanka as a result of the 2004 tsunami had an effective warning protocol been available.

ENVIRONMENTAL CHANGE

Climate change is covered at length in Chapter 7. Here it suffices to say that Earth's climate has been changing rapidly. Global temperatures have been rising on average, tropical storms have increased in frequency and intensity, and polar ice covers are melting (Intergovernmental Panel on Climate Change, 2007). More than 60,000 deaths have been documented as a result of climate-related natural disasters, mostly in developing countries (McMichael et al., 2003). Even though the acute impact of climate change–related incidents may be local, the cause is often global. Whether it is the contamination of international waters by floods, the migration of people across borders in the search for food and shelter, or alterations in disease patterns due to climate change, the impact is felt on a global scale (WHO, 2007).

CHEMICAL, RADIOACTIVE, AND BIOLOGICAL TERROR THREATS _____

Bioterrorism and Biowarfare

The deliberate release of bacteria, viruses, or other agents (collectively called **biological agents**) with the intention of causing illness or death in humans, animals, and/or plants is **bioterrorism**. The use of such an approach during times of war against enemy troops or civilian populations constitutes biowarfare.

Some of the important differences between conventional weapons and attacks and biological attacks are the means by which the latter can affect human life. Unlike conventional weapons of offense, biological agents can be spread through the air, through water, or via food. They may be extremely difficult to detect and may not cause illness for several hours to several days after having afflicted the host. Some bioterrorism agents, such as the smallpox virus, can be spread from person to person and some, such as anthrax, cannot. Depending on the risk they pose to the health and security of nations worldwide, bioterrorism agents have been classified into three categories by the Centers for Disease Control and Prevention (CDC), as shown in **Table 12.1**

> *A bioterrorism attack is the deliberate release of viruses, bacteria, or other germs (biological agents) used to cause illness or death in people, animals, or plants. These agents are typically found in nature, but it is possible that they could be changed to increase their ability to cause disease, make them resistant to current medicines, or to increase their ability to be spread into the environment.*
>
> —Centers for Disease Control and Prevention (2007)

General Characteristics of Biological Agents

Biological agents are usually classified based on their taxonomy, with the most important of these taxonomic groups being fungi, bacteria, and viruses. The usefulness of such classification to the medical services derives from the implications it holds for detection, identification, prophylaxis, and treatment.

Another approach to classifying biological agents is by their utility for hostile purposes, which can be determined by factors such as ease of production or resistance to prophylactic and therapeutic measures. More commonly, however, biological agents can be defined by factors such as **infectivity**, **virulence**, **incubation period**, **lethality**, contagiousness and mechanism of transmission, and **stability**, all of which influence their potential for use as weapons (WHO, 2004b).

- *Infectivity:* A measure of a biological agent's capability to enter, survive, and multiply in a host. It can be quantified as the proportion of persons in a given

TABLE 12.1	CDC Classification of Bioterrorism Agents
Category A	Organisms or toxins (anthrax, botulism, smallpox, etc.) that pose the highest risk to the public and national security because they: • Can be easily spread or transmitted from person to person • Result in high death rates • Have the potential for major public health impact • Might cause public panic and social disruption • Require special action for public health preparedness
Category B	Agents (typhus fever, brucellosis, Q fever, etc.) accorded the second-highest priority because they: • Are moderately easy to spread • Result in moderate illness rates and low death rates • Require specific enhancements of the CDC's laboratory capacity and enhanced disease monitoring
Category C	Agents (hantavirus, Nipah virus, etc.) given the third-highest priority, including emerging pathogens that have the potential of be engineered for mass spread in the future because of their: • Ease of availability • Ease of production and spread • Potential for high morbidity and mortality rates and major health impact

Source: Taken from Centers for Disease Control and Prevention. (2007). *Bioterrorism overview.* Centers for Disease Control and Prevention. Retrieved from http://emergency.cdc.gov/bioterrorism/overview.asp

population exposed to a given dose who become infected. The median infective dose (ID_{50}) is the minimal dose that, under a set of given conditions, will infect 50% of a population exposed to a particular agent. Doses higher or lower than the ID_{50} are expected to infect a larger or smaller proportion of that given population. If the ID_{50} value of a pathogen is low, the implication is that it can be devastating even if introduced in small amounts to a previously unexposed population.

- *Virulence:* The relative severity of the disease caused by a microorganism. Depending on the severity of the disease, one can quantify the virulence of different strains of the same species.
- *Incubation period:* The time elapsing between exposure to an infective agent and the first appearance of the signs of disease associated with the infection.

Multiple variables have the potential to influence the incubation period, including the infective agent, the route of entry, the dose, and specific characteristics of the host.

- *Lethality:* The ability of an agent to cause death in an infected population.
- *Contagiousness:* For those infections that are contagious, a measure of their contagiousness is the number of secondary cases arising under specified conditions from exposure to a primary case.
- *Stability:* The capability of the airborne agent to survive the influence of adverse environmental factors such as sunlight, air pollution, surface forces, and drying while still remaining infective. The term can also refer to stability during production or storage processes.

Chemical Agents

According to the Chemical Weapons Convention (CWC), *chemical weapons* can be defined as follows (WHO, 2004b):

- Toxic chemicals and their precursors, except where intended for purposes not prohibited under this Convention, as long as the types and quantities are consistent with such purposes; some of the purposes not prohibited under the convention are industrial, agricultural, research, medical and pharmaceutical
- Munitions and devices, specifically designed to cause death or other harm through the toxic properties of those toxic chemicals, which would be released as a result of the employment of such munitions and devices
- Any equipment specifically designed for use directly in connection with the employment of munitions and devices

The convention defines **toxic chemical** as

Any chemical which through its chemical action on life processes can cause death, temporary incapacitation or permanent harm to humans or animals. This includes all such chemicals, regardless of their origin or of their method of production, and regardless of whether they are produced in facilities, in munitions or elsewhere.

Chemical agents, like biological agents, can be classified in multiple ways (WHO, 2004). Some of the more common approaches are discussed here. Chemical agents are often classified according to the main intended effect: harassing, incapacitating, or lethal.

- A **harassing agent** disables exposed people for the entire duration of the exposure, but the exposed individuals remain capable of removing themselves from the source of exposure. Recovery from the effects of the agent is usually complete and within a short time, and no medical treatment is needed.

- An **incapacitating agent** also disables individuals, but the exposed individuals may either not be aware of the effects (e.g., exposure to opioids and certain other psychotropic agents) or may be unable to move away from the source of exposure. Effects can be longer than the first category, but recovery is still possible without specialized medical aid.
- A **lethal agent** causes the death of those exposed.

A second means of classification of chemical agents is by the route of entry into the body.

- *Respiratory agents* are inhaled and either cause damage to the lungs or are absorbed there and cause systemic effects.
- *Cutaneous agents* are absorbed through the skin, either damaging it (e.g., mustard gas) or gaining access to the body to cause systemic effects (e.g., nerve agents), or both.
- An agent may also be taken up by both routes, depending on its physical properties or formulation.

Yet another scheme of classification of chemical agents takes the duration of the hazard posed by that agent into consideration.

- **Persistent agents** tend to remain in the area of contamination for prolonged durations. By nature they are substances of low volatility that contaminate surfaces and have the potential to damage the skin if they come into contact with it. The potential danger of inhalation of any vapors that might be released is significant. Mustard gas and VX (a nerve agent) are two examples of persistent agents. Protective footwear or dermal protective clothing, or both, will often be required in contaminated areas, usually together with respiratory protection.
- **Nonpersistent agents** are volatile substances that do not stay long in the area of application and disperse quickly. The primary danger is from inhalation, and surfaces are generally not contaminated. Respirators are the main form of protection required. Protective clothing is not needed if the concentrations are below the skin toxicity levels. Hydrogen cyanide and phosgene are typical nonpersistent agents.

Another way of grouping chemical agents is based on the effect of the agent on the body—for instance, the organ system affected. Such a classification can yield the following division of chemical agents:

- Nerve agents or gases (e.g., sarin)
- Vesicants or skin-blistering agents (e.g., mustard gas, lewisite)

- Lung irritants, asphyxiants, or choking agents (e.g., chlorine, phosgene)
- Blood gases or systemic agents (e.g., hydrogen cyanide)
- Sensory irritants (e.g., CN, CS, CR)
- Psychotropic or other centrally acting agents (e.g., the disabling agent BZ and the fentanyl opioids)

Table 12.2 lists instances in which biological and chemical weapons have been employed post–World War I. Focus Feature 12.1 chronicles the sequence of events that culminated in the infamous sarin nerve gas attacks in subway stations in Japan in 1995. Preparedness and public health initiatives for biological and chemical disasters are discussed in the next section.

TABLE 12.2	Antipersonnel Toxic and Infective Agents Whose Hostile Use Since 1918 Has Been Verified	
Period	**Agent**	**Location of Use**
1919	Adamsite; diphenylchlorarsine; mustard gas	Russia
1923–1926	Bromo methyl ethyl ketone (a tear gas); chloropicrin; mustard gas	Morocco
1935–1940	Chlorine (a choking agent); mustard gas; phosgene	Abyssinia
1937–1945	Omega-chloroacetophenone; hydrogen cyanide; lewisite; mustard gas; phosgene; *Yersinia pestis*	Manchuria
1963–1967	Mustard gas; phosgene	Yemen
1965–1975	2-chlorobenzalmalononitrile	Vietnam
1982–1988	2-chlorobenzalmalononitrile	Iraq
	Mustard gas; sarin; tabun	Iran
1984	*Salmonella enteritidis*	United States
1994–1995	Sarin	Japan
2001	*Bacillus anthracis*	United States

Source: Taken from World Health Organization. (2004b). *Public health response to biological and chemical weapons: WHO guidance* (p. 35). Geneva: Author. Retrieved from http://www.who.int/csr/delibepidemics/biochemguide/en/index.html

FOCUS FEATURE 12.1   The Sarin Gas Attack on the Japanese Subway

On March 20, 1995, a terrorist group (the Aum Shinrikyo cult) launched a coordinated attack with the nerve gas sarin on commuters on the Tokyo subway system. The cult had launched its highly ambitious chemical program in 1993. After experiments with multiple other agents, the cult's final choice was the nerve gas sarin, and a plan was developed for the production of about 70 tons of this substance at facilities in Kamikuisiki, at the foot of Mount Fuji.

On the morning of March 20, 1995, five two-man teams carried out the attack. Around 8:00 AM, the peak commuting time, the five assailants placed their sarin-filled bags on the train floor, pierced them with sharpened umbrella tips, and left the trains several stations away from Kasumi-gaseki, a transit hub for multiple buildings and the Tokyo Metropolitan Police Department that had been selected by the perpetrators as the target.

The Tokyo fire department received the first distress call at 8:09 AM, and the emergency services were soon overwhelmed with calls from numerous subway stations. More than 4,000 people found their own way to hospitals and doctors using taxis and private cars or on foot. The lack of emergency decontamination facilities and protective equipment resulted in the secondary exposure of medical staff (135 ambulance staff and 110 staff in the main receiving hospital reported symptoms).

Having been misinformed that a gas explosion had caused burns and carbon monoxide poisoning, medical centers initially began treating for organophosphate exposure based on the typical symptoms encountered. Only after an official police announcement 3 hours later had clarified the true cause of the disaster were measures directed toward the actual cause instituted.

The attack was serious: 12 people died, 54 were severely injured, and around 980 were mildly to moderately affected. The majority of the 5,000 seeking help, many of them with psychogenic symptoms, were (understandably) worried that they might have been exposed. The toll could have been worse: the sarin had been hastily manufactured and was only 30% pure.

Fortunately, the disaster did not approach the human and environmental toll that has resulted from a number of more recent terrorist strikes using conventional explosives. Despite multiple difficulties, the casualty figures were contained secondary to a remarkably rapid deployment of emergency units and local hospitals. While analysis of the event reveals a number of important lessons for authorities to consider when preparing for such incidents, it also reveals many of the technical difficulties associated with toxic chemicals and their limitations as weapons for use by terrorist groups. Without the prompt and massive emergency response by the Japanese authorities, and some fortunate mistakes by the terrorist group, the incident could have been much more devastating.

TOWARD A SAFER FUTURE

The theme for the 2007 World Health Day and World Health Report was "International Health Security"—the need to reduce the vulnerability of people around the world to new, acute, or rapidly spreading risks to health, particularly those that threaten to cross international borders (WHO, 2007).

The phenomenon of globalization has been dealt with at length earlier. In this era of globalization, health concerns present novel problems and challenges that surpass national borders and have an impact on the collective safety of entire populations around the world. All nations thus share a common interest in preventing the international spread of disease. The spread of diseases, in recent decades, has been hastened by high-speed transit and the exchange of goods and services between nations and continents. The rapid spread of disease is preventable only if there is an immediate alert and response system in place to tackle disease outbreaks and other episodes that could potentially set off epidemics or have global impacts (WHO, 2007). International treaties and regulations binding on all member nations are also necessary to prevent incidents such as the sarin nerve gas attack of 1995 (see Focus Feature 12.1) from happening again.

This section deals chiefly with the global measures and alliances that have been instituted to prevent or limit the effect of potential epidemics, global health disasters, biochemical attacks, and so on. The surveillance networks already in place are also briefly discussed.

Disaster Preparedness

A resolution entitled "Global Public Health Response to Natural Occurrence, Accidental Release or Deliberate Use of Biological and Chemical Agents or Radio Nuclear Material That Affect Health" was passed by the World Health Assembly in May 2002. The World Health Organization then developed a four-pronged strategy to respond to this resolution (WHO, 2004b), namely:

- International preparedness
- Global alert and response
- National preparedness
- Preparedness for selected diseases/intoxication

International Preparedness

The objective of international preparedness is to respond to the increased number of requests by member nations for technical assistance on national chemical and biological warfare preparedness and response programs and training. The Chemical and Biological Weapons (CBW) Scientific Advisory Group has been established as a permanent resource for the WHO Secretariat and its member states.

Global Alert and Response

The primary objective of the **Global Outbreak Alert and Response Network** (GOARN) is the provision of an operational framework to link the expertise and skills needed to keep the international community constantly alert to the threat of outbreaks and ready to respond. WHO's global alert and response activities and operational framework together with the technical resources of the Global Outbreak Alert and Response Network would be vital for effective international containment efforts in responding to the potential use of biological agents in case the intentional release of a biological agent were to happen.

National Preparedness

Guidelines for the assessment of national chemical and biological warfare health preparedness and response plans are being developed according to the recommendations provided by a group of experts that met in Rome, Italy, in 2002 (WHO, 2004b). Training modules on the management of preparedness and response programs for chemical, biological, and radionuclear incidents are also being developed. The laboratory and epidemiology capacities of countries are being strengthened through a program targeting microbiologists and epidemiologists from several countries of the African, eastern Mediterranean, and European regions. Included in this program is a comprehensive review of surveillance systems leading to national plans of action for strengthening surveillance and early warning systems for epidemic-prone diseases, including those associated with deliberate use. Finally, the World Health Organization Biosafety Program contributes to these activities by providing information, training, and advocacy for laboratory biosafety procedures and practices.

Preparedness for Selected Diseases and Intoxications

The objective is to contribute to international preparedness on specific diseases associated with biological weapons by (1) launching global networks of experts and laboratories, (2) laying down standards and procedures and disseminating information, and (3) organizing and implementing training.

Preparedness and Response

In relation to biological and chemical incidents, **preparedness** is best understood as "what needs to be considered long before an incident actually takes place," and **response** is basically defined as "the sequence of events or responses that needs to happen after a warning of a pending release is received, or after the release has actually occurred" (WHO, 2004b). The major steps, in chronological order, that need to be taken for effective preparedness and the ability to mount an effective response are discussed next.

Threat Analysis

The first step, **threat analysis**, is a multidisciplinary endeavor that involves a nation's law enforcement, intelligence, and medical and scientific communities. The idea is to identify individuals or groups who might wish to use biological or chemical weapons against the population, the agents that might be used should an attack actually happen, and the circumstances under which they might be used. This is an exercise with a broad scope and requires active coordination among law enforcement agencies, security agencies, and public health organizations (typically centralized state institutions), along with local authorities. Usually, the identification of the precise nature or likelihood of threat is not possible or realistic, and general preparedness measures need to be instituted depending on an overall appraisal of national or local circumstances.

Preemption of an Attack

The formation of effective biological and chemical response systems is in itself a preemptive risk-reduction strategy. The mere existence of an effective ability to respond to and manage an incident serves to considerably lower the risk of biological or chemical attack in war. If an attacker knows that an attack will be quickly and effectively neutralized or its effects minimized, the incentive to commit such an attack will be considerably weakened. The demonstration of a vigilance and response system can produce negative perceptions regarding the vulnerabilities of a country in the minds of its citizens; therefore, it is advisable to mount such a system only if the need outweighs the costs of having to live with such perceptions. Also, ill-considered publicity given to the perceived threat of biological or chemical terrorism might have the opposite effect to that desired.

Preemption of terrorist use of biological or chemical agents presupposes, first and foremost, accurate and up-to-date intelligence about terrorist groups and their activities. Such intelligence leans heavily on human sources, mainly because terrorist activities may be much less conspicuous than large-scale manufacturing of biochemical weapons and therefore more difficult to detect.

An important prerequisite for preemption is the existence of national legislation that renders the development, production, possession, transfer, or use of biological or chemical weapons a crime, and that empowers law enforcement agencies to act in situations where such activities are suspected before an actual event occurs. For instance, the highly controversial USA PATRIOT Act (Uniting and Strengthening America by Providing Appropriate Tools Required to Intercept and Obstruct Terrorism) passed by the U.S. Congress and signed by President George W. Bush on October 26, 2001, deals chiefly with provisions designed to empower law enforcement and immigration authorities with the intent of preempting any future terrorist scenarios. Concerted national and international efforts to monitor and control dual-use technology and equipment related to chemicals and toxins can also help preempt future threats.

Preparing to Respond

A preparedness program for a possible mishap is needed even if preemptory protocols are in place, because preemptory efforts cannot completely eliminate the possibility of an accident. Such a preparedness program requires the acquisition of equipment and supplies, the development of appropriate procedures, and training. Personnel such as the police, firefighters, emergency medical service personnel, and public health personnel, including physicians, epidemiologists, veterinarians, and laboratory staff, have to be trained and their resources adapted for response to deliberately released biological or chemical agents. Ironically, most civilian health care providers have little or no experience with illnesses caused by biological and chemical weapons and can easily miss the early signs and symptoms of such an incident. There is thus a vital need to train health care workers in the recognition and initial management of both biological and chemical casualties, and for a speedy communication system that allows immediate sharing of information when an unusual incident is suspected.

Typically, education and instruction must cover the general characteristics of biological and chemical agents; the clinical presentation, diagnosis, prophylaxis, and treatment of diseases that may be caused by deliberate release of those agents; and sample handling, decontamination, and barrier nursing (WHO, 2004b). Training, planning, and drills of physicians and staff regarding the management of mass casualties, providing respiratory support to large numbers of patients, the large-scale distribution of medication, and supporting the local authorities in vaccination programs should be conducted. Also, because early diagnosis is essential in the selection of treatment and response, a reference laboratory (or network of laboratories) needs to be established where potential biological and chemical agents can be identified.

It is vital not to make the mistake of assuming that availability of equipment is synonymous with the ability to respond, or that a community without all the latest equipment is doomed to failure. Without cautious establishment of the essential protocols and exhaustive training, the introduction of such equipment can hamper the ability to respond, and can even be counterproductive (WHO, 2004b).

Preparing Public Information and Communication Packages

Demystification of the subject of chemical and biological weapons well before any incident occurs is vital for the success of any plan designed to deal with such incidents. The general public have to be cognizant of their roles and how they are expected to act should an unfortunate incident happen. The communication plan could be dispersed through mass media such as radio and television broadcasts or through the distribution of brochures to the public describing the potential threat in plain, objective language. A well-constructed media plan with unambiguous and extensive instructions on channels of communication and clearance procedures for potentially sensitive information is needed.

Validation of Response Capabilities

Response capabilities that are in place but not being frequently challenged should undergo periodic validations to ensure their potential efficacy. Training simulations can be employed to critically appraise such response capabilities and identify areas that can be strengthened.

Response

If news regarding the potential release of biological or chemical agents is released, a number of steps can and should be taken. The initial indication of such an incident could be the recovery of an unusual device or unusual materials or the discovery of a strange package. **Figure 12.1** illustrates the standard response cascade, which should be refined and modified depending on local conditions and priorities (WHO, 2004b).

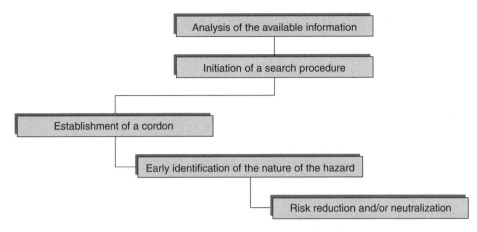

FIGURE 12.1   Response before any overt release of a biological or chemical agent.

After the initial response to the threat or warning of an impending incident is executed, a more definitive, directed reaction to the incident needs to be initiated. This definitive response depends on whether the incident is biological or chemical in nature. **Table 12.3** states some of the major distinguishing features of biological and chemical incidents.

TABLE 12.3 Differentiating Features of Biological and Chemical Attacks		
Indicator	**Chemical Attack**	**Biological Attack**
Epidemiologic features	Unusual numbers of patients with very similar symptoms seeking care at the same time; patient clusters arriving from a single locality; definite pattern of symptoms clearly evident	Rapidly increasing disease incidence (hours to days); atypical increase in febrile, respiratory, or gastrointestinal cases; unusual time/pattern of emergence of an endemic disease; patients with rapidly fatal illness (dependent on agent virulence); relatively uncommon disease with bioterrorism potential
Animal indicators	Not specific; death and disability	Not specific; death and disability
Devices	Suspicious devices or packages; droplets, oily film; unexplained odor; low clouds or fog	Suspicious devices or packages

Source: Taken from World Health Organization. (2004b). *Public health response to biological and chemical weapons: WHO guidance* (p. 66). Geneva: Author. Retrieved from http://www.who.int/csr/delibepidemics/biochemguide/en/index.html

Individual response steps for biological (**Table 12.4**) and chemical (**Table 12.5**) incidents have been proposed by the World Health Organization as part of a broader strategy to address the problem.

INTERNATIONAL PARTNERSHIPS AND REGULATIONS

International Health Regulations

The **International Health Regulations** (IHR) are an international legal instrument, entered into force on June 15, 2007, that is binding on 194 countries across the globe (including all the member states of WHO) and requires member countries to report

TABLE 12.4 Major Response Steps for a Biological Attack	
Risk assessment	Determine that a release has occurred or is taking place
	Identify the nature of the agent involved and case definition
	Evaluate the potential outbreak spread
	Assess current and delayed case-management requirements
Risk management	Protect responders and health care workers
	Introduce infection prevention and control procedures
	Triage cases
	Provide medical care for infected individuals
Activity monitoring	Decide whether international assistance should be sought
	Implement active surveillance to monitor the effectiveness of the prevention and control procedures, follow up the distribution of cases (time, place, and person), and adjust response activities as needed
	Repeat the risk assessment and management process as required
	Implement longer-term follow-up activities
Risk communication	Implement a risk communication program for the affected population that conveys information and instructions as needed

Source: Taken from World Health Organization. (2004b). *Public health response to biological and chemical weapons: WHO guidance* (p. 67). Geneva: Author. Retrieved from http://www.who.int/csr/delibepidemics/biochemguide/en/index.html

TABLE 12.5	Major Response Steps for a Chemical Attack
Risk assessment	Rapid chemical detection and identification techniques to determine the causal agent
	Definitive identification, needed for forensic and legal purposes
Risk management	Protect responders
	Control contamination
	Conduct casualty triage
	Ensure medical care and evacuation of casualties
	Conduct definitive decontamination of the site
Activity monitoring	Decide whether local and national resources are adequate, and whether international assistance should be sought
	Continuously monitor the residual hazard level on the site, and adjust response activities as needed
	Repeat the risk assessment and management process as required
	Implement follow-up activities (e.g., of long-term injuries and rehabilitation)
Risk communication	Risk communication program as previously mentioned (see Table 12.4)

Source: Taken from World Health Organization. (2004b). *Public health response to biological and chemical weapons: WHO guidance* (p. 77). Geneva: Author. Retrieved from http://www.who.int/csr/delibepidemics/biochemguide/en/index.html

specified disease outbreaks and public health events to the World Health Organization (WHO 2005, 2008a).

The primary purpose of the IHR is to assist the international community to avert and counter acute public health risks that have the ability to cross borders and threaten human health internationally. In the globalized era, diseases can spread far via international travel and trade in a fairly short amount of time. A health crisis in one country can potentially influence livelihoods and economies in multiple regions of the globe. Emerging infections; chemical spills, leaks, and dumping; and nuclear meltdowns can each result in such a catastrophe (WHO, 2008a). The IHR seeks to minimize obstruction of international traffic and trade, at the same time ensuring public health through the prevention of disease spread.

Drawing from the rich experience of the World Health Organization in global disease surveillance, alert, and response, the IHR delineates the rights and duties of member nations to report public health events. Member nations are required to strengthen their existing capacities for public health surveillance and response and improve their capacity to detect, assess, notify, and respond to public health threats. Timely and open reporting of public health events is expected to make the entire world more safe and secure. Member nations have two years to evaluate their capacity and activate national action plans, followed by three years to meet the requirements of the regulations regarding their national surveillance and response systems as well as the requirements at designated airports, ports, and certain ground crossings (WHO, 2005, 2008a).

Biological Weapons Convention

The **Biological Weapons Convention** (BWC) was the first multilateral disarmament treaty banning an entire category of weapons. The BWC was opened for ratification in 1972 and entered into effect in 1975. The treaty effectively prohibits the "development, production, acquisition, transfer, retention, stockpiling and use of biological and toxin weapons and is a key element in the international community's efforts to address the proliferation of weapons of mass destruction" (United Nations Office at Geneva, 2008).

> *The Biological Weapons Convention is an abbreviated title for the Convention on the Prohibition of the Development, Production and Stockpiling of Bacteriological (Biological) and Toxin Weapons and on Their Destruction, which is also known as the Biological and Toxin Weapons Convention (BTWC).*
>
> —United Nations Office at Geneva (2008)

State signatories to the convention undertake "never in any circumstances to develop, produce, stockpile or otherwise acquire or retain microbial or other biological agents, or toxins whatever their origin or method of production, of types and in quantities that have no justification for prophylactic, protective or other peaceful purposes; weapons, equipment or means of delivery designed to use such agents or toxins for hostile purposes or in armed conflict."

Chemical Weapons Convention

The **Chemical Weapons Convention** (CWC) is an arms control agreement, signed in 1993 and entered into force on April 29, 1997, that outlaws the manufacturing, stockpiling, and use of chemical weapons. Its full name is the Convention on the Prohibition of the Development, Production, Stockpiling and Use of Chemical Weapons and on Their Destruction. The current agreement is administered by the Organization for the Prohibition of Chemical Weapons (OPCW), which is an independent organization (Organization for the Prohibition of Chemical Weapons, 2008). Presently, the agreement has 165 individual state signatories. The CWC does not prohibit production, processing, consumption, or trade of related chemicals for peaceful purposes, but it does establish a verification regime to ensure that such activities are consistent with the object and purpose of the treaty.

Important Treaties Related to Nuclear Weapons

Nuclear Non-Proliferation Treaty

The **Nuclear Non-Proliferation Treaty** (NPT) is a historic international treaty whose prime objective is to avert the proliferation of nuclear weapons and weapons-related technology, to foster cooperation in the peaceful uses of nuclear energy, and to further the goal of achieving nuclear disarmament. The treaty lays down as an inalienable right the right of all signatories to be able to "develop research, production and use of nuclear energy for peaceful purposes without discrimination." The NPT is, to date, the only binding multilateral commitment that aims at a goal of complete disarmament of states with nuclear weapons. The treaty was opened for signature in 1968, entered into force in 1970, and was extended indefinitely on May 11, 1995. A total of 190 parties have joined the treaty, including the five nuclear-weapon states (United Nations Office for Disarmament Affairs, 2002a).

The most important provisions of this treaty are as follows:

- Each nuclear-weapons state (NWS) undertakes not to transfer, to any recipient, nuclear weapons or other nuclear explosive devices, and not to assist any non-nuclear-weapon state to manufacture or acquire such weapons or devices.
- Each non-NWS party undertakes not to receive, from any source, nuclear weapons or other nuclear explosive devices; not to manufacture or acquire such weapons or devices; and not to receive any assistance in their manufacture.
- Each non-NWS party undertakes to conclude an agreement with the International Atomic Energy Agency (IAEA) for the application of its safeguards to all nuclear material in all of the state's peaceful nuclear activities and to prevent diversion of such material to nuclear weapons or other nuclear explosive devices.
- Each party has the right to withdraw from the treaty giving three months' notice.

Comprehensive Nuclear Test Ban Treaty

The **Comprehensive Nuclear Test Ban Treaty** (CTBT) bans nuclear explosions in all environments whatsoever, for military or civilian purposes (CTBTO Preparatory

Commission, n.d.). Each state that is a party to the treaty "undertakes not to carry out any nuclear weapon test explosion or any other nuclear explosion, and to prohibit and prevent any such nuclear explosion at any place under its jurisdiction or control . . . [and] to refrain from causing, encouraging, or in any way participating in the carrying out of any nuclear weapon tests explosion or any other nuclear explosion" (United Nations Office for Disarmament Affairs, 2002b).

Opened for signature in New York on September 24, 1996, the treaty was signed by 71 states, including five of the eight then-nuclear-capable states. The treaty will enter into force 180 days after the 44 states listed in Annex 2 of the treaty have ratified it. Nine of these have not yet done so, including two nuclear weapon states under the NPT (the United States and the People's Republic of China), as well as all four states outside the NPT (India, Pakistan, Israel, and North Korea).

Surveillance Networks

Global Outbreak Alert and Response Network

The Global Outbreak Alert and Response Network (GOARN) is a "voluntary technical partnership of 140 existing institutions and networks that pool human and technical resources for the rapid identification, confirmation, and response to disease outbreaks of international importance. The Network provides an operational framework to link this expertise and skill to keep the international community constantly alert to the threat of outbreaks and ready to respond" (WHO, 2008b). GOARN's mission is rapid identification and/or confirmation and effective response to disease outbreaks of international public health importance.

Objectives   As outlined on the World Health Organization's Web site, the primary objectives of this international network are threefold: (1) combating the international spread of outbreaks, (2) ensuring that appropriate technical assistance reaches affected states rapidly, and (3) contributing to long-term epidemic preparedness and capacity building.

WHO coordinates international outbreak response using resources from the network. Furthermore, elaborate protocols pertaining to network structure, operations, and communications have been developed to advance coordination between partners.

Guiding Principles for International Outbreak Alert and Response   The Global Outbreak Alert and Response Network has established certain guiding principles and protocols to standardize epidemiologic, laboratory, clinical management, research, communications, logistics support, security, and evacuation and communications systems. These steps maximize the efficiency of the network and help it in realizing its primary objectives (WHO, 2008b). Some of these principles are as follows:

- WHO ensures that outbreaks of potential international importance are rapidly verified and that information is quickly shared within the network.
- There is a rapid response, coordinated by the Operational Support Team, to requests for assistance from affected states.
- The most appropriate experts reach the field in the least possible time to carry out coordinated and effective outbreak control activities.
- The international team integrates and coordinates activities to support national efforts and existing public health infrastructure.
- There is a fair and equitable process for the participation of network partners in international responses.
- Effective coordination of participation and support of outbreak response by participating partners.
- There is commitment to national and regional capacity building as a follow-up to international outbreak responses to improve preparedness and reduce future vulnerability to epidemic-prone diseases.
- Full respect for ethical standards, human rights, national and local laws, cultural sensitivities, and traditions.

HUMAN CLONING AND STEM CELL RESEARCH

Human Cloning

The word *clone* comes from the Greek word for "twig" and denotes identical entities. It has come to refer to an organism that is an identical copy of another. It is also applied by the scientific world to refer to molecules (such as DNA) and cells that are replicas of other molecules. The lamb Dolly, born at a research institute in Scotland in 1996, was the first reported mammalian clone produced by scientists (WHO, 2008c).

Human cloning can be used to refer to two different situations. The term can be applied to the creation of genetically identical siblings, such as those which occur naturally in identical twins or artificially through the splitting of embryos in the laboratory at the two- to eight-cell stage of development. It may also refer to the creation of embryos through **somatic cell nuclear transfer** (SCNT, the transfer of genetic material from one cell to an external controlled environment), not to produce off-spring but for use as a scientific tool. Such nonreproductive use of cloning is often called "research cloning" or "therapeutic cloning" to differentiate it from cloning for reproductive purposes.

SCNT is being employed as a means of producing human embryonic **stem cells** for scientific study and eventually for therapeutic purposes. Once cloned embryos have reached a certain stage of maturation, the embryo can be destroyed and stem cells derived from it. It is this process of salvaging the stem cells that raises a multitude of ethical questions regarding stem cell research.

> *Stem cells have the remarkable potential to develop into many different cell types in the body. Serving as a sort of repair system for the body, they can theoretically divide without limit to replenish other cells as long as the person or animal is still alive. When a stem cell divides, each new cell has the potential to either remain a stem cell or become another type of cell with a more specialized function, such as a muscle cell, a red blood cell, or a brain cell.*
>
> —The National Institutes of Health Resource for Stem Cell Research (2006)

Advocates of human reproductive cloning argue that its use would enlarge the current range of assisted reproductive techniques. In particular, men who do not produce gametes could have children who inherit their genome. In such a case, if the egg came from the wife, the couple would not have to involve a third "parent" (the sperm donor) in producing their child. Other reasons offered for using SCNT to create children include to produce a child with specific genetic features (who could, for instance, provide bone marrow for a diseased sibling), to "replicate" a deceased child, or even to achieve "immortality" by living on through one's clone. It is not surprising that all of these scenarios raise serious ethical, legal, and social issues.

The Big Debate

Although presently there is a widespread international consensus among the scientific community, the public, and policy makers against reproductive cloning, a strong debate does exist. The arguments against any further development of human reproductive cloning are as follows (WHO, 2008c):

- *Physical harm.* Experience with animal cloning has shown substantial risks of debilitating and even lethal conditions occurring in the fetuses produced using these techniques; moreover, these problems cannot be individually predicted and avoided at this time.

- *Research standards.* Traditionally, human research is preceded by thorough laboratory and animal studies and a thorough scientific appraisal of the results of those studies. Such studies are lacking for reproductive cloning.
- *Autonomy.* Any child created through SCNT would be unable to give consent to the experiment. An issue of autonomy would also arise if a person's DNA were used to create one or more copies without that person's permission or perhaps even without his or her knowledge.
- *Psychological/social harm.* The cloned individual may suffer psychological harm from his or her status as a "genetic copy" of somebody else and having been produced through unconventional means.
- *Justice.* If cloning became established as an assisted reproductive technology, it would probably only be available to a small group of privileged individuals with the financial resources to afford it. It would divert resources that could be better used to deal with existing health and socioeconomic issues, especially in the third world.

The main arguments proposed in favor of human reproductive cloning are as follows:

- *Beneficence.* Infertile couples would have another treatment option on the table. Selection of desirable traits and advantages would be possible by predetermining the genetic makeup of children.
- *Autonomy.* State and international organizations do not have the right to interfere with the autonomy of people in making reproductive choices and decisions.

Regulations

The field of human cloning is essentially a gray zone and one that is hotly debated. A multitude of national and international laws and proposed bills exist. Presently, around 35 nations have adopted laws forbidding reproductive cloning. Some, including Germany, Switzerland, and some authorities in the United States, prohibit all forms of human cloning, whereas others, among them the United Kingdom, China, Israel, and other jurisdictions in the United States, prohibit reproductive cloning but allow the creation of cloned human embryos for research.

The United Nations discussed the possibility of an international convention against the reproductive cloning of human beings during the General Assembly in November 2002. That discussion is still ongoing, with the principal issue being whether the ban should include research as well as reproductive cloning (WHO, 2008c).

SKILL-BUILDING ACTIVITY

A bioterrorism attack is the deliberate release of viruses, bacteria, or other agents used to cause illness or death in people, animals, or plants. Contact your local health department and find out the following information regarding its preparations for and response to a potential attack. Then compile the following information in a one-page brochure.

1. What are the provisions in place for controlling the spread of such an attack?
2. Can the local health agencies deal with a mishap of such kind; if not, what referral facilities are available?
3. Are the local measures in compliance with the WHO standards discussed in the text?
4. Is there a protocol in place regarding the evacuation and resettlement of inhabitants if needed?

SUMMARY

Globalization refers to the increased interconnectedness and interdependence of people and countries. The forces that cause globalization also mold it into a phenomenon that extends to political, cultural, and environmental and security issues. Consequently, economic, political, sociocultural, and technological changes have occurred secondary to globalization. Public health threats such as emerging new diseases, international humanitarian crises, biological threats, and environmental change have also happened as a result.

Because of the severity of the effects of possible biological and chemical attacks, multiple global measures and alliances have come into being. The prime purpose of these alliances is to prevent completely or to limit the effect of potential epidemics, global health disasters, biochemical attacks, and so on. Some of the global measures are disaster preparedness initiatives undertaken by the World Health Organization, which include training nations for potential disasters, instituting global surveillance networks, and designing protocols to deal with potential attacks in an effective manner.

The International Health Regulations (IHR) are part of this global preparedness strategy and require member countries to report specified disease outbreaks and public health events to the World Health Organization. The Biological and Chemical Weapons Conventions are international agreements that outlaw the manufacturing, stockpiling, and use of biological and chemical weapons, respectively. Similar treaties that attempt to eliminate the risks posed by nuclear weapons are the Nuclear Non-Proliferation Treaty and the Comprehensive Nuclear Test Ban Treaty.

The Global Outbreak Alert and Response Network (GOARN) is a voluntary technical partnership of 140 existing institutions and networks that pool human and technical resources for the rapid identification, confirmation, and response to disease outbreaks of international importance. It is part of the larger strategy of the World Health Organization to effectively tackle disease outbreaks of global proportions.

The nonreproductive use of human cloning, particularly the use of stem cells, is a hotly debated area with limited international agreement. It raises some very serious ethical questions and remains one of the more important challenges to be faced by the scientific community, and the world at large, in the coming years.

IMPORTANT TERMS

biological agents

Biological Weapons Convention

bioterrorism

chemical agents

Chemical Weapons Convention

Comprehensive Nuclear Test Ban Treaty

globalization

Global Outbreak Alert and Response
  Network

harassing agent

human cloning

incapacitating agent

incubation period

infectivity

International Health Regulations

lethal agent

lethality

nonpersistent agents

Nuclear Non-Proliferation Treaty
  (NPT)

persistent agents

preparedness

response

stability

stem cells

somatic cell nuclear transfer

threat analysis

toxic chemical

virulence

REVIEW QUESTIONS

1. Discuss any two public health threats that have arisen as a consequence of globalization.
2. Define bioterrorism. What are category A, B, and C agents?
3. Differentiate between nonpersistent and persistent agents.
4. Differentiate between a biological and a chemical attack.
5. Enumerate the major response steps for a potential biological attack.

6. What does the acronym GOARN stand for? What mechanisms does GOARN employ to effectively control disease outbreaks?

7. Discuss five different arguments against stem cell research.

WEB SITES TO EXPLORE

CDC Emergency Preparedness and Response Site

http://www.bt.cdc.gov/

This Web site from the Centers for Disease Control and Prevention is designed to increase the nation's ability to prepare for and respond to public health emergencies. *Explore this Web site and prepare an emergency preparedness kit.*

Organization for the Prohibition of Chemical Weapons

http://www.opcw.org/

The Organization for the Prohibition of Chemical Weapons (OPCW) is an international agency, located in The Hague, the Netherlands. It is the mission of this organization to promote membership of the Chemical Weapons Convention treaty, which entered into force in 1997 and mandated the elimination of "the scourge of chemical weapons forever and to verify the destruction of the declared chemical weapons stockpiles within stipulated deadlines." It arranges inspection procedures to ensure compliance with the treaty, and provides technical assistance to countries who have inherited a legacy of chemical weapons stockpiles from previous governments. *Read the section entitled "About the OPCW." Prepare a fact sheet on the OPCW.*

United States Chemical Weapons Convention Website

http://www.cwc.gov/cwc_about.html

The United States is one of 175 states that are party to the Chemical Weapons Convention (CWC), which prohibits the development, production, stockpiling, and use of chemical weapons. The purpose of this site is to inform U.S. industry of its rights and obligations under the CWC regulations. *Read the CWC treaty. Are there any aspects you do not agree with?*

United Nations Office for Disarmament Affairs

http://disarmament.un.org/index.html

Established in January 1998 as part of the UN secretary-general's program for reform, the United Nations Office for Disarmament Affairs (UNODA) promotes the goal of nuclear disarmament and nonproliferation and the strengthening of the disarmament regimes in respect to other weapons of mass destruction, namely, chemical and biological weapons. It also promotes disarmament efforts in the area of conventional weapons, especially land mines and small arms, which are often the weapons of choice in contemporary conflicts. *Review the Web site and prepare a list of disarmament issues.*

United Nations Office at Geneva: The Biological Weapons Convention

http://www.unog.ch/80256EE600585943/(httpPages)/04FBBDD6315AC720C1257-180004B1B2F?OpenDocument

The Biological Weapons Convention effectively prohibits the development, production, acquisition, transfer, retention, stockpiling and use of biological and toxin weapons, and is a key element in the international community's efforts to address the proliferation of weapons of mass destruction. *Read the text of the Biological Weapons Convention. Prepare a summary of its articles.*

REFERENCES

Bhagwati, J. (2004). *In defense of globalization.* New York: Oxford University Press.
Centers for Disease Control and Prevention. (2007). Bioterrorism overview. Retrieved from http://emergency.cdc.gov/bioterrorism/overview.asp
Centre for Research on the Epidemiology of Disasters. (2006). 2006 disasters in numbers. Retrieved from http://www.em-dat.net/documents/Confpress%202006.pdf
CTBTO Preparatory Commission. (n.d.). *The Comprehensive Nuclear Test Ban Treaty.* Retrieved August 10, 2008, from http://www.ctbto.org/the-treaty/the-comprehensivenuclear-test-ban-treaty/
Heymann, D. L. (2003). Emerging infections. In M. Schaechter (Ed.), *The desk encyclopedia of microbiology.* New York: Elsevier/Academic Press.
Intergovernmental Panel on Climate Change. (2007). *Climate change 2007: The physical science basis—summary for policy makers.* Retrieved from http://www.ipcc.ch/SPM2feb07.pdf
McMichael, A., Campbell-Lendrum, D. H., Corvalan, C., Ebi, K., Githeko, A., Scheraga, J., et al. (2003). Climate change and human health: Risks and responses. Retrieved from https://www.who.int/globalchange/publications/climchange.pdf
The National Institutes of Health Resource for Stem Cell Research (2007). *Stem Cell Basics.* Retrieved from http://stemcells.nih.gov/info/basics/basics1.asp
Organization for the Prohibition of Chemical Weapons. (2008). Convention on the Prohibition of the Development, Production, Stockpiling and Use of Chemical Weapons and on their Destruction. Retrieved from http://www.opcw.org/html/db/cwc/eng/cwc_menu.html
Rossi, V., & Walker, J. (2005). *Assessing the economic impact and costs of flu pandemics originating in Asia.* Oxford: Oxford Economic Forecasting.

United Nations Office for Disarmament Affairs. (2002a). Treaty on the Non-Proliferation of Nuclear Weapons (NPT). Retrieved from http://disarmament.un.org/wmd/npt/index.html

United Nations Office for Disarmament Affairs. (2002b). Comprehensive Nuclear-Test-Ban Treaty. Retrieved from http://disarmament.un.org/wmd/ctbt/index.html

United Nations Office at Geneva. (2008). Disarmament: The Biological Weapons Convention. Retrieved from http://www.unog.ch/80256EE600585943/(httpPages)/04FBBDD6315AC720-C1257180004B1B2F?OpenDocument

World Health Organization. (2004a). Avian influenza A (H5N1) in humans and poultry in Vietnam. Retrieved from http://www.who.int/csr/don/2004_01_13/en/index.html

World Health Organization. (2004b). *Public health response to biological and chemical weapons: WHO guidance.* Retrieved from http://www.who.int/csr/delibepidemics/biochemguide/en/index.html

World Health Organization. (2005). *The International Health Regulations.* Retrieved from http://www.whqlibdoc.who.int/publications/2008/9789241580410.pdf

World Health Organization. (2007). *Invest in health, build a safer future.* Retrieved from http://www.who.int/world-health-day/previous/2007/activities/issues_paper/en/

World Health Organization. (2008a). Ten things you need to know about the IHR. Retrieved from http://www.who.int/csr/ihr/howtheywork/10things/en/index.html

World Health Organization. (2008b). Global Outbreak Alert and Response Network. Retrieved from http://www.who.int/csr/outbreaknetwork/en/

World Health Organization. (2008c). A dozen questions (and answers) on human cloning. Retrieved from http://www.who.int/ethics/topics/cloning/en/

World Health Organization. (n.d.). *Trade, foreign policy, diplomacy and health: Glossary of globalization, trade and health terms.* Retrieved July 6, 2008, from http://www.who.int/trade/glossary/story043/en/index.html

Guidelines for Traveling and Working in Developing Countries

Many students and professionals in health fields are interested in either working for international aid agencies or volunteering for work in developing countries. There are both short-term and long-term opportunities available in international health for people desirous of working in these settings. However, traveling and working in developing countries requires mental and physical adjustment and preparation. If one is not prepared, one can experience culture shock. When traveling, one is exposed to a variety of potential risks. Many such risks can be minimized by suitable precautions taken before, during, and after travel. The purpose of this appendix is to offer some guidelines for traveling and working in developing countries.

When traveling from one country to another, there is always some stress and strain. Working in developing countries also involves some special health risks. In the 1980s the U.S. Peace Corps conducted a study to track health conditions affecting over 5,500 Peace Corps volunteers working in development projects in 62 countries all over the world (Bernard, Graitcer, van der Vlugt, Moran, & Pulley, 1989). Results showed that in 1987, the most commonly reported health problems were diarrhea (48 cases per 100 volunteers per year), amebiasis (24 per 100 volunteers per year), injuries (20 per 100 volunteers per year), bacterial skin infections (19 per 100 volunteers per year), and giardiasis (17 per 100 volunteers per year). The health problems with very low rates (<1.0 per 100 volunteers per year) were filariasis, hepatitis, non-*falciparum* malaria, and schistosomiasis. To minimize risks, a set of guidelines are presented here.

PREPARATION BEFORE TRAVEL

In preparing for travel, you must first obtain a passport from the country of which you are a citizen and a visa from the country to which you are traveling. Different categories of visas are issued by different countries. To obtain a visa, you need a valid passport, a letter of invitation or employment from the concerned agency for which you will be working in the foreign country, passport-sized photographs, and a valid travel ticket. The passport should be valid for at least 6 months beyond the date of travel, and the visa must be valid for the duration of the stay. Ideally, the tickets, passport, and visa should be ready at least 4 to 6 weeks before international travel. You should also obtain information about the consulate or embassy of your parent country nearest to the place where you will be staying in the foreign country. This information is essential to have with you in case you have any difficulties, such as a lost passport.

It is also important to have complete medical insurance that will cover you in the foreign country. If you have obtained a job in a developing country, be sure to check with your employer about medical insurance. If you are traveling for a shorter duration, sometimes the sponsoring organization may provide you with insurance. If not, then you must shop for health insurance in your parent country. Be sure to purchase insurance that will cover medical illnesses as well as injuries. Check for exclusions and limits of coverage. Obtain a policy with adequate limits of coverage.

If you plan on driving in the country to which you are traveling, be sure to obtain an international driver's license. Carry both the international driver's license and the license from your country. Become familiar with the driving rules and regulations of the country to which you are traveling. In many countries the traffic drives in the opposite side of the road to which you may be used to in your country of residence. It is also a good idea to locate information about the condition of roads in the country to which you are traveling, as well as local driving customs. For example, in many countries it is customary to sound the horn on the road to let others know that your vehicle is passing and that they should give way, whereas in other countries sounding the horn is done only to show your annoyance.

Travelers heading to developing countries should consult a medical practitioner at least 6 to 8 weeks prior to departure. During this health checkup you should find out about any required vaccinations and about antimalarial medications and other medical items that you should carry. If you have a preexisting condition that requires regular medication, such as a cardiovascular disorder, diabetes, epilepsy, or mental disorder, then you must plan on carrying a sufficient amount of medication for the entire duration of the trip if it will be a short trip. If you will be working abroad for an extended period of time, you must make arrangements with your employer to see a medical practitioner within 4 weeks in the country to which you are traveling. You should carry with you the name and contact information of your physician, along with information about the medical condition and treatment, and details of medication, such as generic drug names and prescribed doses. A physician's letter stating that the medication must be carried is required for satisfying customs officials. While traveling, all medications should be stored in carry-on luggage in their original containers with clear labels. It is also a good idea to keep a duplicate supply of the medication in your checked baggage in the event of theft or loss.

Malaria is a common disease in many countries outside of North America and western Europe. Malaria is transmitted in large areas of Central and South America, the island of Hispaniola (which includes Haiti and the Dominican Republic), Africa, Asia (including the Indian subcontinent, southeast Asia, and the Middle East), eastern Europe, and the South Pacific (Centers for Disease Control and Prevention [CDC], 2006). The chances of developing malaria are higher if you are traveling to rural areas, traveling in the rainy season, and if you do not take preventive measures to protect yourself against mosquito bites. Measures for protection against malaria include taking antimalarial medication 1 week prior to travel if it is chloroquine or 2 to 3 weeks prior if it is mefloquine (for areas where chloroquine-resistant malaria is present), as well as measures for reducing bites by mosquitoes (discussed in the section on precautions upon reaching the destination country). Antimalarial medication should be continued for 4 weeks after leaving the endemic area.

In terms of vaccinations, the first thing that must be checked is whether the routine adult vaccination schedule is complete. These vaccines in the United States include tetanus and diphtheria (Td), which is given every 10 years; three doses of HPV (human papillomavirus) vaccine for women younger than 26 years; one or two doses of MMR (measles, mumps, and rubella) vaccine; two doses of varicella vaccine; one dose annually of influenza vaccine; one to two doses of pneumococcal vaccine; two doses of hepatitis A vaccine; three doses of hepatitis B vaccine; and one dose of meningococcal vaccine (CDC, 2007). Meningococcal vaccination is also required by the government of Saudi Arabia for annual travel during the Hajj.

If any of the required adult vaccines is missing, that vaccine should be administered. In addition, the International Health Regulations require yellow fever vaccination for travel to countries in sub-Saharan Africa and tropical South America. **Table A.1** lists countries that require yellow fever vaccination. There are a number of other countries where yellow fever is endemic besides the countries listed in Table A.1; it is a good idea to get vaccinated if you are traveling to one of those countries. For current information on the list of countries and other details, you should consult a Web site such as the CDC's Traveler's Health site (wwwn.cdc.gov/travel/) prior to your travel. Yellow fever is a viral disease that is transmitted through the bite of infected mosquitoes. The disease ranges in severity from an influenza-like syndrome to severe

TABLE A.1	Countries in Africa and South America Requiring Yellow Fever Vaccination	
Africa		**South America**
Angola		Bolivia
Benin		
Burkina Faso		
Burundi		
Cameroon		
Central African Republic		
Chad		
Congo		
Côte d'Ivoire		
Democratic Republic of the Congo		
French Guiana		
Gabon		
Ghana		
Liberia		
Mali		
Mauritania (for a stay >2 weeks)		
Niger		
Rwanda		
São Tomé and Principe		
Sierra Leone		
Togo		

Source: Centers for Disease Control and Prevention. (2007). Yellow fever. In *Health information for international travel 2008*. Atlanta: U.S. Department of Health and Human Services, Public Health Service. Retrieved from http://wwwn.cdc.gov/travel/yellowbook/Ch4/yellow-fever.aspx

hepatitis and hemorrhagic fever. A single dose of vaccine is administered subcutaneously and is sufficient for protection.

PRECAUTIONS DURING TRAVEL

Air travel is a common means of transcontinental travel, but in some situations it may be contraindicated. Some of the contraindications for air travel include pregnancy after 36 weeks, any active communicable disease, decompression sickness after diving, increased intracranial pressure due to hemorrhage, sinus infection, recent myocardial infarction and stroke, angina pectoris, severe respiratory diseases, sickle cell disease, and uncontrolled psychotic conditions (World Health Organization, 2008).

Certain problems can occur with air travel. The first is that the cabin pressure in airplanes is lower than sea level, which causes hypoxia (less oxygen in the blood). Although most healthy passengers can tolerate this, some people who suffer from heart and lung conditions or blood conditions such as sickle cell anemia need to make arrangements with the air carrier to have an additional oxygen supply during flight.

The second issue is that as the aircraft ascends, gases expand, which causes air to escape from the middle ear and sinuses; as the aircraft descends, air flows back into the ear and sinuses. This is often perceived as a popping sensation and in healthy individuals causes no problems. In individuals with ear or sinus infections, however, it can cause pain and damage. Therefore, if you are suffering from sinus or ear infection, you may want to avoid travel by air. If it is absolutely essential for you to travel, then you should use decongestant nasal drops shortly before the flight and again before descent.

The third issue is that of prolonged immobility, which can cause swelling of feet, stiffness, and discomfort. In rare cases it can lead to a condition called deep vein thrombosis, in which blood clots form and occasionally may travel to the lungs and result in pulmonary embolism, which can cause chest pain, shortness of breath, and even death. The chances of deep vein thrombosis increase with a previous history of deep vein thrombosis or pulmonary embolism, use of oral contraceptives, pregnancy, cancer, obesity, and recent surgery. To prevent this condition, it is important to move around periodically during the flight so that immobility is lessened. Doing exercises while seated is also helpful.

Finally, air travel over long distances causes jet lag, which happens as a result of disruption of the body's circadian rhythm, or internal clock. To prevent jet lag, it is important to sleep during the flight and then adjust to the different time zone in the foreign country. Melatonin is also sometimes helpful in reducing jet lag and is often available as an over-the-counter drug.

PRECAUTIONS UPON REACHING THE DESTINATION COUNTRY _____

You should carry at least two copies of your passport, visa, and other travel documents. Upon arrival in the destination country, keep the original passport and visa in a safe, secure place, and carry a photocopy of the documents with you at all times.

If you are driving in your destination country and will be there for an extended period of time, try to obtain the driver's license of that country. If you are on a shorter trip and using an international driver's license, be sure to follow safety precautions. These include not driving after drinking alcohol, always wearing a seat belt if it is available, driving within the speed limits, and being aware of pedestrians and wandering animals on the roads.

Exposure to violence is a reality in many countries. Foreigners are often targeted by criminals, and one must be watchful both day and night. Do not carry large sums of money or other valuable items with you. These should be kept secured in a safe deposit box or other safe place. You should avoid isolated spots as well as overcrowded spots. Avoid traveling at night, and as far as possible do not travel alone. If possible, have a local person accompany you, especially in the beginning of your stay. When traveling by car, keep your doors and windows shut and do not pick up strangers.

Food and water safety is very important in developing countries. Common foodborne and waterborne illnesses include traveler's diarrhea, hepatitis A, typhoid fever, and cholera. To avoid these illnesses, you should consume only thoroughly cooked food and drink water from a well-sealed bottle. Boiling water is helpful if its safety is questionable. If boiling is not possible, then use a certified filter or a disinfectant.

Travelers to developing countries are often exposed to helminthic (worm) infestations as a result of lower conditions of hygiene and sanitation. Common types of worms to which you might be exposed are as follows:

- Hookworms (*Necator* and *Ancylostoma* species): Larval forms of this worm are found in human and canine feces. The larva penetrates the skin at places where soil is contaminated with feces and one is walking barefoot, such as on beaches.
- Tapeworms (*Taenia saginata* and *Taenia solium*): *Taenia saginata* is often found in raw or undercooked beef, whereas *Taenia solium* is present in raw or undercooked pork.
- Roundworms (*Ascaris* and *Trichuris* species): These parasites are usually transmitted by contaminated foods, such as unwashed fruits and vegetables, and by contaminated hands.

To protect yourself from worm infestation, you should never eat raw food or food from food stalls and street hawkers. If food has to be eaten raw, then you should thoroughly wash it with safe water before consumption. You should eat fruits such as bananas or oranges that can be peeled and consumed. Meat products should only be consumed if they have been thoroughly cooked and the food preparation place is clean. Finally, you should never roam barefoot. Wearing shoes any time you are outside is important to protect against hookworm infestation.

A second set of illnesses that can be acquired are vector-borne diseases transmitted by vectors such as mosquitoes and ticks. Some examples of such diseases are malaria, yellow fever, dengue, Japanese encephalitis, and tick-borne encephalitis. If you are in a malaria endemic zone, measures for protection against malaria should be practiced. These include taking a regular dose of antimalarial medication, using insect repellent, wearing long-sleeved clothing, using a bed net at night, and spraying flying insect spray to keep away mosquitoes. Yellow fever requires vaccination, as explained earlier. For other vector-borne diseases, you should try to minimize contact with the vector.

Acquiring sexually transmitted diseases (STDs) while on a foreign assignment is also a possibility. Common examples of these diseases are HIV/AIDS, syphilis, gonorrhea, and hepatitis B. Sexual contact between project personnel and members of the target population are unethical and should be avoided as far as possible. As a general rule, you should abstain from any casual sex while on a project; this is the best means of protection against acquiring STDs. The only STD for which there is a vaccine is hepatitis B.

REFERENCES

Bernard, K. W., Graitcer, P. L., van der Vlugt, T., Moran, J. S., & Pulley, K. M. (1989). Epidemiological surveillance in Peace Corps Volunteers: A model for monitoring health in temporary residents of developing countries. *International Journal of Epidemiology, 18*(1), 220–226.

Centers for Disease Control and Prevention. (2006). Malaria and travelers. Retrieved from http://www.cdc.gov/malaria/travel/index.htm

Centers for Disease Control and Prevention. (2007). Recommended adult immunization schedule—United States, October 2007–September 2008. *Morbidity and Mortality Weekly Report (MMWR), 56*(41), Q1–Q4.

World Health Organization. (2008). International travel and health. Geneva: Author. Retrieved from http://www.who.int/ith/en/index.html

accessibility: Reasonable access of individuals to medically necessary care.

acculturation: Psychosocial adjustment and adaptation to a new culture for people from another culture.

act of commission: A kind of abuse in which a caretaker actively engages in an action detrimental to the health and development of the child.

act of omission: A kind of abuse in which a caretaker fails to do something he or she is morally, ethically, or legally expected to do for the optimal health and development of the child.

acute gastrointestinal infections: Infections of the gastrointestinal tract caused by bacteria, viruses, or parasites and characterized by diarrhea often accompanied by nausea, vomiting, fever, and abdominal pain.

acute respiratory infections: A myriad of infections of the respiratory tract caused primarily by bacteria and viruses that can affect either the upper respiratory tract, causing rhinitis, sinusitis, ear infections, acute pharyngitis, tonsillopharyngitis, epiglottitis, and laryngitis; or the lower respiratory tract, causing bronchitis, pneumonia, and bronchiolitis.

age cohort: A group of people delimited by an age-based criterion. For instance, the cohort of young sexually active females may include all sexually active females younger than 15 years.

age-specific fertility rate: The number of live births per 1,000 women in a specific age group.

alcohol use: The drinking of beer, wine, spirits, or home-brewed alcoholic beverages. Typically one drink consists of 12 ounces of beer, 5 ounces of wine, or 1.5 ounces of 80-proof distilled spirits.

analytical epidemiology: Studies done to identify determinants of health and health-related conditions and events in populations.

anthropology: Study of humankind from ancient times to the present in terms of biological, linguistic, social, and cultural variations. Anthropology has four major subfields: physical anthropology, archaeology, sociocultural anthropology, and linguistics.

anxiety disorders: An umbrella term for multiple different forms of abnormal anxiety-based conditions. All of these conditions are, however, marked by some degree of pathological anxiety, abnormal fears, or phobias.

avian influenza (bird flu): Disease caused by avian influenza A (H5N1) virus that is transmitted by direct contact with infected birds or with surfaces contaminated by their excretions. It is characterized by influenza-like symptoms (fever, sore throat, cough, myalgia, etc.) and can lead to severe respiratory illness and death.

Ayurveda: Ancient Indian system of medicine that is known as the science of life or health.

Baby-Friendly Hospital Initiative (BFHI): A World Health Organization initiative aimed at reducing infant morbidity and mortality across the globe by creating a health care environment in which breastfeeding is the norm.

behavior: Any overt action, conscious or unconscious, with a measurable frequency, intensity, and duration.

Beveridge model: A system in which health care is provided and financed by the government through tax payments, just like the security forces.

biological agents: Viruses, bacteria, or other germs (agents) used to cause illness or death in people, animals, or plants.

biological psychiatry: An interdisciplinary approach to psychiatry that aims to understand mental disorders in terms of the biological functioning of the nervous system. It is interdisciplinary in that it draws from diverse sciences such as neuroscience, psychopharmacology, biochemistry, genetics, and physiology to form theories about the biological basis of human behavior and psychopathology. Also known as biopsychiatry.

Biological Weapons Convention: The first multilateral disarmament treaty banning an entire category of weapons. The convention, opened for ratification in 1972 and entered into effect in 1975, prohibits the "development, production, acquisition, transfer, retention, stockpiling and use of biological and toxin weapons" and is a key element in the international community's efforts to address the proliferation of weapons of mass destruction.

bioterrorism: The deliberate release of viruses, bacteria, or other germs (agents) used to cause illness or death in people, animals, or plants.

Bismarck model: A system of health care in which there is a partnership between the public (government) and private sectors of the economy with the main motive of ensuring the provision of universal health coverage for all citizens.

brain drain: A large emigration of individuals with technical skills or knowledge, normally because of conflict, lack of opportunity, political instability, or health risks.

breast cancer: The term *cancer* refers to an uncontrolled proliferation or growth of normal human cells. Breast cancer is a special type of cancer that affects the breast tissue, mostly in females, but rarely also in males.

burden of disease: The gap between current health status and an ideal situation in which everyone lives into old age free of disease and disability.

cancers: A diverse group of diseases that have in common an uncontrolled growth of cells and spread of these cells. Cancers are classified according to their organ or tissue of origin and according to their histologic features.

cardiovascular diseases (CVD): Diseases affecting the heart and circulatory system.

carrying capacity: The capacity of the area or environment to support population.

cerebrovascular disease: Ischemic (clogging by thrombus or embolus) or hemorrhagic (rupture) disturbances of the blood vessels of the brain. The most severe form of cerebrovascular disease is stroke; a less severe condition is transient ischemic attack (TIA).

chemical agents: Any chemical that through its chemical action on life processes can cause death, temporary incapacitation, or permanent harm to humans or animals. This includes all such chemicals, regardless of their origin or of their method of production, and regardless of whether they are produced in facilities, in munitions, or elsewhere.

Chemical Weapons Convention: An arms control agreement, signed in 1993 and entered into force in 1997, which outlaws the manufacturing, stockpiling, and utilization of chemical weapons.

child abuse: All forms of physical and/or emotional ill-treatment, sexual abuse, neglect or negligent treatment, or commercial or other exploitation resulting in actual or potential harm to a child's health, survival, development, or dignity in the context of a relationship of responsibility, trust, or power.

chronic obstructive pulmonary disease (COPD): An umbrella term that is used to describe chronic lung diseases that cause limitations in airflow to the lungs, such as chronic bronchitis, bronchial asthma, and emphysema. Common symptoms of COPD include breathlessness, increased sputum production, and an accompanying chronic cough.

Clifford Beers: A Yale graduate and young businessman who was largely responsible for ushering in 20th century reforms in psychiatric care; also credited with the foundation of the Connecticut Society for Mental Hygiene.

climate change: Any significant alteration in the indices used to measure climate (such as temperature, precipitation, or wind) extending for a longer than usual duration.

Codex Hammurabi: A set of more than 200 laws developed by Hammurabi (1810–1750 BCE), king of Babylon, which included the first codification of medical practice. Also known as Hammurabi's Code.

complementary feeding: The addition of complementary foods to the diet of an infant, usually between 18 and 24 months of age, when breast milk is not enough to meet the infant's nutritional demands.

comprehensive neonatal care: Immediate attention to breathing and warmth, hygienic cord and skin care, and early initiation of exclusive breastfeeding after an infant is born.

Comprehensive Nuclear Test Ban Treaty: An international agreement that bans nuclear explosions in all environments altogether, for military or civilian purposes.

Convention on the Elimination of All Forms of Discrimination Against Women (CEDAW): An international agreement, adopted by the United Nations in 1979, that comprehensively addresses women's rights within political, cultural, economic, social, and family life.

Convention on the Rights of the Child: An international treaty, adopted by the United Nations General Assembly in 1989, that lays down the rights of children as equal to those of adults.

coronary heart disease (CHD): Disease characterized by the narrowing and/or blockage of coronary arteries that supply blood to the heart. Also known as ischemic heart disease or arteriosclerotic coronary artery disease.

Corpus Hippocraticum: A body of writings (a compilation of around 70 books) attributed to Hippocrates.

crude birth rate (CBR): The total number of live births in a given year divided by the midyear population of that community and expressed per 1,000 population.

crude death rate (CDR): The total number of deaths in a given calendar year divided by the midyear population of that community and expressed per 1,000 population.

cultural competence: Understanding of another culture, respect for varying cultural perspectives, and effective use of skills in cross-cultural situations.

cultural sensitivity: Incorporation of specific cultural features, practices, behavioral attributes, and values in the design, implementation, and evaluation of health promotion programs and materials.

culture: A shared set of knowledge, beliefs, customs, mores, traditions, practices, and values that are passed on from one generation to another.

culture-bound syndrome: Recurrent, locality-specific patterns of aberrant behavior and troubling experience that may or may not be linked to a particular DSM-IV-TR diagnostic category. Culture-bound syndromes are generally limited to specific societies or culture areas and are folk diagnostic categories that frame coherent meanings for certain repetitive, patterned, and troubling sets of experiences and observations.

deforestation: The conversion of forests to arable land.

deinstitutionalization: The process of transferring formerly committed individuals to sheltered community environments or community homes with a view to facilitating an easy transition to the best possible social functioning possible for those individuals.

delusions: Fixed false beliefs.

demographic transition: A population model that divides the history of population growth into four stages, characterized mainly by changing patterns of birth and death rates, yielding an S-shaped curve.

Department of Child and Adolescent Health and Development: A department created within the World Health Organization for preventing and managing the health problems of infants, children, and adolescents.

descriptive epidemiology: Time, place, and person distribution of health and health-related conditions and events in populations.

diabetes: A chronic disease in which either the pancreas does not produce enough insulin or the body develops resistance to its action. There are two types of diabetes: type 1 (formerly called insulin-dependent or juvenile diabetes), which comprises 10% of all cases, and type 2 (formerly called non-insulin-dependent or adult-onset diabetes), which comprises 90% of all cases.

diffusion of innovations: A theory that explains the adoption of a new idea, practice, or object over a period of time.

diphtheria: An acute communicable disease caused by the bacterium *Corynebacterium diphtheriae* that affects the respiratory system, manifesting as sore throat, difficulty in swallowing, nasal discharge, hoarseness, malaise, fever, and a tenacious gray membrane in the pharynx.

disability-adjusted life expectancy (DALE): A composite indicator that depicts the equivalent number of years of life expected to be lived in full health, taking into account the degree of disability.

disability-adjusted life year (DALY): For a disease or a health condition, DALY is calculated as the sum of (a) the years of life lost due to premature mortality (YLL) in the population and (b) the years of healthy life lost due to disability (YLD) based on the incident cases of the health condition.

disability-free life expectancy (DFLE): Computed by subtracting from the life expectancy the probable duration of bed disability and inability to perform major activities at work, home, or school.

DSM-IV-TR: *The Diagnostic and Statistical Manual of Mental Disorders* (4th ed., text revision), published by the American Psychiatric Association; an American instruction manual for mental health professionals that lists different categories of mental disorders along with the criteria for diagnosing them.

eating disorders: Abnormal eating behaviors, marked by compulsive eating or behaviors targeted toward avoiding eating that negatively affect both one's physical and mental health.

Ebers papyrus: Document from the Egyptian civilization, believed to have originated in 1550 BCE, that deals with medicine and was purchased in 1872 by George Ebers, after whom it was named. It is 110 pages long and has more than 800 paragraphs, each of which deals with a different medical ailment and its management.

Ebola hemorrhagic fever: A viral disease characterized by fever, intense weakness, muscular pain, headache, and sore throat, followed by vomiting, diarrhea, rash, impaired kidney and liver function, and internal and external bleeding.

eclampsia: The onset of fits in a pregnant female with pregnancy-induced hypertension.

ectopic pregnancy: A pregnancy in which the zygote or egg implants outside the uterus.

Edwin Smith papyrus: A document from the Egyptian civilization that dates to around 1700 BCE, but is believed to be a copy of an original written in 3000 BCE. It is considered to be the oldest known surgical text in the history of civilization and is divided into 48 cases, arranged by anatomic region, that primarily describe traumatic injuries and their management.

electroconvulsive therapy: A controversial psychiatric treatment in which seizures are electrically induced in anesthetized patients for therapeutic effect. Also known as ECT or electroshock therapy.

emergency obstetric care: The functions necessary to save the lives of a pregnant woman and her baby. Some of the components of emergency obstetric care are administration of intravenous antibiotics, manual removal of the placenta, assisted vaginal delivery, and occasionally blood transfusions.

emotional abuse: The failure of a caregiver to provide an appropriate and nurturing environment; it includes acts that have an unfavorable effect on the emotional health and development of a child.

EMTALA: The Emergency Medical Treatment and Active Labor Act; a U.S. law that requires hospitals and ambulance services to provide care to anyone needing emergency treatment regardless of citizenship, legal status, or ability to pay.

epidemiology: The study of the distribution and determinants of health and health-related conditions and events in populations to prevent and control health problems.

ethnic shifts: Definitive changes in the overall ethnicity mix of a population in a defined geographic region.

family planning: The ability of individuals and couples to manage their desired number of children and the spacing and timing of births through the use of contraceptive methods and the treatment of involuntary infertility.

female genital mutilation: The partial or total removal of the external female genitalia, or any other injury caused to the female genital organs for nonmedical reasons.

feminist movement: A sequence of campaigns on female-centric issues such as reproductive rights (often including abortion), domestic violence, maternity leave, equal pay, sexual harassment, and sexual violence. Also known as the women's movement or women's liberation.

fetal mortality rate (FMR): Calculated by dividing fetal deaths (deaths that occur at 20 weeks of gestation or later) in a given calendar year by the total number of live births plus fetal deaths in that same year.

gender-based approach: An approach to public health that begins from the recognition of the differences between women and men. It helps health care providers to identify the ways in which the health risks, experiences, and outcomes are different for women and men, boys and girls, and to act accordingly.

gender-based biology: A field of scientific inquiry committed to identifying the biological and physiological differences between men and women.

general fertility rate (GFR): The number of live births per 1,000 women of childbearing age (15 to 44 years) in a given year. Sometimes, the age group that is considered is 15 to 49 years or 10 to 49 years.

germ theory of disease: The theory that microorganisms are responsible for some diseases.

global health: The study of health problems and solutions affecting all people of the world.

Global Outbreak Alert and Response Network: A verification and response program; a voluntary technical partnership of 140 existing institutions and networks that pool human and technical resources for the rapid identification, confirmation, and response to disease outbreaks of international importance.

Global Strategy for Infant and Young Child Feeding: A World Health Organization strategy aimed at rekindling global efforts to guard, foster, and support appropriate infant and young child feeding.

global warming: An average increase in the temperature of the atmosphere near the Earth's surface and in the troposphere.

globalization: The increased interconnectedness and interdependence of people and countries.

greenhouse effect: The retention of solar heat within the Earth's atmosphere by virtue of atmospheric gases, similar to the phenomenon seen within the glass walls of a greenhouse.

gross reproduction rate (GRR): The average number of daughters that would be born to a woman if she experienced the age-specific birth rates observed in a given year throughout her childbearing years and if she did not die during her childbearing years.

Haemophilus influenzae **type b infections:** Disease caused by *Haemophilus influenzae* type b (Hib), a nonmotile, gram-negative bacterium that causes meningitis and pneumonia, especially in children younger than 5 years.

hallucinations: Sensory perceptions in the absence of sensory stimuli.

harassing agent: An agent that disables exposed people for the entire duration of the exposure, but which allows exposed individuals to remain capable of removing themselves from the source of exposure. Recovery from the effects of the agent is usually complete and within a short time, and no medical treatment is needed.

health: A means to achieve desirable goals in life while maintaining multidimensional (physical, mental, social, political, economic, and spiritual) equilibrium that is operationalized for individuals as well as for communities.

health-adjusted life expectancy or healthy life expectancy (HALE): The expected number of years to be lived in terms equivalent of complete health.

health behavior: Actions with a potentially measurable frequency, intensity, and duration performed at the individual, interpersonal, organizational, community, or public policy level for primary, secondary, or tertiary prevention.

Health belief model: Behavioral theory that predicts behavior based on the constructs of perceived susceptibility, perceived severity, perceived benefits, perceived costs, cues to action, and self-efficacy.

health-promoting school: A school that constantly improves its capacity as a healthy setting for living, learning, and working by promoting health and scholarship with its entire capacity.

health system: All organizations, institutions, and resources devoted to producing actions whose primary intent is to improve health.

healthy life year (HeaLY): A composite measure that combines amount of healthy life lost due to morbidity and that attributable to premature mortality.

historic period: History of humankind since the time humans learned to write, which was about 5,000 years ago.

HIV/AIDS Program of the World Health Organization: A program of the World Health Organization, conducted in close collaboration with multiple other United Nation agencies, nongovernmental organizations, health services providers, and health-care institutions across the globe, whose purpose is to reinforce all aspects of the health sector to improve HIV-related services.

human cloning: The creation of genetically identical siblings, such as those which occur naturally in identical twins or artificially through the splitting of embryos in the laboratory at the two- to eight-cell stage of development. Also, the creation of embryos through somatic cell nuclear transfer.

human immunodeficiency virus/acquired immunodeficiency syndrome (HIV/AIDS): Disease caused by a retrovirus and transmitted through sexual transmission through rectal, vaginal, and even oral contact; parenteral transmission through injection, transfusion, or accidental exposure to blood or its components; and perinatal transmission from infected mothers to children before, during, or after childbirth. It is characterized by symptoms that can affect almost all organs of the body.

incapacitating agent: An agent that disables individuals, but the exposed individuals may either be unaware of the effects or unable to move away from the source of exposure.

incidence rate: The number of new cases of a disease occurring in a population during a given time period divided by number of people exposed to the risk of developing that disease in that time period. It is expressed per 1,000 or per 10,000 or 100,000 population.

incubation period: The time elapsing between exposure to an infective agent and the first appearance of the signs of disease associated with the infection.

indoor air quality: An index of air purity based on the content of interior air that could adversely affect the health and comfort of the inhabitants of a particular building.

infant mortality rate (IMR): The total number of infant deaths in a given calendar year divided by the total number of live births in that same year, expressed per 1,000 live births.

infectivity: A measure of the capability of a bacterial agent to enter, survive, and multiply in a host. It can be quantified as the proportion of persons in a given population exposed to a given dose who become infected.

Innocenti Declaration: The Innocenti Declaration on the Protection, Promotion and Support of Breastfeeding was prepared and adopted by participants at a meeting of policy makers jointly sponsored by WHO and UNICEF in Florence, Italy, in 1990. The declaration endorsed breast milk as the ideal nutrition and a contributor to the healthy growth and development of infants.

integrated management of childhood illness (IMCI) strategy: An integrated approach that focuses on the well-being of the child as a whole and strives to reduce death, illness, and disability and to promote improved growth and development among children younger than 5 years. It blends both preventive and curative components of health care.

integrated management of pregnancy and childbirth (IMPAC): The center point of the technical assistance activities offered by the Making Pregnancy Safer department of the World Health Organization. The integrated approach seeks to enhance maternal and newborn health by addressing diverse factors that are vital for the access to skilled care before, during, and after pregnancy and childbirth.

international health: The science and art of examining health problems in multiple countries, primarily those that are developing, and finding population-based solutions.

International Health Regulations: An international legal instrument, entered into force in 2007, that requires member countries to report specified disease outbreaks and public health events to the World Health Organization.

iodine deficiency disorders (IDD): Disorders that result from a deficiency of iodine or deficient synthesis of triiodothyronine (T_3) and thyroxine (T_4) by the thyroid gland.

iron deficiency: A lack of iron that causes anemia characterized by easy fatigability, increased heart rate, palpitations, and breathlessness on exertion.

Kahun papyrus: Document from the Egyptian civilization that dates back to about 1900 BCE and deals primarily with gynecologic matters.

kwashiorkor: A form of protein-energy malnutrition in which there is mainly protein deficiency and edema. The body weight is 60 to 80% of standard for age.

leprosy: A chronic infectious disease caused by the bacterium *Mycobacterium leprae* that affects the skin, peripheral nervous system, eyes, and mucous membranes.

lethal agent: An agent that causes the death of those exposed to it.

lethality: The ability of an agent to cause death in an infected population.

life expectancy at birth: The average number of years of life a newborn can be expected to live if current mortality trends continue.

Making Pregnancy Safer (MPS): A department (originally an initiative) within the World Health Organization that focuses on accelerating the reduction of maternal and newborn mortality and ensuring access to skilled attendance and the highest attainable standards of health for all women and babies.

malaria: A vector-borne disease that is transmitted through the bite of the female *Anopheles* mosquito and caused by protozoa of the genus *Plasmodium*. It is characterized by chills (cold stage), followed by high-grade fever (hot stage) and sweating (sweating stage), with accompanying fatigue, headache, muscle pains, joint pains, and backache.

mammogram: An imaging study of the breasts done with the use of low-dose x-rays.

marasmic kwashiorkor: A form of protein-energy malnutrition in which there is a combination of chronic energy deficiency and chronic or acute protein deficiency with edema. The body weight is less than 60% of standard for age.

marasmus: A form of protein-energy malnutrition in which there is mainly energy deficiency and no accompanying edema. The body weight is less than 60% of standard for age.

maternal mortality rate (ratio) (MMR): Usually defined as the number of maternal deaths per 100,000 live births.

measles: An acute viral infection caused by a paramyxovirus, characterized by high-grade fever, coryza (nasal obstruction, sneezing, and sore throat), Koplik spots (white and irregular specks in the buccal mucosa usually opposite the upper premolars but which may fill the entire inner cheek), and a red rash that appears on the third to fifth day of the fever and begins on the face and proceeds downward and outward, affecting the palms and soles last. Also known as rubeola.

Medicaid: The U.S. health program for eligible individuals and families with low incomes and resources. It is a means-tested program that is jointly funded by the states and federal government and is managed by the states. Among the groups of people served by Medicaid are eligible low-income parents, children, seniors, and people with disabilities.

medical anthropology: A branch of sociocultural anthropology that studies the relationships between culture and disease and culture and health.

medical model: A model associated with diagnosing and treating illnesses in individuals.

Medicare: A social insurance program administered by the U.S. government, providing health insurance coverage to people aged 65 and over, or people who meet other special criteria.

meningococcal meningitis: A disease caused by the bacterium *Neisseria meningitides* and characterized by high fever, chills, headache, nausea and/or vomiting, and neck rigidity.

mental health: An individual's capacity to realize his or her potential to cope with daily life stressors, work productively, and contribute meaningfully to society.

Middle Ages: The time period between 500 CE and 1500 CE in Europe. During this period there was very little progress in medicine and public health; it is therefore also known as the Dark Ages.

Millennium Declaration: The United Nations Millennium Declaration, signed in September 2000, commits world leaders to combat poverty, hunger, disease, illiteracy, environmental degradation, and discrimination against women.

Millennium Development Goals: Eight international development goals that 189 United Nations member states and at least 23 international organizations have agreed to achieve by the year 2015. They include reducing extreme poverty, reducing child mortality rates, and fighting disease epidemics such as AIDS.

mood disorders: States in which the existing emotional mood is unsuitable to the circumstances. Also known as affective disorders.

mumps: An acute viral disease caused by a paramyxovirus and characterized by painful, swollen salivary glands, especially parotid glands; fever; malaise; sometimes meningitis characterized by neck stiffness; headache and vomiting; and sometimes testicular swelling and tenderness (orchitis) or ovarian enlargement (oophoritis), or pancreatitis or encephalitis.

national health insurance model: A health care model that combines elements of both the Beveridge and Bismarck models. Even though it uses private-sector providers, the payment comes from a government-run insurance program into which every citizen pays.

neglect: The failure of a caretaker to provide for the development of the child (provided the caretaker has the capacities of doing so) in one or more of the following areas: health, education, nutrition, emotional development, shelter, and safe living conditions.

neonatal mortality rate (NMR): Neonatal deaths (deaths of infants between the ages of 0 and 28 days of life) in a given calendar year divided by the total number of live births in that same year. The results are shown per 1,000 live births.

net reproduction rate (NRR): The average number of daughters that would be born to a woman if she passed through her lifetime conforming to the age-specific fertility and mortality rates.

noise mitigation: Strategies designed to reduce unwelcome environmental sound. Also known as noise abatement.

nonpersistent agents: Volatile chemicals that do not stay long in the area of application but disperse quickly.

Nuclear Non-Proliferation Treaty (NPT): An international treaty whose prime objective is to avert the proliferation of nuclear weapons and nuclear-weapons-related technology, to foster cooperation in the peaceful uses of nuclear energy, and to further the goal of achieving nuclear disarmament.

obesity: A body mass index of more than 30 kg/m^2.

Obras Sociales: Umbrella organizations that represent Argentine workers' unions.

obstetric fistula: A hole in the vagina or rectum caused by childbirth that is prolonged and unattended by skilled nursing care.

obstructed labor: A discrepancy in the size of the baby and the birth canal leading to a halt in the childbirth process, usually with adverse health consequences for both mother and child.

one-child policy: The controversial nonvoluntary population control policy of the People's Republic of China, introduced in 1979 by the Chinese government as a means to ease the social and environmental problems of China.

oral rehydration solution or salts (ORS): A solution of salts and sugars that is administered orally as a simple, cheap, and effective treatment for dehydration associated with diarrhea, particularly gastroenteritis such as that caused by cholera or rotavirus.

osteoarthritis: A degenerative joint disease in which there are biomechanical alterations in the cartilage and the underlying bone in a joint. It commonly affects the knees, hands, feet, hips, and spine.

osteoporosis: A bone disorder characterized by low bone mass leading to fractures with minimal trauma. The common fractures that occur are of the hip, vertebrae, and distal radius.

out-of-pocket model: A health care system that totally or partially follows the out-of-pocket payment system.

out-of-pocket payment: Payment of the entire cost for any health care service by the individual from his or her own financial resources.

overweight: A body mass index of between 25 kg/m^2 and 29.9 kg/m^2.

Palermo Convention and Protocol: A United Nations convention that laid down the defining criteria for human trafficking in 2000.

passive purchasing: Adherence to a preset budget and paying bills when presented.

PEN-3 model: A health promotion and education planning model in which there are three dimensions: health education (PEN = person, extended family, neighborhood), educational diagnosis of health behavior (PEN = perceptions, enablers, nurturers), and cultural appropriateness of health beliefs (PEN = positive, exotic, negative).

perinatal mortality rate (PMR): Perinatal deaths (deaths that occur at greater than or equal to 28 weeks of gestation and 7 days of birth) in a given calendar year divided by the total number of live births plus fetal deaths in that same year. The results are shown per 1,000 live births plus fetal deaths.

persistent agents: Chemical agents that tend to remain in the area of contamination for prolonged durations.

persistent organic pollutants: Chemical substances that persist in the environment, bioaccumulate through the food web, and pose a risk of causing adverse effects to human health and the environment (e.g., pesticides).

pertussis: An acute communicable disease affecting the respiratory tract that is caused by the gram-negative coccobacillus *Bordetella pertussis*, characterized by a paroxysmal cough with a high-pitched whoop on inspiration that is often followed by vomiting. Also known as whooping cough.

Phillip Pinel: A French physician who first challenged the traditional wisdom of keeping the mentally ill restrained. His theories on mental illness were the first to span both physiological and psychological explanations.

physical abuse: Those acts of commission by a caregiver that either cause actual physical harm or have the potential for the same.

physical inactivity: Not meeting the minimum requirements with regard to physical activity, which is defined as any bodily movement that increases energy expenditure.

poliomyelitis: A viral disease caused by an enterovirus and characterized in some cases by flaccid paralysis of the lower limbs with muscle wasting, or paralysis of the cranial nerves with respiratory paralysis. Also known as infantile paralysis.

pooling: The accumulation and management of revenues in such a way as to ensure that the risk of having to pay for health care is borne by all the members of the pool and not by each contributor individually.

portability: A feature of the Canadian health insurance system that ensures that coverage for insured services is preserved when an insured person travels within or outside of Canada.

postneonatal mortality rate (PNMR): Postneonatal deaths (infant deaths between 28 days and 1 year of age) in a given calendar year divided by the total number of live births in that same year. The results are shown per 1,000 live births.

PRECEDE-PROCEED model: A health promotion and education planning model in which PRECEDE stands for predisposing, reinforcing, and enabling constructs in educational/environmental diagnosis and evaluation, and PROCEED stands for policy, regulatory, and organizational constructs in educational and environmental development.

prehistoric period: Those times (more than 5,000 years ago) during which there were no written records.

preparedness: What needs to be considered long before an incident actually takes place.

prevalence rate: The total number of cases of a disease present in a population during a given time period divided by the number of people exposed to the risk of having that disease in that time period. It is expressed per 1,000 or per 10,000 or 100,000 population.

primary health care: Basic health care comprising education about health problems; provision of food supply and nutrition; safe water supply and basic sanitation; maternal and child health, including family planning; immunization against diseases; prevention of locally endemic diseases; treatment of common diseases and injuries; and provision of essential drugs.

primary prevention: Preventive actions that are taken prior to the onset of disease or an injury with a view of removing the possibility of their ever occurring.

proportion: The relationship of a part to the whole. It is expressed as $[a/(a + b)]c$, where a = number of persons experiencing a particular event during a given period, $(a + b)$ = number of people who are at risk of experiencing the particular event during the same period, and c = multiplier. A proportion is usually expressed as a percentage, with the multiplier being 100.

proportion of 1-year-old children immunized against measles: The percentage of children younger than 1 year who have received at least one dose of a measles vaccine.

protein-energy malnutrition (PEM): A general lack of food, as opposed to deficiency of any one type of vitamin or mineral. Kwashiorkor, marasmus, and marasmic kwashiorkor are forms of protein-energy malnutrition (also known as protein-energy deficiency).

psychotic disorders: Mental states or conditions that involve a loss of contact with reality.

public health: The science and art of disease prevention and health promotion through organized community effort with the aim of ensuring social justice.

purchasing: The process through which pooled funds are remunerated to providers in order to deliver a prespecified or unspecified set of health interventions.

qi: A concept in Chinese medicine; the basis of the activities of body and mind and the primordial entity of both material (body) and nonmaterial (mind) things, gross and subtle.

quality-adjusted life year (QALY): The mathematical product of life expectancy; a measure of the quality of the remaining years of life.

rate: Measures the occurrence of some particular event (development of disease, occurrence of birth, death, etc.) in a population during a given time period; a statement of the risk of developing a condition. The general mathematical formula by which a rate can be expressed is $[a/(a + b)t]c$, where a = number of persons experiencing a particular event during a given time period, $(a + b)$ = number of people who are at risk of experiencing the particular event during the same period, t = total time at risk, and c = multiplier (usually 1,000 but can also be 100, 10,000, 100,000, etc., depending on how frequent the event is).

ratio: A relation in size between two random quantities. It can be depicted by the expression $(a/d)c$, where a = number of persons experiencing a particular event during a given period, c = multiplier, and d = number of persons experiencing some event different from event a but during the same period.

ready-to-use therapeutic food (RUTF): Palatable, soft, and crushable nutrient- and energy-rich foods that can be eaten by children over the age of six months without adding water, thereby reducing the risk of bacterial infection.

response: The sequence of events or responses that needs to happen after a warning of a pending release of biological or chemical agents is received, or after the release has actually occurred.

revenue collection: The process by which a health system generates capital needed to run its operations.

rheumatic heart disease (RHD): A consequence of rheumatic fever that is caused as a delayed immune response to group A beta-hemolytic streptococcal infection of the pharynx. In rheumatic heart disease the valves of the heart become defective; if uncorrected, this leads to heart failure.

rubella: An infectious disease caused by a togavirus and characterized by fever, malaise (pain in the joints), and a pink rash that appears on the face, then the trunk, and then the extremities and usually lasts for one day in each area (total three days' duration). Also known as German or 3-day measles.

Safe Motherhood Initiative: A close collaborative effort of the World Health Organization, the World Bank, and the United Nations Population Fund that seeks to reduce the burden of maternal mortality, particularly in developing countries.

salinization: The accumulation of water-soluble salts in the soil secondary to human activities.

secondary prevention: Actions that block the progression of an injury or disease at its incipient stage.

Securite sociale: The name of the French national health insurance plan that provides health care coverage to all salaried employees.

severe acute respiratory syndrome (SARS): A respiratory disease caused by a coronavirus, the SARS-associated coronavirus (SARS-CoV), that leads to high fever, headache, body ache, and dry cough and can lead to pneumonia.

sex-based biology: See *gender-based biology*.

sexual abuse: The use of a child for sexual gratification.

sexually transmitted diseases (STDs): See *sexually transmitted infections (STIs)*.

sexually transmitted infections (STIs): Diseases that are spread primarily through person-to-person sexual contact and are caused by bacteria, viruses, and protozoa; often characterized by manifestations such as urethral discharge, genital ulcers, inguinal swellings, scrotal swelling, vaginal discharge, and lower abdominal pain.

Sigmund Freud: An Austrian physician who founded the psychoanalytic school of psychology. Freud is best known for his theories of the unconscious mind.

skilled attendance: The presence of midwives and others with midwifery skills at childbirth, as well as an environment conducive to childbirth.

slum: Living conditions marked by deficiency of one or more of the basic facilities needed: durable housing, sufficient living area, access to improved water, access to sanitation, and secure tenure.

social capital: The degree of cohesion and solidarity existing within a community.

Social cognitive theory: Theory that explains human behavior as a triadic reciprocal causation among behavior, environment, and personal factors (expectations, expectancies, self-efficacy, and self-control).

social insurance model: Another name for the *Bismarck model* of health care.

social marketing: Use of commercial marketing techniques to help a target population acquire a beneficial health behavior.

socialized medicine: A health care system in which the government is responsible for both provision and payment of health care.

somatic cell nuclear transfer: The transfer of genetic material from one cell to an external controlled environment.

stability: The capability of an airborne biological agent to survive the influence of adverse environmental factors such as sunlight, air pollution, surface forces, and drying, while still remaining infective. It can also refer to stability during the production or storage processes of agents.

State Children's Health Insurance Program (SCHIP): A component of the American health care system designed to help states provide insurance for children of the working poor, for people with full-time jobs that did not offer employment-based insurance, and for those whose income is too high for Medicaid eligibility, but not high enough to afford private insurance.

stem cells: Cells that have the potential to develop into many different cell types in the body. Serving as a sort of repair system for the body, they can theoretically divide without limit to replenish other cells as long as the person or animal is still alive.

strategic purchasing: An uninterrupted search for the best ways to maximize health system performance by deciding which interventions should be purchased, how the purchase should be done, and from whom those services should be procured.

syndromic approach: A scientifically based method that uses common signs and symptoms as proxies for underlying infection and offers accessible and timely treatment.

Taoism: Chinese philosophy developed by Lao Tse (Lao Tzu) and based on *Tao* (or the *Way*), which refers to a reality that naturally exists from primordial time and gives rise to all other things. *Tao* can be found by experiencing oneness in all things.

Ten Steps to Successful Breastfeeding: The ten specific steps supporting successful breastfeeding that should be implemented by any maternity facility in order to be designated "baby friendly."

tertiary prevention: Those actions taken after the onset of disease or an injury with a view of assisting diseased or disabled people.

tetanus: A disease caused by the neurotoxin (tetanospasmin) produced by the anaerobic, gram-positive bacterium *Clostridium tetani*, which, when introduced into a wound, produces localized spasticity of the muscles, stiffness of the jaw (lockjaw) and neck, spasms of the jaw muscles (trismus) and other muscles of the body, painful convulsions, and respiratory muscle spasms.

theory: Set of interrelated ideas known as constructs that explain or predict events or conditions, including human behavior.

theory of contagion: Theory, propounded by Hieronymus Fracastorius (1478–1553), that the transfer of infection in epidemics occurs via minute imperceptible particles.

Theory of planned behavior: A theory that posits that behavioral intention precedes behavior and is determined by attitude toward the behavior, subjective norms, and perceived behavioral control (how much a person feels that he or she is in command of enacting the given behavior).

Theory of reasoned action: A theory that posits that behavioral intention precedes behavior and is determined by attitude toward the behavior and subjective norms.

threat analysis: A multidisciplinary endeavor, with involvement of a nation's law enforcement, intelligence, and medical and scientific communities, that attempts to identify individuals or groups who may wish to use biological or chemical weapons against the population, the agents that may be used should an attack actually happen, and the circumstances under which they may be used.

three delays model: A model portraying the roles of communities and health systems in the utilization of emergency obstetric care. It postulates that the result of an obstetric emergency is influenced by factors that govern the decision to seek care, reaching the medical facility, and receiving adequate care.

ticiotl: The system of medicine used by the Aztecs, who used plants and herbs in the treatment of diseases.

tobacco use: The smoking of cigarettes, cigars, pipes, bidis or kreteks (clove cigarettes), or hookahs, or the use of smokeless tobacco (snuff and chewing tobacco).

total fertility rate (TFR): The average number of children a woman would bear if she was to live to the end of her childbearing age and bear children at each age in accordance with the age-specific fertility rate.

toxic chemical: Any chemical that through its chemical action on life processes can cause death, temporary incapacitation, or permanent harm to humans or animals. This includes all such chemicals, regardless of their origin or of their method of production, and regardless of whether they are produced in facilities, in munitions, or elsewhere.

trafficking: According to the Palermo Convention, "the recruitment, transportation, transfer, harboring or receipt of persons, by means of the threat or use of force or other forms of coercion, of abduction, of fraud, of deception, of the abuse of power or of a position of vulnerability, or of the giving or receiving of payments or benefits to achieve the consent of a person having control over another person, for the purpose of exploitation. Exploitation shall include, at a minimum, the exploitation of the prostitution of others or other forms of sexual exploitation, forced labor or services, slavery or practices similar to slavery, servitude or the removal of organs."

Transtheoretical model: A model of behavior change that posits that people move through five stages of change: from precontemplation (not thinking about change), to contemplation (thinking about change over the next six months), to preparation (thinking about change in the next month), to action (having made meaningful change but not completed six months), and finally to maintenance (acquisition of the healthy behavior for six or more months).

treatment gap: The absolute difference between the true prevalence of a disorder and the treated proportion of individuals affected by the disorder.

triage: The process of prioritizing patients based on the severity of their condition so as to treat as many as possible when resources are insufficient for all to be treated immediately.

***tridosha* theory of disease:** In the system of Ayurveda, an ancient Indian medical system, diseases were explained as disturbances in the three *doshas*, or humors, which were *vata* (wind), *pitta* (gall), and *kapha* (mucus).

tuberculosis (TB): An infectious disease caused by the bacterium *Mycobacterium tuberculosis* that primarily affects the lungs and upon reactivation produces fatigue, weight loss, anorexia, low-grade fever, night sweats, a cough that is productive with purulent sputum and blood, and chest pain.

Unani **system:** Arabic system of medicine that originated in the Middle Ages and utilizes herbs and folk remedies.

under-5 mortality rate: The probability of a child born in a specific year or period dying before reaching the age of 5, if subject to age-specific mortality rates of that period.

unhealthy eating: Dietary behaviors that are risk factors for several chronic diseases, such as consuming less than 400 g of fruits and vegetables per day; consuming large amounts of saturated fat, dietary cholesterol, and/or red meat; and consuming large quantities of salt.

urbanization: The process of transition from a predominantly rural to an urban society; one of the hallmark trends of contemporary demographics.

varicella: An infectious disease caused by varicella-zoster virus and characterized by fever, malaise, and a rash that looks like dew drops on a rose petal, which becomes pustular and eventually crusts. Also known as chickenpox.

violence against women: Any act of gender-based violence that results in, or is likely to result in, physical, sexual, or mental harm or suffering to women, including threats of such acts, coercion, or arbitrary deprivation of liberty, whether occurring in public or in private life.

virulence: The relative severity of a disease caused by a microorganism.

vitamin deficiency disorders: Disorders caused by a deficiency of vitamins, such as the fat-soluble vitamins A, D, E, and K and the water-soluble vitamins thiamin, riboflavin, niacin, vitamin B_6, folic acid, pantothenic acid, vitamin B_{12}, and vitamin C.

women's health: Health issues specific to the anatomic makeup of a human female. These often pertain to structures such as the female genitalia and breasts and health-related conditions arising from those structures.

World Population Day: An annual event, observed on July 11, whose purpose is to spread awareness of global population issues.

*yang***:** The masculine principle in Chinese medicine. It should be in balance with the feminine principle, *yin*, for good health.

*yin***:** The feminine principle in Chinese medicine. It should be in balance with the masculine principle, *yang*, for good health.

yoga: A practice from Ancient India that attempts to establish balance between body, mind, and environment.

youth bulge: The burgeoning of youth populations in some developing countries (such as Pakistan and Afghanistan) over the next few years, which will have widespread socioeconomic and political repercussions.

INDEX